Introduction

MW01599568

Welcome to the third edition c̲ _____us ʌ̲ourist Attractions & Events of the World, which has been fully revised and updated. This is the only reference work of its kind to cover the world's most important tourist attractions and contains practical and descriptive information on over 500 world tourist attractions.

Tourist Attractions and Events of the World describes well-known landmarks like the Sydney Opera House and Universal Studios Hollywood, alongside lesser-known, though equally dramatic attractions such as the ancient city of Bagan in Myanmar. The title is designed to complement our other travel guides, such as the Columbus World Travel Guide, Columbus City Guide, Columbus World Travel Atlas and Columbus World Airport Guide.

The guide is organised by country and individual attractions are arranged alphabetically. Each entry contains a detailed description of the attraction including its history and highlights, transportation information and a contact address. Each attraction also includes easy to read symbols detailing the available facilities and other practical information.

Individual attraction entries can be found, either by locating the country in which the attraction is found, or by consulting the alphabetical index at the back of the book. Attractions are listed in English (or the most commonly used name) first with the native language translation in brackets. Thus, Prague Castle in the Czech Republic is listed as Prague Castle (Prazsky Hrad), and Angel Falls in Venezuela are listed as Angel Falls (Salto Ángel).

It must be stressed that the attraction entries included in this book are only a selection of the thousands of tourist attractions around the world. Entries have been chosen to reflect a number of different criteria, and those that appear are not necessarily the most popular attractions in their respective countries. In this edition, the number of attractions has again been increased with particular emphasis on the UK and Ireland sections.

The guide covers numerous natural attractions such as Copacabana Beach as well as many manmade attractions such as Alton Towers. Columbus Travel Guides believes that the attractions listed are representative of many of the world's unique places and thus demonstrate some of the motivating factors encouraging today's generation of travellers.

Top cultural and sporting events in major cities around the world have also been revised and updated for this edition of the guide. We have listed over 200 top events and festivals from around the world, ranging from Edinburgh's Hogmanay to India's Pushkar Fair. The list is by no means inclusive of all annual events which take place around the world; it is nonetheless a comprehensive list of major events which take place on an annual basis in some of today's most important tourist destinations.

Columbus Travel Guides would like to thank the many tourist offices, embassies, high commissions, consulates, chambers of commerce and public relations departments that assisted in the preparation of this edition. If there is anything that you would like to see expanded, clarified or included for the first time, or if you come across any information that needs adjustment, please write to:

The Editor
Tourist Attractions & Events of the World
Columbus Travel Guides, Media House, Azalea Drive,
Swanley, Kent BR8 8HU
Tel: +44 (0) 1322 616344   Fax: +44 (0) 1322 616323
E-mail: travel.editor@nexusmedia.com

ISBN: 1-902221-91-5

Columbus Travel Publishing Limited
Media House
Azalea Drive
Swanley, Kent BR8 8HU
Tel: (01322) 616344
Fax: (01322) 616323
E-mail: booksales@nexusmedia.com

Editor:	Dominic Tombs
Editorial Consultant:	Graeme Payne
Research:	Graham Johnson, Gemma Palmer
Sales & Marketing:	Martin Newman
Production:	Mile Budimir, Micheal Popejoy, Nigel Tansley
Cartographer:	David Burles
Publisher:	Pete Korniczky
Printed & bound by	UP Group, Lithuania

Contents

Key to symbols used in all entries:	£.......Entry charged	P.......Parking
	&.......Disabled access	✗.......Restaurant
	▟.......Man-made attraction	⛬.......Shop
	❤ ....Natural attraction	🏛 ......UNESCO site

Contents

Contents

Contents

Contents

Contents

United Kingdom - Isle of Man

United Kingdom - Northern Ireland

United Kingdom - Scotland

Contents

United Kingdom - Wales

USA - Arizona

USA - California

Contents

Contents

Andorra

1 Caldea

Tourist Information

Andorra Tourist Office
Tourist Office of Andorra la Vella, Plaça de la Rotonda, Andorra la Vella, CP: AD500
Tel: (376) 827 117
Website: www.andorra.ad

Andorra Tourist Delegation
63 Westover Road, London SW18 2RF
Tel: (020) 8874 4806
Website: www.andorra.ad

Caldea

Benefiting from its location nestled between Spain and France in the heart of the Pyrenees, Andorra has a world-renowned reputation for its clean mountain air and spa treatments. Built at an altitude of 1,100m (3,600ft) on a site measuring 25,000 sq m (269,100 sq ft), *Caldea* is the largest

spa centre in Southern Europe. Treatments and facilities at the centre include spas, high pressure indoor and outdoor jacuzzis, saunas, hammam, UVA cabins, massages and a whole programme of facial and body treatments. There's also a water bar and a nighttime underwater music and light show. The site also boasts cafes, bars and a gastronomic restaurant. Caldea is open all year round and is a popular place to cool off in the summer and a welcome distraction from the ski slopes in the winter.

Transportation
Air: Barcelona International Airport in Spain and Toulouse-Blagnac Airport and Perpignan Airport in France. **Rail:** There are no direct rail services to Andorra. **Road:** Bus: Daily services from Spain and France to Andorra then public services to Caldea.

Contact Addresses
Caldea, Parc de la Mola, 10 Escaldes-Engordany, Andorra
Tel: (376) 800 995
Website: www.caldea.ad

Caldea

Tourist Office of Andorra la Vella©

Argentina

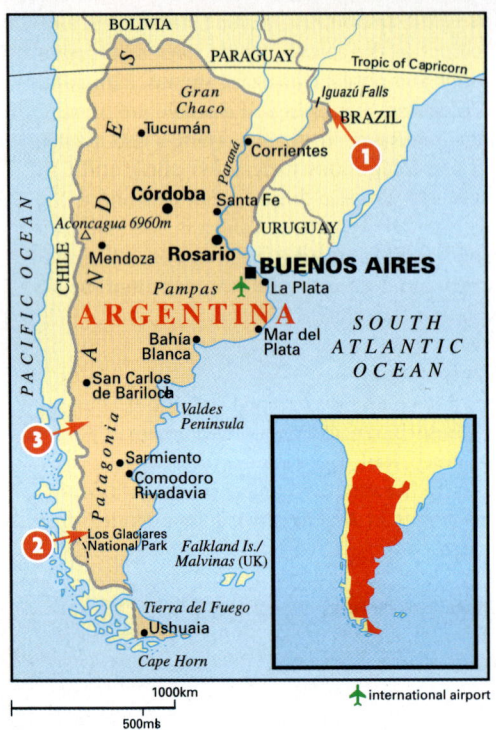

1000km
500mls

✈ international airport

1 Iguazú Falls
  (Cataratas del Iguazú)
2 Los Glaciares National Park (Parque
  Nacional Los Glaciares)
3 Nahuel Huapi National Park
  (Parque Nacional Nahuel Huapi)

Tourist Information

National Tourist Board
(Secretaría de Turismo de la Nación)
Calle Suipacha 1111, 20º, 1368 Buenos Aires,
Argentina
Tel: (011) 4312 5621
Website: www.turismo.gov.ar

Embassy of the Argentine Republic
65 Brooke Street, London W1K 4AH, UK
Tel: (020) 7318 1300
Website: www.argentine-embassy-uk.org

Iguazú Falls
(Cataratas del Iguazú)

The *Iguazú Falls* fittingly receive their name from
the Guarani Indian word meaning 'great waters'.
Surrounded by the virgin jungle of *Iguazú National
Park*, which is home to 2000 species of flora and
400 species of bird, the *Paraná River* divides into
275 separate falls. The highest, the *Garganta del
Diabolo* (Devil's Throat) reaches 70m (230ft),
which is one-and-a-half times the height of the
Niagara Falls. Besides taking in the stunning view
from a series of catwalks, visitors may enjoy
kayaking, canoeing and other watersports. Historic
Jesuit Mission ruins nearby, such as those at *San
Ignacio Miní*, are also popular.

Transportation
Air: Ministro Pistarini Airport (Buenos Aires).
Road: Coach: Services to bus terminal from
Buenos Aires.

Contact Addresses
Iguazú National Park, Victoria Aguirre 66,
3370 Puerto Iguazú, Misiones, Argentina
Tel: (037) 5742 0722 *or* 5742 0180 *or*
5742 0382
Website: www.parquesnacionales.gov.ar

Los Glaciares National Park
(Parque Nacional Los Glaciares)

Los Glaciares National Park is the second largest
in Argentina and runs for 170km (106 miles)
along the border with Chile; it is characterised
by rugged mountains and clear lakes. Some 40
per cent of the Park's 6600 sq km (2548 sq
miles) is covered by vast ice fields that hold 47
major glaciers. The largest glacier is *Upsala*, but
the most popular is the mighty *Moreno* glacier,
where massive chunks of ice shear off and fall
into *Lago Argentino*, the largest lake in
Argentina, to form icebergs. Visitors can view
the advancing Moreno glacier from catwalks and
platforms.

Transportation
Air: Ministro Pistarini Airport (Buenos Aires) or El Calafate International Airport. **Road:** Coach: Services to the bus terminal on Avenida Julia Roca (from El Calafate); services to El Calafate (from Río Gallegos). Car: Provincial Route 5, National Route 40 and Provincial Route 11 (from Río Gallegos).

Contact Addresses
Los Glaciares National Park, 1302, Libertador Avenue, Z94054AHG - Els Calafate, Santa Cruz, Argentina
Tel: (02) 491 005 *or* 491 755 *or* 491 026
Website: www.parquesnacionales.gov.ar *or* www.losglaciares.com

Nahuel Huapi National Park (Parque Nacional Nahuel Huapi)

In 1903 Dr Francisco P Moreno donated 710,000 hectares (1,754,386 acres) of land which became a state national park known as *Nacional del Sur* (Southern National Park). In 1934 it was renamed *Nahuel Huapi National Park* which comes from the Mapuche language, Nahuel meaning 'tiger' and Huapi meaning 'island'. The park offers trekkers and sightseers many areas of natural beauty, including an extinct volcano called *Tronador*, alpine meadows and amazing fauna. The sprawling glacial lake, Lake Nahuel Huapi, stretches over 100km (63 miles) to the border with Chile; the lake contains a nature reserve, the Isla Victoria, which can be reached by private or organised boat trips.

Transportation
Air: Ministro Pistarini Airport (Buenos Aires).
Road: Coach: Services from San Carlos de Bariloche.

Contact Addresses
Nahuel Huapi National Park, 24 San Martin St, (8400) San Carlos de Bariloche, Rio Negro, Argentina
Tel/Fax: (029) 4442 3121/11 *or* 4442 2366
Website: www.parquesnacionale.gov.br

Australia

Map of Australia

INDONESIA

TIMOR SEA

Melville I.

Darwin ✈

Cape York

PAPUA NEW GUINEA

INDIAN OCEAN

Wyndham

Arnhem Land

Katherine

Gulf of Carpentaria

Great Barrier Reef

CORAL SEA

Kimberley

Broome

Halls Creek

NORTHERN TERRITORY

Cairns ✈

Port Hedland

Tennant Creek

Great Sandy Desert

Townsville

Mackay

North West Cape

AUSTRALIA

Mount Isa

Flinders

QUEENSLAND

Tropic of Capricorn

Alice Springs

Rockhampton

Gascoyne

Gibson Desert

△ Uluru (Ayers Rock)

Simpson Desert

Diamantina

Longreach

Fraser I.

Carnarvon

WESTERN AUSTRALIA

Great Victoria Desert

Charleville

Sunshine Coast

Geraldton

Coober Pedy

Lake Eyre

Cooper Ck.

Brisbane ✈

Gold Coast

Kalgoorlie

Nullarbor Plain

SOUTH AUSTRALIA

Darling

Bourke

Port Macquarie

Perth ✈
Fremantle

Port Augusta

Broken Hill

NEW SOUTH WALES

Esperance

Great Australian Bight

Port Lincoln

Barossa Valley

Blue Mtns.

Newcastle
Sydney

Albany

Kangaroo I.

Adelaide ✈

Murray

Wollongong

■**CANBERRA**
AUSTRALIAN CAPITAL TERRITORY

VICTORIA

SOUTHERN OCEAN

Geelong

Melbourne ✈

1000km

Bass Strait

TASMAN SEA

500mls

Launceston

TASMANIA

Hobart ✈

✈ international airport

Northern Territory Rock Art

Tourist Information

Australian Tourist Commission
PO Box 2721, Sydney, NSW 2001, Australia
Tel: (02) 9360 1111
Website: www.australia.com

Tourism Australia
Australia Centre, Australia House, 6th Floor,
Melbourne Place, The Strand, London
WC2B 4LG, UK
Tel: (020) 7438 4601
Website: www.tourism.australia.com *or*
www.australia.com

Key to symbols: £ Entry charged & Disabled access
⌦ Man-made attraction ❤ Natural attraction
P Parking ✕ Restaurant ⌂ Shop 🏛 UNESCO site

Australian Capital Territory

NEW SOUTH WALES
• Hall
Lake George
Murrumbidgee
Bungendore •
CANBERRA ①
Lake Burley-Griffin
Tidbinbilla Deep Space Tracking Station
Queanbeyan
AUSTRALIAN CAPITAL TERRITORY
Molonglo
• Tharwa
Captains Flat
Brindabella Range
Namadgi National Park
△ Bimberi Peak 1910m
Kosciuszko National Park
Michelago •
NEW SOUTH WALES
Queanbeyan
Great Dividing Range

20km
10mls

 airport

1 National Gallery of Australia

National Gallery of Australia

The *National Gallery of Australia* houses many of Australia's finest art collections, and boasts a selection of indigenous works. The gallery, which opened in 1982, has a permanent art collection which is home to more than 100,000 works and is also home to regular international art and photography exhibitions. There is also a beautiful landscaped garden located in the grounds between the gallery and the banks of Lake Burley Griffin, where many sculptures are on permanent display.

Transportation
Air: Canberra International Airport. **Rail:** Train: Canberra Station. **Road:** Car: The gallery is situated in central Canberra, on the banks of Lake Burley Griffin.

Contact Addresses
National Gallery of Australia, GPO Box 1150, Canberra, ACT 2601, Australia
Tel: (02) 6240 6502
Website: www.nga.gov.au

National Gallery of Australia

Tourism Australia©

New South Wales

QUEENSLAND

NEW SOUTH WALES

SOUTH AUSTRALIA

Lismore
Moree
Cofs Harbour
Bourke
Tamworth
Brolen Hill
Dubbo
Port Macquarie
Willandra Lakes
Orange
Hunter Valley
Newcastle
Wentworth
Lachlan
Blue Mtns.
Wyong
Parramatta
Grifith
Sydney
Murrumbidgee
Wollongong
Riverina
Jervis Bay
Murray
Albury
A.C.T.
CANBERRA
△ Mt Kosciuszko 2230m
TASMAN SEA
VICTORIA
Cape Howe
Melbourne
Geelong
Frankston

600km
300mls

✈ international airport
◉ state capital

1 AMP Centerpoint Tower
2 Sydney Harbour Bridge and The Rocks
3 Sydney Opera House

AMP Centerpoint Tower

Standing at 305m (1001ft) high, *Sydney Tower* is the tallest building in Sydney. Located in the Central Business District in the heart of the city, visitors can experience amazing views across *Sydney Harbour* and as far as the *Blue Mountains* from the *Observation Deck*. The tower, which was completed in 1981, also has a revolving restaurant offering 360° views. Visitors can also experience the *OzTrek* attraction, a simulated journey showcasing Australia's culture, history and geography. This experience includes a storytelling room; a room with a small stage with moving

models of Australian landscapes and holograms; and a fake Aboriginal cave with appropriate sounds and melodies. The Sydney Tower itself forms part of the Westfield Centrepoint complex which is home to around 140 shops, as well as the Centrepoint Convention and Exhibition Centre.

Transportation
Air: Sydney (Kingsford Smith) Airport. **Rail:** Monorail: City Centre Station. **Bus:** Public services.

Contact Addresses
Sydney Tower, Podium Level, Westfield Centrepoint, 100 Market Street, Sydney NSW 2000, Australia
Tel: (02) 9223 1341
Website: www.sydneyskytour.com.au

🅿 ✗ 🧺 ♿ £ 🏭

Sydney Harbour Bridge and The Rocks

Sydney Harbour Bridge is one of the most famous man-made structures in the world, and is undoubtedly one of Sydney's most recognisable icons. The bridge, affectionately known as 'the Coathanger', took 1400 workers (16 of whom were killed in the process) eight years to complete and was officially opened in 1932. Thrill-seekers can do the *BRIDGECLIMB* - a guided walk to the top of the 50-storey-high bridge, over the cars and trains rumbling across the deck below. The area at the foot of the bridge is known as *The Rocks* and is recognised as Sydney's historical birthplace. The area was the site of the first landing from

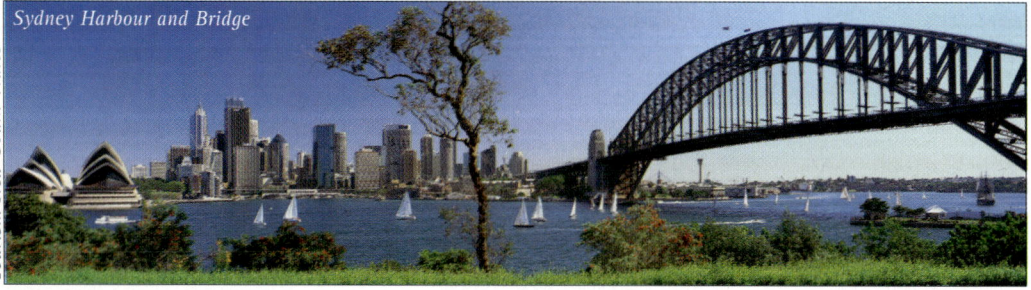

Sydney Harbour and Bridge

Tourism New South Wales©

Sydney Opera House

Tourism New South Wales©

Plymouth, England in 1788; today The Rocks is a busy area consisting of cafés, restaurants, galleries, museums and countless souvenir shops. Historic buildings in the district include the *Museum of Contemporary Art*, *Merchants' House*, *Garrison Church* and *Susannah Place*.

Transportation
Air: Sydney Airport. **Rail:** Train: Circular Quay Station. **Bus:** Public services.

Contact Addresses
BRIDGECLIMB: 5 Cumberland Street, The Rocks, Sydney NSW 2000, Australia
Tel: (02) 8274 7777
Website: www.bridgeclimb.com

Pylon Lookout: South East Pylon, Sydney Harbour Bridge, Sydney NSW 2000, Australia
Tel: (02) 9240 1100
Website: www.pylonlookout.com.au

The Rocks: Sydney Visitor Centre, 106 George Street, The Rocks, NSW 2000, Sydney, Australia
Tel: (02) 9240 8788
Website: www.rocksvillage.com *or*
www.sydneyvisitorcentre.com *or*
www.viewsydney.com

Sydney Opera House

Opened in 1973, the *Sydney Opera House* is the most recognisable symbol of both the city of Sydney and the country of Australia, and is also considered one of the 20th century's great buildings. Revolutionary in concept, the building's Danish architect, Jørn Utzon, designed the building to resemble a ship at sea with its roof appearing as a billowing white sail. It is one of the busiest performing arts centres in the world, housing a large complex of theatres and halls that play host to a wide range of performing arts. Located on Bennelong Point, the Opera House, which offers spectacular views of Sydney Harbour, is visited by more than 4.5 million tourists every year. Various tours – including the Front of House and Backstage areas – can be taken.

Transportation
Air: Sydney Airport. **Rail:** Train: Circular Quay Station. **Road:** Bus: Public services.

Contact Addresses
Sydney Opera House, Bennelong Point, GPO Box 4274, Sydney NSW 2001, Australia
Tel: (02) 9250 7111
Website: www.sydneyoperahouse.com

Northern Territory

TIMOR SEA
Cobourg
Peninsula
ARAFURA SEA
Bathurst I.
Melville I.
Wessel
Islands
Darwin
Maningrida
Nhulumbuy
① Kakadu
Nat.
Park
Gulf of
Carpentaria
Daly
Arnhem
Land
Groote
Eylandt
Katherine
Katherine Gorge
Roper
Ngukurr
Timber
Creek
Mataranaka
Sir Edward
Pellow Group
Victoria
River
Downs
Daly
Waters
Borroloola
Barkly
Tableland
Tanami
Desert
Tennant
Creek
NORTHERN
TERRITORY
Devils Marbles
Lake
Mackay
Ti Tree
Mt Zeil
1510m
Macdonnell Ranges
Alice Springs
Tropic of
Capricorn
Yulara
Mt Olga
1069m
Uluru
(Ayers Rock)
867m
Kulgera
Simpson
Desert
② SOUTH AUSTRALIA
WESTERN AUSTRALIA
QUEENSLAND
Georgina
Victoria
Ord

400km
200mls

✈ international airport
◉ state capital

1 Kakadu National Park
2 Uluru-Kata Tjuta National Park

Kakadu National Park

Located in Australia's tropical Northern Territory and stretching from Arnhem Land in the east to Katherine Gorge in the south, *Kakadu National Park* is one of the few UNESCO World Heritage Sites to be listed for both natural and cultural reasons. Many believe the park has been continuously inhabited for up to 40,000 years, and rock paintings and other archaeological sites testify to the Aboriginal history of the region. Kakadu is also home to many different species of plant and animals. Covering an area of 2 million hectares (4.9 million acres), the park is still home to around 300 Aboriginals today and encompasses river floodplains, savannah woodlands, rich tidal wetlands and sandstone escarpments.

Transportation
Air: Darwin International Airport. **Road:** Coach: Coach tours operate between Darwin, Jabiru and Cooinda. Car: Arnhem Highway off the Stuart Highway leads from Darwin to Jabiru. Kakadu Highway leads into the park (from Jabiru).

Contact Addresses
Kakadu National Park, PO Box 71, Jabiru, NT 0886, Australia
Tel: (08) 8938 1120
Website: www.deh.gov.au/parks/kakadu

Uluru-Kata Tjuta National Park

Uluru-Kata Tjuta National Park is home to one of Australia's most popular tourist attractions and best-known national symbols: *Uluru*, which means 'great pebble' in the Aboriginal language. Formerly known as *Ayers Rock*, Uluru is a 3.6km-long (2.2 mile-), 348m-high (1142ft-) smooth chunk of sandstone that rises abruptly out of the sandy scrubland. It is the world's largest rock monolith and the most famous natural landmark in Australia. The rock also holds deep significance for the local Aboriginal people who believe it was formed during the creation period. The nearby *Kata Tjuta*, meaning 'many heads' and formerly known as *The Olgas*, is a series of 36 massive rock domes and a system of gorges and valleys. Visitors can walk through the *Valley of the Winds* and the *Olga Gorge*, and also visit the *Uluru-Kata Tjuta Cultural Centre*.

Transportation
Air: Darwin International Airport, Connellan Airport. **Rail:** Train: Alice Springs Station. **Road:** Bus: Services from Uluru. Car: Stuart Highway from either Darwin (in the north) or Alice Springs (in the south), then signs to Uluru-Kata Tjuta.

Contact Addresses
Uluru-Kata Tjuta National Park, PO Box 119, Yulara, NT 0872, Australia
Tel: (08) 8956 2299
Website: www.deh.gov.au/parks/uluru

Queensland

1 Fraser Island
2 Great Barrier Reef

Map labels:
Torres Strait
PAPUA NEW GUINEA
Bamag
Cape York Peninsula
Gulf of Carpentaria
Cape Melville
CORAL SEA
Great Barrier Reef
Cooktown
Wellesley Is.
Cairns 2
Mt Bartle Frere 1612m
Hinchinbrook I.
Normanton
Great Dividing Range
Townsville 1
Mount Isa
Whitsunday Is.
Proserpine
Hughenden
Mackay
Georgina
Flinders
Boulia
QUEENSLAND
NORTHERN TERRITORY
Rockhampton
Tropic of Capricorn
Diamantina
Longreach
Thomson
Gladstone
Birdsville
Channel Country
Charleville
Bundaberg
Fraser Island
SOUTH AUSTRALIA
Balonne
Gympie
Sunshine Coast
Lake Eyre
Brisbane
Ipswich
Gold Coast
NEW SOUTH WALES

800km
400mls

✈ international airport
◉ state capital

Fraser Island

Stretching over 120km (75 miles) from tip-to-tip and covering an area of 165,280 hectares (408,423 acres), *Fraser Island* is the largest sand island in the world. Located of Australia's East Coast in the state of *Queensland*, Fraser Island was listed as a UNESCO World Heritage site in 1992. Characterised by its stunning freshwater lakes, coloured sand cliffs, lush rainforests growing in the sand, secluded creeks and long, white sandy beaches, the idyllic island attracts thousands of visitors each year who come on 4x4-led camping trips or to stay in lodges including the new award-winning eco lodge, *Kingfisher Bay*, built on the island's west coast. The island is also famous for its resident populations of dingoes that are said to be Australia's purest breed. Aside from its swimming holes, creeks and stunning natural beauty, other attractions on the island include the rusting wreck of the *Maheno* ship which ran aground during a cyclone in 1935 and the former logging camp of *Central Station* that's now home to an exhibition about the island's unique environment. Day trips to the island are possible but many people choose to spend a few nights on this idyllic natural phenomenon.

Fraser Island

Fraser Coast South Burnett Regional Tourism Board©

Transportation

Air: Brisbane Airport (international arrivals).
Hervey Bay Airport (domestic services) **Water:**
Ferry: Services from Hervey Bay. **Rail:**
Maryborough Station then travel by bus or taxi
on to Hervey Bay. **Road:** Bus: Public services to
Hervey Bay then ferry to Fraser Island.

Contact Addresses

Maryborough Fraser Island Visitor Information
Centre, Maryborough South Travel Shop, Bruce
Highway, Maryborough, Queensland, 4650 Australia
Tel: (07) 4121 4111
Website: www.maryborough.qld.gov.au

Great Barrier Reef

The *Great Barrier Reef* is the most famous marine-
protected area in the world and the largest
UNESCO World Heritage area. Covering a
geographical area of 35 million hectares (86
million acres) and stretching approximately
2300km (1429 miles) along the coast of
northeastern Australia from *Bundaberg* to *Cape
York*, the Reef is bigger in size than the states of
Victoria and Tasmania combined. The Great
Barrier Reef is the largest coral reef system in the
world and home to approximately 400 different
types of coral. It is also an area of outstanding
natural beauty and home to around 1500 different
species of fish, 4000 types of mollusc and many
endangered species. There are also more than 30
historic shipwrecks in the area and a number of
archaeological sites which are of Aboriginal
origin. In 2005, more coral reefs were discovered
in the *Gulf of Carpentaria* off Australia's north
coast.

Transportation

Air: Brisbane Airport, Cairns Airport; many
domestic airlines fly to national airports located
closer to the Reef on the Australian mainland.
Water: The Great Barrier Reef can only be reached
by boat; tour operators can arrange transfer from
mainland Australia to resort islands.

Contact Addresses

Great Barrier Reef Marine Park Authority, 2-68
Flinders Street, PO Box 1379, Townsville,
Queensland 4810, Australia
Tel: (07) 4750 0700
Website: www.gbrmpa.gov.au

The Great Barrier Reef

Tourism Queensland©

Tasmania

1 Port Arthur

Port Arthur

Port Arthur is a former penal colony which originally opened as a timber station in 1830. It became a prison settlement for male convicts in 1833 and quickly gained a reputation for being 'hell-on-earth'. Convicts ranged from boys as young as nine through to hardened criminals. The prison closed in 1877 and was renamed *Carnarvon* in an attempt to lose its former associations; however, in 1927 it was reinstated as Port Arthur. Today, the prison is open to the public and visitors can take part in guided tours and harbour cruises. There is also an interpretation gallery where visitors can find out about some of the convicts that were sentenced there.

Transportation

Air: Hobart International Airport. **Road:** Coach: Tigerline and Experience Tasmania operate day tours (from Hobart). Car: Reached by scenic drive, which takes approximately 1.5 hours along the Tasman and Arthur highways.

Contact Addresses

Visitor Centre, Port Arthur Historic Site, Port Arthur, Tasmania 7182, Australia

Tel: (1800) 659 101
Website: www.portarthur.org.au

Port Arthur Penitentiary

Tourism Australia©

Key to symbols used in all entries:

£ ....Entry charged
& ....Disabled access
🏭 ....Man-made attraction
✓ ....Natural attraction
🅿 ....Parking
✗ ....Restaurant
🏪 ....Shop
🏛 ..UNESCO site

Austria

Tourist Information

Österreich Werbung (Austrian National Tourist Office - ANTO)
Margaretenstrasse 1, 1040 Vienna, Austria
Tel: (01) 588 660 (information)
Website: www.austria.info

Austrian National Tourist Office (ANTO)
9-11 Richmond Buildings, London W1D 3HE, UK
Tel: (0845) 101 1818
Website: www.austria-tourism.at

Belvedere Palace (Österreichishce Galerie Belvedere)

Belvedere Palace, situated right in the heart of Vienna, is Austria's most famous art gallery and home to *der Kuss* (The Kiss) which was painted by Gustav Klimt. There are two permanent collections – *Oberes Belvedere* (Upper Belvedere) and *Unteres Belvedere* (Lower Belvedere) – in the Palace. The palace was built by Lukas von Hildebrandt between 1714 and 1723 as a summer residence for Prince Eugene of Savoy. The two museums house an impressive collection of Austrian art from the Middle Ages through to the 20th century. Today, the Upper Belvedere is home to the Austrian Gallery and works by Renoir, Monet, Klimt,

Belvedere Palace

Österreichische Galerie Belvedere©

Kokoschka and Schiele, whilst the Lower Belvedere houses the Baroque Museum and the Museum of Medieval Austrian Art.

Transportation
Air: Vienna International Airport. **Rail:** Underground: Südtirolerplatz or Taubstummengasse. Tram: Public services. **Road:** Bus: Service to Südbahnhof.

Contact Addresses
Österreichische Galerie Belvedere, Prinz Engen-Strasse 27, 1030 Vienna, Austria
Tel: (01) 7955 7134
Website: www.belvedere.at

Giant Ferris Wheel (Riesenrad)

Located in the giant wooded park and fairground known as the *Prater*, Vienna's *Giant Ferris Wheel* is one of Austria's best-known and best-loved landmarks. The Ferris Wheel was completed in 1897 at a time when other such ferris wheels stood in cities like London, Paris and Blackpool, but it is the only one of its era still surviving. Constructed to celebrate the 50th jubilee of Emperor Franz Joseph I, several unusual events have taken place on the wheel, most notably the suicide of local resident Marie Kindl, who hanged herself from the window of a car in 1898 to draw attention to the economical plight of her family. After dark, the wheel lights up and acts as a giant clock for the city by flashing the correct number of times on the hour.

Transportation
Air: Vienna International Airport. **Rail:** Train: S-Bahn to Wien Nord (Praterstern) from Wien Mitte. Underground: Praterstern. Tram: Public services. **Road:** Bus: Wien Prater. Car: Signs for Vienna city centre, then take Praterstrasse.

Contact Addresses
Wiener Riesenrad, Prater 90, 1020, Vienna, Austria
Tel: (01) 729 5430
Website: www.wienerriesenrad.com

Hofburg Palace (Hofburg)

The *Hofburg Palace* was home to the Austrian Hapsburg emperors until 1918. The palace buildings have been constantly added to for over 800 years, with the first fortifications being erected by King Ottakar Premysl in the 13th century. Today, the palace serves as a repository of Austrian culture and history, embracing 22 separate museums, a 14th-century Augustinian church, the famous *Spanische Hofreitschule* (Spanish Riding School), the *Österreichische Nationalbibliothek* (National Library), as well as the president's offices. The most popular of the museums is the *Kaiserappartements*, which takes visitors on a tour of the Kaiser's Imperial apartments. The *Vienna Boys' Choir* sings Sunday mass at the Royal Chapel.

Transportation
Air: Vienna International Airport. **Rail:** Underground: Herrengasse. Tram: B-line to Burgtor. **Road:** Bus: Services to Michaelerplatz. Car: A1 Westautobahn or A2 Südautobahn to the city centre.

Contact Addresses
Hofburg, Michaelerkuppel, 1010 Vienna, Austria
Tel: (01) 533 7570
Website: www.schoenbrunn.at/en

Mozart's Birthplace and Residence (Mozarts Geburtshaus und Mozarts Wohnhaus)

Born Joannes Christosomos Wolfgang Theophulis Mozart to Leopold and Anna Maria Mozart on January 27 1756, Mozart is one of the most famous musicians of all times. The musical genius was born in *Getreidegasse 9* in Salzburg, known today as *Mozarts Geburtshaus* (Mozart's Birthplace), where the family lived from 1747 until 1773 when the family moved to a house in *Makartplatz* which is known today as *Mozart Wohnhaus* (Mozart's Residence), where they remained until 1787. Both houses are now popular museums. Most of Mozart's Residence was destroyed by a bomb in 1944; the building has however been restored to its original glory by the Mozarteum Foundation.

Museum of Fine Art

Kunsthistorisches Museum©

gallery) contains works by Rubens, Rembrandt, Vermeer, Dürer and Titian, and the largest collection of work by Brueghel in the world.

Transportation
Air: Vienna International Airport. **Rail:** Underground: Volkstheater. Tram: Tram D to Burging/ Kunsthistorisches Museum (from Südbahnof); U3 tram to Volkstheater (from Westbahnof). **Road:** Bus: Public services. Car: A1 Westautobahn or the A2 Sudautobahn to the city centre.

Contact Addresses
Kunsthistorisches Museum, Main Building, Maria-Theresien-Platz, 1010 Vienna, Austria
Tel: (01) 525 24-590
Website: www.khm.at

P ✗ 🧺 ♿ £ 🏭

Schonbrunn Palace (Schloss Schönbrunn)

One of the most renowned Baroque structures in Europe, *Schönbrunn Palace* began life as a hunting lodge during the 16th century, but was turned into a lavish palace by the Empress Maria Theresa in 1750. Home to the Hapsburg emperors from the 18th century to 1918, the palace was built by the architects Johann Bernhard Fischer von Erlach and Nicolaus Pacassi. A tour offers visitors the chance to admire the site's opulent elegance, including the famous ceiling frescoes of the *Great Gallery*, and the *Hall of Mirrors* where Mozart played. The Baroque grounds include a *Flower Garden*, *Tiergarten* (a zoo dating from 1752) and a reproduction of a maze created at the beginning of the 18th century.

Transportation
Air: Vienna International Airport. **Rail:** Train: Schönbrunn Station. Underground: Schönbrunn. **Road:** Bus: Public services to Schönbrunn. Car: Ostautobahn from the airport towards Vienna, then the A23 (Sudosttangente) towards Graz.

Contact Addresses
Schloss Schönbrunn Kultur und Betriebs GmbH, Schloss Schönbrunn, 1130 Vienna, Austria
Tel: (01) 8111 3239
Website: www.schoenbrunn.at

Transportation
Air Salzburg Airport. **Rail:** Train: Salzburg Central Station.

Contact Addresses
Mozarts Geburtshaus, Getreidegasse 9, 5020 Salzburg, Austria
Tel: (06) 6284 4313

Mozart Wohnhaus, Makartplatz 8, 5020 Salzburg, Austria
Tel: (06) 62874 22740

🏛 £ 🏭

Museum of Fine Art (Kunsthistorisches Museum)

Opened in 1891 to house the imperial family's vast art collection, *Vienna's Museum of Fine Art* was designed by Gottfried von Semper and Karl Hasenauer. It was built in the style of the Italian Renaissance to firmly establish the building's link with one of history's great artistic periods. Today, the museum, which is located in *Marie-Theresien-Platz,* holds one of the most important art collections in the world. The *Gemäldegalerie* (picture

P ✗ 🧺 ♿ 🏛 £ 🏭

Azerbaijan

Azerbaijan man with craft items

1 Walled City of Baku

Tourist Information

Azerbaijan Ministry of Foreign Affairs
4 Shykhali Qurbanov Street, 1009 Baku,
Azerbaijan
Tel: (12) 492 9692
Website: http://azerbaijan.tourism.az

Embassy of the Azerbaijan Republic
4 Kensington Court, London W8 5DL, UK
Tel: (020) 7938 3412
Website: http://azerbaijan.tourism.az

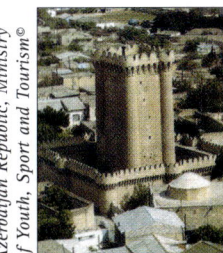

Walled City of Baku

Located on the western shore
of the *Caspian Sea*, the
ancient *Walled City of Baku* in
the Azerbaijani capital of
Baku was inscribed on the
UNESCO World Heritage list
along with the *Shirvanshah's*
Palace and Maiden Tower in 2000. The walled fort
is built on a site inhabited since the Palaeolithic
Period (thought to be between 100,000BC and
30,000BC) and archaeologists have found evidence
of Zoroastrian, Sassanian, Arabic, Persian,
Shirvani, Ottoman and Russian influences. The
Shirvanshah's Palace was built in the 12th century
by the Shirvanshah Dynasty who moved their
capital to Baku from *Shamakha* after an
earthquake. Baku developed as an important
trading port and was captured and conquered by
many warring empires before finally becoming the
capital of Azerbaijan in 1920. The Walled City is
the old part of the Baku and its maze of alleyways
and ancient buildings still thrive with life today
with the modern city fanning out around it.

Transportation
Air: Baku International Airport. **Water:** Ferry:
Passenger ferry. **Rail:** Baku City Train Station.
Underground services. **Road:** Bus: Public services.

Contact Addresses
For more information on the Walled City of Baku,
contact the Ministry of Foreign Affairs (see
Tourist Information above).

Bahrain

1 Bahrain Fort   2 Barbar Temple

Tourist Information

Bahrain Tourism Company
PO Box 5831, Manama, Bahrain
Tel: (17) 530 530
Website: www.alseyaha.com

Embassy of the Kingdom of Bahrain
30 Belgrave Square, London SW1X 8QB
Tel: (020) 7201 9170
Website: www.bahraintourism.com

Bahrain Fort (Qal'at al-Bahrain)

Excavations at the *Bahrain Fort* began in 1950 and uncovered a tell – an artificial mound created by several layers of human occupation. Research at the site has shown that the earliest habitation dates back to approximately 2300BC with evidence of continuous habitation through until the 16th century when the fort was constructed by the Portuguese to protect their island possessions.

The site was once an important trading port and is now a UNESCO World Heritage site.

Transportation
Air: Bahrain International Airport. **Water:** Ferry: Public services. Rail: Currently no rail network but plans to build one are under way. **Road:** Bus: Public services.

Contact Addresses
For more information on the Bahrain Fort, contact the Bahrain Tourism Company (see **Tourist Information** above).

Barbar Temple

Located in the village of *Barbar*, the most recent of the three Barbar temples was rediscovered by a Danish archaeological team in 1954. A further two temples were discovered on the site with the oldest dating back to 3000BC. The three temples were built atop one another with the second built approximately 500 years later and the third added between 2100BC and 2000BC. It's thought that the temples were constructed to worship the God Enki, the god of wisdom and freshwater, and his wife Nankhur Sak. The temple contains two altars and a natural water spring that is thought to have held spiritual significance for the worshippers. During the excavation of the site many tools, weapons, pottery and small pieces of gold were found which are now on display in the *Bahrain National Museum* (www.bnmuseum.com).

Transportation
Air: Bahrain International Airport. **Water:** Ferry: Public services. **Rail:** Currently no rail network but plans to build one are under way. **Road:** Bus: Public services.

Contact Addresses
For more information on the Barbar Temple, contact the Bahrain Tourism Company (see **Tourist Information** above).

Bangladesh

100km
50mls

✈ international airport

NEPAL · Darjeeling · BHUTAN

INDIA · Rangpur · Dinajpur

Bogra · Jamalpur · Mymensingh · Sylhet

BANGLADESH · Rajshahi

Pabna · Brahmanbaria · INDIA

Faridpur · ✈ ■DHAKA · Tropic of Cancer

Jessore · Comilla

Khulna

Calcutta · Barisal · Chittagong

Sundarbans

Mouths of the Ganges

Cox's Bazar

Bay of Bengal · MYANMAR

1 Chittagong

Tourist Information

Bangladesh Parjatan Corporation (National Tourism Organisation)
233 Airport Road, Tejgaon, Dhaka-1215, Bangladesh
Tel: (02) 811 7855-9
Website: www.parjatan.org

High Commission for the People's Republic of Bangladesh
28 Queen's Gate, London SW7 5JA, UK
Tel: (020) 7584 0081

Chittagong

Chittagong, the second largest city in Bangladesh, is a port city, set against the blue waters of the

Bay of Bengal and surrounded by green forests, coconut groves and sandy beaches. Attractions include the *Ethnological Museum*, the 17th-century *Shahi Jama-e-Masjid Mosque*, the colourful multi-domed *Chandanpura Mosque* and the *Tomb of Sultan Bayazid Bostami*. *Foy's Lake*, an artificial lake named after the Englishman responsible for its design, is located 8km (5 miles) from Chittagong, and is a popular picnic site. Chittagong is also a good base from which to explore the *Rangamati Hill District*, famous for its beautiful flora and lakes and the predominantly Buddhist tribal culture. Entrance fees are charged for some of the attractions.

Transportation
Air: Chittagong MA Hannan International Airport.
Rail: Train: Chittagong Station.

Contact Addresses
Tourist Information Centre, Motel Shaikat, Station Road, Chittagong, Bangladesh
Tel: (031) 209 845

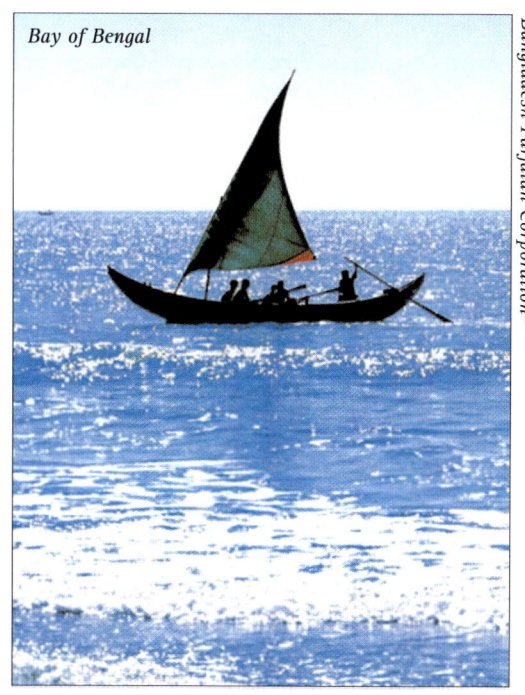

Bay of Bengal

Bangladesh Parjatan Corporation©

Belgium

NORTH SEA
NETHERLANDS
Maas
Zeebrugge
Ostend
Bruges
Antwerp
Ghent
Mechelen
FLANDERS
BRUSSELS
BELGIUM
Liège
Tournai
Meuse
Mons Charleroi
WALLONIA
Namur
Dinant
Ardennes
Arlon
LUX.
FRANCE
GERMANY
Moselle
100km
50mls
✈ international airport

1 Atomium
2 Cathedral of Our Lady (Onze Lieve Vrouwe-Kathedraal)
3 Central Square (Grand' Place)
4 Flanders Fields
5 Statue of the Pissing Boy (Manneken-Pis)

Tourist Information

Belgian Tourist Office – Brussels & Wallonia (Office de Promotion du Tourisme Wallonie-Bruxelles)
30 rue Saint Bernard, 1060 Brussels, Belgium
Tel: (02) 504 0390
Website: www.belgium-tourism.net

Tourism Flanders-Brussels (Toerisme Vlaanderen)
Grasmarkt 63, B-1000 Brussels, Belgium
Tel: (02) 504 0300 or 504 0390
Website: www.visitflanders.com

Belgium Tourist Office – Brussels & Ardennes
217 Marsh Wall, London E14 9FJ, UK
Tel: (0906) 302 0245 (calls cost 60p per minute) or (0800) 954 5245 (brochure request line; toll free UK only)
Tel: (020) 7531 0390
Website: www.belgium-tourism.org
Website: www.belgiumtheplaceto.be

Tourism Flanders-Brussels
1a Cavendish Square, London W1G 0LD, UK
Tel: (0906) 3020 245 (calls cost 60p per minute)
Website: www.visitflanders.co.uk

Atomium

The *Atomium* was designed by engineer André Waterkeyn as a celebration of scientific progress for the 1958 World Fair. The structure stands 102 m (334 ft) high, weighs 2400 metric tonnes (2439 tons), and represents an iron crystalline molecule enlarged 165 billion times. Inside the nine spheres, visitors can see an exhibition showing how the Atomium has been depicted in comic strips through the years and an audiovisual presentation on the construction of the Atomium. There are splendid views across Brussels and the surrounding countryside from the top of the structure.

Transportation
Air: Brussels Airport. **Rail:** Train: Bruxelles Centrale Station. Underground: Heysel. Tram: Public services. **Road:** Bus: Public services. Car: Ring road West (exit 8 Wemmel-Heizel).

Contact Addresses
ASBL Atomium, Atomium Square, 1020 Brussels, Belgium
Tel: (02) 475 47 77
Website: www.atomium.be

Cathedral of Our Lady (Onze Lieve Vrouwe-Kathedraal)

The *Cathedral of our Lady* is the largest Gothic church in the Low Countries and rises to a height of 123m (404ft), piercing the skyline of historic Antwerp. Although construction began on the cathedral in 1352, it was not completed until 1521; the roof and Gothic furniture were then destroyed by fire in 1533. The interior of the cathedral is Baroque in style, the original

Gothic features having been destroyed by religious idealists in the late 16th century. There are many fine works of art in the nave, the most famous being Ruben's 'Descent from the Cross' (1611-14).

Transportation
Air: Brussels Airport or Antwerp Airport. **Rail:** Train: Antwerp Central Station. Tram: Regular public services. **Road:** Car: N1. Bus: Regular public services.

Contact Addresses
Onze Lieve Vrouwe-Kathedraal, Groenplaats 21, 2000 Antwerp, Belgium
Tel: (02) 213 9951
Website: www.dekathedraal.be

Central Square (Grand' Place)

The *Grand' Place* has been at the heart of Brussels' life since the 11th century. Almost totally destroyed by the French bombardment ordered by Louis XIV in 1695, it was later rebuilt in its original architectural style by various workers' guilds. The splendid neo-Gothic and Baroque houses that surround the cobbled square once housed the headquarters of corporations of artists, merchants and tailors; the *City of Brussels Museum* in the former *Maison du Roi* (King's Residence) allows visitors to explore the city's illustrious trading history. Other buildings in the Grand' Place which provide insights into Brussels' traditions are the *Town Hall*, the *Museum of Cocoa and Chocolate* and the *Museum of Brewing*.

Transportation
Air: Brussels Airport. **Rail:** Train: Bruxelles Centrale Station. Underground: Bourse, De Brouckère, Gare Centrale.

Contact Addresses
Office de Tourisme et d'Information de Bruxelles, Hôtel de Ville, Grand-Place, 1000 Brussels, Belgium
Tel: (02) 513 8940
Website: www.belgium-tourism.org

Central Square, Brussels

Corel©

Statue of the Pissing Boy

Belgian Tourist Office©

Flanders Fields

Flanders Fields was the site of around half a million deaths in the horrific trenches of World War I. There are numerous military cemeteries and 'Missing Memorials' in the region commemorating those of all nationalities who fell in battle. Most of the soldiers who perished were the victims of poison gas attacks – the deadly gas *Yperite* was invented in the nearby city of Ypres, which was a renowned trading centre during the Middle Ages but was almost completely destroyed during World War I. At the *In Flanders Fields* museum in Ypres, visitors can discover what it was like to be a soldier in the trenches and learn about major events and aspects of the war such as the first gas attack, the Christmas Truces of 1914, and No Man's Land.

Transportation
Air: Brussels Airport. **Rail:** Train: Ieper/Ypres Station. **Road:** Car: N369 (from Ostend).

Contact Addresses
In Flanders Fields, Lakenhallen – Grote Markt 34, 8900 Ieper, Belgium
Tel: (057) 239 220
Website: www.inflandersfields.be

Statue of the Pissing Boy (Manneken-Pis)

The *Manneken-Pis*, situated in Rue de l'Etuve, is as funny as it is well known. Crowds of tourists patrol the meandering cobbled streets near Brussels' Grand' Place hoping to find this small statuette of a little boy in the midst of a never-ending pee. Sometimes known as 'Little Julian', the statue is, in its own way, a typically Belgian symbol of cultural self-mockery. Since its creation by J Duquesnoy in the 17th century, the Manneken-Pis has attracted a great deal of attention, having been stolen (by the English in 1745 and the French in 1747), vandalised and dressed in over 600 costumes, which are on display at the *City of Brussels Museum*.

Transportation
Air: Brussels Airport. **Rail:** Train: Bruxelles Centrale Station. Underground: Bourse. Tram: Regular services. **Road:** Public services.

Contact Addresses
Office de Tourisme et d'Information de Bruxelles, Hôtel de Ville, Grand-Place, 1000 Brussels, Belgium
Tel: (02) 513 8940
Website: www.belgium-tourism.org

Bolivia

and its shape bears a strong resemblance to this animal when viewed from above. Measuring 194km (121 miles) long and 65km (45 miles) wide, it has been revered in history, featuring prominently in Inca creation myths. There are daily tours to the *Uros* and *Taquile Islands*; the *Uros* people live on floating islands made out of reeds that grow in the lake, while the inhabitants of *Taquile Island* are renowned for maintaining ancient traditions and for their remarkable weaving skills.

Transportation
Air: El Alto Airport (La Paz). **Road:** Bus: Daily services leave La Paz every 30 minutes. Car: From La Paz (journey time: 2.5 hours).

Contact Addresses
For more information on Lake Titicaca, contact the Viceministerio de Turismo (see **Tourist Information** above).

1 Lake Titicaca (Lago Titicaca)

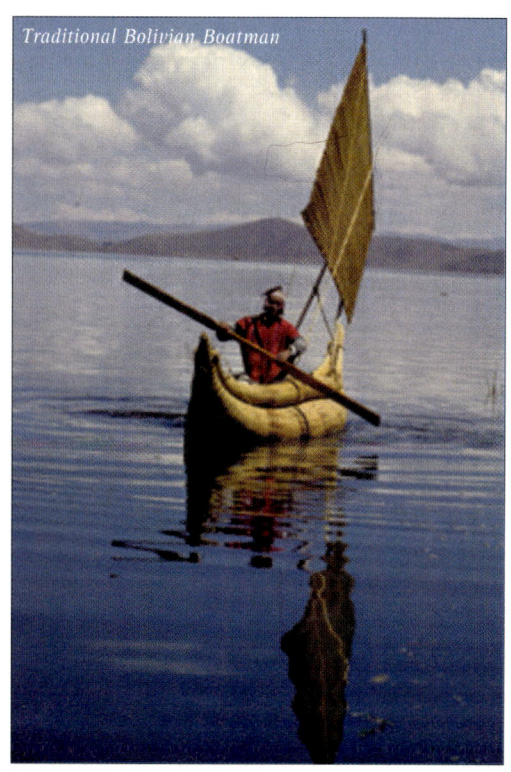

Traditional Bolivian Boatman

Sky Bolivia©

Tourist Information

Bolivian Tourist Board (Viceministerio de Turismo)
Avenida Mariscal Santa Cruz, Palacio de las Comunicaciones, Piso 16, La Paz, Bolivia
Tel: (591) 2 236 6474 or 1665
Website: www.embassyofbolivia.co.uk

Embassy and Consulate of the Republic of Bolivia
106 Eaton Square, London SW1W 9AD, UK
Tel: (020) 7235 4248 or 7235 2257
Website: www.embassyofbolivia.co.uk

Lake Titicaca (Lago Titicaca)

At an elevation of 3810m (12,492ft), *Lake Titicaca* is one of the world's highest navigable lakes. It is named after the native word for 'puma of stone'

Botswana

```
400km
200mls
international airport
```

ZAMBIA

ANGOLA

Okavango   Caprivi Strip   Kasane
Cuando   Zambezi
Mabebe
Depression
Tsodilo
Hills
Okavango
Delta   Maun   ZIMBABWE
Tsau
Ngamiland   Makgadikgadi
Salt Pans
NAMIBIA   Francistown
Ghanzi
B O T S W A N A   Selebi-
Serowe   Phikwe
K A L A H A R I   Palapye   Limpopo
Tropic of Capricorn   Khutse
Tshane   Mochudi
D E S E R T   **GABORONE**
Gemsbok   Kanye
Nat. Park   Lobatse
PRETORIA
Tshabong
Johannesburg
SOUTH AFRICA

1 Moremi Wildlife Reserve

Tourist Information

Department of Tourism

Ministry of Commerce and Industry, Private Bag 0047, Gaborone, Botswana
Tel: 353 024
Website: www.gov.bw/tourism or www.botswanatourism.org.uk

Department of Tourism UK

Representation Office/Botswana Tourism UK c/o Southern Skies Marketing, Old Boundary House, London Road, Sunningdale, Berkshire SL5 0DJ, UK
Tel: (01344) 298 982

Moremi Wildlife Reserve

Botswana's *Moremi Wildlife Reserve* lies in the centre of the Okavango Delta, the largest inland delta in the world. Named after the chief of the Batawana tribe who declared the reserve in 1963, it is characterised by seasonal and permanent swamped areas and covers an area of 3000 sq km (1170 sq miles). The reserve encompasses a wide range of habitats – from wetland, floodplain and reed beds to forest and savannah woodland. The fauna inhabiting the park is abundant and equally diverse, ranging from exotic birds, zebras, buffalo, wildebeest and giraffes to hippos and lions; the only large African mammals not found here are rhino. Boats take visitors to various lagoons, such as Xakanaxa, Gcobega and Gcodikwe, to view game and birdlife. There are many campsites and lodges in the reserve, each with its own viewing possibilities and activities.

Transportation

Air: Maun Airport (internal), Gaborone Sir Seretse Khama International Airport. **Rail:** Train: Francistown Station. **Road:** Car: Main road to Maun, then road to Maqwee via Showobe; from here there are various routes into the park (visitors must have a 4x4 vehicle to enter the reserve and most visitors are accompanied by a qualified guide).

Contact Addresses

Moremi Wildlife Reserve, Department of Wildlife and National Parks, Parks and Reserves Reservation Office, PO Box 131, Gaborone, Botswana
Tel: (267) 598 0774

Aerial view of the Okavango Delta

Botswana Tourism©

Brazil

2000km
1000mls

international airport

1 Copacabana Beach (Praia de Copacabana)

2 Iguazu Falls (Foz do Iguaçú)

3 Statue of Christ the Redeemer (Cristo Redentor)

4 Sugar Loaf Mountain (Pão de Açucar)

Tourist Information

Brazilian Tourist Board (EMBRATUR – Instituto Brasileiro do Turismo)
SCN, Quadra 2, Bloco 'G', CEP 70712-907
Brasília, DF, Brazil
Tel: (061) 429 7773
Website: www.embratur.gov.br

Brazilian Embassy and Tourist Office
32 Green Street, London W1K 7AT, UK
Tel: (020) 7629 6909
Website: www.brazil.org.uk

Copacabana Beach (Praia de Copacabana)

Copacabana Beach is one of the world's most famous beaches. Located right in the heart of Rio de Janeiro, it is also one of the most lively

beaches in the world with thousands of visitors flocking to its 4km (2.5 mile) stretch of sand every year. Located in front of the black and white wavy mosaics on *Avenida Atlântica* which were designed by Burle Max, the area is busy both day and night and lined with shops, bars, restaurants and luxury hotels. There are also fine examples of *Art Deco* architecture in the area, such as the *Copacabana Palace Hotel* which was built in 1923. *Copacabana Fort*, which was built in 1914 to defend Guanabara Bay, is situated at the end of the beach and offers panoramic views of the surrounding area.

Transportation
Air: Rio de Janeiro Galeão Antonio Carlos Jobim International Airport. **Road:** Coach: Novo Rio Coach Station.

Contact Addresses
RIOTUR – City of Rio de Janeiro Tourism Authority, Rua da Assembléia, 10 / 9° Floor, Centro 20011-000, Rio de Janeiro, RJ, Brazil
Tel: (021) 2217 7575
Website: www.rio.rj.gov.br/riotur/en

Iguazú Falls (Foz do Iguaçú)

The *Iguazú Falls* fittingly receive their name from the Guarani Indian word meaning 'great waters'. Surrounded by the virgin jungle of *Iguazú National Park*, home to 2000 species of flora and 400 species of bird, the *Paraná River* divides into 275 separate falls. The highest, the *Garganta del Diabolo* (Devil's Throat) reaches 70m (230ft), which is one and a half times the height of the Niagara Falls. Besides taking in the stunning view from a series of catwalks, visitors may enjoy kayaking, canoeing and other watersports. Historic Jesuit Mission ruins nearby, such as those at *San Ignacio Miní*, are also popular.

Transportation
Air: Ministro Pistarini Airport (Buenos Aires). **Road:** Coach: Services to bus terminal from Buenos Aires

Iguazú Falls

Contact Addresses
Iguazú National Park, Victoria Aguirre 66, 3370
Puerto Iguazú, Misiones, Argentina
Tel: (037) 5742 0722 *or* 5742 0180 *or* 5742 0382
Website: www.parquesnacionales.gov.ar

Statue of Christ the Redeemer (Cristo Redentor)

The *Statue of Christ the Redeemer*, standing 30m
(98ft) tall and overlooking the city of Rio de Janeiro,
is one of the tallest statues in the world. The statue
represents Jesus standing with outstretched arms and
is one of the most famous symbols of this lively city.
Developed by the engineer Heitor da Silva Costa and
originally conceived in 1921, construction started in
mid-1926 and was completed in 1931. The statue sits
on top of *Corcovado Mountain* (Hunchback
Mountain) located in *Tijuca National Park*, a popular
area for picnics and walking. From the statue there
are superb views of Sugar Loaf Mountain, downtown
Rio de Janeiro and Rio's beaches.

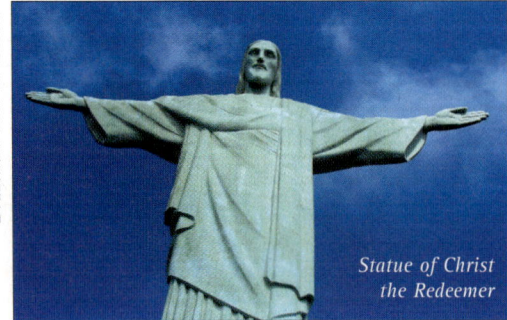

*Statue of Christ
the Redeemer*

Transportation
Air: Rio de Janeiro Galeão Antonio Carlos Jobim
International Airport. **Rail:** Train: Rua Cosme
Velho Station. **Road:** Coach: Novo Rio Coach
Station. Car: Routes to Corcovado.

Contact Addresses
RIOTUR – City of Rio de Janeiro Tourism
Authority, Rua da Assembléia, 10 – 9° Floor,
Centro 20011-000, Rio de Janeiro, RJ, Brazil
Tel: (021) 2217 7575
Website: www.rio.rj.gov.br/riotur

Sugar Loaf Mountain (Pão de Açucar)

Shaped like a Victorian sugar loaf and 396m
(1299ft) tall, *Sugar Loaf Mountain* stands high
above the city of Rio de Janeiro and *Baía de
Guanabara* (Guanabara Bay). The mountain is
one of the most famous in the world and is a
spectacular backdrop to Brazil's most lively city.
Visitors can see excellent views of Rio de
Janeiro from the top of the mountain and
sunsets are particularly spectacular. Cable cars,
which were introduced by the engineer Augusto
Ferreira Ramos in 1912, take visitors to the top
of the mountain, although more adventurous
travellers may choose to make the steep climb
on foot.

Transportation
Air: Rio de Janeiro Galeão Antonio Carlos
Jobim International Airport. **Road:** Bus: Regular
public bus services. Car: Road towards city
centre, then coastal road past Ipanema and
Copacabana beaches to 'Urca' (from the south);
south towards Ipanema and Copacabana
beaches, then the exit marked 'Urca' (from the
city centre).

Contact Addresses
RIOTUR – City of Rio de Janeiro Tourism
Authority, Rua da Assembléia, 10 – 9° Floor,
Centro 20011-000, Rio de Janeiro, RJ, Brazil
Tel: (021) 2217 7575
Website: www.rio.rj.gov.br/riotur

Brunei

1 Omar Ali Saifuddin Mosque (Masjid Omar Ali Saifuddin)

Tourist Information

Brunei Tourism
Ministry of Industry and Primary Resources, Jalan Menteri Besar, Bandar Seri Bagawan 1220, Brunei Darussalam
Tel: 6732 382 822
Website: www.industry.gov.bn

High Commission of Brunei Darussalam
19-20 Belgrave Square, London SW1X 8PG, UK
Tel: (020) 7581 0521

Omar Ali Saifuddin Mosque (Masjid Omar Ali Saifuddin)

Omar Ali Saifuddin Mosque is one of the most spectacular mosques in Asia Pacific and is a magnificent sight. Named after the 28th Sultan of Brunei, the mosque, which is seen as a symbol of the Islamic faith in Brunei, dominates the skyline in the capital city, Bandar Seri Begawan. The golden dome of the mosque stands at 52m (171ft)

high and can be seen from virtually anywhere in the city. The building was completed in 1958 and is an impressive example of Islamic architecture, with magnificent mosaic stained glass, as well as many arches, domes and columns. Marble from Italy, granite from Shanghai and chandeliers from England were all used in the construction of Brunei's most ornate building.

Transportation
Air: Bandar Seri Begawan International Airport.
Road: Taxi: Taxis can be hailed in the city centre to take visitors to the mosque. Bus: A number of bus routes run to the mosque.

Contact Addresses
For more information on Omar Ali Saifuddin Mosque, contact Brunei Tourism (see **Tourist Information** above).

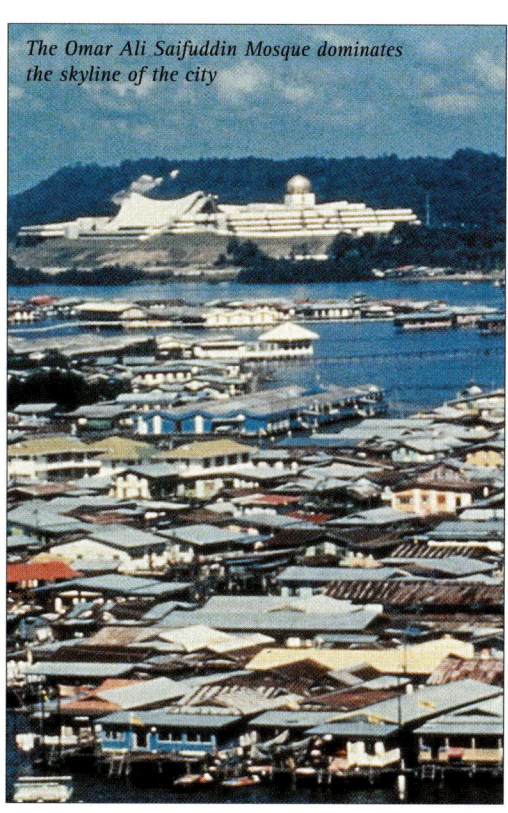

The Omar Ali Saifuddin Mosque dominates the skyline of the city

Royal Brunei Airways©

Bulgaria

ROMANIA

YUGOSLAVIA

SERBIA

Danube • Ruse

Dobrich

Balkan

• Pleven

Mountains

B U L G A R I A

• Varna

Iskur

Nessebŭr

SOFIA   Kazanlŭk

Rila •   Stara Zagora •

Burgas •   *BLACK SEA*

Maritsa

Plovdiv

FYR OF MACE-DONIA   Pirin Mtns.

Rhodope Mo ains

TURKEY

GREECE

Sea of Marmara

AEGEAN SEA

200km
100mls
✈ international airport

1 Baba Vida Castle

2 Rila Monastery (Rilski Manastir)

3 St Alexander Nevski Cathedral
   (Hram-pametnik Aleksander Nevski

4 Trigrad Gorge

Tourist Information

National Information and Advertising Center to the Ministry of Economy
1 St Sophia Street, Sofia 1040, Bulgaria
Tel: (02) 987 9778 *or* 987 1152
Website: www.bulgariatravel.org

Embassy of the Republic of Bulgaria
186-188 Queen's Gate, London SW7 5HL, UK
Tel: (020) 75849 8402
Website: www.bulgarianembassy.org.uk

Baba Vida Castle

Built on the banks of the *River Danube* in the town of *Vidin* in the northwestern tip of the country, *Baba Vida Castle* occupies a commanding position overlooking the town. The present castle is actually built upon the foundations of a Roman fortress known as *Bononia* which marked the Danubian Frontier of the Roman Empire from the first to the seventh centuries. Baba Vida Castle was actually built during the 10th century and is the only medieval fortress to have survived intact to the present day. The castle is protected by inner and outer walls and is ringed by a moat filled with water from the Danube. Today, the castle hosts numerous theatre productions during the summer months and is often used as a historical film set. There's also an onsite museum with exhibitions about the region's history.

Transportation
Air: Sofia International Airport. **Rail:** Vidin Station. **Road: Bus:** Public services to Vidin.

Contact Addresses
For more information on the Baba Vida Castle, contact the National Information and Advertising Center (see **Tourist Information** above).

Rila Monastery (Rilski Manastir)

Rila Monastery, the largest monastery in Bulgaria, is situated in the spectacular *Rhodope Mountains* in *Rila National Park* and is included on the UNESCO list of World Cultural Heritage Sites. Rila was the first Christian monastery to be built in Bulgaria and was founded by followers of John of Rila (the patron saint of Bulgaria) during the 10th century. Rila was damaged by fire several times over the years and was not fully restored to its current state until 1816. The monastery is ornately decorated with murals which were painted by famous artists, including Kosta Valyov and Zahari Zograph, between 1840 and 1848.

Transportation
Air: Sofia Airport. **Road: Car:** E79 south of Sofia

for 100km (62 miles), then a further 21km (13 miles) to arrive at Rila Monastery.

Contact Addresses
For more information on Rila Monastery, contact the National Information and Advertising Center to the Ministry of Economy (see **Tourist Information** above).

St Alexander Nevski Cathedral (Hram-pametnik Aleksander Nevski)

St Alexander Nevski Cathedral is one of Sofia's most famous monuments. This neo-Byzantine structure, which is surmounted by copper and golden domes, was built between 1882 and 1912 in honour of the Russian soldiers who died trying to liberate Bulgaria from Ottoman rule during the War of Liberation in 1878. The cathedral, which is also one of the finest buildings in the Balkan States, takes its name from Alexander Nevski, the patron saint of the family of the Russian Tsar at the time, Alexander II. Visitors can also see the *Icon Museum*, located in the Crypt, which houses around 300 exhibits following the development of Bulgarian icon-painting from the ninth to 19th centuries. Sofia also has many other attractions, including the *Rotunda of St George*, *St Sofia Church*, the *Church of St Nedely*, *Vassil Levski Monument* and the *Dragalevtsi* and *Boyana* churches.

Transportation
Air: Sofia Airport. **Rail:** Train: Sofia Station. **Road:** Public bus and minibus services. Car: Signs for Sofia city centre, then over Orlov Most (Eagle Bridge).

Contact Addresses
For more information on St Alexander Nevski Cathedral, contact the National Information and Advertising Center to the Ministry of Economy (see **Tourist Information** above).

Trigrad Gorge

The spectacular *Trigrad Gorge* is in the *Rhodope Mountains* close to the town of Trigrad in

Southern Bulgaria and is flanked by walls rising to 250m (820ft). One of the most popular sites at the gorge is *Devil's Throat Cave* which formed when layers of the mountain collapsed. From here, visitors can travel through a manmade tunnel to see the highest underground waterfalls in Europe which cascade 42m (138ft) into the abyss below. Nearby is the famous *Haramiiska Cave* where archaeologists discovered evidence of human habitation dating back over 4,000 years. There are over 150 other caves in the region and the area is popular with rock climbers; numerous companies provide guides and tuition. The region is also popular with birdwatchers who come to see Pallid Swifts, Crag Martins, Rock Partridges and the rare Wallcreeper.

Transportation
Air: Sofia International Airport. **Road:** Bus: Public services to Trigrad.

Contact Addresses
For more information on the Trigrad Gorge, contact the National Information and Advertising Centre (see **Tourist Information** above).

Rila Monastery

Cambodia

1 Angkor Temple Complex (Angkor)

Tourist Information

Ministry of Tourism (Krâsuong Teschor)
3 Boulevard Monivong, Phnom Penh, 12258
Cambodia
Tel: (023) 212 837
Website: www.mot.gov.kh

Royal Embassy of Cambodia
28-32 Wellington Road, St. John's Wood,
London NW8 9SP UK
Tel: +44 (0) 20 7483 9063

Angkor Temple Complex

Angkor, the former capital of the ancient Khmer
Empire, is one of the greatest and most
spectacular Hindu religious sites in the world.
Construction of this elaborate temple complex –

built in honour of the god Vishnu – began in AD
879 during the reign of King Suryavarman II and
was completed in 1191. It lay concealed for many
years, however, until the site was discovered by
Frenchman Henri Mahout in 1860. The central
complex, *Angkor Wat* (Angkor Temple), features an
elaborate, unmortared 66m (215ft) central tower
surrounded by four smaller towers. Stretching
around the outside of the temple complex is an
800m-long (2625ft-) bas-relief, the longest in the
world.

Transportation
Air: Siem Reap Airport. **Road:** Car: Route 6 (from
Phnom Penh to Siem Reap). Taxi: Moto-taxi and
tuk-tuk services are available (from Siem Reap).

Contact Addresses
Ministry of Tourism, Boulevard Monivong, Phnom
Penh 12258, Cambodia
Tel: (023) 212 837 *or* 880 623 (Phnom Penh office)
Website: www.mot.gov.kh

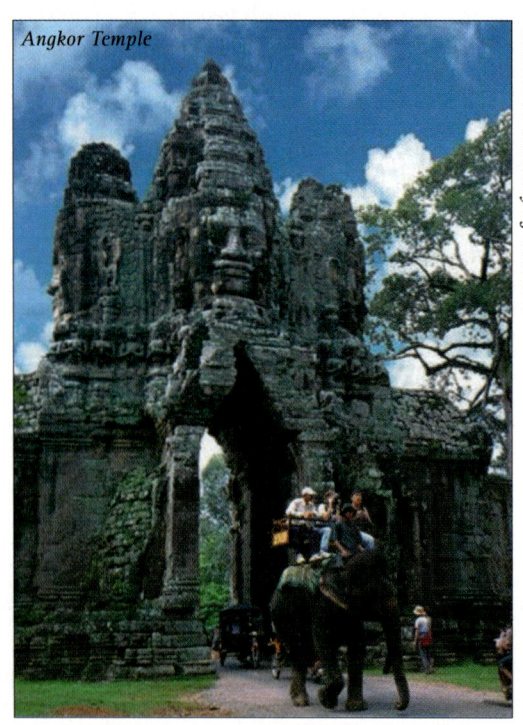

Angkor Temple

Cambodian Ministry of Tourism©

Canada

Map of Canada showing provinces, territories, cities and international airports.

- BEAUFORT SEA
- North Magnetic Pole (1997)
- GREENLAND (Den.)
- ICELAND
- ALASKA (US)
- △ Mt McKinley 6194m
- Banks I.
- Devon I.
- Ellesmere I.
- Baffin Bay
- Qikiqtaaluk (Baffin I.)
- YUKON TERR.
- △ Mt Logan 5959m
- Whitehorse
- Mackenzie
- Great Bear Lake
- Victoria I.
- NORTHWEST TERRITORIES
- Yellowknife
- NUNAVUT
- Southampton I.
- Iqaluit
- LABRADOR SEA
- Great Slave Lake
- Peace
- Lake Athabasca
- Hudson Bay
- Ungava Peninsula
- NEWFOUNDLAND AND LABRADOR
- ROCKY
- Queen Charlotte Is.
- BRITISH COLUMBIA
- ALBERTA
- CANADA
- SASKAT-CHEWAN
- MANITOBA
- Edmonton
- Vancouver I.
- Vancouver
- Victoria
- Calgary
- Saskatoon
- Lake Winnipeg
- ONTARIO
- QUEBEC
- Newfoundland
- Gander
- St John's
- St-Pierre et Miquelon (Fr.)
- PACIFIC OCEAN
- Regina
- Winnipeg
- Lake Superior
- St Lawrence
- PRINCE EDWARD
- NEW BRUNSWICK
- Charlottetown
- Fredericton
- Québec
- NOVA SCOTIA
- Halifax
- Montréal
- OTTAWA
- Toronto
- Hamilton
- L. Ontario
- Lake Huron
- Lake Erie
- ATLANTIC OCEAN
- New York
- Lake Michigan
- UNITED STATES
- MOUNTAINS
- 1000km / 500mls
- ✈ international airport

Travel Manitoba ©

Tourist Information

Canadian Tourism Commission
55 Metcalfe Street, Suite 600, Ottawa, Ontario K1P 6LS, Canada
Tel: (613) 946 1000
Website: www.canadatourism.com

Visit Canada Centre
PO Box 5396, Northampton NN1 2FA, UK
Tel: (0906) 871 5000 (24-hour consumer and tourism enquiries line; calls cost 60p per minute)
Website: www.travelcanada.ca

Alberta

NORTHWEST | TERRITORIES

Wood Buffalo National Park

Rainbow Lake

Fort Chipewyan

Lake Athabasca

L. Claire

Peace River

Fort McMurray

Grande Prairie

Lesser Slave Lake

ALBERTA

Athabasca

Bonnyville

Fort Saskatchewan

② St Albert

Spruce Grove ◎ Edmonton

Leduc

Mt Robson 3954m

Jasper

Wetaskiwin

Camrose

Mt Columbia 3747m

Red Deer

BRITISH COLUMBIA

Lake Louise

Kicking Horse Pass

Airdrie

Drumheller

Banff

Calgary

①

Oldman

Medicine Hat

Lethbridge

UNITED STATES

400km
200mls

♠ international airport
◉ province capital

1 Banff National Park
2 Jasper National Park

Tourist Information

Travel Alberta
PO Box 2500, Edmonton, Alberta T5J 2Z4, Canada
Tel: (403) 297 2700 or (780) 427 4321 or (800) 661 8888 (toll free USA and Canada only)
Website: www.travelalberta.com

Travel Alberta UK
Travel Alberta UK, 11 Cornflour Way, West Sussex RH13 7WB, UK
Tel: (01403) 754 424

Key to symbols: £ Entry charged ♿ Disabled access
⛏ Man-made attraction ♥ Natural attraction
🅿 Parking ✕ Restaurant 🛒 Shop 🏛 UNESCO site

Banff National Park

Banff National Park was created by the Canadian government in 1885 as the country's first national park. The park, which includes the Rocky Mountains, has 6641 sq km (2564 sq miles) of mountains, rivers, forests, lakes, glaciers and hot springs, and is home to wolves, mountain goats, eagles, grizzly bears and elk. The most famous man-made addition to the area is the *Banff Springs Hotel*, completed in 1888. It was built to resemble a baronial Scottish castle and accommodates more than 800 guests. *Lake Louise*, named in honour of Queen Victoria's daughter, Princess Louise Caroline Alberta, is one of the most popular sites in the *Rocky Mountains*.

Transportation
Air: Calgary International Airport. **Road:** Coach: Services from Calgary. **Car:** Trans-Canada Hwy-1.

Contact Addresses
Banff Lake Louise Tourism Bureau, Box 1298, Banff, Alberta T1L 1B3, Canada
Tel: (403) 762 8421
Website: www.bannflakelouise.com

🅿 ✕ 🛒 ♿ 🏛 £ ♥

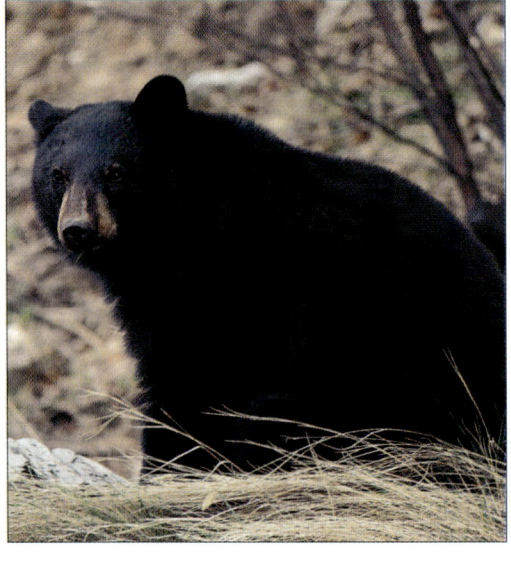

Travel Alberta©

Travel Alberta©

Moraine Lake and the Valley of the Ten Peaks, Banff National Park

Jasper National Park

Jasper National Park was established in 1907 and is the largest of Canada's _Rocky Mountains_ parks, spanning 10,878 sq km (4200 sq miles). The spectacular scenery is characterised by glaciers, rugged mountains, forests and meadows carpeted with alpine flowers. The park protects a range of fragile mountain ecosystems – elk, moose, bear, bighorn sheep and mule deer are regular sights – and is home to the threatened woodland caribou. _Maligne Lake_, 48km (30 miles) southeast of Jasper is surrounded by snow-capped mountains and its crystal clear waters are popular for boating and fishing.

Transportation

Air: Calgary International Airport, Edmonton International Airport. **Rail:** Train: Jasper Station. **Road:** Bus: Jasper Bus Station. Car: Hwy-16 (from Edmonton); Hwy-1 (from Calgary); Hwy-93 (from Lake Louise).

Contact Addresses

Jasper National Park, Visitor Information Centre, PO Box 10, Jasper, Alberta T0E 1E0, Canada
Tel: (780) 852 6176 _or_ (888) 773 8888
Website: www.pc.gc.ca/banff

Ontario

1 Algonquin Provincial Park

2 CN Tower

3 National Gallery of Canada

4 Niagara Falls, Canada

Southern Ontario. It soon became popular with outdoor enthusiasts and canoeists because of its beautiful lakes, forests, bogs, rivers, cliffs and beaches. For campers and day visitors, *Highway 60* is the centre of the park, offering campgrounds, walking trails, conducted hikes and access to public wolf-howling sessions. In winter, cross country skiing trails are popular. Visitors can also soak up the history of the park in the *Logging Museum*, or in the *Algonquin Gallery*, which focuses on the Canadian artist Tom Thomson's (1877-1917) famous group of painters, the *Group of Seven*.

Transportation

Air: Lester B Pearson International Airport (Toronto). **Rail:** Train: Huntsville Station. Road: Coach: Services to Huntsville (from Toronto). **Car:** Hwy-11, Hwy-17 or Hwy-60.

Contact Addresses

Algonquin Provincial Park, PO Box 219, Whitney, Ontario K0J 2M0, Canada
Tel: (705) 633 5572 (information)
Website: www.algonquinpark.on.ca

Tourist Information

Ontario Tourism Marketing Partnership
Tenth Floor, Hearst Block, 900 Bay Street, Toronto, Ontario M7A 2E1, Canada
Tel: (1) 800 668 2746 (toll free USA and Canada only)
Website: www.ontariotravel.net

Ontario Tourism Marketing Partnership
c/o CIB, 1 Battersea Church Road, London SW11 3LY, UK
Tel: (020) 7771 7004 (trade enquiries only) or (01622) 832 288 (brochure request line)

Algonquin Provincial Park

Spanning 7725 sq km (4800 sq miles), *Algonquin Provincial Park* was established in 1893 to develop a wildlife sanctuary in a rugged, beautiful part of

CN Tower

As the world's tallest free-standing structure on land, the *CN Tower* is the defining feature of Toronto's lakefront skyline. Completed in 1976, the 553m (1815ft) tower offers stunning views of Toronto and Lake Ontario. It takes only 58 seconds to reach the LookOut level in a glass-fronted lift which travels at 22km (15 miles) per hour. Once there, visitors can enjoy a meal at the revolving *360° Restaurant*, walk across a glass floor on the 113th storey or get an even better view from the *Sky Pod* that is 447m (1465ft) high. There is also a collection of entertainment attractions at the base of the tower, including two motion simulator rides, and a short documentary film describing the feat of engineering undertaken to build this colossal structure.

Transportation
Air: Lester B Pearson International Airport (Toronto). **Rail:** Train: Union Station. Underground: Union Station. **Road:** Car: Hwy-427 (from the north).

Contact Addresses
CN Tower, 301 Front Street West, Toronto, Ontario M5V 2T6, Canada
Tel: (416) 868 6937
Website: www.cntower.ca

National Gallery of Canada

The *National Gallery of Canada* was founded in 1880 by the Governor General, the Marquess of Lorne and since then has grown to become an internationally-renowned art museum. The permanent collections reflect Canada's diverse history, and includes works by European masters such as Monet, Turner and Di Cosimo, as well as avant-garde Canadian paintings from the 1960s and religious sculptures from Québec. The museum also contains a large collection of Inuit art, including prints, drawings and whale bone sculptures, many of which portray the cultural and social issues that have affected Canada's indigenous population since World War II.

Transportation
Air: Ottawa Macdonald-Cartier International Airport. **Rail:** Train: Ottawa VIA Rail Station. **Road:** Bus: 3. Car: Hwy-417 (Metcalfe exit). Then Metcalfe Street, right onto Wellington Street and left onto Sussex Drive.

Contact Addresses
National Gallery of Canada, 380 Sussex Drive, Box 427, Station A, Ottawa, Ontario K1N 9N4, Canada
Tel: (613) 990 1985
Website: www.national.gallery.ca

Niagara Falls, Canada

Niagara Falls is one of the most popular tourist destinations in North America. The falls are made up of two separate parts, *Horseshoe Falls* on the Canadian side and *American Falls* on the USA side. Although not the highest waterfall in the world they move a staggering 168,000 cubic metres (219,600 cubic yards) of water per minute over a drop of 51m (167ft), making them one of the natural wonders of the world. The surrounding town, a celebrated North American honeymoon destination, offers a wealth of visitor activities including a casino, as well as land and boat tours of the falls.

Transportation
Air: Buffalo Niagara Airport or Lester B Pearson International Airport (Toronto). **Rail:** Train: Niagara Falls VIA Rail Station. **Road:** Bus: Falls Shuttle to the Niagara Falls (from downtown). Coach: Niagara Falls Coach Station. Car: Queen Elizabeth Way (QEW) towards Niagara, then Hwy-420 to Niagara Falls (from Toronto).

Contact Addresses
Niagara Falls Tourism, 5515 Stanley Avenue, Niagara Falls, Ontario L2G 3X4, Canada
Tel: (905) 356 6061
Website: www.niagarafallstourism.com

Niagara Falls

Ontario Tourism©

Quebec

international airport
⊙ province capital

---

1 Old Port of Montréal (Vieux Port de Montreal)
2 Old Québec (Vieux Québec)

Tourist Information

Tourisme Québec

Centre Infotouriste Montréal,
1001 Square Dorchester,
Bureau 100, Montréal, Québec
H3B 4V4, Canada
Tel: (514) 873 2015 or (800) 363 777 (toll free
USA and Canada only)
Website: www.bonjourquebec.com

Destination Québec

Suite 116, Fourth Floor, 35-37 Grosvenor
Gardens, London SW1W 0BS, UK
Tel: (020) 7233 8011
Website: www.quebec4u.co.uk

Old Port of Montréal (Vieux Port de Montréal)

The *Old Port* is located in the historic heart of the cosmopolitan, francophone city of Montréal. It was once the sea-trading hub of North America and in the first half of the 20th century was the second largest port in North America after New York. After port operations declined in the late 1950s, the Canadian government decided to redevelop the area, and it is now a thriving arts and entertainment venue, visited by five million people each year. The port is surrounded by the city's original 17th century walled fortifications and the activities on offer reflect both the area's illustrious past and its modern, forward-looking philosophy. The *Clock Tower* offers excellent views across the city and houses an exhibition tracing the city's history.

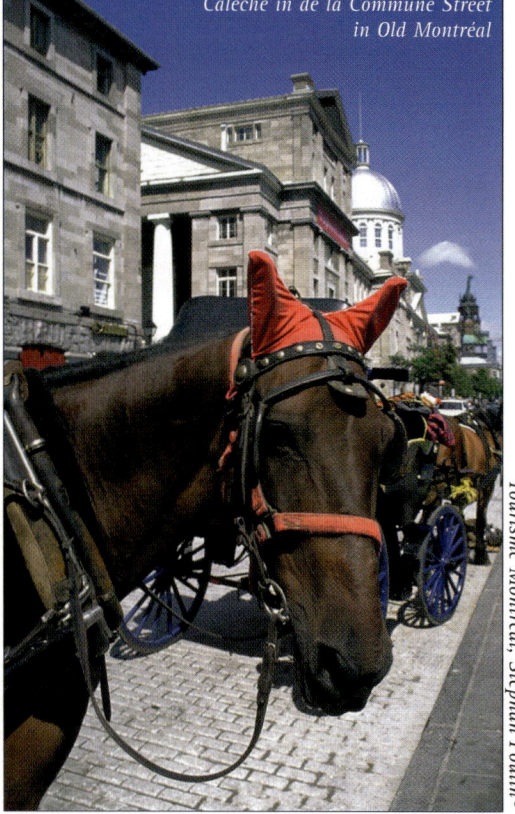

Caleche in de la Commune Street in Old Montréal

Tourisme Montréal, Stéphan Poulin©

Transportation

Air: Montréal Dorval International Airport, Montréal Mirabel International Airport. **Rail:** Train: Montréal Station (Gare Centrale). Underground: Square-Victoria, Champ-de-Mars or Place d'armes. **Road:** Car: Ville-Marie Expressway (Hwy-720).

Contact Addresses

Old Port of Montréal Inc., 333 rue de la Commune Ouest, Montréal, Québec H2Y 2E2, Canada
Tel: (514) 496 7678
Website: www.oldportofmontreal.com

Old Québec (Vieux Québec)

The only walled city north of Mexico, *Québec* was settled in 1608 as a fur trading post. Its fortified exterior and strategic position high above the St Lawrence River is a testament to the historical territorial tensions between France and England that culminated in the Battle of the Plains of Abraham (1759). Divided into two sections, *Haute* and *Basse*, the old town seems more like an island of old Europe, with winding cobblestone streets, 17th- and 18th-century buildings and churches, squares, parks and numerous monuments. The *Château Frontenac*, a Canadian landmark, is its most prominent building – built in 1893, it is now a luxury hotel with views over the St Lawrence River and Old Québec.

Transportation

Air: Jean-Lesage International Airport. **Rail:** Train: Québec Station (Gare du Palais). **Road:** Bus: Gare du Palais. Car: Hwy-20 or Hwy-40.

Contact Addresses

Tourisme Québec, PO Box 979, Montréal, Québec H3C 2W3, Canada
Tel: (514) 873 2015
Website: www.bonjourquebec.com

Cannon and Château Frontenac, Québec

Corel©

Yukon Territory

Tourist Information

Tourism Yukon
PO Box 2703, Whitehorse, Yukon Territory
Y1A 2C6, Canada
Tel: (867) 667 5340
Website: www.touryukon.com

Yukon First Nations Tourism Association
PO Box 4518, Whitehorse, Yukon Y1A 2R8,
Canada
Tel: (867) 667 7698
Website: www.yfnta.org

Key to symbols: £ Entry charged & Disabled access
⌖ Man-made attraction ❤ Natural attraction
P Parking ✖ Restaurant 🛍 Shop 🏛 UNESCO site

Kluane National Park and Reserve

Established in 1972, *Kluane National Park and Reserve* has been the home of the Southern Tutchone First Nations people for thousands of years. The park is a vast expanse of mountains and ice and encompasses the *Icefield Ranges*; the highest mountain in this range, *Mount Logan*, rises to 5959m (19,545ft) and is the highest peak in Canada. Other popular activities on offer in the park include cross country skiing, boating, fishing, snowmobiling, cycling, mountainbiking and horseriding. A rafting trip down the *Alsek River* allows visitors to view the wildlife (including grizzly bears, Dall sheep and golden eagles) and glaciers along the way; however, permits for rafting on this Canadian Heritage river are strictly limited to one departure per day and visitors are advised to arrange their trip well in advance.

Transportation
Air: Vancouver International Airport, then Whitehorse Airport (domestic flight). **Road:** Car: Alaska Highway (from Whitehorse) or Haines Highway (from Haines, Alaska) to Haines Junction.

Contact Addresses
Kluane National Park and Reserve, PO Box 5495, Haines Junction, Yukon Y0B 1L0, Canada
Tel: (867) 634 7250
Website: www.pc.gc.ca/kluane

P ✖ 🛍 & 🏛 £ ❤

Kluane Glacier

Tourism Yukon©

Chile

1000km
500mls

✈ international airport

1 Easter Island (Rapa Nui)

Tourist Information

Servicio Nacional de Turismo (SERNATUR)
Avenida Providencia 1550,
PO Box 14082, Santiago, Chile
Tel: (269) 67141
Website: www.visitchile.org

Embassy and Consulate of the Republic of Chile
12 Devonshire Street,
London W1G 7DS, UK
Tel: (020) 7580 6392 (embassy and tourist office) or 7580 1023 (visa section)
Website: www.echileuk.demon.co.uk

Easter Island (Rapa Nui)

A lonely volcanic island in the middle of the Pacific Ocean, as far away from Chile as from Tahiti, *Easter Island* is famous for its mysterious stone statues, or *moais*, that form an almost unbroken ring around the coast. Three hundred statues and related items of stonework, which were built during the 10th to 16th centuries, grace the island. Scientists are fascinated to learn how native inhabitants designed and forged the massive sculptures from hard volcanic rock, and how they transported them to the coast from inland quarries. Today, about 2000 people inhabit *Easter Island*, most of them living in the town of Hanga Roa.

Transportation
Air: Mataveri International Airport (Easter Island).

Contact Addresses
SERNATUR, Tourist Information, Tuu Maheke s/n, esquina Apina, Easter Island, Chile
Tel: (032) 100 255
Website: www.sernatur.cl

A stone moais on Easter island

Zena Turner©

People's Republic of China

1 Beijing Zoo (Beijing Dongwu Yuan)
2 Forbidden City (Zijin Cheng)
3 Great Wall of China (Wanli Changcheng)
4 Potala Palace (Kukhar Potrang)
5 Summer Palace (Yi He Yaun)
6 Terracotta Army (Bingma Yong)
7 Three Gorges of the Yangtze River (Sanxia)
8 Victoria Peak (Tai Ping Shan)

Tourist Information

China National Tourism Administration (CNTA)
Department of Marketing and Communications, 9A Jianguomennei Avenue, Beijing 100740, People's Republic of China
Tel: (010) 6520 1114
Website: www.cnta.com/lyen/index.asp

China National Tourist Office (CNTO)
71 Warwick Road, London SW5 9H8 UK
Tel: (020) 7373 0888

Tibet Tourism Administration
Yuanlin Road, Lhasa, Tibet 850001, People's Republic of China
Tel: (0891) 683 4313

Beijing Zoo (Beijing Dongwu Yuan)

Beijing Zoo is the oldest zoo in Asia Pacific and home of the world-famous giant pandas. Located in the northwest area of the city, it is home to more than 7000 animals, including golden monkeys from Sichuan, yaks from Tibet, sea turtles from the Chinese sea, Manchurian tigers and snow leopards. The zoo is also famous for being the home of zoological research and for housing many rare birds and animals. During the Qing Dynasty (1644-early 20th century), the zoo was a private garden, but later became an experimental farm and small menagerie. It was first opened to the public in 1908, but was destroyed during the Japanese occupation of Beijing (1937-1945), only to reopen in 1950.

Transportation
Air: Beijing Capital Airport. **Rail:** Train: Beijing Station.

Contact Addresses
Beijing Dongwu Yuan, 137 Xizhimenwai, Xicheng District, Beijing, People's Republic of China
Tel: (010) 6831 4411
Website: www.beijingzoo.com

Forbidden City (Zijin Cheng)

Built in the early 15th century during the Ming dynasty, the 74-hectare (183-acre) *Forbidden City* served as the home for 24 of China's Ming and Qing emperors. The palace drew its name from the fact that vast sections of it were off limits to virtually all save the emperor himself. Its 9000 rooms, filled with paintings, pottery and bronzes, are redolent of China's imperial past, an era of concubines, palace eunuchs and a rigid power structure. Among the Forbidden City's more notable landmarks are the *Meridian Gate*, the *Hall of Supreme Harmony* and the *Imperial Garden*.

Transportation

Air: Beijing Capital Airport. **Rail:** Train: Beijing Station. Underground: Qianmen. **Road:** Bus: Regular public services. Car: Towards Beijing city centre.

Contact Addresses

For more information on the Forbidden City, contact China National Tourism Administration (see **Tourist Information** above).

Great Wall of China (Wanli Changcheng)

One of the only man-made structures visible from space, the *Great Wall of China*, which stretches for some 6700km (4163 miles) through northern China, is the greatest symbol of the country's history and grandeur. Begun in the third century BC, the Great Wall connected a number of earlier walls to create a defence against nomads invading from the north. Although the wall ultimately failed in this regard, it was effective in bringing stability and continuity to Chinese culture. Much of the wall that exists today was rebuilt between the 14th and 18th centuries by the Ming dynasty. Many tourists choose to walk along a stretch of the wall, as it passes through some of China's most spectacular scenery.

Transportation

Air: Beijing Capital Airport. **Rail:** Train: Badaling Station. **Road:** Bus: Tourist bus (from Beijing city centre). Car: Motorway to Badaling (from Beijing).

Contact Addresses

For more information on the Great Wall of China, contact China National Tourism Administration (see **Tourist Information** above).

Potala Palace (Kukhar Potrang)

The *Potala Palace* is the largest monumental structure in Tibet, covering 41 hectares (101 acres). It stands high above the Lhasa Valley and was built in the seventh century AD as a retreat for the local lord, Songtsen Gampo, and his bride Princess Wen Cheng. Thirteen storeys high and perched on a huge cliff face, it is the world's highest palace. The palace complex is made up of two sections, the *Red Palace* and the *White Palace*, which together consist of 1000 rooms. The palace is the headquarters of the Dalai Lama and is a treasure house of traditional Tibetan culture.

Transportation

Air: Gonggar International Airport, Bangda Airport. **Road:** Taxi: From various locations in Lhasa (the palace is located in the centre of Lhasa). Car: Chengdu-Lhasa Highway (from Chengdu); Lhasa-Zham Friendship Bridge-Kathmandu Highway (from Kathmandu, Nepal).

Contact Addresses

Tibet Tourism Bureau, Yuanlin Road, Lhasa, Tibet 85001, People's Republic of China
Tel: (0891) 633 5472 *or* 683 4315

Summer Palace (Yi He Yaun)

Considered to be one of the finest classical gardens in China, the *Summer Palace* was first built in 1153 and served as a retreat for the royal court to escape the heat in the city. The imperial residences are built on the shores of Kunming Lake, which contains small islands, ornamental bridges and a marble boat that was once a teahouse. The palace was rebuilt in 1888 by the Empress Dowager Ci Xi who spent large amounts of money, from a fund intended for building a Chinese navy, on bringing the garden to its present state of glory. Covering an area of 290 hectares (717 acres), the gardens consist of a large lake with halls, towers, galleries, pavilions and bridges dotting the surrounding hilly land.

Transportation

Air: Beijing Capital Airport. **Rail:** Train: Beijing Station. **Road:** Bus: Public services.

Contact Addresses

Summer Palace, Yiheyuan Road, Haidian District
Tel: (010) 6288 114
Website: www.summerpalace-china.com

Terracotta Army (Bingma Yong)

The *Terracotta Army* is an enormous collection of Chinese warriors made out of hardened clay, 40km (25 miles) east of the town of Xi'an. The army, which is set out in rigid columns, was created in the second century BC by the emperor Shih Huang-Ti, the first emperor of a unified China, and was entombed with him upon his death. It was discovered in 1974 during an attempt to dig a well, and since then three separate chambers have revealed over 10,000 figures. The clay figures are all individual, and are made to represent actual members of the imperial army, including both soldiers and officers. Some are armed with real weapons, standing in battle formation next to real wooden chariots. The collection also includes clay horses and is often referred to as 'the eighth wonder of the world'.

Transportation
Air: Xi'an Xianyang International Airport. **Rail:** Train: Xi'an Station. **Road:** Taxi: Services from Xi'an.

Contact Addresses
Terracotta Warriors and Horses Museum, Qinling town, Lintong District, Shanxi Province, Peoples Republic of China.
Tel: (029) 8139 9046
Website: www.bmy.com.cn

Three Gorges of the Yangtze River (Sanxia)

The *Three Gorges of the Yangtze River* are a system of breathtaking gorges on China's longest river, which is also the third longest river in the world (after the Amazon and the Nile), stretching for 6300km (3915 miles). The *Qutang Gorge* is best known for its steep precipices that form an enormous gateway over the river. The *Wu Gorge* is home to the famous 12 peaks of the Wushan Mountains. And the *Xiling Gorge* is known for its hidden reefs, perilous cliffs and tumbling rapids. The controversial Three Gorges Project involves the construction of a dam which will be the largest hydroelectric project in the world. The dam, estimated to have a total cost in excess of $25 billion, is sheduled for completion in 2009.

The first tourist tickets to enable visitors to take a closer look at the dam were sold in the summer of 2005.

Transportation
Air: Beijing Capital Airport, Shanghai Hong Qiao Airport, Shanghai Pudong Airport. **Water:** Ferry: Services from Yichang. **Rail:** Train: Yichang Station.

Contact Addresses
Chongqing Tourism Administration, 50 Jiuchikan, Cangibai Road, Yuzhong District, Chongqing, Peoples Republic of China
Tel: (023) 8903 3037
Website: www.cqta.gov.cn

Victoria Peak (Tai Ping Shan)

At 552m (1514ft) above sea level, *Victoria Peak* is the most conspicuous landmark in Hong Kong. The Peak was rarely visited until 1888, the year the *Peak Tramway* opened, and its popularity has risen steadily since. Today, it is home to Hong Kong's wealthiest executives and bankers who favour the rarefied, natural surroundings. The view from the top is breathtaking even offering views of Macau and mainland China on a clear day. There are many restaurants and attractions, including a *Madame Tussaud's Wax Museum* in the *Peak Galleria* at the summit. Walking trails allow visitors to explore The Peak's natural beauty, including forests of bamboo and fern, stunted Chinese pines and sightings of birds, such as magpies, goshawks and kites.

Transportation
Air: Hong Kong International Airport. **Rail:** Train: MTR Central Station. Tram: Peak Tram (from Garden Road). **Road:** Bus: Public services.

Contact Addresses
Hong Kong Tourism Board, 9-11th Floors, Citicorp Centre, 18 Whitefield Road, North Point, Hong Kong, People's Republic of China
Tel: (852) 2807 6543
Website: www.discoverhongkong.com

Costa Rica

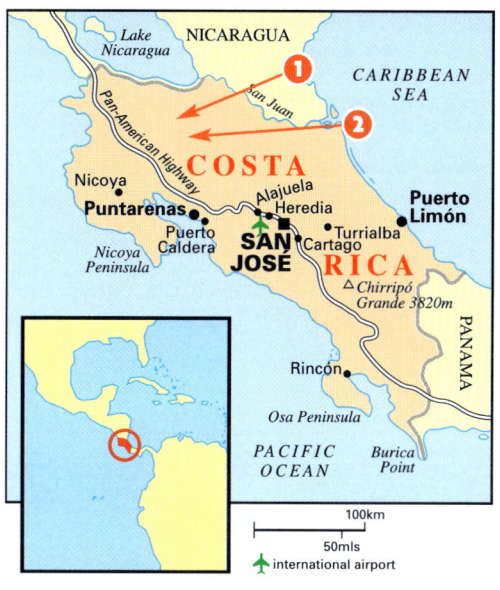

1 Arenal Volcano (Volcán Arenal)
2 Monteverde Cloud Forest (Bosque Nuboso de Monteverde)

National Park offers trails around the slopes and views of the summit; there are also hot spring spas with views over the surrounding area. At night, the view is even more spectacular, as molten rocks and lava tumble down the slopes, creating a dramatic 'firework' display that is fortunately always at least 5km (3 miles) away.

Transportation
Air: Juan Santamaria International Airport (San José) or Daniel Oduber Airport. **Road:** Coach: Services to La Fortuna (from San José and Ciudad Quesada). Car: Pan-American Highway (from San José).

Contact Addresses
Arenal Observatory Lodge, PO Box 321-1007, Centro Colón, Costa Rica
Tel: (506) 290 7011
Website: www.arenalobservatorylodge.com

Tourist Information

Costa Rica Tourist Board (Instituto Costarricense de Turismo)
Apartado 777, 1000 San José, Costa Rica
Tel: (506) 299 5800
Website: www.visitcostarica.com

Embassy and Consulate of the Republic of Costa Rica
Flat 1, 14 Lancaster Gate, London W2 3LH, UK
Tel: (020) 7706 8844
Website: www.embrclon.demon.co.uk

Arenal Volcano (Volcán Arenal)

One of the world's most active volcanoes, *Arenal* can be seen for miles around. The volcano had lain dormant for over 400 years until 1968, when it erupted, forming a lava landscape around the base. Research centre *Arenal Observatory Lodge* provides excellent views and *Arenal Volcano*

Arenal Volcano

ICT – Instituto Costarricense de Turismo©

Monteverde Cloud Forest (Bosque Nuboso de Monteverde)

Straddling the Continental Divide and covering 170 sq km (66 sq miles), this vast forest has its head – and its feet – in the clouds. The ever-present drizzle and mist provide a home to an amazing array of flora and fauna. Trails, overnight shelters for camping and a 91m (300ft) suspension bridge enable visitors to experience the incredible biodiversity of the forest. There is also a *Visitor Centre*, *Butterfly Centre*, *Orchid Garden*, *Serpentarium* and *Hummingbird Gallery*, as well as the *Frog Pond of Monteverde Herpetarium*. Other highlights include the *Sky Trek* and the *Sky Walk*, a series of trails and platforms reaching high into the jungle canopy.

Transportation

Air: Juan Santamaria International Airport (San José). **Road:** Coach: Services to Santa Elena (from Puntarenas) services from Monteverde (from Tilarán); express service to Monteverde (from San José). Car: Pan-American Highway to Kilometre #149 (from San José).

Contact Addresses

Monteverde Cloud Forest Preserve, Apdo 55-5655, Monteverde, Puntarenas, Costa Rica
Tel: (506) 645 5122
Website: www.cct.or.cr *or* www.cloudforestalive.org

P ✕

Monteverde Cloud Forest

ICT – Instituto Costarricense de Turismo©

Croatia

Adriatic'. Founded in the seventh century, *Dubrovnik* reached its heyday as an important sea-trading port in the late Middle Ages, and the proliferation of Gothic, Renaissance and Baroque buildings are a legacy of its rich and glorious past. The most famous sights are the *Franjevaèkog Samostana Mala Braca* (Franciscan Friars Minor Monastery) in the west, which houses one of the three oldest pharmacies in Europe, the 15th-century *Dominikanskog Samostana* (Dominican monastery), located in the east of the city, and the 17th-century *Katedrale* (cathedral). The *Dubrovaèki Muzej* (Dubrovnik Museum) housed in the splendid *Kneažev Dvor* (Rector's Palace) is also worth a visit.

Transportation
Air: Dubrovnik International Airport or Zagreb International Airport. **Water:** Ferry: Services from Bari (Italy). **Road:** Bus: Public services. Coach: Services from Split. Car: Adriatic Coastal Road from Split, Trieste and Zagreb).

Contact Addresses
Dubrovnik Tourist Board, Cvijete Zuzoric 1/ 2, 20000 Dubrovnik, Croatia
Tel: (020) 324 999
Website: http://web.tzdubrovnik.hr

1 Dubrovnik
2 Plitvice Lakes National Park (Nacionalni Park Plitvicka Jezera)
3 Split

Tourist Information

Hrvatska turisticka zajedni (Croatian National Tourist Board)
Iblerov jrg 10/IV, 10000 Zagreb, Croatia
Tel: (01) 455 6455
Website: www.croatia.hr

Croatian National Tourist Office
Croatia House, 162-164 Fulham Palace Road, London W6 9ER, UK
Tel: (020) 8563 7979

Dubrovnik

This small fortified city with a population of about 43,000 lies on the Dalmatian coast in southern Croatia and is often referred to as the 'Pearl of the

Plitvice Lakes National Park (Nacionalni Park Plitvicka Jezera)

Plitvice Lakes National Park in the heart of Croatia consists of 16 beautiful blue-green lakes, linked by a series of waterfalls and cascades to form a chain through a wooded valley. Over thousands of years, the waters that flow through this area have

Plitvice Lakes National Park

passed over limestone and chalk, creating deposits which form natural barriers between the lakes. The lakes range in height from *Proscansko Jezero* at 636.6m (1746ft) above sea level, to the lowest, *Kaludjerovac*, at 505.2m (1386ft), and in surface area from 81 hectares (200 acres) to 1 hectare (2.5 acres).

Transportation
Air: Zagreb International Airport. **Road:** Coach: All coaches on the Zagreb-Zadar route stop at Plitvice; it is also possible to visit Plitvice as a day trip from most coastal resorts between the Kvarner Riviera and mid-Dalmatia.

Contact Addresses
Plitvice Lakes National Park, 53231 Plitvièka jezera, Croatia
Tel: (053) 751 015
Website: www.np-plitvicka-jezera.hr/

Split

Located on Croatia's stunning *Dalmatia Coast*, *Split* is the largest city in the area and cultural centre of the region. The city dates back nearly 2,000 years boasting a variety of architectural styles and historical landmarks. Most famous of these is the *Palace of Diocletian* which is inscribed on the UNESCO World Heritage List. The palace was built in the third century by the emperor Diocletian in the style of a Roman fort around a rectangular plot with turrets and huge palace gates. At the time, Split itself did not exist and the town sprang up around the palace. Other important attractions in Split include the *Museum of Croatian Archaeological Monuments*, the *Museum of Marine History*, the *Museum of Natural Science* and *Split Cathedral's Treasury* containing important sacral works of art dating back to the seventh century. A pleasant 15-minute stroll from the historic city centre is *Marjan Forest Park* which is home to *Split Zoo* and numerous walking trails that offer spectacular views of the peninsular and surrounding area.

Transportation
Air: Split Airport. **Water:** Ferry: Ferry services link Split with Rijeka and Dubrovnik as well as some of the bigger Dalmatia islands. **Rail:** Split Station. **Road:** Bus: Public services. Car: Adriatic Coastal Road.

Contact Addresses
Split Tourist Board, HR-21000 Split, Trg Republike 2
Tel: (021) 348 600
Website: www.visitsplit.com

Split

Cuba

Gulf of Mexico · USA · BAHAMAS · Tropic of Cancer · HAVANA · Varadero · Bahama Sea · Pinar del Río · Matanzas · Santa Clara · Cienfuegos · CUBA · Trinidad · Isle de la Juventud · Camagüey · Holguín · Bayamo · Guantánamo · Pico Turquino △ 2005m · Santiago de Cuba · JAMAICA · HAITI · CARIBBEAN SEA

400km
200mls
✈ international airport

1 Old Havana (Vieja Habana)

Tourist Information

Ministry of Tourism (Ministerio de Turismo)
Calle 19, No 710, Entre Paseo y A, Vedado, Havana, Cuba
Tel: (07) 330 545
Website: cubatravel.cu

Cuba Tourist Board
154 Shaftesbury Avenue, London WC2H 8JT, UK
Tel: (020) 7240 6655 or (09001) 600 295 (24-hour brochure request line)

Old Havana (Vieja Habana)

Old Havana harks back to Cuba's days as a colonial outpost and its subsequent era as a glamorous, sophisticated Caribbean playground. Although some of the crumbling palaces look like they could do with a lick of paint, many of its colonial buildings, majestic boulevards, elegant plazas and side streets have been restored, attracting more and more visitors each year. The *Plaza de la Catedral* (Cathedral Square), dominated by the towers of the 18th-century Baroque *Catedral de San Cristobal de La Habana* (St Cristobal Cathedral), perhaps best captures Old Havana's spirit.

Transportation
Air: Havana Jose Marti International Airport. **Rail:** Train: Miramar Station. **Road:** Bus: Public services. Car: Carreterra Central (across Cuba via Havana); Autopista (from Pinar del Rio or Ciego de Avila to Havana).

Contact Addresses
Infotur, 5ta Avenida esq. 112, Miramar, La Habana, Cuba
Tel: (07) 247 036
Website: www.infotur.com

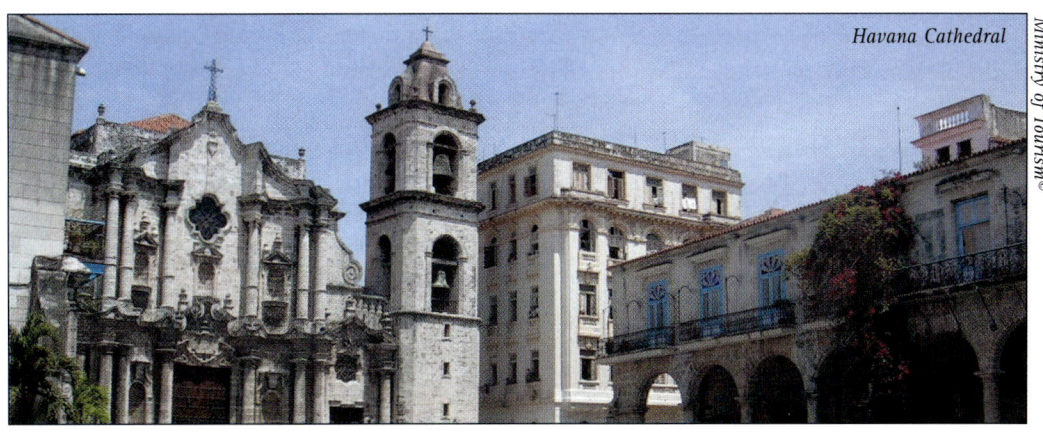

Havana Cathedral

Ministry of Tourism©

Cyprus

1 Kykkos Monastery (Panagia tou Kykkou)
2 Paphos (Pafos)

Kykkos Monastery

Cyprus Tourism Organisation©

Tourist Information

Cyprus Tourism Organisation
PO Box 24535, Nicosia 1390, Cyprus
Tel: (02) 337 715
Website: www.visitcyprus.org.cy

Cyprus Tourism Organisation – UK
17 Hanover Street, London W1S 1YP, UK
Tel: (020) 7569 8800
Website: www.visitcyprus.org.cy

Kykkos Monastery (Panagia tou Kykkou)

Kykkos Monastery is the largest and most famous monastery in Cyprus. Founded in AD 1100 by the Byzantine emperor Alexios Komnenos, the monastery is dedicated to the Virgin Mary and is home to one of the three surviving icons painted by the Apostle Luke. Kykkos Monastery is ornately decorated and covered in a silver gilt, enclosed in a tortoiseshell shrine. It is also famous for its museum, located within the monastery grounds, which houses an impressive collection of icons, woodcarvings and manuscripts, and other Cypriot antiquities. The nearby *Troodos Mountains*, with magnificent hills and valleys, should also be explored as they are home to nine Byzantine churches, included on UNESCO's World Heritage List, and richly decorated with murals and Byzantine paintings.

Transportation
Air: Paphos International Airport. **Road:** Car: Road to Pedoulas which leads to Kykkos (from Troodos); road north towards Platres, past Pedoulas to Kykkos (from Limassol); towards Limassol, then northeast past Kedares to Platres (from Paphos). The monastery is well-signposted.

Contact Addresses
Kykkos Monastery, PO Box 24850, 1304 Nicosia, Cyprus
Tel: (02) 942 736 (museum) *or* 590 768 (office)
Website: www.kykkos-museum.cy.net

Paphos (Pafos)

The town of *Paphos* is famed for being the birthplace of Aphrodite (the Goddess of Love) and home to *Aphrodite's Rock* (Petra Toy Romiou), which was erected by the Myceneans in the 12th century BC. The town also boasts majestic landscapes, lovely coastline, as well as numerous historic sites including the beautiful *Mosaics of Paphos*, the *Tombs of the Kings*, the *Medieval Fort*, the *Paphos District Archaelogical Museum*, the *Byzantine Museum* and the *Ethnographical Museum*. The impressive second century *Odeon*, which was rediscovered in 1973, the 12th-century *Saranta Kolones Castle*, which was built by the Lusignans but virtually destroyed by an earthquake in 1222, and the fifth-century *Panagia Limeniotissa Basilica* are all also worth a visit for their architectural and historical importance.

Transportation

Air: Paphos International Airport. **Road:** Car: Coastal road east to Paphos (from Limassol); coastal road south to Paphos (from the Polis region); road southwest, past Platres and Kedares. Then join coast road east from Limassol (from Troodos).

Contact Addresses

Pafos Chamber of Commerce and Industry (PCCI), 7 Athinon Avenue and Alexandrou Papagou Corner, Tolmi Court, First Floor, Office 101-102, Pafos 8100, Cyprus
Tel: (00357) 269 35115
Website: www.ccci.org.cy

Paphos Odeon

Cyprus Tourism Organisation©

Czech Republic

1 Charles Bridge (Karluv Most)
2 Kutná Hora
3 Old Town Square (Staromestskee namesti)
4 Prague Castle and St Vitus Cathedral

Tourist Information

**Czech Tourist Authority
(Ceská centrála cestovního ruchu)**
Vinohradská 46, PO Box 32,
120 41 Prague 2, Czech Republic
Tel: (02) 2158 0611
Website: www.visitczechia.cz

Czech Tourist Authority
2nd floor, Morley House, 320 Regent Street,
London W1B 3BG
Tel: (020) 7631 0427
Website: www.visitczechia.cz

Charles Bridge (Karluv Most)

The *Charles Bridge* is Prague's most familiar
monument. Built in 1357, this 520m-long bridge
(1770ft) was the only connection between the
two halves of Prague for 400 years. Originally,
the bridge was bare of ornamentation except for
one solitary cross; however, as the Counter
Reformation took hold in Bohemia, the bridge
eventually gained over 30 Baroque statues. The
earliest, erected in 1683, is a bronze statue of
martyr St John of Nepomuk who was thrown off
the bridge. Craft stalls and buskers along the
bridge add to the atmosphere and make it a
popular meeting place.

Transportation
Air: Praha Ruzyně International Airport. **Rail:**
Train: Hlavní nádraží Station (Prague Station).
Underground: Staromestská. Tram: From Karlovy
Lazne. **Road:** Bus: From Staromestská. Coach:
Praha-Florenc Coach Station. Car: E48, E50, E55
or E67 towards Prague.

Contact Addresses
Prague Information Service, Betlémské námistí 2,
116 98 Prague 1, Czech Republic
Tel: (02) 12444
Website: www.prague-info.cz

Kutná Hora

Kutná Hora once rivalled Prague and even
London in terms of size and importance. The
discovery of silver ore here in the 14th century
led to the creation of the Royal Mint and the
town became the political, cultural and
economic centre of Bohemia. The legacy of this
glorious epoch can be seen in the fine Gothic
and Italianate buildings that line the cobbled
streets. The most famous of all is the
magnificent *St Barbara's Cathedral*, built between
1388-1565 by the town's miners (St Barbara is
the patron saint of miners) to rival St Vitus'
Cathedral in Prague. Visitors with a taste for the
macabre should pay a visit to the monastic
church at nearby *Sedlec*, the interior of which is
made entirely of human bones.

Transportation
Air: Praha Ruzynì International Airport. **Rail:**
Train: Kutná Hora Mesto Station. (From Prague,

change at Kolin for Kutná Hora). **Road:** Coach: Kutná Hora Lorecka Bus Station (from Prague Florenc Coach Station). Car: Road to Kolin, then follow signposts for Kutná Hora (from Prague).

Contact Addresses
Information Center, Sankturinovsky dum, Falackého námestí 377 284 01, Kutna Hora, Czech Republic
Tel: (327) 512 378
Website: www.kutnahora.cz

Old Town Square (Staromestské námestí)

Prague's picture-book *Old Town Square*, with its colourful facades and cobbled surface, is perhaps one of the most familiar tourist scenes of Central Europe. Although many of the facades are Baroque in style, the houses actually date from Medieval times when the square was the centre of the Bohemian world, and a meeting place for merchants and traders from across Europe. The square is home to many of Prague's best-loved attractions but perhaps the most famous is the *Astronomical Clock* on the *Town Hall (Staroměstská radnice)* which dates from the 14th century. Much of the original structure was destroyed when the Nazis set fire to it in May 1945 during the Prague Uprising.

Transportation
Air: Prague Ruzyně International Airport. **Rail:** Train: Hlavní nádraží Station (Prague Station). Underground: Staromìstská or Mùstek. **Road:** Bus: Regular public services. Car: E55 (from Dresden/Berlin); E67 (from Warsaw/Wroclaw) or E50 (from Paris). Visitors should note that the historic centre of Prague is pedestrianised.

Contact Addresses
Prague Information Service,
Betlémské námestí 2,
116 98 Prague 1,
Czech Republic
Tel: (224) 371 111
Website: www.prague-info.cz

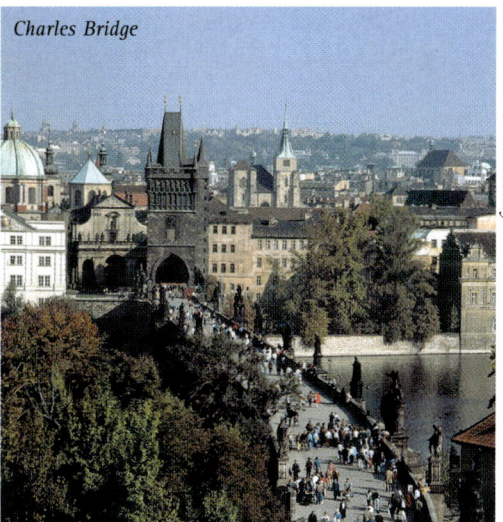
Charles Bridge

Prague Castle and St Vitus Cathedral (Prazsky Hrad and Katedrála sv Vita)

The reaching spires of *Prague Castle*, the seat of Bohemian government for a thousand years, can be seen from virtually anywhere in Prague. It is actually more of a complex than a castle, covering 45 hectares (110 acres) and comprising three courtyards, fortifications and gardens. Its most famous attraction is the Gothic *St Vitus Cathedral*, the country's largest church, which was begun in 1344 under Charles IV but not completed until 1929, and is much loved for its stained glass. *St Wenceslas' Chapel* contains the tomb of the country's most famous patron saint and a cycle of paintings depicting scenes from his life.

Transportation
Air: Praha Ruzyně International Airport. **Rail:** Train: Hlavní nádraží Station (Prague Station) or Praha-Holesovice Station (for some international express trains). Tram: To Prazsky Hrad. **Road:** Coach: Praha-Florenc Coach Station.

Contact Addresses
Prazsky Hrad, 11908 Prague 1, Czech Republic
Tel: (02) 2437 3368
Website: www.hrad.cz

Denmark

200km
100mls
✈ international airport

NORWAY

Skagerrak

Grenen

Frederikshavn

Laesø

Mors

Aalborg

Viborg

SWEDEN

DENMARK

Århus

Jutland

Samsø

Elsinore

Helsingborg

Legoland

Billund

COPENHAGEN

Esbjerg

Roskilde

Malmö

Odense

Zealand

Fyn

Nyborg

Als

Møn

Rønne

Bornholm

Lolland

Falster

Rügen

NORTH SEA

Kattegat

Kiel

Rostock

GERMANY

1 Kronborg Castle (Kronborg Slot)

2 Legoland

3 Little Mermaid (Lille Havfrue)

4 Tivoli

Tourist Information

Danish Tourist Board (Danmarks Turistråd)
Vesterbrogade 6 D, DK-1620 Copenhagen V,
Denmark
Tel: 3311 1415
Website: www.dt.dk or www.visitdenmark.com

Danish Tourist Board
55 Sloane Street, London SW1X 9SY, UK
Tel: (020) 7259 5959

Kronborg Castle (Kronborg Slot)

Strategically located on a site overlooking the
Sound, the stretch of water between Denmark and
Sweden, *Kronborg Castle* at Helsingør (Elsinore) is of
great historical importance playing a key role in the
history of Northern Europe during the 16th to 18th
centuries. Work began on the castle in 1574, with its
defences being reinforced in the late 17th century.
Kronborg, which is one of the most important
Renaissance castles in Northern Europe, is also
famous for being the setting for William
Shakespeare's play *Hamlet* (the Prince of Denmark)
and has staged many performances of the play over
the centuries. Most of the rooms and fortifications in
and around the castle are open to the public, along
with the *Danish Maritime Museum*, which is home to
many temporary and permanent exhibitions.

Transportation
Air: Copenhagen Airport. **Rail:** Train: Elsinore
Station or Grønnehave Station. The castle is
approximately 15 minute's walk from Elsinore
Station. **Road:** Bus: Public services.

Contact Addresses
Kronborg Castle, Kronborg 2c, 3000 Elsinore,
Denmark
Tel: 4921 3078
Website: www.ses.dk/kronborgcastle

Legoland

The renowned 10-hectare (25-acre) amusement
park located north of Billund features attractions
and rides built from no less than 40 million
plastic LEGO blocks. Shows are performed daily
by the Children's Theatre, and there are also circus
acts in high season. Adults and children can
marvel at the detailed LEGO reconstructions of
famous sights from around the world in *Miniland*;
Duplo Land, with its chunkier bricks, is particularly
popular with younger children. Other popular
attractions include *Pirateland* and *Castleland*. The
sophisticated *Port of Copenhagen* exhibit, featuring
electronically controlled trains, cranes and ships,
is also popular. The *Falck Fire Brigade* was a new
attraction added in 2005.

Transportation
Air: Billund International Airport. **Rail:** Train:
Vejle, Kolding or Fredericia stations. **Road:** Bus:

Regular public services. Car: A7/E-45 (exit 63), then route 441 and route 28 (from the south); E-45 (exit 60), then route 28 (from the north); E-20 (exit 61), then route 18 and route 28 (from Copenhagen).

Contact Addresses
Legoland A/S, Nordmarksvej 9, DK-7190 Billund, Denmark
Tel: 7533 1333
Website: www.lego.com

Little Mermaid (Lille Havfrue)

Denmark's most famous cultural symbol comes from a tale told by its most renowned poet, Hans Christian Andersen. In his story the youngest daughter of the Sea King rescues a drowning prince and falls in love, but in the end gets turned into sea foam. The idea for the statue originated in 1909 when brewer Carl Jacobsen saw the ballet version of the *Little Mermaid* and was so impressed that he commissioned sculptor Edvard Eriksen to create a bronze statue on Copenhagen's waterfront. Eriksen modelled the mermaid on his wife and she is now Copenhagen's most famous symbol as she stares dreamily across the water from *Langelinie*.

Transportation
Air: Copenhagen Airport. **Rail:** Train: Copenhagen Central Station or S-Bahn to Østerport. **Road:** Bus: Public services. Car: Signs to København harbour and Langelinie waterfront, then Lille Havfrue.

Contact Addresses
Wonderful Copenhagen Tourist Information, Copenhagen Right Now, Vesterbrogade 4A, 1620 Kobenhavn V
Tel: 7022 2442
Website: www.visitcopenhagen.dk

Tivoli

Opened in 1843 as a theme park and public garden, *Tivoli Gardens* has outlasted the great parks of Europe that were its inspiration – the Tivoli in Paris and Vauxhall Gardens in London. Tivoli Gardens still retains a flavour of that era, seeming more like an open-air garden than it does a theme park. However, there are plenty of rides including the *Golden Tower*, *Valhalla Castle*, a *Ferris Wheel* and a roller coaster. The less daring can enjoy the many concerts, circus acts, and theatrical performances that also find a home at Tivoli. The famous *Copenhagen Christmas market* is held here in November and December, making this a particularly atmospheric time to visit.

Transportation
Air: Copenhagen Airport. **Rail:** Train: Copenhagen Central Station or S-Bahn to København H. **Road:** Bus: Services to Town Hall Square. Car: Signs to the city centre and the Town Hall.

Contact Addresses
Tivoli, Vesterbrogade 3, DK 1631 Copenhagen V, Denmark
Tel: 3315 1001
Website: www.tivolidk.com

The main entrance at Tivoli

Danish Tourist Board/Ireneusz Cyranek©

Dominica (Commonwealth of)

20km
10mls

✈ international airport

Cape Capucin

Cabrits
Peninsula
Prince
Rupert Bay
Portsmouth

Melville Hall ✈ Marigot

Colihaut
Morne Diablotin
△1447m

Carib
Reserve

DOMINICA

ATLANTIC OCEAN

St Joseph
Layou

Morne
Trois Pitons
1387m△
Rosalie

①

✈ Canefield
■ **ROSEAU**

*CARIBBEAN
SEA*

Soufrière
Soufrière Bay
Grand
Bay
Scotts Head

1 Morne Trois Pitons National Park

Tourist Information

**National Development Corporation (NDC) –
Division of Tourism**
PO Box 293, Valley Road, Roseau,
Commonwealth of Dominica
Tel: 448 2045
Website: www.dominica.dm

Dominica Tourist Office
MKI Ltd, Mitre House, 66 Abbey Road, Bush
Hill Park, Enfield, Middlesex EN1 2QE, UK
Tel: (020) 8350 1004

Key to symbols: £ Entry charged ᴅ Disabled access
⚒ Man-made attraction ❤ Natural attraction
🅿 Parking ✕ Restaurant ⚱ Shop 🏛 UNESCO site

Morne Trois Pitons National Park

The *Morne Trois Pitons National Park* encompasses
69 sq km (27 sq miles) of varied landscape – lush
tropicana and rainforests contrast starkly with
volcanic terrain characterised by deep valleys and
bubbling pools. The park was created in 1975 and
is centred around the *Morne Trois Pitons* (meaning
'mountain of three peaks'), a triple-spiked
mountain formed from volcanic remains, which
rises to 1342m (3681ft) above sea level. The *Valley
of Desolation* is a barren area of volcanic rock
which contains over 50 fumaroles (geysers)
emitting sulphurous gases and steam. One of the
most beautiful sites in the park is the *Emerald
Pool*, a waterfall grotto located against a backdrop
of tropical plants and flowers.

Transportation
Air: Melville Hall Airport.
Road: Bus: Regular public services. Car: Imperial
Road to *Emerald Pool* (from Roseau); Trafalgar
Road, then Laudat Road to *Trafalgar Falls* (from
Roseau); Valley Road to *Freshwater Lake* or *Boiling
Lake* (from Roseau).

Contact Addresses
Morne Trois Pitons National Park, Forestry,
Wildlife and Parks Division, Botanical Gardens,
Roseau, 10017 Commonwealth of Dominica
Tel: 448 2401

🅿 ✕   £ 🏛

Morne Trois Pitons National Park

Dominica Division of Tourism, UK office©

Ecuador

PACIFIC OCEAN

COLOMBIA

Caqueta

Esmeraldas   Tulcán

Putumayo

Equator

QUITO   Coca

Cotopaxi △5895m   Napo

Manta

Portoviejo   Ambato   Oriente

Chimborazo△ 6310m   **ECUADOR**

Riobamba

△ Sangay 5230m

Guayaquil

Salinas

Gulf of Guayaquil   Puná I.   Cuenca

Machala   PERU

Loja

Cordillera del Condor

1

200km

100mls

✈ international airport

PACIFIC OCEAN

Sierra

Costa

Vinces

Oriente

Tourist Information

Ministry of Tourism (Ministerio de Turismo)
Avenida Eloy Alfaro N32-300 and
Carlos Tobar, Quito, Ecuador
Tel: (02) 250 7555/9
Website: www.vivecuador.com

Embassy of the Republic of Ecuador
Flat 3B, 3 Hans Crescent,
London SW1X 0LS, UK
Tel: (020) 7584 2648

---

1   Galapagos Islands (Islas Galapagos)

Galapagos Islands (Islas Galapagos)

Straddling the Equator 1000km (622 miles) off the
coast of Ecuador, the *Galapagos Islands* are famous
for being the inspiration for Charles Darwin's
theory of evolution. There are 13 large islands and
six small, which were formed by oceanic
volcanoes some three to five million years ago.
Visitors come to the islands to see the
unparalleled variety of wildlife that flourishes due

to the remote location and temperate climate. The
most famous residents are the giant tortoises after
whom the islands are named, although other
common species include iguana, dolphins, boobies
and cormorants. The animals are so used to
human company visitors can even swim with
penguins and sea lions. Snorkelling and sailing
are also popular.

Transportation
Air: Baltra Airport.

Contact Addresses
Galapagos National Park Service, Puerto Ayora,
Santa Cruz, Galapagos, Ecuador
Tel: (05) 526 189
or
CAPTURGAL, Galapagos Chamber of Tourism,
Puerto Ayora, Santa Cruz, Galapagos, Ecuador
Tel: (05) 526 206
Website: www.galapagostour.org

    £ ✦

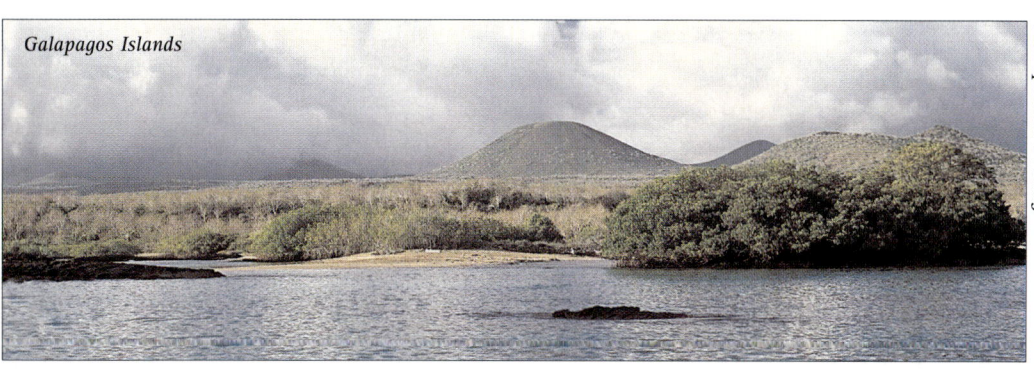

Galapagos Islands

Metropolitan Touring©

Egypt

400km
200mls
✈ international airport

Crete

MEDITERRANEAN SEA

PALESTINE
Nile Delta Port Said
Mersa Matruh **Alexandria** JORDAN
El Alamein **Abu Mena** *Tanta Suez Canal* ISRAEL
Qattara Depression -133m **Giza CAIRO**
Siwa *Giza Pyramids & Sphinx* *Sinai*
El Tur *Gulf of Aqaba*
Minia **Ras Gharib** SAUDI ARABIA
E G Y P T Hurghada *Ras Muhammad*
Asyut *Nile*
RED SEA
Thebes & *Karnak*
Valley of the Kings **Luxor**
El Kharga *Edfu*
The Great Oasis
Aswan
dam *Philae*
Tropic of Cancer
Lake Nasser Admin. bndy.
Abu Simbel Halaib
Political bndy.
LIBYA SAHARA SUDAN

1 Abu Simbel
2 Egyptian Antiquities Museum (El Mathas El Massry)
3 Hatshepsut's Temple (Deir el-Bahri)
4 Karnak Temple (Ipet-Isut)
5 Pyramids at Giza and the Sphinx (Ahramat Al-Jizah and Abu el-Hol)
6 Valley of the Kings and Valley of the Queens (Biban-el-Melouk and Biban-el-Harem)

Tourist Information

Ministry of Tourism (Wezarit El Suaha)
Misr Travel Tower, Abassiya Square, 11381 Cairo, Egypt
Tel: (202) 6845828/4870802

Egyptian State Tourist Office
Egyptian House, Third Floor, 170 Piccadilly, London W1V 9DD, UK
Tel: (020) 7493 5283 or (09001) 600 299 (24-hour brochure service: calls cost 60p per minute)
Website: www.egyptnow.com/english

Abu Simbel

One of the most famous ancient Egyptian sites, the two temples of *Abu Simbel* were carved out of sandstone cliffs high above the River Nile in 1257BC, under the orders of Pharaoh Ramses II (1304-1237BC). The most famous of the two features four colossal 20m-high (65ft) statues of Ramses II flanking the entrance, although they are actually dedicated to the sun god Re-Herakhte. The temples, which were rediscovered by the Swiss explorer Burckhardt in 1813, withstood the passage of time until the construction of the Nasser Dam in 1970, which caused the waters of Lake Nasser to rise significantly. With the support of UNESCO, an international appeal was launched and the temples were gradually relocated to a higher elevation over a four-year period between 1964 and 1968.

Transportation
Air: Luxor International Airport. Internal flights are available to Aswan International Airport and Abu Simbel Airport. **Water:** Boat: Cruise boats and feluccas take visitors to the site. **Road:** Bus: Public services leave from Aswan.

Contact Addresses
For more information on Abu Simbel, contact the Ministry of Tourism (see **Tourist Information** above).

   £

Egyptian Antiquities Museum (El Mathas El Massry)

The 107 halls of the *Egyptian Antiquities Museum* in Cairo were built in 1900 by the French architect Marcel Dourgnon and opened in 1902. The collection itself dates back to 1835, however, when the *Service des Antiques de l'Egypte* (Egyptian Antiquities Service) was set up to protect government-owned artefacts and put a halt to the raiding of archaeological sites. Today, the museum houses a number of ancient Egypt's greatest artefacts, with by far the most popular being the treasures from Tutankhamun's tomb, which include the boy-king's famous golden facemask, as well as approximately 1700 other objects. The museum exhibits around 120,000 objects in total.

Transportation
Air: Cairo International Airport. **Train:** Rail: Ramses Station. Underground: Sadat (Tahrir) Station. **Road:** Bus: Abdel Mouneem Riyad Bus Terminal. Car: Delta Road or Alexandria Desert Road to Cairo (from Alexandria).

Contact Addresses
Tahrir Square, Cairo 11557, Egypt
Tel: (02) 579 6974
Website: www.egyptianmuseum.gov.eg

Hatshepsut's Temple (Deir el-Bahri)

Hatshepsut's Temple is the mortuary temple of Queen Hatshepsut. Located on the West Bank in Luxor, this spectacular temple was built by the Queen's architect, Senenmut, in honour of the only woman ever to reign over Egypt as Pharaoh. Set against towering cliffs in the *Theban Hills*, this unique temple attracts bus loads of tourists every day to see one of the most impressive sites in the *Necropolis*. The temple, with its many monumental ramps, fine terraces, elegant columns and hieroglyphic paintings, also tells the story of Hatshepsut's journey to the *Land of Punt* (which is believed to be modern-day Somalia) to bring back treasures such as ebony, ivory, gold, perfumes and myrrh trees.

Transportation
Air: Luxor International Airport. **Water:** Ferry: A tourist ferry leaves from the East Bank to take passengers across the River Nile. Motor boats can also be hired. **Road:** Coach: The majority of tourists visit the temple as part of an organised coach tour. Taxi: Taxis are available to take visitors to the temple and can be hired on arrival on the West Bank.

Contact Addresses
Luxor Tourist Office, Nile Sreet, Luxor, Egypt
Tel: (095) 382 215 *or* 373 294
Website: www.luxorguide.com

Karnak Temple (Ipet-Isut)

Karnak Temple is a vast complex consisting of three main temples, several smaller enclosed temples, and a number of outer temples. The most spectacular of these is the *Temple of Amun* (*Amun's Precinct*). This is entered via the *Avenue of the Sphinxes* that once connected Karnak and *Luxor Temples*, and led through the ancient city of Thebes, the capital of Egypt during the period of the Middle and New Kingdoms. The whole complex was built over a period of 1300 years and includes several of the finest examples of ancient Egyptian design and architecture. Among them are the *Hypostyle Hall*, considered one of the world's great architectural achievements with around 130 enormous carved columns covering an area of 6000 sq m (64,586 sq ft), and the *Obelisk of Thutmose I*, a 22m (71ft) monument, the only one of four original obelisks that is still standing.

Transportation
Air: Luxor International Airport. **Rail:** Train: Luxor Station. **Road:** Coach: The vast majority of tourists visit the temple as part of an organised coach tour. Bus: Luxor Bus Station. Taxis: Taxis can be hired from the centre of Luxor; alternatively visitors can travel by *caleche* (horse and cart).

Contact Addresses
Luxor Tourist Office, Nile St, Luxor, Egypt
Tel: (095) 382 215 *or* 373 294
Website: www.luxorguide.com

Pyramids at Giza & the Sphinx (Ahramat Al-Jizah & Abu el-Hol)

The *Pyramids* at Giza are among the best-known ancient monuments in the world and the only one of the Seven Wonders of the ancient world still standing. Of the three pyramids, the *Pyramid of Chephren*, which is sometimes known as the *Second Pyramid*, is the most famous due to its imposing size, with its base once covering an area of 216 sq m (2325 sq ft). The famous *Sphinx* stands in front of the Great Pyramid, with the body of a lion joined to the head of a man. There is a Sound and Light show every night at Giza which adds to the atmosphere surrounding these mysterious ancient sights.

Transportation

Air: Cairo International Airport. **Rail:** Train: Ramses Station. **Road:** Bus: From Midan Tahrir. Public buses also run from Ahmed Helmi Bus Station. Taxi: Many visitors take a taxi from Cairo city centre. Car: Sharia al-Ahram (Pyramids Road) (from Cairo city centre).

Contact Addresses

For more information on the Pyramids at Giza and the Sphinx, contact the Ministry of Tourism (see **Tourist Information** above).

Valley of the Kings and Valley of the Queens (Biban-el-Melouk and Biban-el-Harem)

The *Valley of the Kings* is a limestone valley situated in the Theban Hills where the mummified bodies of many Egyptian pharaohs were interred. The area marks a period in ancient Egyptian history in which the pharaohs abandoned the pyramid style and chose instead tombs dug within limestone in order to preserve the mummies for eternity and prevent grave robbing. The tombs, although stripped of many of their contents centuries ago, still display fantastic wall paintings depicting the lives of the pharaohs in ancient Egypt, down to the minutest detail. The most famous tomb is that of Tutankhamun, discovered in pristine condition by Howard Carter in 1922. The many treasures found in the tomb are now exhibited in the *Egyptian Antiquities Museum* in Cairo. Nearby, the wall paintings in the tombs of the *Valley of the Queens* and the *Valley of the Nobles* are equally fascinating. The most famous tomb in the Valley of the Queens is the *Tomb of Queen Nefertari*, the principal wife of Ramses II, which was only opened to the public in 1995.

Transportation

Air: Luxor International Airport. **Water:** Ferry: A tourist ferry leaves from the East Bank to take passengers across the River Nile. Motor boats can also be hired. **Road:** Coach: The majority of tourists visit the temple as part of an organised coach tour. Taxi: Taxis are available to take visitors to the temple and can be hired on arrival on the West Bank. Bicycle: Bicycles can be hired in Luxor.

Contact Addresses

Luxor Tourist Office, Nile St, Luxor, Egypt
Tel: (095) 382 215 *or* 373 294
Website: www.luxorguide.com

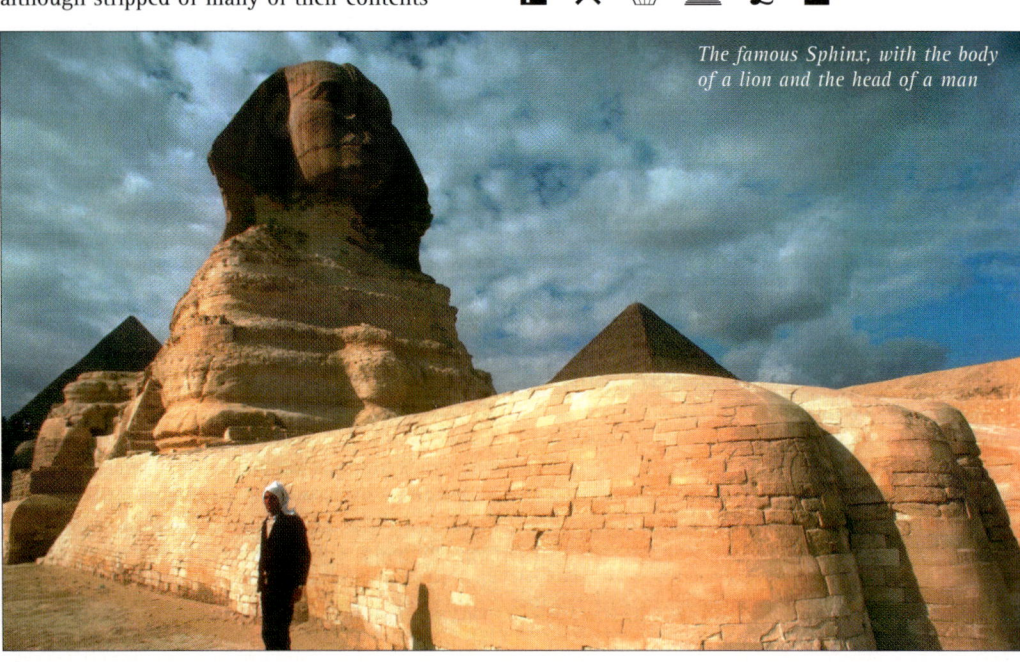

The famous Sphinx, with the body of a lion and the head of a man

Corel©

Estonia

1 Kadriorg Palace and Park
2 Tallinn Town Hall Square (Raekoja Plats)

Tourist Information

Eesti Turismiagentuur (Estonian Tourist Board)
Roosikrantsi 11, Tallinn 10119, Estonia
Tel: (06) 279 770
Website: www.visitestonia.com

Embassy of the Republic of Estonia
16 Hyde Park Gate, London SW7 5DG, UK
Tel: (020) 7589 3428
Website: www.estonia.gov.uk

Kadriorg Palace and Park

The Russian Tsar Peter I began building *Kadriorg Palace and Park* in 1718 in honour of the empress Catherine I. Designed by the Italian architect Niccolo Michetti, the building was inspired by Italian villas and stands as one of the finest examples of Baroque architecture in Northern Europe. By 1921 the palace had become home to the *Estonian Museum of Tallinn* which later became the *Art Museum of Estonia* in

1928. The *Kadriorg Park* was originally 100 hectares (247 acres) and consists of beautiful landscaped gardens, the *Flower Garden* and the popular *Swan Lake*.

Transportation
Air: Tallinn Airport. **Rail:** Tallinn Station. **Road:** Bus: Public services.

Contact Addresses
Kadriorg Palace, 37 Weizenbergi Street, 10127 Tallinn, Estonia
Tel: (06) 066 400
Website: www.ekm.ee/kadriorg

Tallinn Town Hall Square (Raekoja Plats)

With its colourful buildings, turreted walls and gabled roofs, Tallinn is one of the best-preserved historic centres in Europe. All the winding cobbled streets lead on to the *Raekoja plats* (Town Hall Square), which is dominated by the imposing façade of the *Raekoda*, or Town Hall. The building was constructed in the 14th and 15th centuries and is the only surviving late Gothic town hall in Northern Europe. Its soaring steeple bears a 16th-century weather vane portraying the medieval warrior, 'Old Thomas', guardian of the city. Open-air concerts are held here in summer and its many cafés, bars and restaurants make it a bustling meeting place for both tourists and Tallinners alike.

Transportation
Air: Tallinn Airport. **Water:** Ferry: Reisisadam Sea Port (Tallinn). **Rail:** Train: Balti jaam Station. **Road:** Coach: Autobussijaam (Tallinn Bus Station).

Contact Addresses
The Tallinn Tourist Information Centre, Niguliste 2/ Kullassepa 4, Tallin 10146, Estonia
Tel: (06) 457 777
Website: www.tourism.tallinn.ee

Finland

400km
200mls

✈ international airport

Tourist Information

Finnish Tourist Board (Matkailun Edistämiskeskus)
Head Office: Töölönkatu 11, PO Box 625, 00101 Helsinki, Finland
Tel: (09) 417 6911
Website: www.mek.fi
Eteläesplanadi 4, PO Box 249, 00131 Helsinki, Finland
Tel (09) 4176 9300 *or* 4176 9211
Website: www.visitfinland.com

Finnish Tourist Board
PO Box 33213, London W6 8JX, UK
Tel: (020) 7365 2512 (information and brochures only) *or* (020) 8600 5680 (trade and press only)
Website: www.finland-tourism.com *or* www.mek.fi

The wooden rollercoaster at Linnanmäki Amusement Park

Linnanmäki Amusement Park ©

Linnanmäki Amusement Park

Founded in 1950, *Linnanmäki* amusement park is one of the most popular tourist attractions in Finland. This giant theme park was opened by six Finnish child welfare organisations to promote children's events in the country. The *Children's Day Foundation* was set up by these six charities with responsibility for managing the park in 1956. This is still the case today and all profits are donated to charity. Rides include a *Wooden Roller Coaster* which was built in 1951, the *Space Express* roller coaster and the *Space Shot* adventure ride. A *Toy and Play Museum* opened in 1996.

Helsinki Tourist & Convention Bureau©

Suomenlinna Sea Fortress

The maritime barracks at Suomenlinna

Helsinki Tourist & Convention Bureau/Juhhani Sepporaara©

Transportation
Air: Helsinki-Vantaa Airport. **Rail:** Tram: 3T (from Mannerheimintie). **Road:** Bus: Public services from Helsinki city centre.

Contact Addresses
Linnanmäki, Tivolikuja 1, 00510 Helsinki, Finland
Tel: (09) 773 991
Website: www.linnanmaki.fi

Suomenlinna Sea Fortress (Suomenlinna Sveaborg)

Suomenlinna Sea Fortress was built over 250 years ago and once had a population of 4600, larger than the population of Helsinki at the time. Construction began off the coast of Helsinki in 1748, when Finland was part of the Swedish Empire and the Swedes built a fortress on the islands as a counter to the increasing Russian naval strength in Kronstadt. In 1808, the fortress surrendered to the Russians, with Finland becoming part of the Russian empire. The fortress was originally called *Sveaborg*

(literally, 'Sweden's Fortress'), but was renamed *Suomelinna* ('Finland's Fortress') in 1918, one year after Finland finally gained independence from Russia. Today, the fortress is an integral part of the city and home to around 900 inhabitants. There are a variety of attractions on the islands, including guided walks, the *Suomenlinna Museum* (with the *Suomenlinna Experience* multi-media show), the *Ehrensvärd Museum*, the *Doll and Toy Museum*, the *Manege Military Museum*, *Submarine Vesikko*, the *Coast Artillery Museum* and the *Customs Museum*.

Transportation
Air: Helsinki-Vantaa Airport. **Water:** Ferry: Ferries leave from the eastern edge of the main market square, Kauppatori. Waterbuses also operate in summer and leave from their own jetty at Market Square.

Contact Addresses
Suomenlinna Tourist Information, Visitor Centre, Suomenlinna C74, 00190 Helsinki, Finland
Tel: (09) 684 1880
Website: www.suomenlinna.fi

France

1 Arc de Triomphe de l'Étoile

2 Bayeux Tapestry (Tapisserie de Bayeux)

3 Cave of Lascaux (Grotte de Lascaux)

4 Claude Monets House and Water Garden (Maison de Claude Monet et Le Jardin d'eau)

5 D-Day Beaches (Plages du Débarquement de la Bataille de Normandie)

6 Disneyland Resort Paris

7 Eiffel Tower (Tour Eiffel)

8 Louvre (Musée du Louvre)

9 Mont Saint-Michel Abbey (Abbaye du Mont Saint-Michel)

10 Orsay Musuem (Musée d'Orsay)

11 Palace of Versailles (Château de Versailles)

12 Parc Astérix

13 Paris Notre-Dame Cathedral (Cathédrale Notre-Dame de Paris)

14 Popes' Palace (Palais des Papes)

15 Regional Nature Park of the Volcanoes of Auvergne (Parc Naturel Régional des Volcans d'Auvergne)

16 Rocamadour

17 Roman Ampitheatre in Arles (Arénes d'Arles)

18 The Walled Town of Carcassonne (Cité de Carcassonne)

Tourist Information

Maison de la France (French Tourist Office)
20 avenue de l'Opéra, 75041 Paris, Cedex 01, France
Tel: (01) 4296 7000
Website: www.franceguide.com

French Tourist Office
178 Piccadilly, London W1V 0AL, UK
Tel: (09068) 244 123 (information line; calls cost 60p per minute)
Website: www.franceguide.com

Arc de Triomphe de l'Étoile

Commissioned by Napoleon to commemorate the victorious French Army, the *Arc de Triomphe* has been a defining symbol of Paris ever since completion in 1836. Engraved on the arch are numerous names of important and not so important victories and beneath it lies the *Tomb of the Unknown Soldier*. Visitors can reach the 50m-tall (164ft-) top of the arch for stunning views of Paris, including the *Louvre* and the *Champs-Elysées*, or tour the museum inside which charts the history and construction of the arch. The Champs-Elysées is considered to be one of the most elegant boulevards in the world and used to be a showground for Parisian high society. It still retains an air of exclusivity, with luxury boutiques and expensive cafés.

Transportation

Air: Paris Roissy-Charles de Gaulle Airport, Paris Orly Airport. **Rail:** Train: Paris Gare du Nord (Eurostar) Station. Underground: Charles-de-Gaulle-Étoile. RER: Charles-de-Gaulle-Étoile. **Road:** Bus: Regular public services.

Contact Addresses

Centre des monuments nationaux, Arc de Triomphe de l'Étoile, 75008 Paris, France
Tel: (01) 5537 7377
Website: www.monum.fr

Bayeux Tapestry (Tapisserie de Bayeux)

The *Bayeux Tapestry*, which is one of the most historically important, and unusual, chronicles of its day, is now located in the town of Bayeux in Normandy. The 70m-long (231ft-) tapestry offers a splendidly vivid depiction of the events leading up to the Norman Conquest of England in 1066. It begins with Harold of Wessex's visit to Normandy and his meeting with Duke William in 1064, and culminates with the flight of the English army at Hastings. All the main intervening events are covered in painstaking detail. Although it was almost destroyed in 1792 when French revolutionaries used it as a wagon cover, the whole tapestry (with the exception of the final section, thought to have depicted William's coronation in Westminster Abbey on Christmas Day 1066) has survived to this day and can still be viewed by visitors to the town of Bayeux.

Transportation

Air: Caen-Carpiquet Airport. **Rail:** Train: Bayeux Station. **Road:** Bus: Public services. Car: N13, A14, A13, N413, N175, E46, N13 and D6 (from Paris).

Contact Addresses

Tapisserie de Bayeux, Centre Guillaume le Conquérant, 13 bis rue de Nesmond, 14400 Bayeux, France
Tel: (02) 3151 2550
Website: www.normandy-tourism.org

Cave of Lascaux (Grotte de Lascaux)

Discovered by chance in 1940 by a group of teenagers, the cave paintings at Lascaux are considered to be among the world's best examples of prehistoric art. The area around Périgueux features many such cave paintings, although the 15,000-year-old images of bulls, horses and reindeer are believed to be some of the best. After the discovery of the cave, the increasing levels of carbon dioxide emitted by visitors were found to be damaging the paintings and, as a result, the caves were sealed in 1963, following an order from the French Ministry of Cultural Affairs. In order to compensate for the closure, a precise cement replica of the original caves, known as Lascaux II, was opened to the public in 1983; these caves feature the two most important parts of the original caves, the *Great Hall of the Bulls* and the *Painted Gallery*.

Transportation

Air: Périgueux-Basillac Airport. **Rail:** Train: Condat-Le-Lardin Station. **Road:** Bus: Services to Périgueux (from Montignac). Car: D901, D31 and D86 (from Brive-La-Gaillarde) or N21, D705, D4, D75, D7, D31 and D86 (from Périgueux).

Contact Addresses

Grotte de Lascaux, Semitour Périgord, 25 rue du Président Wilson, BP 1024, 24001 Périgueux Cedex, France
Tel: (05) 5335 5010
Website: www.culture.gouv.fr/culture/arcnat/lascaux/en

Claude Monet's House and Water Garden (Maison de Claude Monet et Le Jardin d'eau)

The Impressionist painter Claude Monet, who was born in Paris in 1840, spent the latter part of his life in Giverny in Northern France. Monet purchased a house in the village in 1883 and remained there until his death in 1926. Today, visitors can see the renovated house and wander around the beautiful gardens at Giverny. Inside the house, the walls are filled with a collection of Monet's Japanese prints. Visitors can also see a beautiful display of waterlilies in the gardens which greatly inspired the painter and featured in some of his most famous works.

Transportation
Air: Paris Roissy-Charles de Gaulle Airport. **Rail:** Train: Vernon Station (from St Lazare Station in Paris). **Road:** Bus: Buses from Vernon Station.

Contact Addresses
84 rue de Claude Monet et Le Jardin d'Eau, Fondation Claude Monet, 27620 Giverny, France
Tel: (02) 3251 2821
Website: www.fondation-monet.com

D-Day Beaches (Plages du Débarquement de la Bataille de Normandie)

The Allied Landings that took place at dawn on D-Day, June 6 1944, signalled the beginning of the end of World War II. Some 83,000 British and Canadian and 73,000 US troops landed by sea and air along a 64-km (40-mile) stretch of the Normandy coast in northern France. The horrific conditions, with many of the floating tanks sunk before they even reached the beaches, meant that thousands of soldiers never returned. The war cemeteries where many of the soldiers were laid to rest are open to the public, and some contain chapels and memorials. One of the most famous beaches is Omaha Beach, portrayed in Steven Spielberg's film 'Saving Private Ryan', where there is a large American cemetery overlooking the beach at *Colleville-sur-Mer*.

Transportation
Air: Caen-Carpiquet Airport, Paris Roissy-Charles de Gaulle Airport, Paris Orly Airport. **Water:** Ferry: Services to Cherbourg, Caen and Le Havre (from Ireland and the UK). **Rail:** Train: Caen Station or Bayeux Station (services from Paris St Lazare Station). **Road:** Car: D514 or D513, N158, N13 (to Caen).

Contact Addresses
Comité Régionale de Tourisme de Normandie, 14 rue Charles Corbeau, 27000 Evreux, France
Tel: (02) 3233 7900
Website: www.normandy-tourism.org

Disneyland Resort Paris

Opened in 1992, *Disneyland Paris*, located within the *Disneyland Resort Paris*, was the Walt Disney Company's first attempt to win the hearts of the Europeans. The park is very much like its American cousin, featuring sections like *Mainstreet USA*, *Discoveryland*, *Adventureland*, *Frontierland* and *Fantasyland*, however, enthusiasts rave that the more modern engineering of the French Parks make for a superior experience. Although locals took some time to warm to the park, the resort's success eventually led to Disney opening a second theme park, *Walt Disney Studios Park*, in 2002.

Transportation
Air: Paris Roissy-Charles de Gaulle Airport, Paris Orly Airport; shuttle services are available from both airports to the park. **Rail:** Train: Eurostar, SNCF, Thalys or RER to Marne-la-Vallée/Chessy Station. **Road:** Car: A4, 32km (20 miles) east of Paris (exit 14) (signposted Parcs Disney).

Contact Addresses
Disneyland Paris, Guest Relations, BP100, 77777, Marne la Vallée, Cedex 4, France
Tel: (01) 6030 6053 (in France)
Website: www.disneylandparis.com

Eiffel Tower (Tour Eiffel)

Originally created as the centrepiece of Paris' *Exposition Universelle* in 1889, in commemoration of the centenary of the French Revolution, the *Eiffel Tower* went on to become the centrepiece of the city itself. The tower that has become symbolic of Paris the world over weighs 10,100 tonnes (990 tons) and contains 18,000 pieces of iron, held together by 2,500,000 rivets. At 324m (888ft) high, it was, until 1929, the tallest structure in the world; although that record was broken many years ago, there are still superb views over Paris from the first floor, which can be reached by a stairway, and even better views from the third floor, which is accessible by lift. The tower was designed by architect Stephen Sauvestre and took 2 years, 2 months and 5 days to build.

Transportation

Air: Paris Roissy-Charles de Gaulle Airport or Paris Orly Airport. **Rail:** Train: Paris Gare du Nord (Eurostar). Underground: Bir-Hakeim, Trocadéro or Ecole Militaire. RER: Champ de Mars-Tour Eiffel. **Road:** Bus: Public services.

Contact Addresses

Tour Eiffel, Champ de Mars, 75007 Paris, France
Tel: (01) 4411 2323
Website: www.tour-eiffel.fr

Louvre (Musée du Louvre)

Constructed as a fortress in the Middle Ages and rebuilt in the mid-16th century as a royal palace, it wasn't until 1793 that the *Louvre* became a museum. Today, it is the home of some of the world's most famous works of art, including the *Mona Lisa* and *Venus de Milo*. The rest of the permanent collection includes Greek, Etruscan, Roman, Egyptian and oriental antiquities, as well as sculptures, *objets d'art* and prints and drawings. Entrance to the museum is through the largest of the three glass pyramids that dominate the courtyard. The huge global success of Dan Brown's novel *The Da Vinci Code*, which opens with the murder of the museum's curator, has swelled visitor numbers as literary pilgrims flock to see the places featured in the novel.

Transportation

Air: Paris Roissy-Charles de Gaulle Airport, Paris Orly Airport. **Rail:** Train: Paris Gare du Nord (Eurostar). Underground: Palais Royal-Musée du Louvre. **Road:** Bus: Regular services. Car: A1 (from Lille); A16 (from Boulogne); E60 (from Brussels); A62, then A20, A71 and A10 (from Toulouse); A3 (from Paris Roissy-Charles de Gaulle Airport); A4 (from Strasbourg); A6 (from Lyon and Marseille) or A13 (from Caen).

Contact Addresses

Musée du Louvre, 75058 Paris Cedex 01, France
Tel: (01) 4020 5151 (recorded information)
Website: www.louvre.fr

Eiffel Tower at dusk

Maison de la France©

Mont Saint-Michel Abbey (Abbaye du Mont Saint-Michel)

Mont Saint-Michel (Saint Michael's Mount) is a rocky island surrounded by perilous waters 1km (0.6 miles) off the coast of Normandy. It was founded in 708 by the Bishop of Avranches who built a chapel there after the Archangel Michael appeared to him in a dream. Construction of the spectacular *Abbaye du Mont Saint-Michel* (Mont Saint-Michel Abbey) started in 1023 and finished some 400 years later. Fashioned from granite, its delicate contours are an extension of the shape of the island and encompass a range of architectural styles, from Norman to Gothic. For centuries, the Abbey was a place of pilgrimage but it has also variously served as a prison, a fortress against the English and a monastery.

Contact Addresses

Abbaye du Mont Saint-Michel, 50116 Le Mont Saint-Michel, France
Tel: (02) 3389 8000
Website: www.monum.fr/m_stmichel/indexa.dml

Transportation

Air: Caen-Carpiquet Airport, Paris Roissy-Charles de Gaulle Airport, Paris Orly Airport. **Water:** Sea: Ferry services from the UK and Ireland to Cherbourg, Caen, Le Havre and Dieppe. **Rail:** Train: Pontorson Railway Station; high-speed TGV services from Paris Gare Montparnasse via Rennes. **Road:** Car: N176 (from St Malo and Avranches) or N175 (from Rennes).

Orsay Museum (Musée d'Orsay)

This magnificently restored railway station houses the French national collection of art from 1848 to 1914. Since opening in 1986, the museum has attracted pilgrims from far and wide who come to take in the stunning collection of Impressionist and Post Impressionist art. Paintings include five Monet canvases of Rouen Cathedral, ballet scenes by Dégas, Courbet's shocking *L'Origine du Monde* (the Origins of the World), a hyperrealistic painting depicting a naked woman lying on her back, and works by Cézanne, Van Gogh, Renoir and Toulouse-Lautrec. The museum's collection also contains several fine sculptures as well as examples from the Art Nouveau movement. The museum works upwards in chronological order, and there is a café on the sky-lit upper level, where views of Paris can be enjoyed from behind the original station clock. The museum's restaurant is a finely decorated dining room, preserved in its original state, and popular with its many visitors.

Contact Addresses

Musée d'Orsay, 62 rue de Lille, 75343 Paris, France
Tel: (01) 4049 4872
Website: www.musee-orsay.fr

Transportation

Air: Paris Roissy-Charles de Gaulle Airport or Paris Orly Airport. **Rail:** Paris Gare du Nord (Eurostar) Station. RER: Musée d'Orsay. Underground: Solférino. **Road:** Bus: Public services. Car: A1 (from Lille); A16 (from Boulogne); E60 (from Brussels); A62, then A20, A71 and A10 (from Toulouse); A3 (from Roissy-Charles de Gaulle Airport); A4 (from Strasbourg); A6 (from Lyon and Marseille) or A13 (from Caen).

Palace of Versailles (Château de Versailles)

The *Palace of Versailles* is one of the most visited sites in France and famous for its immense size. The palace began as a 'modest' hunting lodge, built by Louis XIII in 1623, and was transformed by the architect Jules Hardouin Mansart under the guidance of Louis XIII's son, Louis XIV, into a grand palace complex surrounded by lavish gardens designed by André Le Nôtre. Louis XIV was so taken with the palace that by 1682 it had become the official residence of the court of France and a lavish statement of monarchical power. Today, visitors are still able to view much of the palace, including the renowned 75m (250ft) *Galerie des Glaces* (Hall of Mirrors), where the Treaty of Versailles was signed in 1919, signifying the end of World War I.

Transportation

Air: Paris Roissy-Charles de Gaulle Airport or Paris Orly Airport. **Rail:** Train: Versailles-Chantier Station or Versailles-Rive-Droite Station. RER:

Versailles-Rive-Gauche Station on line C. **Road:** Bus: Public services to Versailles-Place d'Armes. Car: A13 towards Rouen, first exit signposted Versailles-Château.

Contact Addresses

Château de Versailles, RP 834, 78008 Versailles, France
Tel: (01) 3083 7800
Website: www.chateauversailles.fr

Parc Astérix

Opened in 1989, *Parc Astérix* is a giant theme park based on the adventures of the popular cartoon character, Astérix. Located in the heart of protected forest, north of Paris, the park takes visitors on a humorous journey through ancient Gaul, the Roman Empire and the Middle Ages to the 21st century. Visitors can meet the Gauls of prehistoric times, step back in time to Le Moyen-Âge (the Middle Ages), travel through Rome and Ancient Greece, and shake hands with the Three Musketeers. There are around 30 permanent rides at the park, as well as regular shows to entertain visitors.

Transportation

Air: Paris Roissy-Charles de Gaulle Airport. **Rail:** Train: Roissy-Charles de Gaulle 2 TGV Station, then bus to Parc Astérix. Underground: Roissy-Charles de Gaulle 1, then bus to Parc Astérix. **Road:** Bus: Public services. Car: A1 Paris–Lille motorway, 35km (22 miles) north of Paris (exit 7-8) (signposted Parc Astérix).

Contact Addresses

Parc Astérix, BP8, 60128, Plailly, France
Tel: (03) 4462 3404 *or* 4462 3030
Website: www.parcasterix.com

Paris Notre-Dame Cathedral (Cathédrale Notre-Dame de Paris)

Begun in 1163 by the architect Maurice de Sully and completed in about 1345, *Notre Dame* ranks as one of France's finest examples of Gothic architecture. During its long life, besides being a resplendent medieval cathedral, Notre Dame was reportedly set on fire during the Commune of 1871, when the Communards rose against the French government in the wake of their defeat during the Franco-Prussian war and was also used to house livestock. It has also been the site of many historical events, including the crowning of Henry VI of England in 1430 and the marriage of the Catholic Marguerite de Valois to the Huguenot (Protestant) Henri of Navarre in 1572, which sparked the St Bartholomew's Day Massacre during the French Wars of Religion. Today, the cathedral still awes visitors with its massive rose windows, its 7800-pipe organ, towering spire and splayed flying buttresses.

Transportation

Air: Paris Roissy-Charles de Gaulle Airport or Paris Orly Airport. **Rail:** RER: Châtelet-Les Halles or St-Michel-Notre-Dame. Underground: Cité. **Road:** Bus: Public services. Car: A1 (from Lille); A4 (from Strasbourg); A16 (from Dunkirk); A13 (from Caen) or A6 (from Lyon). In Paris, from either bank of the River Seine, signs are marked to Ile de la Cité.

Contact Addresses

Cathédrale Notre-Dame de Paris, Ile de la Cité, 6 Place du Parvis, 75004 Paris, France
Tel: (01) 4234 5610
Website: www.cathedraledeparis.com

Paris Notre-Dame Cathedral
Corel©

Popes' Palace (Palais des Papes)

The imposing *Popes' Palace* towers over Avignon and dates back to the time when the Provençal city was the centre of the Christian world after the papacy was moved here from Rome in 1309. Although the papacy moved back to Rome in 1377, Avignon remained the property of the Holy See and was used to house members of the Papacy. Various popes added to the buildings during the Middle Ages, creating the largest Gothic palace in Europe, and today visitors can visit many of the rooms. The *Great Chapel*, also built by Clement VI, is spectacular and is more like a cathedral than a chapel in terms of size. The palace also gave its name to the famous *Châteauneuf-du-Pape* wine, and regular tastings are held in a new wine store located in the heart of the palace.

Transportation
Air: Marseille-Provence Airport. **Rail:** Train: High-speed TGV services to Avignon (from Paris Gare de Lyon, Montpellier, Barcelona and Lyon). **Road:** Car: A7 or A9 (from Lyon, Marseille and Nîmes).

Contact Addresses
Palais des Papes, RMG - 6 rue Pente Rapide Charles Ansidéi, BP 149, 84008 Avignon, Cedex 1, France
Tel: (04) 9027 5074
Website: www.palais-des-papes.com

Regional Nature Park of the Volcanoes of Auvergne (Parc Naturel Régional des Volcans d'Auvergne)

Covering an area of more than 395,000 hectares (976,085 acres), the *Parc Naturel Régional des Volcans d'Auvergne* was created in 1977 and is home to four volcanic massifs: the *Chaîne des Puys* (*Puy de Dôme*, 1465m/4792ft high), *Monts Dore* (*Puy de Sancy*, 1886m/6188ft high), *Monts du Cézalier* (*Signal du Luguet*, 1551m/5089ft high) and *Monts du Cantal* (*Plomb du Cantal*, 1855m/6086 ft high). There are glaciers, lakes and peatland throughout the park, as well as numerous exhibitions of flora, fauna and traditional architecture. Activities include hiking, riding, cycling, hand-gliding and hot-air ballooning. There are numerous other educational centres located within the park.

Transportation
Air: Clermont Ferrand Airport. **Rail:** Train: Clermont Ferrand Station. **Road:** Car: A71 (from Paris); A72 (from Lyon).

Contact Addresses
Regional Nature Park of the Volcanoes of Auvergne Information Centre, Montlosier 63970 Aydat, France
Tel: (04) 7365 6400
Website: www.parc-volcans-auvergne.com

Rocamadour

Built into limestone cliffs, with its medieval houses clinging precariously overlooking the gorge of the River Alzou, *Rocamadour* is a major pilgrimage site. The town is famed for being the site where the body of St Amadour was discovered near the town's chapel in 1166, an event which led to a succession of miracles in the town. Dedicated to the Virgin Mary, the town ranks behind Rome, Jerusalem and Santiago de Compostela as a pilgrimage site. Visitors to the town can climb the *Grand Escalier* (Great Ladder) to the 12th-century *Cité Religeuse* (Religious City) at the top, which consists of seven chapels. Visitors can also climb the *Chemin de Croix* (Way of the Cross) for exceptional views of the Dordogne from the ramparts of the 14th-century château. Other attractions nearby include the *Rocher des Aigles* birds of prey conservation centre, the *Forêt des Singes* monkey sanctuary and the *Grottes de Lacave* underground caves.

Transportation
Air: Bordeaux Airport, Toulouse International Airport. **Rail:** Train: The four levels of the city are connected by a small train and a lift. **Road:** Bus: Public services. Taxis: Available to take visitors from Rocamadour-Padirac Station. Car: Well signposted from all directions. A winding road leads from the village at the base of the hill to the top.

Contact Addresses

Office de Tourisme de Rocamadour, 46500 Rocamadour, France
Tel: (05) 6533 2200
Website: www.rocamadour.com

Roman Amphitheatre in Arles (Arénes d'Arles)

The two-tiered *Roman Amphitheatre* is probably the most prominent tourist attraction in the charming city of Arles, which thrived in Roman times. Measuring 136m (446ft) in length and 109m (358ft) wide, the 120 Romanesque arches date back to the first century BC. The amphitheatre was capable of seating over 20,000 spectators, and was built to provide entertainment in the form of chariot races and bloody hand-to-hand battles. Today, it draws large crowds for a sport only slightly less brutal – bullfighting – as well as plays and concerts in summer.

Transportation

Air: Marseille-Provence Airport. **Rail:** Train: Arles Station. **Road:** Bus: Public services. Car: A54 (exit Arles-Centre).

Contact Addresses

Arènes d'Arles, Rond-Point des Arènes, 13200 Arles, France
Tel: (04) 9049 3686

The Walled Town of Carcassonne (Cité de Carcassonne)

Set on a hillside allowing extensive views over the *Pyrénées* mountains and the surrounding countryside, the medieval town of *Carcassonne*, which is the largest former fortress in Europe, dates back to the Roman Empire. The ramparts were built during the fourth

century, whilst the château was built during the 12th century by Vicomte Trencavel. Because of its strategic importance, the town was attacked and invaded many times over its history. The town was renovated and restored during the 19th century giving it back some of its former glory and importance. Today, the town, which is beautifully lit up at night, remains an impressive site. The main attractions within the city's walls are the *Château Domtal*, the *Cour du Midi* and the torture chamber at the *Exposition Internationale*.

Transportation

Air: Carcassonne Salvaza Airport. **Water:** Boat: Cruise and leisure boats have moorings along the Canal du Midi just after Carcassonne lock. **Rail:** Train: Carcassonne Station. **Road:** Car: N9, D213, A9, A61 and N113 (from Narbonne) or A620, A61, N161, D118 and N113 (from Toulouse).

Contact Addresses

Cité de Carcassonne, Château Vicomtal, Monument National, 11000 Carcassonne, France
Tel: (04) 6811 7077
Website: www.carcassonne.culture.fr

Rocamadour

Germany

NORTH SEA · Helgoland · Frisian Islands · NETHS. · BELG. · LUX. · FRANCE · SWITZ.

DENMARK · Kiel · Rostock · Lübeck · Greifswald · Hamburg · Bremen · Hanover · Münster · Duisburg · Dortmund · Essen · Düsseldorf · Cologne · Aachen · Bonn · Frankfurt-am-Main · Trier · Saarbrücken · Stuttgart · Kassel · Erfurt · Halle · Leipzig · Magdeburg · BERLIN · SAXONY · Dresden · Chemnitz · GERMANY · Nuremberg · Black Forest · BAVARIA · Munich · L. Constance (Bodensee) · AUSTRIA · CZECH REPUBLIC · POLAND · BALTIC SEA · Rügen · Harz · Weser · Elbe · Oder · Rhine · Main · Danube

200km
100mls
✈ international airport

1 Brandenburg Gate (Brandenburger Tor)
2 Checkpoint Charlie Museum (Haus am Checkpoint Charlie)
3 Cologne Cathedral (Kölner Dom)
4 English Garden (Englischer Garten)
5 Freiburg Cathedral (Freiburger Kathedrale)
6 German Parliament (Reichstag)
7 Heidelberg Castle (Schloss Heidelberg)
8 Jewish Museum Berlin
9 Munich Residence (Residenz München)
10 Neuschwanstein Castle (Schloss Neuschwanstein)
11 Pergamon Museum
12 Sanssouci Palace (Schloss Sanssouci)

Tourist Information

German National Tourist Office (Deutsche Zentrale für Tourismus)
Beethovenstrasse 69,
60325 Frankfurt/M, Germany
Tel: (069) 974 640
Website: www.germany-tourism.de

German National Tourist Office
PO Box 2695, London W1A 3TN, UK
Tel: (09001) 600 100 (recorded information and brochure request line; calls cost 60p per minute) or (020) 7317 0908 (general enquiries)
Website: www.germany-tourism.de

Brandenburg Gate (Brandenburger Tor)

Built in 1791 as a triumphal arch, the *Brandenburg Gate*, the only remaining town gate in the country, is an enduring symbol of Berlin. The design, by architect Carl Gotthard Langhans, is modelled on the entrance to the Acropolis in Athens, and is crowned by a statue of a horse-drawn chariot, which symbolises Victory. The overall effect was intended to testify to the might and power of the Prussian Empire. It has survived multiple wars, including the long Cold War, during which it was sealed off in no-man's land by the *Berlin Wall*, and became a symbol of division between east and west. In 1989 it was reopened to the public following the destruction of the Berlin Wall.

Transportation
Air: Berlin Tegel Airport. **Rail:** Train: S-Bahn to Unter den Linden. Underground: Friedrichstrasse, Französische Strasse or Mohrenstrasse. **Road:** Bus: Public services (to Pariser Platz).

Contact Addresses
Berlin Tourism Marketing, Am Karlsbad 11, 10785 Berlin, Germany
Tel: (0)30 2500 2424
Website: www.btm.de

Checkpoint Charlie Museum (Haus am Checkpoint Charlie)

Checkpoint Charlie was the monitoring tower used to control the area around the *Berlin Wall* that divided the city during the Cold War. It was demolished soon after the 1989 revolution, but the *Haus am Checkpoint Charlie* museum that stands in its place is well worth a visit to discover the historic significance of this apparently unremarkable site. A cinema shows films on the Third Reich and the Cold War era, and the museum also details the history of the Berlin Wall, a piece of which still stands a short distance from the museum, complete with decorations on the western side.

Transportation
Air: Berlin Tegel Airport, Berlin Schönefeld Airport. **Rail:** Train: Bahnhof Berlin Zoologischer Garten Station or Lehrter Bahnhof Station. Underground: U6 Kochstrasse or U1 Stadtmitte. **Road:** Bus: Public services. Coach: Zentraler Omnibusbahnhof (ZOB) am Funkturm.

Contact Addresses
Haus am Checkpoint Charlie, Friedrichstrasse 43-45, 10969 Berlin–Kreuzberg, Germany
Tel: (030) 253 7250
Website: www.mauer-museum.com

Brandenburg Gate

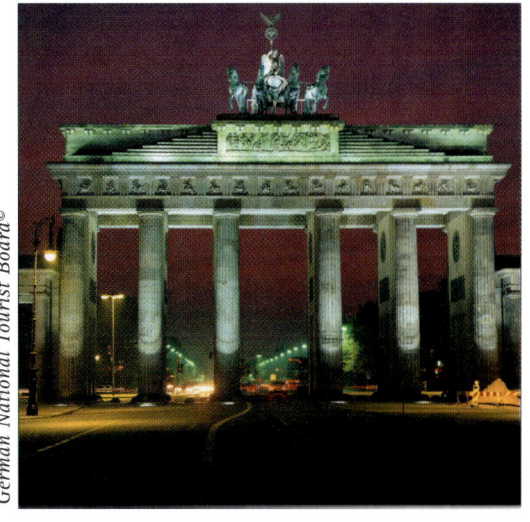

German National Tourist Board©

Cologne Cathedral (Kölner Dom)

Begun in 1248 and completed in 1880, *Cologne Cathedral* is a celebration of the finest aspects of Gothic architecture with intricate detail and elaborate decoration. Its twin towers stand 157m (515ft) above the city, on the left bank of the Rhine, and made the cathedral the tallest structure in the world until the *Eiffel Tower* was built in 1889. The interior is equally impressive, with 14th-century stained glass, a resplendent choir, and a large gold shrine, considered a masterpiece of medieval goldwork. Remarkably the cathedral survived a total of 14 bomb raids during World War II and today visitors can climb the tower for superb views over Cologne and the *Rhineland*.

Transportation
Air: Cologne/Bonn Airport. **Rail:** Train: Cologne Station. Tram: Dom or Hbf (Hauptbahnhof). **Road:** Car: A1, A3, A4, A57 or A555; signs are marked either 'Hauptbahnhof' or 'Dom'.

Contact Addresses
Dompfarramt Domkloster 3, 50667 Köln, Germany
Tel: (0221) 17940 200
Website: www.koelner-dom.de

English Garden (Englischer Garten)

The *Englischer Garten*, measuring 3.7 sq km (1.4 sq miles), is one of Europe's oldest urban landscaped parks, originally laid out in 1789 by American Benjamin Thomson as a garden for the military. It was soon opened to the public, however, and has been popular with locals and visitors ever since due to the natural landscapes and wide open spaces which make it an oasis in the centre of the city. Popular activities include boating on the *Kleinhesseloher Lake* and sunbathing (there is even a special area for naturists). In winter, the garden hosts a Christmas market and in summer there are open-air concerts and plays performed in the amphitheatre.

Transportation
Air: Munich International Airport. **Rail:** Tram: 17 (Tivolistrasse). Underground: U 3/6 to

Universität, Giselastrasse or Münchener Freiheit.
Road: Bus: Public services. Car: A9 to
Schwabing, signs then marked Englischer
Garten.

Contact Addresses
Verwaltung des Englischen Gartens München,
Englischer Garten 2, 80538 Munich, Germany
Tel: (089) 3866 639-0

Freiburg Cathedral (Freiburger Kathedrale)

Consecrated in 1513 and taking over 300 years
to build, *Freiburg Cathedral* is a masterpiece of
Gothic architecture. The 116-m (318-ft) high
west tower, which soars above the jumbled
rooftops of the Black Forest city, was described
by Swiss historian Jacob Burckhardt as 'the
most beautiful spire in Christendom' and
contains the 'Hosanna' bell which dates from
1258. Visitors can climb the tower for excellent
views over Freiburg and the picturesque *Black
Forest*. The interior of the cathedral is just as
beautiful, the highlight being Hans Baldung
Grien's Renaissance *High Altar*, depicting the life
of the Virgin Mary. *Münsterplatz*, the cathedral
square, is a lively venue all year round, but is
particularly atmospheric on long summer
evenings, when people sit outside cafés
enjoying the wine that is produced in local
vineyards.

Contact Addresses
Freiburg Wirtschaft und Touristik GmbH & Co KG,
Rotteckring 14, 79098 Freiburg, Germany
Tel: (0761) 388 1880
Website: www.freiburg.de

Transportation
Air: Euro-Airport Basel-Mulhouse-Freiburg. **Rail:**
Train: ICE (InterCity Express) trains to Freiburg
Hauptbahnhof (from Hamburg, Frankfurt and
Basel) and IC/EC (InterCity and regional) trains to
Freiburg Hauptbahnhof (from Hamburg,
Frankfurt and Cologne). Tram: Bertoldsbrunnen,
Oberlinden. **Road:** Car: A5 Frankfurt-Basel (exit
Freiburg-Mitte).

German Parliament (Reichstag)

The imposing neo-Renaissance *Reichstag*, located
in the heart of Berlin's city centre near the River
Spree and the *Brandenburg Gate*, was completed in
1894. It was home to the *Deutscher Bundestag*
(German Parliament) until 1933, when a huge fire
destroyed the building – an event that coincided
with Adolph Hitler assuming dictatorial control of
the country. In 1999, following the fall of the
Berlin Wall in 1989 and German re-unification, the
parliament moved permanently to a renovated and
renewed Reichstag. A new glass dome symbolises
the transparency of the democratic process, and
visitors can walk along the different levels of the
dome to watch the government in session below.

Transportation
Air: Berlin Tegel Airport. **Rail:** Train: S-Bahn 1, 2
or 25 to Unter den Linden. **Road:** Bus: Public
services to Reichstag/Bundestag. Car: Signs are
marked for the Reichstag in Berlin city centre.

Contact Addresses
Deutscher Bundestag, Besucherdienst (Visitor
Services), Platz der Republik 1, 11011 Berlin, Germany
Tel: (030) 227 73834
Website: www.bundestag.de

Heidelberg Castle (Schloss Heidelberg)

Situated high above the *River Neckar*, *Heidelberg
Castle* is one of Germany's most romantic locations.
It has had a long and turbulent history since it was
first constructed in the early 15th century as a
residence for the Palatine princes, the powerful
secular rulers who presided over this part of
southern Germany during the Holy Roman Empire.
Having been totally destroyed during the Thirty
Years War, and later by the French in 1689 and
1693, the red sandstone building was struck by
lightning in 1764 and even its stones were taken for
use in other building projects. All this rebuilding
has led to a variety of architectural styles and yet
the castle's delapidated air adds to its charm. The
best way to reach the site is by cable car. There are
excellent views over the university city of
Heidelberg and the *Neckar Valley* from the summit.

Transportation
Air: Frankfurt Airport (a coach service runs directly from the airport to Heidelberg). **Rail:** Train: Direct services from across Europe or via Mannheim to Heidelberg Hauptbahnhof. Funicular: Services up to the castle. **Road:** Coach: Heidelberg Busbahnhof. Bus: Public services.

Contact Addresses
Convention and Visitors Bureau, Ziegelhäuser Landstraße 3, 69120 Heidelberge
Tel: (06221) 14220
Website: www.cvb-heidelberg.de

Jewish Museum Berlin

Designed by the Polish-born architect David Libeskind, the *Jewish Museum Berlin* opened in 2001 to worldwide acclaim. Famed for its innovative use of space and challenging designs, the museum site is in the shape disrupted Star of David representing the dislocation and exile of Jews within Europe. The museum explores Jewish history tracing it back from Roman times through to the present day with particular emphasis on the holocaust. One of the most moving areas of the museum is the *Holocaust Tower* in which visitors enter a cold, concrete void where the only source of light, air and sound comes from small shafts at the top representing the isolation and fear of the Nazi extermination camps. The museum is the first Jewish museum in Berlin since the last one was destroyed by the Nazis in 1938.

Transportation
Air: Berlin Tegel Airport and Berlin Schoenefeld Airport. **Rail:** Bahnhof and underground stations. **Road:** Bus: Public services.

German Parliament (Reichstag)

Image supplied by Wikipedia

Contact Addresses
Jewish Museum Berlin Lindenstraße 9-14, 10969 Berlin
Tel: (030) 2599 3300
Website: www.jmberlin.de

Munich Residence (Residenz München)

The *Munich Residence*, located in the centre of the city, is a magnificent complex of buildings constructed by the powerful Wittelsbach family who ruled Bavaria for 800 years. Although originally dating from the 14th century, subsequent additions and alterations gave the Residence a variety of architectural styles, right up until the fall of the Wittelsbach dynasty in 1918. Renaissance features predominate and one of the most impressive rooms in the complex is the *Imperial Hall*. The *Antiquarium*, built in 1571, is the oldest part of the palace and houses the family's collection of antiquities, whilst the *Schatzkammer* (treasury) holds an exquisite array of diamonds, rubies and other precious stones.

Transportation
Air: Munich International Airport. **Rail:** Train: München Hauptbahnhof (Munich Station). Underground: Odeonsplatz or Marienplatz. Tram: 19 (Nationaltheater).

Contact Addresses
Residenz München, Residenzstrasse 1, 80333 Munich, Germany
Tel: (089) 290 671
Website: www.schloesser.bayern.de

Neuschwanstein Castle (Schloss Neuschwanstein)

Neuschwanstein Castle is one of three castles built by 'mad' Ludwig II of Bavaria, who was born in 1845 and died in 1886. This fairytale castle sits perched among the natural splendour of the Alps. Its Neo-Romanesque architecture imitates that of a medieval castle and, in turn, Neuschwanstein was the inspiration for Disney's Magic Kingdom. Built between 1869 and 1886, only about a third of the castle was actually completed as Ludwig II was found to be mentally unfit by a government commission. Nearby *Marienbruecke* (Mary's Bridge), which spans a deep gorge, provides magnificent views of the castle.

Transportation
Air: Munich International Airport. **Rail:** Füssen Station. **Road:** Coach: Services from Füssen to Hohenschwangau. Car: A9 (from Berlin and Nuremberg); A92 (from Passau); A95 (from the Alps); A8 (from Salzburg); B17 (from Munich).

Contact Addresses
Schlossverwaltung Neuschwanstein, Neuschwansteinstrasse 20, 87645 Schwangau, Germany
Tel: (08362) 939880 (admin) 930830 (tickets)
Website: www.schloesser.bayern.de

Pergamon Museum

One of the world's great museums, the *Pergamon Museum* lies on Berlin's *Museumsinsel* (Museum Island) complex, which is situated between the River Spree and Kupfergraben. Five museums were built here between 1824 and 1930 to house archaeological treasures and art collections. The last of the five to be built was the Pergamon Museum which was designed by Alfred Messel and houses spectacular works of architectural antiquities, including collections of Greek, Assyrian, Islamic and Far Eastern art.

Transportation
Air: Berlin Tegel Airport.
Rail: Train: S-Bahn to Friedrichstrasse or Hackescher Markt. Tram: Regular services. Underground: Friedrichstrasse. **Road:** Bus: Regular services.

Contact Addresses
Pergamon Museum, Bodestrasse 1-3, 10178 Berlin, Germany
Tel: (030) 2090 5577
Website: www.germany-tourism.co.uk

Sanssouci Palace (Schloss Sanssouci)

Sanssouci Palace was built for the Prussian emperor Frederick II as his summer retreat. Its name, which literally means 'no worries' in French, reflects the fact that he intended it as an escape from the pressures of Berlin and married life. The real showpiece of Sanssouci, however, is the park. Visitors can wander through a series of beautifully landscaped gardens, including the *Sizilianischer Garten* (Sicilian Garden), which is filled with subtropical plants. A series of fountains and terraces leads to other structures within the park, such as the *Neue Orangerie* (New Orangery) and the *Bildergalerie* (Picture Gallery), which holds paintings by Renaissance artists, including Caravaggio, Rubens and Van Dyck.

Transportation
Air: Berlin Tegel Airport or Berlin Schönefeld Airport. **Rail:** Train: S-Bahn to Potsdam-Hauptbahnhof Bahn (from Berlin Zoo).

Contact Addresses
Stiftung Preussische Schlösser und Gärten, Berlin-Brandenburg, Postfach 60 14 62, 14414 Potsdam, Germany
Tel: (0331) 969 4202
Website: www.spsg.de

Sanssouci Palace

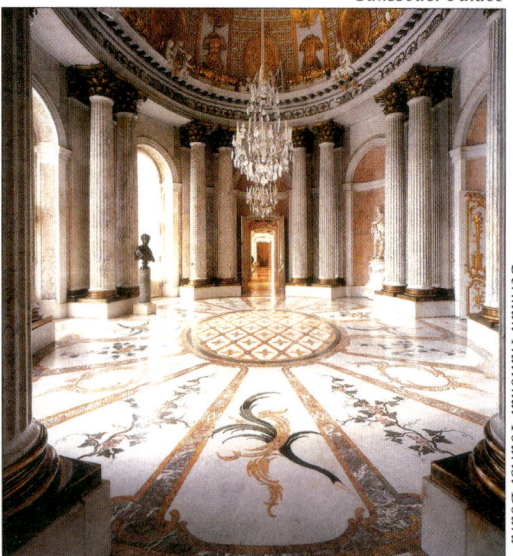

German National Tourist Board©

Gibraltar

SPAIN
North Front
North Mole
Cruise Terminal
Europort
Eastern Beach
Detached Mole
GIBRALTAR
Catalan Bay
Harbour
Cable car
The Rock
Bay of Gibraltar
South Mole
Sandy Bay
100 ton gun
1
426m
Camp Bay
Little Bay
MEDITERRANEAN SEA
Europa Point
1km
½ml
✈ international airport

1 Upper Rock Nature Reserve

Tourist Information

Gibraltar Tourist Board
Duke of Kent House, Cathedral Square, Gibraltar
Tel: 74950
Website: www.gibraltar.gi

Gibraltar Tourist Board
Arundel Great Court, 178/9 The Strand, London WC2R 1EL, UK
Tel: (020) 7836 0777
Website: www.gibraltar.gov.uk

Upper Rock Nature Reserve

The *Upper Rock Nature Reserve* is a protected area of great natural beauty perched about 421m (1380ft) above sea level on the limestone peninsular of Gibraltar. Its most famous residents are the *Barbary Apes*, which have lived on the Rock for hundreds of years as Europe's only free-roaming apes. According to legend, when the apes leave, Gibraltar will cease to be British. The Reserve is also home to many species of bird, such as buzzards and Barbary partridges. Visitors also come to see *St Michael's Cave*, one of a vast warren of caves containing stalagmites and stalactites, and the *Siege Tunnels*, which were used as a defence system by the British in the Great Siege (1779-1783) against the French and Spanish. Another popular site in the Reserve is the 14th-century *Moorish Castle*, which testifies to the diverse history of the peninsular.

Transportation
Air: Gibraltar Airport. **Rail:** Cable Car: From Grand Parade. **Road:** Bus: Public services. Car: Access from the border with Spain at La Linea.

Contact Addresses
For more information on the Upper Rock Nature Reserve, contact the Gibraltar Tourist Board (see **Tourist Information** above).

The famous Rock of Gibraltar

Gibraltar Tourist Board©

Greece

300km
150mls

✈ international airport

1 Acropolis (Akrópoli)
2 Delphi (Delfí)
3 Epidaurus (Epídavros)
4 Knossos
5 Mycenae (Mikines)
6 National Archaeological Museum of Athens (Ethnikó Archaiologiko Mouseio)
7 Olympia (Olimbía)
8 Samarian Gorge (Samaria)

Tourist Information

Ellinikos Organismos Tourismou (Greek National Tourism Organization)
No 7 Tsoha Street, 11521, Athens, Greece
Tel: (210) 870 7000
Website: www.gnto.gr

Greek National Tourism Organization (GNTO)
4 Conduit Street, London W15 2DJ, UK
Tel: (020) 7495 9300 or 7499 8161
Website: www.gnto.co.uk

Acropolis (Akrópoli)

The *Acropolis* is one of the most famous sites of the ancient world and a symbol of Greek civilization. It is the site of three different temples dedicated to Athena Parthenos, the patron goddess of Athens, the most famous of which is the internationally-renowned *Parthenon*. Completed in 438BC, its broad flank of Doric columns is synonymous with ancient culture throughout the world. Built entirely of marble that glows at sunset, the Parthenon once housed a statue of Athena. Visitors can also see the *Propylaea* constructed in 437-432BC, the *Temple of Athena Nike* (the Goddess of Victory), the *Erechtheion Temple*, and the *Acropolis Museum*, which houses many treasures from the Acropolis.

Transportation
Air: Athens International Airport. **Rail:** Underground: Acropolis Station. **Road:** Bus: Plaka

Station. Car: B8A towards Athens and signs for the Acropolis.

Contact Addresses
Acropolis Museum, First Ephorate of Prehistoric and Classical Antiquities, 2-4 Makrygianni Street, 11742 Athens, Greece.
Tel: (010) 321 0219 (Acropolis) *or* 323 6665
Website: www.culture.gr

Delphi (Delfí)

According to Greek mythology, *Delphi* stands at the point where two eagles, released to the east and west by the god Zeus, met, thus marking the centre of the world. Soaring high above the Gulf of Corinth, on Mount Parnassos, it has long been home to the sanctuary of Apollo and the seat of his oracle. Perhaps the best known of Delphi's ancient inhabitants, dating from the second millennium BC, the oracle's predictions affected matters as grand as those of warfare. Today, the ancient site lies in ruins, although visitors still come in their thousands to see the remains. The *Delphi Museum*, which was built in 1903, exhibits various statues and offerings from the sanctuary of Delphi.

Transportation

Air: Athens International Airport. **Road:** Bus: Arahova Bus Stop. Car: Road to Galaxidi, then road to Arahova Acropolis (from Athens).

Contact Addresses

Delphi Museum, 33054 Delphi, Greece
Tel: (026) 5082 313
Website: www.culture.gr

Epidaurus (Epídavros)

The *Sanctuary of Asclepius* at *Epidaurus* was once an important healing centre as well as a religious centre and spa. Built in the fourth century BC, the sanctuary was dedicated to the healer god, Asclepius, and boasts a well-preserved 1400-seat theatre, which was designed by Polycleitus, who built similar buildings at Olympia and Delphi. The theatre is the most famous of all the ancient theatres in Greece and comes alive every summer with theatrical performances. There is also a small excavation museum near Epidaurus, which was built between 1902 and 1909, and contains many remains from the sanctuary.

Transportation

Air: Athens International Airport. **Rail:** Train: Náfplion Station (services from Athens). **Road:** Bus: Public services.

Contact Addresses

Epídavros, Lygourio 21052, Argolis, Peloponnesos, Greece
Tel: (075) 3022 009
Website: www.culture.gr

Knossos

Located on the island of Crete, *Knossos* is the site of the most important palace of the ancient Minoans, the earliest of the Aegean civilisations. It was home to King Minos and, as legend has it, the Minotaur, a giant bull who inhabited the perilous Labyrinth. The Minoan civilisation spread to mainland Greece to form the Mycenaean civilisation, a precursor to the Ancient Greeks. The site was first discovered by Minos Kalokairinos in 1878 and was excavated further by Arthur Evans between 1900 and 1931. Today, Knossos offers the modern-day visitor an abundance of ancient sites, including the *Palace of Knossos*, the *Little Palace*, the *Royal Villa*, the *House of Frescoes* and the *Temple Tomb*.

Transportation

Air: Heraklion Airport. **Road:** Bus: Services to Knossos (from Heraklion Airport). Car: E-75 to Knossos (from Heraklion).

Contact Addresses

Knossos Palace, Heraklion, Crete, Greece
Tel: (081) 231 940
Website: www.culture.gr

Mycenae (Mikines)

Mycenae was first inhabited during Neolithic times and is located between Corinth and Argos, on top of a hill halfway up the Euboea Mountain. It was a citadel palace that included extensive fortifications, shrines and private dwellings. The site continued to be inhabited until the end of the third century AD. Mycenae was first discovered in 1874 by the German archaeologist Heinrich Schliemann, who began excavation in search of gold and believed the site he had found to be the home of Agamemnon, the leader of the Greek assault on Troy. Highlights at Mycenae, which is one of the most popular attractions in Greece, include the *Citadel*, the *Treasury of Atreus*, the *Lion Gate* and the *Royal Cemetery*.

Transportation

Air: Athens International Airport. **Road:** Bus: Public services. Car: E-94 to Corinth, then N-7 (from Athens); N-70 to Árgos, then N-7 (from Náfplion).

Contact Addresses
Mycenae 21200, Argolis, Peloponnesos, Greece
Tel: (075) 1076 585
Website: www.culture.gr

National Archaeological Museum of Athens (Ethnikó Archaiologiko Mouseio)

The most important museum in Athens, the *National Archaeological Museum* houses one of the richest collections of Ancient Greek art in the world. Completed in 1899, the collection includes artefacts from all periods of Ancient Greek civilisation. It is particularly well known for objects found at the ancient city of *Mycenae*, including the *Mask of Agamemnon*, gold vases and elaborate weapons. The museum also has a large collection of Cycladic art on display, as well as the *Statue of Poseidon*, the *Helène Stathatos Collection* of gold jewellery which dates from the ancient and Byzantine worlds.

Transportation
Air: Athens International Airport. **Rail:** Underground: Victoria. **Road:** Bus: Museum Bus Stop. Car: B8A towards Athens, then signs for the city centre.

Contact Addresses
Ethnikó Archaiologikó Mouseio, Patission 44, Athens 10682, Greece
Tel: (010) 821 7717
Website: www.culture.gr

Olympia (Olimbía)

Dedicated to the father of the gods, Olympian Zeus, *Olympia* is the birthplace of the Olympic Games, which were first held here in 776BC. Situated in a Peloponnesus Valley in Southern Greece, the site has been inhabited since prehistoric times and boasts many ancient buildings, including the *Heraeum*, the *Stadium* and the *Hippodrome* where ancient horse races were held. There was also a *Palaestra*, or wrestling school, and a *Gymnasium* where competitors were obliged to train for at least a month. Today, visitors to Olympia come to see the *Temple of Zeus*, which once contained a gold and ivory statue of

Zeus, and the nearby *Archaelogical Museum*, which contains many artefacts from Olympia, including a collection of terracottas, statues and bronzes.

Transportation
Air: Athens International Airport. **Rail:** Train: Train to Pirgos, then change for Olympia (from Athens). **Road:** Bus: Services to Olympia or services via Pirgos. Car: E-65, then E-55 (from Athens).

Contact Addresses
Olimbía, Seventh Ephorate of Prehistoric and Classical Antiquities, 27065, Ancient Olympia, Greece
Tel: (062) 4022 517
Website: www.culture.gr

Samarian Gorge (Samaria)

Regarded as one of Europe's greatest natural wonders, the *Samarian Gorge* is a beautiful 18km- (11 mile-) hike through the *Samaria National Park* in Crete's *White Mountains*. The gorge is believed to be the longest in Europe and is home to beautiful flora and fauna and dramatic rock formations. There are several churches and chapels, including the church dedicated to Saint Maria of Egypt, found in the village of Samaria and dating back to 1379, where the name Sa(int)maria comes from. After a long day's hike, visitors can relax on beaches at the end of the gorge before taking a boat back along the coast to embark on their return journey to Chania.

Transportation
Air: Chania International Airport. **Water:** Boat: Services to Soúyia or Hóra Sfakíon (from Ayía Roúmeli), then bus service back to Chania. **Road:** Coach: Many visitors book trips through tour operators. Bus: Public services. Car: It is not advisable to travel by car to the entrance of the gorge, as visitors must return to their starting point to pick up their car.

Contact Addresses
Samaria, Forest Directorate of Chania, Chania GR 73100, Greece
Tel: (082) 1092 287

Guatemala

200km
100mls
✈ international airport

MEXICO

Palenque

El
Petén • Tikal

Usumacinta

• Flores   BELIZE

• Sayaxché

Pan-American
Highway

Gulf of
Honduras

Puerto
Barrios

GUATEMALA

Lake Izabal

Quiriguá

Ulua

Tajumulco
4220m △

• Utatlán

Motagua

Quezaltenango
• Sololá

HONDURAS

L. Atitlán   Antigua •

**GUATEMALA
CITY** ✈

Mazatenango

Escuintla

Lempa

San José

EL SALVADOR

PACIFIC OCEAN

1 Tikal

Tourist Information

**Instituto Guatemalteco de Turismo (INGUAT)
(Guatemala Tourist Commission)**
7a Avenida 1-17, zona 4, Centro Cívico,
Guatemala City, Guatemala
Tel: 331 1333 or (888) 464 8281 (24-hour toll
free USA only) or (801) 464 8281 (24-hour
toll free Guatemala only)
Website: www.guatemala.travel.com.gt

Embassy of the Republic of Guatemala
13 Fawcett Street, London SW10 9HN, UK
Tel: (020) 7349 0346 (tourism section)

Key to symbols: £ Entry charged & Disabled access
☑ Man-made attraction ♥ Natural attraction
P Parking ✕ Restaurant ⬒ Shop 🏛 UNESCO site

Tikal

Located 548km (341 miles) north of Guatemala
City, the ancient site of *Tikal* was once home to an
estimated 100,000 Maya. Unlike many other
ancient Mayan sites, the wonders of Tikal are
hidden deep within the rainforest. Every year,
visitors come to gaze at its towering 70m- (230ft)
high pyramid and ancient plazas to the
accompaniment of jungle sounds. The site has
more than 3000 structures including temples and
palaces and is located in *Tikal National Park*, which
is listed as a UNESCO World Heritage Site and is
home to many species of wildlife. There is also an
on-site museum, which contains a collection of
objects found during excavations at the site.

Transportation
Air: Guatemala City La Aurora International
Airport. **Road:** Coach: Services to Flores and Santa
Elena, then on to Tikal (from Guatemala city). Car:
CA9 to junction Ruidosa, then the main CA11
road from Flores (from Guatemala city).

Contact Addresses
For more information on Tikal, contact Guatemala
Tourist Commission (see **Tourist Information**
above).

    £

Tikal

Inguat©

Hungary

1 Buda Castle Palace (Budavári Palota)
2 Budapest Central Synagogue (Nagy Zsinagóga)
3 Fisherman's Bastion (Halászbástya)
4 Gellért Bath

Tourist Information

Magyar Turizmus Rt. (Hungarian National Tourist Office – HNTO)
1052 Budapest, Sütö Utcha 2, Hungary
Tel: 800 3600 0000 (call centre info line)
Website: www.hungarytourism.hu

Hungarian National Tourist Office (HNTO)
46 Eaton Place, London SW1X 8AL, UK
Tel: (020) 7823 1032 or 7823 1055
Website: www.hungary.com

Buda Castle Palace (Budavári Palota)

Located in Budapest's picturesque Old Town, *Buda Castle Palace* was first inhabited by King Béla of

Hungary during the 13th century. The king, who fled to the Adriatic Sea in 1241 following the Mongol invasion, returned to live in the palace, building a stronghold to protect the palace from further attack. Over a period of 700 years, the palace was home to many royal residents, including King Lajos the Great, King Matthias I and King Charles III. Today, the palace is home to a number of museums, including the *Ludwig Museum*, the *Hungarian National Gallery* and the *Budapest History Museum*.

Transportation
Air: Budapest Ferihegy Airport. **Rail:** Tram: 18 to Dózsa tér. **Road:** Bus: Public services. Car: M1 to Budapest (from Vienna or Graz). Road signs are then marked for the 'centrum' and the 'citadella'.

Contact Addresses
I Budvári Palota, Dísz tér 17, Budapest, Hungary
Tel: (01) 375 7533
Website: www.budapestinfo.hu

Budapest Central Synagogue (Nagy Zsinagóga)

Budapest Central Synagogue is the largest synagogue in Europe and the second largest in the world after the *Emanuel Synagogue* in New York. Completed in 1859, it was built in a Moorish-Byzantine style by the Austrian architect Ludwig Förster. The building was partly destroyed by bombing campaigns during World War II, but has been the subject of much renovation to restore its two shining Moorish domes to their former brilliance. The *Jewish Museum* next door recounts the horrors of the Holocaust and displays exhibits dating as far back as the Middle Ages. The museum, which was built between 1931 and 1936, stands on the former home of Theodor Herzl, who was the founding father of Zionism and responsible for developing the idea of a modern Jewish state.

Transportation
Air: Budapest Ferighegy Airport. **Rail:** Train: Keleti

Station (East). Underground: Astoria. Tram: Astoria. **Road:** Bus: Public services. Car: M1, M5, M7 or main roads 5, 6, 7, 51 to M0 (circular road around Budapest) or M3 towards Budapest. Follow signs to Astoria (city centre).

Contact Addresses
Nagy Zsinagóga, VII. Dohány utca 2, Budapest, Hungary
Tel: (01) 342 1335
Website: www.budapestinfo.hu

Fisherman's Bastion (Halászbástya)

The *Fisherman's Bastion* was built in 1905 and named after the guild of fishermen responsible for defending this stretch of wall from enemy attack during the Middle Ages. An almost Disney-like tower dominates this stone wall with seven turrets representing the Magyar tribes who once populated the country. Excellent views can be had from the top of the tower across the River Danube to *Margaret Island*, *Parliament*, *St Stephen's Basilica* and the *Chain Bridge*. Visitors can also see the nearby *Nagyboldogasszony Templom* (Church of Our Lady), which was built at the beginning of the 14th century and is more commonly called *Matthias Church* (AD1443-1490) after King Matthias who held both his wedding ceremonies here.

Transportation
Air: Budapest Ferihegy Airport. **Rail:** Underground: Moszka tér. Tram: 18. **Road:** Bus: Public services. Car: No access.

Contact Addresses
1052 Budapest, Sütö Utcha 2, Hungary
Tel: 800 3600 0000 (call centre info line)
Website: www.hungary.com

Gellért Bath

Located next door to the *Danubius Hotel Gellért* in the heart of Budapest, the *Gellért Bath* is a world-famous thermal bath and spa complex that first opened its doors in 1918. Based around the natural hot springs of *Gellért Hill* on the banks of the Danube, Gellért Bath is a traditional thermal bath house that's renowned for its healing properties and consists of 13 indoor and outdoor pools. It's the most famous of Budapest's thermal spas and is admired for its opulent style and baths adorned with tiles, statues and marble pillars. The natural remedies use water that's naturally rich in calcium, magnesium, hydrocarbonate, alkalis, chloride, sulphide and fluoride. It's reputation is international and visitors travel from all over the world for treatments which include physiotherapy, hydrotherapy, balneotherapy and electrotherapy.

Transportation
Air: Budapest Ferihegy Airport. **Rail:** Budapest Station. Tramway: Public services. **Road:** Bus: Public services.

Contact Addresses
Gellért Thermal Bath, Kelenhegyi út 4, H-1118 Budapest, Hungary
Tel: (01) 466 6166
Website: www.spasbudapest.com

Buda Castle Palace and Chain Bridge by Night

Hungarian National Tourist Office©

Iceland

1 Geyser (Geysir)
2 Golden Waterfall (Gullfoss)
3 The Pearl (Perlan)

Strokkur in the Geyser area

Icelandic Tourist Board/Walter Sommerhalder©

Tourist Information

Icelandic Tourist Board (Islenska Tourist Board)
Laekjargata 3, 101 Reykjavik, Iceland
Tel: 535 5500
Website: www.icetourist.is

Geyser (Geysir)

Until 1916, *Geyser*, located 125km (78 miles) northeast of Reykjavik, was one of the world's great geysers, spouting boiling water and steam 60-80m (165-220ft) into the air at three-hourly intervals. Mysteriously, it fell dormant (some say due to hundreds of tourists filling its chamber with objects) and has come to life only once since then, in 1935. The smaller *Strokkur* geyser nearby makes up for its big brother's silence by erupting every five to ten minutes. The entire area is a geothermal park, with belching mud pits, hissing steam vents, hot and cold springs, warm streams and primitive plants. The *Geysir Center* offers visitors year-round exhibitions on geothermal activity, and also contains a folk museum with displays on the history of the area and Icelandic flora and fauna.

Transportation
Air: Reykjavik Keflavik Airport. **Road:** Bus: Public services. Car: Ring road 1, then left near Selfoss to Road 35.

Contact Addresses
Gesyir Center, 801 Selfoss, Iceland
Tel: (354) 480 6800
Website: www.geysircenter.is

Golden Waterfall (Gullfoss)

Located just a few kilometres from Geyser, *Golden Waterfall* (Gullfoss) is the most dramatic section of the *Hvita River* (White River) in southern Iceland. In the midst of lush vegetation, white water thunders down a 32-m (105-ft) drop into a narrow canyon 70m (192ft) deep and 2.5km (1.5 miles) long. The site was bought by the Icelandic government to prevent foreign investors from turning it into a commercial site, and the footpath is opened each morning by a local farmer to allow visitors to see the waterfall from a viewing platform.

Transportation
Air: Reykjavik Keflavik Airport. **Road:** Bus: Public services. Car: Hwy-1, then Road 35 (from Reykjavik).

Contact Addresses
For more information on Gullfoss, contact the Icelandic Tourist Board (see **Tourist Information** above).

The Pearl (Perlan)

The Pearl (Perlan) is as much an architectural masterpiece as it is a feat of engineering. Designed by architect Ingimundur Sveinsson, this awesome 10-storey building opened to the public in 1991. It's geothermally heated by water forced through steel supports and provides a means of water storage and power for the greater Reykjavik region. Excellent views of Reykjavik can be had from the *Viewing Deck* on level four. There is a revolving restaurant in the glass dome at the top of the building. Cocktails are the speciality in the Perlan bar, and art exhibitions and concerts are held regularly.

Transportation
Air: Reykjavik Keflavik Airport. **Road:** Bus: Public services to Perlan. Car: Bustrdrvegur Road towards Perlan (from Reykjavik).

Contact Addresses
Perlan, Post 5252, 125 Reykjavik, Iceland
Tel: 562 0200
Website: www.perlan.is

Restaurant at the Pearl, Reykjavik

India

1 Crown Palace (Taj Mahal)

2 Ellora Temple Caves

3 Ghats at Varanasi (Banaras Ghats)

4 Indian Museum, Calcutta

5 Kaziranga National Park

6 Khajuraho

7 Palace of the Winds (Hawa Mahal)

8 Red Fort (Lal Quila)

Tourist Information

India Tourism
88 Janpath, New Delhi 110 001, India
Tel: (011) 332 0342 or 332 0005 or 332 0008
Website: www.incredibleindia.org

India Tourism
7 Cork Street, London W15 3LH, UK
Tel: (020) 7437 3677 or (0870) 010 2183
(brochure request line)
Website: www.incredibleindia.org

Crown Palace (Taj Mahal)

The *Taj Mahal* has been described as the most extravagant monument ever built for love. It is also India's most emblematic and famous tourist attraction. Renowned for its tree-lined reflective pond leading up to the fabulous domed roof, few know that the Taj Mahal is, in fact, a mausoleum not a mosque. Completed in 1653, it was built by the Emperor Shah Jahan in memory of his second wife, Mumtaz Mahal, who died in childbirth. The elaborate marble designs are inlaid with semi-precious stones such as jade, crystal, turquoise and coral. Many people choose to spend at least several hours here as the changing light and shadows affect the colour and patterns of the Taj Mahal, and it is also possible to picnic in the tranquil gardens.

Transportation
Air: Indira Gandhi International Airport, Agra Airport (domestic flights). **Rail:** Train: Agra Cantt Station. **Road:** Bus: Services to Indian Tourist Office bus stop. Car: NH24, then NH2 (from Delhi); NH11 (from Jaipur); NH25, then NH2 (from Lucknow).

Contact Addresses
India Tourism, 191 The Mali, Agra 282001 Uttar Pradesh, India
Tel: (0562) 363 959
Website: www.incredibleindia.org

Ellora Temple Caves

The *Ellora Temple Caves* consist of 34 separate religious shrines carved into the actual rock of a basaltic hill and containing a wealth of sculptural and architectural treasures. Carved between the fourth and ninth centuries AD, the caves represent three separate faiths: Buddhism, Jainism and Hinduism. The 16 *Buddhist Caves* are the oldest in the group. The *Jain Caves* illustrate the non-violent, ascetic beliefs of this religion, depicting scenes of pastoral beauty and images such as lotus flowers. In terms of stylistic ambition, the *Hindu Caves* outdo their neighbours – one cave alone, the *Temple of Kailasa*, covers twice the area of the *Parthenon* in Athens and took 100 years to complete. Dedicated to Lord Shiva, this temple is the largest monolith in the world and is undoubtedly the most visited site at Ellora.

Transportation
Air: Mumbai Chhaprati Shivaji International Airport, Aurangabad Airport (domestic flights). **Rail:** Train: Aurangabad Station. **Road:** Bus: MSRTC Services to Ellora Temple Caves (from Aurangabad). Car: NH50 towards Nashik and major roads to Ellora (from Pune).

Contact Addresses
India Tourism Aurangabad, Krishna Vilas, Station Road, Aurangabad, 431005, Maharastra, India
Tel: (0240) 331 217
Website: www.incredibleindia.org

many temples lining the riverbank. Huge crowds of pilgrims gather to take part in this ancient ritual which involves making offerings (*puja*) to the rising sun and is often watched by tourists who come to photograph this incredible sight.

Transportation
Air: Indira Gandhi International Airport, Babatpur Airport. **Rail:** Train: Varanasi Station. **Road:** Bus: Main bus stop in Varanasi City Centre. Car: NH2 to Delhi, then NH7 to Kanya and NH29 to Gorakhpur (from Calcutta).

Contact Addresses
India Tourism, 15B The Mall, Cantt, Varanasi 221002, Uttar Pradesh, India
Tel: (0542) 2501784
Website: www.incredibleindia.org

Ghats at Varanasi (Banaras Ghats)

Varanasi, which was created by Lord Shiva, is one of the oldest and holiest cities in India and home to the most famous *ghats* (steps leading down to the river) in the country. Worshippers flock to these *ghats* every day to bathe in the holy River Ganges and then worship at the

Indian Museum, Calcutta

Originally established in 1814, and moved to its present site in 1878, Calcutta's *Indian Museum* is the largest and best museum in the country. Founded by Dr Nathaniel Wallich and housed in a magnificent Italian-style building, the museum has over 60 galleries and is divided into six

Ghats at Varanasi

Ministry of Tourism, India©

different sections: archaeology, art, anthropology, geology, zoology and industry. The art section contains a picture gallery, with Persian- and Indian-style drawings and paintings, and also contains other artefacts and textiles, including silk-woven Tibetan temple banners. Other sections of the museum contain diverse treasures, such as an Egyptian mummy, the skeleton of a whale, rare statues and a collection of meteorites.

Transportation
Air: Calcutta International Airport. **Rail:** Train: Howrah Station or Sealdah Station. Underground: Park Street Station. **Road:** Bus: Jawaharlal Nehru Road. Car: NH2 (from Delhi); NH28A, NH28, NH31 and NH34 (from Kathmandu); NH5 and NH6 (from Bhubaneswar).

Contact Addresses
Indian Museum, 27 Jawaharlal Nehru Road, Calcutta 700016, West Bengal, India
Tel: (033) 22 49 56 99
Website: www.indianmuseum-calcutta.org

Kaziranga National Park

Kaziranga National Park was set aside as a game sanctuary in 1926 and became a national park in 1974. It's made up of 688 sq km (266 sq miles) of breathtaking land containing rainforests, rivers, sprawling grasslands and herds of wild elephant. It is best known for its thriving population of one-horned Indian rhino, which is the largest in the world. The rhino's natural enemy, the tiger, also lives in the park along with many other typical species of Indian wildlife. Visitors can use jeeps or cars to travel around the park; alternatively, opt for a more traditional experience on the back of an elephant. The park has been on the UNESCO World Heritage List since 1985.

Transportation
Air: Indira Gandhi International Airport, Kolkhata International Airport, Gopinath Bordoloi Airport (Guwahati), Jorhat Airport. **Rail:** Train: Furkating Station. **Road:** Bus: Services to Kohara. Car: NH37 to Kohora (from Guwahati). Visitors are advised to travel by air from Guwahati to Jorhat airport and then by bus.

Contact Addresses
Kaziranga National Park, PO Bokakhat 785612, District Golaghat, Assam, India
Tel: (0376) 266 8321

Khajuraho

The famous erotic temples of *Khajuraho* are one of the most popular tourist attractions in India. Built between AD 950 and 1050 by the kings of the Chandela, the site originally possessed 85 temples, of which 20 are still reasonably preserved. Lost for centuries after the decline of the Chandela, the small village of Khajuraho was rediscovered in 1838 by a British army captain. The temples are best known for the erotic friezes on their walls. The name Khajuraho is derived from Khajur, the local word for the date trees which grow in abundance in the region. A *son et lumière* show every evening tells the story of the Chandela Kings and the history of the temples.

Transportation
Air: Indira Gandhi International Airport, Khajuraho Airport (domestic flights). **Rail:** Train: Harpalpur or Jhansi stations. **Road:** Coach: Services from Satna, Harpalpur and Jhansi.

Contact Addresses
Regional Office, Madhya Pradesh State Tourism Development Corporation Ltd, Chandela Cultural Centre, Khajuraho, India
Tel: (0768) 644 051
Website: www.incredibleindia.org

Palace of the Winds (Hawa Mahal)

Built in 1799, *Hawa Mahal* is the most stunning sight in the city of Jaipur. The palace, part of a huge complex, overlooks one of Jaipur's main streets and was originally constructed to offer women of the court a vantage point, behind stone-carved screens, from which to watch the activities taking place in the bazaar and the surrounding streets. For this purpose, it was designed with over 900 niches, and the entire building is shaped like a crown adorning Lord Krishna's head. The site offers superb views of the city, including the many old palaces and houses which were painted ochre-pink, the colour of hospitality, by the Rajputs, for the 1853 visit of Prince Albert.

Transportation
Air: Indira Gandhi International Airport, Sanganer Airport (domestic flights). **Rail:** Train: Jaipur Station. **Road:** Bus: Public services. Car: NH8 (from Delhi); NH11 (from Agra); NH12 (from Bhopal).

Contact Addresses
India Tourism, Khasa-Kothi, Jaipur 302001, India
Tel: (0141) 372 200
Website: www.incredibleindia.org

Red Fort (Lal Quila)

Completed in 1648, the *Red Fort* is the largest of Old Delhi's monuments. Its red sandstone walls dominate Old Delhi's Muslim district, rising above a wide dry moat to a height of up to 33m (108ft), and are lined with turrets and bastions. Today, rather than repel enemy invaders, they keep out the noise of the surrounding city, and the serene gardens and pavilions within the fort hark back to the power and majesty of the Mughal emperors. The main entrance of the Red Fort opens onto a bazaar that was at one time home to the city's most skilled goldsmiths, carpet makers and jewellers. Farther within lies the *Hall of Public Audiences*, where the emperor would listen to the complaints of the common people, and the spectacular *Royal Baths*

Transportation
Air: Indira Gandhi International Airport. **Rail:** Train: Main Delhi Station (Old Delhi). **Road:** Bus: Services to Lal Quila entrance. Car: Grand Trunk Road NH1 (from Amritsar and north); Mathura Road (from Agra and south); NH2 (from Calcutta and east); Gurgaon Road (from Jaipur and west).

Contact Addresses
Government of India Tourist Office (GITO), 88 Janpath, New Delhi 110 001, India
Tel: (011) 332 0005 *or* 332 0342
Website: www.incredinleindia.org

Ministry of Tourism, India©

Khajuraho

Indonesia

1 Prambanan Temple Compounds
  (Loro Jonggrang)

Tourist Information

Indonesian Tourism Promotion Board (ITPB)
Wisma Nugra Santana Building, 9th Floor,
Jalan Jend Sudirman Kav 7-8, Jakarta 10220,
Indonesia
Tel: (21) 570 4879
Website: www.tourismindonesia.com

Indonesian Embassy
38 Grosvenor Square, London W1K 2HW
Tel: (020) 7499 7661
Website: www.indonesianembassy.org.uk

Prambanan Temple Compounds (Loro Jonggrang)

The *Prambanan Temples* form the largest temple complex on the Indonesian island of Java. Constructed around AD 900, the compound was deserted soon after it was completed, possibly due to the eruption of nearby Mount Merapi. The temples were restored in 1953 and now

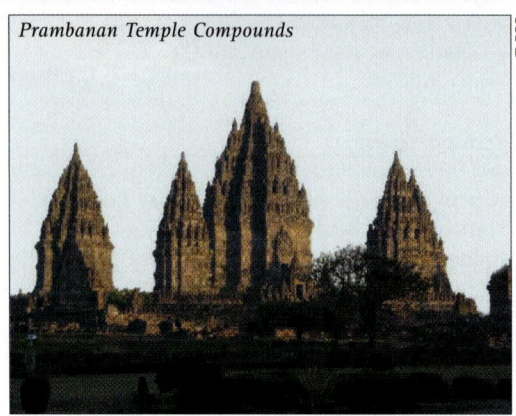

Prambanan Temple Compounds

form one of the world's great Hindu shrines. There are 224 temples in total, but the site is dominated by the imposing figures of the three main temples: the *Brahma Temple*, the *Vishnu Temple* and the *Shiva Temple*. From May to October, the *Ramayana Ballet*, a traditional Indonesian dance based on the Hindu epic, is performed at the open-air theatre.

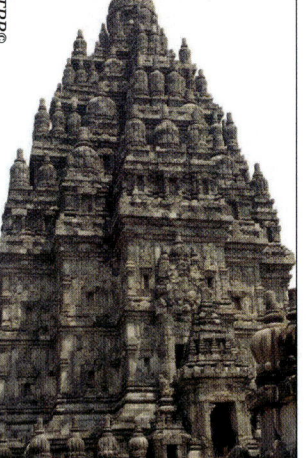

Transportation
Air: Adi Sucipto Airport (Yogyakarta), Jakarta Soekarno-Hatta Airport. **Road:** Coach: Services from Yogyakarta. Car: Signposted Central Java, Yogyakarta, then Prambanan (from Jakarta).

Contact Addresses
The Ministry of Culture and Tourism of the Republic of Indonesia,
JI. Merdeka Barat No.17,
Jakarta 10110, Indonesia
Tel: (21) 3838 436
Website: www.indonesiatourism.go.id

Islamic Republic of Iran

monuments. *Masjid-é Imam*, the Imam Mosque, was built by Shah Abbas the Great during the city's Golden Age in the early 17th century. The women's mosque, the *Sheikh Lotfollah*, is decorated with exquisite Persian tilework and is the highlight of the square for many visitors. The magnificent *Ali Qapu Palace* stands opposite. The central area consists of a formal park and a lake with a fountain and covered bazaar which leads out of the square to the enormous *Masjid-é Jamé* (Friday Mosque).

Transportation
Air: Tehran Mehrabad International Airport, Isfahan Airport (domestic flights). **Road:** Coach: Services from Tehran.

Contact Addresses
Isfahan Tourist Office, Naghsh-é Jahan, Isfahan, Iran
Tel: (0311) 663 5231

1 Imam Square (Naghsh-é Jahan)
2 Persepolis (Takht-é Jamshid)

Tourist Information

Iran Touring and Tourism Organisation (ITTO)
238 Sindhokht Street, Fatemi Avenue, Tehran, Iran
Tel: (021) 643 5650
Website: www.irantourism.org

Embassy of the Islamic Republic of Iran
16 Prince's Gate, London SW7 1PT, UK
Tel: (020) 7225 3000
Website: www.iran-embassy.org.uk

Imam Square (Naghsh-é Jahan)

With its tiled mosques and exotic palaces, the city of Isfahan is considered by many to be the jewel in the Iranian crown. The central square, *Naghsh-é Jahan*, is framed by a series of elegant archways and contains several of the city's most important

Persepolis (Takht-é Jamshid)

Persepolis is thought to have been founded by Darius I in 518BC as the capital city of the vast and powerful Achaemenid Empire. The name Persepolis translates from Greek as 'Persian City' and it was built over a period of 120 years. Set on fire and looted by Alexander the Great in 330BC, it is nevertheless still astounding in its size and splendour; constructed on a large terrace 10m (27ft) high, access is up a wide staircase, and the huge pillars of the *Audience Hall* dwarf the visitors who come to see the impressive ruins.

Transportation
Air: Tehran Mehrabad International Airport, Shiraz Airport (domestic flights). **Road:** Taxi: Services from Shiraz.

Contact Addresses
For more information on Persepolis, contact Iran Touring and Tourism Organisation (see **Tourist Information** above).

Ireland

1 Aran Islands
2 Bantry House
3 Blarney Castle
4 Bunratty Castle and Folk Park
5 Cliffs of Moher
6 Croach Patrick
7 Dingle Peninsula
8 Dublin Castle
9 Dublin Zoo
10 Fota Wildlife Park
11 Glendalough
12 Guinness Storehouse
13 Killarney National Park
14 Kinsale
15 National Gallery of Ireland
16 National Shrine of Our Lady of Knock
17 Phoenix Park
18 RDS Arena
19 Ring of Kerry
20 Rock of Cashel
21 Trinity College Dublin
22 Waterford Crystal Visitor Centre

Tourist Information

Irish Tourist Board (Bord Fáilte Eireann)
Baggot Street Bridge, Dublin 2,
Republic of Ireland
Tel: (01) 525 525
Website: www.failteireland.ie

Irish Tourist Board
150 New Bond Street, London W1S 2AQ, UK
Tel: (020) 7518 0800 *or* (0800) 039 7000
(travel enquiries)
Website: www.irelandtravel.co.uk

Aran Islands

The *Aran Islands* are located approximately 48km (30 miles) out from the mouth of *Galway Bay* in the *Atlantic Ocean*. The largest of the three islands is *Inishmore* (or *Inis Mór*) which measures just 14km (9 miles) from tip to tip and 4.8km (3 miles) at its widest point. The islands are famous for

their prehistoric and Christian monuments including the spectacular *Dún Aengus* fort that is one of best examples of this type of fort in all of Europe. The fortified inner citadel is protected by huge semicircular ringed defences and the *chevaux-de-frise*, a cliff face peppered with sharp shards of rock jutting out intended to impede the advance of an attacking army. Other ancient stone forts worth visiting include *Dún Eoghanachta* and the crumbling *Dún Dúcathair*. The stunning islands are criss-crossed with thousands of miles of stone walls and visitors flock to the islands to enjoy the cliff-top walks and spectacular coastal scenery. The islands are also home to more than 430 different varieties of wild flowers and plants making them popular with botanists. Inishmore can get quite busy during the summer months but the other islands, *Inishmaan* (or *Inis Meáin*) and the smallest, *Inisheer* (*Inis Thiar*, or *Inis Oírr*), are less busy and can offer visitors a more authentic experience. But all three islands have held on to their ancient traditions including the use of Gaelic language (although English is also widely spoken).

Transportation

Air: Knock International Airport and Shannon International Airport. Inverin Airport (domestic flights). **Water:** Ferry: Services from Rossaveal and Doolin on the mainland to Kilronan. **Rail:** Galway Station. **Road:** Bus: Public services.

Contact Addresses

Aran Heritage Centre, Cill Ronain, Inis Mor, Arainn, Co na Gaillimhe
Tel: (099) 61355
Website: www.visitaranislands.com

Bantry House

Overlooking *Bantry Bay* in the south west of *Ireland*, *Bantry House* is a spectacular stately home that's been open to the public since 1946. Originally called *Blackrock*, the house was built in the 17th century as the ancestral home of the Earls of Bantry and is still lived in today by their descendants. The house was extended several times during the 18th century and gradually acquired an extensive collection of tapestries, paintings, furniture and artefacts that had been collected during their travels all over the world. Today, Bantry House consists of approximately 40 hectares (100 acres) of land of which approximately half is landscaped gardens and accessible woodland. Parts of the house can be rented out for weddings and private functions.

Transportation

Air: Cork International Airport. **Water:** Ferry: Services to Ringaskiddy Ferry Port. **Rail:** Killarney Station or Cork Station. **Road:** Bus: Public services. Car: N71.

Contact Addresses

Bantry House, Bantry, Cork, Ireland
Tel: (027) 50047
Website: www.bantryhouse.com

Blarney Castle

Set in idyllic Irish countryside, *Blarney Castle* is home to the famous *Blarney Stone*. Situated high in the battlements of the castle, the stone is thought to be half of the Stone of Scone, an ancient Scottish stone believed to have special powers. Those that kiss the stone are said to inherit the gift of eloquent speech. The castle itself began life as a 10th-century hunting lodge and was rebuilt in stone in 1210, only to be demolished and reconstructed in its original form by Dermot McCarthy, King of Munster, in 1446. Today, much of it lies in ruins.

Transportation

Air: Cork Airport. **Rail:** Train: Cork Station. **Road:** Bus: Regular bus services to Blarney (from Cork Station). Car: N20 (from Cork).

Contact Addresses

Blarney Castle, Blarney, County Cork, Ireland
Tel: (021) 438 5252
Website: www.blarneycastle.ie

Bunratty Castle and Folk Park

Built in 1425 by the McNamara family on the site of an earlier Viking settlement, and later acquired by the Anglo-Irish Studdart family, the spectacular *Bunratty Castle* is one of the finest examples of an Irish tower house still existing today. Inside is a beautifully preserved collection of Medieval furniture which serves as a reminder of Ireland's rich Celtic heritage. A Medieval banquet is served every night on demand to enable guests to experience what it was like to be entertained in the castle's heyday. The adjacent *Folk Park* recreates daily life as it was in 19th-century rural Ireland – farmhouses, shops and cottages have all been reconstructed in detail to provide visitors with an authentic experience.

Transportation

Air: Shannon Airport. **Rail:** Train: Limerick Station. **Road:** Bus: Services from Limerick or Ennis. Car: N18 (from Limerick, Ennis or Galway City).

Contact Addresses
Central Reservations, Bunratty Castle and Folk
Park, Bunratty, County Clare, Ireland
Tel: (061) 360 788
Website: www.shannonheritage.com

Cliffs of Moher

The majestic *Cliffs of Moher* are one of Ireland's
most spectacular and most visited tourist
attractions and tower 213m (700 ft) above the
Atlantic Ocean. The best vantage point from
which to see the Cliffs is *O'Briens Tower*,
constructed in 1835 by Cornelius O' Brien, a local
Member of Parliament who was responsible for
many other local landmarks, and restored in 1970.
The locals know each of the cliffs by name from
north to south: *Aillenasharragh*, *Carrickatreel*,
Knockardachuan, *Branawnmore*, *Stookeen* and *Hag's
Head*. Visitors also go to the cliffs to see the rich
birdlife of the area, including puffins, shags,
kittiwakes and razorbills. Nearby is an area
known as the *Burren* consisting of rolling hills and
cliff faces covered in limestone rock. The area
supports a diverse range of flora and fauna and is
also famous for its megalithic tombs and
monuments that pre-date the Egyptian pyramids.

Transportation
Air: Shannon Airport. **Rail:** Train: Ennis Station or
Galway Station. **Road:** Car: N-85 (from Ennis);
N-67 (from Galway).

Contact Addresses
Cliffs of Moher Centre, Shannon Heritage Visitor
Centre, Liscannor, County Clare, Ireland
Tel: (065) 708 1171 *or* 708 1565
Website: www.shannonheritage.com

Croach Patrick

Situated close to the town of *Westport* in *County
Mayo*, the peak of *Croach Patrick* rises 765m
(2,510ft) and was a sacred pagan site of spiritual
significance for hundreds of years before the
arrival of Christianity. Saint Patrick travelled across

Ireland spreading the word of God and, according
to religious stories, arrived at what is now known
as Croach Patrick in AD 441 where he spent forty
days and forty nights fasting on the summit of the
mountain. By the seventh century, Croach Patrick
had become one of the most important Christian
pilgrimage sites in Ireland. And still today, each
summer millions of pilgrims, many walking
barefoot as a penance for wrongdoings, ascend
Croach Patrick to visit the small church at the
summit. The last Sunday in July is the main
pilgrimage day attracting thousands of pilgrims.
The climb is also popular throughout the year with
walkers who ascend the mountain for the
spectacular views across *Clew Bay* below.

Transportation
Air: Knock International Airport and Shannon
International Airport. **Rail:** Westport Station.
Road: Bus: Public services.

Contact Addresses
Ireland West Tourism, Aras Failte, Forster Street,
County Galway, Ireland
Tel: (091) 537700
Website: www.irelandwest.ie

Dingle Peninsula

Located on the very south-western most tip of
Ireland in *County Kerry*, the dramatic *Dingle
Peninsula* is a popular diversion off the *Ring of
Kerry* tourist trail (see separate entry). The
spectacular peninsula is made up the
Macgillicuddy's Reeks mountain range, a series of
granite peaks that rise out of the *Atlantic*. Also in
and around the town of Dingle are approximately
2,000 archaeological sites. One of the most
famous Christian sites is the *St Gallarus Oratory*
which was thought to have been built between the
seventh and ninth century. Paid-entry attractions
in the region include the ever-popular *Oceanworld
Aquarium* (www.dingle-oceanworld.ie), and the
Blasket Centre, an exhibition celebrating Irish
culture, language and heritage. A popular resident
is *Fungie* the *Dingle Dolphin*. First spotted in *Dingle
Harbour* in 1984, the wild dolphin has returned
from feeding grounds further afield each summer
and can frequently be seen playing in the surf as

boats pass in and out of the harbour. With miles of secluded sandy beaches, rocky outcrops and stunning coastal paths, the Dingle Peninsula is popular with walkers.

Transportation
Air: Kerry Airport (domestic connections). **Water:** Ferry: Services from Europe to Cork. **Rail:** Killarney Station. **Road:** Bus: Public services.

Contact Addresses
Dingle Peninsula Tourism, Dingle, Count Kerry, Ireland
Website: www.dingle-peninsula.ie

Dublin Castle

Located in the heart of historic *Dublin*, *Dublin Castle* was built on the orders of King John, the first Lord of Ireland, in 1210 on the site of a former Danish Viking Fortress. Much of the castle has been rebuilt several times over its history with most of the modern day structure built at points during the 18th century. Of the original structure, only the *Record Tower* still stands today and is now more like a palace than a castle with lavish architecture and opulent rooms. Over the years the castle has been used as a royal residence, court house and prison and the *Irish Crown Jewels* were kept here until they were stolen in 1907. And it was here that on December 6 1921 the Anglo-Irish Treaty was signed effectively ending 700 years of colonial rule and forming what is now the *Republic of Ireland*. Nowadays, the castle is used for ceremonial procedures and to entertain visiting heads of state. It remains one of the most lavish places in all of Dublin.

Transportation
Air: Dublin International Airport. **Water:** Ferry: Services to Dun Laoghaire Port and Dublin Port. **Rail:** Dublin Station. **Road:** Bus: Public services.

Contact Addresses
Dublin Castle, Dublin 2, Ireland
Tel: (01) 677 7129
Website: www.dublincastle.ie

Dublin Zoo

First opened in 1830 with animals supplied by London Zoo, *Dublin Zoo* is one of the city's most popular attractions. It covers a 173-hectare (70-acre) site at *Phoenix Park* in the west of Dublin and houses a wide variety of animals, including red panda, South American birds, arctic fox, otter, elephants, and even a pack of grey wolves. Another popular attraction within the zoo is *City Farm*, which has a special children's corner and a flock of Galway sheep, and the Californian sea lion pool where audiences watch the animals train at regular intervals throughout the day.

Transportation
Air: Dublin Airport. **Water:** Ferry: Services from Holyhead (Wales) and Stranraer (Scotland) to Dun Laoghaire Port and Dublin Port. **Rail:** Train: Heuston Station. **Road:** Bus: Public services. Car: N1 (from Dublin Airport); M11, then N11 (from Wicklow); N7 (from Kildare); N11 (from Dun Laoghaire port), then signs to Dublin city centre and to Dublin Zoo.

Contact Addresses
Dublin Zoo, Phoenix Park, Dublin 8, Ireland
Tel: (01) 474 8900
Website: www.dublinzoo.ie

Dublin Castle
Corel©

Fota Wildlife Park

Located just a few miles outside *Cork*, *Fota Wildlife Park* opened in 1983 as a joint project between the Zoological Society of Ireland and the University of Cork. It's primary objective was the conservation of wildlife and today the zoo is home to over 70 species of exotic wildlife including giraffes, zebra, antelope and ostrich which are all free to roam together within the park as they would in their natural habitats in the wild. Of all the animals in the zoo, only the resident cheetahs are in conventional enclosures. The entrance ticket to Fota Wildlife Park also includes entrance to the *Fota Aboretum* containing a fine collection of plants and trees from around the world.

Transportation
Air: Cork International Airport. **Water:** Ferry: Services to Ringaskiddy Ferry Port. **Rail:** Cork Station then connection to Fota Wildlife Park's own station. **Road:** Bus: Public services.

Contact Addresses
Fota Wildlife Park, Carrigtwohill, County Cork, Ireland
Tel: (021) 481 2678
Website: www.fotawildlife.ie

Glendalough

Known in Irish as 'glenn of the two lakes', *Glendalough* is a glacially sculpted beautiful green valley. During Ireland's 'Golden Age' (AD 500-900) the country flourished as the poetry, music and writing of its missionaries and teachers influenced scholars across Europe. During this time, Glendalough was home to a monastic settlement established by St Kevin, a reclusive monk, who for seven years enjoyed a simple and solitary existence, with animals and birds as his only companions. St Kevin came to the area during the sixth century and founded his monastery in AD 498, remaining there until his death at the grand old age of 120

Transportation
Air: Dublin Airport. **Rail:** Train: Rathdrum Station. **Road:** Bus: Public services. Car: N11 (exit Kilmacanogue), then R755 and R756 to Glendalough (from Dublin).

Contact Addresses
Glendalough Visitor Centre, Glendalough, Co Wicklow, Ireland
Tel: (0404) 45325 *or* 45352
Website: www.heritageireland.com

Guinness Storehouse

Opened in December 2000, the *Guinness Storehouse* is a whole museum dedicated to Ireland's most famous export, Guinness stout. Arthur Guinness first began brewing the 'black gold' on the site in 1759, with the present-day building being designed by the architect A H Hignett in 1904. Used for fermenting and storing Guinness until the 1980s, the Storehouse is a listed building with exhibitions spanning over six floors. Entry to the Guinness Storehouse is through a pint glass-shaped atrium capable of holding 10,000 pints of stout, and there is a free pint of the magic brew for every visitor in the *Gravity Bar* which offers spectacular views across the city.

Transportation
Air: Dublin Airport. **Water:** Ferry: Services from Holyhead (Wales) and Stranraer (Scotland) to Dun Laoghaire Port and Dublin Port. **Rail:** Train: Connolly Station or Heuston Station.

Contact Addresses
Guinness Storehouse, St James's Gate, Dublin 8, Ireland

The Guinness Storehouse

The Guinness Storehouse©

Tel: 353 1 453 8364 (recorded information) *or* 353 1 408 4800 (customer services)
Website: www.guinness-storehouse.com

Killarney National Park

Killarney National Park covers over 10,000 hectares (25,000 acres) of woodland, lakes, mountains, parks and gardens in the far southwest of Ireland. It was Ireland's first national park and was founded in 1932 when the Muckross estate was given to the Irish people by Senator Arthur Vincent. Popular sports include trout fishing in the three lakes, boating at *Ross Castle*, walking and cycling. *Muckross House*, a Victorian mansion completed in 1843, is open to the public as is its working farm and the beautiful landscaped gardens. Other attractions within the grounds of the park include the 15th-century *Muckross Abbey* and the ruined seventh-century monastery at *Inisfallen Island* on *Lough Leane*, where the 'Annals of Inisfallen', detailing Ireland's early history, were written by the monks.

Transportation
Air: Cork Airport. **Road:** Car: Killarney National Park is located 6.5km (4 miles) from Killarney on the N71 (Kenmare Road).

Contact Addresses
Muckross House, Muckross, Killarney, Ireland
Tel: (064) 31440
Website: http://homepage.tinet.ie/~knp

Kinsale

The coastal town of *Kinsale* in the county of *Cork* in the southwest of the country is one of the most picturesque regions in *Ireland*. Two 17th-century forts guard the entrance to the harbour and guided tours are available of the star-shaped *Charles Fort* that was built in 1677. The 15th-century *Desmond Castle* had originally been used as a customs house before being converted to a prison in the 17th century.

Nowadays, it's home to the *International Museum of Wine* that details Kinsale's role in the early international wine trade. Other attractions include an interesting museum housed within the old *Courthouse* and the 13th-century *St Multose Church* that's still in use today. Away from the harbour, visitors can explore the winding cobbled streets through a maze of bars and fine seafood restaurants. A walk away from the town up to the *Old Head of Kinsale* offers stunning coastal views.

Transportation
Air: Cork International Airport. **Water:** Ferry: Services to Ringaskiddy Ferry Port. **Rail:** Cork Station. **Road:** Bus: Public services.

Contact Addresses
Kinsale Tourist Office, Pier Road, Kinsale, Cork, Ireland
Tel: (021) 477 2234
Website: www.kinsale.ie

National Gallery of Ireland

The *National Gallery of Ireland* was founded in 1854 and houses the national collection of Irish art, the national collection of European Old Masters including works by Caravaggio and Rubens, the *National Portrait Collection* and the *Yeats Collection*. The latter features many works by Jack B Yeats, Ireland's most important 20th-century artist. The grand National Gallery building stands in the south of the city and dominates Merrion Square, one of Dublin's finest Georgian squares. The *Millennium Wing* features temporary exhibitions and themed collections. Visitors to the Gallery can take advantage of the free public tours every Saturday and Sunday.

Transportation
Air: Dublin Airport. **Water:** Ferry: Services from Holyhead (Wales) and Stranraer (Scotland) to Dun Laoghaire Port and Dublin Port. **Rail:** Train: Heuston Station, Connolly Station or Tara Street Station. DART (electric rail): Pearse Station. **Road:** Bus: Public services. Car: N1 (from Dublin Airport); M11, then N11 (from Wicklow); N7 (from Kildare); N11 (from Dun Laoghaire port), then signs to Dublin city centre.

Contact Addresses
National Gallery of Ireland, Merrion Square West,
Dublin 2, Ireland
Tel: (01) 661 5133
Website: www.nationalgallery.ie

National Shrine of Our Lady of Knock

Located in *County Mayo* on the *West Coast* of
Ireland, the *National Shrine of Our Lady of Knock*
marks the site where, on August 21 1879, it is
said Our Lady the Virgin Mary appeared in an
apparition. Our Lady is said to have appeared with
St. Joseph and St. John the Evangelist at the
church's south gable on a wet and windswept
evening in August and was witnessed by 15
people. The shrine attracts many visitors
throughout the year but the main pilgrimage
season is from the last Sunday in April until the
second Sunday in October.

Transportation
Air: Knock International Airport. **Water:** Ferry:
Services to Ringaskiddy Ferry Port. **Rail:** Cork
Station then bus services to Knock. **Road:** Bus:
Public services.

Contact Addresses
Shrine Office, County Mayo, Ireland
Tel: (94) 9388 100
Website: www.knock-shrine.ie

Phoenix Park

Dublin's *Phoenix Park* located to the west of the
city centre is one of the largest city parks in
Europe. With a circumference of 11km (7 miles)
and a total area of 712 hectares (1,760 acres),
Phoenix Park is made up of open grasslands,
tree-lined avenues, ornamental gardens, lakes
and nature trails. The park is also home to a
herd of wild deer. *Dublin Zoo* (see separate entry)
is located within the park. Also within the park
grounds is a 63-m (206-ft) obelisk in memory of
the Duke of Wellington who was born in Dublin
in 1769 and the *Phoenix Monument* located in
the very centre of the park. The *Phoenix Park
Visitor Centre* is at Ashtown Castle, a medieval
tower house that is thought to date back to the
17th century, and now houses an excellent
exhibition about the history and wildlife of the
park and surounding region. Access to the park
is free but entry is charged for the Phoenix Park
Visitor Centre.

Rock of Cashel

Corel©

Transportation
Air: Dublin International Airport. **Water:** Ferry: Services to Dun Laoghaire Port and Dublin Port. **Rail:** Dublin Station. **Road:** Bus: Public services.

Contact Addresses
Phoenix Park Visitor Centre, Phoenix Park, Dublin 8, Ireland
Tel: (01) 677 0095
Website: www.heritageireland.ie

RDS Arena

Dublin's *RDS* (*Royal Dublin Society*) *Irish International Convention and Exhibition Centre* is the country's premier venue for meetings, conferences, exhibitions, trade shows, entertainment and sporting events. The Society itself was founded in 1731 to promote the development of agriculture, arts, science and industry in Ireland. The arena measures over 20,000 sq m (215,280 sq ft) and regularly hosts the city's major events and exhibitions.

Transportation
Air: Dublin International Airport. **Water:** Ferry: Services to Dun Laoghaire Port and Dublin Port. **Rail:** Dublin Station. DART connections to the venue. **Road:** Bus: Public services.

Contact Addresses
Merrion Road, Ballsbridge, Dublin 4, Ireland
Tel: (01) 668 0866
Website: www.rds.ie

Ring of Kerry

The famous *Ring of Kerry* is a 170km (106 miles) tourist trail that takes in some of the southwest of Ireland's most spectacular sights along the *Iveragh Peninsula*. Beginning at *Killarney*, visitors can travel in either direction (although tour buses should travel anti-clockwise) on the circular route which passes through *Kenamare*, *Sneem*, *Waterville*, *Cahersiveen*, *Kells*, *Glenbeigh* and *Killorglin* with specific sights of interest in each location.

Highlights of the trail include the *Bog Village*, *Derrynane House* – former home of Daniel O'Connel, the 15th-century *Muckross Abbey*, *Staigue Fort* and *Ross Castle*. Natural attractions along the route include the picturesque *Rossbeigh* beach, the thundering waters of *Torc Waterfall*, and the spectacular *Blue Pool Nature Reserve*. There are also established Ring of Kerry walking and cycling routes that use, where possible, quieter roads and tracks with the cycling route taking in the additional sights of *St Finian's Bay* and the island of *Valentia*. The scenic drive can be comfortably completed in one day but accommodation is available in each location (although this may need to be booked in advance) for visitors who want to spend longer exploring specific attractions.

Transportation
Air: Kerry Airport (domestic connections). **Rail:** Killarney Station. **Road:** Bus: Public services.

Contact Addresses
Killarney Tourist Information Office, Beech Road, Killarney, Country Kerry, Ireland
Tel: (064) 31633
Website: www.corkkerry.ie

Rock of Cashel

Located on a limestone base on the outskirts of the town, the *Rock of Cashel* (also known as the *Cashel of the Kings*) is one of *Ireland*'s most spectacular archaeological sites. The origins of the site date back to the fourth century and the Welsh Eoghachta clan who conquered and became kings of the region building a hilltop stronghold on the site. King Aengus was baptised here by St Patrick, Ireland's patron saint, in the fifth century. A *Cathedral* and *Romanesque Chapel* were added to the compound and the site was eventually given to the church in the 12th century. Visitors also come to the Rock of Cashel to see the *Hall of the Vicars Choral* and the 28-metre (92-foot) *Round Tower*. The Rock sits high on a hill offering good views of the surrounding area and there's also a museum at the site.

Transportation
Air: Shannon Airport, Dublin Airport or Cork Airport. **Water:** Ferry: Accessible from Rosslare Port, Cork Port, Dublin Port and Dun Laoghaire.

Rail: Thurles Station and Limerick Junction Station. **Road:** Bus: Public services.

Contact Addresses
Rock of Cashel, Cashel, Tipperary, Ireland
Tel: (062) 61437
Website: www.heritageireland.ie

Trinity College Dublin

Founded in 1592 by a small group of Dublin citizens who obtained a royal charter from Queen Elizabeth I of England, *Trinity College* is Ireland's most prominent university. It's famous scholars through the years include Samuel Beckett, Jonathan Swift and Oscar Wilde. It has played a somewhat controversial role in Irish politics and religion, since, until 1873, only Anglicans could enrol as full members of the university to obtain degrees and scholarships; Catholics were not even permitted to use the library. Today, as well as strolling through the campus' lush grounds, visitors flock to the *Old Library*. Built in 1732, the Old Library is the largest in Ireland and holds four million volumes and an extensive collection of manuscripts. The most famous work in the collection is the *Book of Kells*, one of the finest examples of medieval decorated manuscripts, which was written in about AD 800. The *Dublin Experience* is a multimedia presentation of Dublin, featuring photographs and music, and provides an excellent introduction to the city.

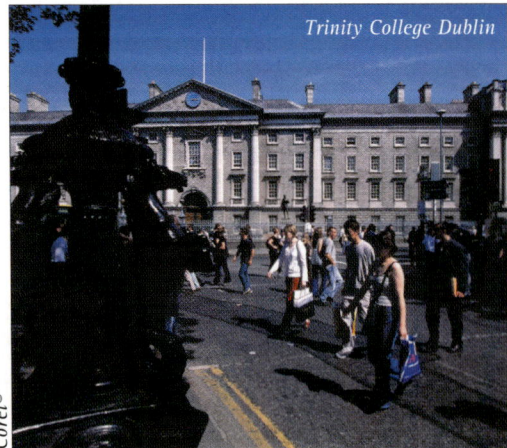
Trinity College Dublin

Corel©

Transportation
Air: Dublin Airport. **Water:** Ferry: Services from Holyhead (Wales) and Stranraer (Scotland) to Dun Laoghaire Port and Dublin Port. **Rail:** Train: Heuston Station, Connolly Station or Tara Street Station. DART (electric rail): Pearse Station. **Road:** Bus: Public services. Car: N1 (from Dublin Airport); M11, then N11 (from Wicklow); N7 (from Kildare); N11 (from Dun Laoghaire port), then signs to Dublin city centre.

Contact Addresses
Trinity College Library, College Street, Dublin 2, Ireland
Tel: (01) 608 2320
Website: www.tcd.ie

   £

Waterford Crystal Visitor Centre

Waterford is famous the world over as the home of beautiful crystal designs. The *Waterford Factory* was opened in 1783 by George and William Penrose, and bowls, vases and ornaments continue to be made on the site. The crystal mix is transformed into glass in a 1200ºC (2192ºF) furnace before being blown and decorated with deep engravings by skilled workers. Visitors to the centre can watch the glass being formed into decanters, bowls and wine glasses and learn about the unique production techniques used at Waterford, through audiovisual displays and chatting to the craftsmen in their workshops. Many of the most prestigious pieces of Waterford Crystal, which have been presented to celebrities and politicians, are on display in the *Gallery*.

Transportation
Air: Shannon Airport, Dublin Airport, Waterford Airport (domestic flights). **Rail:** Train: Plunkett Station (Waterford). **Road:** Bus: Public services. Car: N25 (from Cork).

Contact Addresses
Waterford Crystal Visitor Centre, Kilbarry, Cork Road, Waterford, Ireland
Tel: (051) 332 500
Website: www.waterfordvisitorcentre.com

   £

Israel

1 Dead Sea (Yam Ha-melah)

2 Masada (Horvot Mezada)

3 Temple Mount (Al-Haram al-Sharif)

4 Western Wall (HaKotel HaMaaravi)

Tourist Information

Ministry of Tourism (Misrad Hatayarut)
PO Box 1018, King George Street 24,
Jerusalem, Israel
Tel: (02) 675 4811
Website: www.infotour.co.il

Israel Government Tourist Office
UK House, 180 Oxford Street, London W1D
1NN, UK
Tel: (020) 7299 1111
Website: www.goisrael.com

Dead Sea (Yam Ha-melah)

Lying 400m (1320ft) below sea level and
spanning the border between Israel and Jordan,
the *Dead Sea* is a natural wonder. It contains more
minerals and salt than any other stretch of water
in the world, and thus it is possible to float on
top of the water. Its natural properties make it a
prime centre for spa treatments and relaxation
therapies and there are a number of resorts in the
area. The Dead Sea has strong Biblical
connections: the salt mountain range of *Mount
Sodom* is, according to the Bible, the site of the
sinful city that perished alongside Gomorra. In
turn, the *Dead Sea Scrolls*, the oldest Biblical
documents known to be in existence, were
discovered at *Qumran*, a restored archaeological
site in the north. *Masada* is also located on the
Israeli shores of the Dead Sea. The *Ein Gedi Nature
Reserve and Kibbutz* provides opportunities for
spotting desert wildlife and offers trails to
waterfalls, canyons, caves and shallow pools.
Metzoke Dragot, located in a deep crater, is a
popular site for more adventurous sports such as
abseiling, climbing (with amazing desert views)
and mountain biking.

Transportation
Air: Ben-Gurion International Airport. **Road:**
Coach: Public services. Taxi: Sheshir taxis (from
Ben-Gurion International Airport).

Contact Addresses
Dead Sea Regional Tourist Organization, NP Dead
Sea 86910, Israel
Tel: (07) 668 8808
Website: www.deadsea.co.il

Masada (Horvot Mezada)

Perched high on a sheer-sided plateau, *Masada* is
famous for being the site of a mass suicide by a
group of Jewish people who put their religous
beliefs and cultural pride before their own lives.
Located in the Negev desert on the southern coast
of Israel, the fortress was originally built in

around 35BC as a luxurious refuge for King Herod. But it was seized by the Jewish people following a Jewish revolt in AD 66. In AD 72, the Roman army lay siege to Masada and seeing that the Romans would soon breach their defences, the Jewish people chose to take their own lives rather than being captured alive and becoming slaves. The site was excavated between 1963-65 and today many visitors climb the steep, winding 'snake path' to the fortress to enjoy the beautiful views. A gentler climb from the other side is possible or visitors can opt to take a cable car to the summit. Sunrise ascents are particularly popular.

Transportation
Air: Ovda Airport (Eilat) *or* Ben-Gurion International Airport. **Rail:** Cable Car: A cable car runs from the Masada Cable Car Station at the bottom of the mountain to the summit. **Road:** Bus: Services run from Jerusalem, Tel Aviv and Bersheva. Car: Route 3199 (from Arad).

Contact Addresses
Horvot Mezada, M P Yam Hamelach, Negev, Israel
Tel: (08) 658 4207
www.goisrael.com

Temple Mount (Al-Haram al-Sharif)

Temple Mount, a walled section of the *Old City of Jerusalem*, is a site of tremendous religious significance to Jews, Muslims and Christians. The area, which is one of Jerusalem's most famous landmarks, is believed to be the site of the holy rock where Abraham offered his son Isaac for sacrifice. It is also reputedly the site where Solomon erected the *First Temple* to house the *Ark of the Covenant*, which had been brought to Jerusalem by his father David, and also the area from where Mohammed ascended to heaven. The Babylonians captured Jerusalem in 587BC and burned down the temple, exiling many of the people to Babylonia. A *Second Temple* was subsequently constructed in 515BC, only to be destroyed by the Roman Emperor Titus in AD 70. Today, the site is dominated by the *Dome of the Rock* and is also home to the silver-domed *Al Aqsa*

Mosque, which is a Muslim place of worship, as well as the *Islamic Museum*, which houses a collection of Korans, as well as Islamic artefacts and relics.

Transportation
Air: Ben-Gurion International Airport. **Road:** Bus: Public services to the Dung Gate. Car: Hwy-1 (from Tel Aviv).

Contact Addresses
For more information on Temple Mount, contact the Ministry of Tourism (see **Tourist Information** above).

Western Wall (HaKotel HaMaaravi)

The *Western Wall*, known to non-Jews as the 'Wailing Wall', is a 488-m (1601-ft) stretch of wall which is all that remains of the *Second Temple of Jerusalem*. The most sacred Jewish place in the world, it attracts thousands of devout Jews every year who come to pray, and push prayer notes and messages of goodwill into the cracks of the wall. The wall was built more than two thousand years ago under King Herod, and has been under Israeli control since 1967. It is also sacred to Muslims who believe that the wall marks the place where the prophet Mohammed tied up his winged horse, al-Burak, before ascending to heaven. It has been divided into two sections of prayer, the left for men and the right for women, and forms part of a larger wall surrounding the *Dome of the Rock* and *Al Aqsa Mosque*. Visitors are able to watch the religious ceremonies.

Transportation
Air: Ben-Gurion International Airport. **Road:** Bus: Public services. Car: Hwy-1 to central Jerusalem (from Tel Aviv).

Contact Addresses
Western Wall Heritage Foundation, 2 HaOmer Street, Old City, Jerusalem 97500, Israel
Tel: (02) 627 1333
Website: www.hakotel.org.il

Italy

Tourist Information

Italian State Tourist Office – ENIT (Ente Nazionale Italiano per il Turismo)
Via Marghera 2, 00185 Rome, Italy
Tel: (06) 49711
Website: www.enit.it

Italian State Tourist Office (ENIT)
1 Princes Street, London W1R 8AY, UK
Tel: (020) 7408 1254 or 7355 1557 (trade enquiries only) or (09001) 600 280 (brochure line; calls are charged at 60p per minute)
Website: www.enit.it

1 Colosseum (Colosseo)
2 Doges' Palace (Palazzo Ducale)
3 Florence Duomo (Duomo Santa Maria del Fiore)
4 Leaning Tower of Pisa (Torre Pendente di Pisa)
5 Mount Etna
6 Old Bridge (Ponte Vecchio)
7 Pantheon (Panteone)
8 Pompeii
9 Rialto Bridge
10 Roman Forum (Foro Romano)
11 San Siro Stadium
12 Siena Main Square (Piazza del Campo)
13 Spanish Steps and Keats Shelley Memorial House
14 St Mark's Basilica (Basilica di San Marco)
15 St Peter's Basilica (Basilica di San Pietro)
16 Trevi Fountain (Fontana di Trevi)
17 Uffizi Gallery (Galleria degli Uffizi)
18 Vatican Museums and Sistine Chapel (Musei Vaticani e Capella Sistina)

Colosseum (Colosseo)

The *Colosseum* is arguably ancient Rome's most famous building. This massive structure, with arch upon arch reaching 48m (157ft) into the air and measuring 190m by 155m (620ft by 513ft), used to hold up to 50,000 boisterous Roman citizens. Opened in AD 80 by Emperor Titus in a ceremony that included 100 days of games, the Colosseum played host to Rome's favourite spectator sports – gladiatorial contests, combats between men and wild animals and even mock naval battles. Today, only the shell remains along with a view down to the passages through which slaves and animals were led before entering into battle. Unlike other Roman amphitheatres that are dug into hillsides, the Colosseum is a free-standing structure of stone and concrete and has long served as a model for stadia around the world.

Transportation

Air: Rome Leonardo da Vinci Airport (Fiumicino), Rome Ciampino Airport. **Water:** Ferry: Civitavecchia port, from where there are services to central Rome. **Rail:** Train: Roma Termini Station, Roma Tiburtina Station, Roma Ostiense Station or Roma Trastevere Station. Underground: Colosseo. Tram: Piazza del Colosseo. **Road:** Bus: Regular public services. Car: A12 (from the west); A24 (from the east); SS7 (from Rome Ciampino Airport).

Contact Addresses

Piazza Del Colosseo, Rome, Italy
Tel: (06) 39 96 7700
Website: www.enit.it

Doges' Palace (Palazzo Ducale)

Located in Venice's renowned *Piazza San Marco*, adjacent to the *Basilica di San Marco*, the *Doges' Palace* was home to the government of the former Venetian Republic from AD 697 to 1797. Although the palace was originally built in AD 814, the present structure was completed in the early 15th century. The palace was a showplace for artistry, craftsmanship and architecture, and still exemplifies the splendour of Venetian Gothic style. As well as ruling the city state, the doges (a Venetian word from the Latin *dux*, meaning leader) were great patrons of the arts and the palace is filled with works by Venetian Renaissance masters such as Veronese and Tintoretto. The *Ponte dei Sospiri*, or Bridge of Sighs, is an integral part of the palace and forms the link between the courts and the prisons across the canal. It is named after the noise prisoners used to make as they were led to confinement in the damp and gloomy cells, which can still be visited on a tour of the palace.

Transportation
Air: Venice Marco Polo Airport. **Water:** Ferry: Public services. **Rail:** Train: Venezia Santa Lucia Station (Venice Station). **Road:** Bus: Public services. Car: A4 (from Turin); A13 (from Bologna); A1 (from Rome or Florence); A1, then A13, then A4 (from Naples); SS11 (from Padua).

Contact Addresses
Palazzo Ducale, San Marco 1, 30124 Venice, Italy
Tel: (041) 522 4951

Florence Duomo (Duomo Santa Maria del Fiore)

Florence's *Duomo*, or cathedral, completed in 1466 after 170 years of work and its domed roof is symbolic of the meeting of Renaissance craft and culture. Engineered by the architect and sculptor Filippo Brunelleschi (1377-1446), using specially invented machines, the *cupola* (dome) was one of the greatest achievements of the Italian Renaissance. Its octagonal form has a diameter of 46.5m (153ft) at the base, and was completed in 1434; it is possible to climb to the top of the dome for magnificent views over the city. The vast interior boasts frescoes by Renaissance masters such as Paolo Uccello and Andrea del Castagno, as well as a monument to the poet Dante and his *Divina Commedia* (Divine Comedy). The nearby *campanile* (bell tower) is decorated inside with frescoes and statues by Giotto and Donatello, amongst others.

Transportation
Air: Amerigo Vespucci Airport (Florence), Galileo Galilei Airport (Pisa). **Rail:** Train: Firenze Santa Maria Novella Station (Florence). **Road:** Bus: Public services. Car: A1 (from Milan, Bologna, Rome or Naples); A11 (from Pisa, Lucca, Prato or Siena).

Contact Addresses
Opera di Santa Maria del Fiore, Via della Canonica 1, 50122 Florence, Italy
Tel: (055) 230 2885
Website: www.operaduomo.firenze.it

Leaning Tower of Pisa (Torre Pendente di Pisa)

Constructed in 1174, at a time when the Pisans were enjoying an era of military success, the *Leaning Tower of Pisa*, located in Pisa's *Campo dei Miracoli* (Field of Miracles) is famous not only because of its striking beauty but also because of its awkward geometry. It served as the bell tower of the equally impressive *Cattedrale* (Cathedral) and *Battistero* (Baptistry), and, as a result of the poor swampy soil beneath, has leaned almost since construction first started. Today, one side is 5m (16ft) closer to the ground than the other. Galileo used the tower for experiments to prove his theory of motion whilst he was chair of mathematics at the *Università di Pisa* (Pisa University) in 1589.

Transportation

Air: Pisa Galileo Galilei Airport. **Rail:** Train: Pisa Centrale Station. **Road:** Car: A12 (from Genoa and the north); A11 (from Florence).

Contact Addresses

Opera della Primaziale Pisana, Via B Croce 26, 56125 Pisa, Italy
Tel: (050) 560 547
Website: http://torre.duomo.pisa.it or www.pisae.it

Mount Etna

Mount Etna is one of the most active volcanoes in Europe and is Sicily's best-known natural attraction. It is also the highest mountain on the island currently measuring 3,350m (10,990ft); the height varies each time the volcano erupts. Its mythical importance dates back to the Ancient Greeks who believed it was here that Cyclops helped forge lightning bolts for Zeus, deep within the volcano's core. Mount Etna is situated within the *Etna Regional Park* (Parco Regionale dell'Etna), Sicily's first national park that was established in 1987. The park offers skiing opportunities in the winter and some great hiking trails with mountain refuges during the summer. The park is popular with volcanologists all year round and drew particular attention in 2001, the year of the volcano's last major eruption. The fertile volcanic terrain supports an array of flora and fauna including vineyards and magnificent forests.

Doges' Palace

Archivo Fotografico A.P.T di Venezia©

Transportation

Air: Catania Airport (Fontanarossa Airport) and Palermo Airport. **Rail:** Services from Catania to Riposto. **Road:** Bus: Public services from Catania.

Contact Addresses

Etna Regional Park, Via Etnea 107, Nicolosi, Sicily
Tel: (095) 914 588
Website: www.agriturismosicilia.com

Old Bridge (Ponte Vecchio)

This famous 14th-century bridge, built by Taddeo Gaddi and home to medieval Florence's gold and silversmiths, is still paved with jewellers' shops today. The *Ponte Vecchio*'s genteel atmosphere dates back to the days of Cosimo de' Medici, a member of the city's ruling dynasty in Renaissance times, who threw out a group of butchers who set up shop on the bridge. Above the shops that line the bridge is a secret passageway known as the *Corridoio Vasariano*, linking the *Palazzo Vecchio*, *Uffizi Gallery* and the *Pitti Palace*, and originally built as a private passage for the Medici family. The Ponte Vecchio was the only bridge across the River Arno to be spared German bombing during World War II.

Transportation

Air: Amerigo Vespucci Airport (Florence), Pisa Galileo Galilei Airport. **Rail:** Train: Santa Maria Novella Station.

Contact Addresses

Opera Della Primaziale, Pisa, Piazza Duomo 17, CAP S6126, Pisa, Italy
Tel: (055) 23320
Website: www.firenze.turismo.toscana.it

Pantheon (Panteone)

Considered by many to be the best preserved of all the great classical monuments, the *Pantheon* was dedicated in 27BC by Agrippa, the admiral who defeated Anthony and Cleopatra, and rebuilt by Hadrian in AD 125 after it had been struck by lightning and burnt down sometime between AD 98-117. The Pantheon possesses a dome with a span of 43.2m (142ft), the largest of its kind until the *Duomo* in Florence was built in the 15th century. The bronze and gold décor was stripped away to be used in other Roman monuments, such as *St Peter's Basilica*, but the sheer size and age of the building cannot fail to impress. Inside visitors can see the tomb of the Renaissance master Raphael.

Transportation
Air: Rome Leonardo da Vinci Airport (Fiumicino), Rome Ciampino Airport. **Water:** Ferry: Civitavecchia port, from where there are services to central Rome. **Rail:** Train: Roma Termini Station, Roma Tiburtina Station, Roma Ostiense Station or Roma Trastevere Station. **Road:** Bus: Public services. Car: A12 (from the west); A24 (from the east); SS7 (from Rome Ciampino Airport).

Contact Addresses
Piazza della Rotunda, Panteone 00186, Rome, Italy
Tel: (06) 6830 0230
Website: www.romeguide.it

Pompeii

Once a lavish resort town for wealthy Romans, *Pompeii*, situated 25km (16 miles) south of Naples, was literally buried alive under hot volcanic ash and mud during an eruption of nearby *Mount Vesuvius* in AD 79. The city was eventually forgotten, and it was not until the 16th century that it was rediscovered. Now excavated, it provides an enthralling insight into the everyday lives of the ancient Romans. Visitors can view restored villas complete with erotic and religious wall paintings, temples and the forum, as well as actual brothels and plaster casts of fallen volcano victims. Nearby *Ercolano* (Herculaneum) was also destroyed by Vesuvius, and is a smaller but better-preserved site consisting of villas and shops. From Ercolano, the modern town, it is possible to take a bus to the top of Mount Vesuvius.

Transportation
Air: Naples International Airport. **Rail:** Train: Pompeii FS Station, Pompeii Santuario, Pompeii–Villa dei Misteri Station or Ercolano

Station. Circumvesuviana (Bay of Naples rail system): Pompeii-Scavi-Villa dei Misteri Station. **Road:** Car: A3 to Pompeii (from Naples); S18 to Ercolano (from Naples).

Contact Addresses
Azienda di Cura, Soggiorno e Turismo Pompeii (Pompeii Visitors Centre), Via Satra 1, CAP 80045, Pompeii (NA), Italy
Tel: (081) 850 7255

Rialto Bridge

The foundations for the famous *Rialto Bridge* that crosses the *Grand Canal* were laid in 1588 and today lies at the cultural heart of *Venice*. Completed in 1591, the bridge was built to replace earlier wooden versions that frequently collapsed into the canal. Until the building of the *Accademia Bridge* in 1854, the Rialto Bridge was the only means of crossing the Grand Canal on foot. The bridge was built by Antonio da Ponte who competed for the contract against other acclaimed designers of his day such as Michelangelo and Palladio. Antonio's bridge has a 7.3-metre (24-ft) arch to allow boats to pass beneath it and is wide enough to accommodate shops that predominantly cater to the tourists who flock here each day to see this Venetian landmark.

Transportation
Air: Venice Marco Polo Airport. **Water:** Ferry: Public services. **Rail:** Train: Venice Station (Venezia Santa Lucia Station). **Road:** Bus: Public services. Foot: Follow signs for Rialto.

Contact Addresses
For more information on the Rialto Bridge, contact the Italian State Tourist Office (see **Tourist Information** above).

Roman Forum (Foro Romano)

The *Roman Forum*, located between the Capitoline and Palatine hills in the centre of Rome, was the main focus of the Roman Republic and later the symbolic heart of an empire that stretched from England to Carthage. The religious and political institutions, law courts, shops and markets would have bustled with life, and the temples and imperial monuments were architectural triumphs. Fire, invasions and general decay have all detracted from its former glories and in 1932 the Italian fascist dictator Mussolini ordered a main road to be built straight through the site. Among the best-preserved monuments are the triumphal *Arch of Septimius*, eight columns of the *Temple of Saturn* and the rectangular *House of the Vestal Virgins*.

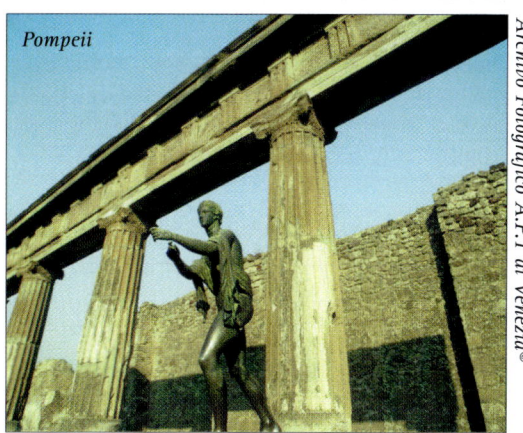

Pompeii

Archivio Fotografico A.P.T di Venezia©

Transportation
Air: Rome Leonardo da Vinci Airport (Fiumicino), Rome Ciampino Airport. **Water:** Ferry: Civitavecchia port, from where there are services to central Rome. **Rail:** Train: Roma Termini Station or Roma Tiburtina Station. Underground: Colosseo. **Road:** Bus: Public services to Piazza del Colosseo or Via dei Fori Imperiali. Car: A12 (from the west); A24 (from the east); SS7 (from Rome Ciampino Airport).

Contact Addresses
Foro Romano, Piazza Santa Maria Nova 53, 00186 Rome, Italy
Tel: (06) 699 0110
Website: www.archeorm.arti.beniculturali.it

San Siro Stadium

The world-famous *San Siro Stadium* (also known as the 'Stadio Giuseppe Meazza') is jointly home to Milan's two main football teams and two of the best teams in Italy's Serie A football league, *AC Milan* (www.acmilan.com) and *Internazionale* (www.inter.it). Both clubs have proud footballing traditions and the *San Siro Museum* tells the histories of both clubs with memorabilia including cups, medals and shirts as well as life-size replicas of some of the clubs' great players including Franco Baresi, Paolo Maldini, Marco Van Basten, Ruud Gullit and Nereo Rocco. Guided tours of this incredible 86,000 capacity ground are available. Both sets of fans are fiercely proud of their clubs and derby games between the two teams often have an electric atmosphere. The San Siro also hosts rock concerts during the closed season.

Transportation
Air: Linate Airport and Malpensa Airport. **Rail:** Milan Centrale Station, Milan Porta Garibaldi Station and Milan Lambrate Station. Metro: Molino Dorino Station. Tram: Line 24. **Road:** Bus: Public services.

Contact Addresses
San Siro Stadium, Via Piccolomini 5, 20151 Milan, Italy
Tel: (02) 4042 432
Website: www.sansirotour.com

Siena Main Square (Piazza del Campo)

The shell-shaped *Piazza del Campo* lies at the heart of Siena and has served as a focus for life in the city for centuries. The *Palazzo Pubblico* (Town Hall), which stands proudly at the top of the piazza, was constructed between 1297 and 1310 as the seat of the *Governo dei Nove*, or Government of Nine, who ruled Siena from 1287-1355. The interior of the building, which is now the *Museo Civico* (Civic Museum), contains many paintings by Sienese masters such as Simone Martini and Ambrogio Lorenzetti, as well as the remains of the *Gaia Fountain*. Next to the Palazzo Pubblico stands the *Torre del Mangia* (Mangia Tower), a belltower which rises to 102m (334ft); visitors can climb to the top for views of the winding cobbled streets which fan out from the piazza, and timeless vistas of the Tuscan countryside.

Transportation
Air: Pisa Galileo Galilei Airport. **Rail:** Train: Siena Station. **Road:** Bus: Public services. Car: A1 (from Rome, exit Valdichiana); Superstrada del Palio (from Florence); A12 (from Genoa). The historic centre of Siena is pedestrianised.

Contact Addresses
Museo Civico, Palazzo Comunale, Piazza del Camponoz, 53100 Siena, Italy
Tel: (057) 7292 263
Website: www.enit.it

Spanish Steps and Keats Shelley Memorial House

Although they have been known as the *Spanish Steps*, after the nearby Spanish Embassy, ever since their construction between 1721-25, the steps that lead up to the rose-coloured *Trinità dei Monti* church were in fact constructed and funded by the French King, Charles VIII. At the bottom of the steps is the *Piazza di Spagna* (Spanish Square), and Pietro Bernini's *Fontana della Barcaccia* (Barcaccia Fountain). The steps have served as a meeting point for generations of travellers, from the English Grand Tourists of the 18th century, to the young people of all nationalities who flock here today. The English Romantic poet, John Keats, spent the last few months of his life in the *Casina Rossa*, or Little Red House, nearby before he tragically died of tuberculosis in 1821. The house was left to go to ruin until it was bought by a group of British and Americans in 1903 and turned into a museum where visitors can learn about the lives of Keats, Shelley, Byron and other English poets who were inspired by Italy.

Transportation
Air: Rome Leonardo da Vinci Airport (Fiumicino), Rome Ciampino Airport. **Water:** Ferry: Civitavecchia port, from where there are services to central Rome. **Rail:** Train: Roma Termini Station, Roma Tiburtina Station, Roma Ostiense Station or Roma Trastevere Station. Underground: Spagna. **Road:** Bus: Publics services. Car: A12 (from the west); A24 (from the east); SS7 (from Rome Ciampino Airport).

Contact Addresses
Keats-Shelley Memorial House, Piazza di Spagna 26, 00187 Rome, Italy
Tel: (06) 678 4235
Website: www.Keats-Shelley-House.org

St Mark's Basilica (Basilica di San Marco)

The glittering facade of *St Mark's Basilica* dominates the vast expanse of *St Mark's Square* and stands as a potent symbol of Venice's status as city state and maritime power in the late Medieval period. The basilica, which was consecrated in 1094, is the third church to be built on the site since the body of St Mark, the city's patron saint, was reputedly brought here to be buried in AD 828. The exotic Byzantine architecture of the basilica reflects the Venetian lagoon's strong trading links with the Orient and the exterior is decorated with marble brought back after the Venetian conquest of Constantinople in 1204; the five vaulted domes which form the roof are set in the shape of a Greek cross There are further displays of riches brought back from foreign crusades in the *Tesoro* (treasury), whilst the *Pala D'Oro* (Golden Altarpiece) is an ornate altar screen in a gilded frame with enamel panels made in Byzantium. Visitors can enter the *Gallerie* to see the four magnificent Horses of St Mark that were brought from the hippodrome in Constantinople in the 13th century, symbolising Venice's links with Byzantium. It is also possible to climb up to the *Loggia* (veranda) on the front of the basilica for views over the lagoon and the surrounding islands, or to ascend the nearby *Campanile* (bell tower) which, at 99m (272ft), is the tallest building in Venice.

Transportation
Air: Venice Marco Polo Airport. **Water:** Ferry: Line 1, 51 or 82. Waterbus (Vaporetto): San Marco or San Zaccaria. **Rail:** Train: Venezia Santa Lucia Station (Venice Station). **Road:** Bus: Public services

Contact Addresses
Basilica di San Marco, Piazza San Marco, 30124 Venice, Italy
Tel: (041) 522 5205 *or* 522 5697

St Peter's Basilica (Basilica di San Pietro)

St Peter's Basilica stands in the Vatican City above the supposed resting place of the remains of St Peter. A church was first built on the site in the fourth century by Constantine but the 16th-century popes decided to build a monument and place of worship that would better reflect the power of the Catholic church. Construction began in 1506 under Pope Julius II, but it was not completed until 120 years later, and the result is awe-inspiring. Michelangelo designed its graceful *cupola* (dome) and the interior is an unbridled display of Renaissance and Baroque grandeur and features Bernini's *Throne of St Peter* made from bronze taken from the *Pantheon*.

Transportation

Air: Rome Leonardo da Vinci Airport (Fiumicino), Rome Ciampino Airport. **Water:** Ferry: Civitavecchia port, from where there are services to central Rome. **Rail:** Train: Roma Termini Station, Roma Tiburtina Station, Roma Ostiense Station or Roma Trastevere Station. Underground: Ottaviano. **Road:** Bus: Public services. Car: A12 (from the west); A24 (from the east); SS7 (from Rome Ciampino Airport).

Contact Addresses

Tourist Information, Vatican City, St. Peter's Square
Tel: (06) 6988 1662
Website: www.roma2000.it

Trevi Fountain (Fontana di Trevi)

Located in the heart of Rome's *centro storico* (historic centre), the *Trevi Fountain* derives its name from its position at the intersection of three roads (*tre vie*). According to legend, anyone who throws a coin into the water is guaranteed to return to the Eternal City. There has been a source of water at this site for over a thousand years, although it was not until 1485 that Pope Nicholas V commissioned Gianlorenzo Bernini to create the actual fountain – and even then the project was abandoned after the death of Pope Urban VIII in 1644. In 1732, Pope Clement XII employed Niccolò Salvi to continue the work, and the result is a Baroque masterpiece that dominates the square. Although the water is no longer safe to drink, the fountain is still a popular place to enjoy an icecream from one of the *gelaterie* in the square.

Transportation

Air: Rome Leonardo da Vinci Airport (Fiumicino), Rome Ciampino Airport. **Water:** Ferry: Civitavecchia port, from where there are services to central Rome. **Rail:** Train: Roma Termini Station, Roma Tiburtina Station, Roma Ostiense Station or Roma Trastevere Station. Underground: Barberini. **Road:** Car: A12 (from the west); A24 (from the east); SS7 (from Rome Ciampino Airport).

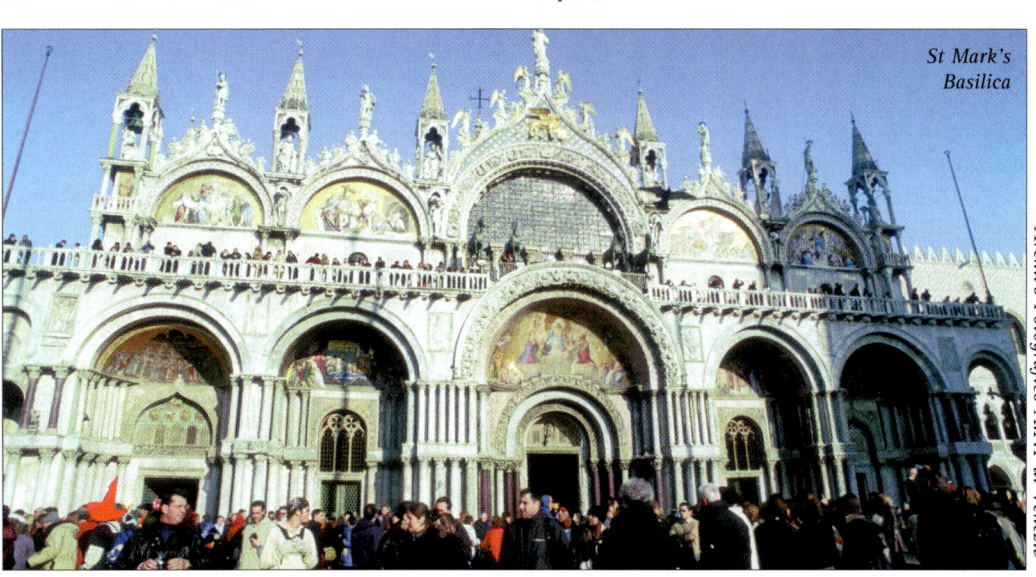

St Mark's Basilica

Archivio Fotografico A.P.T di Venezia©

Contact Addresses
For more information on the Trevi Fountain, contact Ente Nazionale Italiano per il Turismo (see **Tourist Information** above).

Uffizi Gallery (Galleria degli Uffizi)

The *Uffizi Gallery* in Florence houses one of richest and most important art collections in the world. The building, located in the *Piazza della Signoria* close to the banks of the River Arno, was designed in the 16th century by the painter and architect Giorgio Vasari to house Florence's government offices (*uffizi*), and was bequeathed to the gallery as the Medici art collection in 1737, on the condition that it should never leave the city. The museum is a showcase for the Renaissance movement, one of the greatest periods in the history of art, and focuses more specifically on the Florentine School.

Transportation
Air: Amerigo Vespucci Airport (Florence), Pisa Galileo Galilei Airport. **Rail:** Train: Santa Maria Novella Station. **Road:** Bus: Services to Galleria degli Uffizi Castellani. Car: A1 (from Milan, Bologna, Rome or Naples); A11 (from Pisa, Lucca, Prato or Siena), then signs to Centro Storico.

Statue at the Uffizi Gallery

Corel©

Contact Addresses
Loggiato Degli Uffizi, 6-Florence, Italy
Tel: (055) 238 8651 *or* 238 8652
Website: www.arca.net/uffizi

Vatican Museums and Sistine Chapel (Musei Vaticani e Capella Sistina)

The *Vatican Museums* constitute the largest museum complex in the world. Founded in 1506 by Pope Julius II, the collections are staggeringly diverse and are essentially the legacy of the Popes who were not only fabulously rich, but also great patrons of the Arts. Egyptian antiquities, classical statues, Etruscan relics and Byzantine paintings all have their place, but two areas that should not be missed are the *Stanze di Raffaello* (Raphael Rooms) and the *Cappella Sistina* (Sistine Chapel). Renowned equally for the crowds that line up to see it as it is for its breathtaking beauty, the Sistine Chapel was constructed between 1475 and 1480 as the chapel of the papal palace. The painting of its ceiling was charged to a reluctant Michelangelo, whose subsequent depiction of the *Creation of Adam* ranks among the most famous painted images of all time and is considered to be one of the finest achievements of the Renaissance. The *Last Judgement*, also by Michelangelo, hangs behind the altar, while other famous Renaissance works by artists such as Botticelli and Ghirlandaio adorn the rest of the interior.

Transportation
Air: Rome Leonardo da Vinci Airport (Fiumicino), Rome Ciampino Airport. **Water:** Ferry: Civitavecchia port, from where there are services to central Rome. **Rail:** Underground: Ottaviano. **Road:** Bus: Public services.

Contact Addresses
Musei Vaticani, Viale Vaticano, 00120 Vatican City
Tel: (06) 6988 3860 *or* 6988 3332
Website: www.vatican.va

Jamaica

1 Dunn's River Falls

Tourist Information

Jamaica Tourist Board (JTB)
64 Knutsford Boulevard, Kingston 5, Jamaica
Tel: 929 9200
Website: www.jamaicatravel.com

Jamaica Tourist Board
1-2 Prince Consort Road, London SW7 2BZ, UK
Tel: (020) 7224 0505 *or* (0800) 445 533
(brochure request line)

Dunn's River Falls

Located in a dense tropical forest, *Dunn's River Falls* is Jamaica's most famous attraction. This Caribbean paradise consists of a number of waterfalls, which cascade over rock terraces down to the Caribbean Sea below, and beautiful natural pools that have formed in the rockface. The falls are shallow enough to enable visitors to climb the 183m (600ft) limestone tiers to reach a tropical shower, from where they can enjoy panoramic views of the surrounding area. There are beautiful beaches at the bottom of these magnificent falls that are also famous for featuring in the first James Bond film, 'Dr No'.

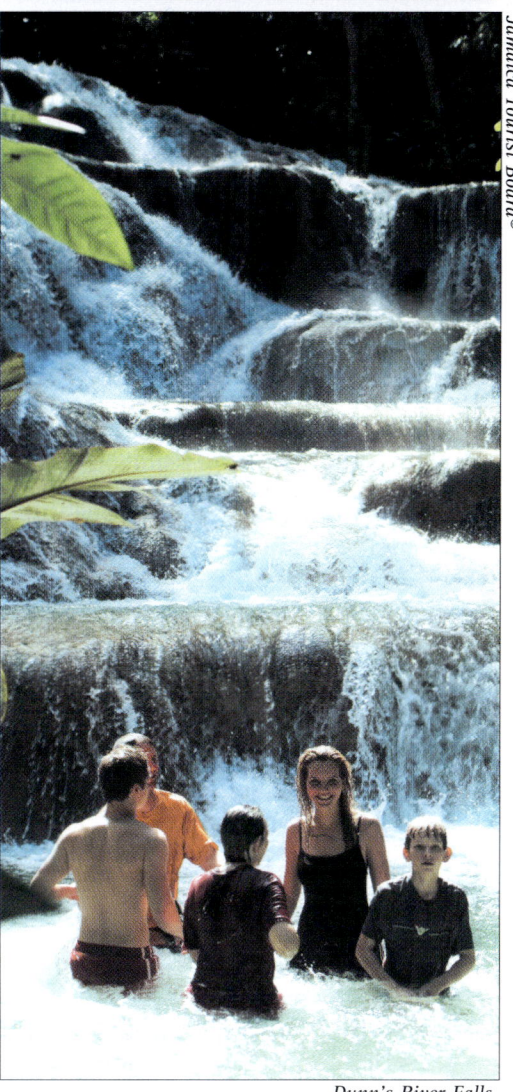

Dunn's River Falls.

Transportation
Air: Norman Manley International Airport. **Road:**
Car: A3 North Coast Highway (from Kingston).

Contact Addresses
Dunn's River Falls and Park, Ocho Rios, St Ann, Jamaica
Tel: 974 2857 *or* 974 4767
Website: www.dunnsriverja.com

Japan

800km
400mls

↑ international airport

RUSSIAN FED.   Sea of Okhotsk

CHINA

Hokkaido
• Sapporo

Hakodate•

Aomori•   ❷ ❻

DPR OF
KOREA   Sea of   Akita•   Honshu
             Japan   Sado I. •Sendai
REP. OF   Niigata•
KOREA   Oki Is.   ❹ ❺   J A P A N
                    Mt. Fuji   TOKYO
         Osaka 3776m •Yokohama
         Kobe   Na goya
Hiroshima   •Osaka
Kitakyúshu   Takamatsu
Fukuoka•   Shikoku
Nágasaki   Kyushu   ❸

East
China
Sea   Southwest Islands   PACIFIC
                          OCEAN   Southern Islands

Amami Is.

Naha• Okinawa

Ryukyu Is.   Iwo Jima

1 Hiroshima Peace Memorial Museum
   (Heiwa Kinen Shiryôkan)
2 Meiji Shrine (Meiji Jingu)
3 Mount Fuji (Fuji-san)
4 Nijo Castle (Nijo-jo)
5 Sanjusangen-do Temple
6 Senso-ji Temple

Tourist Information

Kokusai Kanko Shinkokai
(Japan National Tourist Organisation – JNTO)
10th Floor, Tokyo Kotsu Kaikan Bldg, 2-10-1,
Yurakucho, Chiyoda-ku, Tokyo, Japan
Tel: (0) 3210 3331
Website: www.jnto.go.jp

Japan National Tourist Organisation (JNTO)
Heathcoat House, 20 Savile Row, London
W1S 3PR, UK
Tel: (020) 7734 9638
Website: www.seejapan.co.uk

Hiroshima Peace Memorial Museum (Heiwa Kinen Shiryôkan)

Hiroshima in Western Honshu is known around the world as the city which was destroyed by the world's first atomic bomb on August 6, 1945. Every year, millions of visitors come to the city to pay their respects in the *Hiroshima Peace Memorial Park* and the *Peace Memorial Museum*. The park, which was reconstructed in 1949, is home to many famous monuments and buildings, including the *Children's Peace Monument* and the *A-Bomb Dome*, which was built in 1915 and designed by the Czech architect Jan Letzel. The ruins of the dome, which are included on the UNESCO World Heritage List, have become the symbol of an international desire for peace.

Transportation
Air: Hiroshima Airport. **Road:** Bus: Public services. Streetcar: Direction Ujina via Kamiya-cho, stop marked Chuden-mae. Alternatively direction Koi/Eba/Miyajima, stop marked Genbaku-Dome-mae.

Contact Addresses
Hiroshima Peace Memorial Museum, 1-2 Nakajimamachi, Naka-ku, Hiroshima City, Japan
Tel: (0) 82 242 7798
Website: www.hiroshima-navi.or.jp

Meiji Shrine (Meiji Jingu)

Tokyo's *Meiji Shrine* is one of the holiest and most visited temples in the country. This Shinto shrine is dedicated to the Emperor Meiji, who was credited with opening Japan up to the outside world, and to his wife Empress Shoken. Built in 1920 following their deaths in 1912 and 1914 respectively, the original shrine burnt down during World War II, only to be rebuilt by 1958. Today, as well as the *Naihaiden* (Inner Shrine), which is home to the main shrine, visitors can also see the *Gehaiden* (Outer Shrine), which was completed in 1926. Other highlights are the *Homotsuden* (Treasure Museum), which was built in 1921 and houses photos and personal belongings of the emperor and empress.

Mount Fuji in Spring

Japan National Tourist Organization©

Transportation
Air: New Tokyo International Narita Airport, Haneda Airport (domestic flights). **Rail:** Train: Harajku Station. Underground: Meiji-jingu-mae. **Road:** Bus: Public services. Car: Tomei-Meishin expressway from Kobe (via Nagoya, Kyoto and Osaka); Tohoku expressway (from northern Japan); Chuo expressway (from Nagano and Nagoya).

Contact Addresses
Meiji Jingu, 1-1 Kamizonomachi, Yoyogi, Shibuya-ku, Tokyo, Japan
Tel: (03) 3379 5511
Website: www.meijijingu.or.jp

Mount Fuji (Fuji-san)

This 3776m (12,389ft) volcanic cone is one of the most famous volcanoes in the world and the highest peak in Japan. Of extreme historical and religious importance to the Japanese, *Mount Fuji* is also one of the nation's most significant emblems. Although it has erupted 16 times since AD 781, the mountain is safe and popular for climbing, last erupting in 1707 when it covered the streets of Tokyo in volcanic lava. The summit offers overnight huts, a volcanic crater and unparalleled views of Japan. Although the mountain can be climbed at any time of year, the official climbing season is July-August; outside these months, facilities – including lodging huts – are closed. The *Fuji Five Lakes* located on the northern side of the mountain were created by volcanic eruptions and are fantastic sites from which to see Mount Fuji itself.

Transportation
Air: New Tokyo Narita International Airport, Haneda Airport (domestic flights). **Rail:** Train: Shinjuku (Tokyo) Station to Kawaguchi-ko Station. **Road:** Bus: Public services.

Contact Addresses
Fuji Visitor Center, 663-1 Funatsu Kawaguchi-ko Town, Yamanashi, 401-301, Japan
Tel: (0555) 720 259
Website: www.mt-fuji.com

Nijo Castle (Nijo-jo)

Nijo Castle was built in 1603 by Tokugawa Ieyasu, one of Japan's most powerful shoguns and founder of the Tokugawa Shogunate. The shoguns ruled Japan for a total of 700 years between the 13th and 19th centuries, with Tokugawa Ieyasu founding his dynasty in 1600. Built as a symbol of his power, the castle is filled with many fine works of art, including beautiful paintings of trees and animals by some of Japan's most famous artists of the period. The castle, set in stunning gardens in the old capital of Japan, Kyoto, was built almost entirely of Hinoki wood (Japanese Cypress).

Transportation
Air: Kansai International Airport, Osaka Itami Airport (domestic flights). **Rail:** Underground: Nijo-jo-mae Station. Train: Kyoto Station. **Road:** Bus: Services from Kyoto Station.

Contact Addresses
Nijo Castle Office, Nijojo-cho, Nakagyo-ku, Kyoto, Japan
Tel: (075) 841 0096

P ✕ 🛒 ♿ 🏛 £ 🏭

Sanjusangen-do Temple

Completed in 1266, the *Sanjusangen-do Temple* which is officially called Rengeo-in Temple, is a faithful copy of an original that was built in 1164, but burned down in 1249. Originally built by Taira no Kiyomori for the emperor Go-Shirakawa, the temple is today a national treasure. It is best known for its wooden image of the *Thousand-Armed Kannon* (the Buddhist Goddess of Mercy), a masterpiece of the Kamakura period, which stands surrounded by 1000 smaller statues of the same goddess. The *hondo* (main building) is split into 33 *sanjusan* (bays) that exist between its many pillars to symbolise the 33 incarnations of Kannon, hence the name Sanjusangen-do Temple, which literally means '33 bay hall'.

Senso-ji Temple

Japan National Tourist Organization©

Transportation
Air: Kansai International Airport. **Rail:** Train: Keihan Railway to Shichijo Station. **Road:** Bus: Public services. Car: Hiezan Driveway (from Imazu-cho); Meishin Expressway (from Osaka); Tomei Expressway or Meishin Expressway (from Nagoya).

Contact Addresses
Department of Industry and Tourism, Tourist Section, Kyoto City Government, Kyoto Kaikan, Okazaki, Sayo-ku, Kyoto, Japan
Tel: (075) 752 0215 (administration) *or* 525 0033 (Temple)
Website: http://raku.city.kyoto.jp/sight_e.phtml

P 🛒 ♿ 🏛 £ 🏭

Senso-ji Temple

Tokyo's most revered temple, the *Senso-ji Temple*, was founded in AD 628 to enshrine a gold statuette of the *Kannon Bodhisattva* (the Goddess of Mercy) which, according to legend, was found by two local fishermen. Also known as *Asakusa Kannon* in Japan, the temple and its five-storey pagoda may today be a post-war concrete reconstruction, but nonetheless its precincts are always bustling with worshippers. A huge incense burner at the front of the temple is said to have healing powers. The *Kaminarimon* (Thunder Gate) is one of Tokyo's most recognised sites and is famous for its enormous red paper lantern and guardian statues. There are also many Shinto shrines within the temple's grounds.

Transportation
Air: New Tokyo Narita International Airport, Haneda Airport (domestic flights). **Rail:** Train: Tokyo Station. Underground: Asakusa. **Road:** Bus: Public services. Car: Tomei-Meishin Expressway (from Kobe); Chuo Expressway (from Nagano and Nagoya).

Contact Addresses
Kinryuzan Senso-ji, 2-3-1 Asakusa, Taito-ku, Tokyo 111-0032, Japan
Tel: (03) 3842 0181

✕ 🛒 ♿ 🏭

Jordan

1 Dead Sea (Al-bahr Al-mayyit)

2 Petra

Tourist Information

Jordan Tourism Board
PO Box 830688, Amman 11183, Jordan
Tel: (06) 567 8294 *or* 2314
Website: www.see-jordan.com

Jordan Tourism Board
Kennedy House, 115 Hammersmith Road,
London W14 0QH, UK
Tel: (020) 7371 6496
Website: www.see-jordan.com

Dead Sea (Al-bahr Al-mayyit)

Lying 400m (1320ft) below sea level and spanning
the border between Israel and Jordan, the *Dead Sea*
contains more minerals and salt than any other
stretch of water in the world. Its natural properties
make it a prime centre for spa treatments and
relaxation therapies with three resorts in the area:
the *Movenpick Dead Sea*, the *Dead Sea Spa Hotel* and
the *Dead Sea Rest House*. There are also several
interesting sites around the Dead Sea, including
Bethany, where it is believed Jesus was baptized,
and *Lot's Cave*, where the prophet Lot lived. The
Wadi Mujib Nature Reserve on the eastern shores is a
beautifully preserved area of mountains and rivers,
providing a natural habitat for eagles, vultures,
wolves and the endangered Nubian ibex. There are
many hiking trails within the reserve.

Transportation
Air: Queen Alia International Airport. **Road:** Car:
Desert Highway (from Amman).

Contact Addresses
For more information on the Dead Sea, contact the
Jordan Tourism Board (see **Tourist Information** above).

Petra

Jordan's best-known tourist attraction, *Petra*, is one of
the great wonders of the Middle Eastern world – a
city carved straight into solid rock. It unfolds grandly
after a 2km (1.2 mile) walk through a very narrow
chasm. Built during the fifth and sixth centuries BC,
Petra is the ruined capital of the Nabatean Arabs. Its
immense facades were lost for almost 1000 years
until they were rediscovered by the Swiss traveller
Johann Ludwig Burckhardt in 1812. Today, there are
still many sites to see including the *el Khazneh* (The
Treasury) monument, a giant tomb carved out of
rock, the *Temple of the Winged Lions*, the *al-Deir*
(Monastery) and the *Archaeological Museum*, which
displays artefacts found at Petra during the 19th and
20th centuries.

Transportation
Air: Queen Alia International Airport. **Road:** Coach:
Abdali Bus Station or Wahdat Bus Station. Car:
Desert Highway or King's Highway (from Amman).

Contact Addresses
For more information on Petra, contact the Jordan
Tourism Board (see **Tourist Information** above).

Kenya

1 Amboseli National Park
2 Maasai Mara National Reserve
3 Mount Kenya National Reserve

Tourist Information

Kenya Tourist Board
RE Towers, Ragati Road,
PO Box 30630-00100,
Nairobi, Kenya
Tel: (02) 724 044
Website: www.magicalkenya.com

Kenya Tourist Board
Nottcut House,
36 Southwark Bridge Road,
London SE1 9EU, UK
Tel: +44 (0) 0207 202 6376
Website: www.magicalkenya.com

Amboseli National Park

Amboseli National Park extends across 392 sq km (151 sq miles) of grassland and swamps at the foot of *Mount Kilimanjaro*, Africa's highest peak. It was designated a national park in 1948 and, despite suffering floods in 1993 which caused many of the animals to retreat, it remains one of Africa's best-known game spotting locations. Park residents include baboons, lions, cheetah, black rhinos, wildebeest, hippos, gazelles and large herds of elephant. As well as game-viewing, hiking and camping, bird-watching and camel safaris are also popular and visitors can learn about the culture and way of life of the indigenous Maasai population through homestead visits and lectures. More adventurous travellers can arrange to climb Mount Kilimanjaro with a local guide.

Transportation
Air: Jomo Kenyatta International Airport. **Road:** Coach: Many tour operators provide transport to Amboseli. Car: Via the towns of Namanga and Emali (from Nairobi); via Tsavo West, then through Kimana (Olkelunyiet) Gate (from Mombasa).

Contact Addresses
Senior Warden, Amboseli National Park, PO Box 18 Namanga, Amboseli, Kenya
Tel: (045) 22251
Website: www.kws.org/amboseli.html

Maasai Mara National Reserve

Opened in 1974, the *Maasai Mara National Reserve* is the most popular game park in Kenya. Managed by the Maasai tribe, the area is named after this group of people who first migrated to South Kenya from the Nile Valley in the mid-17th century. The Maasai herdsmen are nomadic people who do not believe in the concept of land ownership and choose instead to live in harmony with the wildlife grazing in the area. The reserve, which occupies a 320 sq km (124 sq miles) chunk of the famous Serengeti plains, is inhabited by many of Africa's most popular wild animals, including lions, cheetahs, elephants, leopards, black rhinos and hippos. There are also over 500 resident birds in the park including ostrich, lark, sunbird and 57 species of birds of prey. The area is famous for rolling grassland and for the Mara River, which runs through the reserve from north to south. It is also the place for one of nature's best spectacles – the annual migration from the dry plains of Tanzania of thousands of wildebeest crossing crocodile-infested waters in order to reach more fertile grazing.

Transportation
Air: Jomo Kenyatta International Airport, Wilson Airport (domestic flights). **Rail:** Train: Naivasha Station (services from Nairobi); visitors must then travel by road into the Maasai Mara. **Road:** Bus: Private tour operators run safaris into the Maasai Mara National Reserve (from Nairobi and Lake Nakura). Car: Nairobi–Naivasha Road to Maai-Mahiu, then B3 to Ewaso Nyiro, then C12 to Aitong, then E177 (from Nairobi); A1 (from Migori).

Contact Addresses
Maasai Mara National Reserve, PO Box 44595, Nairobi, Kenya
Tel: (02) 311 054 *or* 343 968
Website: www.go2africa.com

Mount Kenya National Reserve

Mount Kenya, which is an extinct volcano sitting on the Equator, is Africa's second-highest mountain and stands at a height of 5199m (17,058ft). Opened as the *Mount Kenya National Park* in 1949, the mountain has been revered by local inhabitants for generations and is the official home of 'Ngai', the Kikuyu tribe's Supreme Being. The snowy peak of the volcano was first sighted by an outsider in 1849 – the missionary Johann Ludwig Krapf – although the idea that there could be snow on the Equator was not believed until the British geographer Halford John Mackinder reached the summit in 1899. The park itself, which covers an area of 600 sq km (232 sq miles), offers exotic mountain scenery, starting with upland forest near the bottom and progressing to mountain forest, bamboo forests and glacier peaks. A wide variety of wildlife inhabits the park, some unique to it, including Sykes and Colobus monkeys, buffalo, elephants, black rhinos, leopards, the elusive Bongo antelopes and giant forest hogs. It is also home to many species of birds such as the giant kingfisher, olive pigeons and red-fronted parrots.

Transportation
Air: Jomo Kenyatta International Airport, Wilson Airport. **Rail:** Train: Thika Station. **Road:** Bus: Services to Nanyuki (from Nairobi). Car: A2 heads northwest from Nairobi, by-passing Murunga, before heading west around the base of Mount Kenya to Nanyuki.

Contact Addresses
Senior Warden, Mount Kenya National Park, PO Box 69, Naru Moru, Kenya
Tel: (0171) 2383
Website: www.kws.org/mountkenya.html

Maasai Mara National Reserve
Kenya Tourist Board©

Republic of Korea

DPR OF KOREA
Panmunjom
Demilitarized zone
Sokcho
Kangnung
Kanghwa I.
SEOUL
Inchon
Suwon
Chungju
REPUBLIC OF KOREA
Anmyon I.
Taejon
Kunsan
Chonju
Kyongju
Taegu
Ulsan
Chirisan 1915m△
Kwangju
Masan
Pusan
Mokpo
Koje I.
Chin I.
Tsushima (Japan)
YELLOW SEA
Naktong
Han
Imjin
Taebaek Mtns.
Ullung I.
Cheju
Cheju I.
△*Hallasan 1950m*
EAST CHINA SEA

200km
100mls
✈ international airport

1 Gyeongju
2 Haeinsa Temple

Tourist Information

Korea National Tourism Organization – KNTO (Hangook Kwankwong Kongsa)
40, Cheonggyecheonno, Jung-gu, Seoul, 100-180, Republic of Korea
Tel: (02) 729 9600
Website: www.tour2korea.com

Korea National Tourism Organization (KNTO)
Third Floor, New Zealand House, Haymarket, London SW1Y 4TE, UK
Tel: (020) 7321 2535
Website: www.tour2korea.com

Gyeongju

The city of *Kyongju* was once one of the six largest cities in the world and the capital of the Silla Kingdom, which existed between 57BC and AD 935. Known today as the 'museum without walls' and now spelt *Gyeongju*, the city houses numerous historical sites and relics, and is one of the most important ancient cities in the world, attracting around eight million visitors every year. The city has many royal tombs, museums, temples and monuments and houses an impressive collection of relics from the Silla period in the *Gyeongju National Museum*. Highlights include artefacts found in the *Geumgwanchiong* and *Cheonmachong* tombs, as well

KNTO Korea National Tourist Office©

as the *Seokguram Grotto* and *Bulguska Temple*, which both feature on the UNESCO World Heritage List.

Transportation
Air: Seoul Gimpo Domestic Airport. Internal flights are available to Busan, Ulsan and Daegu airports. Shuttle buses operate from these airports to Gyeongju. **Rail:** Train: Gyeongju Station. **Road:** Bus: Public services. Taxis: Taxis can be hailed in the street.

Contact Addresses
For more information on Gyeongju, contact the Korea National Tourism Organization (see **Tourist Information** above).

Haeinsa Temple

Haeinsa Temple was originally built in AD 802 by two monks, Sunung and Ijong, during King Aejang of the Silla Kingdom's reign. Despite many fires and subsequent reconstructions, the temple remains one of the most beautiful in Korea set in an idyllic location deep in *Gayasan National Park*.

It eventually reached its present-day size during the mid-10th century. The temple is famous for housing the *Tripitaka Koreana* – 80,000 wooden printing blocks carved during the Goryo Dynasty (AD 918-1392), which, together, make up the oldest and best-preserved collection of Buddhist scriptures in the world. The temple also houses a great number of artefacts that have been designated national treasures including the *Seated Stone Buddha*, found at *Cheongyangsa Temple*, and the *Stone Pagoda* at *Wolgwang Temple*.

Transportation
Air: Seoul Gimpo Domestic Airport. **Road:** Bus: Local buses to Haeinsa Temple (from Daego Seobu Bus Terminal) (journey time: 70 minutes); (from Hapcheon Bus Terminal) (journey time: 60 minutes); (from Jinju Bus Terminal) (journey time: two hours 30 minutes). Car: 88 Expressway to Haeinsa Temple (from Seoul).

Contact Addresses
Haeinsa Temple, Information Office, Daegu, Seoul, Republic of Korea
Tel: (055) 931 1001

Latvia

200km
100mls
✈ international airport

BALTIC
SEA

ESTONIA

Gulf
of
Riga

Ventspils

Valmiera

VIDZEME

Sigulda

Jurmala

LATVIA

KURZEME

RIGA

Liepaja

Jelgava
ZEMGALE

Rezekne

LATGALE

Daugavpils

LITHUANIA

BELARUS

RUSSIAN FED.

Daugava

---

1 Riga's Historic Town Centre

2 Rundale Palace

Tourist Information

Latvia Tourism Development Agency
Pils Lauqums 4, LV-1050 Riga, Latvia
Tel: 722 9945
Website: www.latviatourism.lv

Embassy of Latvia
45 Nottingham Place, London W1U 5LY, UK
Tel: (020) 7312 0040
Website: www.london.am.gov.lv

Riga's Historic Town Centre

Situated on the *Daugava River* on the shores of the *Riga Gulf* of the *Baltic Sea*, *Riga* benefits from pleasant coastal air and is the gateway into the Baltic region. Riga came to prominence during the 13th-15th centuries, benefiting from its geographic location as a trade port between Central and Eastern Europe. Riga is particularly renowned for its Art Nouveau structures which many believe is the finest collection of this style of architecture anywhere in Europe. Riga's attractions are numerous and include

Riga Castle, the *Jewish Museum*, *Gauja National Park*, *Riga Zoo* and *St Mary's Dome Cathedral* completed in 1270 with one of the largest organs in the world.

Transportation

Air: Riga International Airport. **Water:** Ferry: Free Port of Riga. **Rail:** Train: Public services to Riga's Central Station. Public Trolley and Tram services. **Road:** Bus: Public services to Riga International Bus Station.

Contact Addresses

For more information about Riga, contact the Latvia Tourism Development Agency (see **Tourist Information** above).

Rundale Palace

Located 79km (49 miles) south of the Latvian capital of *Riga*, *Rundale Palace and Museum* lie just outside the town of *Bauska*. Built as the summer residence of the Duke of Courland Ernst Johann Biron, the opulent palace was completed in two stages from 1736 to 1740 and 1763 to 1768. After many years of neglect, the palace was given to the Republic of Latvia in 1920. Visitors are able to tour the museum that was opened in 1972 and several of the grand rooms are open to the public as well as many in the eastern block, including the *Room of Roses* and the *Duke's Bedroom*. The palace is ringed by a canal, gardens and a hunting park. Some of the palace rooms are also available for hire for wedding ceremonies and private functions.

Transportation

Air: Riga International Airport. **Water:** Ferry: Free Port of Riga. **Rail:** Train: Public services to Bauska (then travel on to Rundale Palace by bus or taxi). **Road:** Bus: Public services.

Contact Addresses

The Rundale Palace Museum, Bauska, 3921 Latvia
Tel: (+371) 3962 274
Website: www.rpm.apollo.lv/engl/

Lebanon

MEDITERRANEAN SEA

Halba
El Mina • • Tripoli   Hermel
Qornet es
Saouda
△ 3087m
Batroun •
Besharre •
Byblos •
Baalbek •
Jounieh •
BEIRUT •①
Chouf
Mtns.   Zahlé •
LEBANON
SYRIA
Sidon •
Mt Hermon 2814m
Tyre •②
Golan
Heights
ISRAEL
60km
30mls
🛬 international airport

1 Jeita Grotto
2 Tyre

Jeita Grotto

Situated under Mount Lebanon in the *Nahr el Kalb (Dog River) Valley*, these caves, which have been known to man since Paleolithic times, consist of a lower and upper gallery. The caves were rediscovered by the American missionary Reverend William Thomson in 1836, who ventured 50m (164ft) underground. In 1873 engineers working for the Beirut Water Company explored a further 1000m (3281ft) into the caves. Today, visitors can explore the 6200-metre deep (20,341ft) lower gallery by boat, whilst the upper gallery, which was not discovered until 1958, can be visited on foot by travelling down a 120m (394ft) tunnel.

Transportation
Air: Beirut International Airport. **Road:** Coach: Many tourists visit the sites as part of an organised tour. Taxi: Taxis can be hired in Beirut to take visitors to the site.

Contact Addresses
For more information on Jeita Grotto, contact the Ministry of Tourism (see **Tourist Information** above). Website: www.jeitagrotto.com

Tyre

The city experienced a golden age during the first millennium BC under Hiram, King of Tyre, but later suffered at the hands of its jealous enemies, including the King of Babylon in the sixth century BC, and Alexander the Great in 332BC. *Tyre* eventually fell under Roman rule in 64BC when, an aqueduct, triumphal arch and hippodrome were built. The impressive 480m (131ft) hippodrome, which once seated up to 20,000 spectators, is one of the main attractions.

Transportation
Air: Beirut International Airport. **Road:** Coach: Many tourists visit the sites as part of an organised tour. Taxi: Taxis can be hired in Beirut to take visitors to the site.

Contact Addresses
For more information on Tyre, contact the Ministry of Tourism (see **Tourist Information** above).

Malawi

1 Lake Malawi National Park
2 Liwonde National Park

Tourist Information

Ministry of Tourism, Parks and Wildlife
Ex-French Embassy, Private Bag 326,
Lilongwe, Malawi
Tel: (0) 771 295 or 772 702

Malawi Tourist Office
33 Grosvenor Street, London W1X 0DE, UK
Tel: (020) 7491 4172

Lake Malawi National Park

Lake Malawi National Park was created in 1980 as the world's first freshwater national park on the southern shore of *Lake Malawi*, Africa's third-largest lake, which stretches for 600km (373 miles) and forms a natural border between Malawi, Tanzania and Mozambique. The lush vegetation is home to a range of wildlife, including many species of bird and fish. The clear blue waters of the lake are popular for snorkelling and scuba diving, as well as sailing, kayaking and swimming.

Transportation
Air: Lilongwe Airport. **Road:** Car: Direct from Lilongwe. Many tour operators provide transport to Lake Malawi National Park.

Contact Addresses
Malawi Tourism Information Service, c/o Geo Group & Associates, 4 Christian Fields, London SW16 3JZ, UK
Tel: (0115) 982 1903
Website: www.malawitourism.com

Liwonde National Park

Due to its unspoilt environment and prolific game, *Liwonde National Park* is generally regarded as the best game reserve in Malawi. It covers 550 sq km (212 sq miles) of mopane and savanna woodland on the floodplains of the *River Shire* and *Lake Malombe* in the south of the country. The river plains are home to many species of bird. Plants and trees found in Liwonde National Park include the baobab, a large native African tree bearing a gourd-like fruit. Despite the incredible sights, the park is still relatively peaceful and uncommercialised.

Transportation
Air: Lilongwe Airport. **Road:** Car: Direct from Lilongwe. Many tour operators provide transport to Liwonde National Park.

Contact Addresses
Central African Wilderness Safaris, PO Box 489, Lilongwe, Malawi
Tel: (0) 771 153
Website: www.wilderness-safarismalawi.com

Malaysia

international airport

THAI-LAND

SOUTH CHINA SEA

PHILIPPINES

Penang

Kota Bharu

Ipoh

MALAYSIA

Kota Kinabalu

BRUNEI

SABAH

KUALA LUMPUR

SARAWAK

Johor Bahru

Kuching

Borneo

INDONESIA

INDONESIA

SINGAPORE

Equator

600km

300mls

THAILAND

Langkawi

Alor Setar

Kota Bharu

SOUTH CHINA SEA

George Town

Penang

Kuala Terengganu

Taiping

Perak

Mt Tahan 2189m

Dungun

Pangkor

Ipoh

PENINSULAR

Cameron Highlands

MALAYSIA

Kuantan

Genting Highlands

Pahang

Port Kelang

KUALA LUMPUR

P. Jaya

Putrajaya

Tioman

Seremban

Port Dickson

Mersing

Malacca

INDONESIA

Johor Bahru

Desaru

200km

SINGAPORE

100mls

1 2

400km

200mls

Kudat

Banggi

Sulu Sea

Kota Kinabalu

Mt Kinabalu △ 4094m

Sandakan

SOUTH CHINA SEA

Labuan

BRUNEI

SABAH

Miri

Tawau

Niah Caves

Celebes Sea

Bintulu

SARAWAK

Sibu

Rajang

Kuching

Borneo

INDONESIA

1 Batu Caves (Gua Batu)
2 Petronas Twin Towers

Tourist Information

Tourism Malaysia
Menara Dato' Onn, 17th, 24-27th, 30th floors, Putra World Trade Centre, 45 Jalan Tun Ismail, 50480 Kuala Lumpur, Malaysia
Tel: (03) 2615 8188
Website: www.tourism.gov.my

Tourism Malaysia
Malaysia House, 57 Trafalgar Square, London WC2N 5DU, UK
Tel: (020) 7930 7932
Website: www.malaysiatrulyasia.co.uk

Batu Caves (Gua Batu)

The *Batu Caves* were discovered over 100 years ago and are now one of Kuala Lumpur's most visited sites. Located in an area of outstanding beauty, the caves contain stalactites and stalagmites, and impressive fauna and flora. There are three main caves and numerous smaller ones. The most famous is the *Temple Cave* and is only accessible by a 272-step climb. Below it is the *Dark Cave*, a vast network of caverns inhabited by several indigenous species of animals. Discovered

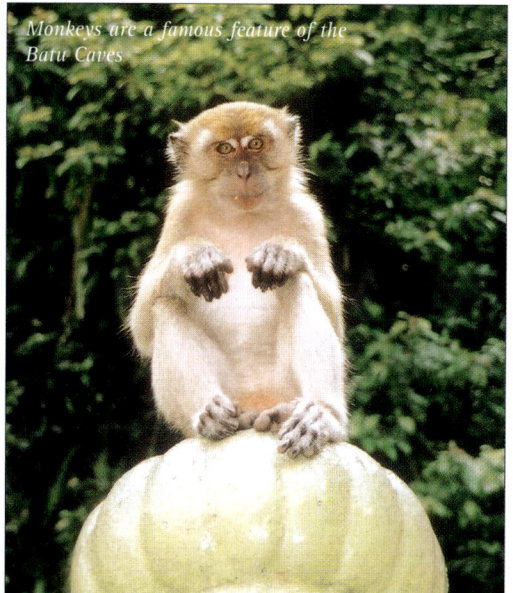

Monkeys are a famous feature of the Batu Caves

Zena Turner©

Petronas Twin Towers

by the American explorer William Hornaby in 1878, the Batu Caves are also an important Hindu shrine, attracting as many as 80,000 devotees during the holy festival of Thaipusam, which takes place in January or February every year.

Transportation
Air: Kuala Lumpur International Airport, then Sultan Abdul Aziz Shah Airport (domestic flights). **Rail:** Train: Kuala Lumpur Station. **Road:** Bus: Public services.

Contact Addresses
For more information on Batu Caves, contact Tourism Malaysia (see **Tourist Information** above).

Petronas Twin Towers

Standing 452m (1483ft) tall, the 88-storey *Petronas Twin Towers* in Kuala Lumpur was the tallest building in the world until Taipei's 101 was built measuring 508m (1666ft). Other projects for even taller buildings are currently underway and are likely to push Petronas further down the list in coming years. Nevertheless, the development also includes a 50 acre (20 hectare) park designed by the late Brazilian landscape artist Roberto Burle Marx, a retail complex and an entertainment centre. Completed in 1997 and designed by Cesar Pelli & Associates, the building consists of two similarly shaped towers joined by a 58m (192ft) *Skybridge* on the 41st and 42nd floors. Entrance is free but visitors do a need a ticket, of which a limited number are issued each day.

Transportation
Air: Kuala Lumpur International Airport, Sultan Abdul Aziz Shah Airport (domestic flights). **Rail:** Train: PUTRA light rail transit to KLCC. **Road:** Bus: Public services.

Contact Addresses
Petronas Twin Towers, Kuala Lumpur City Centre, 50088 Kuala Lumpur, Malaysia
Tel: (603) 2051 5000
Website: www.petronas.com.my *or* www.klcc.com.my

Zena Turner©

Mali

600km

300mls

✈ international airport

WESTERN SAHARA

Tropic of Cancer

S A H A R A

ALGERIA

MAURITANIA

Adrar des Iforas

MALI

Goundam Timbuktu

• Gao

Macina Marshes

• Nioro

Mopti

• Kayes

Djenné • Bandiagara NIGER

SENEGAL

BAMAKO ✈

Ségou • San ①

Niger

BURKINA FASO

Bafing

Niger Bani

NIGERIA

GUINEA

Sikasso •

BENIN

CÔTE D'IVOIRE

GHANA TOGO

1 Djenne Mosque

Tourist Information

Tourist Office of Mali (Office Malien du Tourisme et de l'Hôtellerie)
Rue Mohamed V., Bamako, Mali
Tel: 222 5673
Website: www.malitourisme.com
There is no active Tourist Office for Mali in the UK.

Djenne Mosque

Situated 354 km (220 miles) southwest of *Timbuktu* on the floodplains of the *Bani* and *Niger* rivers, *Old Djenne* is thought to be the oldest known city in Sub-Saharan Africa. Situated along the ancient trans-Sahara trading routes, Djenne had developed into an important settlement in the region and a centre for Islamic learning by the 16th century. Completed in 1907 to replace an earlier mosque, the famous *Djenne Mosque* (also known as the *Grand Mosque*) dominates the old town. Built in the Sudanic style and constructed from sun-baked mud-bricks, each year after the rainy season the entire town turn out to repair the structure at the Spring Festival. Wooden posts that adorn the structure enable workers to scale the walls during the restoration process. A traditional African market is located around the mosque's perimeter. In 1988, Old Djenne and the Grand Mosque were added to the UNESCO list of World Heritage sites.

Transportation
Air: Bamako International Airport. **Water:** River taxis along the Niger River. **Rail:** Train: Bamako Station. **Road:** Bus: Public services or shared bush taxis to Djenne.

Contact Addresses
For more information on the Djenne Mosque, contact the Tourist Office of Mali (see **Tourist Information** above).

Djenne Mosque

Tourist Office of Mali

Key to symbols: £ Entry charged
& Disabled access ◢ Man-made attraction ♥ Natural attraction
P Parking ✕ Restaurant ⊕ Shop
🏛 UNESCO site

Malta

60km
30mls
✈ international airport

Marsalforn
Gozo
•Ggantija
Victoria
Mgarr
Comino
Cominotto
Mellieha Bay
St Paul's Bay
MALTA
St Paul's Bay
Mosta Sliema
Birkirkara **VALLETTA**
Mdina
Rabat Qormi ∴ Tarxien
Malta
△ 253m ✈ Luqa Marsaxlokk
Dingli Cliffs ②
Birzebbuga *Marsaxlokk*
① *Bay*
MEDITERRANEAN
SEA
·Filfla·

1 Blue Grotto (Il-Hnejja)
2 Hagar Qim

Tourist Information

Malta Tourism Authority
Auberge Ditalie, 229 Merchants Street,
Valletta CMR 02, Malta
Tel: 21 22 4444
Website: www.visitmalta.com

Malta Tourism Authority – UK & Eire
Malta House, 36-38 Piccadilly,
London W1J 0LD, UK
Tel: (020) 7292 4900

Blue Grotto (Il-Hnejja)

The *Blue Grotto* is the most famous cave in Malta, with its deep waters displaying magnificent dazzling colours, ranging from turquoise to deep blue. Situated near the village of Zurrieq in southwestern Malta, the cave, which is known as *Il-Hnejja*, meaning 'The Arch', in Maltese, was given its English name by British soldiers who thought that its blue waters resembled the *Grotta Azzurra* (Blue Grotto) in Capri. To get to the grotto,

visitors travel by boat, passing under a massive arch, deep into the 43m (140ft) high cave which is hollowed out of the cliff rockface.

Transportation
Air: Malta International Airport. **Water:** Boat: Boats depart from Wied iz-Zurrieq for the Blue Grotto. **Road:** Bus: Public services. Car: Road to Zurrieq (from Valletta). The Blue Grotto is situated off the southern coast, near Wied iz-Zurrieq and 2.5km (1.6 miles) from Zurrieq.

Contact Addresses
For more information, contact Malta Tourism Authority (see **Tourist Information** above).

Hagar Qim

Discovered under a mound of rubble in 1839, the Neolithic temples of *Hagar Qim*, which date from 300BC, are some of the oldest manmade structures in the world. Reminiscent of England's Stonehenge, the temples are built of limestone rock, some towering 6m (20ft) high, and weighing several tonnes. The complex is an impressive maze of corridors, chambers, niches and altars, carved out of stone using flint. On the morning of the summer solstice, sunlight passes through a hole known as the 'oracle hole' and fills the apse of the temple. The nearby *Mnajdra* temples are included, along with the Hagar Qim, *Tarxien*, *Ta'Hagrat*, *Skorba* and *Ggantija* temple complexes, on the UNESCO World Heritage List.

Transportation
Air: Malta International Airport. **Road:** Bus: Public services. Car: Road towards Wied Zurrieq (from Valletta).

Contact Addresses
Museum of Archaeology, Auberge de Provence, Republic Street, Valetta, Malta
Tel: 2122 1623 *or* 2123 9545
Website: www.heritagemalta.org

Mexico

1000km
500mls
✈ major international airport

UNITED STATES

Colorado

Tijuana
Mexicali
Ciudad Juárez
Hermosillo
Sierra Madre Occ.
Chihuahua
Rio Grande
Torreón
Monterrey
La Paz
2
Baja California
MEXICO
Tropic of Cancer
1
Gulf of Mexico
Léon
Teotihuacán
Tampico
Mérida
Cancún
Guadalajara
Santiago
MEXICO CITY
Toluca
Veracruz
Yucatán Chichén-Itzá
Socorro
Popocatépetl 5452m
Pico de Orizaba 5747m
BEL.
Acapulco
Oaxaca
4
PACIFIC OCEAN
Puebla
3 5 6
GUATEMALA
HON.
7
EL SALVADOR

1 Chichén Itzá

2 Copper Canyon (Barrancas del Cobre)

3 National Museum of Anthropology (Museo Nacional de Antropología)

4 Palenque

5 Parroquia (San Miguel de Allende Parish Church)

6 Teotihuacán

7 White Mountain (Monte Alban)

Tourist Information

Ministry of Tourism (Secretaria de Turismo – SECTUR)
Mariano Escobedo SSO Piso 6 Col. Anzures C.P. 11590 Mexico Df Delagacion Cuauhtemoc
Tel: (055) 278 4200
Website: www.mexico-travel.com

Mexican Tourism Promotion Board
Wakefield House, 41 Trinity Square, London EC3N 4DJ, UK
Tel: (020) 7488 9392
Website: www.visitmexico.com

Chichén Itzá

Located deep within the jungles of *Yucatán,* 193km (120 miles) west of *Cancún,* lies *Chichén Itzá*, one of the most impressive sites of the mysterious Mayan civilisation. Chichén Itzá was the site of countless human sacrifices and flourished until about the year 1200, when it was suddenly abandoned. Today, the old road between Cancún and *Mérida* cuts through the middle of the site, creating two separate ruins, *Chichén Viejo* and *Chichén Nuevo*, which together form the most intact ruins from the Mayan period. Highlights at the complex, which covers an area of approximately 15 sq km (6 sq miles), include the *Kukulcán Pyramid* (also known as the Castle), the *Ball Court* (the largest Mayan ball court ever discovered), the *Thousand Columns* and the *Tzompantli*.

Transportation
Air: Mexico City International Airport, Mérida Airport (domestic flights). **Road:** Coach: Public services. Car: Highway (Autopista) from Cancún or Mérida.

Contact Addresses
Secretária de Turismo de Mérida, Calle 59 #514 entre 62 y 64, Col. Centro, CP 97000 Mérida, Yucatán, Mexico
Tel: (999) 924 9389

Copper Canyon (Barrancas del Cobre)

One of the largest canyon systems in the world, *Copper Canyon* is a land of mountains, rivers, waterfalls, desert and forest. Four of the canyons are deeper than Arizona's famous *Grand Canyon*, although none of them are as wide. Perhaps the most famous attraction for visitors is the *Chihuahua al Pacífico Railway*, a scenic journey that crosses 36 major bridges, travels through 87 tunnels and climbs to a height of 2438m (8000ft) before descending back down to sea level. The *Sierra Tarahumara* mountains are inhabited by

Tarahumara Indians, who live in isolated communities along the railway line.

Transportation
Air: Mexico City International Airport, then Los Mochis Airport or Chihuahua Airport. **Rail:** Train: Copper Canyon Railway to Creel (from Los Mochis or Chihuahua City). **Road:** Coach: Public services. Car: Hwy-16 to Creel (from Chihuahua City).

Contact Addresses
For more information on the Copper Canyon, contact the Secretaria de Turismo (see **Tourist Information** above).

National Museum of Anthropology (Museo Nacional de Antropología)

Mexico's *National Museum of Anthropology* is one of the world's great museums. Opened in 1964, the exhibition halls house Mexico's greatest archaeological collection, celebrating the country's pre-Columbian inhabitants and its existing indigenous peoples. As it is impossible to cover the whole museum at once, it is more rewarding to limit a visit to a few areas of particular interest. Some of the most fascinating rooms are the *Mexica*, which showcases Aztec culture, the *Maya* hall, and the *Teotihuacán* hall. The *Sala de Orientación* provides an overall view of the main Mexican cultures through an audiovisual presentation, and there are also rooms devoted to recent archaeological discoveries.

Transportation
Air: Mexico City International Airport. **Rail:** Underground: Auditorio. **Road:** Car: 57/57D (from the north); 95D (from the south); 150D (from the east); 45D (from the west).

Contact Addresses
Museo Nacional de Antropologia, Paseo de la Reforma, Chapultepec Park, Mexico City, Mexico
Tel: (05) 553 6266
Website: www.mna.inah.gob.mx

Palenque

Located in *Palenque National Park* in the northern *Chiapas* highlands, *Palenque* is one of the grandest of all classical Mayan sites. Situated on a ledge picturesquely overlooking swampy plains to the north, and set against a backdrop of lush, green mountains, Palenque was in its prime between AD 500-700. Visitors can wander from one structure to another amongst waterfalls and jungle, taking in the marvels of this ancient settlement, which is all the more remarkable for having been constructed without the aid of metal tools, the wheel or pack animals. The most notable structures are the *Palace* and the *Temple of Inscriptions* pyramid crypt.

Transportation
Air: Mexico City International Airport, Villa Hermosa Airport (domestic flights). **Road:** Coach: Public services. Car: Main road (from Villa Hermosa or Tuxtla Gutierriz).

Contact Addresses
Chiapas Tourist Board, Blvd. Belisario Dominguez 950 PB, 29060 Tuxtla Gutierrez, Mexico
Tel: (961) 602 5298
Website: www.chiapas.gob.mx

Parroquia (San Miguel de Allende Parish Church)

La Parroquia, a pink, Gothic parish church, is one of *San Miguel de Allende's* most famous landmarks, as well as one of the finest examples of colonial architecture in Mexico. Standing in the city's main square *(El Jardin)*, the church was originally built in 1683 but was given a facelift in 1880. The crypt underneath the main altar contains the remains of Felipe Gonzalez and General Anastasio Bustamante, both of whom were heroes of the Mexican War of Independence (1810-1821) against Spain. There is also a sculpture of Ignacio Allende, who is the city's namesake, displayed on the main altar; he was born in San Miguel in 1779 and became a leader during the Mexican independence movement, with execution in 1811 resulting in his status as a martyr.

Transportation

Air: Mexico City International Airport,
Leon/Guanajuato International Airport. **Road:** Bus:
Public services. Car: Federal Hwy-57 (from
Querétaro); Hwy-49 and Hwy-45D (from Irapuato).
San Miguel de Allende is 274km (171 miles)
northwest of Mexico City.

Contact Addresses

Secretaria de Turismo (SECTUR), San Miguel de
Allende, Guanajuato, Mexico
Tel: (415) 152 0900
Website: www.sanmiguelguide.com

Teotihuacán

Located 50km (31 miles) northeast of *Mexico City*,
Teotihuacán grew to be the largest of Mexico's pre-
Hispanic cities, with an estimated population of
200,000 during its prime in the sixth century AD. Its
greatest building is the *Pyramid of the Sun*, standing
at a height of 63m (207ft). It is joined on the *Avenue
of the Dead*, Teotihuacán's main street, by another
enormous building, the *Moon Pyramid*, which was
originally part of a 'Moon Plaza'. The site was first
excavated in 1884. Visitors can also see the various
palaces once inhabited by the priests who ruled the
city; research has brought to light many of the
rituals of this ancient civilisation, including
ceremonial human sacrifice and elaborate festivals.

Transportation

Air: Mexico City International Airport. **Road:**
Coach: Public services. Car: Main road to Hidalgo
(from Mexico City).

Contact Addresses

Zona Arqueológica de Teotihuacán, Km 22+600
Autopista Ecatepec–Pirámides, CP 55800, Estado
de México, Mexico
Tel/Fax: (594) 956 0276

White Mountain (Monte Alban)

Monte Alban was at one time home to 50,000
Zapotec people. The builders of Monte Alban
artificially levelled the top of the mountain, which
overshadows the three surrounding valleys of
Oaxaca. The site emerged as a political centre in
around 400BC, and later developed as an
important cultural centre between 500BC to AD
700. The site was abandoned by the Zapotecs
when they began to lose political power, which
resulted in conflict between them and the Mixtecs,
who moved into the Valley and used it as a burial
ground. It was later invaded by the Aztecs and
then by the Spanish who gave the site the name
Monte Alban, meaning White Mountain, due to
the white flowering trees that grow in the area.

Transportation

Air: Mexico City International Airport. **Road:**
Coach: Public services. Car: Access from Oaxaca.

Contact Addresses

Monte Alban, Office of Administration,
Archaeological Site, Pino Suarez 715, Centro, CP
68000, Mexico
Tel: (0951) 516 1215

Chichén Itzá

Zena Turner©

Moldova

100km
50mls
✈ international airport

1 Alexandr Pushkin House and Museum
2 Emil Racovita

Tourist Information

Moldova National Tourism Agency
180 Stefan cel Mare Street, Office 901,
Chisinau MD 2004, Moldova
Tel: (22) 210 774
Website: www.turism.md
Embassy of the Republic of Moldova
5 Dolphin Square, Edensor Road, London
W4 2ST, UK
Tel: (020) 8995 6818
Website: www.turism.md

Alexandr Pushkin House and Museum

The famous Russian poet A.S. Pushkin was sent in to exile in Moldova in 1820 for writing subversive poetry and arrived in the Moldovan capital of Chisinau in September of that year. He took up residence in the house of General Iznov in the city which today stands as a popular museum recounting the events of his life. During his time in Moldova, Pushkin wrote many famous poems including 'The Gypsies', 'The Black Shawl' and part of 'Eugene Onegin', one his most celebrated works.

Transportation
Air: Chisinau International Airport. Rail: Train: Chisinau Station. Road: Bus: Public services.

Contact Addresses
A.S. Pushkin House and Museum, 19 Anton Pann Street, Chisinau, Moldova
Tel: (22) 292 685 *or* 242 653

Emil Racovita

Named after the eminent 19th-century Romanian biologist, Emil Racovita, the cave complex in the village of *Criva* in Moldova is one of the biggest in the world. A network of underground galleries stretches over 89,000m (291,991ft) and is split across several levels. Discovered in 1959, the cave is the third-largest gypsum cave in the world and parts of the complex are only accessible via large wells. The huge caves have been given names such as *Cinderella's Hall* and *Dacia's Hall,* reflecting their size and grandeur, and there are also several underground lakes, including the *Blue Lake* and the *Dinosaur Lake*. There are no trail markers but visitors are able to explore the caves in small groups with an experienced guide.

Transportation
Air: Chisinau International Airport. **Rail:** Train: Public services. **Road:** Bus: Public services.

Contact Addresses
For more information on the Emil Racovita Cave, contact the National Tourism Agency (see **Tourist Information** above).

Morocco

1 Fès Medina (Fès el Bali)

2 Hassan Tower (Tour Hassan)

3 Place of the Dead (Djemaa el Fna)

4 Saadian Tombs

Tourist Information

Office National Marocain de Tourisme
22 Avenue d'alger, Rabat, Morocco
Tel: (037) 73 0562
Website: www.tourism-in-morocco.com

Moroccan National Tourist Office
Second Floor, 205 Regent Street,
London W1B 4HB, UK
Tel: (020) 7437 0073
Website: www.visitmorocco.org

Fès Medina (Fès el Bali)

Founded shortly after the Arabs first entered North Africa in the eighth century AD, *Fès* is the oldest of Morocco's imperial cities. Its *medina*, the ancient quarter or the old city, is also the largest medina in Morocco, an enchanting, winding, medieval maze of mosques, food markets and covered bazaars filled with crafts, such as metalwork objects and rugs. The *Souk Dabbaghin* houses the tanneries where leather has been dyed for hundreds of years. Today, this traditional craft is still practised and visitors can see the huge vats of dye and the coloured leather that is laid out to dry in the sun. The medina is also home to the *Al-Qarawiyin Theological University*, founded in AD 857, which is the oldest university in the western world. The *Medersa Bou Inania* was founded in 1350 as a rival to the Al-Qarawiyin University and is a splendid example of Andalusian architecture.

Transportation
Air: Marrakech Ménara Airport. **Rail:** Train: Marrakech Station. **Road:** Coach: Public services.

Contact Addresses
For more information on Fès Medina, contact the Moroccan National Tourist Office in London (see **Tourist Information** above).

Hassan Tower (Tour Hassan)

The *Hassan Tower*, the grandiose minaret of a vast yet incomplete mosque, is Rabat's most famous landmark. Begun in AD 1195, the minaret was intended to be the largest in the Muslim world, soaring 86m (260ft) into the sky. Construction was abandoned, however, upon the death of the sultan, Yacoub al-Mansour, in AD 1199 and the tower instead rises to just 44m (140ft). Two hundred columns mark out the area where the mosque was to stand. Today, the site also houses the *Mosque and Mausoleum of Mohammed V*, the grandfather of the present king of Morocco, which is one of the few sacred sites in the country that non-Muslims are allowed to enter.

Transportation
Air: Casablanca Mohammed V Airport or Rabat Salé Airport. **Rail:** Train: Rabat Agdal Station or Rabat-Ville Station. **Road:** Car: Casablanca-Rabat Highway.

Contact Adresses

For more information on the Hassan Tower, contact the Moroccan National Tourist Office in London (see **Tourist Information** above).

Place of the Dead (Djemaa el Fna)

Djemaa el Fna is the hub of daily life in *Marrakech*, and this town square is as much a focus for the local people as it is for the tourists who flock here to find their bearings and watch the daily spectacle unfold. During the day the square serves more as a thoroughfare for traffic with just a few fresh fruit and juice stalls. The square leads in to the *medina*, or old quarter, where the famous *souks*, or bazaars, can be found. At night, the square really comes alive and turns into an open-air stage filled with acrobats, storytellers, snakecharmers and musicians. There are literally hundreds of food stalls to choose from, selling anything from hearty *harira* soup and couscous to grilled meats and french fries. All this is not merely a show for the tourists either – the entertainers who perform here do so to earn a living, and are carrying on a centuries-old tradition that remains a fundamental part of Marrakech life.

Transportation

Air: Marrakech Ménara Airport. **Rail:** Train: Marrakech Station. **Road:** Coach: Public services.

Contact Addresses

Marrakech Tourist Office, Place Abdelmoumen Ben Ali, Marrakech, Morocco
Tel: (04) 443 6231
Website: www.visitmorocco.com

Saadian Tombs

Situated in the old *Kasbah Quarter* of *Marrakech*, the *Saadian Tombs* were built in the late-16thcentury by the Saadian Sultan Ahmed el Mansour as the final resting place for himself, three other Sultans and 62 of their family members. The series of 66 elaborately decorated indoor tombs were only accessible via the mosque next door but were rediscovered and made accessible to visitors in 1917 and have become one of the city's most visited sites. Famed for their ornate decoration, the central mausoleum known as the *Hall of Twelve Columns* is the most stunning chamber of the complex with high vaulted ceilings, marble columns and intricate mosaics.

Transportation

Air: Marrakech Ménara Airport. **Rail:** Marrakech Station. **Road:** Bus: Public services.

Contact Addresses

For more information on the Saadian Tombs, contact the Moroccan National Tourist Board (see **Tourist Information** above).

Visit Morocco©

Myanmar

1 Bagan

Tourist Information

Myanmar Ministry of Hotels & Tourism
77-91 Sule Pagoda Road, Yagon, Myanmar
Tel: (01) 25 44 17 or 25 28 59
Website: www.myanmar-tourism.com

Embassy of the Union of Myanmar
19a Charles Street, London W1J 5DX, UK
Tel: (020) 7499 43401

plaster carvings and other artefacts from the empire. Many visitors take a river excursion to take in large stretches of the site, which is particularly beautiful at sunset.

Transportation
Air: Yangon International Airport, then Nyaung-u Airport (located 11km (7 miles) from Bagan and next to the archaeological site). **Rail:** Train: Bagan Station. **Road:** Bus: Nyaung-u Bus Station is located 6.5km (4 miles) from Bagan; there are regular buses to/from Yangon and Mandalay. Car: There are road connections to Bagan.

Contact Addresses
Myanmar Travel and Tours, c/o Ministry of Hotels and Tourism, 77-91 Sule Pagoda Road, Yangon, Myanmar
Tel: (01) 283 997 or 252 859

Bagan

The ancient city of *Bagan* (also known as Pagan) was founded in AD 849 by the Myanmar, or Burmans, as the capital of their empire. It is one of the most amazing archaeological sites in the world – 5000 temples, *stupas* (Buddhist dome-shaped monuments believed to contain relics of the Buddha himself) and pagodas lie scattered across an area of 42 sq km (16.2 sq miles) on the eastern bank of the Ayeyarwaddy River, testifying to the power and status of Bagan in bygone times. The most significant pagoda is the golden *Shwezigon Pagoda*, constructed in 1057 by King Anawrahta, the founder of the Myanmar dynasty, as a place of prayer and meditation. The informative *Archaeological Museum* displays murals,

Bagan

Myanmar Ministry of Hotels & Tourism©

Namibia

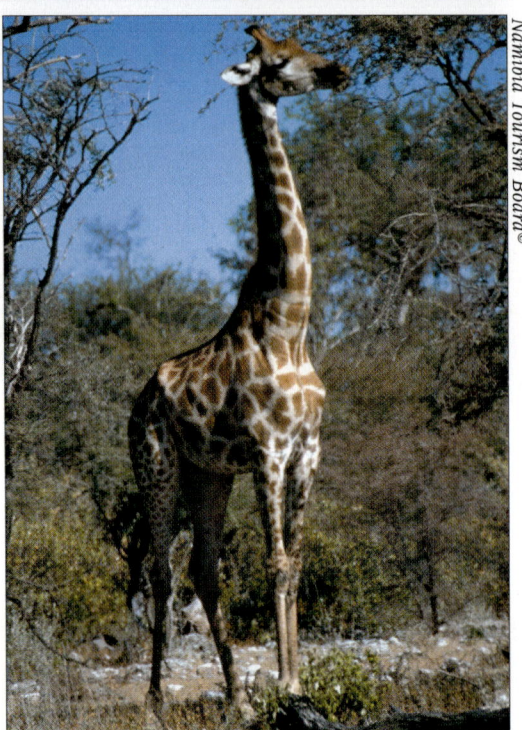

Namibia Tourism Board©

1 Etosha National Park

2 Fish River Canyon

Tourist Information

Namibia Tourism
Ground Floor Sanlam Center, Private Bag
13244, Windhoek, Namibia
Tel: (061) 290 6000
Website: www.met.gov.na

Namibia Tourism
6 Chandos Street, London W1G 9LU, UK
Tel: (0870) 330 9333
Website: www.namibiatourism.co.uk

Etosha National Park

Etosha National Park is located 500km (311 miles) north of Namibia's capital city, Windhoek. It is one of the largest game reserves in the world and famous for its many species of wildlife. Until the 1960s, it was the largest game reserve in the world, when its surface area was reduced due to political reasons. Today, Etosha has three main restcamps – *Okaukejo*, *Namutoni* and *Halali*. Okaukejo is famed for floodlit waterholes that are home to elephants, giraffes, black rhino and lions; Namutoni is centred around a historic fort and Halali is situated halfway between the two and is the quietest. The park has an estimated 300 lions, 2000 giraffes and 1500 elephants and owes its unique landscape to the *Etosha Pan*, a giant clay salt pan forming a shallow depression which allows amazing views of the game.

Transportation
Air: Windhoek International Airport. **Road:** Car: C38 road (from Outjo); C39 road (from Khorixas).

Contact Addresses
Namibia Wildlife Resorts Ltd, Erkrath Building, Independence Avenue, Private Bag 13267, Windhoek, Namibia
Tel: (061) 256 446
Website: www.namibiawildliferesorts.com

www.fotoseeker.com©

Fish River Canyon

Fish River Canyon

Fish River Canyon is the largest canyon in the Southern Hemisphere, second only in the world to the *Grand Canyon*. The whole gorge measures 160km (99 miles) in length and is 127km (79 miles) wide, whilst its impressive inner canyon is an amazing 550m (1804ft) deep. The gorge which has formed over hundreds of millions of years, winds through the arid desert landscape, cutting through the great plateau and surrounded by imposing cliffs and large boulders. The site is the main tourist attraction in the far south of Namibia, popular with hikers who set out on the testing trail through the canyon. At the southern end of the canyon, after a long hike through the desert terrain, weary walkers arrive at *Ai-Ais*

(meaning Burning Water in the local Nama language), a hot water spring which wells from the earth and is believed to cure rheumatism.

Transportation
Air: Windhoek International Airport. **Road:** Car: B4 southwest for around 44km (27 miles), then left onto the C12 (from Keetmanshoop). After 77km (48 miles) a right turn is signposted for Fish River Canyon.

Contact Addresses
Namibia Wildlife Resorts Ltd, Erkrath Building, Independence Avenue, Private Bag 13267, Windhoek, Nambia
Tel: (061) 236 975
Website: www.namibiawildliferesorts.com

Nepal

1 Kathmandu Durbar Square

Durbar Square

Nepal Tourism Board©

Tourist Information

Nepal Tourism Board
Bhrikuti Mandap, PO Box 11018, Kathmandu, Nepal
Tel: (01) 256 909 or 256 229 Website: www.welcomenepal.com

Royal Nepalese Embassy
12a Kensington Palace Gardens, London W8 4QU, UK
Tel: (020) 7229 1594 or 7229 5352
Website: www.nepembassy.org.uk

Kathmandu Durbar Square

Kathmandu's *Durbar Square* is one of three *durbar* (royal palace) squares in the Kathmandu Valley. It is the site of the *Hanuman Dhoka Palace Complex*, which was the royal Nepalese residence until the 19th century and where important ceremonies, such as the coronation of the Nepalese monarch, still take place today. The palace is decorated with elaborately-carved wooden windows and panels and houses the *King Tribhuwan Memorial Museum*

and the *Mahendra Museum*. It is also possible to visit the *State Rooms* inside the palace. At the southern end of Durbar Square is one of the most curious attractions in Nepal, the *Kumari Chowk*. This gilded cage contains the Raj Kumari, a young girl chosen through an ancient and mystical selection process to become the human incarnation of the Hindu mother goddess, Durba. She is worshipped during religious festivals and makes public appearances at other times for a fee paid to her guards.

Transportation
Air: Kathmandu International Airport. **Road:** Coach: Services from Darjeeling, Calcutta and Varanasi (India). Car: Prithvi Highway (from Pokhara).

Contact Addresses
Department of Archaeology, Hanumandhoka Section, Ramshah Path, Kathmandu, Nepal
Tel: (01) 250 683 *or* 250 685

   £

Netherlands

1 Anne Frank House (Anne Frank Huis)
2 Keukenhof Gardens (Keukenhof)
3 Royal Palace (Koninklijk Paleis)
4 State Museum (Rijksmuseum)
5 Van Gogh Museum

Tourist Information

**Netherlands Board of Tourism
(Nederlands Bureau voor Toerisme)**
PO Box 458, 2260 MG Leidschendam,
The Netherlands
Tel: (070) 370 5705
Website: www.holland.com

Netherlands Board of Tourism
PO Box 30783, London WC2B 6DH, UK
Tel: (020) 7539 7950 or (09068) 717 777
(recorded information; calls cost 60p per minute)
Website: www.holland.com/uk

Anne Frank House (Anne Frank Huis)

Anne Frank House is the historic house where Jewish teenager Anne Frank, her family and four other Jews hid from the Nazis during World War II. Anne herself shared a tiny room with family friend Fritz Pfeffer (known to Anne as Albert Dussel). In August 1944, after more than two years living in a cramped secret annex of the canalside townhouse on Prinsengracht in the centre of Amsterdam, they were betrayed to the Germans. Anne died at the Bergen-Belsen concentration camp; however, her father survived and published her diary, which became world famous as testament to one person's courage in the face of persecution. Today, the house is a permanent exhibition dedicated to the memory of Anne Frank, and the place where the original diary is on display. Visitors can see the room where Anne wrote most of her diary and, although the house was stripped by the Nazis after the Franks' arrest, audiovisual presentations document how the rooms would have looked.

Transportation
Air: Amsterdam Airport Schiphol. **Rail:** Train: Amsterdam Centraal Station. Tram: Public services. **Road:** Bus: Public services to Westermarkt. Car: Hwy-A10 (exit Centrum S105).

Contact Addresses
Anne Frankhuis, PO Box 730, 1000 AS Amsterdam, The Netherlands
Tel: (020) 556 7100
Website: www.annefrank.nl

Keukenhof Gardens (Keukenhof)

Located in the town of Lisse, *Keukenhof Gardens* are named after the kitchen gardens where Countess Jacoba of Bavaria grew fruit, vegetables and herbs in the grounds of her estate between 1401-1436 (hence the name Keukenhof, which literally means kitchen garden). Keukenhof was

The Westerkerk (church) neighbouring Anne Frank's House.

Netherlands Board of Tourism & Conventions©

designed as a park by two horticultural architects called Zochter in 1840, with the flower garden opening in 1949 when a bulb-growing consortium acquired the site and decided to develop an open-air flower exhibition. Today, Keukenhof Gardens, which is the largest flower attraction in the Netherlands and the largest display of bulbs in the world, is an impressive and flamboyant example of the Dutch population's love of tulips. Although open daily, the best time of year to visit is between the last week in March and the last week in May when the beautiful bulb flowers are in full bloom.

Transportation
Air: Amsterdam Airport Schiphol. **Rail:** Train: Leiden Central Station or Haarlem Station. **Road:** Bus: Public services.

Contact Addresses
Keukenhof, Stationsweg 166 A, 2160 AB Lisse, The Netherlands
Tel: (0252) 465 564
Website: www.keukenhof.nl

Royal Palace (Koninklijk Paleis)

The *Royal Palace*, which dates from 1648 and was designed by Jacob van Campen, was originally Amsterdam's town hall and is regarded today as the most important cultural and historical building from 17th-century Amsterdam. The building's exterior was originally made of white stone, although none of the white is actually visible today, whilst famous painters including Rembrandt and Ferdinand Bol were brought in to contribute to the interior. Today, the palace, which has been state property since 1936, houses an impressive collection of furniture left behind by Napoleon who made it his home in 1808, as well as chandeliers and clocks from this period. The palace is the official residence of the Dutch Royal Family and the present Queen, Beatrix, still uses the Royal Palace to host official functions such as the Queen's New Year reception and various state visits.

Transportation
Air: Amsterdam Airport Schiphol. **Rail:** Train: Amsterdam Centraal Station. Tram: Public services. **Road:** Signs are marked for Dam Square (from Amsterdam Centraal Station).

Contact Addresses
Ministry of General Affairs (RVD), Binnenhof 19, Postbus 20009, 2500 ea den haag, The Netherlands.
Tel: (0) 70 356 or 4166
Website: www.koninklijkhuis.nl

State Museum (Rijksmuseum)

The largest and most popular museum in the Netherlands, the *Rijksmuseum* was first opened as the *Nationale Konstgallerij* (National Art Gallery) in 1800 in *Huis ten Bosch* in The Hague. The museum houses an impressive collection of 15th- to 19th-century paintings, including work by the Dutch masters Rembrandt, Frans Hals, Jan Steen and Vermeer, and a fine collection of sculpture, furniture and historical items from the Low Countries. Highlights include the museum's most famous piece, Rembrandt's *The Night Watch*, painted in 1642, and *The Kitchen Maid* by Vermeer, dating from 1658. The *Print*

Corel©   *Keukenhof Gardens*

Room is also worth visiting and regularly exhibits famous prints, drawings and photos.

Transportation
Air: Amsterdam Airport Schiphol. **Rail:** Train: Amsterdam Centraal Station. Tram: Public services. **Road:** Car: A10 towards Amsterdam (RAI exit). Signs are marked for the Rijksmuseum (from the city centre).

Contact Addresses
Rijksmuseum, PO Box 74888, 1070 DN Amsterdam, The Netherlands
Tel: (020) 674 7047
Website: www.rijksmuseum.nl

Van Gogh Museum

Opened in 1973, the *Van Gogh Museum* houses some of the painter's most celebrated works. Located in the Museumplein in the centre of Amsterdam, between the Rijksmuseum and the Stedelijk Museum, the modern glass building was designed by the Dutch architect Gerrit Rietveld. It contains the world's largest collection of works by Van Gogh, including some 200 paintings, 500 drawings, 700 letters and the artist's own collection of Japanese prints. Highlights of the Van Gogh collection include his first large-scale painting, *The Potato Eaters* and *The Sunflowers*, one of his most famous pieces, painted in 1889. The museum also houses a large collection of work by Van Gogh's contemporaries, including paintings by Claude Monet and Paul Gauguin.

Transportation
Air: Amsterdam Airport Schiphol. **Rail:** Train: Amsterdam Centraal Station. Tram: Public services to Museum Square. **Road:** Bus: Public services to Museum Square. Car: A10 towards Amsterdam (exit S106). Signs are marked for Museum Square (from the city centre).

Contact Addresses
Van Gogh Museum, PO Box 75366, 1070 AJ Amsterdam, The Netherlands
Tel: (020) 570 5200 *or* 570 5252
Website: www.vangoghmuseum.nl

New Zealand

400km
200mls
✈ international airport

1 Aoraki Mount Cook
2 Fiordland National Park
3 Museum of New Zealand Te Papa Tongarewa
4 Sky City Tower
5 Tongariro National Park

Aoraki Mount Cook

Standing 3754m (12,316ft) high, *Aoraki Mount Cook* is the highest mountain in New Zealand. The mountain, which attracts climbers from all over the world to its snow-covered peaks, stands in *Aoraki/Mount Cook National Park*, on New Zealand's South Island. Aoraki means 'Cloud Piercer' in Maori and the mountain is so called due to its breathtaking peaks which tower high above the clouds. The national park was formally declared in 1953 and covers an area of 70,111 hectares (173,251 acres). There are regular guided tours from Mount Cook to the *Tasman Glacier*,

Tourist Information

Tourism New Zealand
PO Box 95, Wellington, New Zealand
Tel: (04) 917 5400
Website: www.purenz.com *or*
www.tourisminfo.govt.nz
Administrative headquarters only. Trade and consumer enquiries should be directed to TNZ's branches around the world

Tourism New Zealand
New Zealand House, 80 Haymarket, London SW1Y 4TQ, UK
Tel: (020) 7930 1662 *or* (09069) 101 010 (recorded information line; calls cost £1 per minute)
Website: www.purenz.com (consumer information) *or* www.tourisminfo.govt.nz (trade information)

which, at 27km (17 miles) long, 3km (1.9 miles) wide and 600m (1968ft) deep, is New Zealand's largest glacier. Other highlights include the smaller *Hooker Glacier*, *Murchison Glacier Mount Tasman* and *Mount Dampier*. Outdoor activities include helicopter rides, alpine flights, horse trekking, hunting and fishing, mountain biking and hiking through the mountains.

Transportation
Air: Christchurch International Airport, Aoraki/Mount Cook Airport (domestic flights); there are regular shuttle buses from Aoraki/Mount Cook Airport throughout the Mackenzie region.
Road: Bus: Public services.

Contact Addresses
Mackenzie Tourism and Development Board, Lake Pukaki Visitor Centre, State Highway 8, PO Box 68, Twizel, New Zealand
Tel: (03) 435 3280
Website: www.mtcook.org.nz

P

Fiordland National Park

At nearly 1.2 million hectares (3 million acres), *Fiordland National Park* is New Zealand's largest national park – a breathtaking stretch of coastal landscape that typifies the country's natural splendour. Created in 1952, it is a land of ice, beech forests, mountains and waterfalls that tumble into the ocean below. One of the park's most famous sights is *Milford Sound*, which is the largest glacier-carved fiord on New Zealand's coastline and attracts large numbers of sightseers and cruise ships every year. Popular activities in the park include hiking, sea kayaking, diving, cycling, golf, fishing and sailing. The *Milford Track*, which stretches some 53.5km (33 miles) from Glade Wharf to Sandfly Point, has been described as the finest walk in the world, taking visitors on a rugged, alpine journey through the park's most breathtaking scenery. Visitors should, however, note that a permit is required for the track and these must be booked through the Visitor Centre in Te Anau.

Transportation
Air: Christchurch International Airport, Te Anau Airstrip (domestic flights). **Road:** Bus: Public services to Milford Sound and Queenstown.

Contact Addresses
Fiordland National Park Visitor Centre, c/o Department of Conservation, Lakefront Drive, PO Box 29, Te Anau, New Zealand
Tel: (03) 249 7924
Website: www.doc.govt.nz

Museum of New Zealand Te Papa Tongarewa

Te Papa (meaning 'Our Place' in Maori), the national museum of New Zealand, is located on Wellington's waterfront, from where it enjoys magnificent views across the harbour. The museum was opened to enable the people of New Zealand to learn more about their cultural identity and their country's geography and has attracted international acclaim for its ultra-modern and interactive displays. It occupies a floor space measuring 36,000 sq m (387,513 sq ft)

and houses many national artefacts, enabling visitors to learn about the art, history and natural environment of New Zealand. It also has several permanent exhibitions, including the *Time Warp* display, which allows visitors to travel back in time to New Zealand's prehistoric age.

Transportation
Air: Wellington International Airport. **Road:** Bus: Public services. Car: Wellington motorway (Aotea Quay exit), then along Waterloo, Customhouse and Jervois Quay, which leads directly to Cable Street.

Contact Addresses
Museum of New Zealand Te Papa Tongarewa, PO Box 467, Cable Street, Wellington, New Zealand
Tel: (04) 381 7000
Website: www.tepapa.govt.nz

Sky City Tower

The *Sky City Tower* stands at 328m (1076ft) high and is situated in the *Sky City* entertainment complex, which also houses *Sky City Casino*, *Sky City Theatre*, *Sky City Hotel and Conference Centre* and *Sky City Restaurants*. The postmodern Sky City Tower was designed by the architect *Craig Moller* and completed in 1997. The tower has three circular observation levels, the highest of which is the *Sky Deck*, which gives a 360-degree view across Auckland and Waitemata Harbour, over the top of Rangitoto Island to the other islands in the Hauraki Gulf, allowing visitors to see up to 82km (51 miles) on a clear day. Visitors can also eat in the *Orbit* rotating restaurant and travel to the top of the tower in one of six high-tech glass-fronted lifts.

Transportation
Air: Auckland International Airport. **Road:** Bus: Public services.

Contact Addresses
Sky Tower, Sky City, PO Box 90643, Auckland, New Zealand
Tel: (09) 363 6400
Website: www.skycity.co.nz

Auckland with the Sky City Tower

New Zealand Tourist Board©

Tongariro National Park

Originally a gift to Queen Victoria from the Tuwharetoa Maori chief Te Heuheu Tukino IV in 1887, *Tongariro National Park* was the first national park in New Zealand and the fourth oldest in the world. Since its inception, the park has grown to a size of nearly 80,000 hectares (197,688 acres). The area is of religious and cultural importance to the Maoris who first occupied the area in the ninth century when they arrived from Polynesia. In particular, they believed the region's mountains had god-like ancestors, and the core of the park centres around three active volcanoes, *Tongariro*, *Ngauruhoe* and the largest, *Ruapehu*, which erupted in a spectacular fashion in 1995 and again in 1996. Some areas resemble a lunar landscape, which has been created by flowing lava, alongside forests and tussock lands. The *Tongariro Crossing*, completed by about 70,000 hikers every summer, is considered to be one of the best one-day walks in the country, offering magnificent volcanic scenery and fine views of *Lake Taupo* and *Mount Taranaki*.

Transportation
Air: Wellington International Airport, then Taupo Airport. **Rail:** Train: National Park and Ohakune stations (from Auckland and Wellington). **Road:** Bus: Public services. Car: State Hwy-1 (from Auckland in the north or from Wellington in the south).

Contact Addresses
Tongariro National Park, Private Bag, Mt Ruapehu 2650, New Zealand
Tel: (07) 892 3814
or
Tongariro/Taupo Conservancy, Private Bag, Turangi, New Zealand
Tel: (07) 386 8607
Website: www.doc.govt.nz

Norway

400km
200mls
international airport

ARCTIC OCEAN
North Cape
Hammerfest
Kirkenes
Alta
Vesterålen Tromsø
RUSSIA
Lofoten Narvik
Bodø LAPLAND
Arctic Circle
Kjölen Mountains
NORWEGIAN SEA
NORWAY
Kristiansund ②Trondheim
Ålesund Røros
Glittertind 2470m△ Glåma SWEDEN
FINLAND
Gulf of Bothnia
③Bergen ①
OSLO
Stavanger Vänern
Larvik
Kristiansand
Skagerrak Vättern
DENMARK
BALTIC SEA
ESTONIA
LATVIA

1 Hardanger Fjord
2 Nidaros Cathedral (Nidarosdomen)
3 Wharfside (Bryggen)

Tourist Information

Norweigan Tourist Board (Norges Turistrad)
PO Box 722, Santrum 0105, Oslo, Norway
Tel: 2414 4600
Website: www.ntr.no or www.visitnorway.com

Norwegian Tourist Board
Charles House, 5 Lower Regent Street, London
SW1Y 4LR, UK
Tel: (09063) 022 033 (brochure request line)
or (020) 7839 2650 (trade)
Website: www.visitnorway.com

Hardanger Fjord

Hardanger Fjord, which is located 75km (47 miles) east of Bergen, is one of the most popular tourist destinations in Norway. This scenic area offers virtually every kind of natural landscape available in the country, from scenic waterways, apple and cherry orchards, and hiking trails, to mountain plateaux. The area also contains *Hardangervidda*, Norway's largest national park, two of Norway's largest glaciers, *Folgefonna* and *Hardangerjøkulen*, and some of Norway's most popular waterfalls, including *Vøringfossen, Steinsdalsfossen* and *Låtefossen*. There are also various museums in the area, including *Hardanger folkemuseum* (Hardanger Folk Museum) and *Hardanger Fartøyvernsenter* (Hardanger Ships Preservation Centre) treeboat museum.

Transportation
Air: Bergen Flesland Airport. **Rail:** Train: Voss Station. **Road:** Bus: Public services to Norheimsund. Car: Route 7 towards Norheimsund (from Bergen); E-16 and Route 7 (from Oslo).

Contact Addresses
Destination Hardanger Fjord, PO Box 66, 5601 Norheimsund, Norway
Tel: 5655 3870
Website: www.hardangerfjord.com

Nidaros Cathedral (Nidarosdomen)

According to Norwegian history, King Olav Haraldsson, who was killed in the battle of Stiklestad in 1030 and who subsequently became Norway's patron saint several days later, was buried on the exact spot where *Nidaros Cathedral* in Trondheim now stands. Construction of the church began in 1070 after pilgrims began to flock to St Olav's grave, but it was not completed until 1300, when it was widely reputed to be the most beautiful church in Norway. Now restored after fire damage and years of decay and pillage endured during the Reformation, it is particularly renowned for its fine stone statues on the exterior

Nidaros Cathedral

Innovation Norway©

Wharfside, Bergen

founded by a group of northern German towns to protect their mutual trading interests in the 13th to 15th centuries. The buildings were mainly used as warehouses for the dried fish trade, but also contained offices and simple living quarters for merchants, journeymen and apprentices. Today, Bryggen is alive with restaurants, cafés and artists' workshops, and a colourful attraction at the eastern end is *Torget*, a weekday market selling fruit and vegetables, handicrafts and souvenirs.

and the quality and quantity of stained glass in the Gothic interior. Norway's monarchs are still crowned and buried in the cathedral and there are regular music recitals under the high-vaulted arches. Visitors can admire the *Crown Jewels* on display and also climb the tower for fine views over Trondheim.

Transportation
Air: Bergen Flesland Airport, Oslo Gardermoen International Airport, Trondheim Værnes Airport. **Water:** Ferry: Hurtigruten coastal steamer (from Bergen). **Rail:** Train: Trondheim Station. **Road:** Bus: Public services. Car: E6 (from Oslo, Gothenburg or Copenhagen).

Contact Addresses
Nidarosdomen, Nidaros Domkirkes Restaureringsarbeider, Postboks 4447, Hospitalsløkkan, 7418 Trondheim, Norway
Tel: 7353 9160
Website: www.nidarosdomen.no

Wharfside (Bryggen)

Considered by UNESCO to be one of the world's foremost showcases of the Middle Ages, *Bryggen* consists of a series of gabled buildings situated on the old wharf of Bergen. It stands as a reminder of Bergen's prominent role in the days of the Hanseatic League, an organisation

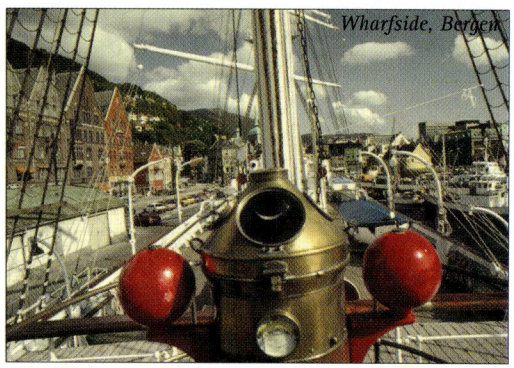
Wharfside, Bergen

Transportation
Air: Bergen Flesland Airport. **Rail:** Train: Bergen Central Station. Road: Bus: Public services. **Car:** E16 (from Oslo); E39 (from Stavanger, Ålesund or Kristiansand, then signs are marked for the city centre).

Contact Addresses
Bergen Tourist Board, PO Box 4055, Dreggen, 5835 Bergen, Norway
Tel: 5531 3860 *or* 5532 1480
Website: www.visitbergen.com

Panama

Locks on the Panama Canal

1 Panama Canal (Canal de Panamá)

Tourist Information

Instituto Panameño de Turismo (IPAT) (Institute of Tourism)
Apartado 4421, Centro de Convenciones ATLAPA, Vía Israel, Panamá 5, Republic of Panamá
Tel: 226 7000 *or* 226 4614/3164
Website: www.ipat.gob.pa

Embassy of Panama
40 Hertford Street, London W1J 7SH, UK
Tel: (020) 7493 4646

Panama Canal (Canal de Panamá)

The idea of building a canal across the Isthmus of Panama dates back to the 16th century when people first recognised the advantage of building a canal which would avoid having to sail around Cape Horn in South America. It was not until 1880, however, that the French made an attempt to build a canal across this stretch of water. Unfortunately the attempt failed miserably due to high costs, with over 22,000 workers dying from malaria and yellow fever. The United States began construction work in 1904, employing nearly 75,000 men and women to build the canal, which opened to traffic ten years later in 1915. Today, the 80km (50 mile) canal still stands as one of the most important engineering feats in the world, providing passage for over 12,000 ships every year. An open-air balcony at *Miraflores Locks* offers visitors good views of the electrical locomotives or 'mules' pulling giant ships through as the water levels are balanced.

Transportation
Air: Tocument International Airport. **Road:** Coach: Many private companies operate coach tours to the canal (from Panama City). Car: Corredor Sur Highway to central Panama City, then through the Albrook Residential and Commercial Area, and right to Miraflores Locks (from Tocument International Airport).

Contact Addresses
Panama Canal Authority, PO Box 5413, Miami, FL 33102, USA
Tel: 272 3165 *or* 272 3202 (in Panama)
Website: www.pancanal.com

Peru

1 Arequipa-Colca Canyon (Cañon del Colca-Arequipa)

2 Lake Titicaca (Lago Titicaca)

3 Machu Picchu

4 Manu National Park (Parque Nacional del Manu)

Tourist Information

PromPerú (Commission for the Promotion of Peru)
Calle 1 Oeste 50, Edificio Mitinci, 13th Floor, Urb. Córpac, San Isidro, Lima 27, Peru
Tel: (01) 224 3271
Website: www.peru.org.pe

Embassy of the Republic of Peru
52 Sloane Street, London SW1X 9SP, UK
Tel: (020) 7235 1917 or 7235 2545
Website: www.peruembassy-uk.com

Arequipa-Colca Canyon (Cañon del Colca-Arequipa)

At a depth of more than 3400m (11,333ft), the *Arequipa-Colca Canyon* is one of the deepest in the world and almost twice the depth of the Grand Canyon (1829m/6000ft). The Rio Colca winds its way through the gorge, with the impressive Sabancaya and Ampato volcanoes looming high in the background. The canyon, which is named after the *Colcas* (warehouses) where the Incas used to store grain in sealed vaults in the canyon walls, is dotted with flora and fauna. A highlight of any trip to the region is a chance to see the giant Andean Condor that inhabits the canyon; visitors can view these great birds soaring into the wind from the *Cruz del Condor* observation point. The valley towns, such as Yanque and Chivay, which have maintained their original appearance for almost 400 years, and the many pre-Inca tombs and ruins in the area, are also of interest.

Transportation
Air: Lima Jorge Chavez International Airport, Cusco Airport (domestic flights). **Rail:** Train: Services to Arequipa. **Road:** Car: Arequipa-Lima road then road from Arequipa to the canyon.

Contact Addresses
Dirección Regional de Industria y Turismo, Jacinto Ibanez 456, Parque Industrial, Arequipa, Peru
Tel: (054) 213 044 or 235 660
Website: www.promperu.gob.pe

Lake Titicaca (Lago Titicaca)

At an elevation of 3810m (12,492ft), *Lake Titicaca* is one of the world's highest navigable lakes. It is named after the native word for 'puma of stone' and its shape bears a strong resemblance to this animal when viewed from above. Measuring 194km (121 miles) long and 65km (45 miles) wide, it has been revered in history, featuring prominently in Inca creation myths. There are daily tours to the *Uros* and *Taquile Islands*; the *Uros* people live on floating islands made out of reeds that grow in the lake, while the inhabitants of

Machu Picchu

Taquile Island are renowned for maintaining ancient traditions and for their remarkable weaving skills.

Transportation
Air: El Alto Airport (La Paz). **Road:** Bus: Daily services leave La Paz every 30 minutes. Car: From La Paz (journey time: 2.5 hours).

Contact Addresses
For more information on Lake Titicaca, contact PromPeru (Commission for the Promotion of Tourism) (see **Tourist Information** above).

Machu Picchu

Located 112km (70 miles) northwest of Cusco and constructed as a refuge against the Spanish in the 16th century, *Machu Picchu* is the most spectacular and best known Inca site in South America. Although it is now of great spiritual and cultural significance to millions of Peruvians, its existence was known only to a few locals until American explorer Hiram Bingham happened upon it on July 24 1911. Machu Picchu also possesses the last *Inihuatana* (sundial) remaining in South America. Located within an incredible cloud forest, the site marks a fitting and dramatic conclusion to the end of the Inca Trail. Due to the high number of visitors, trekking permits are limited and are issued each day and must be applied for in advance.

Transportation
Air: Lima Jorge Chavez International Airport, Cusco Airport (domestic flights). **Rail:** Train: Aguas Calientes Station (from Cusco). **Road:** Coach: Services from Aguas Calientes Station. Car: Hwy-101 (from Lima) then road to Cusco.

Contact Addresses
Dirección Regional de Industria y Turismo Cusco, Avenida de la Cultura 734-3er, Piso, Cusco, Peru
Tel: (084) 223 701
Website: www.promperu.gob.pe

Manu National Park (Parque Nacional del Manu)

Manu National Park covers a staggering 1.5 million hectares (3.7 million acres) of terrain, consisting of successive tiers of vegetation. It is protected by UNESCO as a World Biosphere Reserve, can only be entered as part of a licensed tour, and is so remote that some of the indigenous tribes that live there have had no contact with the outside world. Its unspoiled atmosphere means that it is home to species that are unknown elsewhere in the world; the tropical Amazon jungle in the lower section is home to literally thousands of species of plants, butterfly and bird, and countless reptiles and insects. Further up, the *Andean High Plateau* rises to 4300m (14,100ft) and the *Tres Cruces* lookout on the road from Manu to Cusco offers far-reaching views across the Amazon.

Transportation
Air: Lima Jorge Chavez International Airport, Boca Manu Airstrip (domestic flights). **Water:** Motorised launch: Services from Atalaya to Boca Manu, then down the Madre de Dios river. **Road:** Coach: Services from Cusco to Atalaya; access is then by river.

Contact Addresses
Instituto Nacional de Recursos Naturales (INRENA), Calle Diecisiete 355, Urb, El Palomar, San Isidro, Peru
Tel: (01) 224 3298
Website: www.inrena.gob.pe

Philippines

500km
250mls
international airport

Batan Is.

Luzon Strait

Babuyan Is.

SOUTH CHINA SEA

• Laoag

① • Baguio

Luzon
Mt Pinatubo △ • Angeles
MANILA • Quezon City
Manila Bay **PHILIPPINES**
San Pablo Laguna de Bay
• Calapan
Mindoro
Busuanga • Masbate
Culion • Roxas *Visayas* *Samar*
Panay Iloilo • Cebu
• Bacolod Cebu
Palawan • Negros *Bohol*
• Puerto Princesa
SULU SEA • Iligan
L. Lanao **Mindanao**
Mapin Zamboanga • Davao
Moro Gulf Mt Apo 2954m
Basilan
MALAYSIA *Sulu Archipelago* • General Santos
Jolo
Tawitawi *CELEBES SEA* INDONESIA

PHILIPPINE SEA

Catanduanes

• Legaspi

• Calbayog
Tacloban
Leyte
Dinagat
ⓘ *Siargao*
• Butuan
• Cagayan de Oro

Tourist Information

Philippines Department of Tourism
Department of Tourism Building,
T M Kalaw Street, Rizal Park,
Manila 1000, Philippines
Tel: (02) 523 8411/30
Website: www.wowphilippines.com

Philippine Cultural and Tourism Office
146 Cromwell Road, London
SW7 4EF, UK
Tel: (020) 7835 1100
Website: www.wowphilippines.com

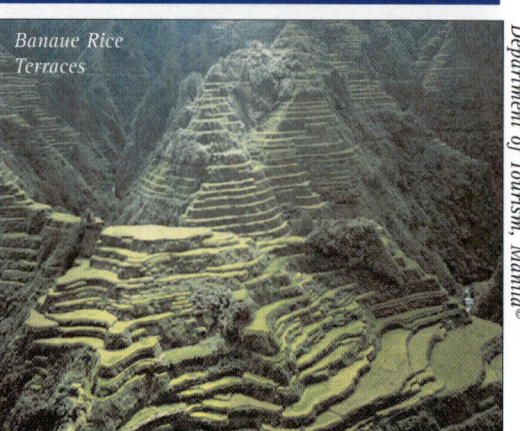

Banaue Rice Terraces

Department of Tourism, Manila ©

Banaue Rice Terraces

Nestled deep in the heartlands of the *Cordilleras* mountains and rising to an altitude of 1525m (5000ft) are the *Banaue Rice Terraces*. The terraces were carved out of the mountain range over 3000 years ago by the *Ifugaos*, the oldest mountain tribe in the area, using only the most primitive tools. The irrigation system uses gravity to harness water from the forests 1800m (2185ft) above thus ensuring a continuous supply of crops. Measured from end to end, the terraces would stretch a total length of 22,400km (13,919 miles), enough to encircle half the globe. They are often dubbed the eighth wonder of the ancient world as their age and scale is comparable to that of the official seven wonders, of which only the Pyramids of Giza remain.

Transportation
Air: Manila Ninoy Aquino International Airport, Baguio Airport (domestic flights), Bagabag Airport (domestic flights). **Rail:** Train: Manila Station. **Road:** Bus: Publice services.

Contact Addresses
Tourism Office, Cordillera Administrative Region, Department of Tourism, DOT Complex, Government Pack Road, 2600 Baguio City, Philippines
Tel: (074) 442 6708 *or* 442 7014
Website: www.tourism.gov.ph

Poland

300km
150mls
✈ international airport

Tourist Information

**Polish Tourism Organisation
(Polska Organizacja Turystyczna)**
4-6 Chalubínskiejo Street, 00-928 Warsaw,
Poland
Tel: (022) 630 1747/8
Website: www.infolinia.pl

Polish National Tourist Office
First Floor, Remo House, 310-312 Regent
Street, London W1B 3AX, UK
Tel: (020) 7580 8811 (tourist enquiries and
brochure request line) *or* 7580 6688 (trade
and press only)
Website: www.visitpoland.org

1 Auschwitz-Birkenau

2 Main Market Square, Krakow (Rynek
Glowny, Krakow)

3 Warsaw Royal Castle (Zamek Królewski
w Warsawie)

4 Wawel Royal Castle (Zamek Królewski
na Wawelu)

Auschwitz-Birkenau

Auschwitz-Birkenau, situated 70km (46 miles) west
of Krakow, is the most infamous and the largest
of the Nazi death camps. It saw the cruel death of
an estimated one million European Jews. Today,
the camp is a museum dedicated to the memory
of those who suffered and perished there. The
forbidding entrance gate, surrounded by barbed
wire, still bears the words *Arbeit Macht Frei* (Work
Brings Freedom) and the railway and gas
chambers remain as they were when the camp

was liberated by Soviet troops in May 1945. The
Museum of Martyrdom shows a film depicting the
nature of the atrocities, and there are further
displays of photos and personal articles, such as
children's shoes, women's hair and toothbrushes,
that were taken from the victims.

Transportation
Air: Krakow-Balice John Paul II International
Airport. **Rail:** Train: Oswiecim Station. **Road:** Bus:
Services to the museum (from Oswiecim). A
shuttle bus runs between the two sites, Auschwitz
I and Birkenau.

Contact Addresses
Auschwitz-Birkenau State Museum, ulica
Wiêzniów Oœwiêcimia 20, 32-620 Oœwiêcim,
Poland
Tel: (033) 843 2022
Website: www.auschwitz.org.pl

Main Market Square, Krakow (Rynek Glowny, Krakow)

Krakow's magnificent *Rynek Glowny* is one of the
largest Medieval squares in Europe and dates from
1257. It is dominated by the *Sukiennice*, the
arcaded Renaissance cloth hall that stands in the
centre, crowned by an elaborate attic construction
known as a Polish parapet, and decorated with

carved masks. The lower part of the building still serves as a market, selling traditional Polish crafts and food, and the upper floor is devoted to an exhibition of 19th-century Polish painting. On the southern side is the copper-domed *Kosciol sw Wojchiecha* (St Adalbert's Church), Krakow's first church, which dates from the 10th century and is the oldest building in the square. The *Ratusz* tower, with its Baroque spire, is all that remains of the 14th-century town hall after it was demolished in 1820 as part of a city development project. There are fine views over Krakow from the top.

Transportation
Air: Krakow-Balice John Paul II International Airport. **Rail:** Train: Krakow Station. Road: Coach: Services from Lviv (Ukraine), Prague (Czech Republic) and Vienna (Austria) to Dworzec PKS (Central Bus Station).

Contact Addresses
Krakowskie Centrum Informacji Turystycznej i Zakwaterowania (Krakow Tourist Information and Accommodation Centre), ulica Pawia 8, Krakow, Poland
Tel: (012) 422 6091
Website: www.krakow.pl

Warsaw Royal Castle (Zamek Królewski w Warsawie)

Set on a plateau overlooking the River Vistula, Warsaw's *Royal Castle* was built in the 14th century as a wooden fortress for the Dukes of Mazovia. It became a royal residence when King Zygmunt III made plans to move the Polish capital to Warsaw from Krakow in 1569 (although the final move to Warsaw was not made until the early 17th century). The castle then remained the seat of the monarchy and the *Sejm* (Polish parliament) for almost 250 years. In 1918, the castle became the official residence of the Polish president but was completely destroyed by the Nazis during World War II. The building that visitors enter today is thus a remarkable reconstruction, carried out in the 1970s, with only a few parts of the interior salvaged from the ruins. Neo-Baroque rooms are filled with museum pieces, including period furniture, porcelain, tapestries, and Oriental rugs.

Transportation
Air: Warsaw-Okecie Airport. **Rail:** Train: Warszawa Centralna (Warsaw Central Station). Tram: Public services. **Road:** Bus: Public services. Car: E30 (from Berlin and Lodz); E67 (from Wroclaw); E77 (from Gdansk and Krakow).

Contact Addresses
Zamek Królewski, Plac Zamkowy 4, 00277 Warsaw, Poland
Tel: (022) 657 2170
Website: www.zamek-krolewski.art.pl

Wawel Royal Castle (Zamek Królewski na Wawelu)

Wawel Royal Castle was the seat of Polish royalty from the 11th century until the early 17th century when King Zygmunt III moved the Polish capital to Warsaw. Today, it functions as a museum, with some of the original Renaissance decoration, including Flemish tapestries, Italian furniture and various Italian and Dutch paintings, still existing. Among its many treasures are the *Crown Treasury and Armoury*, where visitors can see the *Szczerbiec*, a weapon once used to crown Polish monarchs. The *Lost Wawel* exhibition is centred around excavations of Wawel hill's oldest ruins, including the oldest church known to exist in Poland, the Rotunda of St Felix and St Adauctus, which dates from the 11th century. Visitors can also enter the *Dragon's Den*, a cave with karstic limestone features, where, according to Polish legend, a child-eating creature called the Wawel Dragon once lived.

Transportation
Air: Krakow-Balice John Paul II International Airport. **Rail:** Train: Krakow Glowny Station. **Road:** Bus: Public services. Car: A77 (from Warsaw), then signs to the city centre.

Contact Addresses
Zamek Krolewski, Wawel 5, 31-001 Krakow, Poland
Tel: (012) 422 5155
Website: www.cyf-kr.edu.pl/wawel

Portugal

1 Castle of St George (Castelo de São Jorge)
2 Jeronimos Monastery (Mosteiro dos Jerónimos)
3 Maritime Museum
4 Tower of Belém (Torre de Belém)

Tourist Information

ITP Instituto do Turismo de Portugal (National Tourist Office)
Rua Ivone Silva, Lote 6 1050-124, Lisbon, Portugal
Tel: 217 810 000
Website: www.vsitportugal.com

ICEP/Portuguese Trade and Tourism Office
Portuguese Embassy, 11 Belgrave Square, London SW1X 8PP UK
Tel: (0845) 355 1212 (Brochure request line).
Website: www.visitportugal.com or www.icep.pt

Castle of St George (Castelo de São Jorge)

Perched on the highest of Lisbon's seven hills, above the old Moorish quarter, the *Castle of St George* was the royal residence until the late 15th century. Originally built by the Visigoths and later named after King Joao I, the castle, along with much of Lisbon, was severely damaged by a devastating earthquake in 1755. The castle was declared a National Monument in 1910, with rebuilding work starting in 1940 restoring the site to its former state of luxury. Today the castle offers spectacular views of Lisbon from the well-preserved ramparts, as well as beautiful gardens. There is also a giant periscope in the *Torre de Ulisses* (Tower of Ulysses-Camera Obscura), from where visitors can see spectacular, live images of Lisbon below, reflected onto a large screen.

Transportation
Air: Lisbon International Airport. **Rail:** Tram: Public services. **Road:** Bus: Public services. Car: A1 to Lisbon (from Porto); A2 (from the Algarve via Almada); A8 (from Caldas da Rainha in the north).

Contact Addresses
Castelo de São Jorge, Porta de São Jorge, Rua do Chão da Feira, Lisbon, Portugal
Tel: 218 877 244 *or* 218 882 831
Website: www.visitlisboa.com

Jeronimos Monastery (Mosteiro dos Jerónimos)

This 16th-century monastery is one of the few surviving examples of medieval, Manueline architecture. Commissioned by Manuel I (after whom the style of architecture is named), work

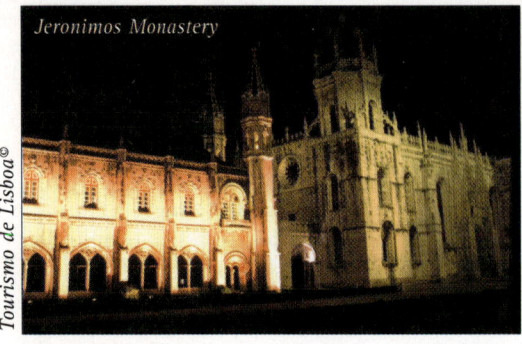
Jeronimos Monastery

Tourismo de Lisboa©

began on the monastery in 1502. It is listed (along with the *Torre de Belém*) as a UNESCO World Heritage Site and is a spectacular building with high arches, impressive columns and ornate spires. It is also the resting place of Vasco da Gama who set sail from Bélem in 1497 to discover India, and of Luís de Camões, Portugal's most famous poet who wrote *Os Lusiadas* (the Lusiads). Other places of interest are the chapels, which house the tombs of royal descendants of Manuel I, and the cloister, which has many impressive galleries.

Transportation
Air: Lisbon International Airport. **Water:** Boat: Bélem River Station (from Trafaria and Porto Brandão). **Rail:** Train: Bélem Station. Tram: Public services. **Road:** Bus: Public services.

Contact Addresses
Mosteiro dos Jerónimos, Praca do Império, 1400-206 Lisbon, Portugal
Tel: 213 620 034/8
Website: www.mosteirojeronimos.pt

Maritime Museum

Originally founded by King Luis in 1863 in the city's *Naval School*, Lisbon's *Maritime Museum* had to be moved in 1916 after the building was gutted by a fire that destroyed many of the exhibits. After resurrection at the *Palace of Count Farrobo*, in 1962, the museum was relocated once more to its present home in the *Jerónimos Monastery*. Today the museum's collection includes over 17,000 items, 30,000 photographs as well as original plans and archives of approximately 1,500 ships. The first of the museum's halls looks at the early days of

Portuguese discovery and colonisation, and examines the impact this had on the formation of the modern world. Other interesting exhibits include the *Deep Sea Fishing Room* which details the history of 15th century Portuguese fleets that went on fishing expeditions in the Atlantic waters off the coast of Newfoundland in Canada.

Transportation
Air: Lisbon International Airport. **Rail:** Belem Station. Tram: Public services. **Road:** Bus: Public services.

Contact Addresses
Maritime Museum, Praça do Império, 1400-206 Lisbon, Portugal
Tel: 213 620 010
Website: www.museumarinha.pt/museu /ENG/Homepage/index.aspx

Tower of Belém (Torre de Belém)

Completed in 1515, the *Tower of Belém* is one of Lisbon's most famous sights. Built under the instruction of the architect Francisco de Arruda, who was greatly influenced by the style of fortifications in Morocco, the tower was intended to provide strategic defence to the River Tagus during Portugal's naval ascendancy in the 16th century. Symbolically, it was also the last sight seen by seafarers leaving the city. The tower has a famous 18th-century statue of Virgin and Child, Our Lady of Safe Homecoming, built into the terrace of the bastion, as well as sentry posts on each corner. Access to the the interesting museum is over a gangway; there is also a drawbridge and bulwark, as well as a terrace that offers superb views across the river and of the western part of Lisbon.

Transportation
Air: Lisbon International Airport. **Rail:** Train: Belém Station. Tram: Public services. **Road:** Bus: Public services.

Contact Addresses
Torre de Belém, Avenida Brasília, 1400 Lisbon, Portugal
Tel: 213 600 34
Website: www.mosteirojeronimos.pt

Romania

300km
150mls
✈ international airport

POLAND
SLOVAK REPUBLIC
Carpathian Mountains
UKRAINE
Tisza
HUNGARY
Baia Mare•
•Moldovita
MOLDOVA
•Oradea
Cluj-Napoca•
Iasi•
Prut
Dniester
MOLDAVIA
•Arad
Mures
ROMANIA
•Bacău
Timişoara•
Moldoveanu 2544m△
•Sibiu
①**Braşov**
•Galaţi
Transylvanian Alps
•Brăila
•Ploieşti
Tulcea• *Danube Delta*
WALACHIA
Olt
BUCHAREST
SERBIA
Craiova•
Danube
•Giurgiu
•**Constanţa**
•Mangalia
BLACK SEA
BULGARIA

1 Bran Castle (Castelul Bran)

Tourist Information

Ministry of Tourism (Ministerul Turismului)
Bd. Dinicu Golescu 38, Mezanin 38, 010867
Bucharest, Romania
Tel: (01) 410 0491
Website: www.mturism.ro *or*
www.MTRomania.ro

Romanian National Tourist Office
22 New Cavendish Street, London W1H 8TT,
UK
Tel: (021) 314 9957

Bran Castle (Castelul Bran)

Perched high on a rock in the midst of
Transylvanian forest, *Bran Castle*, named after the
Romanian word for gate or fortified place, is one
of Romania's most famous attractions, thanks to
its connections with Bram Stoker's novel,
'Dracula' In fact, Stoker cites his further north

than Bran Castle, but its Gothic towers, winding
corridors and labyrinth of secret passages fit the
image of the vampire's home so perfectly that it
has been dubbed *Dracula's Castle*. Built between
1377 and 1382 as a palace and military fortress, it
was once the residence of Queen Maria of
Romania, the granddaughter of Queen Victoria,
whose heart is reputed to have been found hidden
in the castle in a silver box. Nowadays, visitors
who dare enter the eerie chambers can see
collections of furniture, weaponry and armour,
and admire the well-preserved Gothic architecture.

Transportation
Air: Bucharest Otopeni Airport. **Rail:** Brasov
Station. **Road: Coach:** Services to Bran (from
Brasov). **Car:** Drum National Road 1, then
National Road 73A and National Road 73 (from
Bucharest); National Road 71, then National Road
72A and National Road 73 (from Bucuresti).

Contact Addresses
Castelul Bran, 498 Traian Mosoiu Street, Bran,
Romania
Tel: (068) 238 332

Bran Castle

Romanian National Tourist Office©

Russian Federation

international airport

3000km

1500mls

1 Hermitage Museum

2 Kremlin (Moskovksy Kreml)

3 Lake Baikal

4 Red Square (Krasnaya Ploshchad)

5 St Basil's Cathedral (Pokrovsky Sobor)

Tourist Information

Ministry of Tourism (Ministerstvo Turisma)
18 ul. Kazakova, 103064 Moscow, Russian Federation
Tel: (095) 202 7117 or 202 3891

Russian National Tourist Office
70 Piccadilly, London W1J 8HP, UK
Tel: (020) 7495 7555

Key to symbols: £ Entry charged & Disabled access ⛏ Man-made attraction ❦ Natural attraction 🄿 Parking ✘ Restaurant 🛍 Shop 🏛 UNESCO site

Hermitage Museum

Situated in an impressive location on the banks of the *River Neva* in *St Petersburg*, the *State Hermitage Museum* consists of six magnificent buildings housing one of the most important art collections in the world. The origins of the collection date back to 1764 and Catherine the Great who began her own personal collection. The centre point of the Hermitage is the *Winter Palace* that began construction in 1754 as a royal residence. Built by the famous Italian architect Francesco Bartolomeo Rastrelli, visitors will be amazed at the grandeur and extravagance of the three-storey Baroque palace. Other impressive buildings include the *Small Hermitage*, the *Great Hermitage*, the *New Hermitage*, the *Theatre* and the *Menshikov Palace*. Aside from the incredible architecture, the museum houses one of the best displays of art and artefacts in the world, some of which is thought to date back over 500,000 years to Palaeolithic times. Works of art in the collection include masterpieces by such celebrated artists as Michelangelo, Rembrandt, Monet, Renoir, Van Gogh, Matisse and Picasso.

Transportation
Air: Pulvoko Airport, St Petersburg. **Rail:**
Metro: Kanal Griboyedova, Nevsky Prospekt
and Gostiny Dvor stations. Trolley: Public
services. **Road:** Bus: Public services.

Contact Addresses
Hermitage Museum, 2 Dvortsovaya Square,
190000, St Petersburg, Russia
Tel: (812) 710 9625
Website: www.hermitagemuseum.org

Kremlin (Moskovksy Kreml)

The *Kremlin* (literally 'fortified town') is a
walled fortress dating back to the founding of
Moscow in 1147, when it was erected above
the Neglina and Moskva rivers. From 1276 to
1712, it was the seat of government for the
grand princes and tsars of Russia, and from
1917 onwards it has been the seat of power for
the Communist government. The heart of the
Kremlin centres around *Cathedral Square*,
which is surrounded by several important
churches, including the *Cathedral of the
Assumption*, the *Cathedral of the Archangel* and
the *Cathedral of the Annunciation*. The redbrick
walls and towers house many other historic
sights, including the *Armoury Museum*, the
State Diamond Fund, the *Patriarch's Palace*, the
Tsar Cannon and the *Tsar Bell*.

Transportation
Air: Moscow Sheremetyevo International
Airport. **Rail:** Train: Kiev Station.
Underground: Biblioteka imeni Lenina or
Aleksandrovski Sad. **Road:** Trolleybus: Public
services. Car: M1 (from Minsk); M2 (from
Kiev); M7 (from Nizhny Novgorod); M9 (from
Riga); M10 (from St Petersburg). Then,
Moskovskaya Koltsevaya Avtomobilnaya
Doroga (Moscow ring road surrounding the
city).

Contact Addresses
The State Historical-cultural Museum-preserve,
Moscow Kremlin, Moscow 103073, Russian
Federation
Tel: (095) 202 6649 *or* 202 3832
Website: www.kremlin.museum.ru

Lake Baikal

Situated in south-east *Siberia* in southern *Russia*,
Lake Baikal is the oldest freshwater lake in the
world dating back an estimated 25 million years.
It's also the deepest freshwater lake in the world
with a recorded depth of 1,700m (5,577ft) that
contains approximately 20 per cent of the total
unfrozen freshwater in the world. Lake Baikal is
so big, it's estimated that if it was drained it
would take a year for all the world's rivers to
refill it. This incredible natural habitat supports an
array of flora and fauna including the Nerpa – the
only freshwater seal in the world that's unique to
Lake Baikal. During the winter the temperature
plummets and the lake completely freezes over for
approximately two months each year. During the
summer, many visitors choose to take boat tours
out on the lake. Lake Baikal is ringed by stunning
mountain scenery and forests that are home to
bears, elk, lynx, and sables. Lake Baikal has been
protected as a natural park since 1992 and is a
popular trekking destination famed for its natural
beauty.

Transportation
Air: Irkutzk International Airport. **Water:** Ferry
services and boat excursions on Lake Baikal. **Rail:**
Train: Irkutzk Station. **Road:** Bus: Public services.

Contact Addresses
For more information about Lake Baikal, contact
the Russian National Tourist Office (see **Tourist
Information** above).

Red Square (Krasnaya Ploshchad)

Moscow's *Red Square* has seen centuries of
Russian history played out across its vast 700-
metre (2,300-foot) expanse. Laid out during the
reign of Ivan III in the 15th century and
originally serving as a market place, it has borne
the name *Krasnaya*, from the old Russian for
'beautiful', since the late 17th century. Nowadays,
it is framed by three structures of world renown –
the *Kremlin, St Basil's Cathedral* and the *Lenin
Mausoleum*, which contains the embalmed body of
the founder of the Russian Communist Party and
leader of the 1917 Russian Revolution. It has been

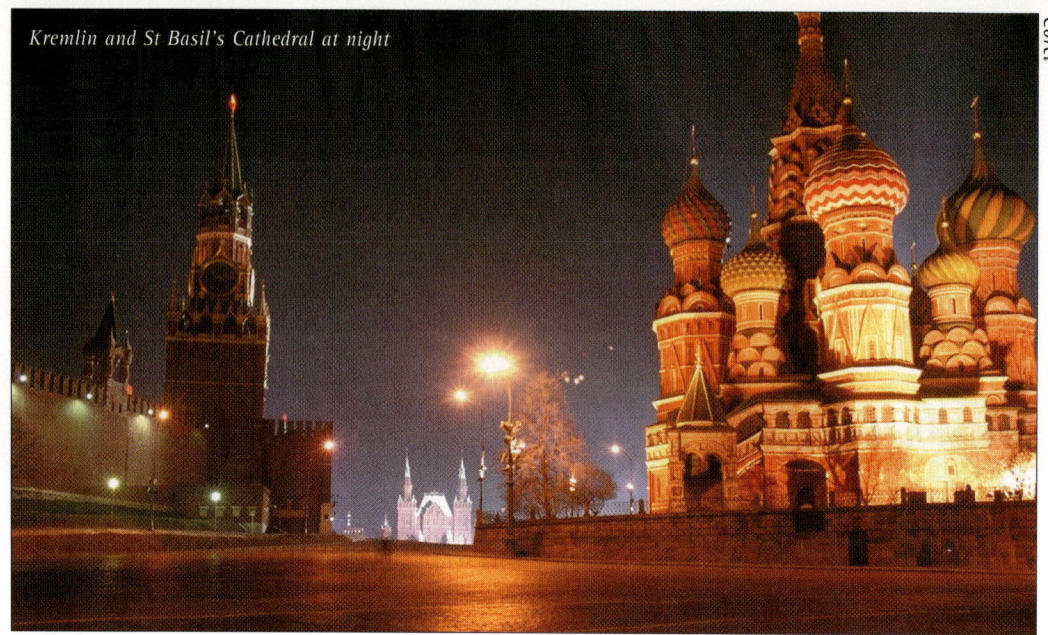

Kremlin and St Basil's Cathedral at night

Corel©

the scene of numerous executions, riots, parades and demonstrations. The square also contains various monuments commemorating Bolsheviks who fell during the 1917 Revolution and past Soviet leaders such as Stalin and Brezhnev.

Tranportation

Air: Moscow Sheremetyevo International Airport. **Rail:** Train: Kiev Station. Underground: Kitay-Gorod. **Road:** Bus: Public services. Car: M1 (from Minsk); M2 (from Kiev); M7 (from Nizhny Novgorod); M9 (from Riga); M10 (from St Petersburg). Then, Moskovskaya Koltsevaya Avtomobilnaya Doroga (Moscow ring road) to the city centre.

Contact Addresses

For more information on Red Square, contact the Ministry of Tourism (see **Tourist Information** above).

St Basil's Cathedral (Pokrovsky Sobor)

The wildly coloured, onion-shaped domes of *St Basil's Cathedral* are one of Russia's most famous images. Situated in Moscow's Red Square, each dome has a distinctive patterning and colour scheme, creating a stunning effect. The cathedral was commissioned by Ivan the Terrible and built during the 1550s to commemorate Russia's military victory over the Khanates of Kazan in 1552. Designed by the architects Postnik and Barma, it has been a branch of the State Historical Museum since 1929. A chapel was added in 1588 to house the tomb of the holy fool Basil (Vasily) the Blessed, after whom the cathedral is now known. Basil, who died in 1552, was a well-known prophet who wandered the streets of Moscow and predicted, correctly, that there would be a fire in the city in 1547.

Transportation

Air: Moscow Sheremetyevo International Airport. **Rail:** Train: Kiev Station. Underground: Kitay-Gorod. **Road:** Trolleybus: Public services to Okhotny ryad. Car: M1 (from Minsk); M2 (from Kiev); M7 (from Nizhny Novgorod); M9 (from Riga, Latvia); M10 (from St Petersburg). Then, Moskovskaya Koltsevaya Avtomobilnaya Doroga (Moscow ring road surrounding the city).

Contact Addresses

Pokrovsky Sobor, Krasnaya ploshchad 4, Moscow, Russian Federation
Tel: (095) 298 3304

Serbia and Montenegro

160km
80mls
✈ international airport

1 Visoki Decani Monastery

Visoki Decani Monastery

Located at the foot of the *Prokletje Mountains* in the western province of *Kosovo*, the *Visoki Decani Monastery* was built in the 14th century for the Serbian King Stefan Decanski. In a picturesque location in a valley surrounded by mountains and the *Bistrica River*, the Decani Monastery is the biggest and best preserved medieval monastery in Serbia. The monastery contains exceptional Byzantine frescoes, Gothic sculptures and the original marble floor is still intact. The monastery is particularly well-known for its *Narthex Room* with its incredible ceiling paintings. Today, the monastery is home to a brotherhood of 30 monks who continue to live according to ancient traditions. The monastery was declared a UNESCO World Heritage site in 2004.

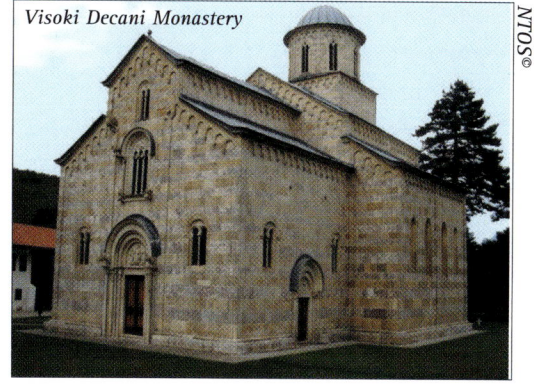

Visoki Decani Monastery

NTOS©

Tourist Information

National Tourist Office of Serbia (NTOS)
Tourist Organization of Belgrade Information Centre, Knez Mihajlova Street 18, 11000 Belgrade, Serbia
Tel: (+381) 11 629 992
Website: www.serbia-tourism.org

National Tourist Office of Serbia (NTOS)
7 Dering Street, London W1R 9AB, UK
Tel: 0207 629 2007
Website: www.serbia-tourism.org

Transportation
Air: Belgrade International Airport or Pristina Airport in Kosovo. **Road:** Bus: Public services to Decani District.

Contact Addresses
For more information about the Visoki Decani Monastery, contact the National Tourist Office of Serbia (see **Tourist Information** above).

Key to symbols:
£ Entry charged & Disabled access ⊞ Man-made attraction
✔ Natural attraction **P** Parking ✖ Restaurant ⊕ Shop 🏛 UNESCO site

Singapore

international airport

---

1 Raffles Hotel

2 Sentosa

Tourist Information

Singapore Tourism Board
Tourism Court, 1 Orchard Spring Lane,
Singapore 247729
Tel: 736 6622
Website: www.stb.com.sg *or* www.newasia-singapore.com

Singapore Tourism Board
First Floor, Carrington House, 126-130 Regent
Street, London W1B 5JX, UK
Tel: (020) 7437 0033 or (08080) 656 565 (toll
free UK only)

Raffles Hotel

Opened in 1887 by four Armenian brothers, the
Raffles Hotel is one of the few remaining original
grand hotels of the East. This world-famous hotel,
which was named after Sir Stamford Raffles, the
founder of modern Singapore, began life as a
modest bungalow. Over the years, it has welcomed
many famous guests, including Rudyard Kipling,
Joseph Conrad and Charlie Chaplin, attracted by
the hotel's luxury and elegance. Today, the hotel
continues to attract the rich and famous, and a
recent S$160-million facelift has ensured that it
has the trappings of modern luxury yet retains the
unique charm of the colonial era. Tourists regularly
flock to drink afternoon tea in the *Tiffin Room* and
enjoy a Singapore Sling in the *Long Bar*. The hotel
was declared a National Monument in 1987.

Transportation
Air: Singapore Changi Airport. **Rail:** Train: City Hall
MRT Station. **Road:** Bus: Public services.

Contact Addresses
Raffles Hotel, 1 Beach Road, Singapore 189673
Tel: 6337 1886
Website: www.raffleshotel.com

Sentosa

A purpose-built island theme park, *Sentosa* (which
means 'peace and tranquility' in Malay) offers history,
golf and gastronomy, as well as a host of themed
attractions, including *VolcanoLand* and *Underwater
World*, one of Asia's largest tropical fish aquariums.
Owned and managed by Sentosa Development
Corporation, Sentosa is Singapore's largest offshore
island and home to beautiful beaches and gardens.
The island's highlights include the *Butterfly Park*,
which houses more than 2500 butterflies, *Fort Siloso*
preserved fortification, which was built in the 1880s,
and the *Images of Singapore Museum*, which exhibits
artefacts from the history of Singapore.

Transportation
Air: Singapore Changi Airport. **Sea:** Ferry: Services
depart from the World Trade Centre in Singapore
City. **Rail:** Cable Car: Services to Sentosa (from
Mount Faber). **Road:** Bus: Public services.

Contact Addresses
Sentosa Development Corporation, 33 Allanbrooke
Road, Sentosa, Singapore 099981
Tel: 275 0388
Website: www.sentosa.com.sg

Slovak Republic

1 Caves of Aggtelek

2 Spiš Castle (Spissky Hrad)

3 Tatrus National Park
(Tatransky Národny Park)

Tourist Information

Slovak Tourist Board (Slovenskej agentúry pre cestovný ruch)
Nám. L Stura 1, PO Box 35, 974 05 Banská Bystrica, Slovak Republic
Tel: (048) 413 6146-8
Website: www.slovakiatourism.sk

Embassy of the Slovak Republic
25 Kensington Palace Gardens, London W8 4QY, UK
Tel: (020) 7313 6470 or (09065) 508 956 (recorded visa information; calls cost £1 per minute).
Website: www.slovakembassy.co.uk

Caves of Aggtelek

The *Caves of Aggtelek* are located in the *Aggtelek National Park* in southeastern Slovak Republic bordering Hungary. Aggtelek was the country's first national park that was set up to protect its geological formations. Formed in shallow seas during the Triassic Period over 200 million years ago, the park lies on limestone bedrock that is prone to karstification – the natural creation of caverns and sinkholes. There are over 260 caves that have been formed in this way in the park. The Aggtelek National Park, which crosses the border into Hungary, also contains the ruins of the *Háromhegyi Pálos* church and monastery near *Martonyi* village. The Pálos were the only religious order to be founded in Hungary whose origins date back to 1308. The Caves were declared a UNESCO World Heritage site in 1995.

Transportation
Air: Kosice International Airport. **Rail:** Train: Kosice Railway Station. **Road:** Coach: Public services to Aggtelek.

Contact Addresses:
For more information about the Caves of Aggtelek, contact the Slovak Tourist Board (see **Tourist Information** above).

Spiš Castle (Spissky Hrad)

Spiš Castle is one of the largest Medieval castles in central Europe. Dating back to the early 13th century, this imposing fortification stands 634 metres (2080ft) above sea level on cliffs dominating the Spišské region in eastern Slovak Republic. It was once one of the most important Gothic castles in Europe and was owned by the Royal Family. It was declared a national monument in 1961 and attempts were made to restore it in order to make it accessible to the public. The castle has a small museum which is open to the public and documents the history of the castle during its prime in the late Middle Ages. Although many parts of the castle's Gothic tower, chapel ramparts and dungeons still stand in ruins, there are fine views of the surrounding countryside from the summit of the hill.

Transportation
Air: Bratislava Airport. **Road:** Car: The castle can be reached from the Šibenik Pass (from the east and from Levoča). Foot: Visitors should approach the castle from the town of Spišské Podhradie.

Tatrus National Park

Contact Addresses

Spissky Hrad, 05304 Spišské Podhradie, Slovak
Republic
Tel: (053) 454 1336
Website: www.spisskyhrad.sk

Tatrus National Park
(Tatranský Národný Park)

Tatras National Park is the oldest national park in the
Slovak Republic and home to the famous *High Tatras
Mountains*. Founded in 1949 and covering an area of
741 sq km (286 sq miles), Tatras National Park is a
hiker's paradise. The landscape incorporates dense
forest on the mountains' lower slopes, as well as
glacial lakes and mountain streams. The High Tatras
is the only alpine mountain range in Eastern Europe
and one of the smallest in the world. The mountains
are also famous for their plant and wildlife, with
chamois (mountain goat), bear and marmot roaming
free on the slopes. Also of interest are the *TANAP
Museum*, which describes the natural history and
ethnography of the region through geology, flora
and fauna displays and exhibits.

Transportation

Air: Bratislava Airport. Special charter flights and
private airplanes land at Poprad-Tary Airport.
Rail: Cable car: Peaks reached by aerial tram
include Skalnate Pleso, Lomnicky Stit, Solisko and
col Lomnicke sedlo. **Road:** Bus: Buses Public
services.

Contact Addresses

Tatranský národný park, Tatranska Lomnica,
Slovak Republic
Tel: (052) 446 7195
Website: www.tanap.sk

Slovenia

1 Lipica Stud Farm (Kobilarna Lipica)

2 Postojana Cave (Postojnska Jama)

Tourist Information

**Slovenian Tourist Organisation
(Slovenska Turisticna Organizacija)**
WTC, Dunajska 156, 1000 Ljubljana, Slovenia
Tel: (01) 589 1840
Website: www.slovenia-tourism.si

Slovenian Tourist Office
49 Conduit Street, London W1R 9FB, UK
Tel: (020) 7287 713
Website: www.slovenia-tourism.si

Lipica Stud Farm (Kobilarna Lipica)

Lipica Stud Farm is the home of one of the world's most famous breed of horses, the Lippizaner. Founded by Archduke Charles of Austria in 1580, the farm has continuously bred the sturdy white horses for over four centuries and some of the best perform at the *Spanish Riding School* in Vienna. As well as watching the horses perform at the *Classical Riding School* at Lipica, visitors can take the reins of a thoroughbred Lippizaner themselves and there are pony rides for children. With its own hotels, swimming pools, fitness centre as well as a wide range of other activities on offer, it is possible to spend an entire holiday on and around the stud farm.

Transportation
Air: Ljubljana Brnik Airport. **Rail:** Train: Divaca Station or Sezana Station. **Road:** Car: A10 (from Ljubljana); A1 (from Klagenfurt, Austria); S14 (from Trieste, Italy).

Contact Addresses
Kobilarna Lipica, Lipica 5, 6210 Sezana, Slovenia
Tel: (05) 739 1580
Website: www.lipica.org

Postojana Cave (Postojnska Jama)

Postojna Cave in western Slovenia is a 20-km (12-mile) labyrinth of subterranean passages, filled with fantastical stalagmites, stalactites and other rock formations. It is considered by experts to be one of the finest examples of karst landscape, where limestone rock has been heavily eroded to form underground streams, a phenomenon that has created several other caves in the area. Postojna Cave is also home to the Proteus Anguinus, a unique creature with no eyes, which can grow up to 30cm (1ft) in length and feeds on snails and worms. Speleological equipment can be provided at the cave for caving enthusiasts.

Transportation
Air: Ljubljana Brnik Airport. **Rail:** Train: Postojna Station. **Road:** Car: E61 or E70 (from Ljubljana); E751 (from Trieste, Italy).

Contact Addresses
Postojna jama – turizem, Jamska c. 30, 6230 Postojna, Slovenia
Tel: (05) 700 0100
Website: www.postojnska-jama.si

South Africa

1 Anglo-Boer War Battlefields
2 Blyde River Canyon Nature Reserve
3 Cape Point
4 Kruger National Park
5 Robben Island
6 Table Mountain

Tourist Information

**South African Tourism Board
(SATOUR)**
Private Bag X10012, Sandton 2146,
South Africa
Tel: (011) 778 8000.
Website: www.southafrica.net

**South African Tourism Board
(SATOUR)**
5-6 Alt Grove, London SW19 4DZ, UK
Tel: (0870) 155 0044 (tourism enquiry
and brochure request line)
Website: www.south-african-tourism.org

Key to symbols: £ Entry charged & Disabled access ☒ Man-made attraction
♥ Natural attraction 🅿 Parking ✗ Restaurant ⛥ Shop 🏛 UNESCO site

Anglo-Boer War Battlefields

The Anglo-Boer War began in 1899 with the British retaliation against President Paul Kruger's refusal to grant political rights to the mainly English outsiders in the gold- and diamond-rich Transvaal. In 1902, after three years of bitter fighting, the British claimed victory, having destroyed Boer farms and sent their occupants to concentration camps where 20,000 people perished. Today, various museums and memorial sites remember those bloody events. The main museum is the *Anglo-Boer War Museum* in Bloemfontein (website: www.anglo-boer.co.za), which displays artwork and artefacts and provides an insight into the horrors of the concentration camps. *Talana Museum* (website: www.talana.ca.za), is located at Talana Hill, near Dundee, the site of the first battle of the Anglo-Boer War on October 20 1899; it is now an eight-hectare (20-acre) heritage park with a cemetery dedicated to those who fought and lost their lives there, and also features displays on local bush traditions.

Transportation
Air: Johannesburg International Airport, Durban International Airport, Cape Town International Airport, Pretoria Airport. **Rail:** Train: Johannesburg Park Station, Durban Station, Cape Town Station, Dundee Station or Pretoria Station.

Contact Addresses
KwaZulu Natal Tourism Authority, PO Box 2516, Durban 400, South Africa
Tel: (031) 304 7144
Website: www.zulu.org.za/kzn

Blyde River Canyon Nature Reserve

Blyde River Canyon provides some of South Africa's most breathtaking scenery and is the third largest gorge in the world, after the Grand Canyon (USA) and Fish River Canyon (Namibia). The 29,000-hectare (71,662-acre) reserve is

South African Tourist Board©

Cape Town

home to a rich variety of wildlife including rare birds and lichens. At the heart of the nature reserve is the *Blyde Dam*, which provides a natural habitat for hippo and crocodile, whilst further afield, in the Lowveld plain at the entrance to the canyon, blue wildebeest, waterbuck and zebra can be seen. Popular activities in the reserve include fishing and hiking to beauty spots such as *God's Window*, which offers unparalleled views across the canyon and the Lowveld. The town of *Pilgrim's Rest* is of particular interest as a former gold-mining town between 1873 and 1972.

Transportation
Air: Johannesburg International Airport. **Rail:** Train: Johannesburg Park Station or Pretoria Station. **Road:** Car: N4 (from Pretoria); N12, then R36, then R532 (from Johannesburg).

Contact Addresses
For more information on Blyde River Canyon, contact the South African Tourism Board (see **Tourist Information** above).

Cape Point

Part of the *Cape Peninsula National Park*, *Cape Point* is an 8000-hectare (19,770-acre) narrow promontory of land jutting into a stretch of open sea popularly believed to be the meeting point of the Atlantic and Indian oceans. The peninsula, situated 60km (37 miles) southwest of Cape Town, is characterised by towering sea cliffs, the highest in South Africa, which reach a height of 249m (817ft). Criss-crossed by spectacular walks and trails, the area also features whale and penguin watching, tidal pools, over a thousand species of indigenous plants and a variety of mammals, such as baboon and buck. Popular activities around Cape Point also include abseiling, parasailing, horseriding and surfing.

Transportation
Air: Cape Town International Airport. **Rail:** Train: Simon's Town Station. **Road:** Bus: Public services. Car: M3 towards Muizenberg (from Cape Town); M4 towards Cape Point (via Simon's Town).

Contact Addresses
Cape Peninsula National Park, PO Box 37,

Constantia, 7848 Western Cape, South Africa
Tel: (021) 701 8692
Website: www.cpnp.co.za

Kruger National Park

At 20,000 sq km (7722 sq miles), *Kruger National Park* is the largest game reserve in South Africa and boasts the world's highest concentration of species. Created in 1898 to protect the flora and fauna of the *South African Lowveld*, the park is named after its original proponent, President Paul Kruger. Today, it is home to a wealth of wildlife, including cheetahs, leopards, lions, rhinos, wildebeest, buffalo, elephants, giraffes, antelope and impala. The park is also renowned for its cultural heritage sites, including many native rock art sites. At *Thulamela Hill*, visitors can see the excavated remains of a late Iron Age settlement, whilst the village of *Masorini* provides an excellent example of the way of life of the Stone Age hunter-gatherers who inhabited South Africa long before the first white settlers arrived.

Transportation
Air: Johannesburg International Airport, Skukuza Airport (domestic flights). **Road:** Coach: Services from Mpumalanga. Car: Mpumalanga Highway.

Contact Addresses
South African National Parks, PO Box 787, Pretoria 0001, South Africa
Tel: (012) 248 9111
Website: www.sanparks.org

Robben Island

Situated 11km (7 miles) north of Cape Town harbour, *Robben Island* is the notorious island prison where thousands of political prisoners were incarcerated between 1961 and 1991 for campaigning against apartheid. Its most famous resident was Nelson Mandela, who referred to it as a 'harsh, iron-fisted outpost'. Used as a prison as far back as 1525, it has also housed the mentally ill and lepers; its long history as a place of cruelty and isolation has turned it into a worldwide symbol of the triumph of the human spirit over oppression. Since 1996, there has been a *National Museum* and cultural centre on Robben Island, where visitors can see, among other things, the cell where Nelson Mandela was imprisoned. Some of the tour guides are former political prisoners, able to provide a personal testimony of the terrible conditions suffered by the inmates.

Transportation
Air: Cape Town International Airport. **Water:** Ferry: From Jetty 1 at the V&A Waterfront (Cape Town) to Autfhumato, Makana.

Contact Addresses
Robben Island Museum, Robben Island 7400, South Africa
Tel: (021) 411 1006
Website: www.robben-island.org.za

Table Mountain

Like Cape Point, *Table Mountain* is part of the strip of land forming *Cape Peninsula National Park*. Table Mountain, however, stands in the middle of Cape Town and defines the downtown area, with the forested ravines of its eastern buttresses flanking the southern suburbs. So named for its flat top, the mountain rises to a height of 1086m (3562ft). Since 1929, a cable car has carried visitors up to the summit, which offers spectacular views of the city and its beaches. The mountain is also home to an indigenous rodent-like creature called the Rock Hyrax or 'dassie', the closest living relative to modern elephants.

Transportation
Air: Cape Town International Airport. **Rail:** Train: Cape Town Station. **Road:** Bus: Public services. Car: N1 (from Johannesburg); N2 (from Overberg and Garden Route); N7 (from West Coast or Namibia).

Contact Addresses
Table Mountain Cableway, PO Box 730, Cape Town 8001, South Africa
Tel: (021) 424 8181 (24-hour information line) *or* 424 0015 (administration)
Website: www.tablemountain.net

Spain

400km
200mls
✈ international airport

1 Alhambra
2 Cathedral of Santiago de Compostela (Santiago de Compostela Cathedral)
3 Caves of Drach (Cuevas del Drach)
4 Expiatory Temple of the Sagrada Familia (Temple Expiatiori de la Sagrada Familia)
5 Güell Park (Park Güell)
6 Guggenheim Museum Bilbao (Museo Guggenheim Bilbao)
7 Monastery of San Lorenzo de El Escorial (Monasterio de San Lorenzo de El Escorial)
8 Nou Camp
9 Pilgrim's Way
10 Prado Museum (Museo del Prado)
11 Roman Aqueduct at Segovia (Acueducto de Segovia)
12 Seville Cathedral (Cathedral de Sevilla)
13 Terra Mítica
14 Universal Mediterranea

Key to symbols: £ Entry charged ⅚ Disabled access
🏭 Man-made attraction ♥ Natural attraction
🅿 Parking ✖ Restaurant 🛍 Shop 🏛 UNESCO site

Tourist Information

Spanish National Tourist Office (Dirección General de Turespaña)
Jose Lázaro Galdiano 6, 28036 Madrid, Spain
Tel: (091) 343 3500 or 343 3689
Website: www.tourspain.es

Spanish National Tourist Office
22-23 Manchester Square, London W1U 3PX, UK
Tel: (020) 7486 8077 or (0906) 364 0630 (brochure request line; calls cost 60p per minute)
Website: www.tourspain.es

Alhambra

Overlooking the city of Granada, the *Alhambra* is the most important and most spectacular piece of Moorish architecture in Spain. The name means 'the red' in Arabic, and the building is so called because of the colour of the bricks forming the outer walls. It was begun in 1238 as both a palace and a fortress by Ibn Ahmar, founder of the Nasrid dynasty (who made Granada the capital of his Moorish kingdom), and it was subsequently elaborated upon by his successors until its completion in 1358. Visitors can explore the *Alcazaba*, or citadel, which is the oldest remaining part of the complex, as well as the *Alhambra Palace*, containing the fabled *Patio de los Leones* (Court of the Lions), an alabaster basin supported by 12 white marble lions. The *Generalife* gardens, dotted with pools and fountains, are located on the neighbouring hill and were laid out in the 14th century.

Transportation
Air: Malaga Airport. **Rail:** Train: Granada Station. Road: **Bus:** Public services. Car: N-IV, then E5, then N323 (from Madrid); N334, then N342 (from Seville).

Contact Addresses
Patronato de la Alhambra y Generalife, Real de la Alhambra s/n, 18009 Granada, Spain
Tel (0958) 220 912 *or* (091) 346 5936 (ticket sales)
Website: www.alhambra-patronato.es

Cathedral of Santiago de Compostela (Santiago de Compostela Cathedral)

According to legend, the *Catedral de Santiago de Compostela* holds the remains of one of Christ's apostles, St James (Santiago in Spanish), who was martyred in Jerusalem around AD 44. King Alfonso II of Asturias built a church over the tomb in the ninth century and this was expanded in later years, making the town the most important place of Christian pilgrimage after Jerusalem and Rome. One of the best, but also most crowded, times to visit the cathedral is during one of the special masses, where priests swing a huge incense-burner on a rope-and-pulley system from one end of the transept ceiling to the other.

Transportation
Air: Madrid Barajas Airport, Santiago de Compostela Lavacolla International Airport. **Rail:** Train: Hórreo Station, Santiago de Compostela. **Road:** Coach: Public services. Car: A52 (from Madrid); A9 (from La Coruña or Ferrol); N-VI, then A9 (from Madrid).

Contact Addresses
Comisión de Cultura, Praza das Praterías s/n, 15704 Santiago de Compostela, Spain
Tel: (0981) 583 548
Website: www.archicompostela.org

Caves of Drach (Cuevas del Drach)

The *Caves of Drach* are the most famous tourist attraction on the island of Mallorca. There are three chambers inside the caves, *Cueva Negra* (Black Cave), *Cueva Blanca* (White Cave) and *Cueva Luis Salvator* (Luis Salvator Cave). The latter is named after the Archduke Ludwig Salvator of Austria who invited Édouard-Alfred Martel to explore the caves in 1896; the caves are also home to *Lago Martel* (Lake Martel), one of the largest subterranean lakes in the world. Visitors can take a boat ride on the lake and see the beautiful limestone formations, including stalagmites protuding from the rockface and stalactites hanging

down from the roof of the cave. As part of their journey underground, they are accompanied by the sound of musicians performing classical music, including compositions by Chopin on a boat.

Transportation
Air: Palma de Mallorca Airport. **Water:** Boat: Services from Cala Ratjada, Canyamel, Cala Millor, Sa Coma and Sillot. **Road:** Car: The caves are located 1.5km (0.9 miles) south of Porto Cristo. Bus: Many hotels and resorts on the island offer a bus service to the caves.

Contact Addresses
Cuevas del Drach, Ctra Cuevas s/n 07680, Porto Cristo, Baleares, Spain
Tel: (0971) 820 753 or 821 617
Website: www.cuevasdeldrach.com

Expiatory Temple of the Sagrada Familia (Temple Expiatiori de la Sagrada Familia)

The *Expiatory Temple of the Sagrada Familia* is the unfinished masterpiece of Barcelona's most celebrated architect, Antonio Gaudí, who began work on it in 1882. Known around the world simply as *La Sagrada Familia*, Gaudí worked on this towering example of Barcelona's modernist architecture for more than 40 years, right up until his death in 1926. Its eerie, snaking lines and omnipresent detail make it unique among Europe's many cathedrals, and its eight spires, which stand 100m (328ft) high, were intended, with the addition of another four, to represent Christ's Twelve Apostles. Despite the fact that work still continues on the cathedral to this day, it lies in a perpetual state of incompleteness, with only one of its three façades actually finished. There is a small Gaudí museum inside the temple, which details Gaudí's life and provides information on the history of the building.

Transportation
Air: Barcelona International Airport. **Rail:** Train: Passeig de Gràcia Station. Underground: Sagrada Familia. **Road:** Bus: Public services. Car: A7 (from France in the north); A2 from (Zaragoza in the south).

Tourist Attractions & Events of the World

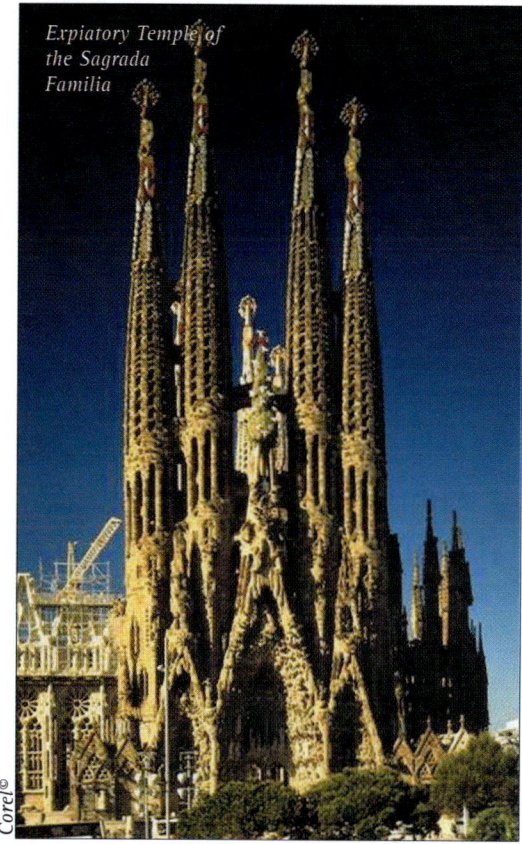
Expiatory Temple of the Sagrada Familia
Corel©

has fantastic pavilions, stairways and columned halls. Highlights include the giant lizard that divides the grand stairway, reputedly the most photographed symbol of the park. Gaudi's former residence in the park, *Casa-Museu Gaudí* houses a collection of Gaudi's furnishings and other memorabilia.

Transportation
Air: Barcelona International Airport. **Rail:** Underground: Vallcarca or Lesseps. **Road:** Bus: Public services.

Contact Addresses
Casa-Museu Gaudí, Park Güell, Carrer del Carmel, s/n 08024, Barcelona, Spain
Tel: (093) 219 3811
Website: www.bcn.es/parcsijardins

Guggenheim Museum Bilbao (Museo Guggenheim Bilbao)

The *Guggenheim Museum Bilbao*, which opened in 1997, has quickly become one of the most famous museums in the world. The museum's collection focuses primarily on American and European art from the 20th century, featuring styles such as Pop Art, Minimalism, Arte Povera, Conceptual Art and Abstract Expressionism, as well as artwork that contemporary European and American artists created specifically for the museum. The building itself was designed by renowned American architect Frank O Gehry and is as well known for its striking architecture as for its collection. Other Guggenheim museums around the world include the *Solomon R Guggenheim* in New York, the *Guggenheim Las Vegas* and the *Guggenheim Hermitage Museum* in Las Vegas, the *Peggy Guggenheim Collection* in Venice and the *Deutsche Guggenheim Berlin* in Germany.

Transportation
Air: Bilbao Airport. **Rail:** Train: Bilbao-Abando Station, Atxuri Station or Santander Station. Underground: Moyua Station. **Road:** Bus: Public services. Car: A8 (from San Sebastian or Santander).

Contact Addresses
Museo Guggenheim Bilbao, Avenida Abandoibarra 2, 48001 Bilbao, Spain

Contact Addresses
Temple Expiatori de la Sagrada Familia, Calle Mallorca 401, 08013 Barcelona, Spain
Tel: (093) 207 3031
Website: www.sagradafamilia.org

Güell Park (Park Güell)

Created by the renowned Spanish architect, Antonio Gaudí between 1900 and 1914, *Parc Güell* is a fantasy land that combines the natural and the man-made. The park was originally conceived as a residential garden city and built for Gaudí's patron, Eusebi Güell Bacigalupi, a textile manufacturer who had a keen interest in the arts and helped develop the architect's career. The project was not a great commercial success, however, and the park became municipal property in 1923. Covering a hill to the north of Barcelona and offering excellent views of the city, the park

Tel: (094) 435 9080 (information) *or* 435 9023 (group admission)
Website: www.guggenheim-bilbao.es

Monastery of San Lorenzo de El Escorial (Monasterio de San Lorenzo de El Escorial)

The *Monastery of San Lorenzo de El Escorial* was built in the latter half of the 16th century by King Philip II of Spain, to commemorate his victory over the French at the battle of San Quentin. Housing a monastery, two palaces and a library, the complex was intended to serve all the functions of church and state. The magnificent interior houses numerous works of art as well as 40,000 volumes in the library that was founded by Philip II himself. The monastery is famous for its symmetrical design, with four towers marking each of the monastery's four corners, and for being the resting place of the remains of many Spanish kings and queens in the *Baroque Royal Pantheon*.

Transportation
Air: Madrid Barajas Airport. **Rail:** Train: El Escorial Station. **Road:** Bus: Public services. Car: M505 (from Las Rozas); N-VI Highway (from Madrid).

Contact Addresses
Monasterio de San Lorenzo de El Escorial, c/Juan de Borbón y Battemberg s/n, 28200 San Lorenzo de El Escorial (Madrid), Spain
Tel: (091) 890 5902 or 890 5903

Nou Camp

Opened for the start of the new season in 1957, the *Nou Camp* (*Camp Nou* in Spanish) is home to *Barcelona Football Club* and is renowned as one of the greatest football stadiums in Europe. Barcelona is one of the most popular teams in Spain's La Liga and the atmosphere at home matches is usually electric. In 1984 the *Nou Camp Museum* was added to the complex which has been extended several times since that date

to accommodate new exhibits and now attracts over a million visitors each year. Guided tours of the ground are available from the museum. The stadium is also used to host other events such as music concerts.

Transportation
Air: Barcelona International Airport. **Rail:** Underground: Public services. **Road:** Bus: Public services.

Contact Addresses
Nou Camp Museum Avenida Arístides Maillol, Barcelona 08028, Spain
Tel. (093) 496 3608
Website: www.fcbarcelona.com

Pilgrim's Way

The *Pilgrim's Way* (also known as *St James' Way*) is in fact a number of different walking trails that all lead to the cathedral of St James in *Santiago de Compostela* in *Galicia* in northwest Spain. It's here where the body of the fisherman and apostle Saint James the Great is said to have been laid to rest in the eighth century. The origins of the trail date back to this time when Christian pilgrims would set off on the annual journey to the saint's final resting place. It is one of the most important Christian pilgrimages alongside those to *Rome* and *Jerusalem*. The Pilgrim's Way still attracts thousands of pilgrims each year in addition to recreational walkers who come to enjoy this popular walking trail. The route is marked with a scallop shell, the symbol of St James. The trail was declared a European Cultural Route in 1987 and a UNESCO World Heritage site in 1993.

Transportation
Air: Vigo Airport or Santiago Airport, Galicia. **Rail:** Train: Vigo Station. **Road:** Bus: Public services.

Contact Addresses
For more information about the Pilgrim's Way, contact the Spanish National Tourist Office (see **Tourist Information** above).

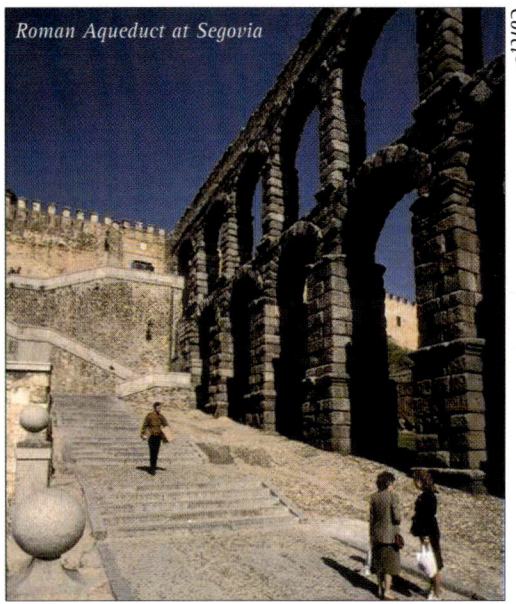
Roman Aqueduct at Segovia

Corel©

Prado Museum
(Museo del Prado)

The *Prado Museum,* which opened to the public in 1819 to house the Royal art collection, is one of Europe's great museums. It houses a collection of over 4000 paintings, emphasising Spanish, Flemish and Italian art from the 15th to 19th century including masterpieces by Titian, Bosch, Botticelli, Rembrandt and Fra Angelico. The museum also possesses a renowned collection of paintings by Francisco de Goya. The museum was originally designed by the architect Juan de Villanueva, with work starting on it in 1785. Today, there are two buildings at the museum, the *Villanueva* and the *Casón del Buen Retiro*, which also house many coins, drawings, etchings and medals.

Transportation
Air: Madrid Barajas Airport. **Rail:** Train: Atocha Station. Underground: Atocha or Banco de España. **Road:** Bus: Public services. Car: N-1 (from Santander); N-2 (from Zaragoza); N-3 (from Valencia); N-4 (from Seville); N-5 (from Badajoz); A6 (from Tordesilos).

Contact Addresses
Museo del Prado, Villanueva Building, Paseo del Prado s/n, 28014 Madrid, Spain
Tel: (091) 330 2800 *or* 330 2900 (information)
Website: http://museoprado.mcu.es

Roman Aqueduct at Segovia
(Acueducto de Segovia)

One of the best preserved Roman constructions, the *Roman Aqueduct at Segovia* was still in use as recently as 50 years ago. Constructed around AD 50 during the reign of the Roman Emperor Trajan out of some 200,400 granite blocks, the aqueduct was made without concrete and stands due to the equal balance of forces. When in use, it carried water from the River Frio to the city of Segovia over a distance of 16km (10 miles). The portion of the aqueduct that is above ground is 728m (2388ft) in length and consists of 165 arches, each over 9m (30ft) high, which are spectacularly illuminated at night. It is possible to climb a staircase next to the aqueduct to get views over the structure itself as well as the city.

Transportation
Air: Madrid Barajas Airport. **Rail:** Train: Segovia Station. **Road:** Bus: Public services. Car: A6, then N603 (from Madrid).

Contact Addresses
Spanish National Tourist Office, Plaza Mayor 10, 40001 Segovia, Spain
Tel: (0921) 460 334
Website: www.turismocastillayleon.com

Seville Cathedral
(Cathedral de Sevilla)

Seville Cathedral, which dates from the 15th century, is located in the city's *Plaza Virgen de los Reyes*, on the site of the *Gran Mezquita* (Great Mosque) originally used by the retreating Moors, who had invaded Spain from North Africa in the eighth century AD. Originally, the mosque was simply converted into a cathedral, but in 1402 the chapter, or ruling body of the cathedral, began plans to construct 'a church so large that everyone who sees it will think we are mad'. Builders retained the minaret and patio from the former mosque, and the cathedral they constructed remains the largest Gothic structure in the world. The main altarpiece, *Retablo Mayor*, is the largest altar in the world and features 45

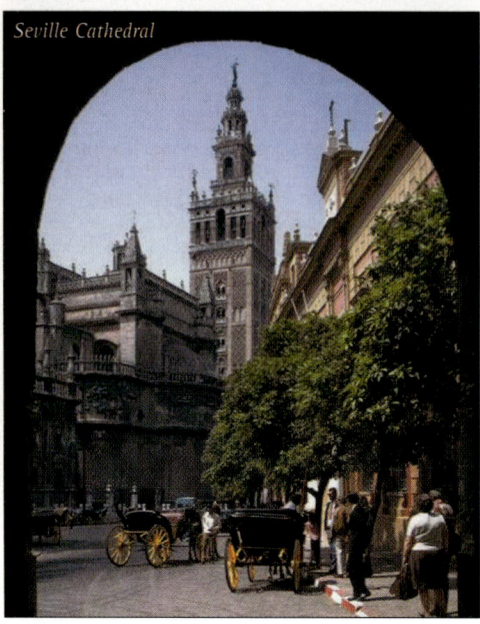
Seville Cathedral

Corel©

scenes from the life of Christ, carved from wood by Pierre Dancart. The cathedral also houses the remains of the world-famous explorer, Christopher Columbus.

Transportation
Air: Seville Airport. **Rail:** Train: Santa Justa Station. **Road:** Bus: 32 to Plaza de la Incarnación, then on foot. Car: N-IV (from Madrid).

Contact Addresses
Cabildo Catedral de Sevilla, Avenida de la Consitución s/n, 41001 Seville, Spain
Tel: (0954) 563 150 *or* 563 321

Terra Mítica

Opened in 2000, Terra Mítica is a giant amusement park located just outside the popular Spanish resort of Benidorm. As well as regular live shows, there are five different areas at the park, all of which are associated with the Mediterranean Sea: *Egypt, Iberia, Greece, Rome* and *The Islands*. At the park, visitors can travel through ancient civilisations and go on the many themed rides. En route, visitors will encounter characters and creatures from many myths and legends, including coming face-to-face with the Minotaur on *El Laberinto del Minotauro* (Minotaur's

Labyrinth) and attempting to rescue Ulysses on the *El Rescate de Ulises* (Ulysses' Rescue) ride.

Transportation
Air: Alicante Airport. **Rail:** Train: Terra Mítica Station. **Road:** Car: A-7 to Terra Mítica's exit which is signposted between Benidorm and Villajoyosa (from Valencia or Alicante).

Contact Addresses
Terra Mitica, Ctra: Benidorm a Finestrat, Camino de Moralet s/n, 3500 Benidorm, Alicante, Spain
Tel: (0902) 020 220
Website: www.terramiticapark.com

Universal Mediterranea

This giant theme park, which opened in 1994, attracts thousands of holidaymakers every year who journey through its five worlds (*Mediterránia, Far West, Mexico, Polynesia* and *China*) on its many rides and attractions. Enjoying an enviable coastal location, between Salou and Vila-seca on Spain's Costa Dorada, this 117-hectare site (289 acre) boasts entertainment aimed at all age groups. There are nightly shows, including *Fiestaventura* in the Mediterranean world, as well as many other attractions, including the *Sea Odyssey* underwater adventure, the *Stampida* roller coaster ride, and the *Grand Canyon Rapids* and *Tutuki Splash* water rides. Visitors who wish to spend a few days in the park can stay in one of the many hotels on site.

Transportation
Air: Barcelona International Airport, Reus Airport. **Rail:** Train: Port Aventura Station. **Road:** Car: Hwy-A7 or Hwy-N340 (from Valencia or Barcelona); Hwy-N240 or Hwy-N420 (from Tarragona).

Contact Addresses
Universal Studios Port Aventura, Avenue Alcalde Pere Molas, Km 2, 43480 Vila-seca, Tarragona, Spain
Tel: (0977) 779 090
Website: www.portaventura.es

Sri Lanka

160km
80mls

✈ international airport

INDIA

Palk Strait

Jaffna
Jaffna Peninsula

Palk Bay
Mullaittivu
Adam's Bridge
Mannar I.
Mannar
Aruvi

Trincomalee • Koddiyar Bay

Anuradhapura
INDIAN OCEAN

Puttalam Lagoon
Puttalam
Sigiriya ①
Dambulla
Polonnaruwa
Kalkudah
Batticaloa

Mahaweli

Gulf of Mannar

SRI LANKA

Kurunegala
Kandy ②
Negombo
Pidurutalagala 2524m
Adam's Peak 2243m
Badulla
Nuwara Eliya
Pottuvil

Colombo
SRI JAYEWARDENEPURA KOTTE

Kalutara

Walawe

Galle • Matara • Hambantota

Dondra Head

---

1 Sigiriya
2 Temple of the Sacred Tooth (Dalada Maligawa)

Tourist Information

Sri Lanka Tourist Board
PO Box 80, Galle Road, Colombo 3, Sri Lanka
Tel: (01) 437 059 *or* 437 060 *or* 427 055
Website: www.srilankatourism.org

Sri Lanka Tourist Board
Clareville House, 26-27 Oxendon Street,
London SW1Y 4EL, UK
Tel: (020) 7930 2627
Website: www.srilankatourism.org

Sigiriya

Taking its name from *giriya* ('jaws and throat') and *sinha* ('lion'), *Sigiriya* is a palace in central Sri Lanka.

It contains the ruins of an ancient royal fortress and city founded in the fifth century AD by King Kasyapa. Three kilometres (1.8 miles) wide and one kilometre (0.6 miles) long, it stands on a steep, large rock, known as *Lion Mountain*, that rises 180m (600ft) above the surrounding plain. The magnificent site also features a series of water gardens, trees and pathways. It is considered one of the best preserved, first-millennium city centres in Asia and is also renowned for its fifth-century rock paintings.

Transportation
Air: Colombo Bandaranayake International Airport.
Rail: Train: Habarane Station. **Road:** Coach: Services from Dambulla. Car: Main road from Colombo.

Contact Addresses
For more information on Sigiriya, contact the Sri Lanka Tourist Board (see **Tourist Information** above).

Temple of the Sacred Tooth (Dalada Maligawa)

Located in Kandy, an ancient religious centre for Buddhism, the octagonal, golden-roofed *Temple of the Sacred Tooth*, built between 1687 and 1707, is a stunning sacred temple, which is believed to house the left upper canine of the Lord Buddha himself. According to legend, the tooth was taken from the Buddha as he lay on his funeral pyre and smuggled to Sri Lanka hidden in Princess Hemamali's hair, where it survived numerous attempts to capture and destroy it. Today, this famous religious relic attracts white-clad pilgrims, bearing lotus blossoms and frangipani, every day.

Transportation
Air: Colombo Bandaranayake International Airport. **Rail:** Train: Kandy Station (from Colombo). **Road:** Bus: Public services. Car: Colombo–Kandy road (from Colombo).

Contact Addresses
For more information on the Temple of the Sacred Tooth, contact Sri Lanka Tourist Board (see **Tourist Information** above).

    £

Sweden

400km
200mls
✈ international airport

1 Drottningholm Palace
   (Drottningholms Slott)
2 Museum of National Antiquities
   (Statens Historiska Museum)
3 Royal Palace (Kungliga Slottet)
4 Vasa Museum (Vasamuseet)

Drottningholm Palace (Drottningholms Slott)

Home to the Swedish Royal Family since 1981, when they moved from the *Kungliga Slottet* (Royal Palace) in Stockholm, *Drottningholm Palace* is one of the most magnificent legacies of Sweden's imperial age. King Johan III first built a palace on the site during the late-16th century; this building was destroyed, however, by fire in 1661 and work began on building a new palace in 1662. Over the years, the interior has been improved upon by successive residents and it is now renowned for its Rococo decorations. The palace was handed over to Princess Lovisa Ulrika of Prussia in 1744 on her marriage to Adolf Fredrik of Sweden. Drottningholm is surrounded by splendid Baroque gardens, including the great English Park and the French formal garden, and is home to many fine buildings such as the *Chinese Pavilion*, the *Court Theatre* and the *Castle Church*.

Transportation
Air: Stockholm Arlanda Airport. **Water:** Boat: Services to Drottningholm (from Stadshuskajen). **Rail:** Underground: Brommaplan. **Road:** Bus: Public services. Car: The palace is located in central Stockholm.

Contact Addresses
Drottningholms Slott, 17802 Drottningholm, Sweden
Tel: (08) 402 6280
Website: www.royalcourt.se

Tourist Information

Swedish Travel & Tourism Council (Sveriges Rese – och Turistråd AB)
PO Box 90, 88122 Solleftea, Sweden
Tel: (08) 725 5500
Website: www.swetourism.se (travel trade) or www.visit-sweden.com (public)

Swedish Travel & Tourism Council
Sweden House, 5 Upper Montagu Street, London W1H 2AG, UK
Tel: (020) 7870 5600 (trade enquiries) *or* (00800) 3080 3080 (consumer enquiries)
Website: www.visit-sweden.com

Museum of National Antiquities (Statens Historiska Museum)

Sweden's *Museum of National Antiquities* traces more than 12,000 years of the nation's history from the Stone Age to the 16th century. Its most famous attraction is the Gold Room, which houses magnificent silver and gold treasures found in Swedish soil from prehistoric times to the Middle Ages. The Viking exhibit features a unique collection of artefacts from the Viking period, whilst the museum also houses one of the world's finest and best preserved collections of Medieval religious art.

Transportation
Air: Stockholm Arlanda Airport. **Rail:** Underground: Karlaplan or Östermalmstorg. **Road:** Bus: Public services.

Contact Addresses
Statens Historiska Museum, Box 5428, 114 84 Stockholm, Sweden
Tel: (08) 5195 5600
Website: www.historiska.se

Royal Palace (Kungliga Slottet)

The *Royal Palace* is the official residence of Sweden's monarch, currently King Carl XVI Gustaf, and houses the offices of the King and Queen and the Duchess of Halland; the latter is the most senior member of the royal family after the King and Queen and their children. A fortress was first built on the site in the 13th century and, as Sweden increased in status, so did the castle, finally becoming the official royal residence in 1521 under Gustav Vasa. The Vasa family developed the palace on a grand scale, adding Renaissance and Baroque features. After fire struck in 1697, much of the interior of the palace was reconstructed over the next 60 years, resulting in a variety of architectural styles. Visitors can view some of the magnificent rooms within the palace, such as the *Royal Apartments*, the *Treasury* and the *Apartments of the Orders of Chivalry* and watch the changing of the guard, which takes place every day.

Transportation
Air: Stockholm Arlanda Airport. **Rail:** Train: Stockholm Central Station. Underground: Gamla Stan. **Road:** Bus: Public services. Car: E4 (from Malmö); E18 (from Oslo, Norway); E20 or E6 (from Gothenburg).

Contact Addresses
Kungliga Slottet, 111 30 Stockholm, Sweden
Tel: (08) 402 6130
Website: www.royalcourt.se

Vasa Museum (Vasamuseet)

The mighty Swedish warship, the *Vasa*, was the most powerful vessel of her day. Commissioned by King Gustavus Adolphus in 1625 as one of a fleet of battleships in the war against Poland, she was constructed by experienced Dutch shipbuilder Henrik Hybertsson who died one year before her completion. The *Vasa* was capable of holding 445 crew and weighed 1210 tonnes (1191 tons). Tragically, due to problems with her stability, the ship keeled over on her maiden voyage on August 10 1628 and sank killing around 40 of the 150 people on board. It was not until 1961 that the remarkably intact wreckage was salvaged by the Swedish Navy and preserved in a temporary museum until the opening of the *Vasa Museum* in 1990. Exhibitions, interactive displays and audiovisual presentations tell of the salvage operation, life on board ship and sea battles of the period.

Transportation
Air: Stockholm Arlanda Airport. **Water:** Ferry: Services from Slussen (all year) and Nybroplan (summer) to Djurgården Island. **Rail:** Train: Stockholm Central Station. **Road:** Bus: Public services. Car: E18 (from Oslo); E20 or E6 (from Gothenburg); E4 (from Malmö).

Contact Addresses
Vasamuseet, Box 27131, 10252 Stockholm, Sweden
Tel: (08) 5195 4800
Website: www.vasamuseet.se

Switzerland

150km
100mls

✈ international airport

1 Chillon Castle
  (Château de Chillion)

2 Jungfraujoch

3 Olympic Museum Lausanne
  (Musée Olympique Lausanne)

4 Water Fountain
  (Jet d'Eau)

Tourist Information

Switzerland Tourism (Schweiz Tourismus)
Tödistrasse 7, 8027 Zürich, Switzerland
Tel: (01) 288 1111
Website: www.myswitzerland.com

Switzerland Tourism
Tenth Floor, Swiss Centre, 10 Wardour Street,
London W1D 6QF, UK
Tel: (00800) 1002 0030 (toll-free Europe only)
or (020) 7292 1550
Website: www.myswitzerland.com

Chillon Castle (Château de Chillon)

Chillon Castle is the most famous castle in Switzerland. It enjoys a spectacular location on the eastern edge of Lake Geneva, near Montreux, with the *Dents du Midi* (literally meaning the Teeth of the South) mountains in the background. Built in the 13th century on Roman foundations, Lord Byron visited the chateau and later wrote the poem 'Prisoner of Chillon' (1816) about the fate of François de Bonivard (1493-1570). Bonivard was the castle's most famous prisoner, incarcerated between 1530 and 1536 for trying to bring protestantism to Switzerland. The castle was once an important medieval fort, strategically located on an island to guard against invasion. Today, visitors can see the castle's famous prison, and also tour the the *Grand Hall*, the *Hall of Justice*, the *Armouries*, the *Grand Hall of the Count*, the *Duke's Chamber* and *Saint George's Chapel*.

Transportation
Air: Geneva International Airport. **Water:** Boat: Boats dock at the CGN jetty next to the castle. **Rail:** Train: Veytaux-Chillon Station. **Road:** Bus: Daily trolley bus service to the castle. Car: A1 and A9 towards Montreux (from Geneva); the castle is within walking distance of Montreux.

Contact Addresses
Association du Château de Chillon, 1820 Veytaux, Switzerland
Tel: (021) 966 8910
Website: www.chillon.ch

Jungfraujoch

The stereotypically Swiss hiking trails and snow-covered Alps of the *Jungfraujoch* have been attracting visitors for hundreds of years. The peak of the Jungfrau is 4158m (13,642ft) high, with the ridge or 'joch' lying below it, where visitors can see the longest glacier in Europe, the 24km (15 miles) long *Aletsch Glacier*. Skiing and alpine activities are immensely popular but one of the best ways to take in the region is by train.

Completed in 1912, the *Jungfraujoch Railway* takes passengers to the mountain's summit where they can get off at the highest railway station in Europe, which reaches an altitude of 3454m (11,333ft).

Transportation
Air: Geneva International Airport, Berne-Belp Airport. **Rail:** Train: Jungfrau Station. **Road:** Car: Via Bern to Interlaken, then Interlaken-Grindelwald Grund exit (from Zurich). Visitors must then take a train (from Grindelwald Grund).

Contact Addresses
Interlaken Tourism, PO Box 369, Hoehweg 37, 3800 Interlaken, Switzerland
Tel: (033) 826 5300
Website: www.interlakentourism.ch
or
Jungfrau Railways, Harderstrasse 14, 3800 Interlaken
Tel: 9033) 828 7111
Website: www.jungfraubahn.ch

Olympic Museum Lausanne (Musée Olympique Lausanne)

Inaugurated in June 1993, the *Olympic Museum* in Lausanne sits on the shores of Lake Geneva. Set in the beautiful *Olympic Park* gardens, the museum displays sport, art and cultural collections from ancient Greece through to modern times. It is the centre of information on the Olympic Movement and preserves the heritage of the Olympic Games. The museum was totally renovated in 2000-2001 and now includes permanent collections, such as The Olympic Adventure, dedicated to the history and origins of the Olympic Movement, and *The Athletes and the Games*, which is fully devoted to the Olympics and athletes' exploits.

Transportation
Air: Geneva International Airport, Zurich International Airport. **Water:** Boat: Steamboats depart from Geneva, Vévey and Montreux and stop in Ouchy. **Rail:** Train: Lausanne Station. Cable Car: Cable train 'La Ficelle' to Ouchy (from Lausanne Station). **Road:** Car: Motorway signs for Lausanne Sud, then the road to Ouchy.

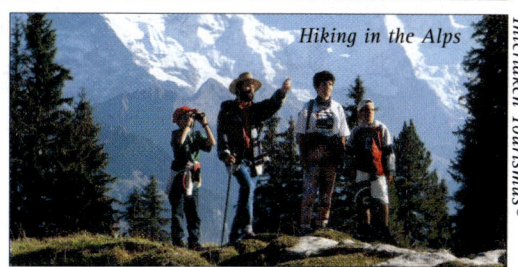
Hiking in the Alps

Interlaken Tourismus©

Contact Addresses
Musée Olympique Lausanne, 1 Quai d'Ouchy, 1001 Lausanne, Switzerland
Tel: (021) 621 6511
Website: www.museum.olympic.org

Water Fountain (Jet d'Eau)

Geneva's *Jet d'Eau* has been breaking the calm of this peaceful city for over a hundred years. The idea that a water fountain might be a tourist attraction came about purely by chance in 1886, when a solution was needed to relieve pressure at the *Forces Motrices* pumping and power station. The water initially reached a height of 30m (98ft), and quickly began to draw large crowds. This led to a more impressive fountain being introduced on Eaux-Vives jetty in 1891 to coincide with the 600th anniversary of the Swiss Confederation and the opening of the Federal Gymnastics Festival. The fountain, which reached a height of 90m (295ft) in 1891, has been technologically improved to spurt water 140m (460ft) into the air. At three times the height of the *Statue of Liberty*, it is now Europe's tallest fountain and today, two electric pumps are used to blast an estimated seven tonnes of water aloft at a speed of 200kmph (124mph).

Transportation
Air: Geneva International Airport. **Rail:** Train: Cornavin Station. Tram: Cours de Rive Station. **Road:** Bus: Eaux-Vives Bus Stop. Car: A1 (from Lausanne).

Contact Addresses
Jet d'Eau, Services Industriéls de Genève, PO Box 2777, 1211 Geneva, Switzerland
Tel: (022) 420 7250
Website: www.sig-ge.ch

Syrian Arab Republic

1 Aleppo (Halab)
2 Palmyra (Tadmor)

Tourist Information

Ministry of Tourism (Wazaretal Siyaha)
Barada Street 14, Damascus, Syrian
Arab Republic
Tel: (011) 221 0122 or 224 6096
Website: www.syriatourism.org

Embassy of the Syrian Arab Republic
8 Belgrave Square, London SW1X 8PH, UK
Tel: (020) 7245 9012 or (09065) 508 935 (recorded
visa information; calls cost 60p per minute)

Aleppo (Halab)

Aleppo vies with Syria's capital Damascus for the
record of the world's oldest continuously inhabited
city. The city's name was first mentioned in texts
as far back as the third millennium BC and has had
a long and extremely rich history under Hittite,
Egyptian, Mitannian, Assyrian, Hellenic, Roman
and Ottoman rule. The legacies that these empires
left behind have provided Aleppo with numerous

attractions, most famously the 12th-century which
served first as a Greek acropolis and later as an
Islamic fortress. Another draw for visitors is the 12
kilometres (8 miles) of covered bazaars, or *souks*.
The *Great Mosque*, or *Ommayad Mosque*, was built
in AD 715 and is one of the best examples of
Islamic architecture in Syria.

Transportation
Air: Aleppo International Airport. **Rail:** Train:
Aleppo Station. **Road:** Coach: Services from
Damascus. Car: Route 5 (from Damascus).

Contact Addresses
For more information on Aleppo, contact the
Ministry of Tourism (see **Tourist Information**
above).

Palmyra (Tadmor)

The ancient city of *Palmyra* rises out of the Syrian
desert 210km (130 miles) northeast of Damascus.
It was originally known as *Tadmor*, meaning 'city
of dates' and its existence was recorded on stone
tablets dating from the 19th century BC. In the
first century AD, Tadmor came under Roman rule
and was renamed Palmyra, meaning 'city of palm
trees'. After a succession of rulers, Palmyra was
captured by the Muslim leader Khalid ibn al-
Walid in AD 634, and its status as a great trading
city and cultural centre declined. Today visitors
can explore the ruins, which include the *Temple of
Bel* and the *Valley of the Tombs*. In the first week
of May, the *Palmyra Festival* is held, featuring
camel races, folk dancing, music, traditional
costume and handicrafts.

Transportation
Air: Damascus International Airport, Aleppo
International Airport. **Road:** Car: Damascus –
Palmyra Highway.

Contact Addresses
For more information on Palmyra, contact the
Ministry of Tourism (see **Tourist Information** above).

Tanzania

1 Kilimanjaro National Park
2 Serengeti National Park
2 Stone Town, Zanzibar

Tourist Information

Tanzania Tourist Board
PO Box 2485, Dar es Salaam, Tanzania
Tel: (022) 211 1244 *or* 213 6105
Website: www.tanzania-web.com

Tanzanian Trade Centre
80 Borough High Street, London SE1 1LL, UK
Tel: (020) 7407 0566
Website: www.tanzania-online.gov.uk

Kilimanjaro National Park

Kilimanjaro National Park is the home of *Mount Kilimanjaro*'s equatorial snow-capped peaks, which form some of the most famous images of Africa. At 5896m (19,340ft), Mount Kilimanjaro, situated

in northeast Tanzania, is the highest mountain in Africa and one of the largest free-standing mountains in the world. It is actually an active volcano and possesses the highest walkable summit in the world, Uhuru Peak, one of six glaciers and volcanic peaks at the top. The scenery is varied and visitors climbing to the summit pass through hot savannah, alpine tropics and finally an arctic moonscape and may even spot elephant wandering the higher slopes. A game reserve since 1921, the area was designated a national park in 1973.

Transportation

Air: Kilimanjaro International Airport, Dar-es-Salaam International Airport. **Rail:** Train: Moshi Station. **Road:** Bus: Services to Moshi Bus Station. Car: North–south route through Chalinze to Moshi (from Dar-es-Salaam).

Contact Addresses

Kilimanjaro National Park, PO Box 96, Marangu, Tanzania
Tel: (027) 275 3195
Website: www.tanzaniaparks.com

Kilimanjaro National Park

Corel©

Serengeti National Park

Made a game reserve in 1921 and a national park since 1951, *Serengeti National Park* is the largest park in Tanzania and one of the most famous in the world. Serengeti fittingly means 'endless plain' in the local Maasai tongue and at 14,763 sq km (5700 sq miles), it features a diversity of environments, ranging from savannah and grass

Corel©

Stone Town, Zanzibar

Zanzibar is situated about 40km (25 miles) off the coast of Tanzania, and is 97km (60 miles) long and 32km (20 miles) wide. *Stone Town* is the old city and cultural centre of Zanzibar, which rose to prominence in the 17th century. The town is made up of narrow streets and winding alleys, bazaars and mosques. It is also home to many grand Arab houses, which were built in the 19th century when Zanzibar was one of the most important trading centres in the Indian Ocean. Key attractions in Stone Town include the *Old Dispensary*, *Livingstone's House*, the *Peace Memorial Museum*, the *Palace Museum*, the *Arab Fort* and the *House of Wonders* (which translates from its local name, *Beit el Jaib*). Zanzibar itself has many breathtaking beaches and is also famed for the rare Kirk's Red Colobus monkey, which can be found in the *Jozani Forest*. As well as Zanzibar, Tanzania boasts many smaller islands which are just a short trip from Stone Town, including *Prison* (*Changu Island*), *Chapwani*, *Chumbe* and *Bawe Islands*.

plains to woodland and black clay plains. The glory of the Serengeti, however, is its wildlife, and the park is most famous for the annual migration of wildebeest, zebra and Thomson's gazelle. It also teems with lions, elephants and ostriches, and is home to around 500 different species of birds. The *Seronera Valley* is popular amongst visitors who come to see the resident prides of lions and photograph the many leopards that can be found in the branches of the acacia and sausage trees. The two saline lakes in the park, the *Lagaja* and the *Magadi*, are famous for attracting flamingos that feed on the lakes' animal and plant life.

Transportation
Air: Kilimanjaro International Airport. Charter flights are available from Arusha, Lake Manyara and Mwanza. **Rail:** Train: Moshi Station. **Road:** Bus: Arusha Bus Station.

Transportation
Air: Zanzibar Airport. **Water:** Ferry: Ferries operate to Zanzibar (from Dar-es-Salaam). **Road:** Car: Stone Town is located on the Western side of Zanzibar and can be reached via the main road (from the airport).

Contact Addresses
Zanzibar Commission for Tourism, PO Box 1410, Zanzibar, Tanzania
Tel: (024) 223 3485/6
Website: www.zanzibartourism.net

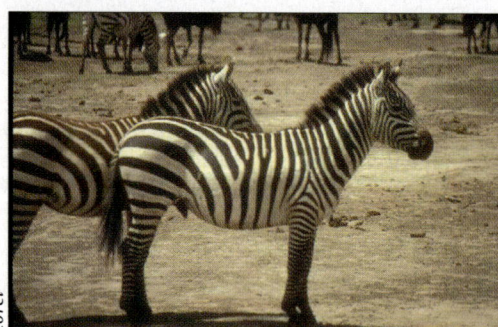

Corel©

Contact Addresses
Serengeti National Park, Tanzania National Parks Authority, PO Box 3134, Arusha, Tanzania
Tel: (028) 262 1569 *or* 262 1510 *or* 262 1504
Website: www.tanzaniaparks.com

Key to symbols:
£ Entry charged
& Disabled access
⚒ Man-made attraction
❦ Natural attraction
P Parking
✗ Restaurant
🛒 Shop
🏛 UNESCO site

Thailand

Tourist Information

**Tourism Authority of Thailand
(Kan Tong Teow Hang Prated Thai)**
Le Concorde Building, 202 Ratchadapisek
Road, Bangkok 10310, Thailand
Tel: (02) 694 1222
Website: www.tat.or.th *or*
www.tourismthailand.org

**Tourism Authority of Thailand
(UK & Ireland)**
49 Albemarle Street, London W1S 4JR, UK
Tel: (09063) 640 666 (consumer enquiries;
calls cost 60p per minute) *or* (0870) 900
2007 (brochure request line) *or* (020) 7499
7679 (trade only).
Website: www.thaismile.co.uk

breaking work under terrible conditions to complete the railway, and large numbers of troops perished during bombing raids on the iron structure by the Allies in 1945. The moving *JEATH War Museum* (JEATH representing the first letter of Japan, England, America, Australia, Thailand and Holland, the countries who lost soldiers in the region) is located in the provincial capital, Kanchanaburi and features photographs and various other memorabilia from World War II.

Transportation
Air: Bangkok International Airport. **Rail:** Train: Services to Kanchanaburi Station (from Bangkok Noi Station). **Road:** Bus: Public services. Car: Hwy-4 (from Bangkok), then Hwy-323.

Contact Addresses
Kanchanaburi Tourist Office: Tourism Authority of Thailand, Region 1, Saeng Chuto Road, Amphoe Mueang, Kanchanaburi 71000, Thailand
Tel: (03) 451 1200 *or* 451 2500

JEATH War Museum: Wat Chaichumpol, Ban Tai, Mueang, Kanchanaburi, Thailand
Tel: (034) 515 203

1 Bridge Over The River Kwai (Menam Kwai)
2 Damnoen Saduak Floating Market (Talat Naam Damnoen Saduak)
3 Phang Nga Bay (Ao Phang-Nga)
4 Royal Barges National Museum (Piphit Thapan Sathan Hang Chart Ruer Pra Raj Pithee)
5 Royal Grand Palace (Phra Barom Maha Rajcha Wang)
6 Temple of the Reclining Buddha (Wat Pho)

Bridge Over The River Kwai (Menam Kwai)

Internationally famous due to the 1957 film the *Bridge Over the River Kwai*, it was constructed as part of the *Japanese Siam-Burma 'Death' Railway* during World War II. An estimated 16,000 Allied prisoners of war died, forced to endure back-

Damnoen Saduak Floating Market (Talat Naam Damnoen Saduak)

Located 80km (50 miles) southwest of Bangkok, *Damnoen Saduak Floating Market* is a daily riot of colour and noise. Farmers and smallholders from the surrounding hills turn up each morning to sell and exchange fruit and vegetables from their heavily-laden barges, as they sail up and down the canals amongst the orchards and vineyards. Trading starts early, at around 0600 and lasts only until 1100, with the main clients being other farmers and the residents of the stilt-houses that line the canals. Visitors can also take boat trips to see the way of life in the many villages up river.

Transportation
Air: Bangkok International Airport. **Road:** Bus: Public services to Damnoen Saduak Bus Terminal. Car: Hwy-4 (from Bangkok), then Bangpae–Damnoen Saduak Road.

Contact Addresses
For more information on Damnoen Saduak Floating Market, contact the Tourism Authority of Thailand (see **Tourist Information** above).

Phang Nga Bay (Ao Phang-Nga)

Phang Nga Bay is one of the world's great scenic wonders. It covers an area of 400 sq km (154 sq miles) and consists of verdant limestone islands, some of which reach 300m (984ft) high. The area is famous for its caves and aquatic grottoes. Apart from the occasional village, few of the islands are densely populated. The most famous of the islands in the bay are *Ko Ping Kan* (more commonly known as *James Bond Island*) and *Koh Pannyi*. The former featured in the James Bond movie 'The Man with the Golden Gun', whilst the latter, which literally means 'Sea Gypsy Island', is a village built out over the water on stilts, guarded by a giant rock monolith. The area suffered badly during the Boxing Day tsunami in 2004 but has recovered well.

Transportation
Air: Phuket International Airport. **Water:** Boat: Many tourists visit Phang Nga Bay by boat; local companies operate day trips to the islands. **Rail:** Train: Surathani Station. **Road:** Bus: Phuket Bus Terminal in Phuket Town. Car: Hwy-402 (Tepkassatri Road, from Phuket), then Route 4.

Contact Addresses
Tourism Authority of Thailand Southern Office, Region 4, 73-75 Phuket Road, Amphoe Mueang, Phuket 83000, Thailand
Tel: (07) 621 1036 *or* 7138 *or* 2213
Website: www.phukettourism.org

Royal Barges National Museum (Piphit Thapan Sathan Hang Chart Ruer Pra Raj Pithee)

The *Royal Barges National Museum* houses several royal barges, which formerly served as war vessels and were subsequently used on royal and state occasions along the Chao Phraya River. The earliest evidence of the use of these decorative barges during royal processions dates back to 1357. The barges are incredibly intricate in design, reflecting Thai religious beliefs and local history. The figure on the bow of each boat signifies whether it carries the King and Queen or other members of the royal family. Today, the royal barges, being so old, are rarely used by the royal family; they were last used at the end of 1999 to celebrate the king's 72nd birthday.

Transportation
Air: Bangkok International Airport. **Rail:** Train: Thonburi Station. **Road:** Bus: Public services from central Bangkok. Car: Hwy-4 (from Hua Hin); Hwy-3 (from Pattaya); Hwy-117 (from Phitsanulok), then Hwy-32. Taxi: Taxis can be hailed in the street to go to the museum.

Contact Addresses
Royal Barges National Museum, Arun Amarin Road, Bangkok Noi, Bangkok 10700, Thailand
Tel/Fax: (02) 424 0004

Damnoen Saduak Floating Market

Tourism Authority of Thailand©

Royal Grand Palace (Phra Barom Maha Rajcha Wang)

The *Royal Grand Palace* is made up of a vast complex of intricate buildings, including *Wat Mahathat* (Palace Temple) and *Wat Phra Keow* (Royal Chapel). Construction of the palace began in 1782 and was completed in time for the coronation of King Rama I, opening in 1785 to signify the end of the Burmese invasion of Thailand. The palace lies in the heart of the old town and covers an area of 218,400 sq m (2,350,857 sq ft). The compound is surrounded by a moat and contains two sections, the former royal residence and the Buddhist temple. The Royal Chapel houses the famous *Emerald Buddha*, which is carved from a single piece of jade, and is the holiest and most revered religious object in Thailand.

Transportation
Air: Bangkok International Airport. **Rail:** Train: Hualamphong Station. **Road:** Bus: Public services. Car: The entrance to the palace is on Na Phra Lan Road, near Sanam Luang in the centre of Bangkok.

Contact Addresses
Phra Barom Maha Rajcha Wang, Bureau of Royal Household, Na Phra Lan Road, Phra Nakhon, Bangkok 10200, Thailand
Tel: (02) 623 5500 *or* 623 5499
Website: www.palaces.thai.net

Temple of the Reclining Buddha (Wat Pho)

Occupying a 20-hectare (50-acre) site next to the *Royal Grand Palace*, *Wat Pho* is the oldest and largest temple in Bangkok. It was built in 1688 during the reign of King Petraja of Ayutthaya and contains one of Thailand's most spectacular sights, a 46m- (150ft) long and 15m- (72ft-) high statue of a reclining Buddha. The statue itself, which is gold-plated and inlaid with mother-of-pearl on the soles of the feet, was not added until 1832 during the reign of King Rama III, and serves to illustrate the passing of Buddha into nirvana (the state of absolute blessedness). Visitors can wander amongst the peaceful rock gardens, chapels and stupas. King Rama III also established Wat Pho as an important centre for Thai medicine and massage and thus founded Thailand's oldest seat of learning. It is still possible to have a massage or learn about the art of Thai massage and medicine at Wat Pho today.

Transportation
Air: Bangkok International Airport. **Rail:** Train: Hualamphong Station. **Road:** Bus: Public services. Car: Hwy-4 (from Hua Hin); Hwy-3 (from Pattaya); Hwy-117 (from Phitsanulok), then Hwy-32.

Contact Addresses
Wat Pho, Thai Wang Rd, Bangkok, Thailand
Tel: (02) 222 0933
Website: www.watpho.com

Tunisia

MEDITERRANEAN SEA

Bizerta
Tabarka   Carthage ❶ a   Cape Bon
                La Goulette
              ■TUNIS
          ✈ Dougg ❸ ✈ Hammamet
        Kairouan   Sousse
                    ✈ Monastir
Jebel Chambi ✈ Sbeitla • Mahdia
  1554m△   • El Jem
ALGERIA   Kasserine Sfax
    Chott el   Kerkenah Is.
      Garsa • Gafsa Gulf
Chott   of Gabès
Melrhir ✈ Tozeur ✈ Jerba
      Chott   ❷
      el Jerid Gabès Ben
          Medenine•   Gardane
          TUNISIA
                Dehiba•
                    LIBYA

300km
150mls
✈ international airport

---

1 Carthage
2 Matmata
3 Medina in Tunis (al-Madinah)

Tourist Information

Tunisian National Tourist Office (Office National du Tourisme Tunisien/ONTT)
1 avenue Mohamed V, 1000 Tunis, Tunisia
Tel: (071) 341 077.
Website: www.tourismtunisia.com

Tunisian National Tourist Office
77a Wigmore Street, London W1U 1QF, UK
Tel: (020) 7224 5561 (enquiries)
Website: www.cometotunisia.co.uk

Carthage

The city of *Carthage*, which is located on the outskirts of Tunisia's capital city, Tunis, was, for many years, the arch-enemy of the ancient Roman empire. Between 264 and 146 BC, the two great cities were embroiled in a series of wars that saw Hannibal's famous attack on Rome, and Rome's subsequent sacking of Carthage in 146 BC. The Romans eventually settled in the conquered city, which went on to become the administrative capital of Roman Africa. Today, it is mainly Roman sites, including theatres, temples, villas and baths, which can be seen by visiting tourists. Many of the sites now stand in ruins, including the *Roman Amphitheatre* and the thermal *Antoine Baths*, which were once the largest baths built by the Romans. Visitors can gain a superb view of Carthage by climbing the nearby *Byrsa Hill*.

Transportation
Air: Tunis–Carthage International Airport.
Water: Ferry: Services from Sardinia, Sicily, Genoa, Naples, Marseille and Malta. **Rail:** Train: TGM (light rail) to Carthage Byrsa Station.
Road: Bus: Public services. Car: Avenue Habib Bourguiba towards Sidi Bou Said (from Tunis city centre).

Contact Addresses
Site de Carthage, Carthage, Tunisia
Tel: (071) 730 036

Matmata

Matmata is one of the most famous villages in Tunisia as it was the setting for the opening scenes of the film 'Star Wars'. The village's lunar-like landscape and subterranean cave dwellings attract hundreds of visitors every day. They come to see the home of the Star Wars characters Uncle Owen and Aunt Beru, which was located in the fictional town of Sidi Driss. The Berber people first dug homes out of the ground over 1000 years ago in order to escape the midday heat. These Troglodyte communities formed craters beneath the earth and constructed tunnels between some of the courtyards to build an underground labyrinth. Today, *Hotel Sidi Driss*, which was the cantina in Star Wars, still stands, and visitors can spend the night in Berber-style accommodation as part of the whole experience.

Matmata

Transportation
Air: Tunis-Carthage International Airport. **Road:** Coach: The majority of tourists visit Matmata as part of an organised coach tour. Bus: Public services. Car: Road southwest out of Gabes, which leads to New Matmata. Camel: Many tourists prefer to hire camels.

Contact Addresses
For more information on Matmata, contact the Office National du Tourisme Tunisien (see **Tourist Information** above).

Medina in Tunis (al-Madinah)

The *medina*, or old quarter, of Tunis was built during the seventh century AD. From the 12th to the 16th centuries, Tunis was considered to be one of the greatest and wealthiest cities of the Islamic world and its medina is testimony to its former grandeur. Today, visitors can step back in time through the maze of narrow, winding streets and barter for souvenirs with the locals; goods on sale include colourful hand-made carpets, hand-crafted jewellery, copper and brassware, pottery and exotic spices. Among the more frequented attractions found within the walls of the medina are: the ninth-century *Ez-Zitouna Mosqu* (*Mosque of the Olive Tree*), the perfume makers' *Souk el Attarine,* the *Bardo Museum*, home to a fine collection of mosaics and Tunis's first Ottoman-style mosque, *Sidi Yousef*, built in the 17th century.

Transportation
Air: Tunis-Carthage International Airport. **Water:** Ferry: Services from Sardinia, Sicily, Genoa, Naples, Marseille and Malta. **Rail:** Train: Tunis Ville Station. Underground: Medina. **Road:** Car: Avenue Habib Bourguiba, Place de l'Independence and Avenue de France (from Carthage).

Contact Addresses
For more information on the Medina in Tunis, contact the Office National du Tourisme Tunisien (see **Tourist Information** above).

Turkey

800km
400mls

✈ international airport

UKRAINE
MOLDOVA
ROMANIA
BULGARIA
Dardanelles
• Edirne Bosporus
BLACK SEA
Sinop
Samsun
Trabzon
Kars • ARM.
GEORGIA
5 **6** Istanbul
• Troy **2** Bursa
ANKARA
Izmir
Ephesus
Konya
Lake Tuz
Antalya
TURKEY
Cappadocia
Elazig Lake Van
Adana Gaziantep
Erzurum
Mt Ararat △
5165m
Sivas
Irmak
Kizil
GREECE
3 aman
Alanya
Iskenderun Euphrates
MEDITERRANEAN SEA
CYPRUS
SYRIA
IRAQ
Tigris
IRAN
1
4

1 Ayasofya (Hagia Sophia)
2 Blue Mosque (Sultanahmet Camii)
3 Ephesus (Efes)
4 Göreme National Park (Göreme Milli Parklar)
5 Topkapi Palace (Topkapi Sarayi)
6 Troy (Truva)

Tourist Information

Ministry of Tourism (Turizm Bakanligi)
Ismet Inönü Bulvar 5, Bahçelievler, Ankara, Turkey
Tel: (0312) 212 8300
Website: www.turizm.gov.tr

Turkish Tourist Office
First Floor, 170-173 Piccadilly, London W1J 9EJ, UK
Tel: (020) 7629 7771 or (09001) 887 755 (brochure request line; calls are charged at the rate of 60p per minute).

Ayasofya (Hagia Sophia)

When the Christian Emperor Justinian inaugurated *Hagia Sophia*, meaning Church of Divine Wisdom, in the year AD 537, it was the most impressive building in the world and remained the crowning achievement of the Byzantine Empire for over a millennium. In the 15th century, Mehmet the Conqueror converted it from a Christian church to a mosque, adding the minarets, tombs and fountains. Turkey became a secular republic in 1923 and Hagia Sophia was established as a museum 12 years later, with many of its Byzantine mosaics revealed from underneath layers of Ottoman plaster. Designed to represent the heavens, visitors marvel at the huge 56m (183ft) high dome.

Transportation
Air: Istanbul Atatürk Airport, Istanbul Sabiha Gökçen International Airport. **Rail:** Train: Sirkeci Station. Tram: Sultanahmet. **Road:** Bus: Public services. Car: E80 or D100 (from Ankara, Izmit and Greece).

Contact Addresses
Museum of Hagia Sophia, Sultanahmet, Istanbul, Turkey
Tel: (0212) 522 0989 or 522 1750

Blue Mosque (Sultanahmet Camii)

With its cascade of opulent domes and slender, balconied minarets soaring towards the sky, Istanbul's *Blue Mosque* is one of the city's most striking images. Construction was begun in 1609 under the Ottoman Sultan Ahmet Khan I, who wished to create a place of Islamic worship to rival the *Aya Sofya*, or Hagia Sophia, constructed under the Roman ruler Justinian II in AD 532 and located across the *Hippodrome*, the old city's central plaza. Completed in 1619, the interior of the mosque features a massive dome supported by four grand columns, 5m (16ft) in diameter, as well as characteristic Ottoman tile patterns and brightly-coloured windows. Hundreds of Muslims still use the mosque for daily prayer and worship. Visitors of all faiths who are modestly dressed may enter the Blue Mosque; special slippers and head and shoulder coverings are distributed at the entrance.

Transportation
Air: Istanbul Atatürk Airport, Istanbul Sabiha Gökçen International Airport. **Rail:** Train: Sirkeci Station. Tram: Sultanahmet. **Road:** Bus: Public services. Car: E-80 or D-100 (from Edirne).

Contact Addresses
Sultanahmet Camii, Sultanahmet Meydani, Istanbul, Turkey
Tel: (0212) 518 1319

Ephesus (Efes)

Ephesus, located 600km (373 miles) southwest of Istanbul, is one of the grandest and best-preserved ruins of the ancient world. According to evidence dating from around 1400BC, the Hittites were the first to settle the site, which they named Apasas. Ephesus first attained importance in the first century BC, due to its position as a sheltered harbour and the starting point of the royal road leading to Susa, the capital of the Persian Empire. The temple was originally founded in the seventh century BC as a shrine to the Anatolian goddess, Cybele. It was destroyed and subsequently rebuilt seven times; the classical marble structure with Ionic columns built around 550BC was one of the seven wonders of the ancient world. The Romans captured the city in 189BC and it continued to flourish, with fountains, pools and the second largest library outside of Alexandria. One of Ephesus' attractions is the fact that so much of it remains intact and little imagination is required to see what the Roman city would have looked like.

Transportation
Air: Istanbul Atatürk Airport, Istanbul Sabiha Gökçen International Airport, Dalaman Airport, Adnanmenderes Airport, Izmir (domestic flights). **Rail:** Train: Selçuk Station. **Road:** Bus: Public services. Car: Selçuk–Kusadasi Road (from Selçuk or Kusadasi).

Contact Addresses
Tourist Information Office, Selçuk, Izmir 35920, Turkey
Tel: (0232) 892 6945
Website: www.ephesusguide.com

Göreme National Park (Göreme Milli Parklar)

Göreme National Park in *Cappadocia*, central Turkey, is home to one of nature's most intriguing phenomena. Commonly referred to as the *Valley of the Fairy Chimneys*, after the strange rock formations that proliferate in the region, this weird and wonderful landscape of 9572 hectares (23,653 acres) was formed when three volcanoes, *Erciyes*, *Hasan* and *Melendiz Dağlari* erupted around 30 million years ago. The deposits they created make up a material called tuff, a soft rock that is easily eroded to form extraordinary table mountains, fairy chimneys and undulating, sand-dune like cliff faces. For hundreds of years, the indigenous population had carved homes out of the rocks, many of which have been turned into comfortable *pansiyon* (guesthouses). St Paul introduced Christianity to the region in the first century AD, and one of Cappadocia's chief attractions is the array of rock churches and monasteries that were hewn out of the landscape, thus being hidden from the pursuing Arab invaders. The town of *Göreme* has an open-air museum where many of these preserved houses and churches, adorned with frescoes, can be seen.

Transportation
Air: Ankara Esenboga Airport, Istanbul Atatürk Airport, Istanbul Sabiha Gökçen International Airport, Nevsehir Airport (domestic flights), Kayseri Airport (domestic flights). **Road:** Coach: Public services.

Contact Addresses
Nevsehir Directorate of Tourism, Atatürk Bulvari 14, Nevsehir, Turkey
Tel: (0384) 213 3659

Topkapi Palace (Topkapi Sarayi)

Topkapi Palace was created on the orders of Mehmed II, the 23-year-old sultan who captured the Roman city of Constantinople in 1453 and made it the capital of his mighty Ottoman empire, under the new name of Istanbul. The palace was constructed between 1459 and 1478 and rapidly grew to become a jumbled complex of elaborate living quarters and administrative offices. The

Blue Mosque

Ruth Blakeborough©

Sultanahmet, Istanbul, Turkey
Tel: (0212) 512 0480 *or* 512 0484
Website: www.kultur.gov.tr

Troy (Truva)

Until 1871, classical scholars the world over had thought the city of *Troy* the stuff of legend. That changed when Austrian millionaire-cum-archaeologist, Heinrich Schliemann, discovered the city that was the site of the famous war between the Greeks and the Trojans in the 12th century BC. According to Homer, war broke out when Paris, the son of King Priam of Troy, eloped with Helen, the beautiful wife of Menelaus of Sparta. An army led by Menelaus' brother, Agamemnon, set out in revenge to attack the Trojans. The ensuing war lasted 10 years, until the Greeks made a pretence of retreating. Instead they hid inside a specially-constructed horse, which the Trojans foolishly believed to be a peace offering and took inside their walls, whereupon the cunning Greeks emerged and ransacked the city. The story was made into a successful Hollywood movie called 'Troy' starring Brad Pitt in 2004.

layout of the palace features a series of interconnected courtyards which progress inwards, from the first, which was open to all citizens, through to the fourth, where the sultans had their gardens and *harem* and private living area. Today visitors can enter the gardens and courtyards, and take a guided tour of the harem to gain an impression of the extravagant lifestyle of the rulers of one of the world's greatest empires.

Transportation
Air: Istanbul Atatürk Airport, Istanbul Sabiha Gökçen International Airport. **Rail:** Train: Sirkeci Station. Tram: Sultanahmet. **Road:** Bus: Public services. Car: E80 or D100 (from Ankara, Izmit or Greece).

Contact Addresses
Topkapi Palace Museum, 34400 Sarayii,

Transportation
Air: Istanbul Atatürk Airport, Istanbul Sabiha Gökçen International Airport, Izmir Adnan Menderes International Airport. **Rail:** Train: Balekesir Station or Bandirma Station. **Road:** Bus: Local Dolmus (minibus) services (from Çanakkale).

Contact Addresses
Canakkale Tourist Informaton Office, Regional Directorate, Valilik Binasi, Kat 1, Canakkale, Turkey
Tel: (0286) 217 5012

Uganda

300km
150mls
✈ international airport

SUDAN
Fola Rapids
Kitgum
KENYA
Arua ● Gulu
Murchison Falls
Moroto
DEMOCRATIC REPUBLIC OF CONGO
UGANDA
L. Kwania
● Soroti
Masindi
L. Kyoga
Lake Albert
Mbale
Mt Elgon 4321m
Owen Falls Dam
Tororo
Margherita Peak △ 5110m
Fort Portal
KAMPALA
Jinja
Buganda
Entebbe
Buvuma I.
L. George
Equator
Lake Edward
Ankole
Sese Is.
❶ Kabale
Masaka
Mbarara
LAKE VICTORIA
Kisoro
Kagera
TANZANIA
RWANDA

| 1 | Bwindi Impenetrable National Park |

Bwindi Impenetrable National Park

Bwindi Impenetrable National Park, located in southwestern Uganda, on the edge of the western Rift Valley, covers an area of 331 sq km (128 sq miles). The forest, which was designated a UNESCO World Heritage Site in 1994, is a sanctuary for around half the world's mountain gorillas, including the Mubare and the Habinyanja groups. It is also famed for being the home of the Colobus monkey, various species of chimpanzee, hundreds of species of birds and many other animals, including forest birds, snakes, lizards, chameleons and butterflies. As well as animals, the park is home to huge trees covered in creepers, a bamboo zone and rare plants, including mistletoe and orchids. Trekking

Tourist Information

Uganda Tourist Board
PO Box 7211, Impala House, Ground Floor, Kimathi Avenue, Kampala, Uganda
Tel: (041) 342 196/7
Website: www.visituganda.com

High Commission for the Republic of Uganda
Uganda House, 58-59 Trafalgar Square, London WC2N 5DX, UK
Tel: (020) 7839 5783

permits for visitors wishing to see the gorillas are strictly limited and must always be booked in advance.

Transportation
Air: Entebbe International Airport. **Road:** Car: Kabale–Buhoma Road to the park headquarters at Buhoma (from Kabale). Four-wheel drive vehicles are advised.

Contact Addresses
Uganda Wildlife Authority, Plot 3, Kintu Road, Nakasero, PO Box 3530, Kampala, Uganda
Tel: (041) 346 287/8
Website: www.uwa.or.ug

Bwindi Impenetrable National Park

UWA – Uganda Wildlife Authority©

Ukraine

1 Saint Sophia Cathedral

Tourist Information

Ministry of Foreign Affairs
Mykhailovska Square 1, 01018 Kyiv, Ukraine
Tel: (44) 238 1777
Website: www.mfa.gov.ua

Intourist Travel Ltd
9 Princedale Road, Holland Park, London W11
4NW, UK
Tel: (020) 7792 5240
Website: www.intouristuk.com

Saint Sophia Cathedral

The outstanding *Saint Sophia Cathedral* in *Kiev*
dates back to 1037 when the foundations were
laid under the orders of Prince Yaroslav the Wise.
The impressive cathedral is characterised by its 13
domes (*cupolas*) that dominate the skyline and the
ornate, gold-topped dome of the *Saint Sophia Bell*

Tower. Inside, much of the Byzantine interior is
intact and the cathedral is famous for its 11th
century mosaics and frescoes. There is now a
museum on the site detailing the cathedral's
spiritual and intellectual influence in the region
and how it contributed to the spread of the
Orthodox faith across Russia from the 17th to the
19th century. Saint Sophia Cathedral and the
related monastic buildings were declared as a
UNESCO World Heritage site in 1990.

Transportation
Air: Boryspil International Airport, Kiev. **Rail:**
Train: Kiev Station. **Road:** Bus: Public services
from Kiev Central Station.

Contact Addresses
Kiev-Pechersk Lavra Monastery, 25 Sichnevogo
Povstannya st., 01015 Kiev, Ukraine
Tel. + 380 (44) 254 2257
Website: www.lavra.kiev.ua

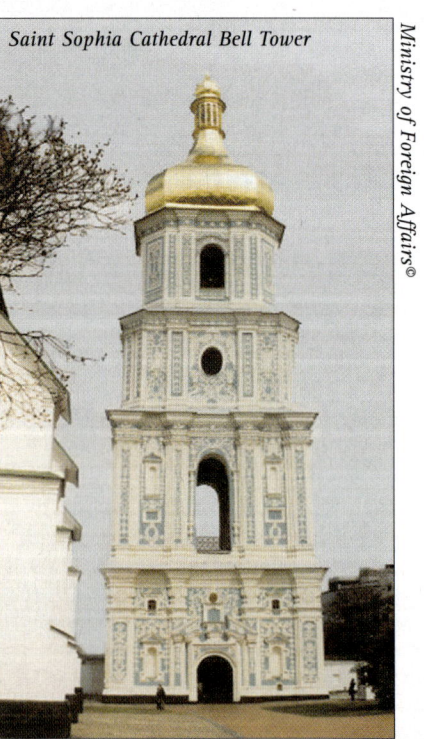

Saint Sophia Cathedral Bell Tower

Ministry of Foreign Affairs©

United Arab Emirates

1 Dubai Creek
2 Jumeirah Archaeological Site

Dubai Spice Souk

Images provided by The Government of Dubai, Department of Tourism and Commerce Marketing©

Tourist Information

Government of Dubai Department of Tourism & Commerce Marketing
National Bank of Dubai Building, 10th-12th Floors, Baniyas Road, Deira, Dubai, UAE
Tel: (4) 223 0000
Website: www.dubaitourism.ae

Government of Dubai Department of Tourism & Commerce Marketing
1st Floor, 125 Pall Mall, London SW1Y 5EA, UK
Tel: (020) 7839 0580
Website: www.dubaitourism.ae

Key to symbols: £ Entry charged ♿ Disabled access 🛠 Man-made attraction ✓ Natural attraction P Parking ✕ Restaurant 🛒 Shop 🏛 UNESCO site

Dubai Creek

The 14km (8.7 mile) *Dubai Creek* is a natural seawater inlet that divides the city of Dubai into two parts – *Deira Dubai* and *Bur Dubai* – and has been the heart and soul of the city ever since it was a center for pearl fishing and the pearl trade. Long established for its ancient sea routes that reached as far as India and the East African coast, the Creek was originally only deep enough to accommodate smaller vessels and goods had to be transferred to traditional Arab sailing dhows at the entrance to the Creek. Recognising the Creek's strategic importance to the region, it was deepened in the 1960s and today functions as a vibrant port and vital part of the city with eight wharfages, each capable of catering to 31 ships of up to 800 tonnes in capacity. Around 720,000 tonnes of cargo pass through the port each year but only wooden ships are allowed to enter the creek in order to maintain its traditional appearance. Abras (small wooden boats) serve as taxis for those who want to cross from the Deira side to the Bur Dubai side. A wildlife sanctuary that's home to over 27,000 birds has been set up at the inland end of

Dubai Creek at night

Image provided by the Government of Dubai, Department of Tourism and Commerce Marketing©

the Creek. Reflecting the wealth of one of the fastest growing economies in the world, boutique hotels, golf courses and yachting clubs have sprung up along the Creek's banks.

Transportation
Air: Dubai International Airport. **Water:** Water taxis operate between Dubai and Deira. **Rail:** Currently no rail network but construction of a rail and underground network is underway. **Road:** Bus: Public services.

Contact Addresses
For more information on the Dubai Creek, contact the Department of Tourism (see **Tourist Information** above).

Jumeirah Archaeological Site

The archaeological site at *Jumeirah* is thought to date back to the sixth century AD and was the site

of a caravan station along an ancient trade route through the desert that linked Iraq to Oman. It's one of the most significant archaeological sites in the United Arab Emirates with sections of walling, a souq and houses – one of which is thought to have been the governor's palace all having been found at the site. Other finds, such as pottery, tools and coins, are on display at the *Heritage Village* in Diera.

Transportation
Air: Dubai International Airport. **Water:** Water taxis operate between Dubai and Deira. **Rail:** Currently no rail network but construction of a rail and underground network are underway. **Road:** Bus: Public services.

Contact Addresses
For more information on the Jumeirah Archaeological site, contact the Department of Tourism (see **Tourist Information** above).

United Kingdom

Channel Islands, Guernsey

Fort Grey Shipwreck Museum

Located on the island's rocky west coast, *Fort Grey Shipwreck Museum* was built in 1804 as part of the island's defences against French attacks. It was restored in 1976 and turned into a popular visitor attraction. Overlooking the *Hanois Reefs*, many ships have sunk off its shores and a small museum housed within the small *Martello Tower* tells the maritime history of the region. The museum is closed during the winter months.

Transportation
Air: Guernsey International Airport. **Water:** Ferry: Services to St Peter Port. **Road:** Bus: Public services.

Contact Addresses
Rocquaine Coast Road, St. Peters, Guernsey
Tel: (0)1481 265 036
Website: www.museum.guernsey.net

German Underground Hospital

The incredible complex of tunnels at the *German Underground Hospital* is the largest construction in the *Channel Islands* and was hewn out of solid rock by forced labourers of many nationalities during the German occupation of the island during the Second World War. Measuring 7,000 sq m (75,348 sq ft), the complex consists of two sets of nine parallel tunnels which were originally built as shelters for the German forces. It was later used as an underground hospital and could house up to 1,000 patients in times of emergency. Visitors enter the complex through an entrance that is barely visible from above ground. The Underground Hospital is only open during the summer months.

Transportation
Air: Guernsey International Airport. **Water:** Ferry: Services to St Peter Port. **Road:** Bus: Public services.

1 Fort Grey Shipwreck Museum
2 German Underground Hospital
3 Oatlands Craft Centre
4 Occupation Museum
5 Victor Hugo's House

Tourist Information

Visit Guernsey
PO Box 23, St Peter Port, Guernsey, Channel Islands GY1 3AN, UK
Tel: (01481) 723 552
Website: www.visitguernsey.com

Jersey Tourism
Liberation Square, St Helier, Jersey JE1 1BB, Channel Islands
Tel: (01534) 500 700 or 500 777 (general visitor enquiries) or 500 800 (brochure line) or 500 888 (accommodation reservations)
Website: www.jersey.com

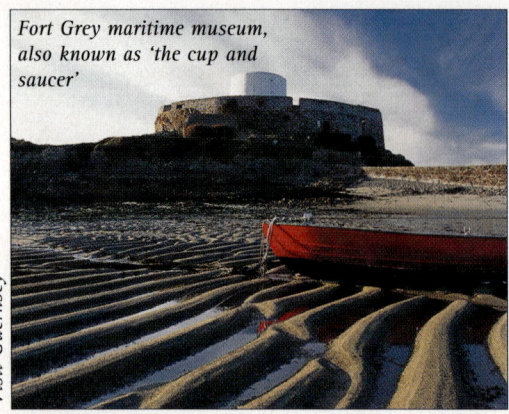
Fort Grey maritime museum, also known as 'the cup and saucer'

Visit Guernsey©

Contact Addresses
Les Eperons, La Vassalerie, Guernsey, GY6 8XR
Tel: (01481) 239100

P   £   ⚒

Oatlands Craft Centre

The *Oatlands Craft Centre* in the north of the island provides visitors with the opportunity to watch local craftspeople at work at a number of different traditional industries. *Guernsey* is famed for its dairy herds and visitors are able to see traditional cheese makers at work and sample some of the famous products. There are also some traditional brick kilns that were built in 1892 and visitors can see how these craftspeople once worked. Other craftspeople exhibiting their work at the centre include glass blowers, potters and silversmiths. There's also a small farm at the centre where visitors can see how a traditional farm was managed and run. There's a children's play area too that's staffed by professional carers.

Transportation
Air: Guernsey International Airport. **Water:** Ferry: Services to St Peter Port. **Road:** Bus: Public services.

Contact Addresses
Les Gigands, Braye Road, St Sampson's, Guernsey
Tel: (01481) 244282

P   ✕   🛒   ♿   ⚒

Occupation Museum

Opened in 1966 by Richard Heaume, a founder member of the *Occupation Society*, the *German*
Occupation Museum has one of the most extensive collections of war memorabilia on the island. The museum has many artefacts and exhibits covering the five years of German occupation during WWII from 1940 to 1945. There are also two fortification sites that are the property of the museum that have been faithfully restored and are open to visitors.

Transportation
Air: Guernsey International Airport. **Water:** Ferry: Services to St Peter Port. **Road:** Bus: Public services.

Contact Addresses
German Occupation Museum, Les Houards, Forest, Guernsey GY8 0BG
Tel: (01481) 238205

P   ✕   🛒   ♿   £   ⚒

Victor Hugo's House

Born in France in 1802, the island's most famous resident was the poet and writer Victor Hugo whose celebrated works include 'Notre Dame de Paris' and 'Les Miérables', the latter which he actually completed in Guernsey. Hugo's outspoken political views led to his expulsion from France and his arrival in Guernsey in 1855. The following year he published a collection of his poetry called Les Contemplations which was a big success. With the money it earned he bought *Hauteville House* which is now a popular visitor attraction on the island. Although legally entitled to return to France in 1859, he chose to reside on the island he adored until 1870 when Louis Bonaparte fell from power. Hauteville House is a large distinctive white building with a commanding position that overlooks the sea. Hugo was an avid collector of eccentric furniture and bric-a-brac and today visitors are able to wander through the house and grounds which has been preserved as it was when Hugo lived there.

Transportation
Air: Guernsey International Airport. **Water:** Ferry: Services to St Peter Port. **Road:** Bus: Public services.

Contact Addresses
For more information about Victor Hugo's House, contact the Visit Guernsey (see **Tourist Information** above).

P   ✕   🛒   ♿   £   ⚒

Channel Islands, Jersey

1 Jersey Zoo
2 Sark

Jersey Zoo

Jersey Zoo was established in 1959 by Gerald Durrell (1925-1995) and is located around his home, *Les Augrès Manor*, where Durrell's widow, Dr Lee Durrell, still lives. The manor is also the headquarters of the *Durrell Wildlife Conservation Trust*. At just 12.55 hectares (31 acres), Jersey Zoo is relatively small but it is still one of the island's most popular attractions focussing as it does on providing safe habitats for some of the world's most endangered species. There's a strong emphasis on education and there are many interactive displays aimed at promoting awareness about animal conservation. Two of the most popular enclosures at the zoo include the orang-utan and gorilla parks. In addition to providing an attraction for visitors, the zoo also manages many research and breeding programmes and is committed to animal conservation. The zoo also has its own organic farm to ensure its animals get chemical-free produce.

Transportation
Air: St Peters International Airport. **Water:** Ferry: Services to Jersey Port. **Road:** Bus: Public services.

Contact Addresses
Durrell Wildlife Conservation Trust, Les Augrés Manor, La Profonde Rue, Trinity, Jersey JE3 5BP
Tel: (01534) 860000
Website: www.durrellwildlife.org

Sark

Located approximately 128.75km (80 miles) south of the English Coast, the island of *Sark* is the smallest of the four *Channel Islands*. Sark stands as the smallest independent feudal state in Europe and has belonged to the British Crown since the time of William the Conqueror when it, along with the other *Channel Islands*, formed part of the *Duchy of Normandy*. King John retained the islands when the Duchy of Normandy was returned to the French in the 13th century. Aside from the island's unique history, Sark is a car-free zone so offers visitors a unique and tranquil experience. Its 65km (40 miles) of dramatic coastline is peppered with caves, bays and picturesque inlets, many of which can be accessed via a network of paths and walkways. The island supports a wide variety of flora and fauna and its spectacular coastal paths are popular with ramblers and bird watchers. Manmade attractions include the *Sark Lighthouse* built in 1912, the *Harbour* and the island *Prison* which was built in 1856 and is still in use today.

Transportation
Air: Guernsey International Airport or St Peters Airport on Jersey then ferry services to Sark. **Water:** Ferry: Services to Sark Harbour. **Road:** Motorised vehicles are banned from the island but bicycles are available for hire.

Contact Addresses
Isle of Sark Tourism
Tel: (01481) 832345
Website: www.sark-tourism.com

England

SCOTLAND

NORTH SEA

NORTHERN IRELAND

Belfast

Scafell Pike 977m ⌃

20

35 Newcastle upon Tyne

Hadrian's Wall

15 Durham

Isle of Man

23

17

Scarborough

64 York

4 **5**

33

Leeds

Kingston upon Hull

Bradford

41

Manchester

44

1

Liverpool

Anglesey

2

30

Sheffield

Grimsby

The Wash

IRISH SEA

E N G L A N D

14

Birmingham

45 Norwich

53

18

WALES

Severn

Coventry

59 **47**

Cambridge

49

9

Felixstowe

Swansea

Oxford

Luton **36**

Stansted

Harwich

Cardiff

LONDON

(London see list)

Lundy

61

Thames

62 **25**

Bristol **39** Bath

Heathrow

42

13

river

12 **63** **28**

Gatwick

24

11

Southampton **52**

Exeter

38

43 Brighton

Folkestone

56

37

Portsmouth

Plymouth

Isle of Wight

16

50

Isles of Scilly

E n g l i s h   C h a n n e l

FRANCE

IRELAND

Pennines

Trent

200km

100mls

✈ major international airport

⊙ capital

Tourist Attractions & Events of the World

Tourist Information

British Tourist Authority
Thames Tower, Black's Road, Hammersmith, London W6 9EL, UK
Tel: (020) 8846 9000
Website: www.visitbritain.com

1   Albert Dock
2   Alton Towers
3   Big Ben and the Houses of Parliament (London)
4   Blackpool Pleasure Beach
5   Blackpool Tower
6   British Airways London Eye (London)
7   British Museum (London)
8   Buckingham Palace (London)
9   Cambridge University
10 Camden Market (London)
11 Canterbury Cathedral
12 Cheddar Caves and Gorge
13 Chessington World of Adventures
14 Drayton Manor Theme Park
15 Durham Castle and Cathedral
16 Eden Project
17 Flamingo Land Theme Park and Zoo
18 Yarmouth Pleasure Beach
19 Greenwich (London)
20 Hadrians Wall
21 Hampton Court Palace
22 Harrods (London)
23 Lake Windermere
24 Leeds Castle
25 Legoland Windsor
26 London Dungeon (London)
27 London Zoo (London)
28 Longleat
29 Madame Tussaud's and Tussaud's London Planetarium (London)
30 Matlock Bath
31 National Gallery (London)
32 National Museum of Photography, Film and Television
33 Natural History Museum (London)
34 Neasden Temple (London)
35 New Metroland
36 Oxford University
37 Poole Harbour
38 Portsmouth Historic Dockyard
39 Roman Baths and Pump Room
40 Royal Academy of Arts (London)
41 Royal Armouries Leeds
42 Royal Botanic Gardens, Kew
43 Royal Pavilion
44 Salford Quays
45 Sandringham Estate
46 Science Museum (London)
47 Shakespeare Houses
48 Somerset House (London)
49 Southwold
50 St Michael's Mount
51 St Paul's Cathedral (London)
52 Stonehenge
53 Swaffam I Ecotech Centre
54 Tate Britain (London)
55 Tate Modern (London)
56 Tintagel Castle
57 Tower of London (London)
58 Victoria and Albert Museum (London)
59 Warwick Castle
60 Westminster Abbey (London)
61 Westonbirt Arboretum
62 Windsor Castle
63 Wookey Hole Caves
64 York Minster

Albert Dock

Recognised for its historic importance, Liverpool's *Maritime Mercantile City* was inscribed onto UNESCO's World Heritage List in 2004 to help preserve one of the world's most recognisable ports as a historic site. In the 19th century, the city of Liverpool was a flourishing export and passenger port that employed thousands of workers from around Britain and Ireland, and it was from here that many set sail for new lives in America. With the decline of the British Empire, the area fell into disrepair until the city council embarked upon a major renewal project in the 1980s. The centrepiece of this project is the *Albert Dock*, 3 hectares (7 acres) of water surrounded by renovated warehouses with iron colonnades. The warehouses have been converted into lively spaces for restaurants, shops and cafés, interspersed with museums chronicling the city's contribution to British history and culture. *The Beatles Story*, dedicated to the famous Fab Four, is one of Liverpool's top attractions, featuring a replica of the Cavern Club where the group performed in the early days alongside posters, personal memorabilia, and other displays. The area is also home to the *Tate Gallery Liverpool*, Britain's largest gallery of contemporary art outside London, featuring displays of art from the Tate museums in London.

Transportation
Air: Liverpool Airport, Manchester Airport. **Rail:** Train: Liverpool Lime Street Station. **Road:** Bus: Public services.

Contact Addresses
22 Edward Pavilion, Albert Dock, Liverpool L3 4AF, UK
Tel: (0151) 708 7334
Website: www.albertdock.com

Alton Towers

Alton Towers is the most popular theme park in the UK. Set on an estate owned by the Earl of Shrewsbury, this amusement park has a wide range of rides and attractions aimed at young and old alike. The park, which opened in 1980, also includes 200 acres (81 hectares) of landscaped gardens, live entertainment and the historic towers building which was the residence of the Talbot family (the Earls of Shrewsbury) until 1923. Today, visitors can explore different kingdoms in the grounds of the estate, such as *Ugland*, the *Forbidden Valley*, *Towers Street* and *Cred Street*. Popular rides include the *Black Hole*, the famous *Corkscrew* and *Nemesis* rollercoasters and the *Log Flume* water slide. New for 2005 is *Rita - Queen of Speed* rollercoaster.

Transportation
Air: Manchester Airport. **Rail:** Train: Alton Towers Station. Buses are available to take visitors to the park. **Road:** Coach: Public services.

Contact Addresses
Alton Towers, Staffordshire, ST10 4DB, UK
Tel: (08705) 204 060
Website: www.altontowers.com

Big Ben and the Houses of Parliament

The elaborate neo-Gothic *Palace of Westminster*, gracefully located beside the River Thames, is one of London's most iconic images. The adjoining clock tower, *St Stephen's*, is often mistakenly assumed to be called *Big Ben*, although this is actually the name of the bell inside. Big Ben rings every hour on the hour and is shown on British television at midnight on December 31 to count in the New Year. The original Palace of Westminster, constructed in the 12th century by Edward the Confessor and enlarged by William the Conqueror, was used as a royal palace until 1512 when it was damaged by fire. It only became the seat of the British government in the mid-16th century, and was rebuilt in its current style, to designs by architect Sir Charles Barry, after it was completely ravaged by fire in 1834. There are special guided tours of the building through August to October but foreign visitors are no longer able to tour the Houses of Parliament during session.

Transportation
Air: London Heathrow Airport, London Gatwick Airport, London Stansted Airport, London Luton Airport. **Rail:** Train: London Victoria Station or London Waterloo Station. Underground:

Westminster (Circle, District or Jubilee lines).
Road: Bus: Public services.

Contact Addresses
House of Commons Information Office,
Westminster, London SW1A 0AA, UK
Tel: (020) 7219 4272
Website: www.parliament.uk

Blackpool Pleasure Beach

The city of Blackpool has been attracting holiday
visitors ever since 1735, when the first guest
house opened. In the 19th century, it became a
popular working-class destination among the
British and, in 1896, *Blackpool Pleasure Beach* was
opened. Today, this American-style amusement
park with a distinctly British feel has a variety of
rides to suit all tastes and ages. Rides suitable for
children include the parks' oldest attraction, a
centrifugal rocket ride called *Flying Machines*.
Valhalla, which opened in 2000, is the world's
biggest ride in the dark. There are also several
shows to entertain visitors, such as *Eclipse at the
Globe*, featuring acrobats, aerialists and dancers,
and a separate *Beaver Creak* theme park with rides
aimed specifically at children. Entrance to the
park is free but rides are paid for.

Transportation
Air: Manchester Airport, Blackpool Airport
(domestic flights). **Rail:** Train: Blackpool North
Station or Blackpool Pleasure Beach Station.
Road: Bus: Public services.

Contact Addresses
Blackpool Pleasure Beach, 525 Ocean Boulevard,
South Shore, Blackpool, Lancashire FY4 1EZ, UK
Tel: (0870) 444 5566
Website: www.blackpoolpleasurebeach.com

Blackpool Tower

The 156-m (518-ft) *Blackpool Tower* houses a
ballroom, an aquarium and play area and
dominates the skyline along Blackpool's lively
promenade. Most visitors head to the top of the
tower for views back across the city or out across

Blackpool Tower

the Irish Sea. The viewing deck includes the *Walk
of Faith*, a clear glass platform enabling visitors to
see the world passing by beneath their feet.
Attractions at the tower include the *Tower Circus*
featuring traditional acts. In 2004, the circus
introduced workshops where children can learn
skills such as plate spinning, juggling and
acrobatics. Also for the younger visitors, *Jungle
Jims* is one of Europe's biggest indoor adventure
playgrounds featuring ball pools, slides and
climbing nets. The famous *Blackpool Tower
Ballroom* hosts dances and concerts in its ornate
halls.

Transportation
Air: Blackpool Airport. **Rail:** Blackpool Station.
Road: Bus: Public services. Car: M55 links
Blackpool with the M6.

Contact Addresses
Blackpool Tower, Promenade, Blackpool,
Lancashire FY1 4BJ, UK
Tel: (01253) 292029
Website: www.blackpooltower.co.uk

*British Airways
London Eye*

The Flat Earth Collection©

British Airways London Eye

At 135m (443ft) tall, the *British Airways London Eye* is the world's largest observation wheel and the fourth tallest structure in London. Designed by Marks Barfield Architects and managed by the Tussaud's Group, the wheel was erected in 1999. It differs from a ferris wheel in that it has an A-frame support structure on only one side, while the pods are located on the exterior. These are stabilised by internal motors that keep them horizontal as the wheel slowly moves around. The structure has 32 separate capsules that rotate and can carry up to 25 people at any one time, taking passengers on a 30-minute trip high above London's skyline. Designed to be visually appealing from the exterior, the wheel provides staggering views of central London to a distance as far away as 40km (25 miles) on clear days. The London Eye continues to be one of the UK's most visited paid for attractions.

Transportation
Air: London Heathrow Airport or London Gatwick Airport. **Water:** The Tate Boat runs along the Thames between Tate Britain, the London Eye and Tate Modern. **Rail:** Train: London Waterloo Station or London Charing Cross Station. Underground: Westminster (Circle and District lines), Waterloo (Bakerloo, Jubilee or Northern lines), Embankment (Bakerloo, Circle, District or Northern lines). **Road:** Bus: Public services for the South Bank.

Contact Addresses
British Airways London Eye, Customer Services, Riverside Building, County Hall, Westminster Bridge Road, London SE1 7PB, UK
Tel: (0870) 500 0600 *or* (0870) 990 8883
Website: www.ba-londoneye.com

British Museum

The British Museum was founded in 1753 to promote a better public understanding of the arts, natural history and science. It contains one of the world's greatest displays of antiquities, documenting the rise and fall of civilisations from all over the world. The museum opened to the public in 1759, with the famous Rosetta Stone being presented to the museum in 1802, along with many other Egyptian antiquities. As well as the Rosetta Stone, the museum also houses many other famous objects including the Elgin Marbles, currently at the centre of debate as to whether they should be returned to Greece. Today, the museum's collection, which is in excess of six million objects, comprises art and antiquities from Egypt, Western Asia, Greece, Rome and Europe, amongst others. The spectacular Great Court, with its impressive glass roof, was opened in 2000, following the relocation of the British Library to St Pancras, and is the largest covered public square in Europe. Entry is free but there is a charge for some temporary exhibitions.

Transportation
Air: London Heathrow Airport. **Rail:** Train: London Kings Cross Station. Underground: Holborn (Central and Piccadilly lines), Tottenham Court Road (Central and Northern lines) or Russell Square (Piccadilly Line). **Road:** Bus: Public services.

Contact Addresses
British Museum, Great Russell Street, London WC1B 3DG, UK
Tel: (020) 7323 8000
Website: www.thebritishmuseum.ac.uk

Buckingham Palace

Work began on *Buckingham Palace* in 1702 and has been the official London residence of the British Royal Family since 1837. After several expansions, the palace now has a total of 52 bedrooms, 78 bathrooms and 92 offices. The palace enjoys an imposing location in the centre of London, opposite *St James's Park*. Every year, millions of visitors come to see the *Changing of the Guard* ceremony, which takes place outside the palace at 1130 daily from April to July and on alternate days at other times of the year. Visitors can also tour the inside of the palace during the summer months. The *Ball Room*, which is the largest room in the palace, opened to the public for the first time in 2000. The 19 *State Rooms* at the palace, which include the *Throne Room* and the *Picture Gallery*, house treasures including English and French furniture, paintings by Rembrandt and Rubens and sculpture by Canaletto. Visitors can also see inside the *Royal Mews*, which is one of the grandest working stables in the world.

Transportation
Air: London Heathrow Airport. **Rail:** Train: London Victoria Station. Underground: St James's Park (District or Circle lines); Victoria (Victoria, District or Circle lines); Green Park (Piccadilly, Jubilee or Victoria lines). **Road:** Bus: Public services.

Contact Addresses
Buckingham Palace, Buckingham Palace Road, London SW1A 1AA, UK
Tel: (020) 7839 1377
Website: www.royal.gov.uk

Cambridge University

Cambridge University is the second oldest university in England, and shares with Oxford University an unrivalled reputation for excellence and tradition. Founded in the 13th century by scholars from universities in Oxford and Paris, its distinguished alumni include Sir Isaac Newton, John Milton and Stephen Hawking. The university's various colleges, many of them architectural masterpieces, are scattered throughout the city. *St John's College* was founded

by Lady Margaret Beaufort, mother of King Henry VII, in 1511 and contains the *New Bridge*, often referred to as Cambridge's *Bridge of Sighs*. *Kings College* is perhaps the most famous of all the colleges due to its magnificent *chapel*, built between 1446 and 1515; the choir's Christmas Eve service of nine lessons and carols is internationally renowned, and constitutes an integral part of the festive season in Britain. *Trinity College*, founded in 1546 by King Henry VIII, who hoped it would produce the future leaders of the reformed Church of England, is the largest college.

Transportation
Air: London Heathrow Airport, London Gatwick Airport, London Stansted Airport, London Luton Airport. **Rail:** Train: Cambridge Station. **Road:** Bus: Public services including Park and Ride.

Contact Addresses
Tourist Information Centre and Shop, The Old Library, Wheeler Street, Cambridge CB2 3QB, UK
Tel: (01223) 322 640
Website: www.tourismcambridge.com

Camden Market

Camden Market is the largest street market in the UK that attracts around 100,000 visitors every weekend. There are various markets located in *Camden Town*, which are collectively known as *Camden Market*; these are *Camden Lock Market*, *Camden Canal Market*, *Inverness Street Market*, *Camden (Bute Street) Market* and *Camden Stables Market*. The area around *Camden Lock* was first developed in around 1791 by the Earl of Camden, with the famous Regent's Canal opening in 1820. The first market to appear in Camden was *Camden Lock Market*, which opened in 1972. Today, there are hundreds of stalls selling a wide array of goods, including arts and crafts, vintage clothes, second-hand household items, records and CDs, jewellery and exotic food.

Transportation
Air: London Heathrow Airport. **Rail:** Train: Camden Road Station and Kentish Town Station. Underground: Camden Town, Chalk Farm or Mornington Crescent (Northern Line). **Road:** Bus: Public services.

Contact Addresses
Camden Lock Limited, 56 Camden Lock Place,
Chalk Farm Road, London NW1 8AF, UK
Tel: (020) 7284 2084
Website: www.camdenlockmarket.com

Canterbury Cathedral

Canterbury Cathedral's history as a religious site
dates back to AD 597 when Pope Gregory's
missionary, St Augustine, was given a church in
the town by King Ethelbert. The cathedral is a
masterpiece of Romanesque and Gothic
architecture. Inside, visitors can see stained glass
windows dating from the 12th century and the
medieval tombs of King Henry IV and Edward the
Black Prince, as well as those of numerous
archbishops. The cathedral is also the former site
of the shrine to the Archbishop Thomas Becket,
who was murdered in the northwest transept in
1170. His shrine, which was desecrated in 1538
during the Reformation, became one of the most
visited by pilgrims during the Middle Ages, many
of whom travelled the famous Pilgrims' Way from
Winchester to see it.

Transportation
Air: London Gatwick Airport. **Rail:** Train:
Canterbury East Station or Canterbury West
Station. **Road:** Bus: Canterbury Bus Station.
Coach: Public services. Car: M26, M20 and A28 or
A2 and M2 (from the M25). There are tourist signs
to the Cathedral.

Contact Addresses
Canterbury Cathedral, Cathedral House, 11 The
Precincts, Canterbury CT1 2EH, UK
Tel: (01227) 762 862
Website: www.canterbury-cathedral.org

Cheddar Caves and Gorge

Parts of the spectacular *Cheddar Caves and Gorge*
complex have been attracting visitors for over
200 years. The largest and most famous cave is
Gough's Cave, so named because it was
discovered by a Sea Captain named Richard
Gough in 1890. It stretches 0.4km (0.25 miles)

underground and is often referred to as a
cathedral because of the vast caverns – such as
the magnificent *Diamond Chamber* and *Solomon's
Temple* – that were carved out by Ice Age melt
waters over a million years ago. When Gough's
Cave was blasted with dynamite to open it up
for further exploration, archaeologists
discovered what's now known as *Cheddar Man*,
the oldest complete skeleton found in Britain
that's thought to date back over 9,000 years.
Other archaeological finds date human
habitation in and around the site back over
40,000 years. The smaller *Cox's Cave* was
discovered by local mill owner George Cox in
1837 when one of his workers fell through a
hole in the roof of the cave whilst collecting
rocks for a new building. Above ground, a series
of 274 steps known as *Jacob's Ladder* take
visitors from the foot of Britain's biggest gorge
to the very top where the *Lookout Tower* and the
cliff top *Gorge Walk* are located. Caving,
climbing and abseiling courses can also be
arranged at the site.

Transportation
Air: Bristol International Airport. **Rail:** Bristol
Station or Weston-Super-Mare Station. **Road:** Bus:
Public services. Car: B3135.

Contact Addresses
Cheddar Caves and Gorge, Cheddar, Somerset
BS27 3QF, UK
Tel: 01934 742343
Website: www.cheddarcaves.co.uk

Chessington World of Adventures

Chessington World of Adventures is the biggest
theme park and zoo in the South of England. The
park began life as a zoo, but was transformed into
a theme park during the late 1980s, with the first
rollercoaster ride opening in 1991. The park
attracts thousands of visitors each day who come
to enjoy the rides and zoo. The latter, which has
been combined with the park, is home to one of
the biggest families of gorillas in Europe and some
of the world's rarest large cats. The *Trail of the
Kings* animal enclosure allows visitors to see
animals safely from behind viewing screens.

Transportation

Air: London Heathrow Airport, London Gatwick Airport. **Rail:** Train: Chessington South Station. **Road:** Bus: Public services. Car: M25, junction 9 and then the A243 towards central London (from the south); A3 to Hook, then A243 to Chessington (from Central London).

Contact Addresses

Chessington World of Adventures, Chessington, Surrey KT9 2NE, UK
Tel: (0870) 999 0045
Website: www.chessington.com

Drayton Manor Theme Park

Drayton Manor Theme Park is set in 280 acres (113 hectares) of lakes and parkland and offers a fun day out for young and old alike. Thrill seekers will enjoy rides such as *Cyclone*, *Shockwave*, *Pandemonium*, *G-Force* and *Apocalypse* – the world's first stand-up drop tower. There's also a zoo that's home to over 100 species from all over the world including big cats, monkeys, reptiles and an exotic creature reserve. In addition to the theme park and zoo, Drayton Manor also hosts wedding receptions and corporate events in its function rooms.

Transportation

Air: Birmingham International Airport. **Rail:** Tamworth Station. **Road:** Bus: Public services. Car: A4091.

Contact Addresses

Drayton Manor Park, near Tamworth, Staffordshire B78 3TW, UK
Tel: 08708 725252
Website: www.draytonmanor.co.uk

Durham Castle and Cathedral

Durham Castle and *Cathedral*, seated high on a peninsula overlooking the River Wear, have been the first sight to greet visitors to this historic city for hundreds of years and were jointly designated a UNESCO World Heritage Site in 1986. Construction on the castle began in 1072, just after

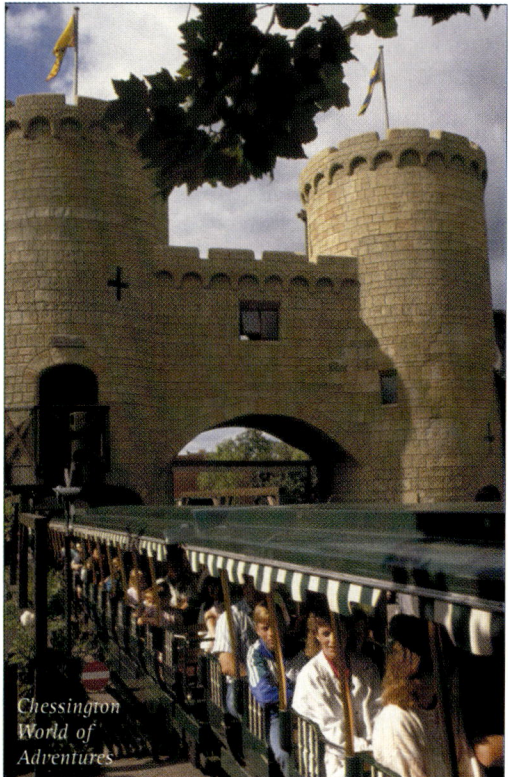

VisitBritain©

Chessington World of Adventures

the Norman Conquest, under the orders of William the Conqueror. From the 11th century onwards it was used as the seat of power of the Prince Bishops appointed by the British Crown to rule the Palatinate of Durham, the remote area of northern England vulnerable to attack from the Scots. In 1837, the last Prince Bishop, Bishop Van Mildert, helped found the *University of Durham* and donated the castle as its first home. It still houses students of *University College*, the oldest of the 14 university colleges, who live in the keep and dine in the wood-panelled Great Hall, containing portraits of the Prince Bishops. Across the lawned area, known as Palace Green, stands the *Cathedral Church of Christ and Blessed Mary the Virgin*, the best example of Norman-style architecture in England.

Transportation

Air: Newcastle Airport. **Rail:** Train: Durham Station. **Road:** Coach: Durham Bus Station. Car: A1 (to Junction 62), then A690 (from London, the Midlands, Scotland or Newcastle). Visitors should avoid driving in the city centre where possible, as the streets are very narrow. The site is a short walk from the bus and train stations.

Contact Addresses

Castle: Durham Castle, Palace Green, Durham DH1
3RW, UK
Tel: (0191) 374 3863
Website: www.durhamcastle.com

Cathedral: The Dean and Chapter of Durham
Cathedral, The Chapter Office, The College,
Durham DH1 3EH, UK
Tel: (0191) 386 4266
Website: www.durhamcathedral.co.uk

Eden Project

Opened in March 2001, the *Eden Project* consists of
two enormous greenhouses built into a 50m- (164ft-)
deep claypit overlooking St Austell Bay in Cornwall.
Through plants, the dome promotes environmental
awareness enabling visitors to understand 'the vital
relationship between plants, people and resources'.
The most impressive of the two giant domes is the
Humid Tropics Biome that's filled with towering plants
from the tropics, including balsa teak and
mahogany, and there is also a Malaysian stilt house
and garden as an example of how one culture uses
its natural resources to survive. The second dome,
the *Warm Temperate Biome*, contains plants from
California, the Mediterranean and South Africa, such
as lemon groves and olive trees. Visitors follow a
path around the biomes, stopping to hear talks and
sketches on the plants and learn about their uses
from interactive displays; for those with a particular
interest, there are themed trails, such as plants and
medicine and plants and sport. Outside, 10 hectares
(25 acres) of landscaped rockeries and gardens
provide the setting for various events, including
puppet shows and storytelling for children; visitors
of all ages can discover more about natural products
through chocolate days, tea-tasting and dyeing
workshops.

Transportation

Air: Exeter International Airport, Southampton
International Airport, Bristol International Airport,
Plymouth City Airport or Newquay Airport.
Rail: Train: St Austell Station. **Road:** Bus: Public
services.

Contact Addresses

Eden Project, Bodelva, St Austell, Cornwall

PL24 2SG, UK
Tel: (01726) 811 911
Website: www.edenproject.com

Flamingo Land Theme Park and Zoo

Flamingo Land in north Yorkshire is one of the
region's biggest theme parks and zoos and
receives over one million visitors each year. The
zoo is home to over 1,000 animals including
White Rhinos, Siberian Tigers, Bactrian Camels,
Humboldt Penguins and meerkats. There is also a
Children's Farm aimed at teaching younger
visitors about the realities of a traditional working
farm. The Theme Park has a wide range of rides
and attractions and a new rollercoaster, Velocity,
opened in July 2005.

Transportation

Air: Leeds Bradford International Airport. **Rail:**
York Railway Station. **Road:** Bus: Publis services.

Contact Addresses

Flamingo Land Holiday Village, Kirby Misperton,
Malton, North Yorkshire YO17 6UX, UK
Tel: 0870 752 8000
Website: www.flamingoland.co.uk

Great Yarmouth Pleasure Beach

Great Yarmouth's *Pleasure Beach* is set along a 3.6
hectare (9 acre) seafront site on the picturesque
East Anglian coastline. The Pleasure Beach is a
traditional seaside resort built around a lively
promenade and is a popular attraction for
families. The Pleasure Beach's attractions include
traditional fairground rides, arcades, flower
gardens, mini golf and candy floss and ice cream
stalls. It may have lost some of its grandeur but it
nevertheless remains one of the most popular
attractions in East Anglia and attracts close to 1.5
million visitors each year.

Transportation

Air: Norwich Airport and Stansted Airport. **Rail:**
Norwich Railway Station with links to Great
Yarmouth Station. **Road:** Bus: Public services.

VisitBritain©

Greenwich Park and the Observatory

Contact Addresses

Great Yarmouth Pleasure Beach, Pleasure and Corporation Plc, South Beach Parade, Great Yarmouth, Norfolk NR30 3EH
Tel: 01493 844 585
Website: www.pleasure-beach.co.uk

Greenwich

The *London Borough of Greenwich*, which is situated on south of the River Thames, is home to a host of attractions, and recognised internationally for its military and naval connections and as the home of Greenwich Mean Time. Famous sites in Greenwich include the *Cutty Sark Clipper Ship* (www.cuttysark.org.uk), built in 1869, *Greenwich Market* (www.greenwich-market.co.uk), and the *Royal Observatory Greenwich*. The latter was designed by the famous architect, Sir Christopher Wren in the 17th century and is home to the *Greenwich Meridian*, the prime meridian of the world, responsible for setting the world clock on zero degrees longitude. The *National Maritime Museum* (www.nmm.ac.uk), the largest maritime museum in the world, and the *Old Royal Naval College*

(www.greenwichfoundation.org.uk), which began life as Greenwich Hospital in 1694 to treat seamen, are also located in Greenwich. The borough has an historic past and was the birthplace of King Henry VIII and Queen Elizabeth I. The area also boasts many open green spaces, including *Greenwich Park* (www.royalparks.gov.uk/parks/greenwich_park), which forms one of eight royal parks in the capital and is the only royal park in East London; it is actually home to the Royal Observatory Greenwich, the National Maritime Museum and the Old Royal Naval College. The *Millennium Dome* (www.millennium-dome.com) is also situated in Greenwich and is visible across London's skyline. Greenwich town centre and park was inscribed as a UNESCO World Heritage Site in 1997, under the name 'Maritime Greenwich'. The whole area boasts a wide selection of restaurants and shops, and is a magnet for shoppers in search of interesting or unusual gifts or souvenirs.

Transportation

Air: London City Airport, London Gatwick Airport, London Heathrow Airport. **Rail:** Train: Greenwich Station or Maze Hill Station. Docklands Light Railway: Cutty Sark Station or Greenwich Station. **Road:** Bus: Public services.

Contact Addresses

Greenwich Tourist Information Centre, Pepys House, 2 Cutty Sark Gardens, Greenwich, London SE10 9LW, UK
Tel: (0870) 608 2000
Website: www.greenwich.gov.uk

Hadrian's Wall

Built by order of the Emperor Hadrian in AD 122, *Hadrian's Wall* is the best known and most important Roman monument in Britain, stretching 117km (73 miles) across the north of England, from Wallsend-on-Tyne to Bowness-on-Solway. The wall was built to mark the northern boundary of the Roman Empire in the British Isles and to keep out the barbarians to the north. After the Empire receded in the fifth century AD, the wall was left to decay, and many of its stones were used in the construction of nearby buildings. Vast sections of the wall still remain and there are many different sites to be visited. *Housesteads Roman Fort and Museum* is an excavated fort located amidst spectacular scenery, and contains the only visible example of a Roman hospital in Britain. *Vindolanda Fort and Museum* is an open-air museum containing reconstructions of the wall, as well as a Roman temple, house and shop. The *Roman Army Museum* at Carvoran provides an insight into the life of a Roman soldier, through models, reconstructions and artefacts. *Chesters Roman Fort and Museum* is an extensively excavated cavalry fort with impressive Roman bathhouse remains.

Transportation

Air: London City Airport, London Gatwick Airport, London Heathrow Airport. **Rail:** Train: Greenwich Station or Maze Hill Station. Docklands Light Railway: Cutty Sark Station or Greenwich Station. **Road:** Bus: Public services.

Contact Addresses

Hadrian's Wall Tourism Partnership, 14b Gilesgate, Hexham, Northumberland NE46 3NJ, UK
Tel: (01434) 602 505 *or* 322 002
Website: www.hadrians-wall.org

Hampton Court Palace

Built by Cardinal Wolsey in the early 16th century and later owned by King Henry VIII (1491-1547), *Hampton Court Palace* occupies a beautiful riverside site 23km (14 miles) southwest of London. The palace was once the centre of royal and political life in England, with many famous monarchs residing there between 1525 and 1737, including King Henry VIII, King William III and Queen Mary during the 17th century, and King George II and Queen Caroline in the 18th century. The palace has been associated with many important events in history: King Henry VIII spent his honeymoon in the palace with Anne Boleyn in 1533 and married his sixth wife Catherine Parr there in 1543, whilst King Charles I was held prisoner in the palace in 1647 by Oliver Cromwell, who came to live there in 1653. The palace was opened to the public in 1838 by Queen Victoria and today, visitors can still see much of the grandeur of this impressive Tudor palace. In the *Palace Gardens*, visitors can happily lose their way in the famous maze which was planted in the North Gardens in 1702.

Transportation

Air: London Heathrow Airport. **Water:** Boat: Services run along the River Thames in the summer (from Westminster, Richmond-upon-Thames and Kingston-upon-Thames). **Rail:** Train: Hampton Court Station. Underground: Wimbledon or Vauxhall, then overland train services to Hampton Court Station. **Road:** Bus: Public services.

Contact Addresses

Hampton Court Palace, Surrey KT8 9AU, UK
Tel: (020) 8781 9500
Website: www.hrp.org.uk

Harrods

Harrods, perhaps London's most famous department store, is named after Charles Henry Harrod, who opened a family grocers shop on the site in 1849. The shop has grown to become a byword for expensive and glamourous shopping,

Corel©

Hampton Court Palace

priding itself on its motto *Omnia Omnibus Ubique*, meaning 'All things, for all people, everywhere'. Bought by Egyptian businessman Mohamed Al Fayed in 1985, the eye-catching seven-storey building, which is illuminated by 11,500 lightbulbs each night, contains over 300 departments selling luxury items, from furniture and ladies fashion to polo mallets and wax coats for dogs. For those on a tighter budget, there is a Harrods gift shop, selling assorted souvenirs such as pencils and teddybears. One department not to be missed is the world-famous *Food Halls*. Harrods also provides banking and real estate services, currency exchange facilities and, for those who want to see the British capital in style, a luxury coach tour of London complete with tea and biscuits.

Transportation
Air: London Heathrow Airport, London Gatwick Airport, London Stansted Airport, London Luton Airport. **Rail:** Train: London's Victoria, Euston, Kings Cross, Liverpool Street or Waterloo Stations. Underground: Knightsbridge (Piccadilly Line). **Road:** Bus: Public services.

Contact Addresses
Harrods Ltd, 87-135 Brompton Road, Knightbridge, London SW1X 7XL, UK
Tel: (020) 7730 1234
Website: www.harrods.com

Lake Windermere

At 17kms (10.5 miles) long and plunging to 61m (200ft) deep in places, *Lake Windermere* is the largest lake in England. It forms part of the *Lake District National Park* and is in an area of outstanding natural beauty with numerous stunning walking trails. Many visitors prefer to explore the lake from the water itself and *Windermere Lake Cruises* (www.windermere-lakecruises.co.uk) operate an extensive network of steamers and launches; a popular trip is the Islands Cruise from Bowness, which passes wooded islands and secluded bays. Other attractions in the area include the *Aquarium of the Lakes*, the *Beatrix Potter Attraction*, the *Lakeside and Haverthwaite Railway*, *Fell Foot Park* and the *South Lakes Wild Animal Park*.

Legoland Windsor

VisitBritain©

Transportation
Air: Manchester Airport, Blackpool Airport and Newcastle Airport. **Rail:** Oxenholme Station (then bus or taxi). **Road:** Bus: Public services. Car: A591.

Contact Addresses
Windermere Tourist Information Centre, Victoria Street, Windermere, UK
Tel: 015394 46499
Website: www.golakes.co.uk

Leeds Castle

Leeds Castle in Kent is built on two islands in a lake. It was originally built as a royal manor in AD 857, but from 1278 onwards was used as a royal palace by King Edward I. Over the centuries, the castle has been home to six Medieval Queens of England. It was also home to Henry VIII and is full of many fine arts, furnishings and tapestries from its illustrious past. The castle was sold to Lady Baillie in 1926 who transformed the interior, filling it with fine furniture, tapestries and paintings. The castle is also famous for its *Aviary*, which is home to many birds including black swans and was built as a memorial to Lady Baillie, opening in 1988. The castle's grounds are also spectacular and include the *Maze*, *Wood Garden*, *Vineyard* and *Culpeper Garden*.

Transportation
Air: London Heathrow Airport, London Gatwick Airport. **Rail:** Train: Bearsted Station (from London Victoria Station) and then connect with a coach service. **Road:** Coach: Public services.

Contact Addresses
Leeds Castle Enterprises Limited, Leeds Castle, Leeds, Maidstone, Kent ME17 1PL, UK
Tel: (01622) 765 400
Website: www.leeds-castle.com

Legoland Windsor

Following on from the success of the original *LEGOLAND* park in Billund, Denmark, *LEGOLAND Windsor* welcomed its first visitors in 1996 and since then has become one of England's most popular theme parks. The park is split into nine different areas, each with its own theme. *Miniland* was the Danish counterpart's founding feature and remains one of the biggest attractions for visitors of all ages, consisting of miniature models of European towns and cities, all created from a total of 35 million LEGO bricks. There are attractions for old and young alike and children can create their own inventions from the thousands of bricks in the *Imagination Centre* workshops, and visitors as young as three can learn to drive around a special LEGO driving track, complete with traffic lights. There are shows every day, including the spectacular live action stunt show at *The Harbour* which is packed with stunning special effects, thrilling gymnastics and hilarious comic routines.

Transportation
Air: London Heathrow Airport, London Gatwick Airport, London Stansted Airport, London Luton Airport. **Rail:** Train: Windsor, Eton Central Station and Eton Riverside Station. **Road:** Bus: Public services.

Contact Addresses
LEGOLAND Windsor, Winkfield Road, Windsor, Berkshire SL4 4AY, UK
Tel: (08705) 040 404
Website: www.lego.com/legoland/windsor

London Dungeon

This horror theme park situated on London's *South Bank* gives visitors the opportunity to explore the darker side of British and European history. The *London Dungeon*, which opened in 1975, is a creepy recreation of many of history's most gruesome events. Visitors can go on various themed rides, which are based around historical murders and executions; they can explore the streets of Victorian London that were home to the serial killer Jack the Ripper, relive the Great Fire of London and take a barge down the *River Thames* to *Traitors Gate*, where they are sentenced to death by an 18th-century judge. The London Dungeons are patrolled by scary characters, dressed in gruesome costumes, who wait in dark corners and jump out at unsuspecting tourists.

Transportation
Air: London Heathrow Airport, London Gatwick Airport. **Rail:** Train: London Bridge Station. Underground: London Bridge or Monument/Bank. **Road:** Bus: Public services.

Contact Addresses
London Dungeon, 28-34 Tooley Street, London SE1 2SZ, UK
Tel: (0870) 846 0666 *or* (020) 7403 7221
Website: www.thedungeons.com

London Zoo

London Zoo, which opened in 1828, is situated on the north side of Regent's Park. The zoo was the site of the world's first children's zoo, which opened in 1838, followed by the first reptile house in 1849, the first public aquarium in 1853 and the first insect house in 1881. Today, the Zoo is home to around 12,000 animals, including Asian lions, Sumatran tigers, Sloth bears, Leadbeater's possums and Death adders. The famous spiral-shaped *Penguin Pool*, which is Grade I listed, is the home of Black-footed penguins, whilst the *Aquarium* houses sharks, piranhas and other sea creatures. The zoo also has beautiful gardens, as well as innovative zoo buildings, designed by architects such as Decimus Burton who designed the *Giraffe House*, Berthold Lubetkin who was responsible for the Penguin Pool and Sir Hugh Casson, responsible for the *Elephant and Rhino Pavilion*.

Transportation
Air: London Heathrow Airport, London Luton Airport. **Rail:** Train: London Euston or London Kings Cross stations. Underground: Camden Town or Regent's Park. **Road:** Bus: Public services.

Contact Addresses
London Zoo, Outer Circle, Regent's Park, London NW1 4RY, UK
Tel: (020) 7722 3333
Website: www.zsl.org/london-zoo/

Longleat

Set in over 3,520 hectares (8,700 acres) of landscaped parkland, woodlands, lakes and farmland, *Longleat* stately home first opened its doors as a safari park nearly 40 years ago. Home to the 7th Marquess of Bath, *Longleat House* dates back to 1580 and is regarded as one of Britain's most beautiful stately homes and a fine example of high Elizabethan architecture. In 1966, Longleat opened the first *Safari Park* outside Africa and provided the concept for many of Britain's successful safari parks that exist today. Visitors to the park drive through a series of separate enclosures including the *East Africa Reserve*, *Monkey Jungle*, *Big Game Park*, *Deer Park*, *Pelican Pond*, *Tiger Territory*, *Lion Country* and *Wolf Wood*. The *Safari Boat* takes visitors on a leisurely cruise to see the *Gorilla Park* and *Hippo Pools*. Attractions specifically for children include an *Adventure Castle* with turrets and rope bridges, the *Blue Peter Maze* and a *Postman Pat Village*. Set amidst beautiful gardens, the *Orangery* is licensed to conduct civil wedding ceremonies. *Longleat House* also hosts corporate functions and wedding receptions.

Transportation
Air: Bristol Airport. **Rail:** Warminster Station or Westbury Station and then taxi to Longleat.

Contact Addresses
The Estate Office, Longleat, Warminster, Wiltshire BA12 7NW, UK
Tel: (01985) 844400
Website: www.longleat.co.uk

Madame Tussaud's and Tussaud's London Planetarium

Over 400 lifesize wax models of the rich and famous are exhibited in *Madame Tussauds*. Lifesize replicas of stars of the stage and screen, musicians and monarchs are displayed alongside footballers and politicians. Madame Tussaud was born in Strasbourg in 1761 and after inheriting a wax museum from Philippe Curtius in 1794, moved to London to set up an exhibition on London's Baker Street. Following her death in 1850, her grandsons moved the display to its present location on Marylebone Road. Today, visitors can have their photo taken with the likes of filmstar Marilyn Monroe, Australian popstar Kylie Minogue, footballer David Beckham and even members of the British Royal Family. They can also descend into the *Chamber of Horrors* to see some of history's most notorious criminals and various torture instruments. *Tussaud's London Planetarium*, which is adjacent to Madame Tussaud's and opened in 1958, enables budding astronomers to see the stars and is one of the largest planetariums in the world.

Transportation
Air: London Heathrow Airport. **Rail:** Underground: Baker Street. **Road:** Bus: Public services.

Contact Addresses
Madame Tussaud's and Tussaud's London Planetarium, Marylebone Road, London NW1 5LR, UK
Tel: (0870) 999 0046
Website: www.madame-tussauds.com *or* www.london-planetarium.com

Matlock Bath

Matlock Bath in the heart of Derbyshire has been attracting tourists since the turn of the 18th century when the wealthy aristocrats of the day would travel to bathe in the warm springs and enjoy its fine climate. A railway line established in the 1840s opened up the area to ordinary tourists and Matlock Bath lost some of its upper-class haughtiness. And nowadays, situated on the A6 that runs through the *Peak District National Park*, visitors still flock here in their thousands each year and is a popular stop-off for cyclists and bikers who come to enjoy the dramatic scenery and wide open spaces. However, Matlock Bath still holds on to some of its gentile charm and there are a number of fine buildings dating back to the 18th century that sit alongside modern day souvenir shops and arcades. Matlock Bath lies at the bottom of *High Tor*, a 137m (450ft) limestone cliff that rises from the *River Derwent*'s eastern bank and is popular with climbers. There are plenty of walking tracks in the area or there's a cable car that takes visitors up to an area known as the *Heights of Abraham* where the *Whistlestop Countryside Centre* is also located. Visitors can also access two old mining caverns, the *Grand Masson Cavern* and the *Great Rutland Cavern*. Other attractions in Matlock Bath include the *Peak District Mining Museum* which tells the story of lead mining in the area that dates back to Roman times. Close by is *Gulliver's* amusement park, a popular day trip for families.

Transportation
Air: Birmingham International Airport and East Midlands Airport. **Rail:** Matlock Bath train station. **Road:** Bus: Public services. Car: A6.

Contact Addresses
Matlock Bath Tourist Information Centre, Pavilion, Matlock Bath, Derbyshire DE4 3NR, UK
Tel: 01629 55082
Website: www.derbyshireuk.net

National Gallery

With its Classical façade gracing the northern side of London's Trafalgar Square, the UK's *National Gallery* possesses one of the world's greatest collections of Western paintings. On display are around 2300 pictures covering every European school of painting from the 13th to the 19th century. Paintings by English masters include Constable's 'The Haywain' and Gainsborough's 'The Watering Place'. There are regular exhibitions at the National Gallery, ranging from displays of schoolchildren's artwork inspired by Hogarth's painting 'The Graham Children', to an exhibition of 19th-century German painting.

Transportation
Air: London Heathrow Airport, London Gatwick Airport, London Stansted Airport or London Luton Airport. **Rail:** Train: London Charing Cross Station.

Underground: Charing Cross, Leicester Square, Embankment or Piccadilly Circus. Road: Bus: Public services.

Contact Addresses
National Gallery, Trafalgar Square, London WC2N 5DN, UK
Tel: (020) 7747 2885
Website: www.nationalgallery.org.uk

National Museum of Photography, Film and Television

Founded in 1983 as part of the *National Museum of Science and Industry*, the decision to locate the *National Museum of Photography*, *Film and Television* outside the capital was based on Bradford's contribution to the development of UK cinema and the city's accessible location. This is an interactive museum and visitors have the opportunity to discover the media world through a variety of hands-on experiences, including reading the news to camera, discovering the workings of a television camera and creating their own animations. The museum reflects ever changing developments within the industry, and contains a gallery devoted to digital media, as well as Europe's first *IMAX* cinema showing 3-D films and two cinemas showing new releases.

Transportation
Air: Leeds/Bradford International Airport or Manchester Airport. **Rail:** Train: Bradford Forster Square Station or Bradford Interchange Station. **Road:** Bus: Public services.

Contact Addresses
National Museum of Photography, Film and Television, Bradford, West Yorkshire BD1 1NQ, UK
Tel: 0870 7010200
Website: www.nmpft.org.uk

Natural History Museum

The *Natural History Museum* in South Kensington began its life as the natural history section of the British Museum, featuring the collections of

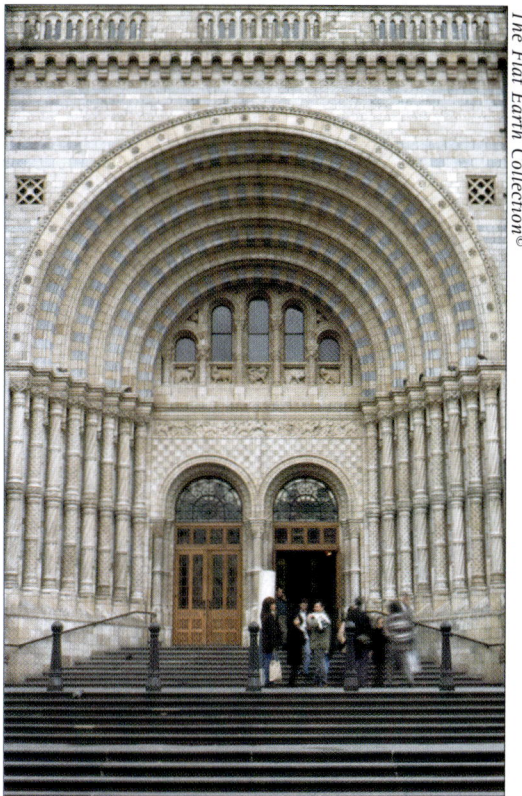

The Flat Earth Collection©

Victorian Doorway to Natural History Museum London

London physician and collector Sir Hans Sloane, who wished his collection to remain together to benefit as many people as possible after his death. Following a competition to choose the architect of the new building, Captain Robert Fowke drew up the original designs, seeing the museum as a cathedral of science, hence its church-like appearance. When he died in 1865, his work was continued by Alfred Waterhouse, who was responsible for the elaborate Romanesque carvings of animals and plants throughout the building. The Natural History Museum moved into its new home in 1883, since which time it has considerably increased the size of its collections, perhaps most famously to include the dinosaur gallery, where visitors can see huge dinosaur skeletons and even an animated T-Rex. The *Earth Galleries* explore the effects human life has on the planet around us and how scientists harness the resources we use in our everyday lives, as well as featuring displays of minerals and gemstones and an earthquake simulator. The *Life Galleries* allow visitors to explore human biology, Darwin's theory

The Gateshead Tyne and Wear MetroCentre shopping complex

VisitBritain©

of natural selection and to see an enormous life-size model of a blue whale. There are also regular exhibitions, and outside the building, the wildlife garden provides an opportunity to discover British wildlife in the heart of London.

Transportation
Air: London Heathrow Airport, London Gatwick Airport, London Stansted Airport, London Luton Airport. **Rail:** Train: London Paddington Station, London Victoria Station or London Waterloo Station. Underground: South Kensington.

Contact Addresses
Natural History Museum, Cromwell Road, London SW7 5BD, UK
Tel: (020) 7942 5000 (Mon-Fri only) *or* 7942 5011 (Sat-Sun)
Website: www.nhm.ac.uk

Neasden Temple

The exotic sight of the Neasden *Shri Swaminarayan Temple* sits alongside suburban houses in Neasden in northwest London. The limestone Hindu temple was inspired by Lord Swaminarayan, an 18th century Indian guru who walked barefoot across the length of India raising awareness about the plight of the country's poor and downtrodden

people. It was built using an estimated 2,000 tons of Italian marble and 3,000 tonnes of Bulgarian limestone which had first been shipped to India where 1,000 local craftsmen volunteered their skills to sculpt the elaborate structure that now stands in West London.

Transportation
Air: Gatwick Airport, Heathrow Airport and London City Airport. **Rail:** Neasden Station. **Road:** Bus: Public services. Car: B453.

Contact Addresses
105 Brentfield Road, Neasden, London NW10 8JP, UK
Tel: (020) 8965 2651

New Metroland

The *New MetroLand* is part of the Gateshead Tyne and Wear *MetroCentre* shopping complex and is Europe's largest indoor funfair, with 12 major attractions on the site. MetroLand first opened its doors to the public in 1988 and has gone on to become one of the region's most popular paying attractions with over 800,000 visitors each year. MetroLand was conceived as a marketing tool that would attract more visitors to the MetroCentre shopping complex and the strategy has been a resounding success; the MetroCentre receives close to 20 million visitors each year. As part of the MetroCentre, visitors are free to walk around the MetroLand complex and rides are paid for on an individual basis or with a wristband giving access to all the rides and attractions. Those travelleing to Tyneside will be greeted by the open arms of Antony Gormley's iconic sculpture, the *Angel of the North*. Situated high on a hill top along the A1, the sculpture towers 20m (65 ft) into the sky and is seen by over 90,000 drivers each day as well as by all rail passengers arriving in the region. Erected in 1998, the Angel of the North has become the quintessential symbol of the region and is now said to be more recognisable than the *Tyne Bridge*.

Transportation
Air: Newcastle International Airport. **Rail:** Metroland has its own station, Newcastle Metro. **Road:** Bus: Public services. Car: Well signposted and large car parks.

Contact Addresses
The New MetroLand, 39 Garden Walk, MetroCentre, Gateshead, NE11 9XY, UK
Tel: (0191) 493 2048
Website: www.metroland.uk.com

Oxford University

As a centre of education dating back to the early 12th century, *Oxford University* ranks as the oldest university in England and one of the most famous in the world. Its extensive list of important past students includes John Locke, Christopher Wren, Lewis Carroll, Jonathan Swift, Oscar Wilde and, more recently, Tony Blair and Bill Clinton. The university itself is made up of a number of colleges, most displaying stunning architecture and trim lawns, situated throughout the city. Of particular interest to visitors are *Christ Church College*, founded in 1524 by Cardinal Wolsey, whose college chapel also serves as Oxford's cathedral; *Merton College*, one of the smaller colleges with only 250 undergraduates and with particularly beautiful gardens and courtyards; and the *Bodleian Library*, the central library of Oxford University, which is the oldest library in Europe and was originally founded in 1320 by Thomas Cobham, Bishop of Worcester.

Transportation
Air: London's Heathrow, Gatwick, Stansted and Luton Airports. **Rail:** Train: Oxford City Station. **Road:** Bus: Public services.

Contact Addresses
Oxford Tourist Information Centre, 15/16 Broad Street, Oxford OX1 3AS, UK
Tel: (01865) 726 871
Website: www.oxford.gov.uk/tourism

Poole Harbour

Poole Harbour is a vibrant quay on England's southern coast that bustles with an array of bars, cafes and restaurants. Visitors wanting to learn more about the history of the region can follow the newly developed *Cockle Trail* discovering myths and legends about Poole's smugglers and ghosts of yesteryear. A series of brass plaques mark the way charting 750 years of Poole's history culminating at the *Waterfront Museum*. Popular sports in and around the harbour include windsurfing, kitesurfing, water-skiing, wakeboarding, surfing, snorkelling and kayaking. Of course, boat trips are popular and visitors can sail out to the National Trust's *Brownsea Island*, protected for its wildlife and peaceful woodland walks. Away from the harbour, nearby *Poole Pottery* (www.poolepottery.co.uk) produces one-off handmade pottery and is famed for its traditional craft that stretches back 130 years. In 2005, it opened its doors for a week for the first time enabling visitors to tour the factory to see how the prize-winning pieces are made.

Transportation
Air: Bournemouth International Airport. **Water:** Ferry: Daily crossings to France and summer sailings to the Channel Islands. **Rail:** Poole Station. **Road:** Bus: Public services.

Contact Addresses
Poole Tourism, Enefco House, Poole Quay, Poole, Dorset BH15 1HJ, UK
Tel: (01202) 253253
Website: www.pooletourism.com

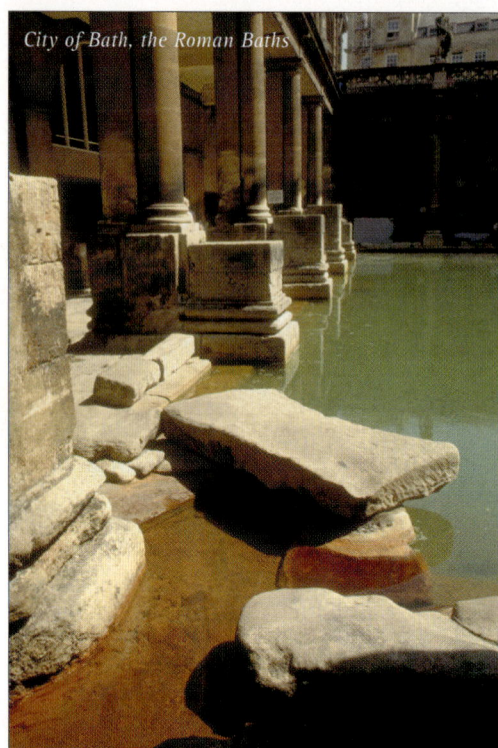

City of Bath, the Roman Baths

VisitBritain©

Portsmouth Historic Dockyard

Portsmouth Historic Dockyard is home to three famous ships: the *Mary Rose, HMS Victory* and *HMS Warrior 1860*. The Mary Rose, which was Henry VIII's favourite warship, sank in 1545, but was raised from the sea in 1982. Today, visitors can enter the *Mary Rose Museum* and *Ship Hall*, where more than 1000 artefacts are on display. They can also see *HMS Victory*, which is the world's oldest commissioned warship, used by Nelson in the Battle of Trafalgar (1805) to defeat the Franco-Spanish fleet. Also on display is the *HMS Warrior 1860*, the world's first iron battleship, one of the largest and fastest warships at the time. The *Royal Naval Museum* is closeby and houses an interactive *Dockyard Apprentice Exhibition*. In 2005 *Flagship Portsmouth* opened a special Trafalgar exhibition commerating the 200th anniversary of the famous battle.

Transportation
Air: Southampton International Airport. **Rail:** Train: Portsmouth Harbour Station. **Road:** Bus: Public services.

Contact Addresses
Flagship Portsmouth Trust, Building 1/7, Porter's Lodge, College Road, HM Naval Base, Portsmouth, PO1 3LJ, UK
Tel: (023) 9286 1512 (24-hour information line) *or* 9286 1533
Website: www.flagship.org.uk

Roman Baths and Pump Room

The ancient Romans were the first to capitalise on the only natural hot spring in Britain, building a temple and bathing complex more than 2000 years ago in the city of Bath. The healing spring, which is located within the bathing complex, produces approximately 2,273,050 litres (500,000 gallons) of water per day at a temperature of 46.5°C (116°F). The baths were once one of the finest in the Roman world, although the Roman structure gradually fell into disrepair. It was not until a visit by the ailing Prince George in 1702 that the baths once again became a popular healing destination. Over the course of the town's redevelopment, the Roman ruins were rediscovered (in 1879) and restored. Visitors can now view the Georgian grandeur of the Pump House and see the remains of the ancient Roman baths and temple.

Transportation
Air: London Heathrow Airport, Bristol International Airport. **Rail:** Train: Bath Spa Station. **Road:** Bus: Public services.

Contact Addresses
Roman Baths and Pumproom, Museum Enquiries, Stall Street, Bath BA1 1LZ, UK
Tel: (01225) 477 785
Website: www.romanbaths.co.uk

Royal Academy of Arts

Located in the historic *Piccadilly* area in the heart of London, the *Royal Academy of Arts* is an independent fine arts institution which supports contemporary artists and promotes interest in the arts through a comprehensive exhibition programme. The Academy is completely independent and as such is a self-funded organisation which is governed by the Royal Academicians – eminent practising painters, printmakers, sculptors and architects who are elected to the position. The Academy has a long history and was founded in 1768 with Sir Joshua Reynolds as its first President. The Academy is located in Burlington House which itself has a long a colourful history with parts of the original structure estimated as dating back to 1664. Today, the Academy attracts well over one million visitors each year making it one of London's top 10 attractions for paying visitors.

Transportation
Air: London's City Airport, Gatwick Airport, Heathrow Airport, Luton Airport and Stansted Airport. **Rail:** Underground: Piccadilly and Green Park or a short walk from Oxford Circus and Bond Street. **Road:** Bus: Public services.

Contact Addresses
Royal Academy of Arts, Burlington House, Piccadilly, London W1J 0BD, UK
Telephone (020) 7300 8000
Website: www.royalacademy.org.uk

Royal Armouries Leeds

The *Royal Armouries* is Britain's national collection of arms and armour, and was moved from its former home in the Tower of London to a specially-created building in Leeds in 1996. Visitors can enter five galleries, each with its own theme covering self-defence, war, armour of the Orient, hunting and tournament. There is a wealth of different objects on display, including over 7500 swords, King Henry VIII's equestrian equipment, several longbows excavated from the sunken British battleship the *Mary Rose*, 50 instruments of torture, and arms and armour from as far afield as central Asia, India, Africa and Japan. The Armouries also hold a variety of events and exhibitions, many of them aimed at children including the popular Easter-egg trails and Hallowe'en stories.

Transportation
Air: Leeds/Bradford International Airport. **Rail:** Train: Leeds Station. **Road:** Coach: Leeds Bus Station.

Contact Addresses
Royal Armouries Museum, Armouries Drive, Leeds LS10 1LT, UK
Tel: 08700 344344 (24-hour information line) or (0113) 220 1916
Website: www.armouries.org.uk/leeds

Royal Botanic Gardens, Kew

Kew Gardens comprise 132 hectares (326 acres) of herbaceous bedding, water features, botanical glasshouses, a large arboretum and historic buildings located on the banks of the River Thames in southwest London. Founded in 1759, this vast oasis on the outskirts of the metropolis has become a favourite with visitors wishing to escape the pressures of the city, and has been extensively developed. Its attractions include an aquatic garden, a bamboo garden, a woodland glade, a conservation area and a Japanese landscape. There are several glasshouses to explore, one of which, *Evolution House*, showcases 3500 million years of plant evolution. *Queen Charlotte's Cottage*, located within the grounds of *Richmond Lodge*, was a wedding gift to Queen Charlotte in 1861 and was also used by Queen Victoria until she presented it to the public upon her Diamond Jubilee in 1897; the building has now been restored to its original state. Visitors to Kew can either join in a guided tour, follow one of several themed trails, or wander around the attractions at their own pace.

Transportation
Air: London Heathrow Airport, London Gatwick Airport, London Stansted Airport, London Luton Airport. **Rail:** Train: Kew Gardens Station (from north and south London); Kew Bridge Station (from London Waterloo Station). Underground: Kew Gardens (District Line). **Road:** Bus: Public services.

Contact Addresses
Royal Botanic Gardens, Kew, Richmond, Surrey TW9 3AB, UK
Tel: (020) 8332 5000 *or* 8332 5655 (24-hour recorded information line)
Website: www.rbgkew.org.uk

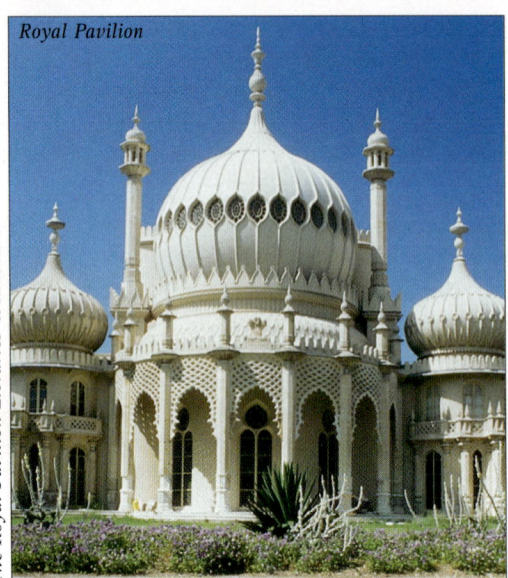

The Royal Pavilion Libraries & Museum©

Royal Pavilion

Royal Pavilion

The *Royal Pavilion*, which is the former seaside home of King George IV, is one of the most exotic-looking buildings in the UK. It was originally a farmhouse, but was transformed into a neo-classical villa in 1787 by the architect Henry Holland. The building was further re-modelled by John Nash in 1820 in the style of an Indian palace. It was also used by George IV's brother, William IV and his niece Queen Victoria, but was sold to the town of Brighton by Victoria in 1850. Today, the exterior of this Regency building still has many domes and minarets, whilst the interior features a huge banqueting room with an impressive chandelier as its centrepiece, as well as a music room with lanterns hanging from a high-domed ceiling. The palace is ornately decorated with an array of Chinese and English furnishing and is set in lavish surrounding gardens.

Transportation
Air: London Gatwick Airport. **Rail:** Train: Brighton Station. **Road:** Bus: Public services.

Contact Addresses
Royal Pavilion, Pavilion Buildings, Brighton BN1 1EE, UK
Tel: (01273) 292 822
Website: www.royalpavilion.org.uk

Salford Quays

Salford Quays is a joint tourism initiative between Salford City Council and Trafford Borough Council and is supported by *The Lowry*, *Imperial War Museum North*, *Manchester United Football Club*, *Lancashire County Cricket Club*, the *Lowry Outlet Mall* and the *Copthorne Hotel* which are private sector partners in the area. The Lowry is one of Manchester's most renowned centres for arts and performance and is the architectural flagship of the redeveloped Salford Quays waterside location. Incorporating two theatres, a range of galleries, as well as restaurants, bars and cafés, the Lowry's eyecatching architecture won it the 2001 building of the year award. The building takes its name from the celebrated painter LS Lowry (who died in 1976) and houses a permanent Lowry exhibition alongside displays of more contemporary artists. In line with regeneration projects throughout the city, Salford Quays has been built around the regenerated docklands and today is a vibrant hub of the city's arts, leisure and sports scenes.

Transportation
Air: Manchester Airport. **Rail:** Services to Manchester Piccadilly or Victoria train stations then services on from there. Tram: Regualar tram services to the Quays. **Water:** During the summer, ferries run between the Quays down the Mersey to Liverpool. **Road:** Bus: Public services and park and ride service from the city.

Contact Addresses
Salford Tourist Information Centre, The Lowry, Pier 8, Salford Quays M50 3AZ, UK
Tel: (0161) 848 8601 or 0870 420 4145
Website: www.thequays.org.uk

Sandringham Estate

Set within beautiful grounds, *Sandringham* was built in 1870 by the Prince and Princess of Wales who later became King Edward VII and Queen Alexandra. Passed down through four generations of British Monarchs, the estate is now the country residence of the Queen and the Duke of Edinburgh. Over the years the estate has acquired many objets d'art and each room is lavishly decorated with fine furniture and paintings. The *Estate Museum* was created by King George V as early as 1928 and visitors can see, amongst other things, the fine collection of Royal Vehicles and Carriages. Visitors are able to enjoy 243 hectares (600 acres) of *Country Park* that lies within the *Norfolk Coast Area of Outstanding Natural Beauty*. Also on the estate are a working sawmill and fruit farm. There's a *Visitor Centre* set within the Country Park with a restaurant, shop and further information about the history of the estate.

Transportation
Air: Norwich Airport and Stansted Airport. **Rail:** Kings Lynn Station. **Road:** Bus: Public services. Car: A148.

Contact Addresses
Estate Office, Sandringham, Norfolk PE35 6EN, UK
Tel: (01553) 772675
Website: www.sandringhamestate.co.uk

Science Museum

Together with the *National Railway Museum* and the *National Museum of Photography, Film & Television*, the *Science Museum* is part of the *National Museum of Science & Industry*. Located in central London, the museum owns an impressive collection of science exhibits, including the Apollo 10 Command Module, the V-2 rocket, which was the world's first long-range missile, and Stephensons' Rocket locomotive. The Science Museum, which originally opened along with the *Victoria and Albert Museum* in 1857 as the *South Kensington Museum*, now houses one of the largest collections of scientific, medical, industrial and technological exhibits in the world. There are numerous interactive displays and permanent exhibitions. Entry to the museum is free but there are charges for some exhibitions.

Transportation
Air: London Heathrow Airport. **Rail:** Train: London Victoria Station. Underground: South Kensington. **Road:** Bus: Public services.

Contact Addresses
Science Museum, Exhibition Road, South Kensington, London SW7 2DD, UK
Tel: (0870) 870 4771
Website: www.sciencemuseum.org.uk

Shakespeare Houses

William Shakespeare, considered by many to be the greatest dramatist and poet the world has ever known, was born in the market town of Stratford-upon-Avon in 1564 and maintained strong links with the town until his death in 1616. His legacy has turned Stratford into a major tourist destination crammed with historic houses relating to the writer's life and that of his family. *Shakespeare's Birthplace* is a half-timbered house in the centre of Stratford, which remained the property of his descendants until 1806, when it was bought by a board of trustees and restored as a museum. The adjacent *Shakespeare's World Museum* guides visitors through the life and times of Shakespeare using drawings, maps, illustrations and audiovisual displays. In 1582, Shakespeare married Anne Hathaway, the daughter of a local farmer, and *Anne Hathaway's Cottage*, is closeby in the hamlet of Shottery, 1.6km (1 mile) from Stratford-upon-Avon. Shakespeare returned from London in 1597 as a successful playwright and bought *New Place*, the second largest house in the town, where he spent the last years of his life. Visitors can also tour the home of Shakespeare's mother, *Mary Arden's House* at *Glebe Farm*, which was fortunately rescued from demolition by the Shakespeare Trust in 1960.

Transportation
Air: Birmingham International Airport. **Rail:** Train: Stratford-upon-Avon Station. **Road:** Bus: Public services.

Contact Addresses
The Shakespeare Centre, Henley Street, Stratford-upon-Avon CV37 6QW, UK
Tel: (01789) 204 016
Website: www.shakespeare.org.uk

Somerset House

Established in 1997 in the heart of London, the *Somerset House Trust* was set up to conserve and develop *Somerset House* and the surrounding areas for public use. The stunning 18th century building has now been renovated and houses celebrated art collections in three exhibition areas: the *Courtauld Institute of Art*, the *Gilbert Collection* and the

Hermitage Rooms. Outside, the redeveloped *Courtyard* is the venue for a summer schedule of concerts and events; during the Christmas and New Year period, the Courtyard is transformed into a popular ice skating rink that provides a welcome distraction for Christmas shoppers. When not holding events, the Courtyard's acclaimed *Safra Fountain Court* bursts into life with daily displays during the summer months.

Transportation
Air: Heathrow Airport, Gatwick Airport and London City Airport. **Rail:** Charing Cross, Waterloo and Blackfriars. Underground: Temple, Covent Garden, Charing Cross and Embankment. **Road:** Bus: Public services.

Contact Addresses
Somerset House Trust, Somerset House, Strand, London WC2R 1LA, UK
Tel: (020) 7845 4600
Website: www.someset-house.org.uk

Southwold

Situated on the north Suffolk coastline, *Southwold* is a traditional seaside town that forms part of the Suffolk Heritage Coast. With its brightly painted beach huts, working lighthouse, harbour and bustling fish markets, Southwold is a quintessential English resort town of yesteryear with none of the razzmatazz of a pleasure beach. Walking south along the pier towards the harbour, visitors can watch sailors navigate their vessels up and down the River Blythe where it joins with the North Sea. A fire destroyed much of the old town in 1659, but some notable buildings survived and are still standing today; St Edmund's Church, which dates back to the 15th century, is well worth a visit. With just one road leading in and out, Southwold retains much of its old charm. However, the area is becoming increasingly popular with visitors and can get quite crowded at weekends during the summer. Nevertheless, its stunning scenery, coastal walks and excellent fish and chip restaurants make Southwold a great place to visit at any time of the year.

Transportation
Air: Norwich Airport or London Stansted Airport. **Rail:** Lowestoft Station then bus or taxi to Southwold. **Road:** Bus: Public services.

Contact Addresses
Tourist Information Centre, 69 High Street, Southwold, Suffolk IP18 6DS, UK
Tel: (01502) 724 729
Website: www.visit-suffolk.org.uk

St Michael's Mount

Perched proudly on a rocky island, *St Michael's Mount* rises 70m (230 ft) from sea level and is one of Cornwall's best-known attractions that dates back to the 12th century. According to legend, it was built by a giant called Cormoran who terrorised local farmers by wading ashore and raiding their flocks for food. A bounty was placed on his head and a local boy named Jack devised a plan to kill the giant. Jack made his way to the island in the dead of night and dug a deep pit, then, waking the giant from his slumber with a blast on his horn, the giant hastily gave chase falling into the pit. Jack became known as Jack the Giant Killer and was the toast of the town. But history tells us that the Abbot of Mont St Michel in Normandy, Bernard of Le Bec, built the Benedictine Priory of St Michael's Mount in 1135 as a dependency of the Norman Abbey. By the early 15th century, Henry V had declared war on France and in 1424 seized St Michael's Mount for the crown. Over the years, the Mount has been a priory, a fort, a site of pilgrimage and eventually became a private residence of the St Aubyn family 1659. In 1954, the St Aubyn's went into partnership with the National Trust opening up the castle and grounds to the public. At low tide it's possible to walk out across the causeway to St Michael's Mount (it's important to check local tide times (tel: 01736 710265 (for tide information only))). During the summer, a ferry service carries people to and from the Mount at high tide.

Transportation
Air: Newquay Airport, Exeter Airport and Plymouth Airport (domestic services). **Rail:** Penzance Station. **Road:** Bus: Public services.

Contact Addresses
St Michael's Mount, Manor Office, Marazion, Cornwall TR17 0EF, UK
Tel: (01736) 710507
Website: www.stmichaelsmount.co.uk

Stonehenge

Corel©

St Paul's Cathedral

Built in 1673, *St Paul's Cathedral* is Sir Christopher Wren's most famous work. Its dome, one of the largest in Europe, stands out as one of the most distinctive features of London's skyline. There has been a cathedral dedicated to St Paul on the site for more than 1400 years, and the present Cathedral stands on the site of an even older medieval cathedral that burned down during the Great Fire of 1666. Decorating the interior of the dome is the *Whispering Gallery*, so named for its incredible acoustics. Contained beneath the main cathedral floor is the *Crypt*, which is the largest in Europe, housing more than 200 tombs, including those of Admiral Nelson and the Duke of Wellington, and the tomb of Sir Christopher Wren himself. Over the years, the cathedral has been the setting for many historic events, including Sir Winston Churchill's funeral in 1965, and the wedding of Prince Charles and the late Princess of Wales in 1981.

Transportation

Air: London Heathrow Airport, London Gatwick Airport, London City Airport. **Rail:** Train: City

Thameslink Station or Blackfriars Station. Underground: St Paul's, Mansion House, Canon Street or Blackfriars. **Road:** Bus: Public services.

Contact Addresses

St Paul's Cathedral, The Chapter House, St Paul's Churchyard, London EC4M 8AD, UK
Tel: (020) 7236 4128
Website: www.stpauls.co.uk

Stonehenge

Erected between 3000 and 1600 BC, *Stonehenge* is a giant stone circle that stands on Salisbury Plain and is considered today to be one of the most famous surviving sites from the ancient world. The stones, which are up to 6.7m (22ft) high, attract hundreds of visitors every day, who come to marvel at the ingenuity of those who engineered the construction of the site and the techniques used to move and position the stones. The first prehistoric structures appeared at the site in approximately 3000BC. However, it was not until 2550BC that the 3.9 ton (4 tonne) bluestones

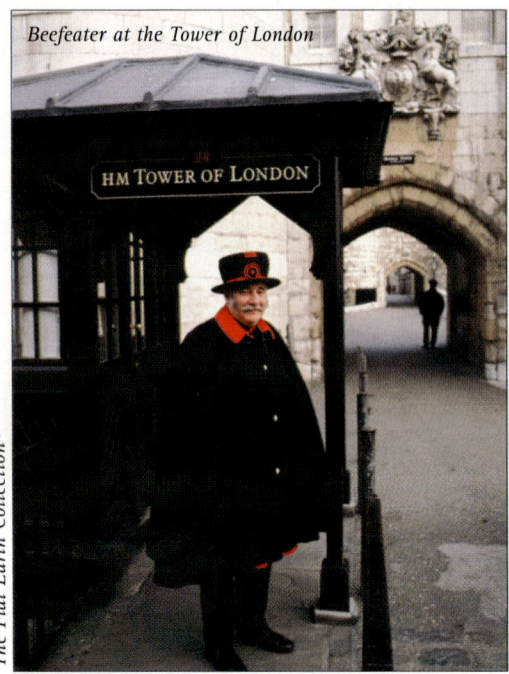

Beefeater at the Tower of London

The Flat Earth Collection©

were brought to Stonehenge from the Preseli Mountains in Pembrokeshire, southwest Wales, using manpower alone. The 30 sarsen stones, which form the Sarsen Circle with raised lintels around the edge, were brought 150 years later from the Marlborough Downs, 32km (20 miles) away, the largest weighing an astonishing 49.2 tons (50 tonnes). *Avebury*, which is located 37km (24 miles) from Stonehenge, is another ancient mystery to modern-day man, and one of the biggest stone circles ever built. There are also many burial mounds nearby, as well as long barrows from the Neolithic Age, the most famous of which is *West Kennet Long Barrow*.

Transportation
Air: London Heathrow Airport. **Rail:** Train: Salisbury Station (from London Waterloo Station). **Road:** Bus: Public services.

Contact Addresses
Stonehenge, English Heritage, First Floor, Abbey Buildings, Abbey Square, Amesbury, Wiltshire SP4 7ES, UK
Tel: (01980) 624 715 (information line)
Website: www.english-heritage.org.uk

Swaffam I Ecotech Centre

Owned and operated by Ecotricity, *Swaffham I* is the first multi-megawatt wind turbine in the UK and is one of a new generation of direct drive, variable speed wind turbines. Located in Swaffham in rural Norfolk, the turbine was installed at the *Ecotech Centre* in 1999 and represents what the future could be like for power generation. A second turbine was built in 2003 and together the two turbines produce enough electricity for approximately 7,000 people – about 75 per cent of the town. The Ecotech Centre is an environmental education centre and Swaffham I includes a viewing platform which is accessed via a 300-step spiral staircase. Since opening, over 50,000 people have visited the site.

Transportation
Air: Norwich Airport. **Rail:** Norwich train station. **Road:** Bus: Public services. Car: A47.

Contact Addresses
Ecotech Centre, Swaffham, Norfolk, UK
Tel: (01760) 726100
Website: www.ecotricity.co.uk

Tate Britain

Tate Britain, which was known as the *Tate Gallery* until *Tate Modern* was opened in 2000, houses the national collection of British art from 1500 to the present day, the largest and most comprehensive collection of British art in the world. Situated on the banks of the River Thames, it houses the art collection of the sugar tycoon Sir Henry Tate and first opened to the public in 1897. Unusually, works from different periods are arranged together according to theme to provide more thought-provoking displays and to enable visitors to see well-known paintings in a new light. The collection includes works by Blake, Constable, Gainsborough, Hogarth, Rosetti and Hockney. The *Clore Gallery*, opened in 1987, houses a magnificent collection of paintings by British Romantic landscape artist JMW Turner. Tate Britain also hosts special events such as themed talks, artists' talks, lectures and films.

Transportation

Air: London Heathrow Airport, London Gatwick Airport, London Stansted Airport, London Luton Airport. **Water:** The Tate Boat runs along the Thames between Tate Britain, the London Eye and Tate Modern. **Rail:** Train: London Victoria Station or London Vauxhall Station. Underground: Pimlico, Vauxhall or Westminster. **Road:** Bus: Public services.

Contact Addresses

Tate Britain, Millbank, London SW1P 4RG, UK
Tel: (020) 7887 8000 *or* 7887 8008 (recorded information)
Website: www.tate.org.uk

Tate Modern

Tate Modern, housed in the former Bankside Power Station on the south bank of the River Thames, opened in 2000. It showcases international modern art from 1900 to the present day and, like its sister museum, *Tate Britain*, it presents visitors with a themed, rather than a chronological, tour of art. Each theme is set in its own set of galleries where a variety of media, including photography, film, sculpture and painting are displayed. The themes are *Nude/ Action/Body*, *History/Memory/Society*, *Still Life/ Object/Real Life* and *Landscape/Matter/Environment*, and feature works by artists such as Dalí, Picasso, Matisse, Warhol, Rothko and Gilbert & George.

Transportation

Air: London Heathrow Airport, London Gatwick Airport, London Stansted Airport, London Luton Airport. **Water:** The Tate Boat runs along the Thames between Tate Britain, the London Eye and Tate Modern. **Rail:** Train: London Blackfriars Station or London Bridge Station. Underground: Southwark or Blackfriars. **Road:** Bus: Public services.

Contact Addresses

Tate Modern, Bankside, London SE1 9TG, UK
Tel: (020) 7887 8000 *or* 7887 8008 (recorded information
Website: www.tate.org.uk

Tintagel Castle

The ruins of the legendary 12th-century *Tintagel Castle* stand on windswept cliffs in North Cornwall on one of England's most dramatic coastlines. The medieval castle was built in around 1250 by Richard, Earl of Cornwall and is believed to be the birthplace of King Arthur who, as legend has it, was protected from the evil magician Merlin by his magical sword, Excaliber. The castle is shrouded in mystery and little is actually known about its history. Today, the remains of the castle stand on rugged cliffs high above the sea. Over the years, the mainland has been eroded by the elements and the castle is now only accessible via a narrow bridge and steep steps. Many claim that Tintagel is one of the most romantic places in the UK, with beautiful walks along the Cornish Coastal Path.

Transportation

Air: Exeter International Airport. **Road:** Bus: Public services. Car: Tintagel Castle is situated on Tintagel Head, 0.8km (0.5 miles) from the main road; it cannot be reached by car. A Land Rover service is however in operation between April and October.

Contact Addresses

Tintagel Castle, Tintagel, Cornwall PL34 0HE, UK
Tel/Fax: (01840) 770 328
Website: www.english-heritage.org.uk

Tower of London

Work began on the infamous *Tower of London* in 1078 on the orders of William the Conqueror, 12 years after his Norman invasion of England. The tower, which is situated on the north bank of the River Thames and once dominated the city of London, is also known as the *White Tower*, after the Central Keep which is made of white Caen limestone. It remained a royal residence until the 16th century and was also a notorious prison where key historical figures, such as Catherine Howard, Sir Walter Raleigh, the two Royal Princes (Edward V and Richard Duke of York) and King Henry VI, lost their lives. Today, it houses the *Crown Jewels* and the *Royal Armouries*, and is also an important museum. The site is guarded by

Statue of King Charles, Windsor Castle

Corel©

Yeoman Warders (or *Beefeaters*, so-called because they used to have to taste the king's food to see if it had been poisoned) and is apparently protected by ravens; according to legend if the ravens ever leave the tower a great disaster will take place in England.

Transportation
Air: London Heathrow Airport. **Rail:** Train: Fenchurch Street or London Bridge stations. Underground: Tower Hill. Docklands Light Railway: Tower Gateway. **Road:** Bus: Public services.

Contact Addresses
HM Tower of London, London EC3N 4AB, UK
Tel: (020) 7709 0765
Website: www.hrp.org.uk

Victoria and Albert Museum

The *Victoria and Albert Museum* is Britain's National Museum of Art and Design. It was first opened in 1852 at *Marlborough House* in central

London as a *Museum of Manufacturers*, following the success of the *Great Exhibition* which had been held in London the previous year. In 1857 it was moved to Brompton in west London, where it was renamed the Victoria and South Kensington Museum. It acquired its current name in 1899 in honour of Queen Victoria (and her beloved husband, Albert) who had laid the foundation stone as her last public appearance. The V&A is the largest museum of decorative arts in the world and highlights include Italian Renaissance sculpture, paintings and drawings by Constable, the *Glass Gallery*, the *Dress Gallery* and the *Canon Photography Gallery*.

Transportation
Air: London Heathrow Airport, London Gatwick Airport, London Stansted Airport, London Luton Airport. **Rail:** Train: London Paddington Station, London Victoria Station or London Waterloo Station. Underground: South Kensington. **Road:** Bus: Public services.

Contact Addresses
Victoria and Albert Museum, Cromwell Road, South Kensington, London SW7 2RL, UK
Tel: (020) 7942 2000
Website: www.vam.ac.uk

Warwick Castle

Warwick Castle ranks amongst the most popular of all Britain's many historic attractions due to its size, picturesque location and turbulent history. The castle was created as a fortification in AD 914, to protect the small hilltop settlement from Danish invaders who posed a threat to the Anglo-Saxon kingdom of Mercia, and was later enlarged by William the Conqueror who turned it into a motte and bailey fort in 1068. Fortifications were added by King Richard III up until his death at the Battle of Bosworth in 1485. Today, visitors can explore the varied history of the castle's dungeons, fortifications and living quarters, as well as the *Rose Garden* and the formal gardens. The *Private Apartments* contain a display of waxwork figures, showing how the rooms would have looked in the late 19th century. Across the River Avon is the *Island*, where jesters, archers and craftsmen show off their skills in the summer months alongside re-enactments of battles and tournaments.

Transportation
Air: Birmingham International Airport. **Rail:** Train: Warwick Station. **Road:** Car: M40 (from London, Birmingham, Manchester, Leeds, Bristol or Stratford-upon-Avon).

Contact Addresses
Warwick Castle, Warwick CV34 4QU, UK
Tel: (0870) 442 2000 (recorded information line)
Website: www.warwick-castle.co.uk

Westminster Abbey

England's most visited religious site, *Westminster Abbey* is a living monument to British history. Inside there are buried kings, statesmen, warriors, scientists, musicians and poets, including Charles Darwin, Geoffrey Chaucer, Charles Dickens, Mary I, James I and Charles II. Initially the site of a Norman abbey, Henry III built the present building in the 13th century to compete with the great European cathedrals of the time. The abbey has seen the coronation of every English monarch since William the Conqueror, with the exception of Edward V and Edward VIII. The abbey continues to play a crucial role in royal state occasions and was the setting for the coronation of the present monarch, Queen Elizabeth II, on June 2 1953, as well as the funerals of the late Princess of Wales on September 6 1997 and Queen Elizabeth the Queen Mother on April 9 2002.

Transportation
Air: London Heathrow Airport. **Rail:** Train: Waterloo Station or Victoria Station. Underground: Westminster or St James Park. **Road:** Bus: Public services.

Contact Addresses
The Chapter Office, 20 Dean's Yard, Westminster Abbey, London SW1P 3PA, UK
Tel: (020) 7222 5152 *or* 7222 7110 (information desk)
Website: www.westminster-abbey.org

Westonbirt Arboretum

Westonbirt - The National Arboretum in Gloucestershire contains some of the country's oldest and rarest shrubs and is famous for its plants, trees and incredible landscaped gardens. Managed by the Forestry Commission, the collection contains over 18,000 specimens across 243 hectares (600 acres) of Grade 1 Listed Landscape. In 2001, Westonbirt was coupled with *Bedgebury* in Kent to form the *National Arboreta*. Visitors are able to enjoy guided walks or they can explore the grounds on their own along marked paths such as the new *Native Tree Time Trail*. Westonbirt also hosts open-air music events throughout the year.

Transportation
Air: Bristol Airport. **Rail:** Stroud Station and then bus or taxi. **Road:** Bus: Public services to Tetbury then taxi. Car: A433

Contact Addresses
Westonbirt, The National Arboretum, Tetbury, Gloucestershire GL8 8QS, UK
Tel: (01666) 880220
Website: www.forestry.gov.uk

Windsor Castle

Windsor Castle, overlooking the Berkshire town of Windsor, is one of the official homes of Queen Elizabeth II and is the largest and oldest occupied castle in the world. It was constructed under William the Conqueror (c. 1028-1087) as a means of guarding the western approaches to London, due to its position high above the River Thames on the edge of a Saxon hunting ground. Since then, it has been continuously inhabited by Britain's monarchs who have created both an impressive fortress and a regal residence. The castle was painstakingly restored after fire swept through more than 100 rooms and *St George's Chapel* in 1992. Visitors can now once again enter many parts of the castle. One of the highlights is St George's Chapel which was founded in 1475 by King Edward IV and completed by King Henry VIII. It is one of the best examples of Perpendicular Gothic architecture in Britain, and contains the remains of numerous British

VisitBritain©

Wookey Hole Caves

sovereigns, including King Henry VIII, Jane Seymour, Charles I and George V. 200 hectares (500 acres) of *Home Park* surround the castle. A popular place to go walking is in the sweeping 700-hectare (1800-acre) expanse of *Windsor Great Park*, which can be accessed by the *Long Walk*, a broad path lined with elm trees planted under the instructions of King Charles II in 1685.

Transportation
Air: London Heathrow Airport, London Gatwick Airport, London Stansted Airport, London Luton Airport. **Rail:** Train: Windsor Central Station (from London Paddington); Windsor & Eton Riverside Station (from London Waterloo). **Road:** Bus: Public services.

Contact Addresses
The Visitor Office, Windsor Castle, Windsor, Berkshire SL4 1NJ, UK
Tel: (01753) 869 898
Website: www.royalresidences.com

Wookey Hole Caves

Situated in the heart of Somerset, evidence of early man inhabiting the site around *Wookey Hole* can be traced back over 50,000 years. As well as human artifacts, the many archaeological finds include the bones of tropical and Ice Age animals such as rhinoceros, bear, mammoth and lion. It's thought that the caves were inhabited alternately by both man and hyenas between 35,000 and 25,000 BC. More recently, the Celts settled and farmed in the area before the Romans arrived approximately 2000 years ago and took over the region for its rich mineral mines. There are other attractions at the site including the *Dinosaur Valley* with life-size models of dinosaurs, a *Victorian Penny Arcade*, a *Mirror Maze* and the *River Axe Pirates* children's play area. There's also a *Victorian Papermill* and *Caves Museum* which are popular with school visits.

Transportation
Air: Exeter Airport and Plymouth Airport. **Rail:** Bristol Station (then bus or taxi). **Road:** Bus: Public services to Wells then taxi. Car: A39 and A371.

Contact Addresses
Wookey Hole Caves, Wookey Hole, Wells,
Somerset BA5 1BB, UK
Tel: 01749 672243
Website: www.wookey.co.uk

York Minster

The largest Gothic cathedral in Northern Europe, the present *York Minster* was constructed in 1220. For hundreds of years before this, however, the site had been of religious and political significance, witnessing numerous battles between the English and the Vikings. Today, half of the surviving medieval stained glass in England is in the minster, with the *Great East Window* displaying over 100 Biblical scenes. The elaborate astronomical clock in the *North Transept* was designed and constructed at the Royal Greenwich Observatory to commemorate 18,000 airmen from Yorkshire and northeast England who lost their lives in World War II. A fire in the South Transept in 1984 led to a £2 million-pound restoration project, and the ceiling now features 62 new bosses decorated with natural and local scenes designed by schoolchildren. There are views of the winding cobbled streets of York and the surrounding Yorkshire countryside from the *Central Tower*.

Transportation
Air: Manchester Airport, Leeds/Bradford International Airport, Newcastle Airport. **Rail:** Train: York Station. **Road:** Bus: Public services.

Contact Addresses
York Minster Visitors Department, St Williams College, 4-5 College Street, York YO1 7JF, UK
Tel: (01904) 557 216
Website: www.yorkminster.org

York Minster

V-sitBritain©

Isle of Man

1 Curraghs Wildlife Park
2 House of Manannan
3 Laxey
4 Manx Museum
5 Rushen Abbey and Castle Rushen
6 Snaefell Mountain Railway
7 St Patrick's Isle

Tourist Information

Isle of Man Government Tourism Department
Sea Terminal Building
Douglas IM1 2RG, Isle of Man
Tel: (01624) 686801
Website: www.gov.im/tourism

Curraghs Wildlife Park

Located at the edge of the *Ballaugh Curraghs*, *Curraghs Wildlife Park* is a wetland wildlife park ('curraghs' being a Manx word for wet) that's made up of boggy woodland and natural enclosures. Visitors are able to walk along designated paths through most of the enclosures with the emphasis being on trying to create environments as close as possible to the animals' natural habitats. Enclosures are based on geographical boundaries and represent the different countries of the world. *Close Beg* is a children's farm area aimed at teaching younger visitors about domestic animals and there are also indoor and outdoor play areas. *The Ark* is another educational attraction where visitors can learn about the problems facing many animals and the need to protect wild habitats. Visitors can also ride a miniature railway line.

Transportation
Air: Isle of Man Airport (Ballasalla). **Water:** Ferry: Douglas Ferry Port. **Rail:** Scenic steam railway travels south from Douglas. The Manx Electric Railway travels north from Douglas. **Road:** Bus: Public services.

Contact Addresses
For more information about Curraghs Wildlife Park, contact the Isle of Man Tourism Department (see **Tourist Information** above).

House of Manannan

Located by the harbour in the city of *Peel*, the award-winning *House of Manannan* is a museum that explores the island's Celtic, Viking and maritime traditions using a series of exhibitions and interactive displays. Manannan is a mythological sea god who was said to be able to blanket the island in a thick fog to protect it from its enemies. The island's history begins with pagan Celts who built wooden roundhouses, many of which have been excavated near the site and a reconstructed version is on display in the museum. Christianity arrived on the island around AD 500 and Viking settlers arrived soon after marrying into the local communities. The *Isle of Man*'s identity, past and present, is intimately linked to the sea and there's a permanent exhibition that explores these links with state-of-the-art displays and interactive exhibits.

Transportation
Air: Isle of Man Airport (Ballasalla). **Water:** Ferry: Douglas Ferry Port. **Rail:** Scenic steam railway travels south from Douglas. The Manx Electric Railway travels north from Douglas. **Road:** Bus: Public services.

Contact Addresses
Manx National Heritage Office, Douglas, Isle of Man, IM1 3LY
Tel: (01624) 648000
Website: www.gov.im/imh

Laxey

Built around a small harbour, the tranquil village of *Laxey* is located along the sides of a glen and dates back to the Viking era. Laxey is famous for the *Great Laxey Mines* which flourished between 1876 and 1882. Close to the hamlet of *Agneash* overlooking Laxey is the *Great Laxey Wheel*. Designed by Robert Casement and built in 1854, the wheel was used to pump water needed for the Great Laxey Mining Company. The wheel, named Lady Isabella after the Governor's wife, was acquired by the Manx Heritage Trust in 1989 and has been restored and still attracts thousands of visitors each year.

Transportation
Air: Isle of Man Airport (Ballasalla). **Water:** Ferry: Douglas Ferry Port. **Rail:** Scenic steam railway travels south from Douglas. The Manx Electric Railway travels north from Douglas. **Road:** Bus: Public services.

Contact Addresses
Manx National Heritage Office, Douglas, Isle of Man, IM1 3LY
Tel: (01624) 648000
Website: www.gov.im/imh

Manx Museum

The origins of the *Manx Museum* date back to 1886 but it was not until 1922 that the museum acquired its first permanent home in what was formerly known as *Noble's Old Hospital*. The

museum set about gathering various historical artefacts from around the island and it quickly became apparent that the museum needed bigger premises. In 1986 the museum underwent extensive development opening a new *Prehistoric Archaeology Gallery* and a film and lecture theatre. The museum is now the biggest museum on the island with award-winning exhibitions. A popular film, *The Story of Mann*, detailing the colourful history of the island is on permanent display at the museum. Other attractions at the museum include exhibitions on maps, geology, the Vikings as well as the renowned *National Art Gallery*.

Transportation
Air: Isle of Man Airport (Ballasalla). **Water:** Ferry: Douglas Ferry Port. **Rail:** Scenic steam railway travels south from Douglas. The Manx Electric Railway travels north from Douglas. **Road:** Bus: Public services.

Contact Addresses
Manx National Heritage Office, Douglas, Isle of Man, IM1 3LY
Tel: (01624) 648000
Website: www.gov.im/imh

Rushen Abbey and Castle Rushen

Situated in the *Silverdale Burn* in what is now known as *Ballasalla*, *Rushen Abbey* is one of the most important medieval structures on the *Isle of Man*. Originally built as a home for monks of the Sauvignac order, the abbey developed into the main religious seat of power on the island and a centre for religious study. The abbey was surrounded by a large estate and the abbey had control of other land holdings making it one of the largest estates on the island at the time. Visitors to the abbey can learn about the archaeological finds in the area and the ongoing excavation projects. Nearby at *Castletown* is *Castle Rushen*, one of Europe's finest medieval castles. The origins of the castle date back to Norse times and it was substantially developed between the 13th and 16th centuries. The oldest part of the structure is thought to be the central Keep and inner courtyard which was probably built by the last Viking King of Mann, Magnus. The imposing

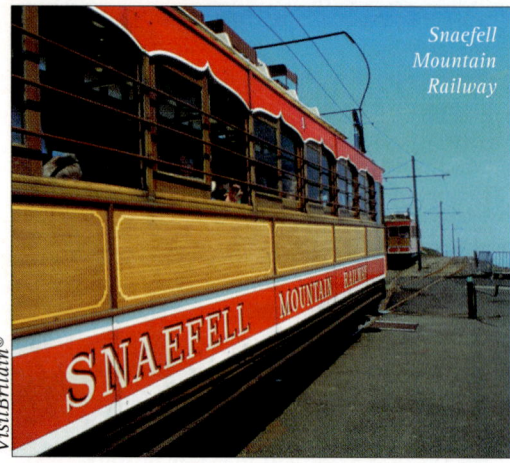

Snaefell Mountain Railway

VisitBritain©

limestone walls would have been visible for miles around as a symbol of the power of the Kings and Lords of Mann.

Transportation
Air: Isle of Man Airport (Ballasalla). **Water:** Ferry: Douglas Ferry Port. **Rail:** Scenic steam railway travels south from Douglas. The Manx Electric Railway travels north from Douglas. **Road:** Bus: Public services.

Contact Addresses
Manx National Heritage Office, Douglas,
Isle of Man, IM1 3LY
Tel: (01624) 648000
Website: www.gov.im/imh

Snaefell Mountain Railway

The *Snaefell Mountain Railway* is an electric railway that first began service in 1895 and today still operates the 6.4-km (4-mile) stretch of track running from the village of *Laxey* (see separate entry) to the top of *Snaefell*, the island's highest peak. The train's only stop en route is known as the *Bungalow* and is midway up the mountain on the *Mountain Road*. The 30-minute journey takes in spectacular views of the surrounding countryside including *Laxey Glen*. A cafe, pub, and small museum are located at the summit stop. On a clear day, it's said that visitors can see across to *Ireland*, *Wales*, *Scotland* and *England*. There is no road access to the summit of Snaefell but there are walking paths.

Transportation
Air: Isle of Man Airport (Ballasalla). **Water:** Ferry: Douglas Ferry Port. **Rail:** Scenic steam railway travels south from Douglas. The Manx Electric Railway travels north from Douglas. **Road:** Bus: Public services.

Contact Addresses
Banks Circus, Douglas, Isle of Man, IM1 5PT
Tel: (01624) 675222 *or* 662525
Website: www.iombusandrail.info

St Patrick's Isle

Dominating *St Patrick's Isle*, *Peel Castle* is one of the *Isle of Man*'s most important historic sites with its origins dating back to the sixth century. Human habitation on the isle goes back much further to the hunter gatherers who were probably attracted by its relative safety and by the abundant fish stocks. But it was St Patrick who is said to have bought Christianity to the isle and established a church. *St Patrick's Church* and the *Round Tower* – one of the oldest surviving parts of the castle – were later ringed by a defensive *Curtain Wall*. The isle was an important site in Manx Christianity and the *Cathedral of St German* was added to the complex during the 13th century. Archaeological finds include the grave of a noble Norse lady who was buried with extravagant jewellery. By the 18th century, Peel Castle's importance was in decline and the buildings were abandoned and left to ruin. Today, the castle ruins are a picturesque attraction on an abandoned rocky outcrop that overlooks the *Irish Sea*.

Transportation
Air: Isle of Man Airport (Ballasalla). **Water:** Ferry: Douglas Ferry Port. **Rail:** Scenic steam railway travels south from Douglas. The Manx Electric Railway travels north from Douglas. **Road:** Bus: Public services.

Contact Addresses
St. Patrick's Isle, Peel Harbour, Peel,
Isle of Man IM5
Tel: (01624) 648000
Website: www.gov.im/imh

Northern Ireland

1 Belfast Zoo (Zoological Gardens)

2 Crawfordsburn Country Park

3 Exploris Aquarium

4 Giant's Causeway

5 Oxford Island National Nature Reserve

6 W5 , Belfast

Tourist Information

Northern Ireland Tourist Board
St Anne's Court, 59 North Street, Belfast BT1 1NB, UK
Tel: (0280) 9023 1221
Website: www.discovernorthernireland.com

Northern Ireland Tourist Board
24 Haymarket, London SW1Y 4DG, UK
Tel: (08701) 555 250 (information) *or* (020) 7766 9920 (trade and marketing)

Belfast Zoo (Zoological Gardens)

The origins of *Belfast Zoo* date back to 1911 with the creation of the *Bellevue Gardens* that were designed to provide the city of Belfast with a recreational area with gardens and a playground for children. In 1934, Bellevue Zoo was added to the site. After some years in decline, in 1974 the area underwent a massive redevelopment project to create the popular zoo that exists today. The zoo has a strong emphasis on conservation and education and zoo works closely with schools and youth groups. Popular sections of the zoo include the *Monkey Island*, the *African* and *Elephant Enclosures*, the *Penguin* and *Sea Lion Pools*, the *Gorilla Enclosure* and the *Children's Farm* where younger visitors can get close to traditional farm animals. The site is located at *Cavehill* which offers stunning views back across the city.

Transportation
Air: Belfast International Airport. **Rail:** Belfast Central Station. **Road:** Bus: Public services. Car: Signposted from the M1 and M2.

Contact Addresses
City of Belfast Zoological Gardens, Antrim Road, Belfast BT 36 7PN, Northern Ireland
Tel: (028) 9077 6277
Website: www.belfastzoo.co.uk

Crawfordsburn Country Park

Located on the southern shores of *Belfast Lough*, *Crawfordsburn Country Park* boasts stunning views along 3.5km (2.2 miles) of rugged coastline. The park includes two great beaches, woodland, ponds and meadows and visitors are able to enjoy three marked trails – the *Coastal Path*, the *Glen Walk* and the *Meadows Walk*. The Glen Walk is the shortest of the three but passes through some spectacular scenery including a five-arched railway viaduct and a beautiful waterfall. The *Coastal Path* is suitable for wheelchair users. Other attractions in the park include the *Grey Point Fort*, a coastal battery and gun emplacement dating from the 1900s. The park offers a series of informative guided walks during the summer months.

Transportation
Air: Belfast International Airport. **Rail:** Bangor Station then taxi or bus services to the park. **Road:** Bus: Public services. Car: Signposted from the A2.

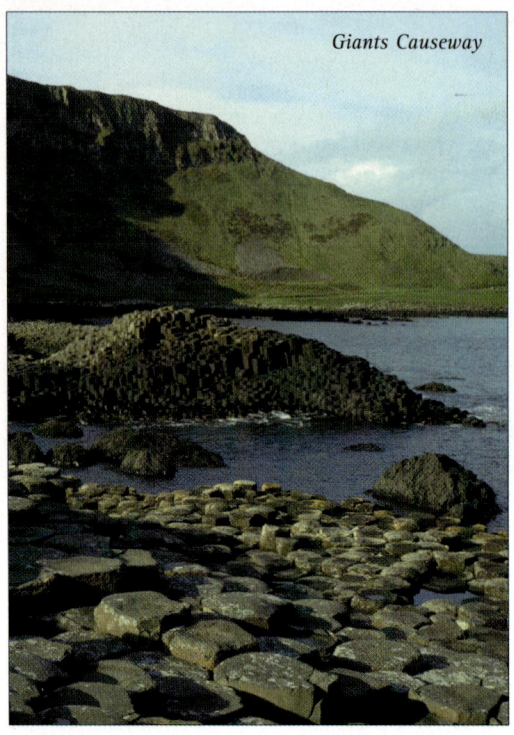

Giants Causeway

Contact Addresses

Crawfordsburn Country Park, Bridge Road South, Helen's Bay, County Down BT19 1LD, Northern Ireland
Tel: (028) 9185 3621
Website: www.ehsni.gov.uk/places/parks/crawfordsburn.shtml

Exploris Aquarium

Situated on the shores of the *Strangford Lough Marine Nature Reserve*, *Exploris* began as the *Northern Ireland Aquarium* which opened in 1987 to enable the public to view and learn more about the diverse marine life that exists in the *Irish Seas*. It underwent significant expansion and reopened in 1994 as Exploris. A new, purpose-built *Seal Sanctuary* was added in 2000 and is now one of the most popular attractions at the site. Holding 250 tonnes of water, the *Open Sea Tank* is the largest tank at Exploris and can be viewed from the bridge that runs over it or from the cave beneath. Species in this tank include shark, conger eels as well as smaller fish such as cod, halibut and bass.

Transportation

Air: Belfast International Airport. **Water:** Ferry: Portaferry. **Rail:** Belfast Central Station then taxi or bus. **Road:** Bus: Public services. Car: A20 from Belfast.

Contact Addresses

Exploris, The Ropewalk, Castle Street, Portaferry, County Down, Northern Ireland
Tel: (028) 4272 8062
Website: www.exploris.org.uk

Giant's Causeway

Situated on the northern coast of Ireland, the *Giant's Causeway* is a unique geological feature consisting of a protrusion of basalt hexagonal columns jutting into the sea. The Causeway was formed an estimated 62-65 million years ago by the cooling of volcanic rock. According to local legend, the Causeway was built by two feuding giants, Finn MacCool in Ireland and Benandonner in Scotland, who needed to travel across the sea in order to do battle. The site was discovered in 1692 by the Bishop of Derry and attracts many visitors every year to see the estimated 40,000 columns. Antrim's coastline and the local scenery are both spectacular, including *Lacada Point* and *Bengore Head*. As well as being an area of outstanding natural beauty, Lacada Point is also famed for being the place where the *Girona*, a Neapolitan galleass which was part of the Spanish Armada, sank in 1588 killing all 1200 men onboard. The Giant's Causeway was declared a UNESCO World Heritage Site in 1986.

Transportation

Air: Belfast International Airport or Belfast City Airport. **Rail:** Train: Portrush Station. **Road:** Bus: Public services.

Contact Addresses

Giant's Causeway Visitor Centre, 44 Causeway Road, Bushmills, County Antrim BT57 8SU, UK
Tel: (028) 2073 1855
Website: www.northantrim.com/giantscauseway.htm

Oxford Island National Nature Reserve

Situated on the southern shores of the large freshwater lake, *Lough Neagh*, the *Oxford Island National Nature Reserve* is a protected area of outstanding natural beauty. The area is made up of a variety of different habitats including reedbeds, woodland, meadows full of wild flowers and ponds that teem with life and is one of the most picturesque regions in *County Armagh*. The reserve includes a number of bird-watching hides, viewing areas, paddling pool and several marked walking trails – some of which are suitable for wheelchair users. The *Lough Neagh Discovery Centre* opened on the shores of the lake in 1993 and provides visitors with information and history about the area.

Oxford Island Lough Neagh Centre

Northern Ireland Tourist Board©

Transportation
Air: Belfast International Airport. **Rail:** Belfast Central Station then taxi or bus. **Road:** Bus: Public services. Car: Signposted from the M1.

Contact Addresses
Lough Neagh Discovery Centre, Oxford Island National Nature Reserve, Craigavon, County Armagh BT66 6NJ, Northern Ireland
Tel: (028) 3832 2205
Website: www.oxfordisland.com

W5, Belfast

W5 is a science and information attraction where visitors can learn more about science and the world around them through the many interactive exhibits. Popular permanent exhibits include the *Fire Tornado*, *Bubble Tubes*, *Cloud Rings*, *Musical Stairs*, the *Sound Wall* and *Tennis Ball Launchers*. Visitors can also learn more about animation with interactive exhibits. W5 also presents a varied programme of temporary exhibitions and events and there is a daily programme of live science demonstrations and shows throughout the day.

Transportation
Air: Belfast International Airport. **Rail:** Belfast Central Station (10-minute walk to W5). **Road:** Bus: Public services.

Contact Addresses
W5, Odyssey, 2 Queen's Quay, Belfast BT3 9QQ, Northern Ireland
Tel: (028) 9046 7700
Website: www.w5online.co.uk

Scotland

ATLANTIC
OCEAN

*Shetland
Islands*
Yell *Unst*
Mainland
Lerwick

Fair Isle

N. Rona
Mainland
Hoy
*Orkney
Islands*
Kirkwall

Flannan Is.
Lewis
Stornoway
St Kilda
Harris
N. Uist
Benbecula
S. Uist
Barra
Rum
Coll
Tiree
Mull
Colonsay
Jura
Islay
Skye

Wick

NORTH
SEA

Ullapool

Moray Firth
Inverness
Peterhead

*Loch
Ness*
Spey
Aberdeen

S C O T L A N D

⑭ ⑩ ①

Ben Nevis
△ *1344m*
Tay
㉒

Oban
*Loch
Lomond*
⑬
Perth
⑦ Dundee
㉓ St Andrews
② ㉔ ④ Stirling *Firth of Forth*
Arran
Ayr ⑮

③ ⑧ ⑪ ⑫ ㉕ **Glasgow** ◎ **Edinburgh**
⑤ ⑥ ⑯ ⑰ ⑱ ⑲ ⑳ ㉑

IRELAND
NORTHERN
IRELAND
Stranraer
Dumfries
⑨
ENGLAND
Belfast

200km
100mls

✈ major international airport
◎ capital

Tourist Information

Visit Scotland
23 Ravelston Terrace, Edinburgh
EH4 3TP, UK
Tel: (0131) 332 2433
Website: www.visitscotland.com

Key to symbols: £ Entry charged & Disabled access ◢ Man-made attraction ♥ Natural attraction ℗ Parking ✗ Restaurant ⑆ Shop �骑 UNESCO site

Balmoral Estate

Balmoral Estate is owned personally by the Queen (rather than as a Sovereign possession) and is a working estate that is closely integrated with the local community. *Balmoral Castle* was first rented by Queen Victoria and Prince Albert in 1948. They loved it so much they bought it four years later and it has been a favourite Royal Residence ever since. Visitors can tour parts of the castle including the famous *Ballroom* which houses several exhibitions including china and silverware from the estate. Visitors can also enjoy guided or marked walks through the gardens and surrounding grounds and there are also opportunities for pony trekking, fishing and Land Rover safaris. The estate rents out holiday cottages and some of the state rooms are available for hire for private functions. The estate is usually closed from August through until the end of March.

Transportation
Air: Aberdeen International Airport. **Rail:** Aberdeen Station then taxi or bus service to the estate. **Road:** Bus: Public services. Car: Located off the A93.

Contact Addresses
The Estates Office, Balmoral Estates, Ballater, Aberdeenshire AB35 5TB, UK
Tel: (01339) 742 534
Website: www.balmoralcastle.com

Blair Drummond Wildlife & Safari Park

Blair Drummond Wildlife and Safari Park opened in 1970 in the grounds of *Blair Drummond House*. The land had been purchased in 1916 by a wealthy Glasgow tea merchant named Sir John Kay. As he himself had no sons, his nephew Sir John Muir inherited the park who was the father of the present owner, Jamie Muir. Today, the safari park attracts thousands of visitors who come to drive through the park enclosures (park buses take visitors that arrived on public transport) to visit crowd-favourites such as elephants, lions, tigers, bears and bison. Visitors can also travel to *Chimp Island* on pleasure boats. In addition to the wildlife, there are also other attractions such as a wooden play castle, adventure play area, boating lake and fairground.

Transportation

Air: Glasgow International Airport or Edinburgh International Airport. **Rail:** Stirling Station. **Road:** Bus: Public services.

Contact Addresses

Blair Drummond Safari Park and Adventure Park, Blair Drummond FK9 4UR, UK
Tel: (01786) 841 456
Website: www.safari-park.co.uk

Celtic Park

Celtic Football Club is one of *Glasgow*'s two top teams, the other being Glasgow Rangers. Celtic moved to its present ground at *Celtic Park* in 1892. The all-seater ground, also known as *Parkhead* and *Paradise* to its fans, has a capacity of 60,500. A double tier rings most of the ground with the single tiered section housing the *Club Museum*. Celtic and Rangers have dominated Scottish football for years and the atmosphere on derby days is passionate and can be quite firey. The ground has good conference and hospitality facilities and is available for private hire.

Transportation

Air: Glasgow International Airport. **Rail:** Train: Glasgow Station then connection to Dalmarnock Station (five minutes walk to ground). **Road:** Bus: Public services. Car: Celtic Park is signposted off the M8.

Contact Addresses

Celtic Football Club, Celtic Park, Glasgow G40 3RE, UK
Tel: (0845) 671 1888
Website: www.celticfc.co.uk

Deep Sea World

Located beneath the famous *Forth Rail Bridge* at *North Queensferry* in *Fife*, *Deep Sea World* is a vast aquarium that's home to thousands of weird and wonderful creatures. Visitors can explore the aquatic world on the *Underwater Safari* via one of the longest underwater tunnels in the world as the impressive marine life – including tiger sharks

and conger eels – swim overhead. There are separate zones such as the *Amazonian Experience* and there's also amphibian and reptile displays. Open to visitors with no previous diving experience, those that want to get closer to the fish are able to take a diving induction course ending with a swim with the ever-popular resident sharks. Deep Sea World has also recently launched its *Shark Awareness* course for qualified divers. The *Seal Sanctuary* is another popular addition which is dedicated to the rehabilitation of orphaned or injured seals. The centre also has conference facilities which are available for private hire.

Transportation

Air: Edinburgh International Airport or Glasgow International Airport. **Rail:** Train: North Queensferry Station (a signposted 10-minute walk from the station). **Road:** Bus: Free shuttle bus operates during July and August with pick ups at the Waverley Bridge. Car: Junction 1 off M90.

Contact Addresses

Deep Sea World, Battery Quarry, North Queensferry, Fife, KY11 1JR, UK
Tel: (01383) 411 880
Website: www.deepseaworld.com

Edinburgh Castle

Edinburgh Castle looks over the city of Edinburgh from its perch on top of an extinct volcano. The oldest building in Edinburgh and its most popular tourist attraction, the castle has served both as fortress and royal residence. Today, it houses the *Scottish Crown Jewels*, the *Stone of Destiny* and *Mons Meg* (a massive 15th-century bombard), as well as the headquarters of the British Army's Scottish Division and a permanent exhibition which depicts the history of Scotland. The castle has had a rich and colourful history, withstanding numerous attacks from Oliver Cromwell's Roundheads in 1650, and William and Mary's army in 1689. It was also the birthplace of James VI of Scotland (who became James I of England in 1603), who was born to Mary Queen of Scots in a tiny room in the *Royal Residence* in 1566. Every day, except Sunday and Bank Holidays, the one o'clock gun is fired from the castle, and for three weeks in August, the annual *Military Tattoo* takes place in the *Castle Esplanade*.

Transportation
Air: Edinburgh Airport. **Rail:** Train: Waverley Station. **Road:** Bus: Public services.

Contact Addresses
Edinburgh Castle, Castle Hill, Edinburgh EH1 2NG, UK
Tel: (0131) 225 9846
Website: www.historic-scotland.gov.uk

Edinburgh Zoo

Founded in 1913 by the Royal Zoological Society of Scotland, *Edinburgh Zoo* is one of the most significant zoos in Europe. It is Scotland's most popular wildlife attraction, with over 1000 animals, including meerkats, pygmy hippos, snow leopards and blue poison arrow frogs. Set in 32 hectares (80 acres) of beautiful parkland on the slopes of Corstorphine Hill, with stunning views of the surrounding countryside, the zoo is famous for having the world's biggest penguin pool, which is home to the largest colony of penguins in Europe. As well as animals, there are many other attractions, such as the *African Plains Experience*, the *Maze*, the *Magic Forest* and the *Hilltop Safari Tour*.

Transportation
Air: Edinburgh Airport. **Rail:** Train: Waverley Station. **Road:** Bus: Public services.

Contact Addresses
Edinburgh Zoo, Murrayfield, Edinburgh EH12 6TS, UK
Tel: (0131) 334 9171
Website: www.edinburghzoo.org.uk

Glamis Castle

Set in the heart of the *Angus Glens*, *Glamis Castle* has been the family home of the Earls of Strathmore and Kinghorne for hundreds of years and has been a royal residence since 1372. It is also famous for being the childhood home of Elizabeth Bowes-Lyon, better known as the Queen

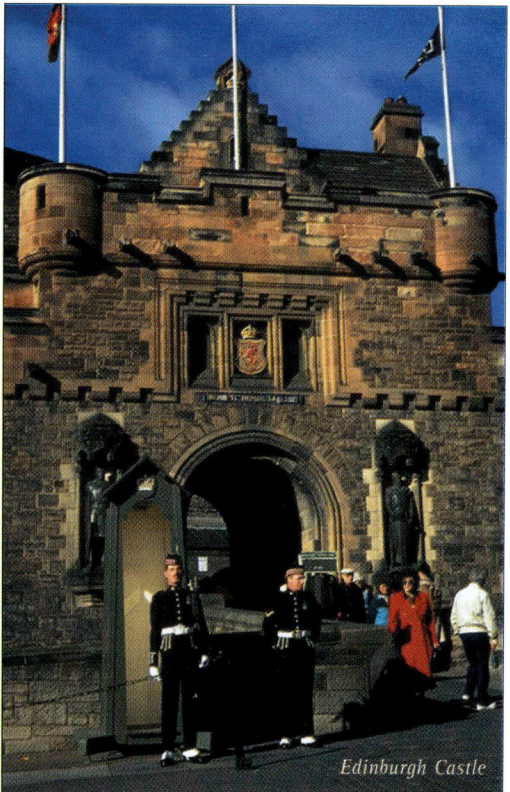

Edinburgh Castle

Mother, and her daughter, Princess Margaret, both of whom passed away in 2002 aged 101 and 71 respectively. The castle is now home to the 18th Earl of Strathmore and Kinghorne. Visitors are able to take a guided tour of the castle and grounds viewing the spectacular *Royal Apartments*. Outside, the *Italian Garden*, *Pinetum* and *Nature Trail* are particularly popular with visitors. Parts of Glamis Castle are available for hire for wedding receptions and private functions. The castle is usually closed from mid-December to mid-March.

Transportation
Air: Dundee Airport. **Rail:** Dundee Station then taxi or bus service to Glamis Castle. **Road:** Bus: Public services. Car: Off the A94.

Contact Addresses
The Castle Administrator, Estates Office, Glamis by Forfar, Angus DD8 1RJ, UK
Tel: (01307) 840 393
Website: www.glamis-castle.co.uk

GOMA (Gallery of Modern Art)

The *Gallery of Modern Art*, which is situated near George Square and Buchanan Street in the centre of Glasgow, is home to the city's principal modern art collection. Glasgow's most recent major art gallery, which opened in 1996, houses an impressive selection of Glasgow's post-war art and design, including work by international artists, such as Andy Warhol and David Hockney, and by Scottish artists, such as Ken Curry and John Bellany. The collection is housed in the Stirling Library in the historic Royal Exchange Square and spread over four floors, encompassing work themed around the four elements: earth, fire, air and water. Highlights include the artist Beryl Cook's paintings 'By the Clyde' and 'Karaoke', and the Scottish artist Avril Paton's painting 'Windows in the West'.

Transportation
Air: Glasgow Airport. **Rail:** Train: Queen Street Station. Underground: St Enoch or Buchanan Street stations. **Road:** Bus: Public services.

Contact Addresses
Gallery of Modern Art, Queen Street, Glasgow G1 3AZ, UK
Tel: (0141) 229 1996
Website: www.glasgowmuseums.com

Gretna Green

Situated on the old coach route that linked London and Edinburgh, *Gretna Green* gained notoriety as the first village across the border from *England* where young lovers would flee to get married due to Scotland's marriage laws. Marriages became a lucrative business and one of the most famous marriage venues was the *Old Blacksmith's Shop*. Owned by a family business called the Gretna Green Group Ltd that was founded in 1886, the site has now been developed into a popular tourist attraction with a museum, restaurant and heritage shops and still retains the feel and values of a small, family business. The centre now attracts thousands of visitors each year and is one of Scotland's most-visited tourist attractions.

Transportation
Air: Newcastle International Airport or Glasgow International Airport. **Rail:** Gretna Green Station. **Road:** Bus: Public services. Car: M4 or A75.

Contact Addresses
Gretna Green Group Ltd, Gretna Green, Dumfries & Galloway DG16 5EA, UK
Tel: (01461) 338441
Website: www.gretnagreen.com

Highland Wildlife Park

The *Highland Wildlife Park* in *Inverness-shire* in the very centre of *Scotland* opened in 1972 and is run by the *Royal Zoological Society* of Scotland. Visitors to this stunning park are able to drive through a series of enclosures and natural habitats of the *Main Reserve*. There are also several walking tracks which visitors can explore. One of the most popular parts of the park is the 2 hectare (5 acre) *Wolf Territory* which is viewable both from cars in the Main Reserve and also from a raised boardwalk *View Point* on one of the walking trails. Other animals at the park include European bison, elk, Highland cattle, red deer and wild sheep. There's also an informative *Visitor Centre*.

Transportation
Air: Aberdeen International Airport and Inverness Airport (domestic services). **Rail:** Kingussie Station then taxi to the park. **Road:** Bus: Public Services. Car: A9 and B9152 to the park.

Contact Addresses
Highland Wildlife Park, Kincraig, Kingussie, Inverness-shire PH21 1NL, UK
Tel: (01540) 651270
Website: www.highlandwildlifepark.org

Ibrox Football Stadium

Inaugurated in 1899, *Ibrox Stadium* is the home of Glasgow Rangers football club, one of the city's two top teams, the other being Celtic. The magnificent all-seater stadium has a capacity of 50,400 and is one of only 12 football grounds in Europe to have been awarded the highest 5-star

VisitBritain©

Loch Lomond

rating by UEFA, footballs' governing body. Visitors can take a tour of the ground as well as viewing the museum and the coveted *Trophy Room* that opened to the public in 1959. The ground itself is a great mix of old and new with visitors being greeted by the famous original red-brick entrance to Ibrox. Inside, the ground boasts executive boxes, conference rooms and hospitality suites and can be hired for corporate functions and wedding ceremonies.

Transportation
Air: Glasgow International Airport. **Rail:** Train: Glasgow Station. Underground: Ibrox Station (Copland Road). **Road:** Bus: Public services. Car: Ibrox is signposted off the M8.

Contact Addresses
The Rangers Football Club plc, Ibrox Stadium, Glasgow G51 2XD, UK
Tel: (0141) 580 8500
Website: www.rangers.premiumtv.co.uk

Kelvingrove Art Gallery and Museum

Kelvingrove Art Gallery and Museum, which is the principal art gallery and museum in the city of Glasgow, is one of Scotland's most popular free attractions. The imposing late-Victorian, red sandstone building, which opened in 1901, houses an impressive display of archaeology, natural history and ethnography, including European armour, prehistoric relics and military weapons. It also houses a wide range of European paintings by Botticelli, Rembrandt, Millet, Monet, Van Gogh, Derain and Picasso. On permanent show is the Glasgow 1900 exhibition which exhibits paintings, furniture and decorative art objects dating from Glasgow at the turn of the 20th century. The main attraction at Kelvingrove is a room dedicated to the works of the 19th-century architect Charles Rennie Mackintosh who studied at the famous Glasgow School of Art.

Transportation
Air: Glasgow Airport. **Rail:** Underground: Kelvinhall Station. **Road:** Bus: Public services.

Contact Addresses
Kelvingrove Art Gallery and Museum, Kelvingrove, Glasgow G3 8AG, UK
Tel: (0141) 287 2699
Website: www.glasgowmuseums.com

Loch Lomond

Loch Lomond Shores is an innovative visitor centre that acts as a gateway to the *Loch Lomond and the Trossachs National Park* (www.lochlomond-trossachs.org) on Scotland's west coast. At the heart of the centre is *Drumkinnon Tower* which was designed by one of Scotland's leading architects, David Page. The building is built in the style of an ancient castle and contains a mix of attractions aimed at offering visitors a greater understanding of the natural and cultural heritage of the Loch Lomond area. The *Legend of Loch Lomond* film tells the story behind the song 'The Bonnie, Bonnie Banks of Loch Lomond' which originated at the time of the 1745 Jacobite rebellion. There's also a family-orientated theatre show narrated by a young otter. The National Park was the first in Scotland and contains the deep waters of Loch Lomond, the glens of the Trossachs, the *Argyll Forest* and the spectacular mountains of *Breadalbane*.

Transportation
Air: Glasgow International Airport. **Rail:** Balloch Station (then bus or taxi to Loch Lomond Shores). **Road:** Bus: Public services.

Contact Addresses
Loch Lomond Shores, Balloch, UK
Tel: (01389) 722406
Website: www.lochlomondshores.com

Loch Ness seen from Fort Augustus

VisitBritain©

Loch Ness

Loch Ness in the heart of Inveness is the largest body of freshwater in the British Isles and has a greater volume than all the lakes and reservoirs in England and Wales. But it is not its size that has gained the loch its worldwide notoriety; Loch Ness is famed for the stories of the *Loch Ness Monster* that is said to live in its murky depths. The first sighting dates back to AD 565 when St Columba is said to have seen a strange 'water beast' on the *River Ness*. The legend of the Loch Ness Monster has endured ever since with images of 'Nessie' apparently caught in now famous photos in 1951 and again in 1955. There are plenty of viewing points around the loch and there's an official *Loch Ness Circular Car Tour* that visitors can take. There's an exhibition dedicated to the myths and legends of the loch at the *Loch Ness Visitor Centre*. The loch is surrounded by some of the finest *Highland* scenery in Scotland that's peppered with castles, forts, waterfalls and stunning valleys.

Transportation
Air: Aberdeen International Airport and Inverness Airport (domestic services). **Rail:** Inverness Station then taxi to the park. **Road:** Bus: Public services. Car: A82 and A321 to the centre.

Contact Addresses
The Original Loch Ness Visitor Centre, Drumnadrochit, Inverness IV63 6TU, UK
Tel: (01456) 450342
Website: www.lochness-centre.com

New Lanark World Heritage Centre

The *New Lanark World Heritage Site* in Southern Scotland is a restored 18th-century cotton mill village. At the award-winning visitor centre visitors can explore what life would have been like for the 18th-century inhabitants of New Lanark which rose to fame in the early 1800s when Robert Owen was manager of the mill. Two of the most popular attractions at the centre are the *Millennium Experience* ride and an audio-visual theatre show called *Annie McLeod's Story* which tells the history of the region through the ghost of a mill-girl. From the centre, visitors can follow the trail to the spectacular *Falls of Clyde* close by where there's also a *Wildlife Centre* that's home to nesting peregrine falcons. The site is one of Scotland's top attractions attracting over 400,000 visitors each year. The visitor centre is closed during December and January.

Transportation
Air: Edinburgh International Airport or Glasgow International Airport. **Rail:** Lanark Station (then bus or taxi to the Visitor Centre). **Road:** Bus: Public services.

Contact Addresses
New Lanark, World Heritage Site, South Lanarkshire ML11 9DB, UK
Tel: (01555) 661345
Website: www.newlanark.org

Palace of Holyroodhouse

The splendid *Palace of Holyroodhouse* in Edinburgh is The Queen's official residence in Scotland in and was originally founded as an Augustinian monastery in 1128 by David I. As the Abbey prospered and Edinburgh became recognised as the Scottish capital, a succession of Royals chose to live here at Holyroodhouse rather than at *Edinburgh*

Castle in the city. James IV added the palace to the abbey during his stay from 1488 to 1513 and his successor, James V, added two massive towers during the early part of the 16th century. The residence has a rich history and was also the home of Mary, Queen of Scots who spent a turbulent time there from 1561 to 1567. After a brief period out of favour with the royals, life at Holyroodhouse was reinvigorated with the arrival of Queen Victoria who initiated an extensive renovation process. Today, the palace is the Queen's official residence in Scotland (with the Queen's official *Holyrood Week* traditionally spanning the end of June and the start of July during which she hosts the annual *Holyrood Garden Party*) that attracts thousands of tourists each year. The largest room in the palace is the spectacular *Great Gallery* used for banquets and official occasions. Other attractions include the *State Apartments*, *Mary, Queen of Scots' Chambers* and the *Queen's Gallery*.

Transportation
Air: Edinburgh International Airport. **Rail:** Edinburgh (Waverley) Station (the palace is a 15-minute walk from the station). **Road:** Bus: Public services from Waverley Bridge.

Contact Addresses
Ticket Sales and Information Office, The Official Residences of The Queen, London SW1A 1AA
Tel: (0131) 556 5100
Website: www.royal.gov.uk

Royal Botanic Garden Edinburgh

Regarded as Scotland's premier garden, the *Royal Botanic Garden Edinburgh* is one of the city's most popular tourist attractions. The garden, which was first opened in 1670 as a small physic (medicinal) garden near Holyrood House, was designed by two doctors, Andrew Balfour and Robert Sibbald. It was moved to its present location during the 1820s and expanded to cover an area of 31 hectares (78 acres). Today, the garden contains a unique collection of plants from around the world, housed in the world-famous *Rock Garden*, the *Chinese Hillside* and the *Glasshouse Experience*. Visitors can also see the *Woodland Gardens & Arboretum* and the *Winter Garden*, as well as enjoy spectacular views across the city of Edinburgh.

Transportation
Air: Edinburgh Airport. **Rail:** Train: Waverley Station. **Road:** Bus: Public services. The Garden lies 1.6km (one mile) north of Edinburgh city centre, off the A902.

Contact Addresses
Royal Botanic Garden Edinburgh, 20A Inverleith Row, Edinburgh EH3 5LR, UK
Tel: (0131) 552 7171
Website: www.rbge.org.uk

Royal Museum and Museum of Scotland

The *Royal Museum* and the *Museum of Scotland* are located on the same site in Edinburgh city centre. The Royal Museum, which has 36 galleries and is well known for its impressive Main Hall, houses an international collection of artistic, archaeological, scientific and industrial exhibits, ranging from Japanese art to natural history. The Museum of Scotland, which opened in 1998, has over 10,000 artefacts detailing the country's history from its geological formation and earliest inhabitants up to the 20th century. Many of Scotland's finest regional treasures are on display, including a communal drinking cup (the *Bute Mazer*), made after the Scots beat the English during the Battle of Bannockburn in 1314. There are also fine views of Edinburgh Castle from the museum's rooftop.

Transportation
Air: Edinburgh Airport. **Rail:** Train: Waverley Station. **Road:** Bus: Public services. Chambers Street is located just off the A7 South Bridge in central Edinburgh.

Contact Addresses
Royal Museum, Chambers Street, Edinburgh EH1 1JF, UK
Tel: (0131) 247 4219
Website: www.nms.ac.uk

Museum of Scotland, Chambers Street, Edinburgh, EH1 1JF, UK
Tel: (0131) 247 4422
Website: www.nms.ac.uk

Royal Yacht Britannia

Launched from *John Brown's Shipyard* in Clydebank in 1953, the *Royal Yacht Britannia* was in the service of the Queen and the Royal Family for over forty years travelling on 968 official voyages as far afield as the South Seas and Antarctica Decommissioned in 1997, the Britannia now resides in the port of *Leith* in *Edinburgh* and is a popular tourist attraction. Visitors to the Britannia are able to board the yacht and view exhibits and displays from the Royal voyages. A multilingual audio headset is also available. Highlights of the Britannia tour include *The Royal Apartments*, *The Sun Lounge*, *The Royal Bedrooms* and *The Drawing Room* – all lavishly furnished with prints, paintings and fine furniture. The *State Dining Room* has hosted many eminent guests over the years including Sir Winston Churchill, Rajiv Ghandi, Nelson Mandela, Bill Clinton, Boris Yeltsin, Ronald Reagan and Margaret Thatcher. Today, it can be hired for corporate functions. Other interesting exhibits onboard include the *Queen's Rolls-Royce Phantom V* worth over £1 million.

Transportation
Air: Edinburgh International Airport. **Rail:** Edinburgh (Waverley) Station. **Road:** Bus: Public services from Waverley Bridge.

Contact Addresses
The Royal Yacht Britannia, Ocean Terminal, Leith, Edinburgh EH6 6JJ, UK
Tel: (0131) 555 5566
Website: www.royalyachtbritannia.co.uk

Scotch Whisky Heritage Centre and Royal Mile

The historic *Royal Mile* in Edinburgh's Old Town leads from *Edinburgh Castle* to the *Palace of Holyrood House* and is actually one mile and 107 yards long. Visitors can tour the *Scotch Whisky Heritage Centre*, situated at the top of the Royal Mile, which allows them to see how whisky is made and is believed to have a resident ghost. The *Camera Obscura* at the top end of the Royal Mile, is also one of Edinburgh's top attractions, where visitors can see a panoramic view of the city reflected onto a white table. *Tron Kirk* is located at

the junction of North Bridge and the Royal Mile and is a traditional place for partygoers to gather and hear the bells toll, ringing in the new year at midnight on Hogmanay (December 31). The long list of other attractions on the Royal Mile include: *Highland Tolbooth Kirk*, *Ramsay Garden*, *Writers' Museum*, *Brodie's Close*, *Parliament Square*, *John Knox's House*, *Museum of Childhood*, *Netherbow Port*, *Huntly House*, *Canongate Kirk*, *Abbey Lairds*, *Gladstone's Land*, *Queen Mary's Bath House* and *St Giles' Cathedral*.

Transportation
Air: Edinburgh Airport. **Rail:** Train: Waverley Station. **Road:** Bus: Public services. The Royal Mile is located in Edinburgh city centre, just off the A7 North Bridge.

Contact Addresses
Edinburgh and Lothians Tourist Board, 3 Princes Street, Edinburgh EH2 2QP, UK
Tel: (0131) 473 3800
Website: www.edinburgh.org

Scotch Whisky Heritage Centre, 354 Castlehill, The Royal Mile, Edinburgh EH1 2NE, UK
Tel: (0131) 220 0441
Website: www.whisky-heritage.co.uk

Scottish Parliament

The original *Scottish Parliament* was abolished in 1707 under the Act of Union to form the Parliament of Great Britain. The Scottish Parliament was reestablished in 1998 under the Scotland Act with the first session of the new Parliament held in 1999 at its brand new *Parliament Building* which lies at the end of Edinburgh's famous *Royal Mile* by *Holyrood Park*. Designed by Enric Miralles who was inspired by the dramatic landscape that surrounds the site, the striking building is made from a mix of steel, oak and granite. Sustainability and minimal impact were key factors in the design, and the building is famed as one of the most progressive and innovative buildings in *Britain* today. Access to the building is free but there is a charge for a guided tour.

Transportation
Air: Edinburgh International Airport. **Rail:** Edinburgh Waverley Station (15-minute walk to

The historic Royal Mile in Edinburgh's Old Town

VisitBritain©

Scottish Parliament). **Road:** Bus: Public services from Waverley Bridge.

Contact Addresses
Public Information Services, The Scottish Parliament, Edinburgh EH99 1SP, UK
Tel: (0131) 348 5000
Website: www.scottish.parliament.uk

Speyside Whisky Trails

Originally celebrated for its apparent medicinal qualities, whisky grew to become an integral part of daily Scottish life, drank for its reviving properties and to warm the body during the long, cold Scottish winters. As its popularity grew, extortionate taxes were imposed on whisky production in the latter stages of the 16th century which drove many distilleries underground, with several establishing themselves in the hills of the *Grampian Highlands* away from the eyes of the excise men. Smuggling became common practice and distilleries would signal from one hilltop to the next when excise men entered the area. In 1823, a new tax system was introduced that made it possible for distilleries to make a profit and pay taxes, and the illegal production of whisky gradually phased out. But many of the old

distilleries remain in their dramatic locations in the hills and today form a popular whisky trail where visitors can tour distilleries and sample a wee dram or two of their favourite malt or scotch whisky. The distilleries on the *Speyside Trail* include *Benromach*, *Cardhu*, *Dallas Dhu*, *Glenfiddich*, *Glen Grant*, *Glenlivet*, *Glen Moray* and *Strathisla*. The award-winning *Speyside Cooperage* and visitor centre is also on the trail where visitors can see how the traditional oak casks used for maturing the whiskies are made. Other popular trails in the Grampian Highlands include the *Castle Trail*, the *Coastal Trail* and the *Victorian Heritage Trail* and the whole area is renowned for its stunning scenery.

Transportation
Air: Aberdeen International Airport. **Rail:** Aberdeen Station. **Road:** Bus: Public Services to Aberdeen. Coach: Many coach tours include the Whisky Trails as part of the their trips. Car: A9 then A95 through Speyside.

Contact Addresses
For more information on the Speyside Whisky Trails, contact Visit Scotland (see **Tourist Information** above) or visit the Speyside Whisky Trails website: www.maltwhiskeytrail.com.

St Andrews Golf Course

St Andrews Golf Course is one of Scotland's finest golf courses and plays host to the prestigious Open tournament every five years in which the world's best golfers compete. The origins of the game are hotly disputed but many believe Scotland and St Andrews to be the true home of the sport. But one thing that cannot be contested is St Andrews' long history and connection with the game; it's thought that golf was first played here in the 1400s before being banned in 1457 allegedly because the men were neglecting archery practice in favour of the sport. James IV acquired a taste for the game and the ban was lifted in 1502 allowing the game to flourish and develop into the international sport it has become today. St Andrews is a 'links' course – the name given to courses in coastal areas which is how the original game is thought to have been played – and is characterised by deep sand bunkers and strong winds. There are now six courses at St Andrews with a seventh due to be added in 2007. Other popular attractions close by include the prestigious *St Andrews University*, *St Andrews Museum*, *St Andrews Botanic Garden* and *Craigtoun Country Park*.

Transportation
Air: Glasgow International Airport or Edinburgh International Airport. **Rail:** Leuchars Station then taxi or bus service to St Andrews. **Road:** Bus: Public Services. Car: M90 then the A91 to St Andrews.

Contact Addresses
St Andrews Links Trust, Pilmour House, St Andrews, Fife KY16 9SF, UK
Tel: (01334) 466666
Website: www.standrews.org.uk

Stirling Castle

The medieval *Stirling Castle*, which is perhaps the finest in Scotland, sits on a rocky outcrop, looking down upon some of the most famous battlefields in Scotland's history. These include *Stirling Bridge*, where William Wallace defeated the English in 1297 during the War of Independence, and

Bannockburn, where Robert the Bruce was triumphant over King Edward II's troops in 1314. Historians are unclear as to the castle's exact date of construction, although it is believed to have been built between 1370 and 1750. Stirling also has famous associations with Mary Queen of Scots, who lived here during her childhood and was crowned in the *Chapel Royal* in 1543. There are many other attractions in or near Stirling, which include *Argyll's Lodging*, the *Wallace Monument*, the *Smith Art Gallery & Museum*, *Alloa Tower* and *Bannockburn*.

Transportation
Air: Glasgow International Airport. **Rail:** Stirling Station. **Road:** Car: M9 (from Edinburgh); A80 and M9 (from Glasgow).

Contact Addresses
Stirling Castle, Castle Wynd, Stirling FK8 1EJ, UK
Tel: (01786) 450 000
Website: www.historic-scotland.net

Waverley Historic Paddle Steamer

The *Waverley* is the last sea-going paddle steamer in the world and provides visitors with the opportunity to sail on scenic cruise journeys throughout the UK. Built on the Clyde in 1945, the Waverley originally sailed the waters between *Craigendorran* and *Arrochar* in West Scotland before falling into disrepair. After a lengthy repair project, the Waverley was fully restored in 2003 and is now docked in Glasgow from where it offers passengers the opportunity to sail on the Clyde as well as on longer voyages throughout the UK. The Waverley is also available for private hire.

Transportation
Air: Glasgow International Airport. **Rail:** Glasgow Station. **Road:** Bus: Public services.

Contact Addresses
Waverley Terminal, Anderston Quay, Glasgow G3 8HA, UK
Tel: (0141) 221 8152
Website: www.waverleyexcursions.co.uk

Wales

Tourist Information

Wales Tourist Board (Bwrdd Croeso Cymru)
First and tenth floors,
Brunel House,
2 Fitzalan Road,
Cardiff CF24 0UY, UK
Tel: (02920) 499 909
Website:
www.visitwales.com

1 Aberystwyth Arts Centre	12 Millennium Stadium
2 Anglesey	13 Museum of Welsh Life
3 Big Pit National Mining Museum of Wales	14 National Museum & Gallery Cardiff
4 Bodnant Garden	15 Oakwood Theme Park
5 Brecon Beacons National Park	16 Penrhyn Castle
6 Caernarfon Castle	17 Portmeirion
7 Cardiff Castle	18 Rhyl Suncentre
8 Chepstow Castle	19 Ruthin Craft Centre Gallery
9 Conwy Castle	20 Snowdonia National Park
10 Great Orme Tramway	21 St David's Cathedral
11 Manor House Wildlife Park	22 Welsh Slate Museum

Aberystwyth Arts Centre

The award-winning *Aberystwyth Arts Centre* is part of the *University of Wales Aberystwyth* and is the largest and busiest arts centre in the whole of Wales *Wales*. It underwent a massive redevelopment project in 2000 and today welcomes over 500,000 visitors each year. The centre hosts a wide-ranging programme of events, activities and workshops from across a variety of art forms. The venue includes the 900-seater *Great Hall* which opened in 1970 and the *Exhibition Gallery* and *Theatre* that was completed two years later. The refurbishment added or updated a number of facilities including a pottery studio, print room, darkroom, video suite, dance studios, studio theatre, recording studio and a new 120-seater cinema.

Transportation
Air: Cardiff International Airport. **Rail:** Aberystwyth Station. **Road:** Bus: Public services.

Contact Addresses
Aberystwyth Arts Centre, The University of Wales, Aberystwyth, Penglais Campus, Ceredigion SY23 3DE, UK
Tel: (01970) 622882
Website: www.aberystwythartscentre.co.uk

Anglesey

Located on the west coast of *Wales*, human habitation on the island of *Anglesey* dates back to 7000BC and the Mesolithic Period. Anglesey was one of the last Celtic strongholds to fall to the Romans during their invasion of Wales in the first century, and many historic sites from this period still exist today. Religious sites on Anglesey include *St Cybi's Monastery* at Holyhead, and *St Seiriol's Monastery* at Penmon that date back to the medieval period and suffered badly at the hands of Viking invaders. As testament to the island's rich history, Anglesey is home to many other historic structures including the *Marquess of Anglesey's Column*, *Plas Newydd* and the splendid *Beaumaris Castle* that was built – although never fully completed – by King Edward I as a sign of his power over the Welsh.

Archaeologists have uncoverd many sites over the years including burial chambers, standing stones and hill forts, and many are in good condition and are open to visitors. Anglesey is also renowned for its natural beauty and is characterised by cliffs, estuaries, dunes, heaths, wetlands, lakes, parks and stunning sandy beaches. The island also lays claim to the first Women's Institute in Britain which was founded in *Llanfairpwllgwyngyllgogerchwyrndrobwllllandysilliog ogogoch,* the Isle of Anglesey village with the longest name in the world.

Transportation
Air: Manchester International Airport. **Rail:** Holyhead Station. **Road:** Bus: Public services.

Contact Addresses
Holyhead Tourist Information, Stenna Line, Terminal 1, Holyhead, Anglesey LL65 1DQ, UK
Tel: (01407) 762622
Website: www.visitwales.co.uk

Big Pit National Mining Museum of Wales

The *Big Pit National Mining Museum* is located on the edge of the town of *Blaenafon* which played a vital role in the industrial revolution and has been awarded World Heritage Status. The Big Pit Museum is at the site of what was one of Britain's biggest coal mines until it closed in 1980. In 1983 it reopened as a museum where visitors can now tour the colliery buildings and venture 91m (300ft) underground with a former miner to see what life would have been like for those that worked in the mines.

Transportation
Air: Cardiff International Airport. **Rail:** Merthyr Tydfil, Newport or Abergavenny Stations. **Road:** Bus: Public services.

Contact Addresses
Big Pit National Mining Museum of Wales, Blaenafon, Torfaen NP4 9XP, UK
Tel: (01495) 790 311
Website: www.nmgw.ac.uk

Bodnant Garden

Situated above the *River Conwy* close to *Colwyn Bay*, *Bodnant Garden* contains plants and trees from all over the world and is regarded as one of the most beautiful gardens in the UK. Measuring 32.4 hectares (80 acres), the garden is made up of two sections. The first is set around Bodnant Hall and is made up of terraced gardens fringed by trees. The second part is lower down and known as the 'Dell' and contains a spectacularly wild garden in the valley of the *River Hiraethlyn*. Visitors are able to explore the grounds at their leisure or guided tours are available. The gardens close from early November to early March each year.

Transportation
Air: Manchester International Airport. **Rail:** Conwy Station. **Road:** Bus: Public services.

Contact Addresses
Bodnant Garden, Tal-y-Cafn, Nr Colwyn Bay, Conwy LL28 5RE, UK
Tel: (01492) 650460
Website: www.bodnantgarden.co.uk

Brecon Beacons National Park

The *Brecon Beacons National Park* is one of Wales's most beautiful outdoor areas. Situated amongst hills and mountains, the park covers an area of 1344 sq km (520 sq miles) and stretches from the Welsh/English border to Llandeilo. The park includes the *Black Mountains*, the *Brecon Beacons* and *Fforest Fawr*, as well as moorland, forests, valleys, waterfalls, lakes, caves and gorges. *Brecon Cathedral*, in the town of Brecon, and *Hay-on-Wye*, with its annual book fair and many bookshops, are also popular tourist attractions. There are also numerous castles in the park, including *Trecastle*, *Tretower*, *Bronllys* and *Morlais*. The *Brecon Beacons Mountain Centre*, which is located 9km (5.5 miles) southwest of Brecon, provides visitors with information on the park and offers a fine view of the surrounding area, including *Pen y Fan* and *Corn Du* peaks. Visitors can also take the *Brecon Mountain Railway*, which runs from near Merthyr Tydfil up into the park, and gives spectacular views across Wales.

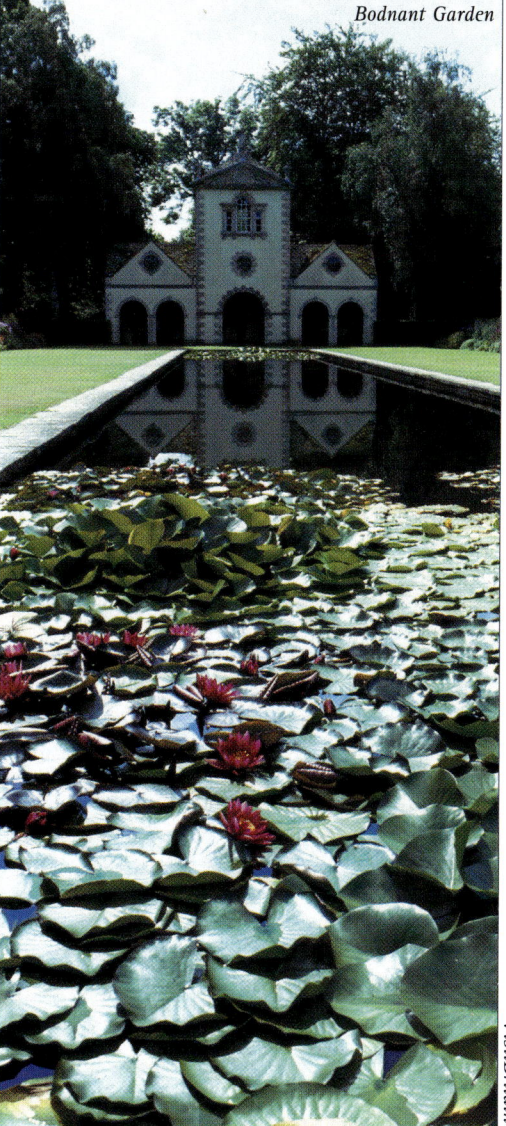

Bodnant Garden

VisitBritain©

Transportation
Air: Cardiff International Airport. **Rail:** Train: Merthyr Tydfil Station or Abergavenny Station. **Road:** Bus: Public services.

Contact Addresses
Brecon Beacons National Park, 7 Glamorgan Street, Brecon, Powys LD3 7DP, UK
Tel: (01874) 624 437
Website: www.breconbeacons.org

Caernarfon Castle

Begun in 1283 by King Edward I, *Caernarfon Castle* is set on a peninsula overlooking the Menai Straits that divide North Wales from the island of Anglesey. The design of the castle, with its high walls marked with arrow slits and its angular towers, is said to have been inspired by the great city of Constantinople (now Istanbul), the former imperial power base of Rome. The castle was built when Edward conquered Wales in 1284 and was intended not only as a military fortress, but also as a royal palace and the English administrative centre of the area. The dual purpose of the castle was demonstrated by the fact that he also founded a town and market within its walls. The future Edward II, son of Edward I, was the first English Prince of Wales, and to this day the ruling British monarch may confer the title of Prince of Wales upon their eldest son. Prince Charles' investiture as the 21st Prince of Wales took place at the castle in 1969. Today, visitors can enjoy informative exhibitions and displays at the castle and walk around the ramparts for fine views over the town and the Menai Straits.

Transportation
Air: Manchester Airport. **Rail:** Train: Bangor Station. **Road:** Bus: Public services.

Contact Addresses
Caernarfon Castle, Castle Ditch, Caernarfon, Gwynedd LL55 2AY, UK
Tel: (01286) 677 617
Website: www.caernarfon.com

Cardiff Castle

Located within easy walking distance of the city centre, the origins of *Cardiff Castle* date back to between AD 55 and AD 400 when the Romans established a fort and trading post in the area. When the Normans invaded in the 11th century, they constructed a typical motte and bailey fortification largely covering up most of the original Roman structure. Robert the Consol, the natural son of King Henry I, became Lord of the Castle in the 12th century replacing the wooden keep with a 12-sided stone one that survives intact to this day. Over the next 500 years,

various medieval lords ruled the region, adding to and modifying the site with each successive reign. It was also a period of great turbulence that saw many civilian revolts and attacks on the castle itself. The Butes were the last of the great families to occupy the castle in the 19th century and employed master architect William Burges to restore the castle with mock-medieval features creating the different styles still apparent to visitors today. One of the most striking features of the castle is the bright clock face of the *Clock Tower* built seven stories high during 1869-1873. Wheelchair users are unable to access the *Castle Apartments* but can access most other parts of the castle.

Transportation
Air: Cardiff International Airport. **Rail:** Cardiff Station. **Road:** Bus: Public services.

Contact Addresses
Cardiff Castle, Castle Street, Cardiff CF10 3RB, UK
Tel: (029) 2087 8100
Website: www.cardiffcastle.com

Chepstow Castle

Located in the *Wye Valley* in picturesque *South Wales*, the *Chepstow Castle* occupies a commanding position on the banks of the *River Wye* guarding what was once a strategically important crossing point on the river. Construction of the castle began in 1066 just after the Battle of Hastings for William the Conqueror, and was the first castle in Britain to be built entirely of stone. The two towers were later added by the Earl of Pembroke around 1200 and his sons added a gatehouse and barbican. During the 16th century, Richard Bigod III added more comfortable living quarters and the place became more like a palace than a castle. It was to later serve as a prison for Henry Marten, a signatory to the death warrant of King Charles I, following the Restoration of Charles II in 1660. The castle opened its doors to tourists for the first time in 1953 and today welcomes guests with life-size models of its former inhabitants and rulers. The award-winning *Chepstow Museum* is in the 18th-century *Town House* located opposite the castle car park and tells the long history of the region.

VisitBritain©

Great Orme Tramway

Transportation
Air: Cardiff International Airport. **Rail:** Chepstow Station. **Road:** Bus: Public services.

Contact Addresses
Chepstow Castle, Bridge Street, Chepstow NP16 5EZ, UK
Tel: (01291) 624065
Website: www.chepstow.co.uk

Conwy Castle

Constructed by the English monarch Edward I between 1283 and 1289, the fortress of *Conwy Castle* was one of a number of castles built in North Wales to subdue the Welsh Princes after a hard fought campaign lasting years and costing thousands of pounds. The castle dominates the town sitting high on a rocky plateau above the *Conwy Estuary* surrounded by the dramatic scenery of *Snowdonia National Park*. It was designed by the master mason of Savoy, James of St George, who was regarded as one of the greatest military architects of his time. It took five years to complete and is remarkable in that it only required a garrison of just 30 men to defend it. It proved to be an indomitable fortress. Visitors can ascend the battlements which offer stunning views of the surrounding area. The town itself is protected by a circuit of walls and 22 towers that add to the medieval feel of this incredible castle.

Transportation
Air: Manchester International Airport. **Rail:** Conwy Station. **Road:** Bus: Public services.

Contact Addresses
Conwy Castle Visitor Centre, Conwy LL32 8LD, UK
Tel: (01492) 592248 *or* 592358

Great Orme Tramway

The *Great Orme Tramway* is a funicular railway consisting of two tramcars which use a system of counterbalanced weights on cables so that as one train descends the hill, it helps to pull the other one up. The cable tramway is over 100 years old and is one of only a few still in operation in the world that today continues to take tourists up *Great Orme*. From the top there are spectacular views across the traditional Victorian seaside town of *Llandudno* with its sandy beaches and promenade. A half way station was added in 2001 where visitors can break their journey with a visit to the nearby *Bronze Age Copper Mine*. At the summit there's a *Visitor Centre* with children's play area. The trams run every 20 minutes, seven days a week from March through to October.

Transportation
Air: Manchester International Airport. **Rail:** Llandudno Station. **Road:** Bus: Public services.

Contact Addresses
Great Orme Tramway, Victoria Station, Church Walks, Llandudno LL30 1AZ, UK
Tel: (01492) 879306
Website: www.greatormetramway.com

Manor House Wildlife Park

Located a few miles outside the coastal town of *Tenby* in the county of *Pembrokeshire*, the *Manor House Wildlife Park* is in beautiful grounds that surround an 18th-century *Manor House*. Paths through the 14-hectare (35-acre) park lead to animal enclosures that are home to animals such as zebras, camels, bison, llamas, antelope and reindeer. Visitors can opt for a tractor and trailer ride through the park that's accompanied by an informative commentary. There's also a picnic site and children's play area.

Transportation
Air: Cardiff International Airport. **Rail:** Tenby Station (then taxi or bus to the park). **Road:** Bus: Public services. Car: B4318.

Contact Addresses
Manor House Wildlife Park, St Florence Parade, Tenby, Pembrokeshire SA70 8RJ, UK
Tel: (01646) 651201
Website: www.safaripark.co.uk

Millennium Stadium

Cardiff's state-of-the-art *Millennium Stadium* opened in 1999 as the premiere sporting arena in the *UK* hosting many major sporting events whilst London's *Wembley Stadium* was being redeveloped (scheduled for completion in 2006). It has been built on the site of the old *National Stadium* at *Cardiff Arms Park* and was the first stadium in the UK with a retractable roof making it suitable for use throughout the year. Part funded by the Welsh Rugby Union, the stadium has a capacity of 74,500 and regularly hosts major football, rugby, athletics and speedway events as well as large music concerts.

Transportation
Air: Cardiff International Airport. **Rail:** Cardiff Central Station. **Road:** Bus: Public services.

Contact Addresses
Millennium Stadium plc, First Floor, Golate House, 101 St Mary Street, Cardiff CF10 1GE, UK
Tel: (0870) 013 8600
Website: www.millenniumstadium.com

Museum of Welsh Life

The *Museum of Welsh Life*, which is located on the outskirts of Cardiff, offers visitors an insight into how life in Wales used to be. Opened in July 1948, this open-air museum explains Welsh history over the past 500 years and allows visitors to imagine how rural life would have been over the centuries. The museum is set in 40 hectares (100 acres) of parkland, on the estate of the Elizabethan mansion, St Fagans Castle, a 16th-century manor house, which was donated to the people of Wales in 1947 by the Earl of Plymouth. Today, St Fagans, which has been refurbished in the style of a late-Victorian Welsh mansion, houses an exhibition on Welsh life through the ages. Other impressive buildings at the site include a chapel, a village store, several 19th-century farmhouses and a Victorian schoolhouse.

Transportation
Air: Cardiff International Airport. **Rail:** Train: Cardiff Central Station. **Road:** Bus: Public services. Car: The museum is signposted from junction 33 of the M4 motorway and can be accessed from the A4232.

Contact Addresses
Museum of Welsh Life, St Fagans, Cardiff CF5 6XB, UK
Tel: (029) 2057 3500
Website: www.nmgw.ac.uk

National Museum & Gallery Cardiff

Cardiff's *National Museum and Gallery* brings together collections and exhibits from the fields of art, science and history. The museum's art collection dates back over 500 years and is one of the finest exhibitions in *Europe* which includes one to the best Impressionist collections outside Paris. The *Natural History – Man and the Environment* display includes the skeleton of a blue whale and the largest leatherback turtle in the world. The popular *Evolution of Wales* display brings visitors face to face with dinosaurs and woolly mammoths in an exploration of evolution in the region. The *Glanely Gallery* is the museum's interactive area that encourages visitors to get closer to the museum's collections with the help of the specialist staff who are able to help with specific questions and research. Visitors are able to wear a headset for an audio tour which gives greater details on 45 of the museum's most popular exhibits.

Transportation
Air: Cardiff International Airport. **Rail:** Cardiff Station (20 minutes walk from station). **Road:** Bus: Public services.

Contact Addresses
National Museum & Gallery, Cathays Park, Cardiff CF10 3NP, UK
Tel: (029) 2039 7951
Website: www.nmgw.ac.uk

Oakwood Theme Park

Located east of *Haverfordwest*, *Oakwood Theme Park* is one of the top paid-entry attractions in *Wales* that receives close to the 400,000 visitors each year. Oakwood is a traditional theme park with rides aimed at all ages. A *Family Zone* includes small scale versions of traditional rides such as the *Pirate Ship* and the *Rollercoaster* as well as more relaxed activities such as *Mini Golf* and the *Boating Lake*. The white knuckle rides include *Megaphobia*, *The Bounce*, *Hydro* and *Vertigo* – a ride in which visitors are harnessed in to a huge 49m (160ft) swing. Indoor attractions include 10-pin bowling and the *Crystal Maze* puzzle area based on the popular television series of the same name.

Transportation
Air: Cardiff International Airport. **Rail:** Narberth Station then taxi. **Road:** Bus: There are no public services directly to Oakwood (except for a summer only service from Swansea). Car: Signposted from the A40 or A48 to Carmarthen.

Contact Addresses
Oakwood Theme Park, Canaston Bridge, Narberth, Pembrokeshire SA67 8DE, UK
Tel: (01834) 891376
Website: www.oakwood-leisure.com

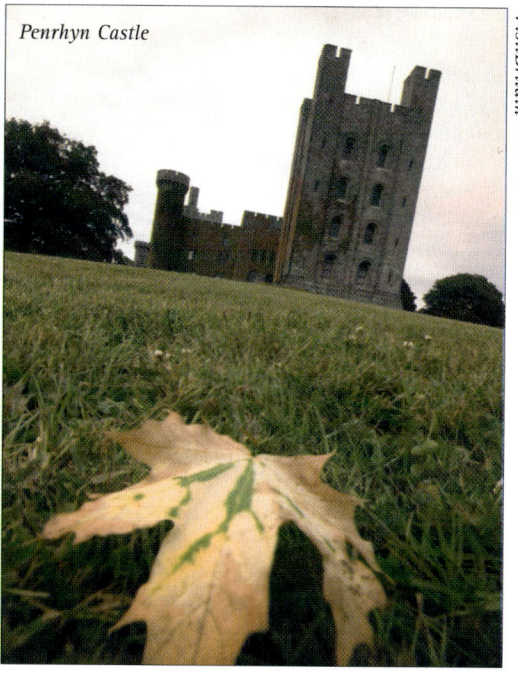

Penrhyn Castle

VisitBritain©

Penrhyn Castle

Built in a dramatic location between *Snowdonia* and the *Menai Strait* by Thomas Hopper from 1820-37, *Penrhyn Castle* was the home of the Pennant family who made a fortune from a local slate quarry. The architecture and much of the interior of the castle has been designed in a mock Norman style and the main entrance to the house opens to a grand staircase adorned with carved stone. The restored Victorian kitchen and domestic rooms are open to the public and an *Industrial Railway Museum* and a *Dolls Museum* are housed in the old stable block. The castle is surrounded by parkland, semi-wooded walks and formal gardens including the famous *Victorian Walled Garden* which contains many exotic plant species.

Transportation
Air: Manchester International Airport. **Rail:** Bangor Station. **Road:** Bus: Public services.

Contact Addresses
Penrhyn Castle, Bangor, Gwynedd LL57 4HN, UK
Tel: (01248) 353084
Website: www.nationaltrust.org.uk

Portmeirion

Located close to the boundary of *Snowdonia National Park*, *Portmeirion* is a quaint holiday village on the Welsh coast. The abandoned site, formerly called *Glacial Estuary*, was bought by the architect Clough Williams-Ellis in 1925 for less than £5,000 and he immediately renamed it Portmeirion. It was to become his personal pride and joy and over the next 50 years he set about redeveloping the peninsula in a way that was sympathetic to the natural surroundings with a strong emphasis on subtle architecture and beautiful landscaping. Today, Portmeirion is owned by *The Second Portmeirion Foundation*, a registered charity that lets out some of the quaint cottages and buildings that characterise the village. Other famous buildings include the *Town Hall*, *Castell Deudraeth*, and the *Bristol Collonade*. A number of traditional industries thrive in the village including *Portmeirion Potteries*, *Pot Jam* selling a range of jams and preserves, and the *Dome Gallery* selling works of art by the local-born artist, Rob Piercy. The area is renowned for its landscaped gardens, woodland walks and long, sandy beaches. Portmeirion also gained notoriety as the location for the filming of the cult 1960s television series, 'Prisoner', which still attracts many fans today.

Transportation
Air: Manchester International Airport. **Rail:** Bangor Station then bus or taxi. **Road:** Bus: Public services. Car: Signposted from the A487 or B4573.

Contact Addresses
Portmeirion, Gwnedd LL46 6ET, UK
Tel: (01766) 770000
Website: www.portmeirion-village.com

Rhyl Suncentre

The *Rhyl Suncentre* is located on the coastal road and has the first indoor surfing pool in Britain. It's one of the most popular paid-entry attractions in Wales and includes the *Buzz* where visitors can ride a 91m- (300ft-) rapid chute on tubes, the 61m- (200ft-) *Black Hole* drop slide, and the *Lagoon Pool* with wave and weather simulators. There's also a rooftop *Monorail* and outdoor decking area with views over the nearby beach and coastline.

Transportation
Air: Manchester International Airport. **Rail:** Rhyl Station. **Road:** Bus: Public services.

Contact Addresses
Rhyl Sun Centre, East Parade, Rhyl LL18 3AQ, UK
Tel: (0)1745 344433
Website: www.rhylsuncentre.co.uk

Ruthin Craft Centre Gallery

The *Ruthin Craft Centre Gallery* is a modern gallery showcasing exhibitions of contemporary artists, many of which have studios on the premises. The centre is dedicated to promoting the local arts scene and has developed a strong programme of workshops aimed at introducing visitors of all ages to the arts through a series of classes and tuition.

Transportation
Air: Manchester International Airport. **Rail:** Chester, Rhyl and Wrexham Stations. **Road:** Bus: Public services.

Contact Addresses
Ruthin Craft Centre Gallery, Park Road, Ruthin, Denbighshire LL15 1BB, UK
Tel: (01824) 703992

Snowdonia National Park

Founded in 1951, *Snowdonia National Park* covers 2180 sq km (840 sq miles) of wild and unspoilt countryside in the western corner of North Wales. Mountain peaks, river valleys and lakes contrast with the 37km (23 miles) of craggy coastline and provide a natural habitat for many species of wildlife, some of which, such as the Snowdon Lily and Rainbow Beetle, are unique to Snowdonia. Much of the dramatic mountainous landscape is the result of millions of years of erosion, with the hanging valleys, moraines and glacial lakes having been formed over 10,000 years ago, during the Great Ice Age. The highest peak is *Mount Snowdon*, which at 1085m (3559ft) is also the highest mountain in Wales. The park's natural attractions have made it a popular place with outdoor enthusiasts, who come to the lakes, mountains and beaches to walk, climb and enjoy watersports. Another way to take in the park's scenery is to ride the *Ffestiniog Narrow Gauge Railway* which runs from *Porthmadog* to *Blaenau Ffestiniog*, stopping off at various beauty spots along the way. There are also many cultural events in the park, focusing on Welsh language and traditions which are very much kept alive in this part of Wales. Visitors to the park should look out for *Eisteddfodau*, which are Welsh cultural festivals featuring choral music, Celtic dancing and readings of poetry and folk tales, and are held in many towns and villages.

Transportation
Air: Manchester Airport. **Rail:** Train: Llandudno Junction Station, Blaenau Ffestiniog Station or Penrhyndeudraeth Station. **Road:** Bus: Public services.

Contact Addresses
Snowdonia National Park Authority, National Park Office, Penrhyndeudraeth, Gwynedd LL48 6LF, UK
Tel: (01766) 770 274
Website: www.eryri-npa.co.uk

St David's Cathedral

The tiny city of St David's, Britain's smallest city with a population of just 1500, is dominated by its cathedral. St David, the patron saint of Wales, was one of the earliest Celtic missionaries who sought to convert the barbaric tribes of western Europe to Christianity. He founded a monastery on the site where the cathedral now stands in AD 589. After Pope Calixtus canonised David (or Dewi as he is known in Welsh) in 1120, the site became a major place of pilgrimage. Bishop Bernard dedicated the cathedral in 1131 and construction work began in 1181. In the south transept there are some fine Celtic carvings on the Abraham Stone, the gravestone of the sons of Bishop Abraham who was killed by Vikings in 1080. Every May and June, the cathedral hosts the St David's Cathedral Festival, featuring nine days of classical music performances.

Transportation
Air: Cardiff International Airport. **Rail:** Train: Haverfordwest Station or Fishguard Station. **Road**: Bus: Public services.

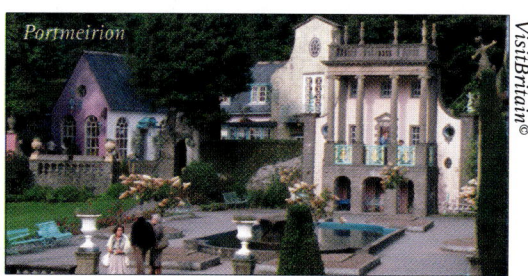

Portmeirion

VisitBritain©

Contact Addresses
St David's Cathedral, St David's, Pembrokeshire SA62 6RH, UK
Tel: (01437) 720 691
Website: www.stdavidscathedral.org.uk

Welsh Slate Museum

The *Welsh Slate Museum* in the *Padarn Country Park* at Llanberis details the history of the slate industry in Wales which was vitally important to the local economy. The mines were at their peak during the industrial revolution when vast quantities of slate was needed to roof the new buildings that were springing up around the country. The museum itself is located in Victorian workshops at the site of the vast *Dinorwig Quarry* with the impressive *Elidir Mountain* in the background. Four quarrymen's houses were saved from demolition in *Blaenau Ffestiniog* and faithfully re-erected at the site and furnished to show four different periods in Welsh history. There's also the largest working water wheel in mainland Britain and visitors can tour the old workshops and foundry. The museum is set in beautiful surroundings on the shores of *Llyn Padarn* at the terminus of the *Llanberis Lake Railway*.

Transportation
Air: Manchester International Airport. **Rail:** Bangor Station. Llanberis Lake Railway Station (scenic railway). **Road:** Bus: Public services.

Contact Addresses
Welsh Slate Museum, Llanberis, Gwynedd LL55 4TY, UK
Tel: (01286) 870630
Website: www.nmgw.ac.uk

USA

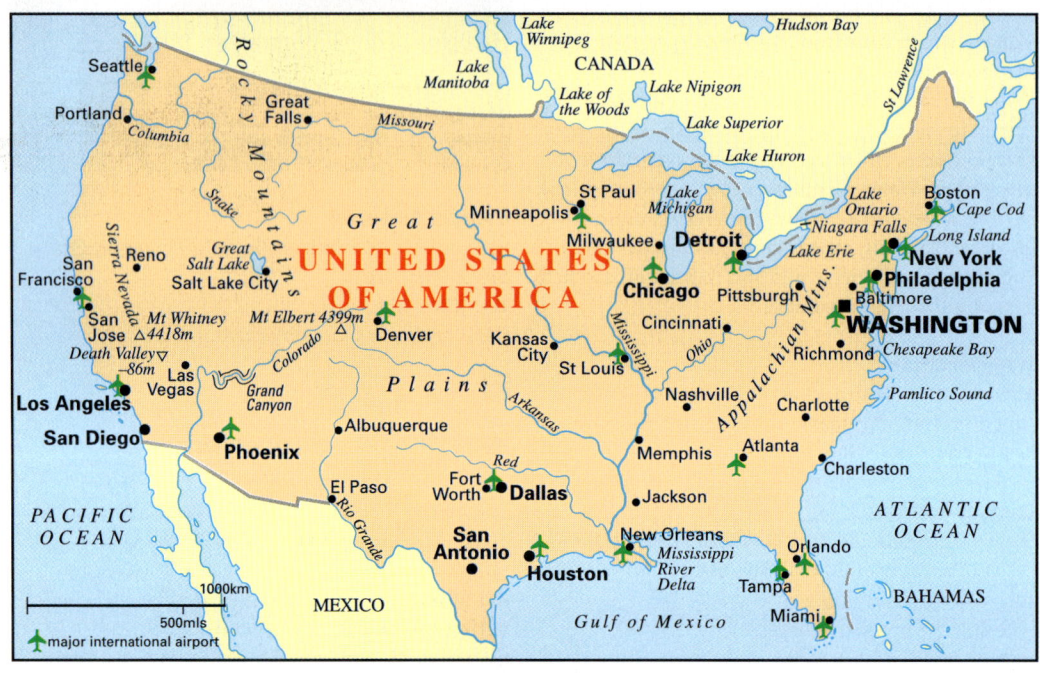

Seattle
Portland
Columbia
Rocky Mountains
Great Falls
Missouri
CANADA
Lake Winnipeg
Lake Manitoba
Lake of the Woods
Hudson Bay
Lake Nipigon
Lake Superior
Lake Huron
St Lawrence
Lake Ontario
Lake Erie
Boston
Cape Cod
Long Island
Niagara Falls
Snake
Sierra Nevada
San Francisco
Reno
Great Salt Lake
Salt Lake City
Minneapolis
St Paul
Lake Michigan
Milwaukee
Detroit
Chicago
Pittsburgh
New York
Philadelphia
Baltimore
WASHINGTON
Richmond
Chesapeake Bay
Great UNITED STATES OF AMERICA
San Jose △4418m
Mt Whitney
Mt Elbert 4399m △
Denver
Kansas City
St Louis
Cincinnati
Ohio
Mississippi
Appalachian Mtns.
Death Valley ▽ −86m
Las Vegas
Grand Canyon
Colorado
P l a i n s
Arkansas
Nashville
Charlotte
Pamlico Sound
Los Angeles
San Diego
Phoenix
Albuquerque
Red
Memphis
Atlanta
Charleston
El Paso
Fort Worth
Dallas
Jackson
Rio Grande
PACIFIC OCEAN
San Antonio
Houston
New Orleans
Mississippi River Delta
Orlando
Tampa
ATLANTIC OCEAN
MEXICO
Gulf of Mexico
Miami
BAHAMAS

1000km
500mls
✈ major international airport

Middleton Evans/Maryland Tourism©

Peter J. Schulz©

Kentucky Department of Travel©

Clockwise from above: the diversity of America shown in the natural splendour of the Great Falls (Maryland), the bustle of Chicago (Illinois) and the mountains of Kentucky

Arizona

1 Grand Canyon National Park

Grand Canyon National Park

Located in the heart of the American West, the *Grand Canyon* is one of the seven natural wonders of the world. The canyon flows (in terms of river miles) for 365km (227 miles), and reaches a vertical depth of 1829m (6000ft) and a width of 29km (18 miles). Activities within the park include hiking, biking, whitewater rafting, cross-country skiing, snowshoeing and fishing. The Grand Canyon is divided into three geographically separated areas: the *South Rim*, the *North Rim* and the *Inner Canyon*. There are three visitor centres in the Grand Canyon National Park providing orientation guides and literature on the park's history and facilities. All three visitor centres offer restroom facilities; those who wish to stay overnight in the park can choose from a variety of lodges, log cabins and campsites (reservations are highly recommended).

Tourist Information

Arizona Office of Tourism
2702 North Third Street, Suite 4015,
Phoenix, AZ 85004, USA
Tel: (602) 230 7733 *or* (888) 520 3434 (toll free USA and Canada only)
Website: www.arizonaguide.com

Arizona Office of Tourism
Ringway House, Bell Road, Basingstoke,
Hants RG24 8FB, UK
Tel: (01256) 316 555

Transportation
Air: Las Vegas McCarran International Airport, Phoenix Sky Harbor International Airport or Grand Canyon Airport (domestic flights). **Rail:** Train: Services from Williams. **Road:** Coach: Services from Phoenix. Bus: Services from Williams and Flagstaff.

Contact Addresses
Grand Canyon National Park, PO Box 129, Grand Canyon, Arizona, AZ 86023, USA
Tel: (928) 638 7888
Website: www.nps.gov/grca

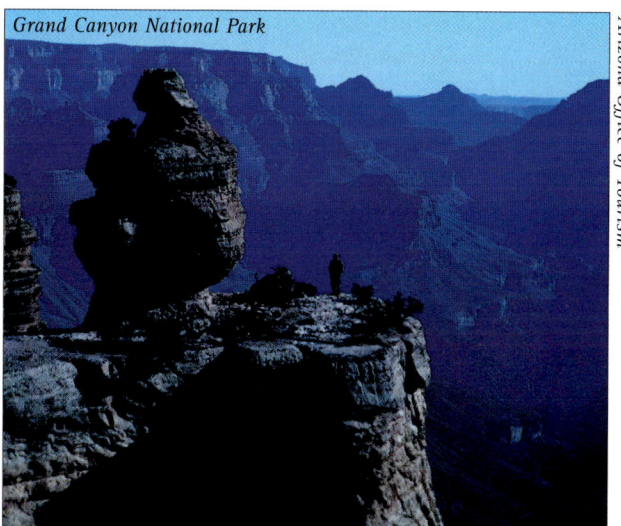

Grand Canyon National Park

Arizona Office of Tourism©

California

OREGON / IDAHO

Klamath Mtns. / Mt Shasta △4317m / Goose Lake / Pit / Humboldt / UTAH

Eureka • Redding • / NEVADA

Mendocino • / Sacramento / Lake Tahoe

Clear Lake / Sierra / Yosemite Nat. Park

Sacramento ⊙ ①⑩ / Santa Rosa • Napa • / ④ Oakland / Stockton • Mono Lake / San Francisco ✈ Fremont • Modesto / Kings Canyon & Sequoia Nat. Parks / San Jose ⑥ / San Joaquin / Mt Whitney △4418m / Badwater Basin -86m / Death Valley Nat. Park / Las Vegas

Salinas • Monterey • / Fresno • / CALIFORNIA / Colorado

San Luis Obispo • / Bakersfield • / ② / Mojave Desert

PACIFIC OCEAN / Santa Barbara • Santa Clarita • ⑤⑧ / Glendale / ③ / San Bernardino / ARIZ.

Oxnard • / Los Angeles Anaheim Palm Springs / Long Beach • Sta. Ana • / Channel Islands / Huntingdon Bch. • Oceanside • / ⑦

San Diego ⑨ / Chula Vista • / MEXICO

400km / 200mls

✈ international airport
⊙ state capital

1 Alcatraz
2 Death Valley National Park
3 Disneyland Resort
4 Golden Gate Bridge
5 Hollywood Walk of Fame
6 Pier 39, Fisherman's Wharf
7 San Diego Zoo
8 Universal Studios Hollywood
9 Venice Beach
10 Yosemite National Park

Alcatraz

Alcatraz, which is also known as '*the Rock*', is the notorious American super-prison located on *Alcatraz Island*, a remote rocky outcrop in San Francisco Bay. It was home to the first lighthouse (1854) and the first US Fort on the West Coast (1859), before being used as a prison between 1934 and 1963. It was home to some famous

Tourist Information

California Tourism
1102 Q Street, Suite 6000, Sacramento, CA 95814, USA
Tel: (916) 322 2881 *or* (800) 862 2543 (toll free USA and Canada only)
Website: www.visitcalifornia.com

California Tourism
Molasses House, Plantation Wharf, Clove Hitch Quay, London SW11 3TN, UK
Tel: (020) 7978 5233

criminals including Al Capone, George 'Machine Gun' Kelly and Robert 'The Birdman' Stroud. Between 1969 and 1971, the island was taken over by Native Americans, when, under the leadership of Richard Oakes, they tried to lay claim to it for themselves. This led to the establishment of the US policy of self-determination for Indian tribes. Today, the whole island is preserved as part of the National Park system and is a venue for tourists rather than criminals, although a few former prisoners and guards can be heard on the prison's audio tour of the famous *Cell House*.

Transportation
Air: San Francisco International Airport. **Water:** Ferry: The only access to Alcatraz Island is by Blue and Gold Fleet Ferry from Pier 41, Fisherman's Wharf.

Contact Addresses
National Park Service, Alcatraz Island, Golden Gate National Recreation Area, Fort Mason, Building 201, San Francisco, CA 94123, USA
Tel: (415) 561 4900 *or* (415) 705 5555 (reservations only)
Website: www.nps.gov/alcatraz

Death Valley National Park

Although only a national park since 1994, *Death Valley* was established as a national monument in 1933 and has long been prized for its unique wildlife and desert beauty. Today, the park covers

13,500 sq km (5212 sq miles), the majority of which is wilderness. Although there are occasional winter storms, Death Valley's summers are notorious for temperatures in excess of 48°C (120°F). Despite this, the park attracts many visitors who come to see rugged canyons, craggy peaks, sand dunes and abandoned mines. One of the most famous sites in Death Valley is *Badwater*, a salty spring which lies 86m (282ft) below sea level and said to be the lowest point in the western hemisphere. From the pool, there are spectacular views of Death Valley's mountains, including *Telescope Peak*, which reaches to 3368m (11,049ft), as well as the surrounding desert

Transportation
Air: Las Vegas McCarran International Airport, Furnace Creek Airport (domestic flights). **Road:** Car: California Hwy-190 (runs through the park from east to west); US Hwy-95 (from Las Vegas); I-15 (from California, Nevada or Utah).

Contact Addresses
Death Valley National Park, PO Box 579, Death Valley, CA 92328, USA
Tel: (760) 786 3200
Website: www.nps.gov/deva

Disneyland Resort

Walt Disney first conceived the idea for the park in 1948 and had originally intended to call it 'Mickey Mouse Park'. *Disneyland* welcomed its first guests in 1955 and celebrated its 50th anniversary in 2005. Today, the park is one of America's most famous attractions and undoubtedly California's most visited theme park. There are eight 'lands' in total: *Main Street USA*, *Tomorrowland*, *Frontierland*, *Fantasyland*, *Adventureland*, *Critter Country*, *Mickey's Toontown* and *New Orleans Square*. Some of the most popular rides include the *Haunted Mansion*, *Space Mountain* and *Buzz Lightyear Astro Blasters*. There are also regular shows featuring such favourites as Mickey Mouse, Donald Duck and Goofy.

Transportation
Air: John Wayne Airport, Los Angeles International Airport, Burbank Airport. **Rail:** Metro Bus: Public services. **Road:** Bus: There are shuttle buses from the majority of hotels in the vicinity of the park.

Contact Addresses
Disneyland Resort, PO Box 3232, 1 313 South Harbor Boulevard, Anaheim, CA 92803, USA
Tel: (714) 781 4565 (recorded information) *or* 781 7290 (operator)
Website: www.disney.go.com

Golden Gate Bridge

Completed in 1937, San Francisco's best-known landmark, the *Golden Gate Bridge*, stretches 2737m (8981ft) across San Francisco Bay, connecting the city with Oakland Bay and the Northern Counties. The elegant suspension towers reach a height of 227m (746ft) and the clearance over the channel below is 67m (220ft). For those who wish to walk the 2.7km (1.7 miles) across the bridge, access is from the Joseph B Strauss statue (on the southeast side), although the bridge can also be accessed from the northeast side. Other viewing areas are located at the north and south ends of the pedestrians' east sidewalk. *Fort Point*, located south of the bridge, is a military defence, constructed between 1853 and 1861 to protect San Francisco Bay from hostile attack. It was also occupied by US federal troops during the American Civil War (1861-65), but the last troops were withdrawn in 1886. Nowadays, visitors can explore the fort itself, as well as learn about the history of the American Civil War and the construction of the Golden Gate Bridge through displays and video presentations in the *Fort Point Bookstore Visitor Center*.

Transportation
Air: San Francisco International Airport. **Rail:** Train: Caltrain Station. **Road:** Bus: Golden Gate Transit bus stop or Muni bus stop.

Contact Addresses
Golden Gate Bridge, PO Box 9000, Presidio Station, San Francisco, CA 94112, USA
Tel: (415) 921 5858
Website: www.goldengatebridge.org

Hollywood Walk of Fame

In 1958, the *Hollywood Walk of Fame* was envisioned as a means of enshrining the memory of the Hollywood greats, with the first star being laid for the actress Joanne Woodward on February 9 1960. Today, it is the defining emblem of Los Angeles and one of its most popular tourist attractions. Two hectares (five acres) of bronze stars, embedded in pink and charcoal terrazzo squares, honour famous luminaries from the world of cinema, including Elvis Presley, John Travolta, Elizabeth Taylor and Frank Sinatra. The Walk of Fame takes visitors on a tour of Hollywood's entertainment industry, passing in front of the famous *Mann's Chinese Theatre*, where stars have literally made their mark, with their hand- and footprints. Visitors to Hollywood will undoubtedly also want to see the famous *Hollywood Sign*. Standing some 15m (50ft) tall and 137m (450ft) wide, this internationally renowned sign, which is located in the Hollywood Hills, was erected in 1923 by a property developer who wanted to advertise new homes in the area. It is one of the most photographed structures in the world, symbolising for many people all the glitz of the Hollywood film industry.

Transportation
Air: Los Angeles International Airport. **Rail:** Metrorail: Redline Station. **Road:** Bus: Public services.

Contact Addresses
Hollywood Chamber of Commerce, 7018 Hollywood Boulevard, Hollywood, CA 90028, USA
Tel: (323) 469 8311
Website: www.hollywoodchamber.net

Pier 39, Fisherman's Wharf

Claiming to be the most visited tourist attraction in the USA, *Fisherman's Wharf* is a bustling area located on San Francisco's waterfront. Developed solely to attract tourists, the area was once a working fishing port. Today, visitors throng the piers along Fisherman's Wharf, to buy souvenirs, eat in bay-side restaurants and visit the numerous attractions located along Embarcadero. *Pier 39*, which opened in 1978, is one of 29 piers located on the waterfront, and is San Francisco's number one attraction. It hosts daily street performances and is home to many attractions, including *Turbo Ride* and *The Great San Francisco Adventure*. There are also the world-famous resident sea lions, which crowd onto pontoons and bask in the midday sun. Visitors can take sightseeing boats from Pier 39 and from neighbouring *Pier 41*, and enjoy fabulous views of the bay area and *Alcatraz* island.

Transportation
Air: San Francisco International Airport. **Rail:** Muni: Streetcar on the F-line to Beach Street. Cable Car: Bay Street on the Powell–Mason line. **Road:** Bus: Public services.

Contact Addresses
Fisherman's Wharf Merchants Association, 1873 Market Street, #3, San Francisco, CA 94103, USA
Tel: (415) 626 7070
Website: www.fishermanswharf.org

Pier 39, PO Box 193730, San Francisco, CA 94119, USA
Tel: (415) 705 5500
Website: www.pier39.com

San Diego Zoo

San Diego Zoo is undoubtedly the city of San Diego's most famous attraction. Located in the beautiful *Balboa Park*, just northeast of the city centre, the zoo is considered to be one of the most impressive in the world with the largest collection of animals, birds and reptiles in North America. Today, the San Diego Zoo houses more than 4000 animals from 800 different species and also has a large collection of more than 6500 species of plants. Balboa Park itself is home to one of the largest groups of museums in the United States, including the *Museum of Man*, *San Diego Museum of Art*, the *Museum of San Diego History*, the *National History Museum* and the *Aerospace Museum*. There are around 15,000 trees in the park, including palms, pines and eucalyptus, the most famous tree in the park is the Moreton Bay fig, located near the National History Museum and planted in around 1915.

Transportation
Air: San Diego International Airport. **Road:** Bus: Public services. Car: The zoo entrance is located off Park Boulevard at Zoo Place.

Golden Gate Bridge

Corel©

Contact Addresses
San Diego Zoo, PO Box 120551, San Diego, CA 92112, USA
Tel: (619) 234 3153 *or* 231 1515
Website: www.sandiegozoo.org

P ✗ 🛒 ♿ £ 🏭

Universal Studios Hollywood

Universal Studios Hollywood is reputedly the world's largest film studio and theme park, and one of the most popular tourist attractions in Los Angeles. The park opened to the public in 1964, allowing the public to see behind the scenes of the film world. Today, a visit to the park, which attracts around 35,000 visitors per day, begins with an exciting behind-the-scenes tram tour of famous film sets, with a simulated earthquake, a collapsing bridge, and several surprise attacks from key Hollywood film characters, such as the shark 'Jaws' and the famous giant gorilla 'King Kong'. The park features the latest in state-of-the-art video and audio technology, and uses impressive special effects and stunt shows to entertain visitors. It also provides musical entertainment and a variety of thrill rides, such as *Back to the Future*, *Jurassic Park* and *Revenge of the*

Mummy - The Ride. Guests can also see TV shows being filmed for free by obtaining tickets from the Audiences Unlimited Ticket Booth, which is located next to the *Wild, Wild, Wild West Stunt Show*. Universal Studios has other theme parks around the world, including *Universal Mediterránea*, *Universal Studios Japan* and *Universal Orlando*.

Transportation
Air: Los Angeles International Airport, Burbank Airport. Airport buses operate from Los Angeles International Airport to Universal Studios Hollywood. **Rail:** Metro: Universal City (Red Line). **Road:** Bus: Public services. There is also a free shuttle bus from hotels in Anaheim on presentation of a Universal Studios Hollywood ticket.

Contact Addresses
Universal Studios Hollywood, 100 Universal City Plaza, Universal City, CA 91608, USA
Tel: (818) 622 3735 *or* (800) 8648 37725 (24-hour recorded information line; toll free USA and Canada only)
Website: www.universalstudios.com

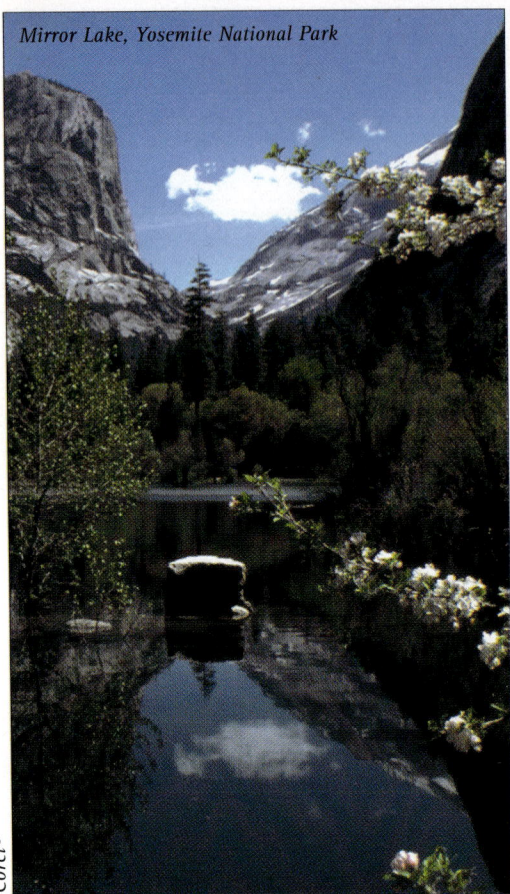
Mirror Lake, Yosemite National Park

Corel©

Venice Beach

Originally developed in 1905 by Abbot Kinney, an ex-cigarette manufacturer who relocated to Los Angeles, the area around *Ballona Creek* was intended to attract Los Angeles's urban populace to live by the ocean. Based on the canals in Venice, the developers hoped to create a European/Bohemian atmosphere by the sea. It's now incredibly popular and the area around *Venice Boardwalk*, which is locally-known as *Venice Beach*, attracts thousands of Angelenos and tourists every week who come to soak up the party atmosphere. Venice Boardwalk is also known as the *Ocean Front Walk*, and is home to hundreds of street performers, including jugglers, palm readers, buskers, snake charmers, fire-eaters, cyclists and roller skaters. *Muscle Beach*, which is situated close by, is just as famous for its legendary weightlifters who work out daily in the sun.

Transportation
Air: Los Angeles International Airport. **Road:** Bus: Public services.

Contact Addresses
Los Angeles Convention & Visitors Bureau, 633 West Fifth Street, Suite 6000, Los Angeles, CA 90071, USA
Tel: (213) 624 7300
Website: www.lacvb.com

Yosemite National Park

Designated a national park in 1890, *Yosemite National Park* stretches along California's eastern flank and covers almost 3108 sq km (1200 sq miles) of alpine meadows, rivers, lakes, cliffs and waterfalls in the central Sierra Nevada mountain range. The park is well known for its giant sequoia trees, particularly in *Mariposa Grove* where some of the trees are over 3000 years old and reach 80m (219ft) in height. Until 1969, when the tree fell during a heavy storm, it was possible to drive through the 3.4m (11.2ft) tunnel carved through the trunk of the famous Wawona Tunnel Tree. Other scenic highlights include *Yosemite Falls*, which cascade 739m (2425ft) into the valley below and *Glacier Point*, which offers spectacular views of the park. The area is also home to abundant wildlife and provides a natural habitat for approximately 250 species of bird, 80 species of mammal – including black bears, squirrels and chipmunks – and 24 species of amphibian and reptile. Visitors can stay at lodges and campsites situated around the park and enjoy activities such as hiking, fishing, climbing, horseriding and cross-country skiing.

Transportation
Air: Fresno Yosemite International Airport, Merced Air Terminal, Modesto City-County Airport. **Rail:** Train: Merced Amtrak Station. **Road:** Bus: Public services.

Contact Addresses
Yosemite National Park, PO Box 577, Yosemite, CA 95389, USA
Tel: (209) 372 0200
Website: www.nps.gov/yose

Florida

Tourist Information

Visit Florida
PO Box 1100, Tallahassee, FL 32302-1100, USA
Tel: (850) 488 5607
Website: www.flausa.com

Visit Florida (UK)
Roebuck House, First Floor Mezzanine, Palace Street, London SW1E 5BA, UK
Tel: (020) 7630 6602 *or* (09001) 600 555 (24-hour information hotline; calls cost 60p per minute)

Everglades National Park

Florida's *Everglades* make up the largest sub-tropical wilderness on the United States mainland and were designated a national park in 1947. Both temperate and tropical plant communities are represented in the park's 610,684 hectares (1,509,000 acres), including cypress swamps, pinelands and sawgrass prairies. *Florida Bay* is the largest body of water within the park, covering 2072 sq km (800 sq miles). The park is particularly well known for its abundant birdlife. Other endangered species protected in the park are the Green turtle, the Key Largo Cotton mouse, the American crocodile and the Schaus swallowtail butterfly. The park's five visitor centres provide information on the flora and fauna in the Everglades, as well as details of various park trails. Hiking and canoeing trails start at *Flamingo Visitor Center*, *Gulf Coast Visitor Center* and *Shark Valley Visitor Center*. Shark Valley Center also hires out bicycles and offers narrated tram and boat tours.

Transportation
Air: Miami International Airport or Southwest Florida International Airport (Fort Myers). **Rail:** Train: Miami Amtrak Station.

Contact Addresses
Everglades National Park, 40001 State Road 9336, Homestead, FL 33034, USA
Tel: (305) 242 7700
Website: www.nps.gov/ever

Kennedy Space Center Visitor Complex

Visitors to the *Kennedy Space Center Visitor Complex* at Cape Canaveral in Florida find a mix of space-age technology and nature. The attraction is primarily known as the home of the *Space Shuttle*, where spectacular launches can be viewed from a safe distance. The centre has been pioneering space exploration since the success of the Apollo lunar programme in the late 1960s. Visitors can also tour the *Apollo/Saturn Visitor Center* to see an actual Saturn V moon rocket, which stands a staggering 111m (363ft) high, and experience *Astronout Encounter*, an interactive show hosted by real astronauts. Other facilities include a *Rocket Garden* and an *IMAX* cinema. The Kennedy Space Center's location on *Merritt Island National Wildlife Refuge*, home to bald eagles, alligators, otters and sea turtles, means that visitors can also enjoy wildlife walks or drives and learn about the animals that inhabit the area.

Kennedy Space Center Visitor Complex

Kennedy Space Centre Visitor Complex©

pools, slides, water mazes, tunnels and other exciting attractions.

Transportation
Air: Orlando International Airport. **Rail:** Train: Orlando Amtrak Station. **Road:** Car: I-4 (from Orlando or Tampa).

Contact Addresses
SeaWorld Orlando, 7007 SeaWorld Drive, Orlando, FL 32821, USA
Tel: (800) 327 2424 (toll free USA and Canada only)
Website: www.seaworld.com

Universal Orlando

Universal Orlando is a 364 hectare (900 acre) entertainment complex, encompassing two theme parks, a dining and entertainment complex, and on-site hotels. *Universal Studios Florida*, the original theme park which opened in 1990, includes modern TV- and movie-making facilities alongside its ever-popular rides and attractions based on films and television, such as 'Men in Black', 'Back to the Future' and 'Shrek'. *Universal's Islands of Adventure* is one of the world's most technologically advanced theme parks with many themed rides. *Universal CityWalk*, a dining and entertainment complex, features restaurants, nightclubs, cinemas, street entertainers, shopping, live concerts and festivals. Both Universal Studios and Islands of Adventure also have many rides suitable for younger children, such as the interactive *ET Adventure*, part-designed by Steven Spielberg himself who is actually creative consultant for the entire complex.

Transportation
Air: Orlando International Airport. **Rail:** Train: Orlando Amtrak Station. **Road:** Bus: Public services. Car: Hollywood Way.

Contact Addresses
Universal Orlando, 1000 Universal Studios Plaza, Orlando, FL 32819, USA
Tel: (407) 363 8000
Website: www.universalorlando.com

Transportation
Air: Melbourne International Airport, Orlando International Airport, Orlando Sanford Airport, Miami International Airport, Fort Lauderdale Hollywood International Airport. **Road:** Coach: Services from Orlando.

Contact Addresses
Kennedy Space Center Visitor Complex, Delaware North Park Services, Mail Code DNPS, Kennedy Space Center, FL 32899, USA
Tel: (321) 449 4444
Website: www.kennedyspacecenter.com

SeaWorld Orlando

SeaWorld Orlando is the most popular marine theme park in the world. It has attracted over 80 million visitors since opening in 1978 and offers rides, shows and various other ocean-themed attractions. The site covers an area of 494 hectares (200 acres) and aims to educate visitors as well as entertain. *Terrors of the Deep* is an underwater ride past live sharks, eels, pufferfish and lionfish from the safe environment of an acrylic tunnel, whilst braver visitors can experience *Journey to Atlantis*, an 18m (60 ft) high roller coaster ride through a large-scale version of the mythical underwater city. Shows include the *Cirque de la Mer* (Circus of the Sea), featuring athletes, acrobats, singers and dancers together with comedy based on South American folklore. Children will particularly enjoy games such as *Shamu's Happy Harbor*, where they can explore a tropical paradise incorporating ball

Walt Disney World

Disney Enterprises, Inc.

Walt Disney World Resort

The world's largest theme park, *Walt Disney World Resort*, covers a space twice the size of Manhattan, delivering the Disney promise of magical escapism and thrilling rides. It is divided into four theme parks, alongside water parks, restaurants, theatres and hotels. The best-known of the theme parks is the *Magic Kingdom*, which provides traditional Disney rides and attractions and allows visitors to meet their favourite Disney characters. *Disney's Animal Kingdom* is an animal park, where visitors can learn about the animal kingdom, enjoy shows such as the 'Festival of the Lion King', and go on an animated jungle trek or African-style safari. *Disney-MGM Studios* is a Hollywood-inspired theme park featuring rides, shows and tours of Hollywood sets, both real sets and reconstructions, including a children's playground adventure based on the film 'Honey, I Shrunk the Kids'. *Epcot* is a science-based park which explores the earth's natural phenomena and the human anatomy, as well as taking visitors on virtual trips around countries such as China and France (in *World Showcase*) and offering a glimpse into the technology of the future (in *Future World*).

Transportation
Air: Orlando International Airport. **Road:** Car: I-95, then I-4 (from New York, Jacksonville, Miami, Fort Lauderdale, Richmond, Baltimore or Washington, DC); I-4 to Osceola Parkway West (exit 3) (from Orlando International Airport).

Contact Addresses
Walt Disney World Resort, PO Box 10040, Lake Buena Vista, FL 32830, USA
Tel: (407) 824 2222 *or* 934 7639 (tickets)
Website: www.disneyworld.com

Hawaii

200km
100mls

↑ international airport
◉ state capital

1 Hawaii Volcanoes National Park

Tourist Information

Hawaii Tourism Authority
Hawaii Convention Centre, 1801 Kalakaua
Avenue, Honolulu, HI 96815, USA
Tel: (808) 973 2255

Hawaii Visitors & Convention Bureau
2270 Kalakaua Avenue, Eighth Floor,
Honolulu, HI 96815, USA
Tel: (808) 923 1811 or (800) 464 2924
(brochure line; toll free Canada and USA only)
Website: www.gohawaii.com

**Hawaii Visitors & Convention Bureau
(UK Office)**
PO Box 208, Sunbury-on-Thames,
Middlesex TW16 5RJ, UK
Tel: (020) 8941 8166 (trade enquiries)
or (8941) 4009 (consumer enquiries)
Website: www.gohawaii.com

Hawaii Volcanoes National Park

Hawaii Volcanoes National Park is located on the
Big Island of Hawaii, which is 800,000 years old.
Established in 1916, the park spans 878 sq km
(339 sq miles) and ranges from sea level to the top
of *Mauna Loa*, the world's tallest volcano at
4169m (13,677ft) high. The result of 70 million

years of volcanic activity is on display,
encompassing the creation of Hawaii out of the
ocean to the evolution of its complex and unique
ecosystems. Many rare species of plant have
flourished in the volcanic landscape, of which 90
per cent of the park's flora and fauna, including
10,000 species of insects and spiders, is unique to
Hawaii. Hiking trails are a popular way of seeing
the wildlife and also the dramatic lava fields and
steam vents surrounding *Kilauea*, the world's most
active volcano.

Transportation
Air: Honolulu International Airport, Hilo Airport,
Kino Airport (domestic flights). **Road:** Bus:
Services from Hilo. Car: Hwy-11 (from Hilo and
Kailua-Kona); Hwy-11 or Hwy-19 (from Waimea).

Contact Addresses Hawaii Volcanoes National Park,
PO Box 52, Hawaii National Park, HI 96718, USA
Tel: (808) 985 6000
Website: www.nps.gov/havo

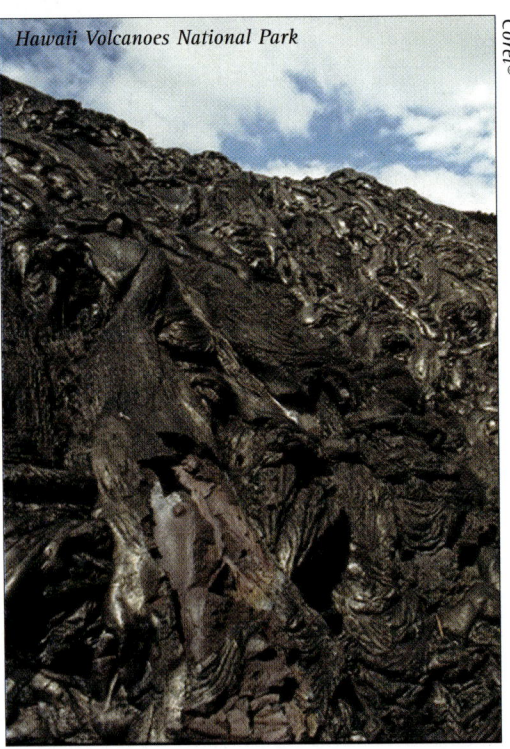

Hawaii Volcanoes National Park

Corel©

Illinois

WISCONSIN
Lake Michigan

Cedar Rapids
Galena
△Charles Mound 376m
Freeport
Waukegan
Rockford
Chicago
Iowa
Rock
Aurora
1
Davenport
Rock Falls
Moline
Ottawa
Joliet
Gary
IOWA
Galesburg
Kankakee
Peoria
Des Moines
Mississippi
Macomb
Bloomington
Illinois
Champaign
Quincy
I L L I N O I S
INDIANA
Decatur
Springfield
Mattoon
Kaskaskia
Effingham
White
Vandalia
Missouri
Centralia
St Louis
East St Louis
Mount Vernon
Wabash
MISSOURI
Chester
Evansville
Ohio
Carbondale
Shawnee Nat. Forest
Mississippi
Metropolis
KENTUCKY

200km
100mls

✈ international airport
◉ state capital

1 Sears Tower

Tourist Information

Illinois Bureau of Tourism
James R Thompson Center, Suite 3-400, 100 West Randolph Street, Chicago, IL 60601, USA
Tel: (312) 814 4732 or (800) 226 6632 (toll free USA and Canada only)
Website: www.enjoyillinois.com

Chicago and Illinois Tourism Office
c/o Global Enterprise Marketing, 15 Nonsuch Estate, Kiln Lane, Epsom, Surrey KT17 1DH, UK
Tel: (01372) 729 140 (trade enquiries) or 726 928 (consumer enquiries)
Website: www.chicago-illinois.co.uk

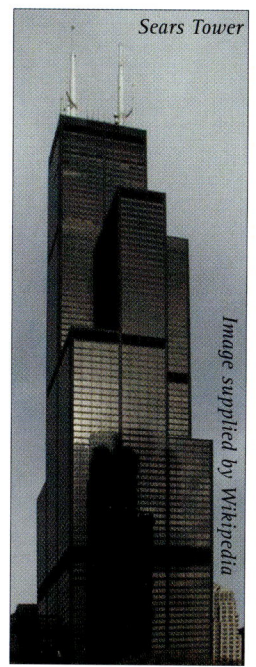

Sears Tower

Image supplied by Wikipedia

Sears Tower

Soaring 443m (1454ft) into the air above the 'Windy City' of Chicago, *Sears Tower*, opened in 1973 after a three-year building project. It was the world's tallest building until it was overtaken by Kuala Lumpur's *Petronas Towers* in 1996 (which itself has since been overtaken). It consists of 110 floors of black aluminium and bronze-tinted glass. The lift takes visitors up to the Skydeck on the 103rd floor in just seven seconds for spectacular views that can stretch as far as 80km (50 miles) to the surrounding states of Michigan, Illinois, Wisconsin and Indiana on a clear day. Although the tower is a working office building – it is owned by real estate and property management company TrizecHahn – there are various visitor attractions and entertainment facilities on the Skydeck. Attractions include interactive multimedia displays showcasing Chicago's history, music, literature and sport, with special knee-high versions for children, and several restaurants.

Transportation
Air: Chicago O'Hare International Airport, Midway Airport (domestic flights). **Rail:** Train: Chicago Union Station. Underground: Quincy Station. **Road:** Entrance to the car park is on Jackson Boulevard in central Chicago.

Contact Addresses
Sears Tower Skydeck, Sears Tower, 233 South Wacker Drive, Suite 3530, Chicago, IL 60606, USA
Tel: (312) 875 9696
Website: www.sears-tower.com or www.the-skydeck.com

Louisiana

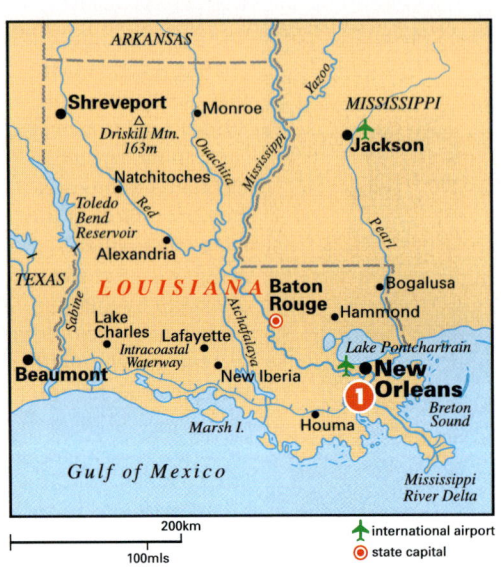

200km
100mls

✈ international airport
◉ state capital

1 New Orleans' French Quarter

Tourist Information

Louisiana Office of Tourism
Department of Culture, Recreation & Tourism, PO Box 94291, Capitol Station, Baton Rouge, LA 70804, USA
Tel: (225) 342 8100 *or* (800) 227 4386 (toll free USA and Canada only)
Website: www.crt.state.la.us/crt/tourism.htm *or* www.louisianatravel.com

Louisiana Office of Tourism
33 Market Place, Hitchin, Hertfordshire SG5 1DY, UK
Tel: (01462) 458 696

New Orleans' French Quarter

New Orleans' French Quarter covers a grid of 98 square blocks stretching back from the *Mississippi River* in downtown New Orleans. It was known to the French, who colonised the state of Louisiana in 1718, as *Vieux Carré*, or Old Square, and

contains some superb examples of 18th- and 19th-century architecture. It was in fact the Spanish, who gained control of Louisiana in 1762, who constructed many of the buildings that are still there today after most of the original French buildings were destroyed by fire in the late 18th century. The focal point of the French Quarter is *Jackson Square* which is home to several monuments and churches including *St Louis Cathedral*, the oldest cathedral in the USA, and the *Cabildo*, which was the meeting place of the Spanish council in colonial times and now home to the *Louisiana State Museum*. *Bourbon Street* is famous for its many jazz clubs and bars. In February each year, the French Quarter plays host to the city's colourful *Mardi Gras* celebrations, one of the world's most famous carnivals, with music, dancing, food, floats and parades.

Transportation
Air: New Orleans International Airport. **Rail:** Train: New Orleans Union Passenger Terminal. **Tram:** Riverfront Streetcar. **Road:** Car: I-10 (from Houston, Los Angeles or Jacksonville); I-55 (from Memphis, Chicago or St Louis); I-59 (from Birmingham or Chattanooga).

Contact Addresses
New Orleans Metropolitan Convention and Visitors Bureau Inc, 1520 Sugar Bowl Drive, New Orleans, LA 70112, USA
Tel: (504) 566 5011
Website: www.neworleanscvb.com

New Orleans' French Quarter

Louisiana Travel & Tourism Marketing©

Massachusetts

1 Freedom Trail

Tourist Information

Massachusetts Office of Travel & Tourism
State Transportation Building, 10 Park Plaza,
Suite 4510, Boston, MA 02116, USA
Tel: (617) 973 8500 *or* (800) 227 6277 (toll
free USA and Canada only)
Website: www.massvacation.com

**Massachusetts Office of Travel & Tourism
(UK Office)**
c/o First Public Relations, Molasses House,
Clove Hitch Quay, Plantation Wharf, York
Place, London SW11 3TN, UK
Tel: (020) 7978 7429

Freedom Trail

The *Freedom Trail* consists of a 4km- (2.5 mile-)
walking tour of historic Boston and Charlestown,
encompassing 16 sites and structures of historical
significance. Highlights include the *USS
Constitution* (website:
www.ussconstitution.navy.mil), the world's oldest
commissioned warship still afloat, which was used
in battle against France and Britain. Visitors can
tour *Paul Revere House* (website:
www.paulreverehouse.org), the one-time home of
the quintessential 'American Patriot', who was a
key figure in the Boston Tea Party and fought for

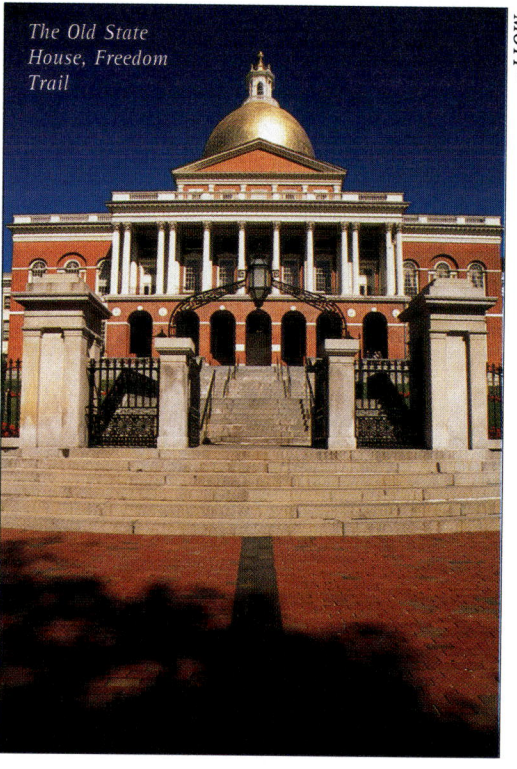

The Old State
House, Freedom
Trail

MOTT©

American independence. Also open to the
public is the *Old State House* (website:
www.bostonhistory.org), built in 1713, which was
once the seat of the British government in Boston.
Nearby is the 18th-century *Old South Meeting
House* where protesters gathered to challenge
British rulers in the years leading up to the
American Revolution. The trail begins at *Boston
Common* in the centre of the city.

Transportation
Air: Boston Logan International Airport. **Rail:**
Train: South Station. Underground: Park Street.
Road: Bus: Public services to South Station.

Contact Addresses
Freedom Trail Foundation, 3 School Street,
Boston, MA 02108, USA
Tel: (617) 227 8800
Website: www.thefreedomtrail.org

Minnesota

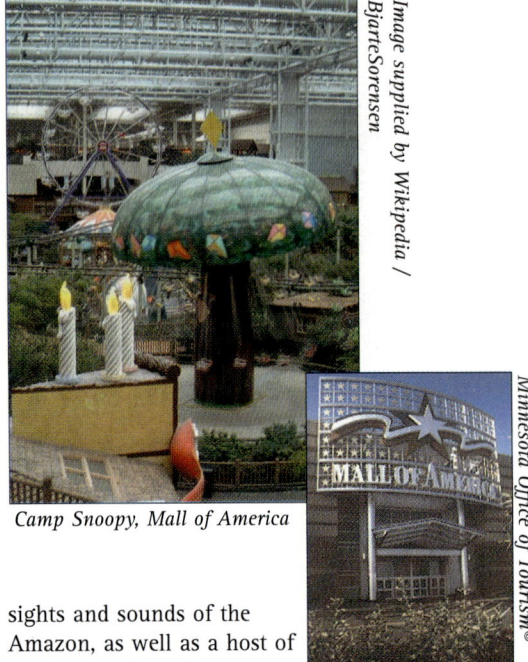

Image supplied by Wikipedia / BjarteSorensen

Camp Snoopy, Mall of America

Minnesota Office of Tourism©

1 Mall of America

Tourist Information

Minnesota Office of Tourism
Suite 100, 121 Seventh Place East, St Paul, MN 55101-2146, USA
Tel: (651) 296 5029 *or* (800) 657 3700 (toll free USA and Canada only)
Website: www.exploreminnesota.com

Mall of America

The *Mall of America*, opened in 1992, is the world's largest undercover shopping centre, covering 32 hectares (78 acres) of land just outside Bloomington. It houses over 520 shops, including American giants such as *Macy's*, *Bloomingdale's*, *Nordstrom* and *Sears*, and attracts more visitors each year than *Disney World Resort*, the *Grand Canyon* and *Graceland* combined. In addition to the shops, there are 14 cinema screens, eight nightclubs, and over 50 restaurants, including the *Rainforest Café*, complete with all the sights and sounds of the Amazon, as well as a host of other attractions. *Camp Snoopy* is a three-hectare (seven-acre) indoor theme park, featuring roller coasters, a ferris wheel and 26 other rides. At *Underwater Adventures*, a huge aquarium, visitors come face to face with 300,000 sea creatures, whilst the *LEGO Imagination Center* contains LEGO models and thousands of LEGO bricks for children to play with. Entrance to the Mall is free but some rides and attractions charge on an individual basis.

Transportation
Air: Minneapolis-St Paul International Airport. **Rail:** Train: Merced Amtrak Station. **Road:** Bus: Public services. Car: I-94, then I-494 (from the east); I-35, then I-35W, then I-94 (from the north or south); I-94, then I-494, then Hwy-77 (from the west).

Contact Addresses
Mall of America Management, 60 East Broadway, Bloomington, MN 55425, USA
Tel: (952) 883 8800
Website: www.mallofamerica.com

Nevada

1 Hoover Dam
2 Las Vegas Strip

Tourist Information

Nevada Commission on Tourism
401 North Carson Street, Carson City,
NV 89701, USA
Tel: (775) 687 4322 *or* (800) 237 0774
(toll free USA and Canada only)
Website: www.travelnevada.com

**Nevada Commission on Tourism
(UK Office)**
c/o Cellet Travel Services Ltd, Brook House,
47 High Street, Henley-in-Arden,
Warickshire B95 5AA, UK
Tel: (01564) 794 999

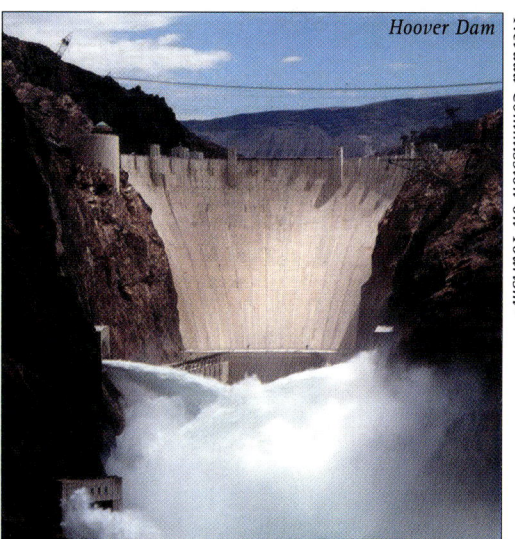

Hoover Dam

Nevada Commission on Tourism©

Hoover Dam

Completed in 1935, after five years of intensive construction, the *Hoover Dam* is a modern engineering marvel. It stretches 380m (1247ft) across the Colorado River, holding in *Lake Mead* the equivalent volume of two years' worth of the river's flow. Thousands of workers were involved in the project, which provided much needed employment during the Great Depression, although tragically 96 men died in industrial accidents during its construction. The dam contains 2,486,250 cubic metres (3,250,000 cubic yards) of concrete. It provides flood control and functions primarily as a storage reservoir, supplying water to southern Nevada, southern California and Arizona. A natural by-product is power generation, with electricity transmitted to Nevada, as well as nearby California and Arizona. Visitor tours examine the construction of the dam and explore its hydroelectric generating facilities, whilst the *Hoover Dam Visitor Center* features displays on the engineering process and the operation of the dam.

Transportation
Air: Las Vegas McCarran International Airport.
Road: Coach: Chartered services from Las Vegas.
Car: US Hwy-93 (from Las Vegas).

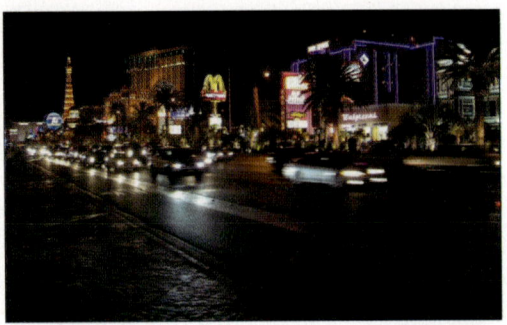

Image supplied by Wikipedia / Marcin Klapczynski

Las Vegas Strip

Contact Addresses

DOI Bureau of Reclamation, Visitor Services, PO Box 60400, Boulder City, NV 89006, USA
Tel: (702) 294 3524
Website: www.usbr.gov/lc/hooverdam/

Las Vegas Strip

The *Strip* in Las Vegas (officially known as *Las Vegas Boulevard*) is, perhaps, the defining symbol of American excess. Every year, millions of people descend upon the city, the vast majority of whom come with the sole intention of gambling. In 2004, nearly 38 million visitors came to Las Vegas and brought in US$6.8 billion in gaming revenue to the city. Nevada is the only state in the USA where gambling is legal, and nowhere is this more evident than on the Las Vegas Strip, where there are more slot machines and roulette wheels than anywhere else in the world. Here, massive neon casino-hotel complexes vie for supremacy in an ongoing competition to be the biggest and the best. In order to attract trade, many of them have turned into brightly-lit mini-theme parks, open 24 hours a day. World-famous hotel-casinos include the *Luxor*, *Paris Las Vegas* and the legendary *Caesar's Palaces*. The whole place is a non-stop cabaret of glitz and extravagance, with nightly performances in all the big hotels, featuring dancing girls, stand-up comedians and live music to keep the punters entertained. The city is also famous as a place to get hitched, with around 200,000 couples visiting Las Vegas every year to get married. Ceremonies range from the kitsch, complete with Elvis impersonator in the *Graceland Wedding Chapel* to ultra-quick drive-in weddings at the *Little White Chapel*, open 24 hours a day. If all this is not enough, there are also numerous museums in the area including *Madame Tussaud's Wax Museum*, *Guinness World of Records Museum*, the *Elvis-A-Rama Museum* and the *Liberace Museum*.

Transportation

Air: Las Vegas McCarran International Airport.
Road: Bus: Public services; Las Vegas Strip Trolley runs along the Strip. Car: I-15 into the centre of Las Vegas, then Spring Mountain Road, Desert Inn Road or Flamingo Road to join Las Vegas Boulevard (from the north or south).

Contact Addresses

Las Vegas Convention and Visitors Authority, 3150 Paradise Road, Las Vegas, NV 89109, USA
Tel: (702) 892 0711
Website: www.lvcva.com

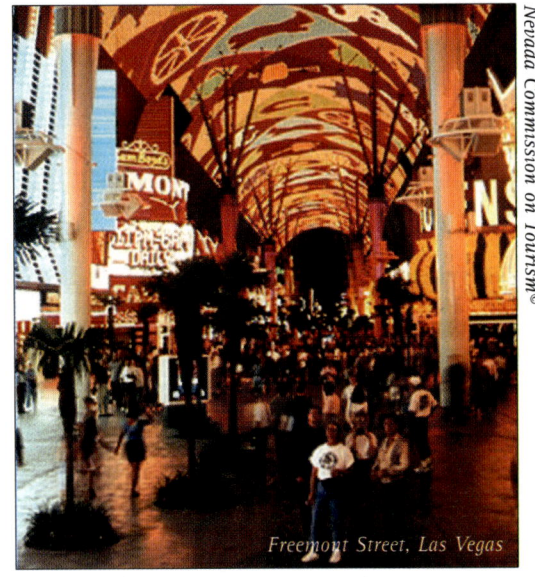

Nevada Commission on Tourism©

Freemont Street, Las Vegas

Key to symbols used in all entries:		
£........Entry charged		P........Parking
♿........Disabled access		✗........Restaurant
⛰........Man-made attraction		🛒........Shop
♥ ....Natural attraction		🏛 ......UNESCO site

New York

CANADA
St Lawrence
Ogdensburg
Lake Champlain
VERMONT
Watertown
Adirondack Mtns.
Mt Marcy 1629m
N.H.
Lake Ontario
Niagara Falls
Niagara Falls
Rochester
Seneca Falls
Rome
Utica
Saratoga Springs
Schenectady
Lake Erie
Buffalo
Finger Lakes
Syracuse
Mohawk
Troy
Albany
MASS.
Springfield
Jamestown
Watkins Glen
Ithaca
Elmira
Woodstock
Catskill Mtns.
Binghampton
Poughkeepsie
Newburgh
CONN.
PENNSYLVANIA
Tarrytown
White Plains
New York
Yonkers
Newark
Hempstead
Long Island
Philadelphia
N.J.
ATLANTIC OCEAN

300km
150mls
✈ international airport
◉ state capital

1 Central Park
2 Empire State Building
3 Greenwich Village
4 Metropolitan Museum of Art
5 Niagara Falls, USA
6 Statue of Liberty
7 Times Square

Tourist Information

New York State Division of Tourism
PO Box 2603, Albany, NY 12220-0603, USA
Tel: (518) 474 4116 *or* (800) 225 5697 (toll free USA, Canada and US External Territories)
Website: www.iloveny.com

New York State Department of Economic Development (Tourism Division)
Media House, 4 Stratford Place, London
W1C 18T, UK
Tel: (020) 7629 2720
Website: www.empire.state.ny.us

Key to symbols: £ Entry charged & Disabled access
⚒ Man-made attraction ❤ Natural attraction
🅿 Parking ✗ Restaurant ⛲ Shop 🏛 UNESCO site

Central Park

Completed in 1873, *Central Park* was designed to provide New York with 341 hectares (843 acres) of rural paradise in what was, at the time, the out-of-the-way northern reaches of Manhattan. Now, located almost in the dead centre of New York due to urban expansion between 59th and 110th streets, Central Park is very much an integral part of the city's landscape. Apart from being a refreshing area of greenery in the middle of a very dense and busy city, Central Park has a cultural side, with public programmes offered by the Central Park Conservancy, as well as a small zoo, a dairy, fountains and an ice-skating rink. The park has featured in many films over the years and is also home to statues of famous people (real and fictional), including Ludwig Van Beethoven, Alice in Wonderland, Hans Christian Anderson and Robert Burns. It is also home to the Strawberry Fields Memorial, dedicated to the late John Lennon who was shot dead in the city on December 8 1980. The park attracts joggers, rollerbladers and buskers every day, as well as thousands of tourists who come to see the most famous urban park in the USA.

Transportation
Air: New York La Guardia International Airport, New York John F Kennedy International Airport. **Rail:** Train: Grand Central Station. Underground: A, B, C, D, N, R, 4, 5 or 6 trains to Fifth Avenue or 59th Street/Columbus Circle. **Road:** Bus: Public services.

Contact Addresses
Central Park Conservancy, 14 East 60th Street, New York, NY 10022, USA
Tel: (212) 310 6600
Website: www.centralparknyc.org

Empire State Building

Completed in 1931 during the Great Depression at a cost of over US$40 million, the *Empire State Building* is an enduring symbol of New York City and the USA. It was built during an era of skyscraper wars, and at 443.2m (1454ft) tall, the Empire State Building defeated the world's then tallest building and fellow Art Deco gem, the nearby *Chrysler Building*. The developers, Empire State Inc, initially struggled to find any tenants for the gigantic office block, due to its size, although it was eventually leased to various companies. Visitors can access the observatory on the 86th floor for spectacular views over the Big Apple. In addition, there is a virtual-reality movie theatre with *NYSkyride* attraction (www.skyride.com) located on the second floor. The tower has also featured in numerous films, such as 'An Affair to Remember', 'When Harry Met Sally', 'King Kong', 'Independence Day', 'Taxi Driver' and 'Sleepless in Seattle'.

Transportation
Air: New York La Guardia International Airport, New York John F Kennedy International Airport. **Rail:** Train: Grand Central or Penn stations. Underground: 34th Street/Penn or Path to 34th Street/Avenue of the Americas. **Road:** Bus: Public services. Coach: Port Authority Bus Terminal.

Contact Addresses
Empire State Building, 350 Fifth Avenue, New York, NY 10118, USA
Tel: (212) 736 3100 *or* (888) 759 7433 (*Skyride*) (toll free USA and Canada only)
Website: www.esbnyc.com

Greenwich Village

Greenwich Village is one of the liveliest and trendiest districts of New York City. Originally a tobacco plantation located towards the tip of *Manhattan Island*, it was given its name by British naval commander, Sir Peter Warren who purchased a farm there in the early 18th century. It was not until New York's yellow fever outbreak in 1822 that people began to move here to escape the disease-ridden conditions of the city, and Greenwich quickly flourished, as banks and businesses sprang up alongside the elegant houses of their wealthy owners. By the turn of the last century, New York's richest residents had begun to move to more fashionable areas of town, such as *Fifth Avenue*. This exodus meant that the

houses were populated by struggling artists and writers, who spent their time in the Village's many bars and coffee houses, discussing political ideals. Greenwich thus gained its reputation as New York's Bohemian, anti-establishment quarter, as well as a centre for women's liberation. The Village also gained a reputation as the focus of the gay rights movement after the infamous Stonewall Riots that followed the police raid on the Stonewall Inn, a gay bar in Greenwich Village, in 1969. The area's reputation as a Bohemian melting pot has stuck, despite the fact that it has once again become home to the city's well-heeled professionals since the sharp rise in property prices during the 1980s economic boom forced writers and artists out. *Christopher Street*, which runs through the centre of the district, is the hub of New York's gay scene, whilst *Greenwich Avenue* is a good place to shop, with plenty of bookstores and second-hand clothes shops. Greenwich Village also has a thriving nightlife, with many of its lively cafés and bars staying open later than those elsewhere in Manhattan.

Transportation
Air: New York La Guardia International Airport or New York John F Kennedy International Airport. **Rail:** Train: Grand Central Station. Underground: Christopher Street or West 4 Street–Washington Square. **Road:** Bus: Public services. Coach: Port Authority Bus Terminal.

Contact Addresses
NYC & Company, 810 Seventh Avenue, Third Floor, New York, NY 10019, USA
Tel: (212) 484 1200
Website: www.nycvisit.com

Metropolitan Museum of Art

With a diverse collection embracing over two million works of art, the *Metropolitan Museum of Art* ranks as one of the world's great museums. The museum houses particularly impressive collections of work by Monet, Cézanne, Vermeer and Giovanni Battista Tiepolo. The modern art section comprises paintings by a wide variety of artists including Modigliani, Picasso, Braque and Charles Rennie Mackintosh. As would be expected,

New York State Division of Tourism©

Niagara Falls

there are also fine displays of American art, from colonial times to the present day; these include pieces of decorative art, such as ceramics and Tiffany glass. *The Cloisters* is a separate branch of the museum, located in Ford Tryon Park in north Manhattan overlooking the Hudson River, and is considered to be one of the greatest collections of Medieval art in the world.

Transportation
Air: New York La Guardia International Airport, New York John F Kennedy International Airport. **Rail:** Train: Grand Central Station. Underground: 77th Street, 86th Street or Fifth Avenue. **Road:** Bus: Public services.

Contact Addresses
Metropolitan Museum of Art, 1000 Fifth Avenue, New York, NY 10028, USA
Tel: (212) 535 7710
Website: www.metmuseum.org

Niagara Falls, USA

Niagara Falls is one of the most popular tourist destinations in North America, made up of two separate parts, *Horseshoe Falls*, on the Canadian side and *American Falls* on the US side. Although not the highest waterfall in the world (that record goes to the *Angel Falls* in Venezuela), they move a staggering volume of 168,000 cubic metres (219,600 cubic yards) of water per minute over a drop of 51m (167ft), making them one of the natural wonders of the world. In the past, people have attempted numerous daring stunts here, including dropping over the edge in a barrel. The most famous daredevil was the Frenchman Jean Francois Gravelot (known as The Great Blondin) who crossed the Niagara Falls on a tightrope in 1859 and lived to tell the tale. The town surrounding Niagara Falls, a celebrated North American honeymoon destination, offers a wealth of visitor activities including a casino, as well as land and boat tours of the falls.

Transportation
Air: Buffalo Niagara Airport or Pearson International Airport (Toronto). **Rail:** Train: Amtrak Station. **Road:** Bus: Public services. Car: Queen Elizabeth Way (QEW) towards Niagara, then Hwy-420 to Niagara Falls (from Toronto); I-190 (from Buffalo); I-81, I-90, I-290 and I-190 (exit 22) (from Syracuse).

Contact Addresses
Niagara Falls Convention and Visitors Bureau, 310 Fourth Street, Niagara Falls, NY 14303, USA
Tel: (716) 285 2400
Website: www.buffalocvb.org

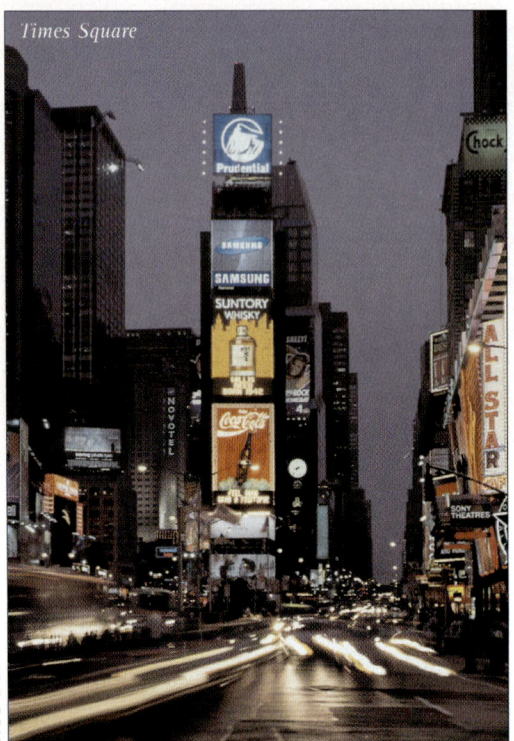

Times Square

NYS DED©

or Newark International Airport. **Rail:** Underground: Bowling Green. **Water:** Ferry: The Statue of Liberty/Ellis Island Ferry departs from Battery Park (New York City) and Liberty State Park (Jersey City, New Jersey). **Road:** Bus: Public services to ferry terminal.

Contact Addresses
Statue of Liberty National Monument and Ellis Island, Liberty Island, New York, NY 10004, USA
Tel: (212) 363 3200
Website: www.nps.gov/stli

Statue of Liberty

A gift to the USA from France in 1886 to celebrate the 100th anniversary of American independence, the *Statue of Liberty* greeted millions of immigrants during the 19th century who came to America to seek a better life. Enjoying a fine position in New York Harbour, this world-famous statue, which was originally called *Liberty Enlightening the World*, has become a defining American symbol of freedom and democracy. This 45m (151ft) statue of a woman holding a torch aloft, was designed by the French sculptor Frédéric-Auguste Bartholdi, and was modelled on the Colossus of Rhodes. A limited number of time passes are issued on the day allowing people to enter the monument. The grounds are still open to the public without a ticket and offer visitors the opportunity to see the statue up close. Nearby Ellis Island, part of the Statue of Liberty National Monument, houses a museum devoted to the history of immigration.

Transportation
Air: New York La Guardia International Airport, New York John F Kennedy International Airport

Times Square

Located just north of 42nd Street, *Times Square* has long been associated with theatre and nightlife and all the excitement and glitz of New York City. There is no better way to discover the Big Apple than by going to see a show in a Broadway theatre, located just off Times Square; the area is home to over 50 theatres, around 30 hotels, cinemas, shops, restaurants and bars. Often referred to as the 'Crossroads of the World', the city's theatre district is alight with neon signs and giant TV screens. Always buzzing with energy, it is an ideal place to experience the atmosphere of life on New York's busy streets. Attracting over 30 million tourists every year, Times Square can be a daunting experience to first time visitors due to the constant stream of traffic and huge crowds. The square is a popular place to spend New Year's Eve when over half a million people gather to join in the festivities.

Transportation
Air: New York John F Kennedy International Airport, New York LaGuardia Airport or Newark International Airport. **Rail:** Underground: 15 subway lines go to Times Square; Amtrak and the Long Island Rail Road companies have services to Penn Station. **Road:** Bus: Public services.

Contact Addresses
Times Square Business Improvement District, 1560 Broadway, Suite 800, NY 10036, USA
Tel: (212) 768 1560
Website: www.timessquarenyc.org

Ohio

Ann Arbor, MICHIGAN
Detroit, CANADA
Lake Erie
Bass Is., Lakewood, Mentor
Toledo, Lorain, Euclid
Maumee, Sandusky, Parma, Cleveland
Defiance, Cuyahoga Valley Nat. Rec. Area, Aurora, Warren
Fort Wayne, Findlay, Youngstown
Lima, Mansfield, Akron, Canton
Marion
Campbell Hill △472m
OHIO, PENNSYLVANIA
Upper Arlington, Columbus, Newark, Zanesville
Dayton, Springfield, Lancaster, Ohio
Kettering, Scioto, Muskingum
Miami, Middletown, Chillicothe, Athens, Marietta
Hamilton, Pomeroy
Cincinnati
Ohio, Portsmouth, WEST VIRGINIA
Ironton, Kanawha
KENTUCKY

200km / 100mls
✈ international airport
◉ state capital

1 Rock and Roll Hall of Fame

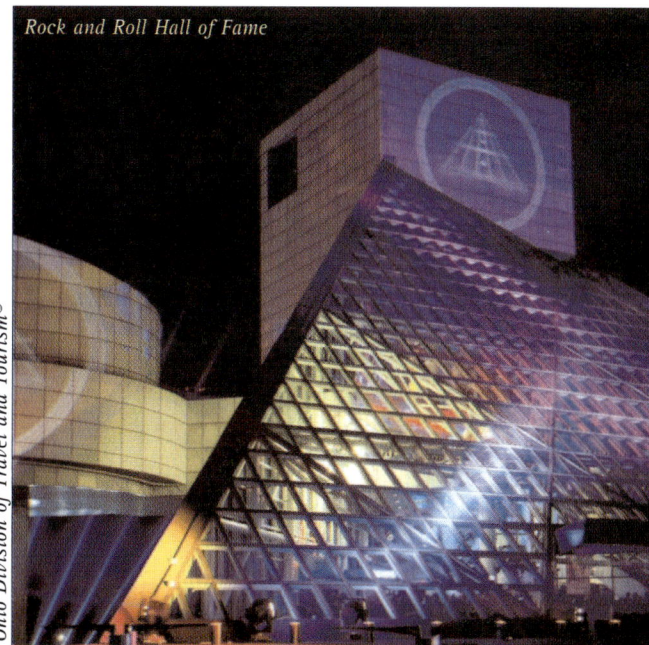

Rock and Roll Hall of Fame

Ohio Division of Travel and Tourism©

Tourist Information

Ohio Division of Travel & Tourism
77 South High Street, 29th Floor, PO Box 1001, Columbus, OH 43216-1001, USA
Tel: (614) 466 8844 *or* (800) 848 1300 (toll free USA and Canada only)
Website: www.ohiotourism.com

Rock and Roll Hall of Fame

The *Rock and Roll Hall of Fame* celebrates the American rock music by honouring its most popular and influential performers, producers, songwriters and djs. The phrase 'rock and roll' was coined by the Cleveland dj Alan Freed in 1951, so it somehow seems fitting that Cleveland should have been chosen as the home of this attraction. Opened in 1995 and designed by the renowned Chinese architect I M Pei, the building is a 13,935 sq m (150,000 sq ft) modern structure with bold designs and a dramatic location on the shores of Lake Erie. The museum features a *Hall of Fame* exhibit, which includes a computerised juke-box containing nearly every song by performers featured, their signatures etched in glass, film exhibits and displays of artefacts. Exhibitions cover different musical genres focusing on icons from the world of rock and pop, including the Beatles, Elvis Presley and the Rolling Stones.

Transportation
Air: Cleveland Hopkins International Airport. **Rail:** Rapid: Downtown to Public Square. Waterfront Rapid: North Coast Harbour Station. **Road:** Bus: Public services.

Contact Addresses
Rock and Roll Hall of Fame, 1 Key Plaza, Cleveland, OH 44114, USA
Tel: (888) 764 7625
Website: www.rockhall.com

South Dakota

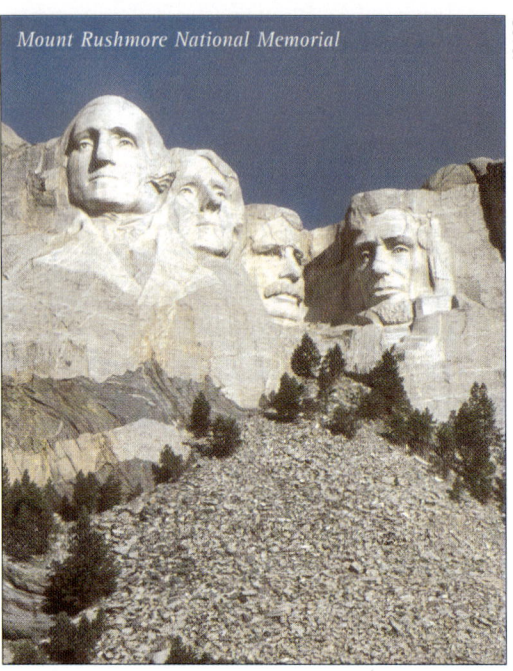

Mount Rushmore National Memorial

Corel©

1 Mount Rushmore National Memorial

Tourist Information

South Dakota Department of Tourism
711 East Wells Avenue, Pierre, SD 57501-3369,
USA
Tel: (605) 773 3301 *or* (800) 732 5682 (toll
free USA and Canada only)
Website: www.travelsd.com

Rocky Mountain International
PO Box 214, Fareham, Hampshire PO14 2TD,
UK
Tel: (01329) 665 111 (trade enquiries only) *or*
(09063) 640 655 (customer request line; 60p
per minute)
Website: www.rmi-realamerica.com

Mount Rushmore National Memorial

Mount Rushmore National Memorial is one of the
USA's most renowned national monuments. The
site in South Dakota is home to 18m-tall (60ft)
faces of four US presidents – George Washington,
Thomas Jefferson, Theodore Roosevelt and
Abraham Lincoln – perched 152m (465ft) in the
air. These giant faces are carved into solid rock
and stand as a gateway to America's majestic
west. Originally called *The Shrine of Democracy*,

the idea to build a monument of this size was
conceived by the historian Duane Robinson and
the sculptor Gutzon Borglum in 1923. Work began
on the monument, which is surrounded by the
Black Hills National Forest, in 1927, and took over
14 years to complete the fundraising and carving.
Today, the memorial is an internationally
recognised symbol of the first 150 years of
America's history and the part the four presidents
played in founding it. The memorial hosts many
exhibits, walks and lectures during the summer
months.

Transportation
Air: Rapid City Regional Airport. **Road:** Car: Hwy-
16 and Hwy-244 (from Rapid City).

Contact Addresses
Mount Rushmore National Memorial, PO Box 268,
Keystone, SD 57751, USA
Tel: (605) 574 2523 *or* 574 3171 (recorded
information)
Website: www.nps.gov/moru

Tennessee

1 Graceland
2 Grand Ole Opry

Tourist Information

Tennessee Department of Tourism Development
Rachel Jackson Building, 320 Sixth Avenue
North, Fifth Floor, Nashville, TN 37243, USA
Tel: (615) 741 2159 *or* (800) 836 6200 (toll
free USA and Canada only)
Website: www.tnvacation.com

Tennessee Tourism (UK)
Lofthouse Enterprises, Woodland Park Street,
Hitchin, Herts SG4 9AH, UK
Tel: (01462) 440 784
Website: www.deep-south-usa.com/tenn.html

Graceland

Graceland is America's monument to one of its
favourite musicians and icons, Elvis Presley. The
'King' bought the colonial-style mansion in 1957
and lived there until his death in 1977. The
house has been open to the public since 1982,
becoming a shrine to his music and his legacy.
At the site, which is located 16km (10 miles)
from Memphis, visitors can enter the rooms
where the star and his family lived, tour Elvis'
jet planes, shop at *Graceland Plaza* or stay at the
Heartbreak Hotel. Highlights include the *Trophy
Building* and the *Meditation Garden* where Elvis
was buried.

Transportation
Air: Memphis International Airport. **Rail:** Train:
Memphis Central Station. **Road:** Bus: Public
services. Car: I-55 (exit 5-B) (from St Louis,
Chicago or New Orleans); I-240 (from Memphis
International Airport).

Contact Addresses
Graceland, Elvis Presley Enterprises Inc, PO Box
16508, 3734 Elvis Presley Boulevard, Memphis, TN
38186-0508, USA
Tel: (901) 332 3322
Website: www.elvis.com

Grand Ole Opry

Grand Ole Opry is the world's longest running live
radio show. It was first broadcast as a weekly barn
dance show on November 28 1925, at a time
when the radio was fast growing in popularity. In
the early days, the show followed a classical music
program, and radio announcer George D Hay joked
that the Grand Opera that listeners had just heard
would be followed by performances of the 'Grand
Ole Opry' – Hay adopted this impromptu name
and it stuck. Within a few years the show became
so popular that thousands of fans flocked to see it
performed live. After a succession of venues, it
finally settled in the specially designed 4400 seat
Grand Ole Opry House in Nashville in 1974, from
where it has been broadcast ever since.

Transportation
Air: Nashville Airport. **Rail:** Train: Memphis
Amtrak Station. **Road:** Car: Hwy-40 (from
Knoxville or Memphis); Hwy-65 (from Louisville
or Birmingham); Hwy-24 (from Chattanooga or
Paducah).

Contact Addresses
Grand Ole Opry, 2802 Opryland Drive, Nashville,
TN 37214, USA
Tel: (615) 871 6779
Website: www.opry.com

Texas

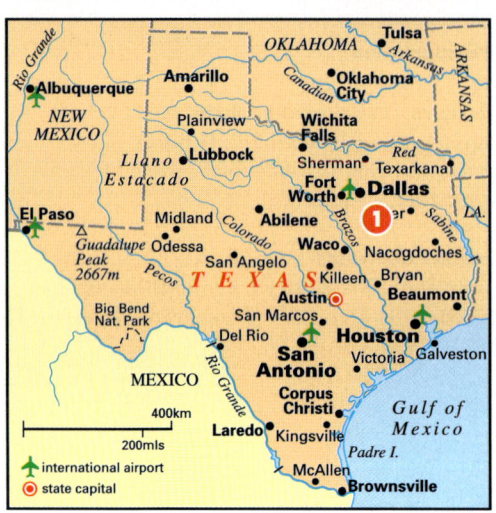

Tourist Information

Texas Economic Development, Tourism Division
1700 North Congress, Suite 200, PO Box 12728, Austin, TX 78711-2728, USA
Tel: (512) 462 9191 *or* (800) 888 8839 (toll free USA and Canada only)
Website: www.traveltex.com

State of Texas Tourism Office
c/o First Public Relations, Molasses House, Clove Hitch Quay, Plantation Wharf, London SW11 3TN, UK
Tel: (020) 7978 5233

Sixth Floor Museum

The *Texas School Book Depository* was a rather ordinary building in downtown Dallas until the infamous assassination of US President John F Kennedy on November 22 1963 as he travelled in an open limousine through Dallas on a pre-election visit. Lee Harvey Oswald, the 24-year-old Dallas citizen who was accused of the crime, and was himself shot dead by nightclub owner Jack Ruby just two days later, had a filing job at the depository. The deadly shot was fired from the

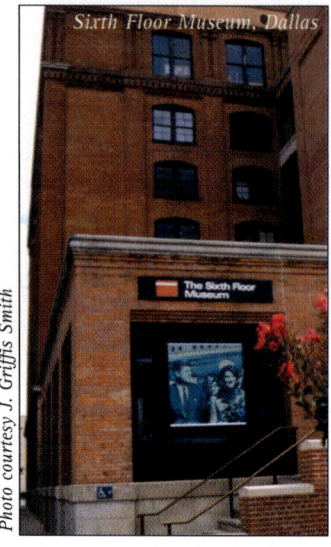

Photo courtesy J. Griffs Smith

sixth floor of the building, which is now the *Sixth Floor Museum at Dealey Plaza* documenting both the assassination itself and the life and times of JFK. Visitors can immerse themselves in the events of the fateful day, with a minute-by-minute account of the action as well as recordings of news broadcasts and even material showing mourning vigils in India and Germany. Other exhibitions focus on the four investigations into the crime, the legacy of Kennedy's administration, and the various theories on who carried out the assassination. The corner staircase where the rifle was found, and down which the assassin is thought to have escaped, has been reconstructed according to official police photographs. Background information to the shooting is provided through displays on the 1960s political, cultural and social movements, and visitors can add their own comments to memorial books which are kept as part of the museum archives.

Transportation
Air: Dallas-Fort Worth International Airport, Dallas Love Field Airport (domestic flights). **Rail:** Train: Union Station. DART (Light Rail System): West End Station or Union Station. **Road:** DART Trolleybus: Route 706 to Union Station or West End Station. Bus: Public services.

Contact Addresses
Sixth Floor Museum at Dealey Plaza, 411 Elm Street, Dallas, TX 75202, USA
Tel: (214) 747 6660
Website: www.jfk.org

Washington, DC

1 Lincoln Memorial
2 Smithsonian Institution
3 White House

Tourist Information

Washington, DC Convention & Tourism Corporation
1212 New York Avenue, Suite 600, NW, Washington, DC 20005, USA
Tel: (202) 789 7000
Website: www.washington.org

Washington, DC Convention & Tourism Corporation
c/o Representation Plus, 11 Blades Court, 121 Deodar Road, London SW15 2NU, UK
Tel: (020) 8877 4521

Lincoln Memorial

Modelled upon a Doric temple, the *Lincoln Memorial* is a tribute to President Abraham Lincoln and the nation he fought to preserve during the Civil War (1861-1865), the nation's bloodiest conflict. Enclosed by a colonnade and complemented by a reflecting pool in front, a large statue of President Lincoln, sculpted by Daniel Chester French, sits in solemn thought, grasping the arms of his throne-like chair. The monument has the Gettysburg Address inscribed on its southern wall and a mural painted by Jules Guerin above it, showing the angel of truth liberating a slave. As a symbol of freedom and racial harmony, the Lincoln Memorial was the site of Martin Luther King's 'I Have a Dream' speech in August 1963.

Transportation
Air: Washington Dulles International Airport, Washington Ronald Reagan National Airport, Baltimore-Washington Airport. **Rail:** Train: Union Station. Underground: Foggy Bottom. **Road:** Bus: Public services.

Contact Addresses
Lincoln Memorial, 900 Ohio Drive South West, Washington, DC 20024, USA
Tel: (202) 426 6841
Website: www.nps.gov/linc

Smithsonian Institution

The *Smithsonian Institution*, established in 1846 with money left to the United States by the English scientist James Smithson, is the largest museum complex in the world. It is composed of 16 museums and the National Zoo in Washington DC, as well as two museums in New York City. One of the most famous is the *National Air and Space Museum*. Opened in 1976, the National Air and Space Museum celebrates the history and evolution of air and space technology. Exhibits include the Wright Brothers' 1903 *Flyer*, Charles Lindbergh's *Spirit of St Louis*, and moon rock collected by the Apollo astronauts (Neil Armstrong and Buzz Aldrin) from the lunar surface, when they touched down on July 20 1969. Other museums in Washington include the *Anacostia Museum and Center for African American History and Culture*, *Arthur M Sackler Gallery*, *Art and Industries Building*, *Freer Gallery of Art*, *Hirshhorn Museum and Sculpture Garden*, *National Museum of African Art*, *National Museum of American History*, *National*

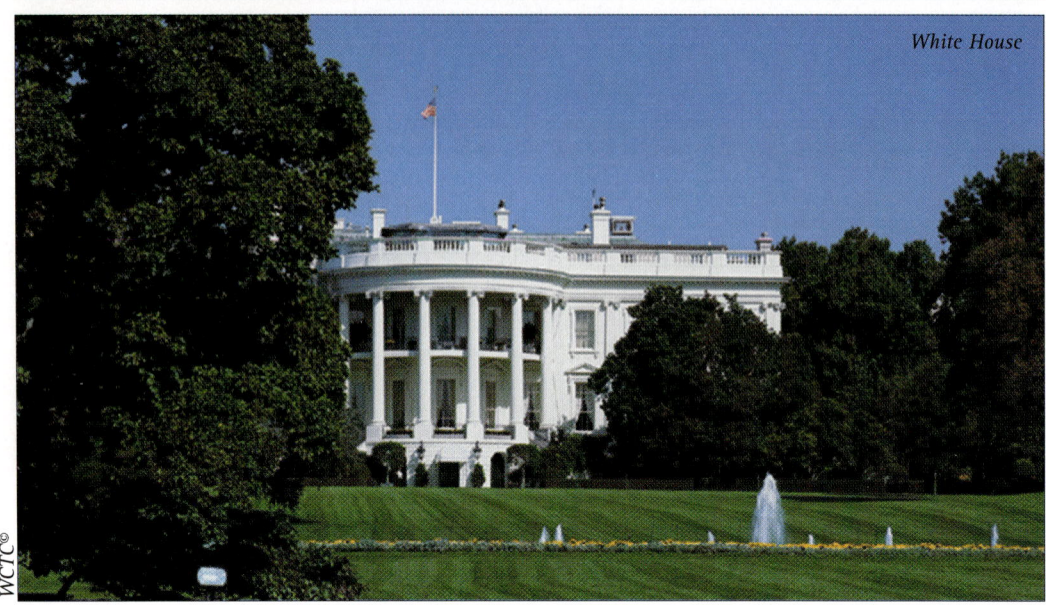

White House

WCTC©

Museum of Natural History, *National Portrait Gallery*, *National Postal Museum*, *Renwick Gallery*, *Smithsonian American Art Museum* and *Smithsonian Institution Building*. The New York museums include the *Cooper-Hewitt*, *National Design Museum* and the *National Museum of the American Indian*.

Transportation
Air: Washington Dulles International Airport, Washington Ronald Reagan National Airport. **Rail:** Train: Union Station. Metrorail: Smithsonian. **Road:** Bus: Public services.

Contact Addresses
Smithsonian Information Center, SI Building, Room 153, Washington, DC 20560, USA
Tel: (202) 357 2020
Website: www.si.edu

White House

The *White House* is where the President of the United States of America lives and carries out official duties as Head of State. It is the most famous building in Washington, DC and was built between 1792 and 1800 by the Irish-born architect James Hoban. Although commissioned during President George Washington's lifetime, the first residents of the White House were President John Adams and his wife who moved into the house in 1800. The building has had a colourful past. It burned down during the War of 1812 (which is often called America's second War of Independence) between America and Great Britain which lasted until the end of 1814, and was rebuilt in 1815, only to endure (and survive) another fire in the West Wing in 1929. Self-guided tours of certain areas of the White House are possible but must be arranged in advance.

Transportation
Air: Washington Dulles International Airport, Washington Ronald Reagan National Airport. **Rail:** Train: Union Station. Metrorail: Federal Triangle (blue or orange lines), Metro Center (blue, orange or red lines) or McPherson Square (blue or orange lines). **Road:** Bus: Public services.

Contact Addresses
President's Park, White House Liaison, 1100 Ohio Drive, SW, Washington, DC 20242, USA *or*
White House Visitor Center, National Park Service, 1450 Pennsylvania Avenue, NW, Washington, DC 20230, USA
Tel: (202) 208 1631 *or* 456 7041 (24-hour information line)
Website: www.nps.gov/whho *or* www.whitehouse.gov

Washington State

```
300km
150mls
```
✈ international airport
◉ state capital

1 Space Needle

Tourist Information

Seattle's Convention & Visitors Bureau
520 Pike Street, Suite 1300, Seattle, WA 98101, USA
Tel: (206) 461 5800 (administration) *or* 461 5840 (visitor information)
Website: www.seeseattle.org

Washington State Tourism Office
PO Box 42500, Olympia, WA 98504-2500, USA
Tel: (360) 725 5051 *or* (800) 544 1800 (toll free USA and Canada only)
Website: www.experiencewashington.com

Washington State Information Office
c/o First Public Relations, Molasses House, Clove Hitch Quay, Plantation Wharf, London SW11 3TN, UK
Tel: (020) 7978 5233

Space Needle

Standing at 185m (605ft) high, Seattle's most famous building is a great place from which to enjoy outstanding 360-degree views across the city and Washington State, including the *Cascade* and *Olympic* mountain ranges, Puget Sound and Mount Rainier. The *Space Needle* is the most recognised landmark in Seattle, and visitors can also eat in its famous revolving restaurant. Designed by Edward E Carlson and completed in 1961 for US$4.5 million, the top of this Space Age tower can be reached in just 43 seconds by a futuristic glass lift. The tower is located at the *Seattle Center*, a 30-hectare (74-acre) site built for the 1962 World Fair, which is also home to the *Pacific Science Center*, offering laser and hologram exhibits, the *Boeing IMAX Theater* and the *Children's Museum*.

Transportation
Air: Seattle-Tacoma International Airport. **Road:** Monorail: A monorail service operates from Westlake Center and stops near the Space Needle. **Road:** Coach: Coaches set down on Broad Street, west of Fifth Avenue. Bus: Public services.

Contact Addresses
Space Needle, 400 Broad Street, Seattle, WA 98109, USA
Tel: (206) 905 2100
Website: www.spaceneedle.com

Space Needle

Wyoming

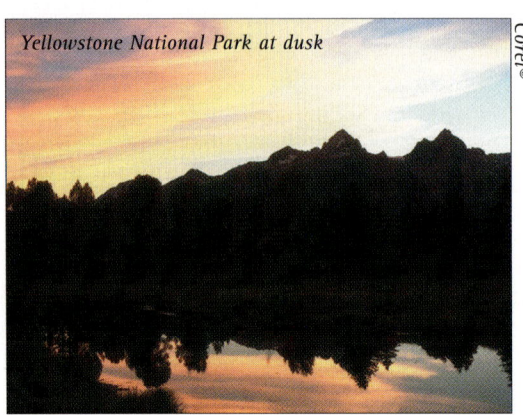

Yellowstone National Park at dusk

Corel©

300km
150mls

⊙ state capital

---

1 Yellowstone National Park

Tourist Information

Wyoming Business Council – Tourism Office
I-25 at College Drive, Cheyenne, WY 82002,
USA
Tel: (307) 777 7777 *or* (800) 225 5996 (toll
free USA and Canada only)
Website: www.wyomingtourism.org

Rocky Mountain International
PO Box 214, Fareham, Hampshire PO14 2TD,
UK
Tel: (01329) 665 111 (trade enquiries only) *or*
(09063) 640 655 (customer request line; calls
cost 60p per minute)
Website: www.rmi-realamerica.com

Yellowstone National Park

Established in 1872, *Yellowstone National Park* is
the first and oldest national park in the world.
Renowned for its geothermal phenomena, the park
has more geysers and hot springs than the rest of
the world combined. The mineral waters of
Mammoth Hot Springs in the northwest of the park,
have long been attracting visitors seeking a natural
cure for various ailments. Other natural attractions
include the *Grand Canyon of the Yellowstone River*
(not to be confused with the *Grand Canyon* in
Arizona), fossil forests and *Yellowstone Lake*.
Natural wildlife, such as bears, wolves, elk, bison
and trout, abound and can often be seen from the
road. Evidence of human activity in the park,
dating back as far as 12,000 years, has also been
found and visitors can learn more about the area's
history at the *Albright Visitor Center Museum*. The
Canyon Visitor Center also features displays on the
culture and wildlife of Yellowstone. Visitors who
wish to stay overnight in the park can take
advantage of the many inns, lodges and campsites
located within the park boundaries.

Transportation
Air: Denver International Airport, Cody Airport
(domestic flights), Jackson Airport (domestic
flights), Bozeman Airport (domestic flights),
Billings Airport (domestic flights), Idaho Falls
Airport (domestic flights), West Yellowstone
Airport (open Jun-early Sep) (domestic flights).
Road: Bus: Services to West Yellowstone (from
Bozeman); summer services to West Yellowstone
(from Idaho).

Contact Addresses
Yellowstone National Park, Visitor Services Office,
PO Box 168, Yellowstone National Park, WY
82190, USA
Tel: (307) 344 7381
Website: www.nps.gov/yell

Venezuela

Tourist Information

Venezuela Tourism Board
(Corporación de Turismo de Venezuela)
Avenida v. Lecuna, Parque Central, Torre
Oeste, Piso 37, Caracas, Venezuela
Tel: (02) 574 1968

Embassy of the Republic of Venezuela
1 Cromwell Road, London SW7 2HW, UK
Tel: (020) 7584 4206 or 7581 2776
Website: www.venezlon.demon.co.uk

Angel Falls (Salto Ángel)

At 988m (3212ft), *Angel Falls* is the tallest waterfall
in the world. To many it is also the most stunning,
with water spilling into a freefall of nearly 1km
(0.6 miles) before crashing into a pool. Double
rainbows can often be seen in the spray-drenched
air above. Located in *Canaima National Park*,

600km (373 miles) south of Ciudad Bolívar and
50km (30 miles) southeast of Canaima village, the
waterfall was made public to the wider world in
1937 by American pilot Jimmie Angel, who was
searching for gold in the area. Angel Falls used to
be a holy site for the Incas, and is still sacred to
the local Venezuelan tribes today. Tours to the
falls can be arranged from the nearest town,
Ciudad Bolívar, by boat or plane.

Transportation
Air: Caracas Simon Bolivar International Airport
or Ciudad Bolívar Airport to Canaima Airport;
then private tour operator's plane or boat. **Water:**
Boat: Motorised canoe services from Ciudad
Bolívar (Jun-Dec). **Road:** Bus: Services from
Caracas or Ciudad Bolívar.

Contact Addresses
For more information on Angel Falls, contact
Corporación de Turismo de Venezuela (see **Tourist
Information** above).

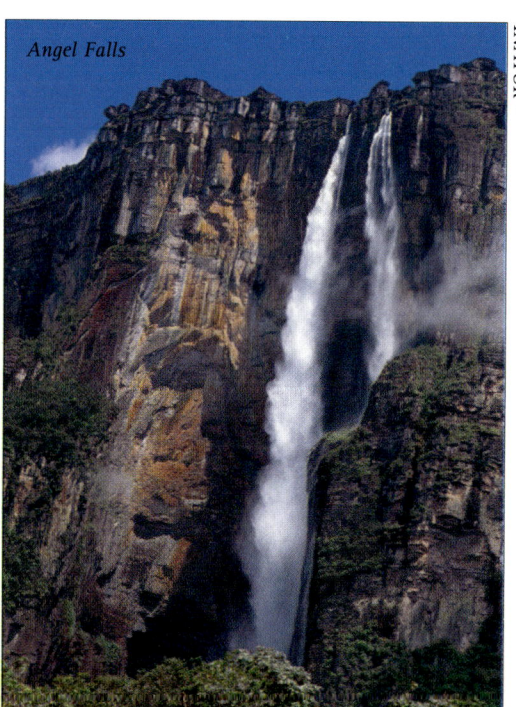

Angel Falls

INATUR®

Vietnam

1 Cu Chi Tunnels (Cu Chi Diadao)
2 Hué Imperial Palace (Hué Cung Vua)

Tourist Information

Vietnam Tourism
30a Ly Thuong Kiet Street, Hanoi, Vietnam
Tel: (04) 825 7532 *or* 826 4154
Website: www.vn-tourism.com

Embassy of the Socialist Republic of Vietnam
12 Victoria Road, London W8 5RD, UK
Tel: (020) 7937 1912 *or* 7937 3222 (visa section)

Cu Chi Tunnels (Cu Chi Diadao)

The *Cu Chi Tunnels* is an underground network excavated by the Vietnamese and used by the Viet

Cong during both the French-Indochina War (1946-1954) and the Vietnam War (1955-1975). Stretching for over 200km (124 miles) and connecting numerous villages in the provinces, the tunnels once housed mini-hospitals, store rooms and factories, and were used as living quarters by both Vietnamese fighters and local villagers.

Transportation
Air: Tan Son Nhat International Airport. **Road:** Coach: Daily coach trip.

Contact Addresses
For more information on Cu Chi Tunnels, contact Vietnam Tourism (see **Tourist Information** above).

Hué Imperial Palace (Hué Cung Vua)

Hué was the political, cultural and religious capital of unified Vietnam between 1802 and 1945. Today, the imperial city is home to many important sites, the most famous of which is the *Imperial Palace* (or *Citadel*) situated on the north banks of the Perfume River. Surrounded by a wall and a moat, the Citadel can be entered via one of 10 gates and contains the *Nine Holy Cannons* that used to defend the palace, the *Imperial Enclosure* where the Emperor carried out his official business, the *Palace of Supreme Harmony* and the *Hall of the Mandarins*. It was also home to the *Purple Forbidden Palace* which was reserved for use by the Emperor himself. The whole city was recognised as a UNESCO World Heritage Site in 1993.

Transportation
Air: Phu Bia Airport. **Rail:** Train: Reunification Express train to Hanoi (from Ho Chi Minh City). **Road:** Bus: Dong Ba Bus Station. Coach: Private tour operators organise trips to Hué.

Contact Addresses
Vietnam Tourism, 14 Ngguyen Van Cu, Hué, Vietnam
Tel: (054) 828 316
Website: www.vn-tourism.com

Yemen

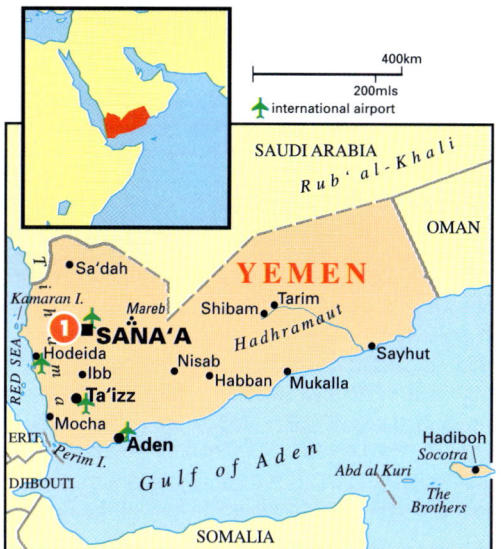

1 Old City of Sana'a (al-Medina al-qadima)

Tourist Information

Ministry of Tourism and Environment
PO Box 5607, 48 Amman Street, Sana'a,
Republic of Yemen
Tel: (01) 252 319
Website: www.yenet.com/tourism

Embassy of the Republic of Yemen
57 Cromwell Road, London SW7 2ED, UK
Tel: (020) 7584 6607

Old City of Sana'a (al-Medina al-qadima)

The UNESCO-preserved site of the *Old City of Sana'a* is the largest preserved old city in the Arab world. Sana'a, which translates from Arabic as 'fortified place', has been the political capital of Yemen since the unification of the Yemen Arab Republic and the People's Democratic Republic of Yemen in 1990. It is one of the oldest continuously inhabited cities in the world, and according to Yemeni legend was founded by Shem, one of the three sons of Noah, possibly as

early as the second century BC. Once an Arabian centre for Christians and Jews, the city was converted to Islam in AD 632. Apart from brief periods of Ottoman control – in the 16th century and between 1872 and 1940 – members of the Zaydi dynasty thereafter ruled Sana'a more or less continuously until 1962, when it became the capital of the newly founded Yemen Arab Republic. Surrounded by ancient clay walls which stand 6m to 9m (20ft to 30ft) high, the old city is a wonderland of over 100 mosques, 12 hammams (baths) and 6500 houses. Most of the buildings date back to the seventh and eighth centuries BC, when the city achieved prominence as an important centre for Islam, and were constructed from dark basalt stone and brick. One of the most popular attractions is the 1000-year-old *Suq al-Milh* (Salt Market), where it is possible to buy not only salt but also bread, spices, raisins, cotton, copper, pottery, silverware, antiques, and a host of other goods. The seventh century *al-Jami'al-Kabir* (Great Mosque) is one of the oldest in the Muslim world and its Persian-style minarets pierce the city's skyline. The *Liberty Gate*, formerly known as *Bab al-Yaman* (Yemen Gate) until the 1962 revolution, is one of the many points of entry through the city walls and is over 700 years old. The *National Museum* consists of three floors of displays and exhibitions, including ancient Yemeni writings, coins, jewellery and traditional costume.

Transportation
Air: Sana'a International Airport. **Road:** Car: Hodeida Way (from Hodeida); Aden Way (from Aden); Ta'izz Way (from Ta'izz); Marib Way (from Marib); Sa'dah Way (from Sa'dah).

Contact Addresses
For more information of the Old City of Sana'a, contact the General Authority of Tourism, Yemen (see **Tourist Information** above).

Key to symbols: £ Entry charged & Disabled access ◢ Man-made attraction ♥ Natural attraction P Parking ✗ Restaurant ☲ Shop 🏛 UNESCO site

Zambia

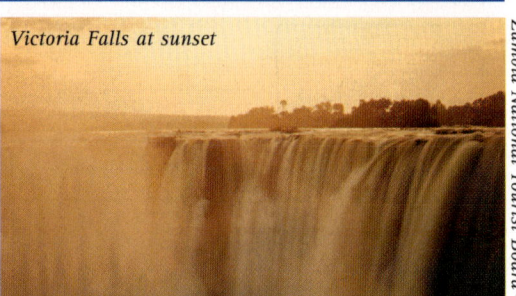

Victoria Falls at sunset

1 Victoria Falls, Zambia

Tourist Information

Tourism Council of Zambia
PO Box 36561, Lusaka, Zambia
Tel: (01) 251 666
Website: www.zambiatourism.com

Zambia National Tourist Board
2 Palace Gate, London W8 5NG, UK
Tel: (020) 7589 6655

Victoria Falls, Zambia

Made known to the wider world by the famous British explorer Dr David Livingstone in 1855, the *Victoria Falls*, which form a natural border between Zimbabwe and Zambia, are one of Africa's best-known natural wonders and one of the world's most impressive waterfalls. The falls, which Livingstone named after Queen Victoria, were known to native Kololo tribes in the 18th century as *Mosi-oa-Tunya*, meaning 'the smoke that thunders', and the spray that they generate can be seen for miles around. The cascade is formed as the calm, 2km- (1.2 miles-) wide *Zambezi River* spills out of a flat basalt lip and plunges into the gorge below. At their highest, the Victoria Falls drop a distance of 108m (345ft), almost twice as far as the *Niagara Falls*. As much as 546,000,000 cubic metres (713,725,490 cubic yards) per minute plummet over the edge at the height of the flood season. Viewing the falls from the Zambia side means that visitors can follow a path that goes right up to the falling water. An alternative view can be had from the *Boiling Pot*, right in the depths of the gorge at the bottom of the falls. The 111m- (364ft-) high *Victoria Falls Bridge*, commissioned by British statesman Cecil Rhodes in 1900 as a railway crossing, is now a popular place for bungee jumping, and can be crossed by foot for excellent views of the falls and the winding blue-green waters of the Zambezi River. It is also possible to see an aerial view of the falls from a Micro-light or fixed-wing plane. The area around the falls is a prime game-viewing location. The best time to view the Victoria Falls is between December-July when the water levels are high.

Transportation
Air: Lusaka International Airport, Harare International Airport, Livingstone Airport (domestic flights). **Rail:** Livingstone Station. **Road:** Coach: Services from Lusaka. Car: Victoria Falls border road (from Zimbabwe); from the south on Mosi-oa-Tunya Road (from Livingstone).

Contact Addresses
Tourist Centre, Mosi-oa-Tunya Road, Livingstone, Zambia
Tel: (03) 321 404

Zimbabwe

ZAMBIA

MASHONALAND

MATABELELAND

MOZAMBIQUE

BOTSWANA

SOUTH AFRICA

300km
150mls
✈ international airport

1 Great Zimbabwe
2 Victoria Falls, Zimbabwe

Tourist Information

Zimbabwe Tourism Authority (ZTA)
PO Box CY286, Causeway, Harare, Zimbabwe
Tel: (04) 758 730
Website: www.zimbabwetourism.co.zw

Zimbabwe Tourism Office
Zimbabwe House, 429 Strand, London
WC2R 0QE, UK
Tel: (020) 7240 6169

Great Zimbabwe

Great Zimbabwe was a large iron-age settlement that existed from the 13th to 15th centuries and lent its name to modern-day Zimbabwe, which derives from a Shona word meaning 'house of stone'. The *Great Enclosure*, with its 250m (820ft) wide and 11m (36ft) high perimeter wall, is the largest single ancient structure south of the Sahara Desert, while the *Hill Complex* rises 79m (260ft) above the surrounding area on a steep, granite hill. For many years, the origins of Great Zimbabwe and its inhabitants were the subject of much debate; various claims for it were made by different groups of white colonisers following its discovery in the 1870s, who raided it for its many treasures and gold. However, archaeologists have proved that it is actually an authentic native African site, developed by a long-dead civilisation advanced enough to trade with people as far away as China.

Transportation

Air: Harare International Airport, Masvingo Airport (domestic flights). **Rail:** Train: Masvingo Station. **Road:** Bus: Services to Morgenster Mission which is one kilometre (0.6 miles) from Great Zimbabwe (from Masvingo). Coach: Services to Great Zimbabwe (from Harare and Bulawayo).

Contact Addresses

For more information on Great Zimbabwe, contact Zimbabwe Tourism Authority (see **Tourist Information** above).

Victoria Falls, Zimbabwe

Made known to the wider world by the famous British explorer Dr David Livingstone in 1855, the *Victoria Falls*, which form a natural border between Zimbabwe and Zambia, are one of Africa's best-known natural wonders and one of the world's most impressive waterfalls. The Falls, which Livingstone named after Queen Victoria, were known to native Kololo tribes in the 18th century as *Mosi-oa-Tunya*, meaning 'the smoke that thunders', and the spray that they generate can be seen for miles around. The cascade is formed as the calm, 2km- (1.2 miles-) wide *Zambezi River* spills out of a flat basalt lip and plunges into the gorge below. At their highest, the Victoria Falls drop a distance of 108m (345ft), almost twice as far as the *Niagara*

Victoria Falls

Corel©

Falls. As much as 546,000,000 cubic metres (713,725,490 cubic yards) per minute plummet over the edge at the height of the flood season. The 111m- (364ft-) high *Victoria Falls Bridge*, commissioned by British statesman Cecil Rhodes in 1900 as a railway crossing, is now a popular place for bungee jumping, and can be crossed by foot for excellent views of the falls and the winding blue-green waters of the Zambezi River. It is also possible to see an aerial view of the falls from a Micro-light or fixed-wing plane. The area around the falls is a prime game-viewing location.

Transportation
Air: Lusaka International Airport, Harare International Airport, Victoria Falls Airport (domestic flights). **Rail:** Train: Victoria Falls Station. **Road:** Bus: Services to Victoria Falls Bus Station.

Contact Addresses
For more information on Victoria Falls, contact Zimbabwe Tourism Authority (see **Tourist Information** above).

Calendar of Events

January

Australia Day	Australia
Australian Open	Australia
Brussels on Ice	Belgium
Burns' Night	United Kingdom
Celtic Connections	United Kingdom
Daily Telegraph Adventure Travel & Sports Show	United Kingdom
Festival in the Desert	Mali
Hogmanay	United Kingdom
Krakow Christmas Crib Contest	Poland
London Parade	United Kingdom
Mummers Parade	United States of America
Munich Carnival	Germany
National Western Stock Show & Rodeo	United States of America
New Year	Russian Federation
New Year's Eve	Brazil
Perth International Arts Festival	Australia
Sydney Festival	Australia
Thorri Feast	Iceland
Three Kings Parade	Spain

February

Berlin International Film Festival	Germany
Chinese New Year	United Kingdom
Dubai Shopping Festival	United Arab Emirates
Hong Kong Arts Festival	People's Republic of China
Krakow Christmas Crib Contest	Poland
Lisbon Carnival	Portugal
Madrid Carnival	Spain
Mardi Gras	United States of America
Munich Carnival	Germany
Perth International Arts Festival	Australia
Rio de Janeiro Carnival	Brazil
Sydney Gay and Lesbian Mardi Gras	Australia
Thorri Feast	Iceland
Toronto Winterfest	Canada
Venice Carnival	Italy

March

Budapest Spring Festival	Hungary
Daily Mail Ideal Home Show	United Kingdom
Dubai World Cup	United Arab Emirates
Explosion of the Cart	Italy
Festival of the Historic Centre	Mexico
Hong Kong Arts Festival	People's Republic of China
International Motor Show	Switzerland
Rio de Janeiro Carnival	Brazil
Singapore Food Festival	Singapore

Calendar of Events

St Patrick's Day Parade ....United States of America
St Patrick's Festival...Ireland
Sydney Gay and Lesbian Mardi Gras ....Australia
Ueno Cherry Blossom Festival ....Japan
Venice Biennial ....Italy

April

Boston Marathon ....United States of America
Budapest Spring Festival ....Hungary
Daily Mail Ideal Home Show ....United Kingdom
Edinburgh International Science Festival ....United Kingdom
Flora London Marathon..United Kingdom
Grand National..United Kingdom
Hong Kong International Film Festival ....People's Republic of China
Lisbon Half Marathon ....Portugal
Queen's Day..The Netherlands
Rand Easter Show ....South Africa
Royal Easter Show ....New Zealand
Singapore Food Festival ....Singapore
Singapore International Film Festival ....Singapore
Songkran Festival...Thailand
Ueno Cherry Blossom Festival ....Japan
Venice Biennial ....Italy
Zurich Spring Festival ....Switzerland

May

Atlanta Jazz Festival ....United States of America
Bergen International Festival. ....Norway
Bergen Night Jazz Festival...Norway
Cannes Film Festival ....France
Cape Gourmet Festival ....South Africa
Chelsea Flower Show ....United Kingdom
Festimad Alternative Music Festival ....Spain
French Tennis Open (Roland Garros) ....France
Heineken Green Energy Festival ....Ireland
National Windmill and Pumping Station Day ....The Netherlands
Prague International Marathon ....Czech Republic
Rand Easter Show ....South Africa
San Isidro Festival ....Spain
Sanja Festival ....Japan
Vancouver International Children's Festival..............................Canada
Venice Biennial ....Italy
Vienna Festival..Austria

June

Barcelona Summer Festival (GREC) ....Spain
Bergen International Festival ....Norway
Bergen Night Jazz Festival...Norway
Bloomsday Festival ....Ireland
Cardiff Festival ....United Kingdom
Carnival of the Cultures..Germany

Christopher Street Day ....Germany
City Foundation Day ....Germany
Festival of Music ....France
French Tennis Open (Roland Garros) ....France
Grant Park Music Festival ....United States of America
Historical Soccer Tournament...Italy
Holland Festival ....The Netherlands
Jewish Culture Festival ....Poland
Lisbon Festivities ....Portugal
Montréal International Jazz Festival ....Canada
Queen's Birthday Parade – Trooping the Colour ....United Kingdom
Roskilde Festival ....Denmark
Royal Highland Show ....United Kingdom
San Isidro Festival ....Spain
Swedish National Day ....Sweden
TT Races ....United Kingdom
Vancouver International Children's Festival......................................Canada
Venice Biennial ....Italy
Vienna Festival..Austria
Vienna Music Film Festival ....Austria
Warsaw Mozart Festival...Poland
Wimbledon Championships ....United Kingdom
Zurich Festival ....Switzerland

July

Arrival of the Tour de France ....France
Athens Festival ....Greece
Avignon Festival..France
Barcelona Summer Festival (GREC) ....Spain
Bastille Day ....France
Calgary Stampede ....Canada
Cardiff Festival ....United Kingdom
Copenhagen Jazz Festival ....Denmark
Geneva Festival ....Switzerland
Grant Park Music Festival ....United States of America
Havana Carnival..Cuba
Independence Day ....United States of America
Jewish Culture Festival ....Poland
Krakow International Street Theatre Festival....................................Poland
Light Nights ....Iceland
Love Parade ....Germany
Montréal International Jazz Festival ....Canada
Ommegang Royal Pageant ....Belgium
Rockwave Festival ....Greece
Roman Summer ....Italy
Roskilde Festival ....Denmark
Running of the Bulls (San Fermin Festival) ....Spain
Salzburg Festival ....Austria
Summer Arts Festival ....France
Tokyo Fireworks Festival ....Japan
Venice Biennial ....Italy
Vienna Music Film Festival ....Austria

Calendar of Events

Warsaw Mozart Festival	Poland
Wimbledon Championships	United Kingdom
WOMAD Festival	United Kingdom
Zurich Festival	Switzerland

August

Amsterdam Gay Pride	The Netherlands
Avignon Festival	France
Cardiff Festival	United Kingdom
Copenhagen International Ballet Festival	Denmark
Edinburgh Fringe Festival	United Kingdom
Edinburgh International Festival	United Kingdom
Edinburgh Military Tattoo	United Kingdom
Elvis Week	United States of America
Geneva Festival	Switzerland
Grant Park Music Festival	United States of America
Havana Carnival	Cuba
Helsinki Festival	Finland
Jaffa Nights	Israel
Light Nights	Iceland
Notting Hill Carnival	United Kingdom
Queen's Birthday Celebrations	Thailand
Roman Summer	Italy
Salzburg Festival	Austria
Summer Arts Festival	France
Swiss National Day	Switzerland
Venice Biennial	Italy
Vienna Music Film Festival	Austria

September

Athens Festival	Greece
Autumn Festival	France
Avignon Festival	France
Berlin Marathon	Germany
Côtes du Rhône Grape Harvest	France
Dublin Fringe Festival	Ireland
Edinburgh International Festival	United Kingdom
Helsinki Festival	Finland
Istanbul Biennial	Turkey
Moscow International Peace Marathon	Russian Federation
October Festival	Germany
Our Lady of Mercy Festival	Spain
Prague Autumn International Music Festival	Czech Republic
Roman Summer	Italy
Stockholm Beer & Whisky Festival	Sweden
Venice Biennial	Italy
Vienna Music Film Festival	Austria

October

Autumn Festival	France
Budapest Autumn Festival	Hungary

Diwali ....India
Dublin Fringe Festival ....Ireland
Frankfurt Marathon ....Germany
International Festival of Authors...........................Canada
Istanbul Biennial ....Turkey
Lord of Miracles ....Peru
Madrid Autumn Festival ....Spain
Melbourne Festival ....Australia
October Festival..Germany
Prague Autumn International Music Festival ....Czech Republic
Pushkar Fair...India
Rome Jazz Festival ....Italy
Venice Biennial ....Italy

November

Athens Marathon ....Greece
Autumn Festival ....France
Budapest Autumn Festival ....Hungary
Ellerslie Flower Show ....New Zealand
International Festival of Advent & Christmas Music ....Czech Republic
International Film Festival of Wales ....United Kingdom
Istanbul Biennial ....Turkey
Lord Mayor's Show ....United Kingdom
Macy's Thanksgiving Day Parade ....United States of America
Madrid Autumn Festival ....Spain
Magic of Advent in Vienna ....Austria
Melbourne Festival ....Australia
Pushkar Fair...India
Rome Jazz Festival ....Italy
Stockholm International Film Festival ....Sweden
Strasbourg Christmas Market................................France
Venice Biennial ....Italy

December

Autumn Festival ....France
Boston Tea Party Re-enactment ....United States of America
Brussels on Ice...Belgium
Christmas Market ....Germany
Christmas Mass in St Peter's Basilica ....Italy
European Christmas Market ....Belgium
Festival of Lights ....France
Hogmanay ....United Kingdom
International Festival of Advent & Christmas Music ....Czech Republic
Krakow Christmas Crib Contest ....Poland
Magic Night ....Portugal
Magic of Advent in Vienna ....Austria
New Year ....Russian Federation
New Year's Eve ....Brazil
New Year's Eve Gala and Ball at the Opera ....Hungary
Rome Jazz Festival ....Italy
Strasbourg Christmas Market................................France

Australia

Melbourne

Tourist Information
Tourism Victoria
GPO Box 2219T, 55 Swanston Street, Melbourne,
VIC 3001, Australia
Tel: (03) 9653 9777
Website: www.visitvictoria.com

• January

Australian Open

The *Australian Open*, which is Australia's main
tennis tournament, forms part of the Grand Slam
competition, which also encorporates the
Wimbledon Championships, the *United States
Open* and the *French Open*. The record attendance
for the event was set in 2005 when 60,669 people
attended on the middle Saturday of the
tournament. The first tennis tournament in
Australia was held in Warehouseman's Cricket
Ground in Melbourne in 1905 when the Australian
Rodney Heath won the men's singles title. The first
woman to win the women's single title was
another Australian, Margaret Molesworth, in 1922.
Over the years, the tournament has been played
across Australia, however in 1972 it was decided
to hold the tournament permanently in Melbourne.
The event has grown in popularity and as a result,
moved to a bigger venue at Flinders Park in 1988,
with the name changing to Melbourne Park in
1996.

Event Organiser
Australian Open, Private Bag 6060, Richmond,
South Victoria, VIC 3121, Australia
Tel: (03) 9286 1355
Website: www.ausopen.org

Venue
Melbourne Park.

Transport
Air: Melbourne Airport. **Rail:** Train: Richmond,
Flinders Street or Jolimont stations. Tram: Public
services. **Road:** Car: Melbourne Park is located on
Bateman Avenue; there is, however, no public
parking during the tournament and visitors are
advised to use public transport.

• October-November

Melbourne Festival

Melbourne Festival is one of the most important
arts festivals in Australia with performances from
the worlds of dance, theatre, music, opera, visual
arts and film. The event runs for 17 days each
October and November and was first held in 1986,
when it was headed by the composer Gian Carlo
Menotti, responsible for the Spoleto Festival series,
also held in Italy and the USA. The festival in
Australia was originally known as the *Melbourne
Spoleto Festival*, but changed its name to the
Melbourne International Festival of the Arts in
1990 and to Melbourne Festival in 1997.

Event Organiser
Melbourne Festival, PO Box 10, Flinders Lane,
Melbourne, VIC 8009, Australia
Tel: (03) 9662 4242
Website: www.melbournefestival.com.au

Venue
Theatres, cinemas and cathedrals in and around
Melbourne.

Transport
Air: Melbourne Airport. **Rail:** Train: Spencer Street
Station. **Road:** Coach: Greyhound Pioneer runs
services to the Melbourne Transit Centre (from
across Australia). Car: Western Highway (from
Adelaide); Hume Highway (from Sydney).

Perth

Tourist Information
Western Australian Tourism Commission
First Floor, 16 St Georges Terrace, Perth, WA 6000,
Australia
Tel: (08) 9270 331
Website: www.westernaustralia.com.au

• January-February

Perth International Arts Festival

Perth International Arts Festival is one of the
highlights of Perth's cultural events calendar.
Every year, the whole city comes alive with
national, international and aboriginal dance,
music and visual art performances. Past highlights
included performances by the Perth Theatre
Company and the Merce Cunningham Dance
Company, as well as concerts from the WA
Symphony Orchestra. This internationally-
acclaimed festival has won the Western Australian
Tourism Award for Best Major Festival and Special
Event on three occasions (1996, 1998 and 1999)
and is the longest-running and biggest
international arts festival in the Southern
Hemisphere.

Event Organiser

Perth International Arts Festival, UWA Festival Centre, 3 Crawley Avenue, Crawley WA 6009, Australia
Tel: (08) 6488 2000
Website: www.perthfestival.com.au

Venue

Various venues across Perth.

Transport

Air: Perth International Airport. Rail: Train: Perth Station or East Perth Terminal. Road: Coach: Greyhound and Westrail operate services to the East Perth Terminal (from across Australia).

Sydney

Tourist Information

Sydney Visitor Centre
106 George Street, The Rocks, Sydney, NSW 2000, Australia
Tel: (02) 9255 1788 *or* 132 077
Website: www.visitnsw.com.au

• January

Australia Day

Australia was formally colonised by the British First Fleet, which arrived at Sydney Cove, led by Captain Arthur Phillip, on January 26 1788. By the early 19th century there are records of celebratory events being held to mark the occasion, including formal dinners, bonfires and the consumption of large amounts of alcohol. The first official national celebrations were held on January 26 1818, the 30th anniversary of formal colonisation, when a salute of 30 guns was fired from Dawes Point, followed by a ball at Government House. Since then, the celebrations have expanded to encompass the whole nation, although Sydney remains the focal point. In the last few decades, the more formal, imperialistic *Australia Day* celebrations, such as the military parades and the re-enactment of the First Fleet landing, have been replaced with more light-hearted events recognising Australia's cultural heritage and multicultural population. Typical Sydney celebrations are many and varied, and range from free access to the city's museums to citywide galas, parades, concerts and street theatre. *Hyde Park* is the focus for family events, featuring music, wine tasting, face painting and children's entertainment, whilst The Rocks play host to jazz and blues concerts and puppet shows.

The grand finale is the *Australia Day Fireworks Spectacular* which takes place at Cockle Bay, Darling Harbour at 2100.

Event Organiser

Australia Day Council of New South Wales, PO Box 5341, Sydney NSW 2001, Australia
Tel: (02) 9513 2000
Website: www.adc.nsw.gov.au

Venue

Various locations across Sydney.

Transport

Air: Sydney Kingsford Smith International Airport. Rail: Train: Sydney Central Station. Cityrail: Circular Quay (to The Rocks), Town Hall (to Darling Harbour), St James (to Hyde Park), Martin Place (to Hyde Park). Road: Bus: Public services.

Sydney Festival

The *Sydney Festival* has been a leading light in the Australian and international arts scene for over 25 years. Every year over 2 million spectators flock to venues as diverse as the *Sydney Opera House*, the *Royal Botanic Gardens* and the *Museum of Sydney* to enjoy hundreds of performances of theatre, jazz, classical music, dance, opera, cinema and puppet shows. There are also visual art exhibitions, complemented by events ranging from guided tours of Sydney's corporate art collections to lectures by visiting artists. Past performers at the Sydney Festival have included an eclectic mix of performers ranging from Nick Cave and Beth Orton to Nederlands Dans Theater, the Russian Philharmonic Orchestra and the Catalan theatre group Els Comediants. The Sydney Festival lasts for three weeks and incorporates elements of the city's *Australia Day* celebrations, such as the free concerts in *Hyde Park* and the fireworks display in *Darling Harbour* on January 26.

Event Organiser

Level 2, 10 Hickson Road, The Rocks, Sydney, NSW 2000, Australia
Tel: (02) 8248 6500
Website: www.sydneyfestival.org.au

Venue

Various venues across Sydney.

Transport

Air: Sydney Kingsford Smith International Airport. Rail: Train: Sydney Central Station. Cityrail: Circular Quay (to Museum of Sydney, Sydney Opera House or Royal Botanic Gardens); Town Hall (to Darling Harbour); St James (to Hyde Park or Royal Botanic Gardens); Martin Place (to Hyde Park or Royal Botanic Gardens). Road: Bus: Public services.

• February-March

Sydney Gay and Lesbian Mardi Gras

Sydney Gay and Lesbian Mardi Gras began in 1978 as a parade down the city's Oxford Street to mark *International Gay Solidarity Day* (in commemoration of the famous Stonewall Riots in New York's Greenwich Village). The Mardi Gras name was adopted the following year and the event steadily grew in size and status during the 1980s and 1990s to become the largest gay carnival in the world, lasting for three weeks and attracting hundreds of thousands of revellers. Over 150 gay and lesbian community groups spend months creating the colourful floats and outrageous costumes for the Oxford Street parade on the final Saturday. Concerts, art exhibitions and theatre performances, all showcasing gay and lesbian talent and highlighting issues relating to sexuality, are held throughout the three weeks.

Event Organiser
Sydney Gay and Lesbian Mardi Gras, 297-299 Trafalgar Street, Petersham, NSW 2049, Australia
Postal address: PO Box 956, Petersham NSW 2049, Australia
Tel: (02) 9568 8600
Website: www.mardigras.org.au

Venue
Various venues across Sydney.

Transport
Air: Sydney Kingsford Smith International Airport. **Rail:** Train: Sydney Central Station. **Road:** Bus: Public services.

Austria

Salzburg

Tourist Information

Salzburg Tourist Board (Tourismus Salzburg GmbH)
Auerspergstraße 6, A-5020 Salzburg, Austria
Tel (43) 662 88 9870
Website: www.salzburg.info

• July-August

Salzburg Festival

Over five or six weeks each summer, the internationally-acclaimed *Salzburg Festival* brings together a programme of opera, plays and concerts that are staged at venues across the city. In 2006, the 250th anniversary of Mozart's birth, the Salzburg Festival will perform all 22 of the composer's stage works which he created in his short but artistically incredible life.

Event Organiser
Salzburg Festival (Salzburger Festspiele), Hofstallgasse 1, PO Box 140, A-5010 Salzburg, Austria
Tel: (43) 662 80 4550
Website: www.salzburgfestival.at

Venue
Various venues across Salzburg.

Transport
Air: Salzburg WA Mozart Airport. **Rail:** Train: Salzburg Central Station. **Road:** Bus: Public services.

Vienna

Tourist Information

Vienna Tourist Board (Wien Tourismus)
Obere Augartenstrasse 40, 1025 Vienna, Austria
Tel: (01) 2111 4222
Website: www.vienna-tourism.at

• May-June

Vienna Festival

The *Vienna Festival* comprises performances of dance, music and theatre, as well as displays of visual art. The festival is renowned for its thought-provoking programmes and in the past has tackled topics such as xenophobia, national identity and the existential struggle of the individual in a socially and culturally foreign environment. Other acclaimed past performances have included Peter Brook's 'Tragedy of Hamlet', a production of the South African drama 'Le Costume', by Can Themba, and Luc Bondy's production of Händel's Baroque masterpiece. Musicians from around the world, including the Arnold Schoenberg Choir and the Vienna Symphony Orchestra, open the festival with a free concert in the *Rathausplatz* (Town Hall Square).

Event Organiser
Vienna Festival Office (Wiener Festwochen), Lehárgasse 11/1/1/6, 1060 Vienna, Austria
Tel: (01) 589 220
Website: www.festwochen.at

Venue
Various venues across Vienna.

Transport
Air: Vienna International Airport. **Rail:** Train: Westbahnhof Station. Underground: Rathaus (to Rathausplatz). **Road:** Bus: Public services.

• June-September

Vienna Music Film Festival

This highly popular film festival, which was first held in 1991, brings the very best in music cinema to Vienna each summer. The open-air programme includes dance, music and opera films, many of which are shown in Austria for the first time at the festival, and every year there are new innovations as well as old favourites. Recent festivals have also seen the introduction of a larger screen with improved audiovisual quality. Films begin at dusk (around 2100) every evening. Many food stalls are set up around the auditorium as part of the festival to enable filmgoers and passers-by to enjoy mouth-watering dishes from around the world.

Event Organiser
Stadt Wien Marketing Service GmbH, Kolingasse 11/13, 1090 Vienna, Austria
Tel: (01) 3198 2000
Website: www.wien-event.at

Venue
Town Hall Square (Rathausplatz).

Transport
Air: Vienna International Airport. **Rail:** Train: Westbahnhof Station. Underground: Rathaus (to Rathausplatz). **Road:** Bus: Public services..

• November-December

Magic of Advent in Vienna

Vienna's Christmas market, held each year in front of the town hall, is the perfect way to stock up on presents and soak up the festive atmosphere. There are over 140 stalls to browse and plenty to eat and drink, including candied fruit, candyfloss, maroni (roasted chestnuts) and the traditional Austrian winter warmer, *Glühwein* (mulled wine). Children will enjoy the Christmas workshop in the Volkshalle (assembly hall) of the town hall, where they can bake Christmas cookies and make their own gifts, or try out the latest games. There is an exhibition on Christmas traditions in other European countries, as well as a life-size nativity scene, and every Sunday during Advent, choirs from around the world sing Christmas carols inside the town hall. In the park next to the town halls there are pony rides

and a merry-go-round to enjoy. All the attractions are open 0900-2100 Monday-Sunday until December 23 and 0900-1700 on December 24.

Event Organiser
Wienwerbepool-City Marketing, Breitenfurter Strasse 513, 1230 Vienna, Austria
Tel: (01) 888 9933
Website: www.christkindlmarkt.at

Venue
Town Hall Square (Rathausplatz).

Transport
Air: Vienna International Airport. **Rail:** Train: Westbahnhof Station. Underground: Rathaus. **Road:** Bus: Public services.

Belgium

Brussels

Tourist Information

Tourist Information Brussels (TIB)
Hôtel de Ville, Grande-Place, 1000 Brussels, Belgium
Tel: (02) 513 8940
Website: www.brusselsdiscovery.com

• December-January

Brussels on Ice

The *Grand Place* has been the social and economic heart of Brussels since the Middle Ages and is flanked by lavish Gothic and Renaissance buildings which once served as guildhouses and now house museums, coffee shops and restaurants. It is turned into a giant ice rink over the Christmas period, allowing visitors and locals to skate in a magical open-air setting to the sounds of festive music.

Event Organiser
VO Communication, 342 chaussée d'Alsemberg, 1190 Brussels, Belgium
Tel: (02) 346 5949
Website: www.vocommunication.com

Venue
Grand Place.

Transport
Air: Brussels International Airport. **Rail:** Train: Bruxelles-Central, Bruxelles-Midi or Bruxelles-Nord stations. Underground: De Brouckère or Gare Centrale/Centraal Station. Tram: Public services to Bourse. **Road:** Bus: Public services.

• July

Ommegang Royal Pageant

Ommegang is a colourful reconstruction of the pageant held in 1549 in honour of Emperor Charles V, his son Don Philip and his sisters Eleanor of Austria and Mary of Hungary. Although the festival was essentially a religious event in Medieval Brussels, today's Ommegang celebrations are resolutely secular. The action starts in the *Grand Place* in the centre of Brussels as the royal guests, some of whom are descended from those present in 1549, take their places and the crossbow men surround the statue of *Notre Dame du Sablon*, their patron saint. Once the peasant dancers and performers have led the way, the Emperor walks the streets past the Gothic and Renaissance façades of the old guildhouses surrounded by horses, dogs, flagbearers, ladies-in-waiting and a falconry train. The costumes, which are lavish reproductions of the originals, can be up to 6m (23 feet) in height and the whole event has all the pomp and ceremony of the original pageant. The parade leaves the Sablon statue in the Grand Place at 2050 and parades through rue Lebeau and other streets until it reaches rue Charles Buls.

Event Organiser
Ommegang-Brussels, rue des Tanneurs 180, 1000 Brussels, Belgium
Tel: (02) 512 1961
Website: www.ommegang-brussels.be

Venue
Sablon statue (Grand Place) at 2050, then parades through rue Lebeau, rue Marché aux Herbes, rue Tabora, rue Midi, rue Lombard, rue Etuve and rue Charles Buls.

Transport
Air: Brussels International Airport. Rail: Train: Bruxelles-Central, Bruxelles-Midi or Bruxelles-Nord stations. Underground: De Brouckère or Gare Centrale/Centraal Station. Tram: Public services to Bourse. Road: Bus: Public services.

• December

European Christmas Market

The *Grand Place* has been Brussels's main square since the Middle Ages. For one week in December each year, the square has a very special atmosphere and a truly European flavour with the arrival of the *Christmas Market*. There are hundreds of stalls to browse, with gift ideas from many countries. The culinary choices are endless – visitors can feast on Italian *panettone* (Christmas cake) or German speciality sausage, whilst enjoying any number of variations on mulled wine: Scandinavian *glögg*, Austrian *Glühwein* or French *vin chaud*. Alternatively, there are numerous varieties of Belgian beer available at the many bars surrounding the Grand Place. There is also entertainment from choirs from around Europe who perform traditional festive songs. The market is open 1100-1900 Monday to Thursday and 1100-2100 Friday to Sunday.

Event Organiser
For more information on the European Christmas Market, contact Tourist Information Brussels (see **Tourist Information** above).

Venue
Grand Place.

Transport
Air: Brussels International Airport. Rail: Train: Bruxelles-Central, Bruxelles-Midi or Bruxelles-Nord stations. Underground: De Brouckère or Gare Centrale/Centraal Station. Tram: Public services to Bourse. Road: Bus: Public services.

Brazil

Rio de Janeiro

Tourist Information

RioTur, City of Rio de Janeiro Tourism Authority (Empresa de Turismo do Município do Rio de Janeiro SA)
Rua da Assembléia, 10-9º andar, 20119, Centro, Rio de Janeiro, Brazil
Tel: (021) 217 7575
Website: www.riodejaneiro-turismo.com.br

• December-January

New Year's Eve

Rio de Janeiro is said to be one of the most exciting and happening places in the world at New Year (known locally as *Reveillon*). Hundreds of thousands of people gather on the city's beaches every year on December 31 to watch the giant firework display at midnight and to dance the night away. The main festivities take place on Copacabana Beach, with live music and DJ sets continuing through the night. There are also events in major hotels in the city, as well as in the many bars and restaurants. The dancing and partying goes on into the small hours, with many people staying up all night to drink a champagne breakfast at dawn.

Event Organiser
For more information on New Year's Eve, contact RioTur (see **Tourist Information** above).

Venue
The main focus is Copacabana Beach.

Transport
Air: Rio de Janeiro International Airport. **Rail:** Train: Estacao D Pedra II or Estacao Barao de Maua stations. **Road:** Coach: Novo Rio Rodoviaria Coach Station.

• February-March

Rio de Janeiro Carnival

Rio de Janeiro Carnival is one of the biggest festivals in the world, attracting hundreds of thousands of tourists and locals every year who come to participate in this incredibly lively event. Carnival is undoubtedly the biggest cultural event in Rio and an annual orgy of over-the-top fun and frivolity. The event originates from the Easter revelry tradition that took place in Portugal in the 15th century. Its date varies from year to year, usually ranging from late February to early March. It starts officially on a Saturday and goes through to the following Wednesday (*quarta-feira de cinza* – Ash Wednesday). There are many events across the city, including street parades, carnival balls and the samba school parade.

Event Organiser
For more information on Rio de Janeiro Carnival, contact RioTur (see **Tourist Information** above).

Venue
Various venues across Rio de Janeiro.

Transport
Air: Rio de Janeiro International Airport. **Rail:** Train: Estacao D Pedra II or Estacao Barao de Maua stations. **Road:** Coach: Novo Rio Rodoviaria Coach Station.

Canada

Calgary

Tourist Information
Calgary Convention & Visitors Bureau
Suite 200, 238 11th Avenue, SE Calgary, AB T2G 0X8, Canada
Tel: (403) 263 8510
Website: www.tourismcalgary.com

• July

Calgary Stampede

Calgary Stampede is one of the world's biggest celebrations of the cowboy way of life and attracts well over one million visitors each year. The event lasts for 10 days in July and includes an annual rodeo, with bull riding, bareback bronco riding and wild horse racing, as well as various stage performances, chuckwagon (chariot) races, agriculture and livestock displays and live music on the Coke Stage. This annual event dates back to 1886 and has grown to become an enormous celebration of all things related to being a cowboy.

Event Organiser
Calgary Stampede, 1410 Olympic Way SE, Calgary, AB T2P-2K8, Canada
Tel: (800) 661 1260 (toll free USA and Canada only)
Website: www.calgary-stampede.com

Venue
Stampede Park, Calgary.

Transport
Air: Calgary International Airport. **Rail:** Train: C-train routes 201 to Brentwood in the north (from Anderson Road in the south) or 202 to Tenth Street in the west (from Whitehorn in the east). **Road:** Bus: Public services.

Montréal

Tourist Information
Montréal Tourist Information
(Centre Infotouriste Tourisme Montréal)
1001 rue du Square-Dorchester, Montréal H3B 1G2, Canada
Tel: (514) 873 2015
Website: www.tourisme-montreal.org

• June-July

Montréal International Jazz Festival

The first jazz festival was held in Montréal in 1980 and attracted 12,000 spectators. Today, the event is one of the biggest jazz festivals in the world, attracting over 100,000 spectators every year to see over 120 concerts, ranging from traditional jazz through to blues and reggae.

Event Organiser
Montréal International Jazz Festival, 822 Sherbrooke Street East, Montréal, Quebec H2L 1K4, Canada
Tel: (514) 871 1881
Website: www.montrealjazzfest.com

Venue
Concert halls and cafés across Montréal.

Transport
Air: Montréal Dorval International Airport. Rail: Train: Gare Centrale (Central Station). Road: Bus: Public services.

Toronto

Tourist Information

Tourism Toronto
PO Box 126, 207 Queens Quay West, Toronto, Ontario M5J 1A7, Canada
Tel: (416) 203 2600
Website: www.toronto.com

• January-February

Toronto Wintercity Festival

Every year, Toronto organises 14 days of entertainment in celebration of Toronto's cultural diversity with a mix of free shows and events held both indoors and outside including circus acts, storytelling, musical concerts, theatre productions, ice-skating shows, dance and cultural exhibitions. There are creative hands-on activities for both children and adults at the Civic Centre and the Toronto Public Library Auditorium, including colouring contests, baking cookies, origami and pyjama parties. Winterlicious is the festival's culinary celebration where customers can enjoy the fine cuisine at over 100 of Toronto's top dining establishments.

Event Organiser
Toronto City Hall, 100 Queen Street, Ninth Floor East Tower M5H 2N2, Toronto, Canada
Tel: (416) 395 0490
Website: www.city.toronto.on.ca/special_events

Venue
Various venues across Toronto.

Transport
Air: Toronto Lester B Pearson International Airport. Rail: Train: Union Station. Underground: North Yorke Centre (to Mel Lastman Square or Civic Centre); Queen Station (to Nathan Phillips Square); Bloor (to Toronto Public Library). Road: Bus: Public services.

• October

International Festival of Authors

Toronto's *International Festival of Authors* is a literary treat for both adults and children. Every year, writers of poetry, fiction, drama and biography converge on the city's Harbourfront Centre to give readings, lectures, talks and seminars and to chat with audiences. The festival invites both new writers and international celebrities; past attendees include J K Rowling, Joanna Trollope, Candace Bushnell, Margaret Atwood, Maeve Binchy, Carlos Fuentes, Susan Sontag, Jonathan Safran Foer and David Baddiel.

Event Organiser
Harbourfront Reading Series, 235 Queens Quay West, M5J 2G8 Toronto, Canada
Tel: (416) 973 4760
Website: www.readings.org

Venue
Various venues across Toronto.

Transport
Air: Toronto Lester B Pearson International Airport. Rail: Train: Union Station. Tram: 510 (from Union Station). Road: Bus: Public services.

Vancouver

Tourist Information

Tourism Vancouver – Tourist Information Centre
Waterfront Centre, Plaza Level, 200 Burrard Street, Vancouver, BC V6C 3L6, Canada
Tel: (604) 683 2000
Website: www.tourismvancouver.com

• May-June

Vancouver International Children's Festival

Vancouver International Children's Festival was first held in 1977 to entertain, educate and inspire children and young people from Vancouver and the surrounding area. It comprises seven days of activities and events in Vanier Park, a scenic setting on Vancouver's waterfront. Every year, artists come from across Canada and around the world to entertain visitors through performances of theatre, circus, puppetry, jazz and pop music. There are colourful daily parades, as well as interactive exhibitions and a variety of hands-on activities such as kite-making, music sessions, exotic crafts, stilt-walking workshops, pottery classes and imaginative games for younger children. Special performances are staged for older children and young people, encouraging them to think about the world they live in and their place in society, whilst younger children can play in a giant sandbox full of toys.

Event Organiser
Festival Communications, 402–873 Beatty Street, Vancouver, BC V6B 2M6, Canada
Tel: (604) 708 5655
Website: www.vancouverchildrensfestival.com

Venue
Vanier Park.

Transport
Air: Vancouver International Airport. **Water:** Ferry: False Creek services (from Granville Island, Aquatic Centre or Science World along the waterfront). **Rail:** Train: Pacific Central Station. **Road:** Bus: Public services.

People's Republic of China

Hong Kong

Tourist Information
Hong Kong Tourism Board
9-11th Floor, Citicorp Centre, 18 Whitfield Road, North Point, Hong Kong, People's Republic of China
Tel: 2807 6543
Website: www.discoverhongkong.com

• **February-March**

Hong Kong Arts Festival

Hong Kong Arts Festival is one of the most important cultural events in Southeast Asia. The festival, which is the leading arts event in Hong Kong, features numerous performances from international stars of theatre, opera, art, dance and classical and popular music. Past highlights include performances by the legendary Russian dancer Mikhail Baryshnikov, the Blind Boys of Alabama and performances by the National Theatre Company of China. Every year, artists from around the world flock into Hong Kong to take part in this internationally-renowned event.

Event Organiser
Hong Kong Arts Festival Society Ltd, 12/F Hong Kong Arts Centre, 2 Harbour Road, Wanchai, Hong Kong, People's Republic of China
Tel: 2824 3555
Website: www.hk.artsfestival.org

Venue
Various venues across Hong Kong including Hong Kong Cultural Centre, Hong Kong City Hall, Hong Kong Academy for the Performing Arts (HKAPA), Hong Kong Arts Centre, Sha Tin Town Hall, Tsuen Wan Town Hall, Tuen Mun Town Hall and Kwai Tsing Theatre.

Transport
Air: Hong Kong International Airport. **Rail:** Train: Hong Kong Station. **Road:** Bus: Public services.

• **April**

Hong Kong International Film Festival

Hong Kong International Film Festival, which was first held in 1977, is an enormous annual event in Hong Kong's calendar. Over 200 films are screened each year at the festival including a mix of global premieres. The festival is a non-competitive event which comprises of four main areas: Asian Cinema, Hong Kong Panorama, World Cinema and Special Section Contributed by Hong Kong Film Archive. The annual event now attracts approximately 150,000 visitors each year, a substantial increase on the 18,624 people who attended the first film festival in Hong Kong in 1977.

Event Organiser
Hong Kong International Film Festival Society Office, 21/F, Sunshine Plaza, 353 Lockhart Road, Wan Chai, Hong Kong, People's Republic of China
Tel: 2970 3300
Website: www.hkiff.org.hk

Venue
Various cinemas across Hong Kong.

Transport
Air: Hong Kong International Airport. **Rail:** Train: Hong Kong Station. **Road:** Car: The most accessible places to drive to are Lantua Island, Macau and Guangzhou; from here visitors must take a ferry trip to get to Hong Kong.

Cuba

Havana

Tourist Information

Ministry of Tourism (Ministerio de Turismo)
Calle 19, No 710, Entre Paseo y A, Vedado, Havana, Cuba
Tel: (07) 330 545
Website: www.cubatravel.cu

• **July-August**

Havana Carnival

The Cuban capital is well known for its party spirit, and carnival time, which has been reinstated after the hardships suffered by the communist country since the collapse of the USSR, promises particularly colourful celebrations as the Cuban holiday period begins in earnest. The festivities begin on a Friday night in late July with a gun salute fired from the San Pedro de la Cabana fortress. The event then continues every weekend until mid-August, with shows, dancing, fireworks, floats and parades, food and drink all accompanied by traditional Cuban rhythms and Latino pop. Each Havana neighbourhood spends months designing costumes and floats for its own parties and parades, whilst the *Malecón* (seafront) is the venue for fairs and concerts.

Event Organiser
For more information on the Havana Carnival, contact the Ministry of Tourism (see **Tourist Information** above).

Venue
Malecón (seafront) and across Havana.

Transport
Air: José Marti International Airport. **Rail:** Train: Central, Egido y Arsenal Station. **Road:** Bus: Public services.

Czech Republic

Prague

Tourist Information
Prague Information Service (PIS – Pražské informační služby)
Betlemske namesti 2, 116 98 Prague 1, Czech Republic
Tel: (02) 264 022
Website: www.pis.cz

• May

Prague International Marathon
Prague International Marathon was first held in 1995, with 980 runners taking part in the main event and 10,000 runners taking part in a non-competitive race. More than 3000 runners take part in the marathon every year, with a further 13,000 and 12,000 respectively taking part in a City Run and Family Run. The marathon is billed as the most international in the world with approximately two thirds of runners coming from overseas. Spectators line the historic streets of Prague during the event, cheering on the competitors. There are also

concerts and street entertainment, with music including jazz, classical, blues, reggae and rock and roll. The marathon starts at 0900 in Paríz̆ská Street and finishes in Old Town Square.

Event Organiser
Prague International Marathon, Záhoranského 3, 120 00 Prague 2, Czech Republic
Tel: (02) 2491 9209
Website: www.pim.cz

Venue
Streets of Prague, passing over Charles Bridge.

Transport
Air: Prague Ruzyne International Airport. **Rail:** Train: Hlavní nádraží Station (Prague Station). Underground: Staroṁestká. **Road:** Bus: Public services.

• September-October

Prague Autumn International Music Festival
Prague Autumn International Music Festival, which takes place in Prague every year, is one of the most important classical music events in Eastern Europe and always attracts thousands of visitors from across Europe. The city is famous for its orchestras and boasts two of the finest in the world: Prague Philharmonic Orchestra and Prague Symphony Orchestra. Many of the festival's events take place in Dvorak Hall in Rudolfinum, which is home to Prague Philharmonic Orchestra, and overlooks the River Vltava. Located next to the famous *Mánesuv Bridge*, the venue is regarded by many to be one of the most beautiful concert venues in Eastern Europe.

Event Organiser
Prague Autumn Musical Management, Príbenická St 20, 13000 Prague 3, Czech Republic
Tel: (02) 540 484
Website: www.pragueautumn.cz

Venue
Various venues and concert halls in Prague, including Dvorak Hall in Rudolfinum, Smetana Hall in the Municipal House, State Opera Prague, St Simon and Judas Church, Lucerna and Grand Hotel Pupp Karlovy Vary.

Transport
Air: Prague Ruzyně International Airport. **Rail:** Train: Hlavní nádraží Station (Prague Station). Underground: Staromestská or Námesti Republiky. **Road:** Bus: Public services.

• November-December

International Festival of Advent & Christmas Music

The *International Festival of Advent & Christmas Music*, which was first held in Prague in 1990, begins each year on the first weekend during Advent. During the festival, there are usually a number of performances by various amateur choirs, including entries to the competition from women's choirs, men's choirs, small mixed chamber choirs, large mixed choirs and children's choirs. The choirs perform Advent and Christmas music of their choice, either a capella or with instrumental accompaniment. The competition is judged by experts in the field, both from the Czech Republic and abroad. Winners are judged on their choice of compositions and programme structure, technical level of interpretation and general artistic impression. At the end of the competition, there is singing in the *Old Town Square*, where Christmas and Advent songs are sung. There is also a competition to win the Petr Eben Prize; entrants perform a composition which has been written especially for the occasion by Petr Eben himself, who is one of the main judges.

Event Organiser
Or Fea AS, Dlouhá 10, Prague 1 110 00, Czech Republic
Tel: (02) 232 1949
Website: www.orfea.cz

Venue
Old Town Square in the centre of Prague.

Transport
Air: Prague Ruzyně International Airport. **Rail:** Train: Hlavní nádraží Station (Prague Station). Underground: Staromestká. **Road:** Bus: Public services

Denmark

Copenhagen

Tourist Information

Wonderful Copenhagen Tourist Information
Gl Kongevej 1, 1610 Copenhagen V, Denmark
Tel: 7022 2442 *or* 3325 7400
Website:
www.woco.dk

• June-July

Roskilde Festival

The annual *Roskilde Festival* is one of the biggest rock and pop music festivals in Europe. The festival began in 1971, when it featured approximately 20 bands and about 10,000 visitors. Today, as many as 170 bands perform at the event on a total of seven stages, and is watched by over 75,000 spectators. Highlights of past festivals include performances from Bob Dylan, Beck, P J Harvey, Queens of the Stone Age, Robbie Williams, Neil Young, Blondie, David Bowie, Blur, REM, Primal Scream and Cold Play. Any profit made by the festival organisers is donated to support humanitarian, cultural and non-profit making initiatives.

Event Organiser
Roskilde Festival, Havsteensvej 11, 4000 Roskilde, Denmark
Tel: 4636 6613
Website: www.roskilde-festival.dk

Venue
Roskilde Festival ground, which is 35km (20 miles) from Copenhagen city centre.

Transport
Air: Copenhagen Airport. **Rail:** Train: Trains to the festival's own train station which is located in the middle of the festival grounds (from Roskilde Station). **Road:** Bus: Public services to the festival grounds (from Roskilde Station).

• July

Copenhagen Jazz Festival

Copenhagen Jazz Festival sees around 600 concerts by Danish and international jazz artists in the city. Many concerts are performed in the city's most historic streets and squares, as well as along the banks of the canals. Clubs and small cafés in the city play host to a varied programme, ranging from New Orleans jazz and swing to experimental music. 'Giant Jazz', which is held in the old Circus Building, is one of the main events of the festival. There are also concerts at the Tivoli Gardens which attract a large audience. As well as performances from top artists there are also street parades every day, concerts and workshops for children, and other events such as midnight concerts at the National Museum. Over 100,000 attend the event in the city.

Event Organiser
Copenhagen Jazz Festival, Nytorv 3, 1450

Copenhagen, Denmark
Tel: 3393 2013
Website: www.jazzfestival.dk

Venue
Various venues in Copenhagen, including
Copenhagen JazzHouse, Circus Building and Tivoli
Gardens.

Transport
Air: Copenhagen Airport. **Rail:** Train: Copenhagen
Central Station. **S-Bahn:** Services to København H
Station. **Road:** Bus: Public services.

• August

Copenhagen International Ballet Festival

The annual *Copenhagen International Ballet Festival* is held in Frederiksberg just outside
Copenhagen. This summer festival features both
classic and new performances from the
Copenhagen International Ballet Group, which
was founded by Danish ballet dancer Alexander
Kølpin. The group consists of principals and
members from the New York City Ballet, Ballet
Béjart, Lyon Opera Ballet, Royal Danish Ballet,
Momix and Hamburg Ballet. The ballets are
staged in beautiful outdoor settings, including
the courtyard of the *Royal Veterinary and
Agricultural University*, where audiences can
watch performances under the night sky.

Event Organiser
Copenhagen International Ballet, Stranezejen 451,
2938 Klanpenborg, Denmark
Tel: 3963 4900 or 3325 2107
Website: www.copeninternationalballet.com

Venue
Various outdoor venues in Frederiksberg.

Transport
Air: Copenhagen Airport. **Rail:** Train: Copenhagen
Central Station. **Road:** Bus: Public services.

Finland

Helsinki

Tourist Information
Helsinki City Tourist & Convention Bureau
(Helsingin kaupungin matkailu – ja
kongressitoimisto)
Pohjoisesplanadi 19, 00100 Helsinki, Finland
Tel: (09) 169 3757
Website: www.hel.fi/tourism

• August-September

Helsinki Festival

Helsinki Festival is a giant performing arts
festival, which is held during three weeks in
August and September every year. The festival
hosts an extensive programme of orchestral and
chamber music, opera, dance, theatre, jazz, rock,
art exhibitions and film. The festival reaches its
climax with the 'Night of the Arts', when art
galleries, museums and bookshops open their
doors, free of charge, into the small hours. A
marquee called the Huvila Festival Tent hosts
many performances and music, poetry and songs
are performed in restaurants and bars around the
city. Visitors can also try local food during the
'Piazza of Tastes' in the Senate Square, when tents
are erected, offering a range of menus, with music
playing in the background.

Event Organiser
Helsinki Festival, The Lasipalatsi, Mannerheimintie
22-24, 00100 Helsinki, Finland
Tel: (09) 6126 5100
Website: www.helsinkifestival.fi

Venue
Various venues, including Aurora Park, Finlandia
Hall, The Alexander Theatre, Helsinki City Theatre,
Senate Square, Huvila Festival Tent, The Savoy
Theatre, Kunsthalle Helsinki, Cinema Orion, Bio
Rex, Atemeum Hall and Temppeliaukio Church.

Transport
Air: Helsinki-Vantaa Airport. **Rail:** Train: Helsinki
Station. **Road:** Bus: Public services.

France

Avignon

Tourist Information
Avignon Tourist Board (Office de Tourisme
d'Avignon)
41 cours Jean Jaurès, 84000 Avignon, France
Tel: (04) 3274 3274
Website: www.ot-avignon.fr

• July-September

Avignon Festival

The *Avignon Festival* began in 1947 when French
actor and director Jean Vilar staged three works
that were previously unknown to the French
public in the *Palais des Papes* (Popes' Palace) in

the historic centre of the city. Since then the festival has become a major cultural event, attracting thousands of visitors and performers from all corners of the globe. The emphasis is on experimental theatre and presenting new theatrical works to the public, many of which then go on tour in France and abroad. Dance and musical theatre also feature in the programme. Avignon is worth visiting at this time of year just for the atmosphere created by the festival – colourful and bizarre parades wind their way through the crowds in the Place du Palais and fire eaters and jugglers entertain visitors and locals in the streets from morning until night. A parallel event called the *Festival Off* allows performers to set up stage wherever they can find space (with permission from the city council), providing an alternative theatre scene.

Event Organiser
Festival d'Avignon, 8 bis rue de Mons, 84000 Avignon, France
Tel: (04) 9027 6656
Website: www.festival-avignon.com

Venue
Various venues across Avignon.

Transport
Air: Marseille-Provence Airport, Avignon-Caumont Airport or Nîmes-Arles-Camargue Airport. **Rail:** Train: Avignon Station (high-speed TGV services from Paris Gare de Lyon, Montpellier, Lyon and Barcelona, Spain). **Road:** Bus: Public services.

• September

Côtes du Rhône Grape Harvest

Avignon is the capital of the Côtes du Rhône, one of the most well-known French wine-producing regions. The wine is harvested at the beginning of September and visitors and locals can taste the results at the many stalls in the square in front of one of the city's most spectacular buildings, the *Palais des Papes* (Popes' Palace). Entertainment is provided around the city as folk groups, jugglers and actors perform for the crowds, and at 1700 the Bacchic confraternities (wine guilds or organisations) parade through the streets in costume, followed by floats bearing barrels of wine. There are also parachutists, films, concerts, shows and exhibitions of painting and crafts to accompany the bacchanalian festivities.

Event Organiser
Compagnons du Ban des Vendanges, Hôtel de Ville, 84045 Avignon, France
Tel: (04) 9016 0032

Venue
Palais des Papes and various locations across Avignon.

Transport
Air: Marseille-Provence Airport, Avignon-Caumont Airport or Nîmes-Arles-Camargue Airport. **Rail:** Train: Avignon Station (high-speed TGV services from Paris Gare de Lyon, Montpellier, Barcelona and Lyon). **Road:** Bus: Public services.

Cannes

Tourist Information
Cannes Tourist Board (SEMAC)
Esplanade Georges Pompidou, BP 272, 06403 Cannes, France
Tel: (04) 9299 8422
Website: www.cannes-on-line.com

• May

Cannes Film Festival

In 1939, the French government chose Cannes as a suitably sunny and enchanting location for its international film festival. Initially it was merely a chance for wealthy tourists to attend the many parties organised in the luxury villas of Cannes and in the hotels and palaces along La Croisette (the main boulevard), and all films shown at the festival received a prize. Nowadays, an award at Cannes can set actors, producers and directors on the path to fame and fortune, as the festival is one of the premier events in the cultural calendar and the annual rendezvous of the international film industry. Only film professionals and journalists may attend the actual festival; however, the original air of glamour and prestige is still felt in Cannes during the two weeks, and for many it is a chance to spot the many stars and millionaires who pose in restaurants and along the expensive private beaches of La Croisette.

Event Organiser
Cannes Film Festival, 3, rue Amélie 75007 Paris, France
Tel: (01) 5359 6100
Website: www.festival-cannes.org

Venue
Palais des Festivals et des Congrès.

Transport
Air: Nice-Côte d'Azur International Airport. **Rail:**
Train: Cannes Ville Station. **Road:** Bus: Public
services.

Lyon

Tourist Information
Lyon Convention and Visitors Bureau (Office du
Tourisme et des Congrès du Grand Lyon)
Place Bellecour, BP 2254, 69214 Lyon cedex 02,
France
Tel: (04) 7277 6969
Website: www.lyon-france.com

• December

Festival of Lights
The *Festival of Lights* takes place every year in
Lyon, when residents hang lights from their
balconies and place candles in their windows,
lighting up the city with a thousand lights. The
locals congregate in the streets to admire the
spectacle on December 8, which is a religious
celebration dating back to 1852 honouring the
statue of the Virgin Mary on *Fourvière Hill*. The
festival is one of Lyon's most popular and
traditional events. During the festivities, there are
also a number of music performances throughout
the city which is dominated by the *Fourvière
Basilica*. During the Franco-Prussian war, Catholics
in Lyon promised to build a giant church on
Fourvière Hill in honour of the Virgin Mary, if she
spared the city from the Prussian enemy. The city
was spared and so the church was built in 1896.

Event Organiser
For more information on the Festival of Lights,
contact Lyon Convention and Visitors Bureau (see
Tourist Information above).

Venue
Fourvière Hill and various venues across Lyon.

Transport
Air: Lyon-Saint Exupéry Airport. **Rail:**
Underground: Fourvière. **Road:** Bus: Public
services.

Paris

Tourist Information
Paris Central Tourist Office (L'Office de Tourisme
et des Congrès de Paris)
127 avenue des Champs-Elysées, 75008 Paris,
France

Tel: (08) 3668 3112
Website: www.parisinfo.com

• May-June

French Tennis Open (Roland Garros)
Tennis first came across the Channel to France at
the end of the 19th century and was a popular
pursuit among the French upper classes. Various
clubs were formed, such as the Racing Club de
France and the Stade Français; the first national
competition was held in 1891, with the ladies
competition following in 1897. Since then, *Roland
Garros* (named after a French engineer and fighter
pilot shot down during World War I) has become
increasingly more commercial. This is one of the
grand slam championships and the hall of fame
includes most of the big names in the sport. The
international prestige of this tournament and its
importance to world tennis, particularly in the
run-up to Wimbledon a few weeks later, create an
exciting atmosphere.

Event Organiser
Fédération Française de Tennis, 2 avenue Gordon
Bennett, 75016 Paris, France
Tel: (01) 4743 4800
Website: www.frenchopen.org

Venue
Roland Garros Stadium (Stade Roland Garros) on
the edge of the Bois de Boulogne.

Transport
Air: Paris Roissy-Charles de Gaulle Airport or
Paris Orly Airport. **Rail:** Train: Paris Gare du Nord
(Eurostar). Underground: Porte d'Auteuil. **Road:**
Bus: Public services.

• June

Festival of Music
The *Festival of Music* (*Fête de la Musique*) is a
nationwide event, although most of the major
concerts take place in Paris. The city's huge variety
of venues makes it an excellent place to catch a
performance of virtually any style ranging from
classical to reggae. The main events take place in
Place de la Bastille in the fourth *arrondissement*
(district), the Hôtel des Invalides in the seventh,
Place de la République in the third and Parc de la
Villette in the 19th. Just wandering the streets is
probably the best way to enjoy this festival
however, as there is music everywhere – even the
métro stations have bands playing, as do parks,
street corners, churches, cafés and museums.

Event Organiser
ADCEP (Association pour le développement de la création, études et projets), 30 rue René Boulanger, 75010 Paris, France
Tel: (01) 4003 9470
Website: www.fetedelamusique.culture.fr

Venue
Various venues across Paris.

Transport
Air: Paris Roissy-Charles de Gaulle Airport or Paris Orly Airport. **Rail:** Train: Paris Gare du Nord (Eurostar). **Road:** Bus: Public services.

• July

Arrival of the Tour de France

The *Tour de France* is widely acknowledged as the world's toughest cycling competition. Started in 1903 by Henri Desgrange, a French cyclist and journalist, the race covers both flat and mountainous terrain and travels through different regions every year in 20 stages. The 20 teams each consist of nine cyclists and the famous yellow jersey is awarded to the cyclist who has the lowest cumulative time for the race at the end of each day. In recent years the race has been dominated by American Lance Armstrong who first won the race in 1999 after overcoming cancer and went on to win the event for a record seventh consecutive time in 2005. Thousands of spectators, including film stars and celebrities, line the Champs-Elysées to see the winners speed towards the end of their three-week journey. The end often turns into a nerve-wracking sprint, followed by the cracking open of champagne and huge celebrations.

Event Organiser
La Société du Tour de France, 2 rue Rouget de Lisle, 92130 Issy-Les-Moulineaux, France
Tel: (01) 4133 1500
Website: www.letour.fr

Venue
Champs-Elysées.

Transport
Air: Paris Roissy-Charles de Gaulle Airport or Paris Orly Airport. **Rail:** Train: Paris Gare du Nord (Eurostar). Underground: Charles-de-Gaulle-Étoile, Georges V or Franklin D Roosevelt. RER: Charles-de-Gaulle-Etoile. **Road:** Bus: Public services.

Bastille Day

Towards the close of the 18th century, disenchantment with Louis XVI's monarchy, the aristocracy and the church had spread across France and was expressed, increasingly, in acts of civil unrest. On July 14 1789, several hundred ordinary Parisians marched to the Bastille prison, killed the governor and triggered the revolution that signalled the end of the monarchy in France with the pronouncement of *liberté, egalité, fraternité* (freedom, equality and brotherhood). To this day, the storming of the Bastille is commemorated across France as the *Fête de la Bastille.* The biggest celebrations are on the Champs-Elysées, with around 6000 people marching down the tree-lined avenue accompanied by military bands playing rousing music. At night there is a huge fireworks display over the city, as well as special entertainment and singing in bars and cafés throughout Paris. This is a national holiday in France, and the sense of pride that the French still feel for their republic is particularly evident on this day.

Event Organiser
For more information on Bastille Day, contact the Central Tourist Office (see **Tourist Information** above).

Venue
Champs-Elysées and various locations across Paris.

Transport
Air: Paris Roissy-Charles de Gaulle Airport or Paris Orly Airport. **Rail:** Train: Paris Gare du Nord (Eurostar). Underground: Charles-de-Gaulle-Étoile, Georges V or Franklin D Roosevelt. RER: Charles-de-Gaulle-Etoile. **Road:** Bus: Public services.

• July-August

Summer Arts Festival

For one month each summer the *Summer Arts Festival* (*Quartier d'Été*) transforms the streets of Paris into a huge open-air venue for the performing arts. Lovers of opera, jazz, theatre, classical music, circus, film and dance will all find something to entertain them – there are over 90 different events with a focus on several different countries each year. Venues range from cinemas in the bohemian Latin Quarter to the elegance of the *Jardin des Tuileries.* Parisians traditionally escape the capital for their summer holiday at this time of year, leaving more space for visitors to enjoy the show.

Event Organiser
Festival Paris Quartier d'Été, 5 rue Boudereau, 75009 Paris, France
Tel: (01) 494 9800
Website: www.quartierdete.com

Venue
Various locations across Paris.

Transport
Air: Paris Roissy-Charles de Gaulle Airport or Paris Orly Airport. Rail: Train: Paris Gare du Nord (Eurostar). Road: Bus: Public services.

• September-December

Autumn Festival

The Paris *Autumn Festival* (*Festival d'Automne*) presents a cultural mélange of literature, film, poetry and theatre from around the world. Each year a different country provides the focus for the festival with poetry, art and writing from that country. Past events have included Peter Brook's adaptation of 'Hamlet' and a staging of Boccaccio's Medieval 'Decameron' tales.

Event Organiser
Festival d'Automne, 16 rue de Rivoli, 75001 Paris, France
Tel: (01) 5345 1700
Website: www.festival-automne.com

Venue
Various venues across Paris.

Transport
Air: Paris Roissy-Charles de Gaulle Airport or Paris Orly Airport. Rail: Train: Paris Gare du Nord (Eurostar). Road: Bus: Public services.

Strasbourg

Tourist Information

Strasbourg Central Tourist Office (Office de Tourisme de Strasbourg)
17 place de la Cathédrale, 67082 Strasbourg, France
Tel: (03) 8852 2828
Website: www.strasbourg.com

• November-December

Strasbourg Christmas Market

Strasbourg Christmas Market is the biggest of its kind in France, and one of the most famous in Europe. It was first held in 1570 and is known in the local Alsatian dialect as *Christkindelsmärik*. There are hundreds of stalls selling gingerbread, spicy sausages, *vin chaud* (mulled wine), crafts and Christmas decorations around the beautiful Cathédrale Notre-Dame and along Place Broglie. A fir tree from the Vosges mountains is erected in Place Kléber in the heart of the city. There are over 50 concerts

and shows, providing musical accompaniment, and there is also an ice rink and a Christmas trail, where visitors can discover local crafts and traditions and the history of the festive season in Alsace. Children will enjoy 'chocolate cruises', which are boat rides through the city with entertainment and sweets.

Event Organiser
For more information on the Strasbourg Christmas Market, contact the Central Tourist Office (see **Tourist Information** above).

Venue
Place de la Cathédrale and various locations across Strasbourg.

Transport
Air: Euro-Airport Basel-Mulhouse-Freiburg. Rail: Train: Strasbourg Station. Tram: Homme de Fer or Langstrosse/Grande Rue. Road: Bus: Public services.

Germany

Berlin

Tourist Information

Berlin Tourist Office (Berlin Tourismus Marketing GmbH)
Am Karlsbad 11, 10785 Berlin, Germany
Tel: (030) 250 025
Website: www.btm.de

• February

Berlin International Film Festival

The *Berlin International Film Festival* was founded in 1951 as the result of an American Cold War initiative and quickly grew to become a well-established and important cultural event both in Berlin and worldwide. Film directors including Ingmar Bergman, Roman Polanski, Jean-Luc Godard and François Truffaut have all enjoyed considerable success with their films at the festival. It features an international competition, numerous film screenings, the Forum of Young Cinema and a children's film festival.

Event Organiser
International Film Festival, Potsdamerstrasse 5, 10785 Berlin, Germany
Tel: (030) 259 200
Website: www.berlinale.de

Venue
Various cinemas across Berlin.

Transport
Air: Berlin Tegel Airport. **Rail:** Train: S-Bahn trains serve the whole of Berlin. Underground: U-Bahn trains operate across Berlin. **Road:** Bus: Public services.

• June

Carnival of the Cultures

Carnival of the Cultures is a four-day street festival celebrating Berlin's cultural diversity and its ethnic communities. The carnival was established in 1996 and has grown to become one of the most important cultural events in Berlin. This huge annual street party sees thousands of performers, jugglers, musicians, dancers and DJs parade through the city's streets. The highlight of the weekend is the giant Whitsum street parade bringing together thousands of participants from around the world as they dance through the streets of the Kreuzberg district. There is also a giant programme of events during the festivities, with approximately 750 artists playing on four giant stages, and a children's party in *Goerlitzer Park*. International food, drinks and handicrafts are on sale at over 200 stalls during the four days, giving visitors the chance to sample international cuisine. Over half a million people attend the festival each year.

Event Organiser
Werkstatt der Kulturen, Wissmannstrasse 32, 12049 Berlin, Germany
Tel: (030) 6097 7022
Website: www.karneval-berlin.de

Venue
Various streets in Berlin, including Blucherplatz, Zossenerstrasse, Blucherstrasse and Gneisenaustrasse.

Transport
Air: Berlin Tegel Airport. **Rail:** Underground: Lines U1, 6 or 15 to Hallesches Tor or lines U6 or 7 to Mehringdamm. **Road:** Bus: Public services.

Christopher Street Day

Christoper Street Day is an enormous outdoor gay and lesbian party, which has been held every June in Berlin since 1979. Every year around 400,000 visitors join in the festivities, which rival gay and lesbian festivals in London, Amsterdam and San Francisco. The parade finishes at Siegessäule with a giant party and live music and DJs. Every year, there is a gigantic firework display at the end of the night, which brings the festivities to a spectacular close.

Event Organiser
Berliner CSD eV, Geschäftsführung, Michael Schmidt, Fuggerstrasse 7, 10777 Berlin, Germany
Tel: (0177) 277 3176
Website: www.csd-berlin.de

Venue
Various outdoor venues across Berlin, with parades setting off from Kurfürstendamm in the city centre.

Transport
Air: Berlin Tegel Airport. **Rail:** Underground: U9 or U15 to Kurfürstendamm. **Road:** Bus: Public services.

• July

Love Parade

The annual *Love Parade* takes place in Berlin in July (although it was cancelled in 2005 due to problems financing the huge free event). The festivities usually start at 1400 when a precession of 'lovetrucks' – many with DJs and onboard sound systems – set off on a giant parade from both *Ernst-Reuter-Platz* and *Brandenburg Tor* to Siegessäule, promoting the 'one world, one Love Parade' idea. Once they reach Siegessäule they turn around before setting off again on the big rally of the day at 1900. The first Love Parade took place on Berlin's Kurfürstendamm in 1989, when German DJ Dr Motte promoted an acid house party in the streets of Berlin to promote love and peace, and respect and understanding between nations; the event attracted 150 partygoers. The Berlin Love Parade has since grown into one of the biggest street parties in the Western world, with well over one million people attending the parade every year to watch the floats parade along the Strasse des 17 Juni, past some of Germany's most important monuments.

Event Organiser
Berlin Love Parade GmbH, Alexander Platz, 5, 10178 Berlin, Germany
Tel: (030) 284 620
Website: www.loveparade.de

Venue
Berlin city centre, starting at the Golden Angel monument in the middle of the Tiergarden and continuing down to Brandenburger Tor.

Transport
Air: Berlin Tegel Airport. **Rail:** Train: For Brandenburg Tor, S-Bahn S3, S5, S7, S9 or S75 to Friedrichstrasse Station. Underground: For Ernst-Reuter-Platz, U-Bahn 2 or 12 to Ernst-Reuter-Platz Station. **Road:** Bus: Public services.

• September

Berlin Marathon

The *Berlin Marathon* is an annual event which first took place on October 13 1974, with 284 runners from four nations starting the race. The event now attracts close to 30,000 participants. The race starts in Strasse des 17 Juni, at the *Charlottenburg Tor*, near *Ernst-Reuter Square* and ends in Kurfürstendamm. The participants run through 10 districts of Berlin: Charlottenburg, Tiergarten, Mitte, Friedrichshain, Kreuzberg, Neukölln, Schöneberg, Steglitz, Zehlendorf and Wilmersdorf, passing the *Brandenburg Gate*, the *Victory Column*, the *State Opera*, *Berlin Cathedral* and the *Botanical Gardens*. Over 60 bands and one million spectators line the streets to cheer on participants and create a truly exciting atmosphere.

Event Organiser
Berlin Marathon, SCC Running, Glockenturmstr 23, 14055 Berlin, Germany
Tel: (030) 3012 8810
Website: www.real-berlin-marathon.com

Venue
Streets of Berlin, starting at Charlottenburg Tor and ending at Kurfürstendamm.

Transport
Air: Berlin Tegel Airport. Rail: Train: S-Bahn S5 or S75 to Charlottenburg (start). Underground: U9 or U15 to Kurfürstendamm (finish). Road: Bus: Public services.

Frankfurt

Tourist Information

Frankfurt Tourist & Congress Board (Tourismus+Congress GmbH Frankfurt am Main) Kaiserstrasse 56, 60329 Frankfurt/Main, Germany
Tel: (069) 2123 8800
Website: www.frankfurt.de

• October

Frankfurt Marathon

The *Frankfurt Marathon* traditionally takes place on the last Sunday in October on a route that takes runners through the centre of the city. The marathon, which was first held in 1981, is the oldest city marathon in Germany, leading through the city centre, on to the west of the city and back through Sachsenhausen to the finish at the *Frankfurt Trade Fair Centre*. As well as the annual 42.2km (26.2 miles) marathon, there is also a 4.2km (2.6 miles) mini marathon for children and a breakfast run. The latter starts at *Frankfurt Römer*, one of the main sights in Frankfurt, and leads 5km (3.1 miles) through the city centre to the city's fairground. Visitors and spectators can also take part in a pasta party, a marathon breakfast and marathon buffet. In addition to this, there is a sportswear and sports equipment exhibition, a presentation ceremony and various course parties.

Event Organiser
Euro Marathon Frankfurt GmbH, 60135 Frankfurt am Main, Germany
Tel: (069) 9717 6330
Website: www.frankfurt-marathon.com

Venue
Starts and finishes at the Frankfurt Trade Fair Centre, in the centre of Frankfurt.

Transport
Air: Frankfurt Airport. Rail: Train: S-Bahn S3, S4, S5 or S6 to Messe Station. Road: Bus: Public services.

Munich

Tourist Information

Munich Tourist Office (Fremdenverkehrsamt München)
Fraunhoferstraße 6, 80469 Munich, Germany
Tel: (089) 230 0180
Website: www.muenchen-tourist.de

• January-February

Munich Carnival

Munich Carnival (or *Fasching* as it is known in Germany) is held every year in the city, with major celebrations taking place during Germany's carnival period; this is known as the 'Fifth Season' or the 'Season of Fools', when Germans let their hair down before Lent. The first Fasching Ball was held in Munich in 1829 and was soon followed by many more masquerades and balls. Their popularity led to the establishment of a Munich carnival society in 1839 to organise annual events, marking the beginning of Fasching as it is known today. Every year, partygoers can choose from thousands of parties, balls and other festivities, which take place in the city, ranging from fancy-dress parties through to black-tie affairs. The climax of the carnival, *München Harrisch* (Mad Munich) costume parade, takes place on the

Sunday before Shrove Tuesday, with revellers partying in the streets and passing through the crowds on floats. Thousands of dancers and musicians congregate in *Marienplatz* after the parade to fill the city's beer halls. Fasching is also celebrated in other parts of Germany, such as Mainz and Düsseldorf, although Munich's Fasching lasts the longest and is the most famous.

Event Organiser
For more information on the Munich Carnival, contact the Munich Tourist Office (see **Tourist Information** above).

Venue
Various dance halls in hotels and breweries in Munich.

Transport
Air: Munich International Airport. Rail: Train: S-Bahn to Marienplatz. Underground: U-Bahn U3, U4, U5 or U6 to Marienplatz. Road: Bus: Public services.

• June

City Foundation Day

City Foundation Day is held every year to celebrate the founding of Munich, which took place on June14 1158 by the German prince, Henry the Lion, who also held the titles Duke of Saxony (1142-1180) and Duke of Bavaria (1156-1180). Every year, in commemoration, the locals drink beer and eat vast quantities of sausages during this giant street party. The festivities are accompanied by music from local bands and street performances. The event is held betweeen *Marienplatz* and *Odeonsplatz* in Munich's city centre. Many attractions, such as the *Neues Rathaus* (New Town Hall), built in the 19th century, *Altes Rathaus* (Old Town Hall), which houses a delightful toy museum, and *Frauenkirche* – Munich's cathedral, are located nearby and are well worth a visit whilst in the city.

Event Organiser
For more information on the City Foundation Day, contact the Munich Tourist Office (see **Tourist Information** above).

Venue
Between Marienplatz and Odeonsplatz in Munich city centre.

Transport
Air: Munich International Airport. Rail: Train: S-Bahn to Marienplatz. Underground: U-Bahn to Marienplatz. Road: Bus: Public services.

• September-October

October Festival

The Munich *October Festival* (or *Oktoberfest* as it is known in Germany) starts at the end of September and is one of the world's biggest public festivals. The event began in 1810 to celebrate the marriage of King Joseph Maximiliam of Bavaria to Princess Theresa of Saxony. The event was such a huge success that it has taken place ever since. The event now attracts over six million partygoers who drink around five million litres of beer. Events include the *Grand Entry of the Oktoberfest Landlords and Breweries*, the *Costume and Riflemen's Procession*, performances by Oompah bands, dancing and a giant funfair at the foot of the *Bavaria Statue*. The festivities take place in beer tents in the Theresienwiese district (a district named after Princess Theresa of Saxony).

Event Organiser
For more information on the October Festival, contact the Munich Tourist Office (see **Tourist Information** above).

Venue
Theresienwiese District.

Transport
Air: Munich International Airport. **Rail:** Underground: U-Bahn U4 or U5 to Theresienwiese. **Road:** Bus: Public services.

• December

Christmas Market

Every year, thousands of people crowd into Marienplatz to watch the Lord Mayor open the *Christmas Market* (known as *Weihnachtsmarkt* in German). This event occurs at 1700 on the Saturday before the first day of Advent, when the mayor switches on the Christmas lights on a 30m-high (98ft) Christmas tree. The market's origins can be traced back to Nicholas Market, which started in 1310, with people shopping in Nenhauserstrasse, buying toys for Christmas. In 1597, the market moved location; changing its name to Christmas Market in 1805. Since 1972, the market has taken place in Marienplatz in the centre of Munich. Every year, gifts are on sale at more than 140 market stalls. Craftsmen can also be seen at work, making gifts such as Christmas baubles and candles. There is also a *Crib Market*, based on the Nativity Crib in the Town Hall Courtyard. Folk music is played at 1730 every evening and Santa Claus greets children in the square on December 5 and 6.

Event Organiser
For more information on the Christmas Market, contact the Munich Tourist Office (see **Tourist Information** above).

Venue
Marienplatz in Munich city centre.

Transport
Air: Munich International Airport.
Rail: Train: S-Bahn to Marienplatz.
Underground: U-Bahn to Marienplatz. **Road:**
Bus: Public services.

Greece

Athens

Tourist Information
Hellenic Tourism Organisation
(Ellinikos Organismos Tourismou)
7, Tsoha, 11521 Athens, Greece
Tel: (210) 870 7000
Website: www.gnto.gr

• July

Rockwave Festival
This is Greece's major rock music event, featuring performances by groups from around the world. The festival first took place in 1996 and has attracted many big name bands since then, including Moby, Pulp, Prodigy, Blur, Garbage, Marilyn Manson and The Fun Lovin' Criminals. The event now attracts well over 50,000 people each year and there are other activities to entertain the crowd including bungee jumping, simulators and circus acts. There are also merchandise stalls and food and drink available, and festivalgoers can take time out to relax in the park.

Event Organiser
Didi Music, 3 Eptanisou Street – 2 Pipinou Street, 11257 Athens, Greece
Tel: (210) 882 0426
Website: www.didimusic.gr

Venue
Varies annually. Contact the Hellenic Tourism Organisation for more details.

Transport
Air: Athens International Airport. **Rail:** Train: Larissa or Pelopónnisos stations. Underground: Monastiraki or Theseion. **Road:** Bus: Public services.

• July-September

Athens Festival
In AD 161 the Roman ruler Herodes Atticus commissioned the *Odeon* amphitheatre at the foot of the *Acropolis* in memory of his wife, Rigilla. Decorated in marble and seating 5000 spectators, this beautiful auditorium has been used to stage performances since ancient times, when musicians, actors, poets and dancers performed to gain the favour of the gods. Since 1955, the Odeon has provided a splendid setting for the *Athens Festival*, an international celebration of theatre, music, dance and literature. The starry night sky above the amphitheatre provides the perfect backdrop for a magical evening's entertainment. Anyone wishing to try a more unusual performance might like to watch a poetry reading or avant-garde musical recital at the *Pnyx*, at the entrance to the Acropolis.

Event Organiser
Athens Festival, Athens Festival Box Office, 4 Stadiou Street, Athens, Greece
Tel: (01) 928 2900
Website: www.hellenicfestival.gr

Venue
Odeon of Herodes Atticus (at the foot of the Acropolis).

Transport
Air: Athens International Airport. **Rail:** Train: Larissa or Pelopónnisos stations. Underground: Monastiraki or Theseion. **Road:** Bus: Public services.

• November

Athens Marathon
Almost every major city in the world has its own marathon, but only Athens can claim to have the original. The event is so called after the legendary 40.2km (25 mile) journey undertaken by the messenger, Phiedippes, when he brought news of the Athenian victory over the Persians at the *Marathon* battlefield in 490 BC. The first marathon event took place at the 1896 Olympic Games in Athens and the winner was a Greek, Spyridon Louis. Today, runners must follow in the footsteps of Phiedippes, to complete a route over 42.2km (26 miles 385 yards) between the ancient battlefield in the village of Marathon and the historic *Olympic Stadium* in the centre of Athens. The standard distance for a marathon event was set in 1924, when the British Olympic Committee decided that

the route for the London Games should lead from *Windsor Castle* to the royal box in the *London Olympic Stadium.*

Event Organiser

SEGAS, 137 Syngrou Avenue, 171 21 N Smirni, Athens, Greece

Tel: (01) 935 1888

Website: www.athensmarathon.com

Venue

Starts at the village of Marathon and ends at the Olympic Stadium.

Transport

Air: Athens International Airport. **Rail:** Train: Larissa or Pelopónnisos stations. **Road:** Bus: Public services.

Hungary

Budapest

Tourist Information

Tourism Office of Budapest (Budapesti Turisztikai Hivatal)

1364 Budapest PF 215, 1052 Budapest, Hungary

Tel: (01) 266 0479

Website: www.budapestinfo.hu

• March-April

Budapest Spring Festival

Although classical music predominates, the *Budapest Spring Festival* encompasses music for most tastes, as well as cinematic and theatrical events. It is the largest cultural festival in Hungary and has a growing reputation abroad. Performances take place in beautiful locations around the city including open-air events such as the *Celebration of Spring* parade. There is a vast array of classical concerts, ranging from piano recitals and string quartets to evenings of French Baroque music. Those interested in discovering traditional Hungarian culture can enjoy performances by the 100-member Budapest Gypsy Orchestra. Jazz, films, exhibitions and children's activities are also on offer each year.

Event Organiser

Budapest Festival Centre (Budapest Fesztiválközpont KHT), Egyetem tér 5, 1053 Budapest, Hungary

Tel: (01) 486 3300

Website: www.festivalcity.hu

Venue

Various locations across Budapest.

Transport

Air: Budapest Ferihegy Airport. **Rail:** Train: Eastern, Western or Southern stations. **Road:** Bus: Public services.

• October-November

Budapest Autumn Festival

The *Budapest Autumn Festival* is an experimental arts festival that aims to highlight new forms within the contemporary arts scene. Variety is the key – visitors can explore almost any genre, from high-brow literary readings and classical orchestral concerts to fun circus acts and eclectic art exhibitions. Children can join in play workshops and there are coffee shop concerts where live music can be enjoyed alongside the mouthwatering Budapest tradition of coffee and cakes. Hungarian folk dancing, jazz, film premieres, clown shows and literary sightseeing tours are also on offer.

Event Organiser

Budapest Festival Centre (Budapest Fesztiválközpont KHT), Egyetem tér 5, 1053 Budapest, Hungary

Tel: (01) 486 3300

Website: www.festivalcity.hu

Venue

Various locations across Budapest.

Transport

Air: Budapest Ferihegy Airport. **Rail:** Train: Eastern, Western or Southern stations. **Road:** Bus: Public services.

• December

New Year's Eve Gala and Ball at the Opera

This ball has taken place every year for the past decade in the opulent surroundings of the *Hungarian State Opera* House in central Budapest and is open to everyone. The Opera House was built in Italian neo-Renaissance style to designs by Miklós Ybl and was first opened in 1884. It was reopened on its 100th birthday in September 1984 after undergoing extensive restoration to return it to its former glory. Those who take part in the New Year's Eve festivities can expect to be richly entertained, with a gala concert of music and dance performed by the resident Opera House ensemble, Hungarian food and drink served on the stage and in the box areas, and old-style Viennese ballroom dancing. For those who prefer something more contemporary, there is a piano bar and disco.

Event Organiser
Organisational Department of the Opera House, 24 Andrássy Street, VI Budapest 1061, Hungary
Tel: (01) 332 7914
Website: www.opera.hu

Venue
Hungarian State Opera House.

Transport
Air: Budapest Ferihegy Airport. **Rail:** Train: Eastern, Western or Southern stations.
Underground: Opera. **Road:** Bus: Public services.

Iceland

Reykjavik

Tourist Information
(Icelandic Tourist Board) Islenska Tourist Board
Laekjargata 3, 101 Reykjavik, Iceland
Tel: 535 5500
Website: www.visiticeland.com

• January-February

Thorri Feast

Thorri is the Icelandic name for the fourth month of winter. Every year in February, Icelanders continue the ancient Viking tradition of celebrating the end of winter and the coming of spring with dancing, singing and huge feasts. The tradition all but disappeared with the advent of Christianity, but was revived in 1873 during Iceland's struggle for independence from Denmark. Traditional delicacies include *slatur* (a type of black pudding), *svith* (boiled sheep's head), *hakarl* (rotten shark meat) and *hrutspungar* (ram's testicles). For the less adventurous there are other specialities on offer, such as various kinds of bread, *lundabaggar* (lamb meatballs), *hardfiskur* (dried fish with butter) and *skyr* (curds and fresh blueberries). Restaurants in Reykjavik offer their own *Thorri Feasts*, usually as a buffet to allow guests to sample as many dishes as they can manage. This is a popular festival giving visitors the chance to experience Icelandic culture.

Event Organiser
For more information on the Thorri Feast, contact the Icelandic Tourist Board (see **Tourist Information** above).

Venue
Various locations across Reykjavik.

Transport
Air: Keflavik International Airport. **Road:** Car: Hwy-1 (from all coastal towns in Iceland, including Akureyri, Höfn and Isafjördur).

• July-August

Light Nights

In the 12th century, *sagnaskemmtun* (saga entertainment) was a popular way of spending evenings on Icelandic farms. Stories were passed on from generation to generation and many have been recorded in writing, although the identity of many of the authors remains a mystery. The sagas are based on legends, historical events, secular fiction and the lives of the saints, and tell the story of everyday people in a bid to give Icelanders an awareness of themselves and the society around them through the tales of their ancestors. The saga remains an important cultural tradition in Iceland and every year the audience is taken on a two-hour journey through several centuries of Icelandic history with storytelling, slides, folksongs and chants. This is a unique theatrical and cultural experience, and performances are held every Thursday, Friday and Saturday at 2100.

Event Organiser
The Travelling Theatre, Baldursgata 37, 101 Reykjavik, Iceland
Tel: 551 9181 (summer months only)
Website: www.lightnights.com

Venue
Tjarnarbió Theatre (next to the City Hall).

Transport
Air: Keflavik International Airport. **Road:** Bus: Public services.

India

Delhi

Tourist Information
Government of India
Tourist Office
88 Janpath, New Delhi 110011, India
Tel: (011) 332 0005
Website: www.tourisminindia.com

• October

Diwali

Diwali is one of the most well-known Hindu festivals and is celebrated throughout India. According to Hindu legend, King Dashratha wished for his son Rama, born to his wife Queen Kaushalaya, to be the heir to his throne. Another of his wives, Queen Keykayee, used the two wishes granted to her by her husband to send Rama into exile for 14 years so that her son, Bharat, would be the future king instead. Rama is believed to have spent his years in exile in the southern tip of the Indian sub-continent killing the king of demons before returning to rule over his kingdom of Ayodhya. Diwali thus symbolises the victory of good over evil and the lifting of spiritual darkness. The Sanskrit name, 'Deepavali', is derived from two words – 'deepa', meaning 'light' and 'avali', meaning 'row', thus 'row of lights'. Diwali is commonly referred to as the 'festival of lights', and many Indians place small oil lamps, or *diyas*, outside their homes, while candles light up the city centres to welcome Lakshmi, the goddess of wealth and prosperity. Firecrackers are also burned and Hindu families hold huge feasts in their homes. Sweets are traditionally given as presents and Delhi stages its own festivities at *Lal Quila* (Red Fort) with fireworks and a funfair.

Event Organiser
For more information on Diwali, contact the Government of India Tourist Office (see **Tourist Information** above).

Venue
Various locations across Delhi with the main focus at Lal Quila (Red Fort).

Transport
Air: Indira Gandhi International Airport. **Rail:** Train: New Delhi or Old Delhi stations. **Road:** Bus: Public services.

Rajasthan

Tourist Information

Government of India
Tourist Office
Tourist Reception Centre, (RTDC), Hotel Saras, Agra Road, Rajasthan, India
Tel. (011) 22542
Website: www.incredibleindia.org

• October/November

Pushkar Fair

The spectacular *Pushkar Fair* is the largest camel fair anywhere in the world at which thousands of camels are bought, traded and paraded for the amassed crowds at this incredible week-long festival. Camels are brought from miles around, many having trekked through the hot, arid desert for several weeks to get to the festival or 'mela'. The festival also has religious significance as one of Hinduism's five major pilgrimages. As the serious business of camel trading draws to an end, the final days of the festival are devoted to fun and games including camel races and a camel beauty pageant. The festival closes with the symbolic washing in the bathing ghats of Pushkar Lake. Over 10,000 foreign tourists travel to witness the incredible festival at what is truly an awe-inspiring event.

Event Organiser
For more information on the Pushkar Fair, contact the Government of India Tourist Office (see **Tourist Information** above).

Venue
Pushkar, Rajasthan.

Transport
Air: Jaipur International Airport. **Rail:** Train: Ajmer Station. **Road:** Bus: Public services.

Ireland

Dublin

Tourist Information
Dublin Tourism
Tourism Centre, Suffolk Street, Dublin 2, Ireland
Tel: (01) 605 7700
Website: www.visitdublin.com

• March

St Patrick's Festival

St Patrick's Festival takes place in Dublin every year to remember St Patrick, who is the Patron Saint of Ireland. St Patrick was born around AD 387 and died on March 17 AD 461. He was the second bishop of Ireland and was most famous for using the shamrock to show how the Father, Son and Holy Ghost can exist as separate parts of the same body, leading to the shamrock becoming the national emblem of Ireland. Patrick is also believed to have given a sermon that drove all snakes from Ireland. To commemorate his life, there is a parade through Dublin city centre on March 17, as well as a giant carnival and celebrations during the four days of festivities. The parade begins at 1100 at *Christ Church Cathedral* and ends in O'Connell Street. St Patrick's Day, on March 17, is a bank holiday in Ireland, when the Lord Mayor of Dublin is driven through the streets in a horse-drawn carriage and is cheered on by spectators. Other events include the *Fanfare Celebration* of marching bands and the *St Patrick's Eve Night Parade* on March 16, the *Ceili Mor Celebration* of Irish dance on March 17 and *The Big Day Out* on March 19, The Big Day Out consists of more than 100 events, including street theatre, magic shows, comedy shows, puppet shows and parades. The festivities end with a giant fireworks display on March 19. St Patrick's Day celebrations take place around the world, with many major cities, including New York, Boston and Chicago, hosting their own Irish celebrations.

Event Organiser
St Patrick's Day Festival Office, St Stephens Green House, Earlsfort Terrace, Dublin 2, Ireland
Tel: (01) 676 3205
Website: www.stpatricksday.ie

Venue
Various locations across Dublin, centred around Christ Church Cathedral and O'Connell Street.

Transport
Air: Dublin Airport. Road: Bus: Public services.

• May

Heineken Green Energy Festival

The annual *Heineken Green Energy Festival* takes place over the May Bank Holiday weekend and showcases a host of unsigned and international bands playing in venues across the city. Over 50,000 people attend the festival each year to see a wide range of acts. Past performers have included the Black Eyed Peas, Paddy Casey and Faithless. Big names play at *Dublin Castle*, the *Olympia Theatre* and *Temple Bar Music Centre*. As well as performances from well-known international artists, unsigned groups also play gigs in Dublin and compete in the festival's band challenge.

Event Organiser
For more information on the Heineken Green Energy Festival, contact the Dublin Tourism (see **Tourist Information** above).

Venue
Various locations across Dublin, including Temple Bar Music Centre, Dublin Castle and Olympia Theatre.

Transport
Air: Dublin Airport. **Rail:** Train: Connolly or Heuston stations. **Road:** Bus: Public services.

• June

Bloomsday Festival

The *Bloomsday Festival* celebrates the life of James Joyce, who was born in 1882 and died in 1941. James Joyce is one of Ireland's most famous writers, responsible for works that include 'Ulysses' and 'Portrait of the Artist as a Young Man'. Events include a re-enactment of Paddy Dignam's funeral in Ulysses, walking tours around Dublin and various talks on James Joyce, Ulysses and Bloomsday. The actual Bloomsday celebration takes place on June 16, starting with the *Guinness Bloomsday Breakfast* which consists of 'eating with relish the inner organs of beasts and fowls', washed down with the 'foaming ebon ale', and listening to readings from the book of the day. The event is named Bloomsday after Leopold Bloom, the main character in 'Ulysses', and takes place on this day as the book was set on June 16 1904. The annual *Bloomsday Lecture & Walking Tour* also takes place on June 16, with talks by Ken Monaghan, Cultural Director of the Centre and nephew of James Joyce, and a walking tour through the city, with characters from 'Ulysses' popping up along the way. Other events include the Riverrun which celebrates the River Liffey and the women in Joyce's books and involves a bus trip to the mouth of the river and Howth Head, rounded off with readings and refreshments in the *Bloody Steam Pub*.

Event Organiser
The James Joyce Centre, 35 North Great George's Street, Dublin 1, Ireland
Tel: (01) 878 8547
Website: www.jamesjoyce.ie

Venue
Various locations across Dublin, including North Great George's Street, Westland Row train station, Temple Bar, National Library and the James Joyce Centre.

Transport
Air: Dublin Airport. **Rail:** Train: Tara Street or Connolly stations. **Road:** Bus: Public services.

• September-October

Dublin Fringe Festival

Dublin Fringe Festival first took place in 1995 and now takes place every year at the end of September. The festival, which lasts for three weeks, incorporates the best of theatre, dance, comedy and visual arts and is now Ireland's largest performing arts festival. The Fringe aims to challenge convention through exploring new ways of looking at the world through performance art and each year the Fringe venues come alive attracting thousands of visitors.

Event Organiscr
Dublin Fringe Festival, 12 East Essex Street, Temple Bar Dublin 2, Ireland
Tel: (01) 679 2320
Website: www.fringefest.com

Venue
20 locations in Dublin, including Civic Theatre, Samuel Beckett Theatre, Temple Bar Square and The Crypt at Dublin Castle.

Transport
Air: Dublin Airport. **Rail:** Train: Connolly or Heuston stations. **Road:** Bus: Public services.

Israel

Tel Aviv

Tourist Information
Tel Aviv-Jaffa Tourist Information Office
New Central Bus Station, Sixth Floor, Room 6108, Tel Aviv, Israel
Tel: (03) 639 5660
Website: www.goisrael.org

• August

Jaffa Nights

Jaffa Nights is held annually in the city of Tel Aviv during mid-August. Lasting for four days, it comprises over 70 music, theatre, dance and art exhibitions, and is Israel's largest street-staged event. In the evenings, the streets of the Old Jaffa area are closed to traffic, during which time the streets come alive with music and dance performed on stages erected in the city's various squares and alleys. Tens of thousands of visitors attend the festival every year.

Event Organiser
Tel Aviv Municipality, Events Department, Tel Aviv 64162, Israel
Tel: (03) 521 8264
Website: www.tel-aviv.gov.il/english

Venue
Old Jaffa area of Tel Aviv.

Transport
Air: Ben-Gurion International Airport. **Train:** Rail: Tel Aviv Central Station. **Road:** Bus: Public services.

Italy

Florence

Tourist Information
Florence Tourist Board (Azienda di Promozione Turistica di Firenze)
Via Cavour 1r, 50129 Florence, Italy
Tel: (055) 290 832
Website: www.firenze.turismo.toscana.it

• March

Explosion of the Cart

The origins of this ritual, which is known as the *Scoppio del Carro* in Italian, go back to the time of the first Christian crusade to seize control of the Holy City of Jerusalem from the Muslims in 1095. A valiant soldier called Pazzino dei Pazzi fought bravely and was the first to scale the walls of Jerusalem, where he raised the Christian flag. For this he was rewarded with some stones from the Holy Tomb. The hero took these with him to Florence to be used by the bishop to light the fire in the cathedral on Easter morning; this fire was then distributed to every Florentine citizen. The Pazzi family then began to build a cart (or *Brindellone*, as it is called in Italian), which has been burned at this annual event for many centuries. On Easter Sunday, starting at 0950, two separate processions transport the stones and the cart (which is led by oxen) from the *Chiesa dei Santi Apostoli* (the Church of the Holy Apostles) throughout the city to the *Piazza del Duomo* (Cathedral Square), where they meet. A special Easter mass then takes place inside the cathedral. During the Gloria (the second element of Catholic mass) at 1100, a rocket, in the form of a dove, which is connected to the car, is set alight. This in turn causes the cart, which is loaded with fireworks, to explode in a mass of colour and light, watched by hundreds of spectators. According to tradition, if the ceremony goes smoothly Florence will have good harvests and a prosperous year.

Event Organiser

For more information on the Explosion of the Cart, contact the Florence Tourist Board (see Tourist Information above).

Venue

Piazza del Duomo in central Florence.

Transport

Air: Amerigo Vespucci Airport (Florence) or Galileo Galilei Airport (Pisa). Rail: Train: Firenze Santa Maria Novella Station (Florence). Road: Bus: Public services.

• June

Historical Soccer Tournament

Costumed football matches (now known as *Calcio Storico Fiorentino* in Italian) have long been played in the *Piazza Santa Croce* in the historic heart of Florence. The origins of the game date back at least to Roman times, with the moves involved in the game being similar to the battle order of the Roman army. It was not until centuries later that football migrated north to England and evolved into the modern game known today. The game was characterised by fights and locked battles for possession of the ball, all of which were meant to strengthen both the body and the mind of the civilians and soldiers who played. Famous players included members of prestigious Renaissance families such as Lorenzo de' Medici and Vincenzo Gonzaga. Matches were played at Carnival time and throughout the year until the end of the 18th century; the tradition was revived in 1930, the 400th anniversary of the siege of Florence, as a means of celebrating the city's resilience in the face of adversity through the centuries. Nowadays, three matches are held on the city's patron saint's day in June and players wear medieval costumes representing the four districts of the city: white for Santo Spirito, blue for Santa Croce, red for Santa Maria Novella and green for San Giovanni. The backdrop to this colourful spectacle is the celebrated Franciscan church of Santa Croce.

Event Organiser

Calcio Storico Fiorentino – Segretaria, Piazzetta di Parte Guelfa 1, 50123 Florence, Italy
Tel: (055) 261 6050
Website: www.globeit.it/caf/info.html

Venue

Piazza Santa Croce in central Florence.

Transport

Air: Amerigo Vespucci Airport (Florence), Galileo Galilei Airport (Pisa). Rail: Train: Firenze Santa Maria Novella Station (Florence). Road: Bus: Public services.

Rome

Tourist Information

Azienda di Promozione Turistica di Roma (Rome Tourist Office)
Via Parigi 11, 00185 Rome, Italy
Tel: (06) 4889 9253
Website: www.romaturismo.com

• July-September

Roman Summer

Rome's summer arts festival (*Estate Romana* in Italian) is a three-month extravaganza encompassing all manner of events. Balmy summer evenings can be spent watching some of the many Italian and foreign films showing at the open-air cinema in *Piazza Vittorio*, or enjoying a live classical music concert in one of the city's parks. The programme features a huge variety of performances including celebrating culture through classical concerts, dance, music, food and drink. The Italians are renowned for their love of children, and younger visitors will find plenty of distractions to amuse them, from sports competitions to games and cartoons.

Event Organiser

For more information on the Roman Summer, contact the Rome Tourist Office (see Tourist Information above).

Venue

Various locations across Rome.

Transport

Air: Rome Leonardo de Vinci Airport (Fiumicino) or Rome Ciampino Airport. Water: Ferry: Civitavecchia port, from where there are services to central Rome. Rail: Train: Roma Termini, Roma Tiburtina, Roma Ostiense or Roma Trastevere stations. Road: Bus: Public services.

• October-December

Rome Jazz Festival

Throughout its history, the *Rome Jazz Festival* has featured many prominent artists, including the Steve Lacy Quartet, Cuban jazz player Gonzalo

Rubalcaba, guitarist John McLaughlin and the Brad Mehldau Trio. Venues range from *Big Mama*, Rome's premier blues club, which has earned the nickname 'Home of the Blues in Rome', to *Auditorium del Massimo*, an historic cultural institute now housed in the city's ultra-modern EUR business district. Jazz and Latin American music have long been popular in Italy's capital and this festival brings together the best of both.

Event Organiser

Rome Jazz Festival, Via Salaria 292, 00199 Rome, Italy

Tel: (06) 5630 5015

Website: www.romajazzfestival.it

Venue

Various venues across Rome.

Transport

Air: Rome Leonardo de Vinci Airport (Fiumicino) or Rome Ciampino Airport. **Water:** Ferry: Civitavecchia port, from where there are services to central Rome. **Rail:** Train: Roma Termini, Roma Tiburtina, Roma Ostiense or Roma Trastevere stations. Underground: EUR Palasport (to Auditorium del Massimo). **Road:** Bus: Public services.

• December

Christmas Mass in St Peter's Basilica

One of the most moving ways to celebrate Christ's birthday is by attending this mass in the second largest church in the Christian world. Work on the *Basilica di San Pietro*, or St Peter's Basilica (so named as it is said to stand on the burial site of St Peter), was begun in 1506 during the time of Pope Julius II, and completed in 1615 under Pope Paul V. Artists and architects involved in its design and construction include famous Renaissance names such as Raphael, Bramante and Michelangelo. The fruits of their labour are awe-inspiring, with the huge interior filled with works of Renaissance and Baroque art, among them Michelangelo's 'Pietà'. Visitors who wish to join the crowds for this special occasion must book in advance by contacting the Prefettura della Casa Pontificia and stating the number of tickets they require.

Event Organiser

Prefettura della Casa Pontificia, 00120 Vatican City, Italy

Tel: (06) 6988 3114

Website: www.vatican.va

Venue

Basilica di San Pietro (St Peter's Basilica).

Transport

Air: Rome Leonardo de Vinci Airport (Fiumicino) or Rome Ciampino Airport. **Water:** Ferry: Civitavecchia port, from where there are services to central Rome. **Rail:** Train: Roma Termini, Roma Tiburtina, Roma Ostiense or Roma Trastevere stations. Underground: Ottaviano-San Pietro. **Road:** Bus: Public services.

Venice

Tourist Information

Azienda di Promozione Turistica (Venice Tourist Board)

Calle dell'Ascensione 71C, Venice, Italy

Tel: (041) 529 8711

Website: www.turismovenezia.it

• February

Venice Carnival

The wearing of masks has been a Venetian tradition since the 13th century. It was particularly popular with gamblers as a means of disguising their identity from their creditors, although the law stated that masks were not allowed during religious festivals, including Lent. They were, however, permitted from San Stefano's Day (December 26) until Shrove Tuesday and this period, the *Carnevale* (as it is known in Italian), saw huge celebrations across the city, with masked balls in the *palazzi* lining the Grand Canal and bullfights and cart-racing in the streets. Nowadays, although it does not start until February, *Venice Carnival* is one of the most famous in Europe and the age-old traditions continue to thrive. Visitors to the city can see actors and ordinary Venetians posing in opulent costumes around *Piazza San Marco* (St Mark's Square), and there are still masked balls in the historic buildings, or *palazzi*, along the canals; tickets for the *Golden Night Ball* in the Palazzo Ca' Zenobio on the last night of the carnival cost about L520,000 (£170) and, as for all balls, guests must arrive in costume. A cheaper option is to enjoy the long-standing tradition of hot chocolate and cakes in one of the city's many cafés, or listen to one of the concerts that take place during the event. Many visitors are content just to mix with the crowds and take in the festive atmosphere. On the first day of the carnival, the *Festa delle Marie* (Festival of the Brides) takes place – seven young women, representing seven brides who were kidnapped and robbed by pirates in AD 948, travel from *San Pietro di Castello* to St Mark's Square where dancing and street entertainment follow. The real climax of the carnival is the last Saturday, when thousands of people flock to the city; many of the balls take place on this night and there are concerts in St Mark's Square.

Event Organiser
Comitato per il Carnevale di Venezia Consortium, Piazzale Roma, Santa Croce 473, 30133 Venice, Italy
Tel: (041) 717 065
Website: www.carnivalofvenice.com

Venue
Various locations across Venice with the focus on St Mark's Square.

Transport
Air: Marco Polo Airport (Venice). **Water:** Waterbus (*Vaporetto*): 1 or 82 (from Piazzale Roma to San Zaccaria for St Mark's Square). **Rail:** Train: Venezia Santa Lucia or Mestre stations. **Road:** Bus: Public services.

• March-November

Venice Biennale

Founded in 1895, the *Venice Biennale* is a major cultural institution aimed at promoting contemporary art and culture to a wider audience by setting up permanent workshops and projects. Every two years, the Biennale presents a varied programme of art exhibitions, dance, music, cinema and theatre in the city, attracting worldwide interest and often provoking controversy. Past exhibitors have included Benetton designer Oliviero Toscani and American artist Robert Rauschenberg. The dance element of the festival (June, July and September) includes pieces choreographed by artists from Egypt, Turkey and Morocco, amongst others. The Biennial also incorporates the *Festival of Music* (May and September), the *International Film Festival* and the *International Theatre Festival* (March, May, July and September).

Event Organiser
Venice Biennale Cultural Corporation, Events Office, Palazzo Querini Dubois, San Polo 2004, 30125 Venice, Italy
Tel: (041) 272 8318
Website: www.labiennale.org

Venue
Various venues across Venice.

Transport
Air: Marco Polo Airport (Venice). **Water:** Waterbus (*Vaporetto*): 1 or 82 (from Piazzale Roma to San Zaccaria for St Mark's Square). **Rail:** Train: Venezia Santa Lucia or Mestre stations. **Road:** Bus: Public services.

Japan

Tokyo

Tourist Information
Tokyo Tourist Information Center (TIC)
Tokyo International Forum, 3-5-1 Marunouchi, Chiyoda-ku, Tokyo, Japan
Tel: (03) 5221 9084
Website: www.tcvb.or.jp

• March-April

Ueno Cherry Blossom Festival

Every year thousands of people gather in *Ueno Park* in Tokyo to see over 1300 beautiful cherry blossom trees come into bloom. Cherry blossoms (or *sakura* in Japanese) are the national flower in Japan and are believed to represent beauty, as well as signifying the end of winter and the beginning of spring. During the annual *Ueno Cherry Blossom Festival*, Ueno Park is lit by lanterns every evening. People hold various parties to admire the cherry blossoms and also gather in *Sumida Park* along the Sumida River to see even more cherry blossom trees bloom.

Event Organiser
For more information on the Ueno Cherry Blossom Festival, contact the Tokyo Tourist Information Center (see **Tourist Information** above).

Venue
Ueno Park, Tokyo.

Transport
Air: New Tokyo Narita International Airport or Haneda Airport (domestic flights). **Rail:** Train: Tokyo Station. **Underground:** Ueno Station. **Road:** Bus: Public services.

• May

Sanja Festival

First held more than 200 years ago, *the Sanja Festival* is one of Tokyo's biggest festivals when the city's residents carry *Mikoshi* (mini-shrines) through the crowded streets surrounding the *Asakusa Shrine*. The shrine (*Asakusa-jinja* in Japanese) was founded during the 17th century and is housed in the grounds of the famous *Senso-ji Temple* in Tokyo. It is dedicated to the two fishermen who discovered the Kannon statuette, which is also housed in the Senso-ji Temple, whilst fishing in the Sumida River.

Today, the festival sees around two million people gather in Tokyo to watch the festivities, which include annual music performances, and to carry around one hundred shrines through the city to honour the famous shrine.

Event Organiser
For more information on the Sanja Festival, contact Tokyo Tourist Information Center (see **Tourist Information** above).

Venue
The streets of Asakusa, surrounding the Asakusa Shrine in Sensoji Temple.

Transport
Air: New Tokyo Narita International Airport or Haneda Airport (domestic flights). **Rail:** Train: Tokyo Station. Underground: Asakusa. **Road:** Bus: Public services.

• July

Tokyo Fireworks Festival

Tokyo Fireworks Festival, which is known as *Sumida-gawa Hanabi Taikai* in Japanese, was first held in the city in 1733 by Shogun Yoshimune who organised the display to pay respects to those who had died during a famine in 1732. It has since grown to become firmly established as Tokyo's main summer fireworks event. Around 20,000 *hanabi* (flower-fires) light up the night skies and up to one million people line the streets and river banks to watch the displays. The event is usually held on the last Saturday in July every year.

Event Organiser
For more information on the Tokyo Fireworks Festival, contact the Tokyo Tourist Information Center (see **Tourist Information** above).

Venue
Along the banks of the Sumida River.

Transport
Air: New Tokyo Narita International Airport or Haneda Airport (domestic flights). **Rail:** Train: Tokyo Station. Underground: Asakusa. **Road:** Bus: Public services.

Mali

Tourist Information
Tourist Office Mali (Office Malien du Tourisme et de l'Hôtellerie)
Rue Mohamed V., Bamako, Mali
Tel: 222 5673
Website: www.malitourisme.com

• January

Festival in the Desert

The desert Tuareg people of Mali have come together for desert gatherings for hundreds of years but it was only with the official end of the Tamashek war in 1996 that the seeds an official festival were sewn. A ceremonial burning of weapons was held to mark the end of the war and a large festival including dancing and music ensued. The first official Festival in the Desert was held in 2001 and despite the event still being in its relative infancy, it has quickly grown into a popular annual event that attracts an international crowd of revellers and curious travellers. Internationally-renowned musicians such as Robert Plant have taken part in the past but the emphasis is very much on musicians from the Sahara creating a truly unique festival experience.

Event Organiser
Festival in the Desert
Email: info@festival-au-desert.org
Website: www.festival-au-desert.org

Venue
Essakane, Mali.

Transport
Air: Bamako International Airport. **Road:** Bus: Public services.

Mexico

Mexico City

Tourist Information
Mexico City Tourist Office (Oficina de Turismo de la Ciudad de México)
Mariano Escobedo 550, Piso 7, Col Anzures, 11590 Mexico City, Mexico
Tel: (05) 2581 0941
Website: www.visitmexico.com

• March

Festival of the Historic Centre

The *Festival del Centro Histórico* (as it is known in Spanish), first held in 1985 to promote Mexico City's old quarter, is a two-week festival celebrating the best in Mexican and international culture. It has become increasingly popular and now attracts nearly 1,000,000 visitors over the two-week festival. A wide variety of events are held in churches, cloisters, squares and concert halls around the historic centre, ranging from performances of theatre, dance and opera to food and drink tastings and children's activities. There are also film screenings, art exhibitions, cultural seminars and guided tours of the historic centre, with themes such as 'Prehispanic times' and 'Jewish Life'.

Event Organiser
Festival del Centro Histórico de la Ciudad de México AC, Avenida Benjamin Franklin 176, Col Escandón, Mexico DF, 11800 Mexico
Tel: (0525) 277 9757
Website: www.fchmexico.com

Venue
Various locations across Mexico City.

Transport
Air: Mexico City International Airport. **Rail:** Train: Buenavista Station. **Road:** Bus: Public services.

The Netherlands

Amsterdam

Tourist Information
Amsterdam Tourist Office (VVV Amsterdam Kantoor Stationsplein)
Stationsplein 10, 1012 AB Amsterdam, The Netherlands
Tel: (020) 201 8800
Website: www.holand.com

• April

Queen's Day

On *Queen's Day* (which is known as *Koninginnedag* in Dutch), Amsterdamers take part in a giant street party to celebrate the Queen's birthday. Every year on April 30, people take to the streets to join in the festivities on what has been a national holiday since the end of World War II. The festivities kick off around 1800 on April 29 and last well into the small hours of the next day. People consume large amounts of alcohol and dress up in orange clothes, as the Queen is from the House of Orange; some of them even paint their faces orange in order to join in the celebrations. Queen's Day actually takes place on the Queen Mother's (Juliana) birthday as Queen Beatrix's birthday is January 31 and considered too cold for any festivities. On April 30, people also

attempt to sell their unwanted household items in the street when the city turns into a giant flea market. There is a chance to pick up a real bargain, although much of what's on sale could easily be classed as junk. Amsterdam becomes extremely crowded on Queen's Day, particularly if it is sunny, and visitors are advised to get there early.

Event Organiser
Rijks Voorlichtings Dienst (RVD), Debennenhof 20, 20001 The Hague, The Netherlands
Tel: (070) 356 4000
Website: www.koninginnedag.nl

Venue
Various locations across Amsterdam and Holland.

Transport
Air: Amsterdam Airport Schiphol. **Rail:** Train: Amsterdam Centraal Station. **Road:** Bus: Public services.

• May

National Windmill and Pumping Station Day

National Windmill and Pumping Station Day is organised every year on the second Saturday in May. Approximately 650 watermills and windmills across Holland open their doors free of charge to visitors. Many windmills also put on exhibitions and demonstrations to explain a miller's work to the general public. Mills which take part in the event can be recognised easily as they have large blue banners on display and they also all turn their sails. There are over 1000 windmills in Holland, although there are only four working windmills in Amsterdam itself. Windmills in Amsterdam include De Rieker, on the banks of the Amstel, two windmills on Haarlemmerweg (1200 Roe and De Bleom), De Gooyer, 1100 Roe and d'Admiraal.

Event Organiser
De Hollandsche Molen, Zeeburgerdijk 139, 1095 AA, Amsterdam, The Netherlands
Tel: (020) 623 8703
Website: www.molens.nl

Venue
Windmills across Amsterdam and Holland.

Transport
Air: Amsterdam Airport Schiphol. **Rail:** Train: Amsterdam Centraal Station. **Road:** Bus: Public services.

• June

Holland Festival

The *Holland Festival* takes place in Amsterdam every June and focuses on the performing arts, including opera, theatre, music and dance. The festival has grown each year and now attracts well over 100,000 visitors, with more than 50,000 attending the popular *Amsterdam Roots Festival* in the city. The festival includes numerous performances by groups from all around the world.

Event Organiser
Stichting Holland Festival, Kleine Gartmanplantsoen 21, 1017 RP, Amsterdam, The Netherlands
Tel: (020) 530 7110
Website: www.hollandfestival.nl

Venue
Across Amsterdam, in various theatres and concert halls, including the Paradiso, Theater Bellevue and the festival centre, Stadsschouwburg. There are also events around Leidesplein.

Transport
Air: Amsterdam Airport Schiphol. **Rail:** Train: Amsterdam Centraal Station. **Road:** Bus: Public services.

• August

Amsterdam Gay Pride

Amsterdam Gay Pride is one of Europe's largest gay and lesbian events and takes place in the city in the middle of summer. There is an enormous *Canal Parade*, when the city's gay and lesbian community takes to the canals in boats, wearing fancy dress and playing music. There are also numerous sport and cultural events throughout the city, as well as huge weekend parties. As well as the parade itself and the numerous parties and club nights, sports and film events also play a key part of the celebrations.

Event Organiser
Siep de Haan, Lange Niezel 7, Amsterdam, NH 1012 GS, The Netherlands
Tel: (020) 620 8807
Website: www.amsterdamgaypride.nl

Venue
Various locations across Amsterdam city centre, including festivities on the canals.

Transport
Air: Amsterdam Airport Schiphol. **Rail:** Train: Amsterdam Centraal Station. **Road:** Bus: Public services.

New Zealand

Auckland

Tourist Information

Tourism Auckland
PO Box 5561, Wellesley Street, Auckland, New Zealand
Tel: (09) 979 7070
Website: www.aucklandnz.com

• April

Royal Easter Show

The first *Royal Easter Show* was held in 1843 by the newly-formed Auckland Agricultural and Horticultural Society to promote the advantages the town could offer to prospective settlers. It has grown from its origins as a small livestock show to incorporate sporting events, family entertainment, animal shows and commercial exhibits, attracting thousands of visitors throughout the 10 days. There are equine events such as showjumping and dressage, displays of rare sheep breeds, a 'New Zealand's Strongest Man' competition, junior sporting championships including basketball and karate, craft demonstrations and exhibits featuring ceramics, photography, Chinese art and painting by mouth and foot. Various stalls are situated in the Commercial Exhibit Halls, and feature food and wine, home improvements and information and technology. Musicians, acrobats and theatre groups travel from as far afield as England to entertain the crowds, and there is also a special children's theatre, a children's art workshop and the opportunity for visitors to try their hand at milking cattle or shearing sheep.

Event Organiser
Auckland Show Grounds, PO Box 26014 Auckland, New Zealand
Tel: (09) 623 7724
Website: www.royaleastershow.co.nz

Venue
Auckland Showgrounds.

Transport
Air: Auckland International Airport. **Rail:** Train: Auckland Station. **Road:** Bus: Public services.

• November

Ellerslie Flower Show

Every summer, Auckland's 64-hectare (160-acre) *Regional Botanic Gardens* host the largest gardening and outdoor show in the Southern

Hemisphere, the *Ellerslie Flower Show*. Some 65,000 visitors come from New Zealand and around the world to enjoy floral displays, plant stalls, fruit and vegetable markets, musical concerts, food and drink and garden sculptures by top New Zealand artists, situated around the lake. Gardening enthusiasts can pick up tips from lectures and demonstrations and, on the last Sunday, materials used in the exhibits, such as paving stones and exotic flowers, are sold off to the public.

Event Organiser
Ellerslie Flower Show, PO Box 11340, Ellerslie, Auckland, New Zealand
Tel: (09) 579 6260
Website: www.ellerslieflowershow.co.nz

Venue
Auckland Regional Botanic Gardens.

Transport
Air: Auckland International Airport. **Rail:** Train: Auckland Station. **Road:** Bus: Public services.

Norway

Bergen

Tourist Information
Bergen Tourist Information
(Turistinformasjonen)
Slottsgarten 1, 2nd Floor, 5835 Bergen, Norway
Tel: (055) 552 010
Website: www.visitbergen.com

• May-June

Bergen International Festival

Bergen International Festival features numerous music, ballet and theatre performances and is the largest event of its kind in Norway and one of the premier international performing arts festivals in Europe. The festival's extensive music programme focuses primarily on Norwegian music. Over the 12 days of the festival there are close to 200 individual performances.

Event Organiser
Bergen International Festival, Box 183 Sentrum, 5084 Bergen, Norway
Tel: (055) 210 630
Website: www.fib.no

Venue
Various venues in the Bergen area, including the

Grieg Hall, the Hakon Hall, the Masonic Lodge and the houses of three local composers: Edvard Grieg, Ole Bull and Harald Sæverud.

Transport
Air: Bergen Airport. **Rail:** Train: Bergen Station. **Road:** Car: E16 (from Voss); E18, E16 and E39 (from Oslo). **Bus:** Public services.

Bergen Night Jazz Festival

Bergen Night Jazz Festival (known as *Nattjazz* in Norway) takes place every year and is one of the longest jazz festivals in Northern Europe which lasts for almost two weeks. The festival plays host to a wide range of performances, ranging from traditional jazz to world music, rock, folk, bebop, hard pop, jazz rock, fusion and funk. The majority of events take place in venues at the *Kulturhuset USF* (*United Sardines Factory*), which can hold approximately 1600 people; they include Røkeriet USF, Sardinen USF and Scene USF. Previous artists have included John Scofield Quartet, Cesaria Evora, Kari Bremnes, Gli Impossibli and Anneli Drecker.

Event Organiser
Natt Jazz, PO Box 1957, Nordnes 5817 Bergen, Norway
Tel: (055) 307 250
Website: www.nattjazz.no

Venue
Held in an area reserved for the festival, as well as at other venues in the city. The festival area is an old sardines factory, called Kulturhuset USF, which is now used for concerts, exhibitions, theatre and cinema.

Transport
Air: Bergen Airport. **Rail:** Train: Bergen Station. **Road:** On foot: Kulturhuset USF is located on Sergels torg square in the centre of the city and can be reached easily on foot from the city centre. **Bus:** Public services.

Peru

Lima

Tourist Information
PromPeru
Edificio Mitince, Calle 1, 13th and 14th Floor, San Isidro, Lima 27, Peru
Tel: (01) 224 3131
Website: www.peru.info

• October

Lord of Miracles

The *Lord of Miracles* festival is the most important cultural event in Lima's calendar and the largest religious procession in the Americas. Hundreds of purple-clad worshippers carry an image of a black Christ through the city's streets every day during the festival to the sound of chanting and church bells. The image has hung in Lima's Church and Convent of the Nazarenes since it was painted in 1665. It is known as *Neustro Señor de los Milagros* (Our Lord of Miracles) since it survived several earthquakes remarkably intact. Concerts and firework displays also form part of the celebrations, which are followed throughout November by Lima's bullfighting season at *Plaza de Acho*, the oldest arena in the Americas dating back over 200 years.

Event Organiser
For more information on the Lord of Miracles, contact PromPeru (see **Tourist Information** above).

Venue
Various locations across Lima.

Transport
Air: Jorge Chavez International Airport (Lima). Road: Car: Pan-American Highway (from Arequipa, Trujillo, Talara or coastal cities in Chile and Ecuador).

Poland

Krakow

Tourist Information

Tourist Information Centre (Centrum Informacji Turystycznej)
ulica Pawia 8, 31-154 Krakow, Poland
Tel: (012) 422 6091
Website: www.krakow.pl

• December-February

Krakow Christmas Crib Contest

The *szopki* (nativity crib) is very much a part of the Polish Christmas tradition. The first ever crib was made by Jan Velita in Italy on the instruction of St Francis of Assisi three years before his death in 1225. From its simple origins, the idea was taken up by the rich merchants and noblemen who commissioned artists to create ever more elaborate versions. Krakow cribs, which can be up to 1.8m

(6ft) tall, maintain this tradition and are modelled on local buildings with their Gothic towers, Baroque onion domes and Renaissance façades. The city's first crib contest was held in 1937 and the event is organised annually by the Krakow Ethnography Museum. All entries, made by both professional craftsmen and amateurs, are put on show at the *Adam Mickiewicz Monument* in the Old Market for several days, and are then taken to the *Ethnography Museum* where they are judged; the prizewinners are announced in early December. The most exquisite and beautifully crafted cribs are then displayed in the museum for the next two months.

Event Organiser
Museum of History (Muzeum Historyczne), Rynek Gÿówny 35, Krakow, Poland
Tel: (012) 422 9922

Venue
Plac Wolnica (Wolnica Square) and Muzeum Etnograficzne (Museum of Ethnography).

Transport
Air: Krakow-Balice John Paul II International Airport. **Rail:** Train: Krakow Station. Tram: 10 (from Main Market Square). **Road:** Bus: Public services.

• June-July

Jewish Culture Festival

For centuries the *Kazimierz* district of Krakow provided a haven for persecuted Jews in Europe. Professional, middle-class Jews contributed a lot to Polish cultural life, particularly in the fields of music and literature, and Jews were free to worship and set up their own organisations and societies. Steven Spielberg's film 'Schindler's List' famously depicts the destruction of Kazimierz during World War II, when Jewish businesses and institutions were razed to the ground and the Jews were deported from the ghetto to the concentration camps, where they were tortured and murdered. Kazimierz is once again a thriving centre for Jewish culture, and the *Jewish Culture Festival* has grown to become an internationally-recognised event. The streets, theatres and synagogues of Krakow host a range of events including film, dance, theatre, the visual arts, lectures and music, with the Jerusalem Jazz band, the Klezmatics and Double Edge Theatre all having performed at the festival in the past. Workshops enable visitors to learn about Jewish traditions such as paper cutting, Hebrew calligraphy, dance and cookery; the workshops are led by instructors who earn a living from such skills. This is a particularly poignant and triumphal celebration of Jewish culture and a chance for visitors to Krakow to learn more about the rich heritage of this remarkable people.

Event Organiser
Jewish Culture Festival Society, 36 Józefa Street, 31-056 Kraków, Poland
Tel: (012) 431 1517
Website: www.jewishfestival.pl

Venue
Various locations across Kazimierz.

Transport
Air: Krakow-Balice John Paul II International Airport. **Rail:** Train: Krakow Station. Tram: 13, 19 or 10 (from Krakow Station or Main Market Square). **Road:** Bus: Public services.

• July

Krakow International Street Theatre Festival

Krakow's main market square, *Rynek Glówny*, is the biggest Medieval square in Europe and every July it is the venue for the city's street theatre festival. Theatre groups from around Europe entertain the crowds each evening against the backdrop of period houses and pavement cafés. The programme for 2001 included shows from France, Poland and Ukraine, with several experimental theatre groups taking part. Performances take place between 1800 and 2200 each day.

Event Organiser
KTO Theatre, ulica Gzymsikow 8, 30-015 Krakow, Poland
Tel: (012) 623 7300
Website: www.teatrkto.pl

Venue
Rynek Glówny in Krakow's Old Town.

Transport
Air: Krakow-Balice John Paul II International Airport. **Rail:** Train: Krakow Station. Tram: 10 (from Krakow Station). **Road:** Bus: Public services.

Warsaw

Tourist Information
Tourist Information Centre
(Centrum Informacji Turystycznej)
Aleja Jerezolimsie 54, Warsaw, Poland
Tel: (022) 635 1881
Website: www.warsawtour.pl

• June-July

Warsaw Mozart Festival

Warsaw Mozart Festival began in 1991, when all 24 of the great composer's stage pieces were performed, and is the largest festival of its kind in the world. Mozart enthusiasts are able to hear oratorio, chamber, symphony and stage pieces in the Warsaw Chamber Opera Theatre. Mozart's connections with Warsaw date back to 1783, when 'Die Entführung aus dem Serail' ('Abduction from the Seraglio') was performed by the German theatre troupe Gottlieb Lorenz.

Event Organiser
Warsaw Chamber Opera, Aleja Solidarnosci 76B, Warsaw, Poland
Tel: (022) 831 2240 *or* 621 9383
Website: www.wok.pol.pl

Venue
Warsaw Chamber Opera Theatre, Solidarnosci Avenue (near Bankowy Square).

Transport
Air: Warsaw (Okecie) International Airport. **Rail:** Train: Warsaw Central Station. Tram: 17, 29 or 33. **Road:** Bus: Public services.

Portugal

Lisbon

Tourist Information
Lisbon Tourist Association
(Associação Turismo de Lisboa)
15 Rua do Arsenal, 1100-038 Lisbon, Portugal
Tel: (021) 312 700
Website: www.atl-turismolisboa.pt

• February

Lisbon Carnival

Carnival signals the end of winter and the beginning of Lent and is celebrated in Lisbon with colourful costume parades and copious amounts of food and drink. In recent years, the Portuguese festivities have taken on a Latin American flavour and many Brazilian TV stars cross the Atlantic to join in the fun. One of the best places to go to watch the celebrations is the *Parque das Naçoes*.

Event Organiser
Lisbon City Council (Câmara Municipal de Lisboa), Paços do Concelho, Praça do Município, 1100-365 Lisbon, Portugal

Tel: (021) 322 7000
Website: www.cm-lisboa.pt

Venue
Parque das Naçoes and across various locations across Lisbon.

Transport
Air: Lisbon International Airport. **Rail:** Train: Santa Apolónia, Rossio, Barreiro or Cais do Sodré stations. Tram: Estação do Oriente. **Road:** Bus: Public services.

• April

Lisbon Half Marathon

The *Lisbon Half Marathon* is watched with particular interest by those in the athletic field as it determines the world's top long distance runners before the major marathons in Boston and London later in the month. The overall race winner takes home over US$100,000 in prize money. There is a party atmosphere in the streets, with live music and entertainment. In addition, free ice cream and gifts are provided by the race sponsors at the finish line.

Event Organiser
Maratona Clube de Portugal, Bàrro Francisco Sà Caraeiro, Av. João Freitas Branco 10, Caxias, 2780 Paço de Arcos, Portugal
Tel: (021) 441 3182
Website: www.lisbon-half-marathon.com

Venue
Starts at the 25 April suspension bridge across the River Tejo and finishes at the Mosteiro dos Jeronemos in Belém via the city centre.

Transport
Air: Lisbon International Airport. **Rail:** Train: Santa Apolónia, Rossio, Barreiro or Cais do Sodré stations. Tram: 15 or 17 (to Belém). Underground: Belém. **Road:** Bus: Public services.

• June

Lisbon Festivities

Lisbon celebrates its patron saint (St Anthony) in a three-week spectacular of street parties, fireworks and entertainment known as the *Festas de Lisboa* in Portuguese. The *Marchas Populares* in mid-June are a chance to see thousands of people from the different neighbourhoods of the city march down the Avenida da Liberdade, displaying colourful costumes and banners that have taken many months to create. The festivities continue long into the night, with music, dancing and sardine barbecues. The best place to go to join one of these parties, or *arraiais*, is the *Alfama* district of the city. Throughout the whole three-week period, both visitors and locals can enjoy theatre, circus, mime and all kinds of music, from pop and ethnic to classical and jazz, in Lisbon's many squares.

Event Organiser
Empresa de Gestão de Equipamentos e Animação Cultural, Palácio Marquês de Tancos, Calçada Marquês de Tancos, 1100-340 Lisbon, Portugal
Tel: (021) 882 0090
Website: www.egeac.pt

Venue
Alfama district and various locations across Lisbon.

Transport
Air: Lisbon International Airport. **Rail:** Train: Santa Apolónia, Rossio, Barreiro or Cais do Sodré stations. **Road:** Bus: Public services.

• December

Magic Night

Magic Night (*Noite Mágica* in Portuguese) aims to create a New Year's Eve party with a difference. There is a 10-minute firework display over the *River Tejo*, which is choreographed to a specially-created musical soundtrack featuring Portuguese bands past and present. Once the show is over, there is a Latin American disco and live music that continues long into the early hours of New Year's Day. Many hotels in Lisbon also organise their own events featuring food, wine and live entertainment. The *Casino Estoril* (Estoril Casino), located 18km (11 miles) outside Lisbon, hosts various shows and an outdoor party.

Event Organiser
Lisbon City Council (Câmara Municipal de Lisboa), Paços do Concelho, Praça do Município, 1100-365 Lisbon, Portugal
Tel: (021) 322 7000
Website: www.cm-lisboa.pt

Venue
Along the River Tejo between Parque das Nações and the district of Algés.

Transport
Air: Lisbon International Airport. **Rail:** Train: Santa Apolónia, Rossio, Barreiro or Cais do Sodré stations. Tram: 15 or 17. Underground: Belém. **Road:** Bus: Public services.

Russian Federation

Moscow

Tourist Information
Ministry of Tourism (Ministerstvo Turisma)
18 ul. Kazakova, 103064 Moscow, Russian
Federation
Tel: (095) 207 7117 *or* 207 3891
Website: www.rossport.ru

• December-January

New Year

On December 31 every year, revellers party in the
streets of Moscow to see in the *New Year.*
Traditionally Moscovites used to celebrate New
Year's Eve (which is known as *Noivy God* in
Russian) at home before taking to the streets after
midnight to visit friends and neighbours and drink
vast amounts of alcohol until the early hours.
Increasingly, more and more people gather in Red
Square to hear the stroke of midnight from the
Kremlin, and to drink champagne in the city
centre. Many people also dress in fancy dress,
either as 'Grandfather Frost' or the 'Snow Maiden',
as they go about the city wishing a happy new
year to fellow revellers.

Event Organiser
For more information on New Year, contact the
Ministry of Tourism (see **Tourist Information**
above).

Venue
Red Square and across the city.

Transport
Air: Moscow Sheremetyevo International Airport.
Rail: Train: Kiev Station. Underground: Kitay-
Gorod. **Road:** Bus: Public services.

• September

Moscow International Peace Marathon

The annual *International Peace Marathon* takes
place in September on the streets of Moscow,
starting at 1100 at Red Square in front of St
Basil's Cathedral. The course runs along the
Moscow River, past many of the city's finest
historic monuments, including the Kremlin, the
Cathedral of Christ the Saviour and the Peter the
Great Monument in Gorky Park. The event
finishes in front of the Rossya Hotel, near St
Basil's Cathedral. On the day before the
marathon, there is a *Marathon Expo* conference

for runners and a lottery draw. In the evening,
there is a pasta party at the Golden Hill
restaurant in the Rossya Hotel, with musical
performances from folk bands.

Event Organiser
For more information on Moscow International
Peace Marathon, contact the Ministry of Tourism
(see **Tourist Information** above).

Venue
Starts at Red Square through the streets of
Moscow, and finishes at the Rossya Hotel, near St
Basil's Cathedral.

Transport
Air: Moscow Sheremetyevo International Airport.
Rail: Train: Kiev Station. Underground: Kitay-
Gorod. **Road:** Bus: Public services.

Singapore

Singapore

Tourist Information
Singapore Tourism Board
Tourism Court, 1 Orchard Spring Lane, Singapore
247729
Tel: (65) 736 6622
Website: www.visitsingapore.com

• March-April

Singapore Food Festival

First held in 1994, *Singapore Food Festival* is a
giant culinary event that allows visitors to taste
food from around the world. During the month-
long event, visitors can sample culinary delights
from as far afield as Italy, Turkey and Japan, as
well as taste the best of Chinese and Asian cuisine.
They can also take part in food tours and wander
through the streets of Singapore, which are filled
with the aromatic smells of different dishes. The
festival usually kicks off with a three-day opening
celebration which is a carnival of food and
entertainment, featuring live music, as well as
food and drink from around the world.

Event Organiser
Singapore Tourism Board, Events Marketing
Division, Tourism Court, 1 Orchard Spring Lane,
Singapore 247729
Tel: (65) 6780 4681
Website: www.singaporefoodfestival.com.sg

Venue
Various locations across Singapore.

Transport
Air: Singapore Changi Airport. **Rail:** Train:
Singapore Station. **Road:** Bus: Public services.

• April

Singapore International Film Festival

Singapore International Film Festival is one of the
most important celebrations of Asian cinema in the
world, with more than 300 films from over 45
countries shown in Singapore during the event. The
festival was first held in 1987 to allow film
enthusiasts to view films which would not normally
be given a mainstream release. The festival also
awards Silver Screen Awards which were introduced
in 1991 and are given to the best Asian film, as well
as to the best actor, actress and director.

Event Organiser
Film Festival Pte Ltd, 45A Keong Saik Road,
Singapore 089149
Fax: 6738 7578
Website: www.filmfest.org.sg

Venue
Golden Village (GV) cinemas in the city, such as
Golden Village Grand, as well as the Goethe
Institut and Alliance Française de Singapour.

Transport
Air: Singapore Changi Airport. **Rail:** Train:
Singapore Station. **Road:** Bus: Public services.

South Africa

Cape Town

Tourist Information

Cape Town Tourism
103 Louis Building, 4 Regent Road, Sea Point,
Cape Town, South Africa
Tel: (021) 434 1750
Website: www.cape-town.org

• May

Cape Gourmet Festival

Every May, Cape Town plays host to two weeks of
events celebrating the indulgent world of food and
wine. The central focus is the Good Food and
Wine Show on the last weekend of the festival,
with culinary demonstrations and masterclasses,
wine-tasting sessions, stalls selling olive oil,
cheeses and local wines and appearances by
celebrity chefs. Chefs come from around the world
to exchange ideas and prepare gastronomic

delights in the city's restaurants, and a whole host
of hotels and eating establishments organize their
own special menus and events, from international
food-tasting evenings to jazz concerts.

Event Organiser
Cape Gourmet Festival, 50 Tennant Road,
Kenilworth, Cape Town 8001, South Africa
Tel: (021) 797 4500
Website: www.gourmetsa.com

Venue
Good Hope Centre (Good Food and Wine Show)
and various venues across Cape Town.

Transport
Air: Cape Town International Airport. **Rail:** Train:
Cape Town Station. **Road:** Bus: Public services.

Johannesburg

Tourist Information

Tourism Johannesburg
Upper Shopping Level, Village Walk Shopping
Centre, corner of Rivonia Road and Maud Street,
Rosebank, Johannesburg, South Africa
Tel: (011) 784 1354
Website: www.joburg.org.za

• April-May

Rand Easter Show

The *Rand Easter Show* is one of the biggest
exhibitions in Southern Africa, attracting around
half a million visitors each year. The show has
developed from its origins as an agricultural event
in 1894, when it was hosted by Witwatersrand
Agricultural Society, to become a giant consumer
fair and entertainment show. As well as
merchandise on display from almost 600 South
African exhibitors and over 100 foreign exhibitors
from nine different countries, the show also
features live music, as well as sporting events and
an amusement park.

Event Organiser
Kagiso Exhibitions Pty Ltd, Private Bag X 383,
Cresta, 2118, South Africa
Tel: (011) 661 4000
Website: www.randshow.co.za

Venue
Expo Centre, which is located in the Nasrec area of
Johannesburg.

Transport
Air: Johannesburg International Airport. **Rail:**
Train: Trains stop at the grounds (from Park
Station). **Road:** Bus: Public services.

Spain

Barcelona

Tourist Information

Barcelona Tourist Office (Turisme de Barcelona)
Plaça de Catalunya 17-S, 08008 Barcelona
Tel: (093) 368 9740
Website: www.bcn.es

• January

Three Kings Parade

The story of the Three Kings is recorded in the
Bible, in St Matthew's Gospel, and tells of three
wise men who travelled from the east to
Bethlehem to present gifts of gold, frankincense
and myrrh to the infant Jesus. Epiphany, as
Twelfth Night (January 5) is known in the
Christian church, commemorates the journey of
the Three Kings and is widely celebrated
throughout Europe. At the end of each year,
Catalan children post their wish lists to the Three
Kings in special boxes in stores around Barcelona.
On the night of January 5, they then place a shoe
on the balcony of their house for the Three Kings
to fill with sweets, as well as a bucket of water
and food for the camels. Every January 5, for the
Cabalgata de los Reyes Magos, or *Three Kings
Parade*, the Three Kings arrive at the harbour at
Moll de Fusta with their entourage and sacks full
of presents, and are greeted by city officials and
excited children before going about their annual
duties. The kings arrive at 1800 in the harbour and
it is advisable to arrive as early as possible to get
the best view.

Event Organiser

For more information on the Three Kings Parade,
contact Barcelona Tourist Office (see **Tourist
Information** above).

Venue

The stalls are mainly located along Gran Vía; the
Three Kings arrive at the harbour.

Transport

Air: Barcelona Airport. **Rail:** Train: Central-Sants
Station. Underground: Tetuan or Monumental (to
Gran Vía); Drassanes or Barceloneta (to harbour).
Road: Bus: Public services.

• June-July

Barcelona Summer Festival (GREC)

The *Teatre Grec* amphitheatre, built into the

mountainside at *Montjuic*, is the birthplace of
the *Barcelona Summer Festival* (popularly
known as GREC), which started when a group
of disillusioned actors and directors got
together to produce a small fringe theatre
festival in 1976. It has since grown to become
the biggest and most popular festival in
Barcelona. Every summer for around six weeks,
tourists and locals are treated to a huge variety
of events, from theatre, dance and cinema to
classical music, rock and circus. The venues are
just as varied, with Gothic chapels, vast
modern theatres and concert halls all hosting
events. At the open-air *Picornell* swimming
pool it is even possible to watch a film whilst
relaxing in the water.

Event Organiser

For more information on the Barcelona Summer
Festival, contact Barcelona Tourist Office (see
Tourist Information above).

Venue

Various venues across Barcelona (for further
information, contac the Spanish Tourist Office (see
Tourist Information above).

Transport

Air: Barcelona International Airport. **Rail:** Train:
Central-Sants Station. **Road:** Bus: Public services.

• September

Our Lady of Mercy Festival

According to legend, *La Mercé* (Our Lady of
Mercy, or the Virgin Mary) once saved
Barcelona from a plague of locusts, and thus
became the patron saint of the city. A wide
range of activities takes place during the
festival, such as musical concerts and theatre
performances in outdoor theatres, food and wine
fairs, and sports activities. The main events are
a huge fireworks display, the *Dance of the
Giants* and the *Correfac*, when demons, dragons
and other devilish creatures run amock through
the streets of the city's old quarter, throwing
firecrackers.

Event Organiser

For more information on the Our Lady of Mercy
Festival, contact Barcelona Tourist Office (see
Tourist Information above).

Venue

Various locations across Barcelona.

Transport

Air: Barcelona Airport. **Rail:** Train: Central-
Sants Station. **Road:** Bus: Public services.

Madrid

Tourist Information

City Tourist Office (Oficina Municipal de
Turismo)
Plaza Mayor 3, 28012 Madrid, Spain
Tel: (091) 588 2900
Website: www.esmadrid.com

• February

Madrid Carnival

In February each year, before the beginning of
Lent, a week of festivities brightens up the streets
of the Spanish capital as the centuries old
tradition of *Carnaval* (Carnival) comes to town.
There is a procession of carriages and a costumed
parade through the streets of Madrid with a fancy
dress competition adding to the fun. The party
ends with a peculiar ritual known as *El Entierro de
la Sardina* (the Burial of the Sardine). This ritual
involves people in black cloaks and top hats
following a coffin that contains an effigy of a
sardine, which is then buried at the 18th-century
hermitage of *San Antonio de la Florida* near the
city centre. However, the mood is not entirely
sombre as the procession stops at *tavernas* on the
way for a drink or two.

Event Organiser
For more information on the Madrid Carnival,
contact the City Tourist Office (see **Tourist
Information** above).

Venue
Calle de Cádiz, San Antonio de Florida and
various locations across Madrid.

Transport
Air: Madrid Barajas Airport. **Rail:** Train:
Chamartín or Atocha stations. **Road:** Bus: Public
services.

• May

Festimad Alternative Music Festival

Visitors to *Festimad* can catch the latest in the
alternative music scene in a beautiful 350 sq
metres (325 sq ft) of parkland. The two days of
events that have been held each summer since
1995 attract over 20,000 spectators who come to
be entertained by a whole host of rock and indie
bands, DJs and other performers. Concerts in the
past have featured groups such as Metallica,
Marilyn Manson and the Black Crowes. The site is
turned into a music village with facilities

including bars, restaurants, a supermarket and
showers for those who wish to camp.

Event Organiser
Festimad, Gran Vía 68, 5E 28013 Madrid, Spain
Tel: (091) 547 2385
Website: www.festimad.es

Venue
El Soto de Móstoles, which is located 20km (12.4
miles) from central Madrid.

Transport
Air: Madrid Barajas Airport. **Rail:** Train:
Chamartín or Atocha stations. Underground: El
Soto (the festival site can then be accessed on
foot). **Road:** Bus: Public services.

• May-June

San Isidro Festival

San Isidro is the patron saint of Madrid and every
year, from mid-May to mid-June, festivities
known as the *Fiestas de San Isidro* in Spanish,
take place throughout the city. According to
tradition, all those from Madrid must make a
pilgrimage to the shrine on the banks of the River
Manzanares on the spot where the saint is said to
have miraculously caused a spring to open up
from the ground. Traditional dress is worn and
specialities such as *barquillos* (rolled wafers),
buñuelos (fritters) and *rosquillas* (doughnuts) are
sold throughout the city. The famous *taurina*
(bullfighting fair) is part of the Fiestas and fights
take place every day at the historic *Plaza
Monumental Las Ventas* bull ring.

Event Organiser
Plaza Monumental Las Ventas, Calle Acalá 237,
28028 Madrid, Spain
Tel: (091) 356 2200
Website: www.las-ventas.com

Venue
Various locations across Madrid.

Transport
Air: Madrid Barajas Airport. **Rail:** Train:
Chamartín or Atocha stations. Underground:
Ventas (to Plaza Monumental Las Ventas). **Road:**
Bus: Public services.

• October-November

Madrid Autumn Festival

This festival brings a huge variety of cultural
performances to Madrid and encompasses theatre,
jazz, musical theatre, dance, literature and art.
Groups come from as far afield as Cuba, India and

the USA to take part, and the festival offers a welcome diversion for *Madrileños* and visitors alike as the nights grow darker and the weather colder.

Event Organiser
For more information on the Madrid Autumn Festival, contact City Tourist Office (see Tourist Information above).

Venue
Various locations across Madrid.

Transport
Air: Madrid Barajas Airport. Rail: Train: Chamartín or Atocha stations. Road: Bus: Public services.

Pamplona

Tourist Information
Navarra Tourist Office
Servicio de Turismo Gobierno de Navarra, Edificio Fuerte del Principe 2, 4a Planta, Plaza Tomás Caballero 1, 31005 Pamplona, Spain
Tel: (948) 20 70 35
Website: www.navarra.es

• July

The Running of the Bulls (San Fermin Festival)
Made famous by Ernest Hemingway who wrote about the Running of the Bulls in his cult 1926 novel, 'Fiesta: The Sun Also Rises', the event is a central part of the nine-day *San Fermin Festival* that's celebrated each July in Pamplona. The festival begins on July 6 and ends on July 14 each year with the traditional bull run taking place at 0800 each day from the second day onwards. The city of Pamplona is packed out to celebrate the festival of St Fermin, the town's patron. Locals and visitors alike take to the streets to run with the bulls dressed in the traditional white clothing with red neckerchiefs. Copious amounts of alcohol are consumed during the festival and parties usually continue late into the night. Fatal gorings have happened in the past and the very real danger involved in the run is not to be taken lightly. In 2005, the town's authorities coated the streets in a non-slip paint to try and minimise the risk of serious injury to the thousands of revellers who flock here to take part in the festival each year.

Event Organiser
For more information about the Running of the Bulls, contact the Navarra Tourist Office (see Tourist Information above).

Venue
San Fermin.

Transport
Air: Bilbao Airport. Water: Ferry: Bilbao Port. Rail: Train: Pamplona Station. Road: Bus: Public services.

Sweden

Stockholm

Tourist Information
Stockholm Information Service
Hamngatan 27, Kungsträdgården, 10327 Stockholm, Sweden
Tel: (08) 508 28508
Website: www.stockholmtown.com

• June

Swedish National Day
Every year on June 6, Skansen Open-air Museum in the heart of Stockholm hosts the *Swedish National Day* celebrations. The event is attended by the Swedish Royal family: King Carl XVI Gustaf, Queen Silvia, Crown Princess Victoria, Prince Carl Philip and Princess Madeleine. King Carl XVI Gustaf is the 74th King of Sweden who came to the throne in 1973. On this patriotic day, when Swedes remember their heritage, highlights include songs, speeches and flag-waving. The festivities are transmitted live on Swedish national television, allowing an even wider audience to see the day's events.

Event Organiser
Stiftelsen Skansen, Post Box 27807, 115 93 Stockholm, Sweden
Tel: (08) 442 8000
Website: www.skansen.se

Venue
Skansen Open-air Museum in Stockholm city centre.

Transport
Air: Stockholm Arlanda Airport. Rail: Train: Stockholm Central Station. Tram: From Norrmalmstorg to Skansen. Road: Bus: Public services.

• September

Stockholm Beer & Whisky Festival

The annual *Stockholm Beer & Whisky Festival* takes place in Stockholm in September. The festival, which began in 1992, is the leading festival for beer, cider and whisky in Scandinavia. Approximately 500 different varieties of beer are available for the public to sample and vote for in an awards ceremony, with a further 100 varieties of whisky and cider also on offer. Every year, more than 150,000 visitors attend the festival to taste different varieties of beer, whisky and cider. Highlights of the event include beer tastings, tutorings and the annual beer awards. Awards are given to the best fresh beer, best blond lager, best porter, best ale and best Swedish beer.

Event Organiser
Stockholm Öl & Vin AB, Karlavägen 75B, 114 49 Stockholm, Sweden
Tel: (08) 662 9494
Website: www.stockholmbeer.se

Venue
Nacka Strand in Stockholm.

Transport
Air: Stockholm Arlanda Airport. Road: Bus: Public services.

• November

Stockholm International Film Festival

The *Stockholm International Film Festival*, which is one of the most important film festivals in Northern Europe, takes place in the city each November. The festival, which was set up in 1990 by two Swedish film enthusiasts, is attended by more than 70,000 people every year who view some 150 films on offer. Many entries are received from directors making their first, second or third film, as well as from directors of short films. The festival also focuses on different regions and screens films ranging from American independent films through to Asian cinema. Many famous names have attended the festival in previous years, including Dennis Hopper and Quentin Tarrantino.

Event Organiser
Stockholm International Film Festival, PO Box 3136, 103 62 Stockholm, Sweden
Tel: (08) 677 5000
Website: www.filmfestivalen.se

Venue
Various cinemas in Stockholm.

Transport
Air: Stockholm Arlanda Airport. Rail: Train: Stockholm Central Station. Road: Bus: Public services.

Switzerland

Geneva

Tourist Information

Geneva Tourism (Genève Tourisme)
Rue du Mont-Blanc 18, PO Box 1602, 1211 Geneva 1, Switzerland
Tel: (022) 909 7070
Website: www.geneva-tourism.ch

• March

International Motor Show

The *International Motor Show* takes place in Geneva every March. Over 700,000 visitors attend the annual event which first began in 1930. Leading car manufacturers, including BMW, Audi, Ferrari, Ford, Jaguar, Mercedes-Benz and Porsche, are all present at the fair, eager to show off their new cars to the world. Around 900 makes of car are exhibited, from over 35 different countries, by 275 exhibitors. Cars are exhibited in numerous sectors, which include cars, fun cars, converted cars, special bodywork, equipment, accessories and components for cars, garage equipment and electric vehicles.

Event Organiser
ORGEXPO, Foundation for the promotion and organization of exhibitions and conferences – PO Box 112, 1218 Grand-Saconnex, Geneva, Switzerland
Tel: (022) 761 1111
Website: www.salon-auto.ch

Venue
PalExpo Exhibition Centre in Geneva.

Transport
Air: Geneva International Airport. Rail: Train: Cornavin Station to Geneva Airport Station, which is 300m (328 yards) from PalExpo Hall 7. Road: Bus: Special buses run from Geneva city centre during the exhibition.

• July-August

Geneva Festival

The *Geneva Festival* begins at the end of July and is one of Switzerland's biggest parties, with street parades, floats, techno parties and theatre performances. There are also various performances by folk groups and live concerts featuring international stars, as well as numerous operatic shows. Children are kept entertained by a giant clown parade, as well as a funfair on children's day at the end of July. Food from around the world is also on sale at street stalls during the festivities. More than 1,500,000 visitors attend the annual festivities and join the great outdoor party which also includes spectacular firework displays over Lake Geneva.

Event Organiser
For more information on the Geneva Festival, contact Geneva Tourism (see **Tourist Information** above).

Venue
In and around Geneva harbour, Parc des Eaux-Vives, Théâtre de Verdure and Grand Casino de Genève.

Transport
Air: Geneva International Airport. **Rail:** Train: Cornavin Station. **Road:** Car: N1 (from Lausanne).

• August

Swiss National Day

Swiss National Day takes place on August 1 every year to celebrate the union of three former Swiss states, Uri, Schwyz and Unterwalden on this date in 1921. Every year, Geneva holds celebrations, which include fireworks at the *Mur des Réformateurs*, a traditional bonfire and dancing after dark in the streets. On this day, which has been a national holiday since 1993, the Swiss drink large amounts of wine and eat local sausages cooked on barbecues. There are also plenty of speeches and a rendition of the national anthem. Other celebrations take place at the *Parc des Bastions* in Geneva's Old Town. In villages throughout Switzerland, the locals also join in the festivities to celebrate their national day, with children lighting coloured lanterns and parents dancing around the bonfire.

Event Organiser
For more information on Swiss National Day, contact Geneva Tourism (see **Tourist Information** above).

Venue
Mur des Réformateurs and the Parc des Bastions in Geneva. Celebrations also take place across Switzerland.

Transport
Air: Geneva International Airport. **Rail:** Train: Cornavin Station. Underground: Place Neuve Station. **Road:** Bus: Public services.

Zurich

Tourist Information
Zurich Tourist Office (Zürich Tourismus)
Bahnhofbrücke 1, 8023 Zurich, Switzerland
Tel: (01) 215 4000
Website: www.zuerich.com

• April

Zurich Spring Festival

Zurich Spring Festival, which is known locally as *Sechseläuten*, celebrates the end of the cold winter weather and the start of spring. The festival begins with a children's parade on April 22, with more than 2000 children taking part. This is followed by the main events on April 23, when members of various guilds (or societies) eat a midday meal at their respective Guildhouses, before taking part in the *Parade of the Guilds* at 1515. Thousands of spectators line the streets of the city's Old Town to watch more than 7000 participants parade through the city. The highlight of the festival, the *Burning of the Böögg*, begins on the stroke of 1800 on April 23. At the moment the bells of St Peter signal an end to winter in the city, a giant Böögg bonfire (in the shape of a snowman, representing the figure, Old Man Winter) is lit on Sechseläuten Field.

Event Organiser
Zentralkomitee der Zünfte, Herr Pit Wyss, Gumpenwiesenstrasse 13, 8157 Dielsdorf, Switzerland
Tel: (01) 853 1777
Website: www.sechseläeuten.ch

Venue
Sechseläutenwiese (Sechseläuten field) at Bellevue.

Transport
Air: Zurich Airport. **Rail:** Tram: Opernhaus or Bellevue Tram to Sechseläutenwiese, which is in front of Zurich's opera house. **Road:** Car: A1 (from Geneva).

• June-July

Zurich Festival

Every summer, Zurich's three main arts institutions – the *Opera*, the *Tonhalle* (concert hall) and the *Kunsthalle* (art gallery) – join forces to transform the city into a hive of cultural activity, with high-quality performances of opera, jazz, classical music, theatre, cinema and ballet, alongside exhibitions of art and literature. The main events are staged at the Zurich Opera House and the city's chapels and churches host smaller concerts.

Event Organiser

Zürcher Festpiele, Falkenstr 1, 8008 Zürich, Switzerland
Tel: (01) 269 9090
Website: www.zuercher-festspiele.ch

Venue

The Opera House, the Kunsthalle, the Tonhalle, and various other venues across Zurich.

Transport

Air: Zurich Airport. **Rail:** Train: Zurich Station. Tram: Opernhaus or Bellevue (to Opera House). Road: Car: A1 (from Geneva).

Thailand

Bangkok

Tourist Information

Tourism Authority of Thailand (Kan Tong Teow Hang Prated Thai)
1600 New Phetburi Road, Makkasan, Rajatevee, Bangkok 10310, Thailand
Tel: (02) 250 5500
Website: www.tourismthailand.org

• April

Songkran Festival

Songkran, meaning 'to pass' or 'to relocate', heralds the arrival of the Thai New Year (when the sun exits Pisces and enters Aries), which is celebrated throughout the country. Bangkok festivities are centred on *Sanam Luang* (Royal Palace Ground), close to *Phra Barom Maha Rajcha Wang* (Royal Grand Palace), where an image of the Buddha is worshipped and bathed by religious elders and devotees; *Wat Phra Kaeo* (Temple of the Emerald Buddha) is another important site where worshippers gather during Songkran to receive blessings from elders. Water fights take place throughout the city, in particular in the old commercial district of *Bang Lamphu*. There are concerts and other forms of cultural entertainment on offer along the Khao San Road, where a *Miss Songkran* beauty pageant is also held.

Event Organiser

For more information on Songkran, contact the Tourism Authority of Thailand (see **Tourist Information** above).

Venue

Various locations across Bangkok.

Transport

Air: Bangkok International Airport. **Rail:** Train: Hualampong Station. **Road:** Bus: Public services. Taxi: Taxis or *tuk tuks* (three-wheeled taxis) are the best way to get around Bangkok.

• August

Queen's Birthday Celebrations

Thailand's present queen, Queen Sirikit, was born M R Sirikit Kitiyakara on August 12 1932. She enjoys a great deal of popularity in the country due to her humanitarian approach and the projects she has established to revive traditional arts and crafts. Every year, Thais celebrate her birthday by erecting portraits decorated with flowers on Ratchadamnoen Avenue near the *Royal Grand Palace* (Phra Barom Maha Rajcha Wang). The palace itself is festooned with coloured lights and other decorations, as are many other public buildings and private homes.

Event Organiser

For more information on the Queen's Birthday Celebrations, contact the Tourism Authority of Thailand (see **Tourist Information** above).

Venue

Various locations across Bangkok. For further information, contact the Tourism Authority of Thailand (see **Tourist Information** above).

Transport

Air: Bangkok International Airport. **Rail:** Train: Hualampong Station. **Road:** Bus: Public services. Taxi: Taxis or *tuk tuks* (three-wheeled taxis) are the best way to get around Bangkok and can be haled from the street.

Turkey

Istanbul

Tourist Information

Tourism Bureau (Turizm Danisma Burosu)
Sultanahmet Square, Istanbul, Turkey
Tel: (0212) 518 1802
Website: www.turizm.gov.tr

• September-November

Istanbul Biennial

The first *Istanbul Biennial* was organised in 1987 by the Istanbul Foundation for Culture and the Arts, and every two years presents a showcase of international contemporary art. The works of art are displayed in a variety of venues across the city, which have in past years included the beautiful *Topkapi Palace* gardens, the historic *Yerebatan Cisterns*, Ottoman warehouses and even Istanbul Atatürk Airport. Past exhibitors at the festival included British Turner Prize winners Gillian Wearing and Gavin Turk.

Event Organiser
Istanbul Foundation for Culture and Arts, Istiklal Caddesi 146, Beyoglu 34435, _Istanbul, Turkey
Tel: (0212) 334 0700
Website: www.iksv.org

Venue
Various venues across Istanbul. For further information, contact the Istanbul Foundation for Culture and Arts (see above).

Transport
Air: Istanbul Atatürk Airport or Istanbul Sabiha Gökçen International Airport. **Rail:** Train: Sirkeci or Haydapasa stations. **Road:** Bus: Public services.

United Arab Emirates

Dubai

Tourist Information

Department of Tourism and Commerce Marketing (DCTM) Welcome Bureau
Beni Yas Square, Deira, Dubai, UAE
Tel: (04) 228 5000
Website: www.dubaitourism.co.ae

• February

Dubai Shopping Festival

Dubai has established itself in recent years as a mecca for duty-free shopping, and every March, visitors to the glittering Arab city can find even more bargains. The *Dubai Shopping Festival* features special discounts on a whole host of goods, from Rolls Royce cars to perfumes and jewellery, in shops across the city. In addition, visitors have the opportunity to win hundreds of prizes in shopping malls and department stores. There is also a Global Village, with pavilions selling goods from countries including Bangladesh, Vietnam and the Czech Republic. Once the purse is empty, there are many events and shows on offer, such as street theatre, fireworks and fashion shows.

Event Organiser
Dubai Shopping Festival Secretariat, PO Box 25425, Dubai, UAE
Tel: (04) 223 5444
Website: www.mydsf.com

Venue
Various venues across Dubai.

Transport
Air: Dubai International Airport. **Road:** Coach: Public services to Gold Souk Bus Station or Al-Ghubaiba Bus Station.

• March

Dubai World Cup

The *Dubai World Cup*, held in late March each year, is one of the most glamorous events in the sporting calendar, and certainly the richest. The two-kilometre (1.3-mile) sand and dirt track is floodlit for the thousands of spectators who come to watch the thoroughbred horses and their jockeys compete for the million dollar prize money. Unsurprisingly, the race attracts some of the best in the field and is closely watched by all involved in the sport. The total prize money for the race exceeded US$15 million at the 2005 event.

Event Organiser
Dubai Racing Club, Suite 206, City Tower 1, PO Box 9305, Dubai, UAE
Tel: (04) 332 2277
Website: www.dubaiworldcup.com

Venue
Nad Al Sheba Race Track.

Transport
Air: Dubai International Airport. **Road:** Coach: Public services to Gold Souk Bus Station or Al-Ghubaiba Bus Station.

Need More Information on UAE /Consult the World Travel Guide

United Kingdom

Cardiff

Tourist Information

Cardiff Visitors Centre
16 Wood St, Cardiff CF10 1ES, UK
Tel: (029) 2022 7281
Website: www.visitcardiff.info

• June-August

Cardiff Festival

The seven-week *Cardiff Festival* takes place in Wales's capital city with events taking place from June through until August. This giant outdoor event attracts hundreds of thousands of people every year to its various free events. The festival features the best in street theatre, live music and comedy in numerous events which take place across the city. The festivities kick off with *Celtic Food & Drink* in Cardiff Bay's Oval Basin. There are various concerts from the Welsh Proms, and the city's streets around Queen Street are brought to life with *Fiesta Nights*, which sees street performances from international artists. There's also a *Children's Festival* in June. Queen Street is the scene of more celebrations at the end of July when the *International Street Festival* brings the best of street theatre to the city. One of the most popular events during the festival is *MAS Carnival* which usually takes place on the last Saturday in July when hundreds of partygoers, including stilt walkers, dancers and samba bands from all over the world join in the celebrations. The festival comes to a climax at the beginning of August, with the free, open-air *Big Weekend*, which attracts more than 750,000 visitors. Highlights of the weekend festival include a free music festival, free entry to the National Museum's exhibitions, the Lord Mayor's Parade, a giant funfair and a dance party.

Event Organiser

Cardiff County Council, County Hall, Atlantic Wharf, Cardiff CF10 4UW, UK
Tel: (029) 2087 3690 (festival information hotline)
Website: www.cardiff.gov.uk

Venue

Various locations across the city. The festival ends in the city's Civic Centre with the Big Weekend.

Transport

Air: Cardiff International Airport. **Rail:** Train: Cardiff Central Station. **Road:** Car: M4 (from London, Reading, Swindon, Bath, Bristol and Swansea).

• November

Cardiff Screen Festival

The *Cardiff Screen Festival* (formerly *International Film Festival of Wales*) takes place each year in November. During the event, more than 100 short, feature-length and animated films are screened in various venues across the capital. The festival attracts thousands of visitors every year, including members of the public, industry professionals and film enthusiasts, and there are many film premieres during the event. The festival culminates in the presentation of the prestigious DM Davies Short Film Award, one of the largest prizes for a short film competition in Europe.

Event Organiser

Cardiff Screen Festival, 10 Mount Stuart Square, Cardiff CF10 5EE, UK
Tel: (029) 2033 3324
Website: www.iffw.co.uk

Venue

Various cinemas and other venues across Cardiff, including Chapter Canton, Chapter Globe and UCI cinemas.

Transport

Air: Cardiff International Airport. **Rail:** Train: Cardiff Central Station. **Road:** Car: M4 (from London, Reading, Swindon, Bath, Bristol and Swansea). **Bus:** Public services.

Edinburgh

Tourist Information

Edinburgh and Lothians Tourist Board
3 Princes Street, Edinburgh EH2 2QP, UK
Tel: (0131) 473 3800
Website: www.edinburgh.org

• December-January

Hogmanay

Edinburgh is undoubtedly one of the most exciting cities in the world to be at New Year, with celebrations taking place throughout the city over a five-day period. Traditional *Hogmanay* celebrations in Scotland date back to 1560 when the Protestant Reformation meant that many religious events, including Christmas, were banned. This meant that the Scots focused on celebrating non-Catholic days, such as New Year, as these were spared a religious ban. Edinburgh's Hogmanay celebrations began in 1992 when the Summit in the City and the European Union Heads of State Conference were held in the city. The festival has grown to be one of the world's largest New Year celebrations, attracting over half a million visitors, with performances from over 400 artists in around 60 venues. Edinburgh's Hogmanay mixes tradition with modern performances and appeals to all age groups. Highlights include the *Concert in the Gardens*, the *New Year Revels*, the *Winter Wonderland* ice rink in West Princess Street Gardens and the *Candlelit Concert* in the Cathedral. Fireworks are let off around the city every year at midnight to celebrate Hogmanay.

Event Organiser

Edinburgh's Hogmanay Box Office, The Hub, Castle Hill, Royal Mile, Edinburgh EH1 2NE, UK
Tel: (09069) 150 150 (information; calls cost £1 per minute) *or* (0131) 473 2000
Website: www.edinburghshogmanay.org

Venue

Various locations across Edinburgh, with the main festivities taking place in the area around Princes Street and Edinburgh Castle.

Transport

Air: Edinburgh International Airport. **Rail:** Train: Waverley or Haymarket stations. **Road:** Bus: Public services.

• January

Burns' Night

Every year, Scotsmen and women around the world gather to eat a traditional Burns' Supper to celebrate the life and works of the great Scottish poet, Robert Burns. He was born on January 25 1759 and died on July 21 1796. The National Bard of Scotland is most famous for poems which include 'To a Haggis', 'To a Daisy', 'Halloween' and 'To a Mouse'. He is also famous for writing the traditional New Year's Song, 'Old Langs Syne', as well as 'Scots Wha Hae', 'A Red, Red Rose' and 'Comin' Through the Rye'. On his birthday, people around Scotland remember his life and celebrate Scottish culture by eating a traditional meal of tatties (potatoes), neeps (turnip) and haggis (a mutton, oatmeal and onion mix, cooked in a sheep's stomach bag) and by consuming large quantities of Scotch whisky. It is customary to hear 'To a Haggis' recited during the celebrations; this famous poem is read by the evening's host. As he reads the line 'an cut you up wi' ready slight', he cuts open the haggis and the meal begins. *Burns' Night* celebrations range from formal

gatherings, where Burn's most well-known poems are recited, to informal parties, where drunken revellers sing his most famous songs.

Event Organiser

For more information on Burns' Night, contact the Edinburgh and Lothians Tourist Board (see **Tourist Information** above).

Venue

Various venues, restaurants and bars across Scotland.

Transport

Air: Edinburgh International Airport or Glasgow International Airport. **Rail:** Train: Waverley Station (Edinburgh) or Glasgow Central Station (Glasgow). **Road:** Bus: Public services.

• April

Edinburgh International Science Festival

The *Edinburgh International Science Festival* takes place in April each year. The festival celebrates all aspects of science and technology, and has a wide appeal to all age groups. Visitors can take part in many interesting events, including lying on a bed of nails and floating in the Dead Sea Loch. Every year, approximately 175,000 visitors enjoy shows, workshops, exhibitions, talks and tours across Edinburgh. At the beginning of the 1990s, there were around 100 events at the festival, which attracted approximately 60,000 visitors. Today, there are around 300 events, attracting visitors from the UK and across Europe.

Event Organiser

Edinburgh International Science Festival, 4 Gayfield Place Lane, Edinburgh EH1 3NZ, UK
Tel: (0131) 558 7666
Website: www.go-edinburgh.co.uk/science

Venue

Various venues, including many of Edinburgh's art galleries.

Transport

Air: Edinburgh International Airport. **Rail:** Train: Waverley or Haymarket stations. **Road:** Bus: Public services.

• June

Royal Highland Show

The *Royal Highland Show* takes place every year in June, just outside Edinburgh. The show attracts approximately 160,000 visitors who come to see over 5000 livestock and 2000 exhibitors. The highlights of the show are the displays of cattle, sheep and horses, as well as the *Food From Scotland* exhibition, which is the largest display of Scottish food and drink in the world. There is also a giant flower display, a crafts show and one of the largest displays of agricultural machinery in the UK.

Event Organiser
Royal Highland & Agricultural Society of Scotland, Royal Highland Centre, Ingliston, Edinburgh EH28 8NF, UK
Tel: (0131) 335 6200
Website: www.rhass.org.uk

Venue
Royal Highland Centre, outside Edinburgh.

Transport
Air: Edinburgh International Airport. There is a free bus service to the show (from the airport). **Rail:** Train: Waverley Station. **Road:** Bus: Public services. Car: M9 or M90 (from the north); M8 (junction 2) (from Glasgow); A8 via Gogar Roundabout (from the east and south).

• August

Edinburgh Fringe Festival

The *Edinburgh Fringe Festival* is held in August every year in parallel with the *Edinburgh International Festival*. The first Edinburgh Fringe Festival was held in 1947 and has since grown to become one of the largest arts festivals in the world. In 1947, eight theatre groups turned up uninvited to the Edinburgh International Festival, but were unable to perform at the event. Finding themselves on the 'fringe' of the event, they found alternative venues at which to perform. The Fringe Festival has continued every year and has developed into an enormous festival where amateur and unknown artists are able to perform. The festival sees many performances in unconventional locations in the city by any artist who is prepared to hire a venue for the night.

Event Organiser
The Fringe Office, 180 High Street, Edinburgh EH1 1QS, UK
Tel: (0131) 226 0026
Website: www.edfringe.com

Venue
Various venues in Edinburgh city centre, including Holyrood Park, La Belle Angele, George Square Theatre, Randolph Studio and Edinburgh College of Art.

Transport
Air: Edinburgh International Airport. **Rail:** Train: Waverley Station (Edinburgh). **Road:** Bus: Public services.

Edinburgh Military Tattoo

The *Edinburgh Military Tattoo* is a well-established, world-renowned event, attracting visitors from around the globe. The Tattoo was first performed in 1950 as the Scottish Army's contribution to the *Edinburgh International Festival*. The word 'tattoo' comes from the cry used by innkeepers in the Low Countries in the 17th and 18th centuries to signal closing time. Every year, hundreds of performers from more than 30 countries, including India, the USA, Norway, Australia and Pakistan, take part in this event, which is watched by an audience of 200,000. The Tattoo is also shown on television in around 30 countries to an annual television audience of 100 million. The event sees international musical performances, theatre and dance, as well as marching by the Army in the spectacular grounds of Edinburgh Castle. Other highlights include the sounds of the Massed Pipes and Drums, music from the Massed Military Bands, the Guards of His Majesty The King of Norway and a Highland Dance display. At the end of each day's events, a lone piper plays a haunting lament on the castle's ramparts, before all the day's performers march off the *Esplanade* to the sounds of the famous pipe melody 'The Black Bear'.

Event Organiser
Edinburgh Military Tattoo, The Tattoo Office, 32 Market Street, Edinburgh EH1 1QB, UK
Tel: 08707 555 118
Website: www.edinburgh-tattoo.co.uk

Venue
Castle Esplanade, Edinburgh Castle.

Transport
Air: Edinburgh International Airport. **Rail:** Train: Waverley Station. **Road:** Bus: Public services.

• August-September

Edinburgh International Festival

The *Edinburgh International Festival* provides audiences with impressive arts performances, ranging from theatrical productions through to opera, dance and music. Every year, this giant festival attracts visitors from all over the globe to see many of the world's greatest artists perform at this renowned festival. The first Edinburgh International Festival took place in 1947 to celebrate the end of World War II.

Event Organiser
Edinburgh International Festival, The Hub,

Castlehill, Edinburgh EH1 2NE, UK
Tel: (0131) 473 2001 (bookings) *or* 473 2099
(administration)
Website: www.eif.co.uk
Venue
Various venues across Edinburgh, including Usher
Hall, Festival Theatre and The Hub.

Transport
Air: Edinburgh International Airport. **Rail:** Train:
Waverley or Haymarket stations. **Road:** Bus: Public
services.

Glasgow

Tourist Information
Greater Glasgow & Clyde Valley
Tourist Board
11 George Street, Glasgow G2 1DY, UK
Tel: (0141) 204 4400
Website: www.seeglasgow.com

• January

Celtic Connections

Celtic Connections is a celebration of traditional
and contemporary Celtic music and culture
from Scotland, Ireland and Brittany, as well as
other Celtic places around the world. The event
takes place across Glasgow during January. The
festival first took place in 1993 to fill a
scheduling gap in the Glasgow Royal Concert
Hall's winter season and has grown into a 19-
day event taking place at venues across the
city. The festival focuses predominantly on
Scottish traditional music but is truly
international with performances by artists from
all over the world.

Event Organiser
Glasgow Royal Concert Hall, 2 Sauchiehall Street,
Glasgow G2 3NY, Scotland
Tel: (0141) 353 8000
Website: www.celticconnections.com
Venue
Venues across Glasgow, including the Piping
Centre, Old Fruitmarket, Tron, Glasgow Cathedral,
St Aloysius Church, St Mary's Cathedral and the
Central Hotel; many events take place in Glasgow
Royal Concert Hall.

Transport
Air: Glasgow International Airport. **Rail:** Train:
Glasgow Central Station. **Road:** Bus: Public
services.

Isle of Man

Tourist Information
Isle of Man Department of Tourism and Leisure
Sea Terminal Buildings, Douglas, Isle of Man IM1
2RG, UK
Tel: (01624) 686 801
Website: www.visitisleofman.com

• June

TT Races

The origins of the legendary *TT Races* date back to
1904 when the isle hosted the Gordon Bennett car
trials because it was not possible to close public
roads to allow racing in England. New legislation
was brought in to make this a regular event and
three years later in 1907 the first TT Races involving
motorbikes were held. The event has grown over the
years and many see the Isle of Man as the Road
Racing Capital of the world which attracts
thousands of visitors each year. In 1988 race
organisers also introduced the Pre-TT Classic Races
where motorbikes of yesteryear race along the 6.8-
km (4.25-mile) Billown Course in May each year.

Event Organiser
For more information on the TT Races, contact the
Isle of Man Department of Tourism and Leisure
(see **Tourist Information** above).
Venue
Courses on the Isle of Man.

Transport
Air: Isle of Man Airport (Ballasalla). **Water:** Ferry:
Douglas Ferry Port. **Rail:** Scenic steam railway
travels south from Douglas. The Manx Electric
Railway travels north from Douglas. **Road:** Bus:
Public services.

Liverpool

Tourist Information
Liverpool Tourist Information Centre
Queen Square Centre, Queen Square, Liverpool L1
1RG, UK
Tel: (0845) 601 1125
Website: www.visitliverpool.com

• April

Grand National

The *Grand National* at *Aintree Racecourse* is one
of the best-known and best-loved horse racing
meets in the UK. The first races at Aintree date

back to 1829 but the first Grand National (now often abbreviated to the National) wasn't held until 1839 in which Lottery became the first horse to win the National. A maximum of 40 riders race in the Grand National which traditionally is the final race in the three-day meeting. The course is notorious for its 16 fences and the 494-yard (452m) sprint to the finish line. The Grand National is one of the most prestigious meetings on the horse racing calendar which has traditionally been the biggest day in the year for British betting. Aintree itself is currently undergoing a £30m renovation project due for completion in 2007.

Event Organiser
Aintree Racecourse, Ormskirk Road, Aintree, Liverpool L9 5AS, UK
Tel: (0151) 523 2600
Website: www.aintree.co.uk

Venue
Aintree Racecourse, Liverpool.

Transport
Air: Liverpool John Lennon Airport or Manchester Airport. Rail: Train: Mainline services to Liverpool Lime Street Station then local services to Aintree from Liverpool Central Station. Road: Bus: Public services. Car: Aintree is signposted from the M6.

London

Tourist Information
London Tourist Board & Convention Bureau Accommodation Booking Service
1 Warwick Row, Victoria, London SW1E 5ER, UK
Tel: (020) 7932 2020
Website: www.visitlondon.com

• January

Daily Telegraph Adventure Travel & Sports Show

The *Daily Telegraph Adventure Travel & Sports Show* began in 1995 and has grown into one of the leading travel shows in the UK bringing together tour operators, travel gear stockists and adventure companies under one roof at the Olympia exhibition hall in London. In addition to over 250 exhibitors there's also a packed programme of lectures and personal appearances by well-known explorers, adventurers, travel writers and presenters. There are also usually live demonstrations, simulators and an indoor climbing wall where visitors can try their hand at new sports. The show also usually features a team of travel experts who can help visitors plan their trip details.

Event Organiser
Ats Events Limited, Lower Dane, Hartlip, Kent ME9 7TE, UK
Tel: (01795) 844400
Website: www.adventureshow.co.uk

Venue
Olympia Exhibition Centre, Hammersmith Road, Kensington, London W14 8UX, UK

Transport
Air: London Heathrow Airport. Rail: Train: Kensington Olympia Station (mainline). Underground: Kensington Olympia underground station (District Line). Road: Bus: Public services.

• January

London Parade

The *London Parade* takes place in central London on January 1 each year. During this giant, free party, spectacular marching bands parade through the streets, along with thousands of cheerleaders, clowns and vintage cars. The parade first took place in the city in 1987, when a few hundred performers from the USA and the UK paraded through London's streets to celebrate the New Year. The event was first called the *Lord Mayor of Westminster's Big Parade*, but was renamed the London Parade in 1994, by which time thousands of professional cheerleaders from the USA had joined the procession. Today, the parade features almost 10,000 participants from all over the world and attracts around one million spectators who line the streets of central London to watch the show. Every year, the event raises large amounts of money for charity. The parade sets off from Parliament Square at 1200 and continues for 3.5km (2.2 miles) through the streets of central London, finishing in Berkeley Square, off Piccadilly and Regent Street.

Event Organiser
London Parade, Research House, Fraser Road, Greenford, Middlesex UB6 7AQ, UK
Tel: (020) 8566 8586
Website: www.londonparade.co.uk

Venue
Central London, beginning in Parliament Square and finishing in Berkeley Square.

Transport
Air: London Heathrow Airport. Rail: Train: London Charing Cross Station. Underground:

Westminster (start); Piccadilly Circus (Piccadilly or Bakerloo lines) or Green Park (Jubilee, Piccadilly or Victoria lines) (finish). **Road:** Bus: Public services.

• February

Chinese New Year

Chinese New Year festivities take place every year in London's Chinatown, which is located in the Soho district of the city. The festival, which is known as *Spring Festival* in its native country, is the oldest and most important festival in China. The Chinese New Year takes place on a different date every year as the Chinese calendar is based on lunar and solar movements. A leap month is added in every couple of years, thus changing the date of the New Year, which takes place on the first day of the new moon every year. The Chinese use 12 animals to represent a 12-year cycle, with a different animal representing each Chinese Year. In London, New Year festivities take place in Gerrard Street, between Soho and Leicester Square, and also spread into nearby *Covent Garden*. There are numerous parades during the festivities, as well as music, Chinese opera, kung fu, and lion and dragon dances. There are also many food stalls in the area selling traditional Chinese cuisine, as well as around 60 Chinese restaurants located in Soho.

Event Organiser
For more information on Chinese New Year, contact the London Tourist Board & Convention Bureau (see **Tourist Information** above).

Venue
Gerrard Street, between Leicester Square and Soho.

Transport
Air: London Heathrow Airport. **Rail:** Train: London Victoria Station. Underground: Leicester Square (Piccadilly and Northern lines) or Piccadilly Circus (Piccadilly and Bakerloo lines). **Road:** Bus: Public services.

• March–April

Daily Mail Ideal Home Show

The *Daily Mail Ideal Home Show* is a major event in the UK calendar, taking place every year in London's Earls Court. The show, which began in 1908, attracts thousands of keen homemakers every year, who are drawn to see inspirational homes from both the past and future. One of the most famous features of the show is the *House of the Future* display which sees leading designers give their impressions of the shape of things to come. Homes from previous decades are also on display and attract huge crowds of people.

Event Organiser
Daily Mail Ideal Home Show, Dmg World Media, Equitable House, Lyon Road, Harrow, Middlesex HA1 2EW, UK
Tel: (020) 8515 2000
Website: www.idealhomeshow.co.uk

Venue
Earls Court Exhibition Centre, SW5, London.

Transport
Air: London Heathrow Airport. **Rail:** Train: West Brompton Station (from Clapham Junction). Underground: Earls Court (District or Piccadilly lines) or West Brompton (District Line). **Road:** Bus: Public services.

• April

Flora London Marathon

The *Flora London Marathon* is a 42.2km (26.2 mile) race, which first took place on March 29 1981. Around 7750 runners took part in the first London Marathon, with approximately 6250 completing the race successfully. The event takes place around the streets of central London, starting in Greenwich Park and ending in the Mall. Runners pass many major London sites, including the Cutty Sark, Canary Wharf, the Tower of London, Buckingham Palace and Big Ben. Nearly 100,000 people applied to run the race in 2005 with more than 30,000 competitors eventually taking part, including top athletes from around the world, as well as thousands of fun runners. The majority of amateur competitors also raise money for charity and many of them take part in fancy dress. Spectators line the streets, joining in the festivities and cheering on the runners, in what has become one of London's biggest street parties.

Event Organiser
Flora London Marathon, Suite 3, Waterloo Court, 10 Theed Street, London SE1 8ST, UK
Tel: (020) 7902 0200
Website: www.london-marathon.co.uk

Venue
Central London, starting in Greenwich Park and ending in the Mall.

Transport
Air: London Heathrow Airport. **Rail:** Train: Greenwich, Maze Hill or Blackheath stations (start), Charing Cross Station (finish). Docklands Light Railway: Cutty Sark or Greenwich (start)

(from Bank). Underground: Charing Cross (Bakerloo or Northern lines), Green Park (Jubilee, Piccadilly or Victoria lines) or St James's Park (District or Circle lines) (finish). **Road:** Bus: Public services.

• May

Chelsea Flower Show

The *Chelsea Flower Show* is one of the most famous garden displays in Europe. Every year, visitors from all over the world flock to London to see this spectacular event which was first held in 1913. Displays range from modern sculptured displays through to wild, untamed gardens. The show includes a *Lifelong Learning in the Garden* feature, explaining how gardens grow, and Royal Horticultural Society experts are on hand to offer advice about gardening to visitors.

Event Organiser
Royal Horticultural Society, 80 Vincent Square, London SW1P 2PE, UK
Tel: (020) 7834 4333
Website: www.rhs.org.uk

Venue
Showgrounds at the Royal Hospital, Chelsea.

Transport
Air: London Heathrow Airport. **Rail:** Train: Victoria Station. Underground: Sloane Square (District or Circle lines). **Road:** Bus: Public services.

• June

Queen's Birthday Parade – Trooping the Colour

Trooping the Colour takes place every year in central London to celebrate the Queen's birthday. The ceremony takes place on *Horse Guards Parade* in Whitehall and is watched by thousands of spectators, as well as invited guests and members of the Royal Family. Queen Elizabeth II was actually born on April 21, although her birthday is officially celebrated in summer. Troops from the Household Division parade down the ranks, escorting regimental colours, before giving the Queen a royal salute at *Buckingham Palace*. A musical 'troop' is also performed, prior to the Queen carrying out an inspection of the troops. The word 'trooping' can be dated back to the origins of the ceremony in the early 18th century, when the colours of the battalion were carried (or trooped) down the

ranks on parade to the soldiers. The parade has been a celebration of the Sovereign's official birthday since 1748, although the Sovereign has officially only taken part in the ceremony since the time of Edward VII's reign.

Event Organiser
Household Divisions Headquarters, Horse Guards, Whitehall, London SW1A 2AX, UK
Tel: (020) 7414 2479.
Website: www.royal.gov.uk

Venue
Horse Guards Parade, London SW1.

Transport
Air: London Heathrow Airport. **Rail:** Train: London Charing Cross Station. Underground: Charing Cross (Bakerloo or Northern lines) or Westminster (District, Circle or Jubilee lines). **Road:** Bus: Public services.

• June-July

Wimbledon Championships

The *Wimbledon Championships* is an internationally-renowned tennis tournament, which attracts leading tennis professionals from around the world. The first *Lawn Tennis Championships* was held at The All England Croquet and Lawn Tennis Club in 1877, with the introduction of the Men's Singles which was won by Englishman Spencer Gore. The first Ladies' Singles event was held in 1884 and was won by Englishwoman Maud Watson; the Men's Doubles was also started in the same year. Every year the event is attended by thousands of spectators, as well as by members of the British Royal Family. Traditionally the event is plagued by rain, with play called off due to the weather; it is also traditional to eat strawberries and drink champagne. The youngest man to win the championships was Boris Becker of Germany in 1985, who at 17 was also the first German to win the title. The youngest female to win the title was Martina Hingis of Switzerland, who was just 16 years old when she won the Ladies' Singles event in 1996.

Event Organiser
The All England Lawn Tennis & Croquet Club, Church Road, Wimbledon, London SW19 5AE, UK
Tel: (020) 8944 1066
Website: www.wimbledon.org

Venue
All England Lawn Tennis & Croquet Club Grounds, Wimbledon, SW19

Transport
Air: London Heathrow Airport. **Rail:** Train: Wimbledon Station (from Waterloo Station). Underground: Southfields (District Line). **Road:** Bus: Shuttle buses from Southfields Station, Victoria Station and Marble Arch.

• August

Notting Hill Carnival

The *Notting Hill Carnival* takes place every year in West London. The first Notting Hill Carnival took place in 1964, when Caribbean immigrants introduced the Carnival to London to unite the inhabitants of the area, which had suffered racial tensions. The event has grown from its origins as a small procession of people in costume carrying steel drums to an enormous multicultural festival which is attended by more than two million people every year. There are five disciplines to the carnival; these are Mas, Steelband, Calypso, Soca and static sound systems. There is a procession of costumes, soca and steel bands along a 4.8km (3 miles) route and 40 licensed static sound systems, playing different types of music, including jazz, soul, funk and reggae. Hundreds of street stalls sell food from around the globe, as well as numerous arts and crafts. There are two live stages, featuring local bands and international artists, which have in the past included Eddie Grant, Jamiroquai, Wyclef Jean, Burning Spear and Finley Quaye. The motto of the carnival is 'Every Spectator is a participant – Carnival is for all who dare to participate'.

Event Organiser
The Notting Hill Carnival Trust, 332 Ladbroke Grove, London W10 5AH, UK
Tel: (020) 8964 0544
Website: www.mynottinghill.co.uk

Venue
Streets around Ladbroke Grove and Notting Hill.

Transport
Air: London Heathrow Airport. **Rail:** Train: London Victoria Station. Underground: Westbourne Park (Hammersmith & City Line), Notting Hill Gate (Central, District or Circle lines) or Latimer Road (Hammersmith & City Line). Ladbroke Grove (Hammersmith & City Line) is usually closed during the weekend and other underground stations close if they become overcrowded. **Road:** Bus: Public services.

• November

Lord Mayor's Show

The *Lord Mayor's Show* takes place in the City of London every year when the Lord Mayor of London parades through the streets as a show of allegiance to the Crown. The position of Lord Mayor of London was created by King John in 1215, as a way of showing thanks to the City for its support. The City is an area around the Bank of England covering 1.6 sq km (one sq mile) which was developed by the Romans and is today the financial heart of the capital. The Lord Mayor (not to be confused with the new title Mayor of London) was originally selected by the people of London in 1215, making this one of the first elected posts in the world. Every year the Lord Mayor must swear loyalty to the Crown in person; the show is a celebration which evolved from his journey. In the evening, fireworks are launched by the Lord Mayor over the River Thames, bringing a spectacular end to the day's festivities.

Event Organiser
Lord Mayor's Show, PO Box 270, Guildhall, London EC2P 2EJ, UK
Tel: (020) 7332 1456
Website: www.lordmayorsshow.org

Venue
Central London parade route between Mansion House and Aldwych.

Transport
Air: London Heathrow Airport or London City Airport. **Rail:** Train: London Blackfriars or London Bridge stations. Underground: St Paul's (Central Line), Mansion House (District or Circle lines), Bank (Central, District, Circle or Northern lines) or Blackfriars (District or Circles lines). **Road:** Bus: Public services.

Reading

Tourist Information

Reading Visitor Centre and Travel Shop
Church House, Chain Street, Reading RG2 7HD, UK
Tel: (0118) 956 6226
Website: www.readingtourism.org.uk

• July

WOMAD Festival

The *WOMAD Festival* (World of Music, Art and Dance) began back in 1990 as an alternative to the UK's mainstream music festivals showcasing the very best acts and performers from the world music scene. The three-day event usually takes place over the last weekend in July each year and attracts thousands of revellers. The festival has a strong family emphasis and there's a children's fun park and area with a circus feel and face painting tents. Past performers have included Robert Plant, Asian Dub Foundation, Youssou N'Dour and reggae legend Jimmy Cliff. WOMAD host similar festivals around the world throughout the year.

Event Organiser
WOMAD, Millside, Mill Lane Box, Wiltshire SN13 8PN, UK
Fax: (01225) 743481
Website: www.womad.org

Venue
The Rivermead, Richfield Avenue, Caversham, Reading RG1 8EQ, UK

Transport
Air: London Heathrow Airport or London City Airport. **Rail:** Train: Reading Station. **Road:** Bus: Public services. Car: Signposted from the M4 and car parking facilities at the festival site.

United States of America

Atlanta

Tourist Information
Atlanta Convention & Visitors Bureau
Suite 100, 233 Peachtree Street NE, Atlanta, GA 30303, USA
Tel: (404) 521 6600
Website: www.atlanta.net

• May

Atlanta Jazz Festival
The month-long *Atlanta Jazz Festival* is a music event featuring many of the world's great jazz legends, as well as rising international stars. The festival, which has been running for nearly 30 years and is the largest free jazz festival in the USA, sees hundreds of entertainers perform every year at the festival in Piedmont Park. There are also concerts in various other parks across Atlanta, as well as night performances in local bars and clubs. A wide selection of food is on sale in Piedmont Park and a large arts and crafts market is held during the festival. Up to 50,000 people attend the festival each year.

Event Organiser
Atlanta Jazz Festival, City Hall East, Fifth Floor, 675 Ponce de Leon Avenue, Atlanta, GA 30308, USA
Tel: (404) 817 6851
Website: www.atlantafestivals.com

Venue
Piedmont Park and various other venues in Atlanta.

Transport
Air: Hartsfield Atlanta International Airport. **Rail:** Train: Brookwood Station. **Road:** Bus: Public services.

Boston

Tourist Information
Greater Boston Convention & Visitors Bureau
2 Copley Place, Suite 105, Boston, MA 02116, USA
Tel: (617) 536 4100
Website: www.bostonusa.com

• April

Boston Marathon
The *Boston Marathon* is the world's oldest annually contested marathon and was first held in 1897 by the Boston Athletic Association, who were inspired by the revival of the marathon event at the 1896 Olympic Games in Athens. The winner of the 1897 marathon was John J McDermott of New York, who completed the 39.4-km (24.5-mile) route from Boston's Irvington Oval to Metcalf's Mill in Ashland in 2 hours, 55 minutes and 10 seconds to earn his place in marathon history. The standard distance of 42.2km (26 miles 385 yards) for a marathon event was set in 1924, when the British Olympic Committee decided that the route for the London Games should lead from Windsor Castle to the royal box in the London Olympic Stadium. The Boston Marathon is held on Patriot's Day, the third Monday in April and a Massachusetts public holiday, which gives the event a party atmosphere. The liveliest places with the best views for spectators are at Boston College or Beacon Street before the race ends at Boylston Street.

Event Organiser
Boston Athletic Association, 40 Trinity Place, 4th Floor, Boston, MA 02116, USA
Tel: (617) 236 1652
Website: www.bostonmarathon.org

Venue
The marathon starts at Irvington Oval and finishes at Metcalf's Mill, Ashland passing through the streets of central Boston.

Transport
Air: Boston Logan International Airport. Rail: Train: South or Back Bay stations. Underground: Boston College or Cleveland Circle. Road: Bus: Public services.

• December

Boston Tea Party Re-enactment

On the night of December 16 1773, a group of American patriots, called the Sons of Freedom, disguised themselves as Mohawk Indians and boarded three tea clippers – Eleanor, the Dartmouth and the Beaver – belonging to the ailing British East India Company. They then threw the cargo into the waters of Boston Harbour in protest at the taxes levied upon tea and other goods by the British colonists and the perceived monopoly granted to the East India Company by the British Parliament. Every year, visitors to Boston can see a re-enactment, performed by the Massachusetts Council of Minutemen and Militia, of what is generally considered to be the single most important event leading up to the American Revolution. The events start with a recreation of the town meeting in the city's South Meeting House where the Tea Party was planned. From there, the band of actors, accompanied by cheers from the assembled crowd, proceed down Congress Street to Beaver II, the replica of one of the original East India Company ships that now serves as a permanent Tea Party Museum, where they ceremonially throw tea chests into the water.

Event Organiser
Boston Tea Party Ship and Museum, 380 Dorchester St., Boston, MA 02127, USA
Tel: (617) 269 7150
Website: www.bostonteapartyship.com

Venue
Various locations in central Boston, focusing on the South Meeting House and Boston Tea Party Ship.

Transport
Air: Boston Logan International Airport. Rail: Train: South or Back Bay stations. Underground: South Station. Road: Bus: Public services.

Chicago

Tourist Information
Chicago Office of Tourism
78 East Washington Boulevard, Chicago IL 60602, USA
Tel: (312) 744 2400 or (0800) 487 2446
Website: www.cityofchicago.org/tourism

• March

St Patrick's Day Parade

Chicago is well known for its parades, and the city's large Irish population means that the St Patrick's Day Parade is one of the biggest and the best. The parade, which features floats decorated with huge shamrocks and leprechauns, live bands, Irish step dancers in traditional costume and even Irish dog and horse breeds, begins at 1200 at Balbo Drive and ends at Monroe Street at around 1700. Other activities, which last well into the evening, include Celtic dancing in churches, and pipe bands by the Chicago River.

Event Organiser
St Patrick's Day Parade Committee, 1340 West Washington Boulevard, Chicago IL 60607, USA
Tel: (312) 942 9188
Website: www.chicagostpatsparade.com

Venue
Balbo Drive to Monroe Street.

Transport
Air: Chicago O'Hare International Airport or Midway Airport (domestic flights). Rail: Train: Chicago Union Station. Underground: Balbo. Road: Bus: Public services.

• June-August

Grant Park Music Festival

Grant Park Music Festival was founded by the Chicago Park District in 1935. The concept grew from a desire to allow Chicagoans of all backgrounds to enjoy live classical music and for professional live musicians, who were suffering due to the rise in popularity of recorded music, to gain secure employment. Today, the festival is the only free, municipally funded, outdoor classical music festival in the USA, and continues to offer an excellent opportunity to enjoy symphonic concerts in a beautiful open-air setting in the heart of the 'Windy City'. Over 40 performances are held for two months each year, mainly at the Petrillo Music Shell (named after

James C Petrillo, the former president of the Chicago Federation of Musicians who convinced the park authorities to hold the event on an annual basis) on the Lake Michigan side of Grant Park, but also in churches and community centres around Chicago. The Grant Park Orchestra and Chorus and Chicago Children's Choir perform a variety of concerts most Wednesdays and Sundays, including opera, folk music, classical music made popular by films, songs from musicals and jazz. Composers featured include Beethoven, Strauss, Rachmaninoff, Sibelius, Rodrigo, Verdi and Britten.

Event Organiser
Grant Park Music Festival, 205 E. Randolph Drive, Chicago, IL 60601, USA
Tel: (312) 742 7638
Website: www.grantparkmusicfestival.com

Venue
Grant Park.

Transport
Air: Chicago O'Hare International Airport or Midway Airport (domestic flights). Rail: Train: Chicago Union Station. Underground: Jackson. Road: Bus: Public services.

Denver

Tourist Information
Denver Metro Convention & Visitors Bureau
1555 California Street, Suite 300, Denver, CO 80202, USA
Tel: (303) 892 1112 or (800) 233 6837 (toll free USA and Canada only)
Website: www.denver.org

• January

National Western Stock Show & Rodeo

Denver's *National Western Stock Show & Rodeo* attracts over 400,000 cowboys every year and is the largest festival in Colorado. It was first held in 1907 in a tent; it has since grown, however, to become a huge annual event which now attracts more than 630,000 visitors. The show aims to preserve the western lifestyle through a giant agricultural festival, which includes livestock displays and an annual horse show. Every year, there are events for all the family, including the *Indoor Rodeo of the Year* event and *The Super Bowl of Cattle Shows*, when cattle are judged to win the *National Western Grand Champion* prize.

Event Organiser
National Western Stock Show, 4655 Humboldt Street, Denver, CO 80216, USA
Tel: (303) 297 1166
Website: www.nationalwestern.com

Venue
National Western Complex, off I-25 and I-70.

Transport
Air: Denver International Airport. Rail: Train: Union Station. Road: Bus: Public services.

Memphis

Tourist Information
Memphis Convention & Visitors Bureau
47 Union Avenue, Memphis, TN 38103, USA
Tel: (901) 543 5300
Website: www.memphistravel.com

• August

Elvis Week

Elvis Week, which takes place in Memphis every August, is a celebration of the music and life of the late Elvis Presley. Every year, fans of the singing legend gather in Memphis to take part in this major event and pay homage to the star. During the week-long festival, there are many concerts and individual events around Memphis. There are also events at Elvis's former home, *Graceland*, the highlight of which is the *Candlelight Vigil* on August 15, the anniversary of his death in 1977, where fans have the chance to pay their respects to 'The King'.

Event Organiser
Elvis Presley Enterprises Inc, PO Box 16508, 3734 Elvis Presley Boulevard, Memphis, TN 38186, USA
Tel: (901) 332 3322 or (800) 238 2000 (toll free USA and Canada only)
Website: www.elvis.com

Venue
The main festivities take place at Graceland, the former home of Elvis.

Transport
Air: New Orleans International Airport. Rail: Train: Memphis Central Station. Road: Bus: A free shuttle bus departs from Elvis Presley's Memphis (a downtown restaurant) daily from 1130 onwards.

New Orleans

Tourist Information

New Orleans Metropolitan Convention & Visitors Bureau Inc
1520 Sugar Bowl Drive, New Orleans, LA 70112, USA
Tel: (504) 566 5011
Website: www.neworleanscvb.com

• February

Mardi Gras

Mardi Gras, which was first held in New Orleans in 1837, is today a giant celebration, with elaborately decorated floats, marching bands, parades, parties and lots of live music. The day itself, Mardi Gras (or *Fat Tuesday*), takes place on a different date each year, although it always ends on Mardi Gras day (46 days before Easter) with enormous parades through the streets. Every year, hundreds of thousands of visitors descend upon the city to join in the festivities, which also include private masked balls. Many partygoers dress up in fancy dress costumes during Mardi Gras, often wearing the official festival colours – purple, green and gold. These colours, which represent justice, faith and power respectively, were chosen by the King of the Carnival (known as Rex today) in 1872. This started a carnival tradition and every year a King and Queen is chosen to ride on the largest float, dressed in flamboyant costumes.

Event Organiser
For more information on Mardi Gras, contact New Orleans Metropolitan Convention & Visitors Bureau Inc (see **Tourist Information** above).

Venue
New Orleans Convention Centre and various venues across the city.

Transport
Air: New Orleans International Airport. **Rail:** Train: New Orleans Station. **Road:** Coach: Public services.

New York

Tourist Information

NYC & Company
810 Seventh Avenue, between 52nd and 53rd Streets, New York NY 10019, USA
Tel: (212) 484 1200
Website: www.nycvisit.com

• November

Macy's Thanksgiving Day Parade

Macy's Thanksgiving Day Parade is one of the Big Apple's most dynamic and colourful events. Its origins can be traced back to the 1920s when the city's European immigrant population decided to celebrate the American *Thanksgiving Day* holiday (which celebrates the harvest) with the sort of festivities they had known in their homelands. Hundreds of immigrant workers marched from 145 Street to 34th Street in costume, accompanied by floats, live animals on loan from Central Park Zoo and music bands. The parade attracted over 250,000 spectators and the Thanksgiving Day Parade quickly became a New York institution. Trademark giant balloons of cartoon characters were introduced for the first time in 1927, with Felix the Cat. The only interruption to the tradition came during World War II, but the festivities were soon revived and are now as popular as ever, with millions of people lining the streets from 0900-1200 to see the balloons, floats, marching bands and clowns and enjoy the holiday atmosphere.

Event Organiser
For more information on Macy's Thanksgiving Day Parade, contact NYC and Company (see **Tourist Information** above).

Venue
West 77th Street and Central Park West to Macy's Department Store, 34th Street and 6th Avenue.

Transport
Air: New York La Guardia International Airport or New York John F Kennedy International Airport. **Rail:** Train: Grand Central Station. Underground: West 81st Street (for West 77th Street) or 34th Street (for Macy's). **Road:** Bus: Public services.

Philadelphia

Tourist Information

Philadelphia Visitors Center
Love Park, 1515 Market Street, Philadelphia, PA 19103, USA
Tel: (215) 636 1666
Website: www.phillyvisitor.com

• January

Mummers Parade

Philadelphias's extravagant *Mummers Parade* heralds the New Year and, like *Macy's Thanksgiving Day Parade* in New York, can trace its origins back to customs and traditions brought over from Europe by the city's immigrant workers. Mummers plays were performed at Christmas time by troupes of actors in towns and villages in Medieval England and told the story of a dead warrior brought back to life by a doctor, loosely based on the story of St George and the Dragon. 'Momerie' was also a popular form of winter entertainment in Europe from the 13th to the 16th century, where groups of masked performers would enter houses to dance or play dice, and the German word for mask, 'Mumme' is thought to derive from this practice. The earliest known Philadelphia mummers band was the Chain Gang, formed in the 1840s and other bands soon formed in other parts of the city. In 1876 these bands of mummers staged their own individual parades, and marched to *Independence Hall* in the heart of the city; it was not until 1901, however, that the first official Mummers Parade was organised. Today's Parade lasts for 11 hours, and the city's various troupes of mummers start their lively march down Market Street or Broad Street at around 0800. There are four divisions: 'Comics' (clowns who impersonate public figures); 'Fancies' (fancy dress costumes developed around a given theme); 'String Bands' (combining fancy dress and music); and 'Fancy Brigades' (mummer troupes who give indoor performances at City Hall and Philadelphia Convention Center). There are prizes for the best costumes and music, awarded by a panel of judges, guaranteeing high standards and plenty of imagination.

Event Organiser
Mummers Museum, 1100 S. 2nd Street, Philadelphia, PA 19147, USA
Tel: (215) 336 3050
Website: www.mummers.com

Venue
Fifth & Market Street to City Hall.

Transport
Air: Philadelphia International Airport. **Rail:** Train: 30th Street Station. Underground: 5th & Market Street, 15th Street or City Hall. **Road:** Bus: Public services.

• July

Independence Day

Philadelphia, founded by Quaker William Penn in 1682, is regarded as the birthplace of the United States. It was here that the Declaration of Independence was signed in 1776 and the city also served as the country's first capital from 1790-1800. It is therefore fitting that the city's *Independence Day* celebrations should be some of the most impressive and significant in the USA, starting with the presentation of the Liberty Medal in *Independence Hall* where the Declaration was first adopted on July 4 1776 (but not signed until July 8). The Liberty Medal is presented to foreign or US citizens who have advanced the cause of freedom; past recipients include Polish trade unionist, Solidarity leader and former president Lech Walesa and former South African president and freedom fighter Nelson Mandela. The commemoration of the importance of this day in American history continues, when at 1300 a group of descendants of the signatories of the Declaration attend a simple ceremony at the Liberty Bell. After this, the fun begins, in the form of parades, concerts and picnics, as Philadelphia celebrates its place in American history and indulges in proud displays of patriotism. A fireworks display over the Delaware River lights up the evening sky to provide a magnificent finale.

Event Organiser
For more information on Independence Day, contact the Philadelphia Visitors Center (see **Tourist Information** above).

Venue
Independence Hall and various locations across Philadelphia.

Transport
Air: Philadelphia International Airport. **Rail:** Train: 30th Street Station. Underground: Fifth Street. **Road:** Coach: Public services.

Index